Fortresses and Icebergs
The Evolution of the Transatlantic Defense Market and the Implications for U.S. National Security Policy

By
Jeffrey P. Bialos
Christine E. Fisher
Stuart L. Koehl

Co-Editor and Co-Contributor
Christer L. Mossberg

Co-Contributors
Giovanni Gasparini
Andrew D. James

Volume II
Country Studies

Bialos, Jeffrey P., *Fortresses and Icebergs—The Evolution of the Transatlantic Defense Market and the Implications for U.S. National Security Policy, Volume II* (Washington, D.C.: Center for Transatlantic Relations, 2009).

Center for Transatlantic Relations
The Paul H. Nitze School of Advanced International Studies
The Johns Hopkins University
1717 Massachusetts Ave., NW, Suite 525
Washington, D.C. 20036
Tel. (202) 663-5880
Fax (202) 663-5879
Email: transatlantic@jhu.edu
http://transatlantic.sais-jhu.edu

ISBN 13: 978-0-9841341-2-0

Table of Contents

Volume I
Study Findings and Recommendations

Volume I
Study Findings and Recommendations

Volume II
Country Studies

VOLUME II

Country Studies

Chapter 7

Accessing the French Defense Market

Like the United Kingdom (UK), France is one of the few European nations that seek to maintain full spectrum military capabilities and related defense technologies and production capabilities—due primarily to the longstanding strategy of military and political independence put in place by Charles de Gaulle. Under Gaullism, France was firmly in the Western bloc but not fully integrated into the North Atlantic Treaty Organization (NATO) Alliance. France only recently moved to rejoin NATO's military command. Despite internal controversy that such a policy change would undermine France's military and diplomatic independence, NATO re-integration won a vote of confidence by the French Parliament in March 2009. Prime Minister François Fillon announced that, in exchange for returning to the Alliance's military command, France would "doubtless" be given a key command in Norfolk, Virginia. "We want to take our place where the future of NATO is discussed," Fillon said.[211]

Consistent with its strong Gaullist policy, France developed and produced its own military platforms—often to specifications not necessarily compatible with NATO standards. While France and the United States have a long and deep history of military cooperation and coalition operations, they have not engaged in extensive defense trade. France was highly dependent on U.S. military assistance and Foreign Military Sales (FMS) financing in the early post-World War II era, but thereafter developed its own defense industrial base to maintain a high degree of autonomy in defense matters and to strengthen its largely stated-owned industry. As a result of this policy, today the United States and France have limited defense product or company presence in each other's markets. As discussed in Chapters 4 and 14, however, French ownership of U.S. defense firms and the French market position in the United States have increased modestly in the last decade.

The French government, focused on maintaining its defense autonomy, has generally not sought to achieve Transatlantic integration of defense markets. Overall, the French government has not acted overtly to either facilitate or hinder the evolution of more Transatlantic defense firms. In the past, the French government at times exerted some pressure behind the scenes to discourage acquisitions or joint ventures with U.S. firms that it felt might bring French industry too close to the U.S. orbit. In recent years, however, the French government has not interfered as French firms increasingly sought to acquire holdings in the United States. Still, several factors, including Franco-American geopolitical disputes and French policies on third-country exports have over the years limited prospects for technology sharing and more in-depth defense cooperation.

In recent years, France has shifted from its traditional Gaullist policy of *National Autonomy* to a neo-Gaullist policy of *Strategic Autonomy* centered on building a stronger *European* defense capability. Under Strategic Autonomy, France seeks to ensure its ability to choose where and when to operate militarily and its ability to operate independently if necessary. But this policy does not mean all industry sources must be French; only a few select areas must remain national (e.g., nuclear weapons capability). Strategic Autonomy is supported by

---

[211] Associated Press, March 17, 2009. Available at: http://www.cbc.ca/world/story/2009/03/17/sarkozy-nato-france.html.

an industrial policy of *Competitive Autonomy* wherein France establishes formal agreements of mutual interdependence and supply security with European partner states for certain defense capabilities, and will allow competitive bidding by other European firms within this framework.

Consistent with this Euro-strategic thrust, French officials assert that it is time for the European Union (EU) to strengthen its own technology and industrial base in order to stand on a more equal footing with the United States. To implement this goal, France will increasingly share its armaments acquisition resources, programs and industrial base with European partners. The new French White Paper on Defence and National Security of June 17, 2008, underscores and amplifies these trends. While reluctant to cede some controls, France strongly supports the EU moves toward a more integrated EU defense marketplace. The White Paper argues for a trans-European industry, the rationalization of its underutilized capabilities (i.e., to eliminate duplication and promote efficiency) and the creation of European centers of excellence. For the future, while the French government turns increasingly to Europe, the French *industry* seeks very much to play three hands: the French, EU and U.S. markets.

Another sustained pillar of French defense industrial policy is *ownership matters*. France must know on whom it can rely for support (both strategic and economic) and refuses to risk its national security by allowing firms motivated solely by financial considerations, or foreign firms with different security interests, to steward its major defense companies. Since France relies on arms exports not only to sustain its domestic industrial base but also as an instrument of foreign policy, it also seeks to maintain export flexibility and avoid the need to get permission from another nation to modify, deploy or export systems and/or technologies.

Consistent with this desire for freedom of operation, the French government is reluctant to buy or employ U.S. International Traffic in Arms Regulations (ITAR) controlled systems and technologies, and strongly prefers ITAR-free solutions unless no alternative is available. Consistent with French government attitudes, French industry in practice seeks work-arounds to ITAR-controlled subsystems and components. French firms doing a considerable business with the United States are more accommodating. As they seek to sell in the U.S. market and meet U.S. customer demands, they are used to dealing with ITAR restrictions. Overall, however, the implications of this French "ITAR-free preference" for U.S. defense trade with France are self-evident.

Historically, the French defense market has been difficult for U.S. firms to access; there are few U.S. defense firms with significant activities or operations in France. In many ways the French market is similar to the U.S. market—each side finds the other's market somewhat challenging to penetrate.

A number of factors point to the possibility of improved U.S. market access in the future: 1) new leadership in France and the United States; 2) the resulting prospect of a closer U.S.-France strategic relationship; and 3) changes in France's defense acquisition policies—with its shift to greater competition in order to promote better value solutions. However, to enhance their access going forward, U.S. firms must play by the "rules of the road" well known to U.S. commercial aerospace firms in France: 1) partner or team with strong local French or European firms; 2) demonstrate strong stewardship by investing locally (e.g., through work share opportunities); 3) develop a presence and trust over time; and 4) work to avoid reliance on ITAR in product solutions and design choices.

All this said, French President Nicolas Sarkozy's return to full NATO participation certainly is a clear turn toward the United States, and an opportunity that the United States should seize upon to improve our defense market relationship with one of the primary European Allies with both the political will and capabilities to participate in coalition expeditionary operations.

Market Background

A. France's Changing Strategic Context and Military Strategy

France's current strategic and defense posture is an outgrowth of the Gaullist policy of strategic autonomy adopted during the Cold War. From 1958 on, France took steps to reestablish itself as a *world* power, capable of its own defense, equal to other nations, and not subordinate to another nation's foreign and security policies.

> General de Gaulle's attitude to NATO, progressing from overt mistrust even before 1958 to his decision in 1966 to withdraw French forces from the integrated military structure, was part of his plan to provide France with an independent defence policy…, while his relations with successive American governments evolved, General de Gaulle judged it time for France to reclaim its independence: the country was now in a position to act alone in Europe and worldwide, and would develop "a nuclear force such that none shall dare attack us without fear of suffering the most terrible injuries."[212]

This independent posture at times created significant tension, and even conflict, with the United States. The fracture between France and NATO has been a strong force in shaping the U.S. and French relationship in defense matters to this day. Despite its withdrawal from the integrated military organization, over the decades that followed France continued to participate in and generally work cooperatively in other ways with NATO. France, like its NATO and other European Allies, focused its Cold War military strategy on territorial defense against Soviet attack. However, France also had to deal with expeditionary operations in former colonies, as well as ongoing bouts of domestic terrorism.

Toward the end of Cold War era, President François Mitterand, (1981-1995) began seeking increased European integration and collective security policies. With the emergence of the European Union and the Common Foreign and Security Policy (CFSP) in the 1992 Maastricht Treaty, France's national security shifted to greater interdependence with its EU partners.

The fall of the Soviet Union, the emergence of new missions replacing the Cold War view, and budgetary pressures all worked to encourage downsizing and reconfiguration of French forces. Under President Mitterand, a 1994 *Livre Blanc* (White Paper) laid out a strategy to restructure the French military—although the strategy did not have the sweep or effectiveness needed for a real transformation.

Thereafter, beginning in May 1995, new "neo-Gaullist" President Jacques Chirac began some military reductions and post-Cold War transformations. To meet the stringent

---

[212] See Charles-De-Gaulle.org, *DeGaulle and NATO* section. Available at: http://charles-de-gaulle.org.

finance commitments of the 1992 Maastricht Treaty, President Chirac undertook a "recasting" of French military that reduced its size, capabilities and budget. Reportedly based on the British military model, Chirac's reforms began to transform the French military from a defensive force focused on Europe to a rapid reaction force capable of "out of area" operations. To improve professionalism, Chirac instituted an all-voluntary military. Chirac was also influenced by the perception that France had been humiliated in the 1991 Gulf War, where the French contingent's lack of combat power and interoperability with other Coalition forces relegated it to a secondary role on a remote front.[213]

The results of these changes were gradual and incremental, not rapid and bold. As several French experts observed:

> Though some steps have been taken to reorient French conventional forces away from Continental war and toward an overseas projection, France's military equipment and capabilities remain the product of decisions made in the 1980s and even 1970s—decisions that reflect both the traditional Gaullist strategy of independence through nuclear deterrence and the assumption of a regular, symmetric enemy.[214]

Post-September 11—New National Security Dynamics

Changes in the global and domestic security environment since the September 11 attacks continue to drive the evolution of French defense policy away from its Gaullist autonomy and toward greater interdependence. France has recognized the change in warfare away from high intensity conventional threats to a range of low intensity and asymmetric threats, including terrorism. As several French analysts noted:

> *There has been a shift from the need to plan for a "virtual" total war in Europe to the need to fight real yet far more limited wars, often far afield. On another level, today's limited wars come in a wide variety of forms, from asymmetric wars like Iraq and Afghanistan to hi-tech, coercive operations like NATO's air campaign against Serbia in 1999. It is difficult to prepare for all forms at once.[215]*

France has recognized that the growth of these wide-ranging threats far afield requires increasing EU and international coordination, and are not missions for a single nation.

At home, the strains on the French economy, including high systemic unemployment, stagnant economic growth and an extensive and unsustainable social welfare system have created pressure to limit or reduce defense spending.[216] With the increasing complexity and cost of modern weapon systems and the high operations and maintenance (O&M) costs

---

[213] For more detail on post-Cold War policies of Presidents Mitterand and Chirac, see R. Tiersky, *French Military Reforms and Strategy*, National Defense University, Institute for National Strategic Studies, November 1996.

[214] C. Chivvis and E. de Durand, *Political and Strategic Consequences of the French White Paper*, French Institute of International Affairs, March 28, 2008. This article can be found at: http://www.brookings.edu/papers/2008/spring_france_chivvis.aspx.

[215] Chivvis and de Durand, Ibid.

[216] Real French GDP increased 2.2 percent in 2006 but GDP growth in 2007 decreased to 1.9 percent and, according to initial projections, will drop to 1.5 percent in 2008, according to the U.S. Department of Commerce. See U.S. Commercial Service website on France. Available at: http://www.buyusa.gov/france/en/doingbusinessinfrance.html.

associated with fielding and supporting expeditionary forces, France finds it increasingly difficult to meet both its defense commitments and its defense modernization plans. With little public support for significant defense spending increases, France simply cannot afford a policy of strategic independence.

The "Livre Blanc"—*A New Neo-Gaullist Defense and National Security Strategy*

On June 17, 2008, President Sarkozy announced the findings of a 35-person Presidential *Commission on the Livre Blanc (White Paper)*.[217] The White Paper sets forth a new comprehensive security strategy that deploys a full spectrum of military and civilian tools to address the range of risks France faces. This more holistic approach highlights the risks of terrorism associated with radical jihadism that "aims directly at France and Europe."[218] It also recognizes that potential adversaries will use asymmetric warfare and exploit vulnerabilities to the French homeland.

The White Paper sets forth key elements of French strategy, including the importance of "knowledge" as the "first line of defense" to enable France's strategic position and the continued importance of the French nuclear deterrent.[219] Under the White Paper, intelligence and information dominance are now essential military capabilities and homeland security is now a major element of French defense strategy in the age of terrorism, cyber-attacks and natural disasters.

The White Paper also highlights a regional sphere of interest—a "priority geographical axis"—from the Atlantic to the Mediterranean, the Arab-Persian Gulf and the Indian Ocean.[220] The White Paper explains that this axis "corresponds to the areas where the risks related to the strategic interests of France and Europe are the highest."[221] Included in this sphere of interest is Africa, and France seeks partnership with Africa in defense and security in order to strengthen African peace-keeping capabilities.

Of most relevance here, a central "priority" of the new strategy is the "European ambition."[222] As it states, "[m]aking the European Union a major player in crisis management and international security is one of the central tenets of our security policy." In effect, the White Paper sets forth a new Eurocentric national security strategy and changing force structure to address the new range of threats. In effect, the new strategy confirms the gradual changes underway since the last White Paper in 1994 and effectively adopts a neo-Gaullist approach that focuses on maintaining an autonomous military capability—but through the EU rather than on a go-it-alone national basis. Thus, if fully implemented, the White Paper will move France from a national-independent strategy to a European-interdependent defense strategy and supporting industry.

---

[217] "New French White Paper on Defence and National Security," June 17, 2008, Présidence de la République Française (English language summary) at: http://www.ambafrance-uk.org/New-French-White-Paper-on-defence.html?var_recherche=sarkozy%20speech%20livre%20blanc%20defense. The Livre Blanc may also be found in its full French text as well as in the English summary form at: http://www.premier-ministre.gouv.fr/information/les_dossiers_actualites_19/livre_blanc_sur_defense_875/.

[218] Ibid., p. 5.

[219] Ibid., pp. 5-6.

[220] Ibid., p. 6.

[221] Ibid.

[222] Ibid., p. 7.

Figure 58   French Defense Budget, 1999-2008 (Billions of Euros – €)

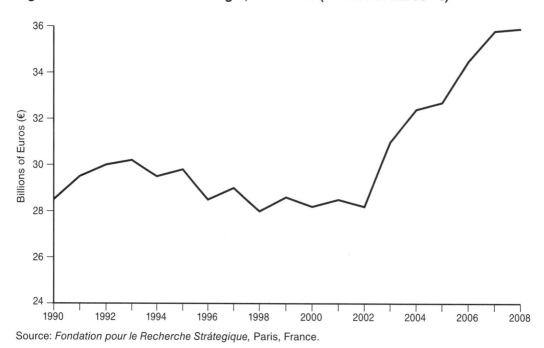

Source: *Fondation pour le Recherche Strátegique,* Paris, France.

French Military Spending and Forces Today

Consistent with its Gaullist approach, France developed a full-spectrum force across all mission areas in sea, air and ground—today sustained by the largest all-volunteer military force on the European continent. Under the 2008 White Paper, the French forces, which today consist of some 320,000 volunteers, will be cut by 54,000 (with most of the cuts coming from support and administrative staff, and effected largely through non-replacement of retirees).[223]

The 2007 French Defense Budget was about €35 billion (about $50 billion) overall, and about $40 billion excluding pensions. The White Paper also calls for sustained and eventually increased defense spending as well as a refocusing of resources.

From 1992 to 2000, the French Defense Budget declined by approximately 3.7 percent per annum (see Figure 58). However, since 2001 its defense spending has risen by 23.5 percent—in part to help fund international deployments, as discussed below.

In Europe, France is second only to the UK in defense spending. Both France and the UK each spend nearly 2.5 percent of gross domestic product on defense overall as compared

---

[223] Unless otherwise noted, French MoD and military force size and deployment numbers are from the French Embassy in the United States augmented by information from the French MoD website, and generally reflect 2007 figures. Available at: http://france.usembassy.gov/. However, these figures cannot be compared on an "apples to apples" basis with the U.S. military because 28 percent of French defense forces are composed of the *Gendarmerie*—a paramilitary national police force under the control of the Ministry of Defense. While some gendarmes are focused on internal threat-oriented activities such as anti-terrorism and even deploy abroad for force protection services, most provide police functions in various localities.

to about 4 percent in the United States. However, if one excludes pensions and the cost of the *gendarmerie*, France spends about 1.7 percent on its defense forces.[224] Together France and the UK account for nearly 60 percent of European defense spending, and upwards of 60 percent of turnover for European defense firms.[225] France and the UK also account for roughly 70-75 percent of European-wide research and development (R&D) spending.

The White Paper calls for sustained and eventually increased defense spending as well as a refocusing of resources. In introducing the White Paper, President Sarkozy promised that the current defense budget would not be cut and would start to rise in 2012 (including an increase of more than 20 percent in the equipment budget). In fact, on October 29, 2008, the French government announced it would increase military spending by an average of $1.8 billion a year as part of an effort to:

> [f]ield a trimmer but better-equipped army to safeguard France's role in world affairs. The defense planning law, which the government's parliamentary majority is likely to pass unaltered, provided for $230 billion through 2014. It listed as priority expenditures the launching of reconnaissance satellites, increasing by 700 the number of intelligence agents and buying anti-missile alert systems. In deference to the economic slowdown, however, it mandated holding firm on expenditures for the first three years and then piling the increases into the last two years.[226]

Following through on this budget increase may prove challenging, given France's other fiscal needs (exacerbated by the current recession). Given the EU's Stability and Growth Pact, which limits member countries' budget deficits, France's defense spending can rise only at the expense of other French budget priorities or increased taxes. This makes the move toward European cooperation in programs and operations an increasing imperative.

From a restructuring standpoint, the White Paper also upgrades the spending and priority for transformation of forces for network-centric warfare and intelligence, surveillance and reconnaissance (ISR). Notably, it calls for doubling the intelligence budget for new satellites, drones and other surveillance equipment.

French Global Commitments

Consistent with the changing threat profile, France today has nearly 36,000 French troops deployed in a range of stabilization and humanitarian missions—under United Nations (UN), NATO and EU mandates. Its forces are engaged in coalition operations in Afghanistan, the Balkans, Lebanon and Africa, where it has longstanding interests and influence in its former colonies. This latter will likely be of interest to the U.S. government

---

[224] The French defense budget is therefore closer to a "national security budget"; to arrive at an analogous figure for the United States, one would have to add the budgets of the FBI, the Department of Homeland Security, and the nuclear operations of the Department of Energy to the budget of the Department of Defense.

[225] France's spending compares favorably with the non-U.S. NATO nation level of about 1.74 percent, but it is substantially less than U.S. spending, which is now at about 4 percent of GDP. European nations' defense spending data can be found in many sources, including data publicly released by each nation. Compiled data is at Stockholm International Peace Research Institute (SIPRI), Wikipedia and several other web sources.

[226] Edward Cody, Washington Post Foreign Service, Oct. 30, 2008; Page A18. Available at: http://www.washington-post.com/wp-dyn/content/article/2008/10/29/AR2008102902589.html.

agencies involved in the nascent U.S. African Command(AFRICOM), as it builds partnerships, interagency and international, to support its mission.

France also views itself as a strong U.S. deployment partner. There are about 7,600 French troops in the Caribbean and Guyana, with the U.S. Joint Inter-Agency Task Force South, countering drug trafficking. There are 10,000 French forces in the Pacific region and Southern Indian Ocean helping to control sea lanes—notably attached to Task Force 150.[227]

France also has announced it will increase its troop presence in Afghanistan (from current levels of 1,500 to 2,000) to support both the NATO International Security Assistance Force and the American-led Operation Enduring Freedom. This increase, coming after months of U.S. encouragement, is unpopular with the French public.[228] Hence, President Sarkozy's decision reflects a clear intent to develop closer relations with the United States. As he said:

> We the French want to strengthen our Euro-Atlantic community because it is built on shared values, democratic principles, human rights… Afghanistan is a strategic issue for international security. It's [a] central issue for relations between Islam and the West…. It's essential for the alliance.[229]

Sarkozy's decision to augment troops in Afghanistan received further public criticism after 10 French troops were killed and 21 wounded in a Taliban ambush on August 19, 2008. Recognizing the sensitivity of these losses, President Sarkozy personally went to Kabul to bring home the bodies and held a special memorial service for the families at the Elysée Palace on August 21, 2008.[230] Yet Sarkozy has continued to support enhanced Afghanistan engagement since that time.

B. The Evolving Franco-American Relationship

The Franco-American relationship has been complex. On the one hand, the United States and France are longstanding allies with congruent interests, and work together on a broad range of geopolitical, trade and security issues.[231] On the other hand, a central thrust of Gaullism in both its traditional and Eurocentric permutations has been autonomy and independence from the United States. This has led to periodic bouts of cool relations and sharp differences on core foreign policy issues, including most notably the U.S.-French divide during the Bush Administration over the 2003 invasion of Iraq.[232] In general, U.S.

---

[227] Force deployment information is from the French Embassy to the U.S. website and so is only as current as the posted information.

[228] An April 5, 2008 posting on the World Socialist Web Site reports on French polls that show 68 percent of the French public disapproves of the Afghan Deployment. Available at: http://www.wsws.org/articles/2008/apr2008/fran-a05.shtml.

[229] "Bush calls Sarkozy the 'French Elvis' after France announces it WILL send more troops to Afghanistan," Mail Online (April 3, 2008). Available at: http://www.dailymail.co.uk/news/article-555748/Bush-calls-Sarkozy-French-Elvis-France-announces-WILL-send-troops-afghanistan.html.

[230] BBC News, Aug. 19, 2008. See http://news.bbc.co.uk/2/hi/south_asia/7569942.stm.

[231] U.S. Commercial Service website, *Executive Summary on France*, U.S. Department of Commerce. Available at: http://www.buyusa.gov/france/en/doingbusinessinfrance.html.

[232] It should be noted, though, that even as public relations between the two countries deteriorated, cooperation in intelligence and counter-terrorism activities became much closer and more extensive—a reflection of the ambivalence that has long characterized the relations between the United States and France.

and French defense establishments and military forces have had a more cooperative relationship than do the politicians.

The election of President Sarkozy in 2007 has led to the tangible prospect of closer Franco-American alignment and engagement. Sarkozy opened this door carefully when, on his election victory, he said "I'd like to appeal to our American friends to say that they can count on our friendship… But I would also like to say that friendship means accepting that your friends don't necessarily see eye to eye with you."[233]

In the latest positive step in this relationship, the new White Paper—and Sarkozy's plans to implement it—will bring France back fully into the NATO integrated command structure, albeit with two clear caveats: 1) French soldiers will not be permanently assigned under other nations' military commanders; and 2) France will continue its independent nuclear deterrence policy.[234] Despite these caveats, the new attitude reflected in the White Paper marks a major sea change in French policy and opens the door for a closer bilateral relationship.

U.S.-France Defense Trade and Industrial Cooperation: A Record of Limited Participation

Not surprisingly, the United States and France have had limited engagement in defense trade and industrial cooperation (both in absolute terms and relative to either country's relationship with other mutual allies). The trade flow among France, other European nations and the United States is described in detail in Chapter 4. This is consistent with the longstanding French autonomy in defense and resulting French preferences for national and increasingly European solutions. The legal frameworks for defense cooperation in place are more limited than with other allies; the United States has established few cooperative programs with France;[235] and there are relatively low levels of defense trade compared to other allies.

Legal Frameworks for Defense Industrial Cooperation

On May 22, 1978, the U.S. Department of Defense (DoD) and French Ministry of Defense (MoD) entered into a Procurement Memorandum of Understanding (MOU), which has been renewed continuously since that time. The MOU provides, in principle, that U.S. firms are afforded access into the French defense markets and treated no less favorably than are domestic firms (and provides reciprocal treatment in the United States for French firms). As reflected below, however, the reality of access to each other's markets is more complex.

More recently, the DoD has entered into Declarations of Principles (DoPs), which are non-binding bilateral agreements on reciprocity and cooperation on defense export, supply and industry, with the MoDs of all countries in the LOI 6 nations—the largest defense producers in Europe—with the exception of France. The United States based its willingness to enter into DoPs—thereby signaling deepened defense industrial cooperation—on

---

[233] J. Anderson and M. Moore, *Washington Post Foreign Service*, May 7, 2007.

[234] French *Livre Blanc*, English Summary, op. cit.

[235] To some extent, the limits on defense cooperation between the United States and France put the military forces of both sides in opposition to their political and civil service leaders. French and U.S. military and service representatives both reported a strong desire for closer cooperation for a wide range of reasons, but suggest opposition from political and bureaucratic interests that made such cooperation extremely difficult at the present time. Despite this, a number of low-level initiatives are being pursued to open up new areas and modalities of cooperative development, particularly in armaments development and technology exchange.

a country's approach to the so-called "Five Pillars of Compatibility and Confidence"—that is, five factors that describe the willingness of the United States to engage in deepened defense industrial relationships with other countries: 1) export controls commonality and reciprocity; 2) industrial security commonality and reciprocity; 3) intelligence cooperation; 4) law enforcement cooperation; and 5) guaranteed reciprocity of access to defense markets.

Over the years since the first DoPs were signed in 2000, France has sought a similar agreement, and the United States and France have had periodic dialogues on broadening cooperation. However, the DoD has been reluctant to commit to a similar agreement because a lack of policy congruence in the "Five Pillars" policy areas. Specifically, in addition to periodic clashes over major policy issues (witness Iraq), the United States has been concerned over the French approach to third-country exports (where France has been viewed by the United States as more permissive in regard to sales to certain countries such as Iran and China) and industrial security (where there have been longstanding U.S. concerns over alleged French industrial espionage).

In June 2007, as Franco-American relations improved, the United States and France entered into a Joint Statement of Intent on Armaments Cooperation. Signed by the senior acquisition officials of each country, this Joint Statement outlined areas for broadened cooperation in research, development and testing and the intent to meet regularly to encourage more congruence in projects and interoperability. The statement did not outline specific programs or spending that would result, but established a process and commitment for follow-on milestones and specific activities to be developed over time. While less forward-leaning than a DoP, this agreement signals the prospect of closer ties and a better environment for defense industrial cooperation in the future—especially as France realigns its policy in key areas.

French government and industry officials interviewed all expressed a desire for a stronger agreement to allow more technology sharing, one such as the U.S.-UK treaty on defense currently pending before Congress. Further, an informal proposal was made to the United States to consider either a trilateral U.S.-UK-FR arrangement in specific defense areas (e.g., aircraft carriers), or a defense export agreement that, given the increase in multinational joint ventures, would ease third-party transfer issues among NATO partners. The French felt this type of arrangement would open markets both ways and strengthen defense ties. In the end, the degree of closer defense industrial cooperation will be heavily dependent on changes in French policy and practices in the "Five Pillars" policy areas noted above and the American perceptions of such changes.

Cooperative Programs. Historically, there has been little noteworthy joint or cooperative armaments development between France and the United States. France is not a participant in the Joint Strike Fighter program and there are no other major bilateral cooperative programs ongoing with the United States (although French firms do participate in NATO programs). There is some chance that the United States and France may participate in a satellite-based security network focused on Eastern Africa, an area of concern for piracy and illegal arms flow. This would fit within the Joint Statement topics of cooperation outlined above.

While there are a number of private cooperative Franco-American defense industrial ventures, they are few and far between. Most notable are the following:

- **GE/SAFRAN (former GE/SNECMA) CFM 56.** The well-known GE engine joint venture operation located in France has been a huge success for nearly four decades: the firms have sold more than 18,000 engines. This is a model based on localized selling and modifications of products that are based on core commercial engine products of GE. The number one end-user in the United States is the U.S. Air Force, followed internationally by Boeing. Airbus purchases are nearly equal to Boeing's.

- **ThalesRaytheon Systems, Ltd.** This joint venture, begun in the late 1990s and finalized in December 2000, is a strategic effort designed to promote cross-marketing of their radar and command and control products. Despite initial start-up difficulties, cultural differences and different market dynamics in the two countries, the parties indicate that the venture has been successful. Among the programs in which it has a role are: the Active Layered Theater Ballistic Missile Defense System; the MPQ-64 Ground-Based Sensor; the Battle Control System-Fixed (BCS-F); the German Improved Air Defense System; the Mobile Multifunctional Modular Radar (M3R); the TRS-2630 Gerfaut Radar; and the Sentry Air Defense System.

Limited U.S. Sales and Market Presence. France has historically bought few defense platforms/systems or major subsystems from the United States and, as a consequence, U.S. defense firms have limited on-the-ground presence in France. Thus, the total U.S. defense trade with France (based on U.S. government data and French MoD data on imports and exports) was only on the order of $2.6 billion for the years 2002-2006 (see Figure 59). In contrast, U.S. defense trade flow with the UK was approximately $18.4 billion for the same period. Among the smaller European countries, trade flow with Germany was $11 billion; with Italy, $4.4 billion; with Sweden, $2.1 billion; and with Poland, more than $4.5 billion. See Figures 37 to 42 in Chapter 4 for a comparison of defense trade flow among the European countries analyzed under this study.

According to French *Délégation Générale pour l'Armement (DGA)*[236] and industry officials, the French typically buy U.S. products when: 1) the U.S. offers an off-the-shelf (non-developmental) or especially attractive technology solution that could not be found in Europe; or 2) the product is needed for compatibility for NATO or other shared U.S./European operations. These categories include the U.S. E-2C Hawkeye and the E-3F airborne warning and control system surveillance aircraft. Two of the former were purchased in 1995, followed by orders for more advanced E-2 Hawkeye 2000 aircraft in April 1999—all operated from the French aircraft carrier *Charles de Gaulle*. France also purchased four E-3s from Boeing between 1987 and 1991 to support the Armée de l'Air. The French military has progressively upgraded these aircraft, in both cases relying almost exclusively on the U.S. prime contractor.

In general, as observed by French DGA officials, the French buy more in defense goods from European partners than they buy from the United States. The United States consistently sells more defense goods to France than France does to the United States—although the gap has closed in recent years.

However, the critical point is the small volume of trade in either direction—typically less than $500 million per annum. This stands in contrast to the relatively high volume of trade between the United States and UK, with UK sales to the United States averaging $1 bil-

---

[236] The *Délégation Générale pour l'Armement (DGA)* of the French Ministry of Defense is the organization responsible for MoD acquisition policies and oversight. Details on the DGA, its mission and programs, may be found at http://www.defense.gouv.fr/dga.

Figure 59   U.S.-France Defense Trade Flow (Millions of Dollars – $)

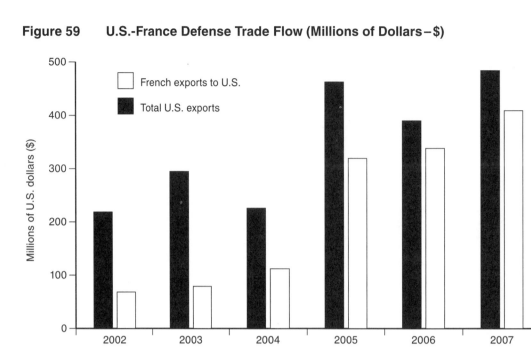

Millions of U.S. dollars ($)

	2002	2003	2004	2005	2006	2007
FMS Sales to France	206.1	276.0	98.9	69.2	42.7	47.0
Commercial Sales to France	12.6	18.9	126.9	393.5	347.1	437.1
Total U.S. Exports	218.7	294.9	225.8	462.7	389.8	484.1
French Exports to U.S.	68.5	79.3	112.1	319.4	338.1	409.2

Source: DSCA and French Export Control Reports.

lion a year, and the U.S. sales to the UK averaging some $2-3 billion. The fact is the United States and France do not presently have a high level of bilateral defense trade despite a very robust overall trade relationship with large trade flows in both directions and an ongoing French trade surplus in the wider economy (see Figure 60).

Platforms/Systems. Large U.S. defense primes have sold few platforms to France and, hence, have little or no permanent on-the-ground presence in France. Most large U.S. defense firms do not even have permanent employees in the country. Rather, they use local representatives to work on specific engagement opportunities and perform market monitoring (e.g., Lockheed Martin, Raytheon and Northrop Grumman). Boeing probably has the most presence, with a business office in Paris and employees in various French locations; it also has a small permanent staff assigned to defense. Boeing's French operations support its platform presence, which is mostly in commercial aerospace products but also includes some military platforms. Boeing also works to build relations and market reach in France via strategic *buying* of components for their commercial systems. Boeing sources roughly some few billion dollars a year in components from France.

Overall, the limited and mostly legacy U.S. platform presence in France is as follows:

Figure 60   **Total U.S.-France Balance of Trade, 2001-2007 (Billions of Dollars–$)**

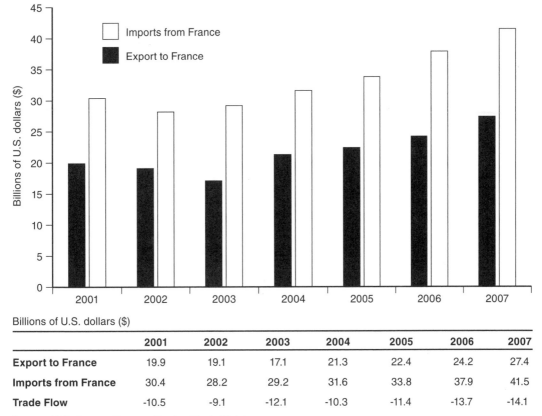

Billions of U.S. dollars ($)

	2001	**2002**	**2003**	**2004**	**2005**	**2006**	**2007**
Export to France	19.9	19.1	17.1	21.3	22.4	24.2	27.4
Imports from France	30.4	28.2	29.2	31.6	33.8	37.9	41.5
Trade Flow	-10.5	-9.1	-12.1	-10.3	-11.4	-13.7	-14.1

Source: U.S. Census Bureau, Foreign Trade Division.

- **Military**—France operates fourteen KC-135s Stratotankers, four E-3F AWACS, and three E-2C Hawkeye AEW aircraft—all sold years ago (more than 40 in the case of the KC-135s). Boeing has not had a significant military platform sale in roughly 20 years. Northrop Grumman has not sold a new aircraft to France since the late 1990s (though there is the potential for follow-on E-2 orders depending on the continuation of the second French aircraft carrier). Both Northrop and Boeing have won major modification or upgrade programs for the E-2 and E-3, usually awarded on a sole source basis. Boeing is also working in business development in several new military product areas, principally via strategic teaming with French firms.

- **Commercial**—Air France owns Boeing 777 airliners, which Boeing supports in extensive modification and upgrade programs.

Smaller Systems, Subsystems and Components. With few exceptions (e.g., Rockwell Collins, as discussed below) U.S. firms providing smaller systems, subsystems and components are generally selling in the French market via agents and by specific opportunity, and do not have long-term presence or operating locations there. Firms selling subsystems, components and materials are generally selling to European primes or lead firms directly, and not to the MoD. While there are few contracts for large purchases such as platforms, U.S.

firms have had somewhat more success in subtier markets, particularly where products are commercial or dual-use or address a special technology niche. The following are examples:

- **Raytheon** has sold some missile systems/munitions in France over the years, including Paveway (formerly Texas Instruments) laser-guided bombs sold throughout the 1990s over seven contracts. Raytheon has been actively marketing a tactical missile product for an upcoming French MoD requirement. Raytheon has representatives working in France to assess and guide Raytheon opportunities or products there, but does not have any operating locations or facilities in France.

- A **Lockheed Martin-Raytheon** team was awarded a contract for AGM-114 Hellfire II anti-tank missiles for use with France's forty Eurocopter Tiger attack helicopters. DGA selected Hellfire in June 2007, in large part because of the failure of the multinational Euromissile TriGAT-LR originally proposed for the Tiger.

- A **Lockheed Martin-Raytheon** team is marketing the Javelin anti-tank missile for use by France's ground forces. DGA is running a competition between Javelin, the Rafael EuroSpike (Israel), and the MBDA Milan-ER (France). The final decision has been postponed, but is currently anticipated in 2009.

- **Rockwell Collins** has won several competitions in France. Where possible, Rockwell has bid with products that are dual-use and customized for Europe (i.e., that had no ITAR components in order to avoid ITAR as a market access barrier). Thus, Rockwell provides several products for the A400M, all bid through various branches of European Aeronautical, Defence and Space Company (EADS). Rockwell also won a competition against Thales for a 1 MW Very Low Frequency radio for submarine transmission because they had an "attractive technology nugget" at a good price. Given its level of business, Rockwell Collins France SA has a robust presence with 645 people and €143 million in sales in France. The firm maintains a French headquarters at Toulouse-Blagnac (the location of Airbus Industries), which includes some technical support and manufacturing. Rockwell also has three other technical sites in France, mainly for product servicing, customer support and marketing.[237]

- **Alcoa** has significant sales in France in forgings, in castings and in other material-based products (e.g., alloys) for aerospace. Alcoa is a partner to Airbus on the A380, and has 2 operating locations and 13 offices throughout France.

---

[237] Detailed information quoted on Rockwell Collins is from their Rockwell Collins France website; see http://www.rockwellcollins.com/about/locations/france/index.html.

II. The French Defense Market: Supply and Demand Dynamics

The degree of U.S. engagement in French defense markets in the future will in large measure be a function of the evolving Franco-American geopolitical relationship, the French impulses toward Eurocentrism, and the dynamics of the French defense market itself. Thus, it is important to understand market access for U.S. firms in the context of the evolving supply-and-demand trends in France set forth below.

A. Evolution of French Defense Industry: Independence and the European Paradox

France is the nation that most strongly underlines the national interest of a strong defense industry. At the same time, it is the European Nation that most strongly has incorporated strategic parts of its defense industry into shared European Structures.... This duality is to some non-French analysts seen as a paradox.[238]

Because of its longstanding policy of strategic independence, France developed a full-spectrum defense industry, producing platforms in many capabilities areas—aircraft, ships, submarines, C4ISR (command, control, communications, computers, intelligence, surveillance and reconnaissance), ground armored vehicles, and importantly for France, in nuclear capabilities and space and ballistic missiles. France's long history of innovation in engineering and science has also resulted in a strong defense technology base in electronics, aviation, software, optics, nuclear engineering and many other areas. With its breadth of sectors, France did not have one national champion, but numerous national firms serving its various needs. The French state historically always played a controlling role in this industry, owning all or a good share in its defense firms (termed "golden shares" by industry officials). To quote European analyst Martin Lundmark, "the central role of the [French] state in shaping the defense industry has never been questioned."[239]

By the mid-1990s, France effectively pursued a three-part industrial strategy to meet its national security needs. First, given its industrial strength and breadth, during the Cold War and into the 1990s, France pursued the development and production of many of its own national platforms (e.g., the Rafale Multi-Role Combat fighter, the *Charles de Gaulle* aircraft carrier, the Exocet missile, and the Leclerc Main Battle Tank). Second, during the post-Cold War era—particularly given post-Maastricht budget realities—President Chirac began to move away from "100 percent reliance" on French industry by participating in several European multinational programs and operations, notably in the very expensive area of space and in areas where France saw an advantageous bilateral opportunity for cooperative development (e.g., the 1988 launch of the French/German Tiger Helicopter development program). Finally, throughout the 1980s and 1990s, the French state has had a strong defense export policy that helped foster defense sales and political influence beyond national boundaries (except in the nuclear and other sensitive areas).

---

[238] Martin Lundmark, Executive Summary, *To Be or Not To Be, The Integration and the Non-Integration of the French Defense Industry*, July 2004, The FIND program, Defense Analysis Stockholm, based on research Mr. Lundmark performed at *Fondation pour la Recherche Stratégique*, Paris. Available to: http://www.frstrategie.org/test/barreCompetences/DEFind/politiquesIndustrielles.php

[239] M. Lundmark, Ibid.

French Defense Industrial Consolidation in the Late 1990s

The 1990s post-Cold War decline in defense budgets in France and Europe more generally, with EU nations down more than 20 percent in the same period,[240] resulted in the consolidation, downsizing and partial privatization of the French defense industry. (See Figure 58 for French budget declines.)

For example, the employment base of *Direction des Constructions Navales Services* (DCNS),[241] the state-owned naval shipyard, declined from 20,000 in 1997 to only 12,500 in 2005; similarly, the combat vehicle firm Nexter (formerly GIAT) declined from 10,000 employees in 1998 to under 2,500 today.[242] Decreased demand and a shrinking program portfolio also drove the consolidation of the larger French and other European national aerospace and defense firms across national boundaries—notably Thales, EADS, MBDA, and later the SAFRAN Group (formed by a combination of Sagem and Snecma).

French Industry Today: Continued Consolidation, Downsizing and Reshaping[243]

Today, France still retains some of the broadest defense industrial capabilities within Europe, with a leadership role in core sectors (electronics, space and missiles) and strong capabilities in other areas (aeronautics and naval).[244]

The French defense industry had turnover of €14.6 billion in 2005 (€10.8 billion for national needs, €3.8 billion for export delivery),[245] employing about 165,000 people in France.[246] These numbers represent thousands of firms, large and small, operating in every sector of defense.

As domestic defense spending declined or became flat, French industry has had to become more export-oriented, as shown in Figures 61 and 62. Specifically, during the period 1996-2005, armament export represented around 30 percent of French defense industry turnover.[247] French armament material orders for export were €5.8 billion in 2006, up from €4.2 billion in 2005.[248]

---

[240] F. Heisbourg, H. Masson, M. Lundmark, et al., *Prospects on the European Defense Industry*, Defense Analysis Institute, Athens Greece (2003), in cooperation with the *Fondation pour la Recherche Stratégique*, Paris, and the German Institute for International and Security Affairs..

[241] The firm was formerly known as *Directions des Constructions Navales* (DCN).

[242] C. Paulin, *French Defense Industry: at a Crossroads*, Part 2, *Fondation pour la Recherche Stratégique*, 2007.

[243] *The Fondation pour la Recherche Stratégique* has published a number of reports and essays that describe all aspects of the consolidation of the French industry and implications of closer European industry integration. English language versions of several of these are on the FRS website. Available at: http://www.frstrategie.org.

[244] DGA Briefing on "Defense Industrial Policy" (unpublished).

[245] SGA, *Annuaire statistique de la défense 2007-2008*.

[246] Note this turnover number does not represent global sales or employees of all French located firms operating in various nations; e.g., this includes the portion of EADS operating in France. The global revenues of major French firms are set forth in the text below.

[247] Export data provided by French MoD DGA/D4S. This percentage is also reflected in the annual public DGA report. Available at: http://www.defense.gouv.fr/dga.

[248] French MoD, *Report to the French Parliament regarding defense equipment exports in 2006*, Point of contact Monsieur Patrick Blanc-Brude.

Figure 61   French Armament Material Orders for Export (Billions of Euros–€)

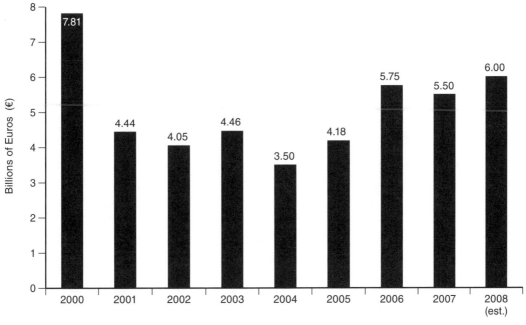

Source: DGA, *Bilan d'activité 2007.*

Figure 62   French Defense Industry Sales, 1996-2005 (Billions of Euros–€)

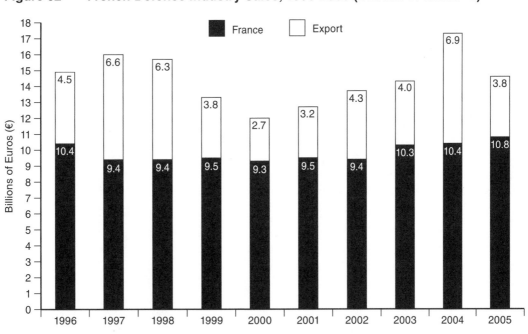

Sources: SGA, *Annuaire statistique de la défense 2007-2008.* DGA, *Direction des systemes de forces et des strategies industrielles, technologie et de cooperation.*

The reshaping of the industry has had a number of significant consequences. First, the increasing privatization of French firms—the reduction of a French state role and their participation in public capital markets—has led to larger French firms with better capabilities to compete internationally—including in the U.S. defense market.

Second, the French firms interviewed by this study team expressed an energetic desire and plan to expand their presence in the U.S. defense and security markets. As global firms, they see this strong U.S. presence as absolutely essential. The French government, focused on maintaining its defense autonomy, has generally not sought to achieve Transatlantic integration of defense markets or acted overtly either to facilitate or hinder the evolution of more Transatlantic defense firms. Rather, when the French government has acted in the past, it has been to use its influence to champion defense industry consolidation within France itself, e.g., forming today's Thales, EADS and SAFRAN. In the past the French government at times exerted some behind-the-scenes pressure to discourage acquisitions or joint ventures with U.S. firms that it felt might lead French industry too close to the U.S. orbit. However, in recent years the French government has not interfered as French defense firms have modestly increased their U.S. holdings.

Notwithstanding the downsizing, there remain a number of sectors where there is insufficient national demand to support the current domestic industrial capabilities and further consolidation is needed. The low volume of purchases, declining program needs and other factors are creating a supply-and-demand imbalance. The DGA recognizes that it faces a risk of gradual decline in these sectors and understands the need for some adjustment.

The Shift Toward European Defense Cooperation and a More "European" Industry

The economics of defense in Europe—shrinking budgets, growing weapons systems costs and consolidating firms—has increasingly led to more cooperative European defense projects and programs where developments can be shared and sales can be more widespread. Joint ventures and joint projects, coupled with the pan-European industry consolidation, are forming an increasingly shared European defense technology and industrial base (DTIB)—albeit with a long way to go to become fully integrated.

Consistent with its growing focus on European defense, France has actively invested in many European joint projects and developments. France and other European governments have taken actions to foster these developments and European firms have increasingly formed joint ventures and other types of collaboration. For example, one major French firm estimates it has about 17,000 employees involved in joint ventures today.

Today, the growing role of European cooperative programs is clear. France is a leader in cooperative engagement within Europe—with the largest spending on cooperative programs of any country studied in recent years. A snapshot of the French procurement and R&D budgets shows some 65 percent in national programs, 31 percent in European cooperative programs, and the remainder divided between U.S. and other countries. The data is supported by interviews with French-based firms that estimated about 30 percent of their program base is European cooperative (France plus one or more European partners). Of the six major programs under OCCAR (Organization for Joint Armament Cooperation) oversight today, France is a key partner in five of them. These include:

- A400M Transport Aircraft (Germany, Spain, Turkey, Belgium and Luxembourg)
- FREMM European Multi-Mission Frigate (Italy)
- COBRA Counter Battery/Missile Radar (UK, Germany and Turkey)
- FSAF Shipboard Surface to Air Missile (Italy and UK)
- TIGER Attack Helicopter (Germany and Spain)

French cooperation with European partners extends beyond development or production programs. France and the UK signed an agreement in early 2008 to share R&D costs for future modular missiles and they are currently discussing sharing carriers between their Navies (i.e., making carrier air groups interoperable so that British aircraft can fly from French carriers and vice versa). Further, in recent years, France has also emphasized cooperative technology demonstrators with European partners, including areas such as radar, optics, unmanned aerial vehicles (UAVs), and chemical-biological defense. Approximately 15 percent of French research and technology funds today are applied to such international or cooperative projects.

France has been one of the most aggressively "pro-EU" nations. It has had a leadership role in promoting the creation of an overall EU defense identity and the European Defence Agency (EDA). France also has been supportive of strengthening the EU's role in creating a European, as distinct from national, defense procurement system.

Additionally, the French government has helped orchestrate and support intra-European transactions—notably the creation of EADS from leading German, French and Spanish firms. This approach is consistent with the French view that these consolidations allow security autonomy and create stronger firms from a technological and financial standpoint that can better compete with American defense firms.[249]

The recent French White Paper confirms and accelerates this Europeanization trend. It states that the defense industry "must be European" and that "individual European countries can no longer master every technology and capability at national level."[250] Consistent with this goal, it calls for the restructuring of the European defense industry. While France has increasingly placed some of its scarce defense resources into European cooperative or joint programs, the question still remains of how far France will go in sending resources and jobs out of national boundaries and into neighboring EU Member States. Analysts frequently note that France is concerned about the potential that the EU's growing authority may conflict with national goals.

---

[249] François Lureau, former Chief Executive of DGA, French MoD, Speech to the Royal United Services Institute for Defence and Security Studies (RUSI), London, Nov. 19, 2004 ("[T]he complexity of our defence system makes it essential for companies to be able to embrace the whole scope of technologies and to be of a financial strength large enough to contract with governments on large systems."). Monsieur Lureau was succeeded as Chief Executive by Laurent Collet-Billon on June 28, 2008.

[250] French White Paper, Ibid., p. 7.

Principal French Defense Firms

Table 28　French Defense Companies in Global Top 100

Company Name	Global Rank	Defense Revenues (Billions of Dollars–$)	Total Revenues (Billions of Dollars–$)	Main Business Areas
EADS*	7	12.24	57.60	Aircraft; Space; Communications; Electronics; Ground Combat Systems; C4I
Thales Group	11	7.25	18.60	Electronics; Communications; Information Technology
DCNS	18	4.16	4.16	Shipbuilding
SAFRAN	22	3.16	17.70	Aerospace Propulsion
Dassault Aviation	28	2.53	5.89	Combat Aircraft

*EADS is a multinational consortium headquartered in the Netherlands but has a substantial French presence, and is considered by many to be mainly a French company.

Source: Defense News Top 100 Rankings for 2007 and Groupe SNPE.[251]

As shown in Table 28, three of the five largest defense firms operating in France—EADS, Thales, and SAFRAN—have global sales and operations and were formed through consolidations over the past decade.

Thales. Consolidation has built Thales into a multisector, multicountry player and one of the largest defense firms in France and in the world, with an estimated €14 billion in turnover in 2008. Thales considers itself a multidomestic firm (not solely a "French" firm), as about half of its 68,000 employees are in 13 nations outside France. Of course, the largest concentration of Thales employees (roughly 35,000) is still in France. But ten years ago *100 percent* of Thales employees were in France. Thales' business is roughly 50 percent defense, 25 percent civil aerospace and 25 percent security. Because Thales has approximately 3,000 employees (including joint ventures) in the United States and considers the United States a critical market, it values highly its relationships, product and technology access with U.S. defense customers and industry. The French state continues to hold a golden share in Thales, and the "public sector" owns 27.3 percent (this concept of public sector ownership is not technically state ownership but does not exist in the United States).

EADS. The largest global defense firm operating in France, European Aeronautical, Defence and Space Company (EADS) has a core presence in four European countries: Germany, France, the UK and Spain. EADS worldwide had €39 billion in sales in 2007, and 116,000 employees (about 44,500 in France). EADS had upwards of €10 billion in defense sales in 2007 (if relevant aspects of A400M military transport and space are included). About 50 percent of EADS defense work is located in Germany, making the German government more often a customer of EADS than of Thales. But since EADS is the parent company of Airbus, a large portion of its aerospace sales and aerospace work is carried out in France (note also that EADS is 100 percent owner of Eurocopter). EADS has about 17,000 employees in the UK, of which 12,000 are also in civil aerospace. The French government owner-ship fractions of EADS are complex and are outlined in detail in the discussion on Government Ownership under III. Evaluation of Market Access Metrics later in this chapter, and in Table 30.

SAFRAN. Created through the merger of Sagem and SNECMA, SAFRAN is a global firm with €12 billion in sales in 2007 and 57,000 employees (mostly in France). Half of its sales are in aerospace and defense propulsion (former Snecma aerospace), and 50 percent of those propulsion sales are in Europe and about 30 percent are in North America. The French State owns 35 percent of SAFRAN, and there is 7.4 percent public sector ownership.

Dassault Aviation, the fourth largest firm also has global sales (€4 billion, 2007). Its primary business is military aircraft and executive jets, UAVs, and some space work. Dassault has a U.S. operating arm in Falcon Jet, a commercial business jet business. It is privately held (ownership is 50.55 percent by Groupe Industriel M. Dassault, 46.3 percent EADS and 3.15 percent free float) but has not participated notably in the consolidation.

More national-centric firms: Nexter, DCNS and SNPE. The French ground vehicle, naval and nuclear sectors remain more national in character—that is, not as consolidated with other sector capabilities and subject to more state control. These French firms still have large or full national ownership stakes: DCNS (Naval), which is 75 percent state-owned, and Nexter (former-GIAT, ground vehicles and ammunition) and SNPE (energetic materials, chemicals), which both are essentially 100 percent state-owned. SNPE has been in the process of selling its business units, effectively reducing the French State ownership of some parts of this business. Given limited demand for new national level systems, upwards of 25 percent of Nexter sales today are export. Note that of these, only DCNS ranks among the top 100 defense companies worldwide. GIAT, which once competed globally with GDLS, BAE and other companies in the ground combat systems market, has lost much of its market share and is no longer a major player in that market.

B. The Re-Shaping of French Acquisition and Defense Industrial Strategy to Meet New National Security Needs—From National to Strategic Autonomy

On the demand side, the changing threat environment and France's growing role in expeditionary operations have caused a realignment in its acquisition system and defense industrial policy. In particular, the fundamental shift from national to strategic (i.e., Euro-centric) autonomy drives changes in procurement and industrial policies. France may no longer need to procure all its products nationally, but it must have the secure ability to access the products and services it needs for autonomous European operations.

Within this framework, the new defense procurement and industrial strategies (supply and demand) focus on "competitive autonomy," including:

- Better value buying (economic efficiency);

- A new security of supply construct that limits the defense industrial sectors that must be retained on a national basis and broadens France's willingness to rely on "secure" sources outside of France; and

- A thrust for European solutions where possible consistent with its shift toward Eurocentric rather than national defense autonomy.

Competitive Autonomy: A Better Value Buying Strategy

French officials note that France long has had an image as a protectionist and relatively closed market—and they note the United States has a similar reputation. However, French acquisition policy is undergoing a sea change. It is gradually shifting from a system based on national buying on a largely non-competitive basis to a somewhat more open system of buying the best performing and most cost-effective solutions on a competitive basis, rather than relying on national favorites.

Specifically, in November 2004, DGA's Chief Executive, François Lureau, described the new "Competitive Autonomy" as having two goals:

> The first one is to optimise the economic efficiency of investments made by the Ministry of Defence to meet Armed Forces' requirements. The second one is to guarantee access to the industrial and technological capabilities on which the long-term fulfillment of these requirements depends, to make it short: the security of supply issue. To obtain the best return on investments in terms of the national defence system's efficiency, priority shall be given to market rules and competitive biddings. The Ministry of Defence must therefore seek to maintain and develop an industrial and technological base which degree of autonomy at the national and European levels should guarantee secure supply sources for the Armed forces, unrestricted use of equipment procured and the possibility of exporting arms to friendly nations and allies.[252]

The French MoD/DGA has been implementing this policy, which it officially defines as: "Maintaining an autonomous capability of design and realization of key armament systems at national and cooperative levels to enable France's:

- Security of supply
- Freedom of use of equipment procured
- Possibility to export to allies and partner countries."[253]

In short, this policy reflects economic and industrial realities: France alone simply cannot sustain a level of investment to maintain full capabilities across defense industry sectors. Complex products designed and developed for France alone cannot be cost-effective for the French budget, or cost-competitive in export markets. Thus, this new policy, if fully implemented, produces a "better" if not best value buying strategy. There is more competition, but not all programs will be competitive and nationality still matters but less so than in the past.

C. French Defense Industrial Policy: Applying Competitive Autonomy

France's core acquisition strategy drives its industrial policies. The central principle is that since secure European sources of supply can meet France's need for strategic autonomy, France does not have to maintain a full-spectrum national defense industry in all areas. France's new buying policy thus would no longer develop French new systems or prefer French systems as a default position. Rather, France will use a sectoral approach. Specifi-

---

[252] F. Lureau, Speech to RUSI, Nov. 19, 2004, Ibid.

[253] French MoD, DGA/D4S.

Figure 63   DGA Competitive Autonomy Strategy by Sector

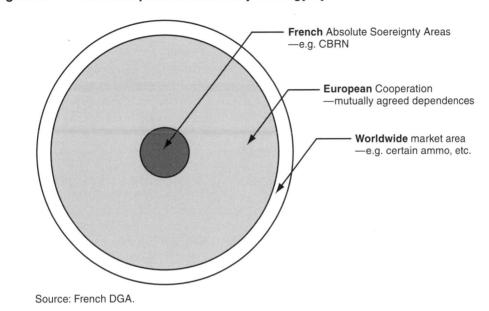

French Absolute Soereignty Areas
—e.g. CBRN

European Cooperation
—mutually agreed dependences

Worldwide market area
—e.g. certain ammo, etc.

Source: French DGA.

cally, DGA has prioritized the degree of national autonomy using a series of concentric circles, illustrated in Figure 63.

1. **French Sovereign Capabilities:** The small center of the circle includes those limited areas of capability that France believes must remain national in character because they are vital to national sovereignty. These include only strategic nuclear systems; chemical, biological and radiological (CBRN) defense; and certain intelligence functions.

2. **European Shared Dependencies.** A second concentric circle—the largest—includes equipment sectors that can be acquired through cooperation with European partner nations or allies. Equipment in this category can be procured on the European market or manufactured through European cooperation. This approach envisages stronger defense industrial cooperation between Member States within a framework of mutually accepted interdependence; the LOI Framework Agreement, for example, has security of supply provisions that would support this interdependence and protect each nation's sovereign interests. The White Paper describes most industry sectors as "European cooperative markets." On the supply side, it calls for less fragmentation in European markets, stating directly that the space industry in Europe must be rationalized. The idea is to gradually develop widely accepted European centers of excellence (such as the agreement being negotiated with Sweden and Finland on explosives).

3. **Worldwide Market.** The third concentric circle, which appears very narrow in scope, represents equipment for which the MoD will turn to the global marketplace—i.e., including the United States and Israel, an increasing competitor in French markets. By way of illustration, these products include 5.56mm ammunitions, camouflage systems, and specific products to be procured in very limited

quantities. According to DGA officials, this category is for procurements where there is no specific interest in strategic autonomy at the European level or where relying on European sources of supply would not be cost-effective.

In essence, under this concentric circle strategy, France will rely on both European cooperative programs and more competition involving foreign suppliers to sustain a vibrant European DTIB. Significantly, for France, this expressly means relying on other European partners even for some core capabilities. Therefore, security of supply from these other nations is a critical underlying condition for France. DGA explains that this is carried out by European industrial reciprocal agreements and formal mutual interdependence. To some extent new European Commission (EC) Directives or laws, as they evolve, could also be a help.

Finally, this strategy places export sales in an increasingly critical position for the national firms in France. As part of its investment strategy, the DGA has examined the range of sectors and capabilities France needs *vis-à-vis* which of those sectors is dual-use or defense unique, combined with which is attractive for export sales (e.g., transport aircraft or C4ISR products) or strongly dependent on domestic buying (e.g., nuclear submarines or heavy armored vehicles). The French DGA views exports as one way to help preserve needed defense capabilities across buying cycles and system/product generations.

Will the Shift From National to European Preferences Be Real?

Analysts in France believe it is too soon to tell if France can move dramatically away from national defense preferences. Market participants interviewed in other countries also expressed some skepticism that France would truly change and open its markets to other European firms. A key indicator is where France is willing to put its resources over time. The most likely scenario is seen in the preference for bilateral agreements and dependences between relative peers in capability that France already has shown—rather than pushing French funds to broad EU-wide initiatives.[254]

A concept in investigation between the UK and France today is called "Domain Pooling." This idea is to put together two strong but complementary capabilities between firms in France and the UK and work to strengthen technology and products out of their combined work. The March 2008 summit between French President Sarkozy and UK Prime Minister Brown agreed on some initial areas for such joint investment.

France's competitive autonomy policy has already had some results. As discussed in-depth below, *France is gradually becoming an increasingly open, competitive market in defense*. This is the message received from every interview—industry, government, academics and analysts. To be sure, this change is evolutionary in nature; the legacy systems that dominate the market still tend to look French and single-sourced. And the move may not be fast and it is not always what all U.S. or other nations' firms might wish, but it is nonetheless the overriding message.

---

[254] Some more cynical observers see French self-interest at the core of the French drive for a Eurocentric market. If successful, France would have much to gain from an economic, industrial and international prestige standpoint. "Who better to lead than France?" This attitude, mirrored by U.S. unilateral global behavior, is often the source of the friction in the Franco-American relationship: each side sees their own position of leadership as legitimate.

For example, U.S. companies are being encouraged to bid on the new Scorpion next-generation land vehicle program (analogous to the U.S. Future Combat Systems family of vehicles), which will be awarded based by a competition involving European, U.S. and Israeli firms. These types of programs would appear to be the types that would be European focused and not open to U.S. and Israeli competitors. Yet, DGA officials noted that not all elements of this program would be in the second (European) circle and that considerations such as interoperability and affordability were relevant in determining whether non-European firms could compete. *In effect, France will probably evolve a preference to buy European but only where it is available, capable and affordable.*

> The key open question for the United States is whether this market opening extends only to Europe and or perhaps primarily to large, peer European nations. On this question, only time will tell. In this regard, it should be recognized that the outer circle, labeled "Worldwide market area," appears very small in the DGA charts. The overall policy thrust appears in this direction of better value European buying. For example, DGA sources indicated that they might try to organize a European effort to develop a next generation fighter aircraft or surveillance UAV. Nevertheless, as market participants have noted, budgetary and economic realities suggest that the category of buying open to the United States may in practice prove broader.
>
> Simply put, French aspirations for a European DTIB and European procurement may very well be subordinated to best value considerations of cost and capability in cases when France faces a choice between an existing, highly capable and affordable U.S. system and an undeveloped or more costly, less capable European alternative.

Ownership Does Matter, and "European Means European"

Both the French White Paper and the DGA's Competitive Autonomy policy reflect a desire to maintain a strong DTIB, but one increasingly European rather than solely French in focus. As noted above, the White Paper states and French DGA officials confirmed that the Competitive Autonomy policy means significant further European rationalization—and hence additional consolidation of European ownership.

Under the DGA vision, this primarily European consolidation would result in the creation of European "centers of excellence" that would presumably gain more work over time as they compete in their areas of expertise, driving out lesser capabilities or excess capacity. While French government officials are quick to note there are no *formal* exclusions of responsible non-European (i.e., U.S.) owners of defense firms, there plainly appears to be an informal European ownership preference going forward (see discussion of foreign investment metric below).

To quote a DGA official, a core precept of French industrial policy is that "*ownership matters*" when it comes to firms critical to national security. DGA officials expressed concerns of the potential for harm that foreign companies or financial buyers could pose in acquiring French defense firms. The concerns fall broadly into two categories:

1. **Stewardship for National Security vs. Maximizing Efficiency/Profitability.** One concern is whether firms' stewardship of defense businesses meet long-term critical national security needs. A new owner might rationalize a defense firm or reduce investments in low or cyclic volume businesses to seek more profit, but result in less ability to meet French defense needs over time. And this issue extends beyond development or production into a large number of fielded systems for which the French military must have assured support for many years to come. In upgrade and logistics support contracts, the MoD needs firms who understand their weapon and logistics systems, force concepts, fielding and fighting needs—all critical to effective military forces. For example, how might a new buyer view the need to maintain the Leclerc Main Battle Tank? The buyer would need to retain the skills and experience, data and capital equipment held today by Nexter. The MoD could not allow a simple shutdown of such under-capacity facilities and outsource these military needs—this would take careful planning and long-term support assurances that might not be attractive to a buyer who was predominantly financially motivated.

2. **Concern over Reliance on ITAR-Controlled Articles That Limit French Flexibility.** As discussed earlier, French policy continues to seek flexibility and independence with respect to the fielding, use and export of French defense systems and subsystems. Hence, there is a concern that foreign (including U.S.) ownership could lead to reliance on ITAR-controlled articles that could limit its freedom of action. The White Paper and evolving French policy and practice plainly include a preference for autonomous European systems with no strings attached.

III. Evaluation of Market Access Metrics

Generally, France is considered an excellent environment for trade and investment with the United States. With the sixth largest economy in the world, it has an advanced defense technology and industrial base. France also has a well-developed, predictable and largely transparent legal system that provides certainty for U.S. investors and U.S. firms doing business there.[255]

As discussed below, however, the picture is different in the French defense marketplace, which has been emerging from a history of being largely national in its orientation.

Tariff Barriers

By and large, tariffs are not significant barriers between France and the United States. All of the countries studied are members of the World Trade Organization (WTO) and thus must provide most-favored-nation and national treatment to imported goods from every other country included in the study. Although defense products are generally exempt from WTO rules governing tariffs and trade, reciprocal procurement MOUs between the United States and France generally provide duty-free treatment for imported defense products procured from the other countries.

---

[255] See U.S. Department of Commerce Foreign Commercial Service, France, website. Available at: http://www.buyusa.gov/france/en/112.html.

However, the MOUs do not apply to dual-use products and technologies such as general aerospace systems that have both military and civil applications. Thus, as more military programs rely on commercial off-the-shelf (COTS) technology, this would tend to put U.S. companies at a competitive disadvantage *vis-à-vis* European firms that get the benefit of the lower intra-European rates that apply under EU rules unless specific exemptions are negotiated on a bilateral basis.

Competition in Procurement

While France is making changes in law and policy designed to create greater openness and more competition in defense procurement, the French market at this point still remains very difficult for all foreign firms, including American firms, to penetrate.

French Procurement Policy: A Shift Toward Competitive Autonomy

As discussed above, there is a significant evolution in French acquisition policy underway, as reflected in the 2008 *Livre Blanc* and actual practices being implemented in specific procurements. Under the new Competitive Autonomy policy, there is a clear shift away from reliance on sole source French suppliers toward more European solutions and competition. Competition will now be open to other European firms for strategic purchases, and to firms from the United States and other foreign countries for non-strategic purchases, where economics is the dominant consideration in purchasing. As noted above, France put in place in 2004 a new law requiring competition of new buys unless a specific exception applies. The new law also extends to upgrades of existing platforms. For example, Boeing provided a common technical data package on its KC-135 in France that the French MoD uses to compete upgrade programs on that platform.

There also is growing anecdotal evidence of this policy shift toward more open and competitive procurement:

- French government officials and executives at French and U.S. firms active in France consistently reported that France is becoming a more open and competitive defense market today than in previous history. Some U.S. firms reported that France's procurement practices are notably less national in tone and attitude today. For example, at times French officials alert them of bid opportunities. They find France interested in U.S. products where they represent a good value solution (best for the price) or have a special technology niche or advantage at a good price.

- Specific reports of active competitions were provided by various defense firms, including programs and concept studies for new Army ground architecture and related systems, a vertical takeoff and landing UAV, and a heavy lift helicopter.

- American firms (especially at the subsystem level) note that they meet more competition than ever in France. Ironically, in some respects, they might be worse off than in the past, when they sold items on a sole source or directed basis. Today, the larger, global firms formed from the European consolidation—e.g., Thales, EADS, MBDA, SAFRAN—have competitive products or find a teammate that does (e.g., Israeli firms). These firms/teams can meet U.S. firms' performance offerings more closely than in the past, and do not have the ITAR limits (see discussion below).

Hence, American firms understand the need to increasingly focus their efforts on products where they have better capabilities, which of course are more likely to run into ITAR restrictions.

- French support for the EDA Code of Conduct on Defence Procurement and the draft EC Defense Procurement Directive indicate support for open competition.

- France has been among the most active users of the EDA's Electronic Bulletin Boards (see discussion in Chapter 5), according to EDA officials, and from July 2006 to April 2008 posted 78 contract opportunities—more than any other EU Member State.[256]

Small and Medium-Sized Enterprises. Unlike U.S. law, the French *Code des Marchés Publics* (Public Procurement Code) does not allow France DGA to set aside certain quotas for small and medium-sized enterprises (SMEs). DGA is taking other steps to support this SME sector by facilitating their access to business opportunities. The DGA seeks a robust SME sector and is wary of larger defense firms using "vertical integration" and possibly overtaking roles that may be served by SMEs.

French Procurement Practice: A Lag Between Policy and Practice

While the stated new policies of the DGA in recent years and available anecdotal evidence of change are quite promising, the data by and large does not reflect a major sea change in French acquisition practices to date. Moreover, as noted above, interviewees in a number of countries outside of France (representatives of non-French, European defense firms) were skeptical that France would award significant systems contracts to non-French firms.

In practice, as shown below, the available data continues to show substantial reliance on sole source national buying in France. However, there is a very sizable and growing reliance on European buying (primarily through cooperative programs) and some evidence of new competitive buying (with both European and U.S. firms winning some awards). U.S. firms have a minor market share in France today. Prospects for the future will also be limited if the new policy is fully implemented—given the clear policy preference for European solutions under Competitive Autonomy. The specifics are as follows:

French Buying of Major Weapons Systems: The Limited Role of Competition. As shown on Table 29, a review of the top 72 French defense programs by value[257] during the period 2006-2008 shows that only 8 programs worth $1 billion (3 percent by value) were awarded competitively. Fifty two programs worth $17.5 billion (65 percent) were awarded sole source, while the remaining eleven programs worth $8.5 billion (31 percent) were European multinational cooperative programs in which work share was negotiated in advance as an element of intergovernmental MOUs (see Figure 64). This data generally confirms observations of market participants interviewed (although some would suggest a lower percentage of sole source sales). Several other observations about overall French buying are worth noting:

- **Sole Source Awards Are Larger Than Competitive Awards.** At $339 million, the average sole source contract was considerably larger than the average com-

---

[256] Based on data provided to the study team by EDA.

[257] The data set includes French RDT&E and Procurement programs in the five sectors included in this study totaling more than $50 million during 2006-2008. See Chapters 2 and Appendices for detailed methodology.

Table 29   **France—Leading Defense Programs by Value (Millions of Constant 2008 Dollars—$)**

System Supplier	System Supplier Full Name	Item Name	Program 2006	Program 2007	Program 2008	Program TOTAL	Procurement Type	Legacy
Airbus	Airbus Industrie	A400M	2,569.39	2,569.39	856.46	5,995.24	Multinational	No
DCNS Group	DCNS Group	S619 Le Terrible	1,549.93	1,559.18	1,568.42	4,677.53	Sole Source	Yes
Dassault	Dassault Aviation	Rafale Multi-Role Fighter	1,623.16	1,132.48	1,366.62	4,122.26	Sole Source	Yes
EADS	European Aeronautical Defense and Space Company NV	Tiger	264.72	526.21	354.86	1,145.79	Multinational	No
DCNS Group	DCNS Group	S620 Suffren	220.54	384.11	385.09	989.74	Sole Source	Yes
MBDA	MBDA	ASMP - A / Air-to-Surface Medium-Range	428.23	240.88	240.88	909.99	Sole Source	Yes
DCNS Group	DCNS Group	Porte-avions 2 (PA2)	73.51	110.27	407.20	590.98	Sole Source	No
DCNS Group	DCNS Group	D617 Chevalier Paul	191.15	192.29	193.42	576.86	Sole Source	No
Armaris	Armaris	FS Aquitaine (FREMM)	131.71	207.10	181.00	519.81	Multinational	No
Nexter	Nexter	Leclerc	158.38	160.35	162.33	481.05	Sole Source	Yes
DCNS Group	DCNS Group	D616 Forbin	193.42	99.54	100.11	393.07	Sole Source	Yes
DCNS Group	DCNS Group	SSN Support	125.58	125.58	125.58	376.75	Sole Source	Yes
SAFRAN	SAFRAN	GFE Acft Engine set for Rafale F2B	153.85	105.99	98.25	358.09	Sole Source	Yes
DCNS Group	DCNS Group	SSBN Engr Service (France)	90.87	90.87	90.87	272.61	Sole Source	Yes
General Electric	General Electric	Vehicle Services	0.00	120.00	120.00	240.00	Competitive	No
Volvo Group	Volvo Group	RGBC 180	66.41	68.06	69.71	204.18	Competitive	No
EADS/Thales	European Aeronautical Defense and Space Company NV	MOIE SIC	60.00	72.00	72.00	204.00	Directed	No
MBDA	MBDA	Apache-EG/Scalp EG	89.29	119.42	94.45	187.43	Multinational	No
FranceCarrier Tm	French New Carrier Team	Porte-avions 2 (PA2) Design	102.10	79.64	0.00	181.74	Competitive	No
DCNS Group	DCNS Group	S616 Le Triomphant	20.69	75.08	74.34	170.11	Sole Source	Yes
SAFRAN	SAFRAN	SITEL	35.13	65.10	66.70	166.94	Sole Source	No
SAFRAN	SAFRAN	French FELIN C2 SDD & Prod.	14.48	71.60	72.93	159.01	Sole Source	No
MBDA	MBDA	MICA-EM	58.25	54.23	44.90	157.39	Multinational	Yes
Nexter	Nexter	VBCI/VCI	14.08	16.39	119.05	149.51	Sole Source	No
Thales Alenia Sp	Thales Alenia Space	Syracuse III Mil. Comm Payload	0.00	147.36	1.04	148.40	Sole Source	Yes
Thales	Thales Group	Syracuse 3 Services/Support	36.74	52.48	52.48	141.69	Sole Source	Yes

Table 29   France—Leading Defense Programs by Value (Millions of Constant 2008 Dollars—$ continued)

System Supplier	System Supplier Full Name	Item Name	Program 2006	Program 2007	Program 2008	Program TOTAL	Procurement Type	Legacy
DCNS Group	DCNS Group	S618 Le Vigilant	46.22	46.22	46.22	138.66	Sole Source	Yes
DCNS Group	DCNS Group	Brest Warship Maintenance	45.95	45.95	45.95	137.84	Sole Source	Yes
DCNS Group	DCNS Group	L-9014 Tonnerre	95.70	39.72	2.25	137.67	Sole Source	Yes
Nexter	Nexter	Caesar	8.56	54.98	73.32	136.86	Sole Source	No
MBDA	MBDA	MICA-IR	53.85	39.57	40.40	133.82	Multinational	Yes
EADS	European Aeronautical Defense and Space Company NV	SIR Dev. and Support	42.82	42.82	42.82	128.47	Sole Source	Yes
DCNS Group	DCNS Group	French Frigate Maintenance	50.03	50.03	25.53	125.58	Sole Source	Yes
Alcatel-Lucent	Alcatel-Lucent	Systeme Preparatoire Infra-Rouge pour l'Alerte	1.02	1.02	104.14	106.18	Sole Source	No
EADS	European Aeronautical Defense and Space Company NV	AS.532 Mk II/EC225	47.92	49.10	8.24	105.26	Sole Source	No
Thales	Thales Group	Arabel	41.84	43.32	19.54	104.70	Sole Source	No
AUVERLAND	Societe Nouvelle des Automobiles Auverland (SNAA)	ERC 90 "Sagaie"	0.00	50.39	50.86	101.25	Sole Source	Yes
Thales	Thales Group	French BOA C2 Risk Reduction	60.00	40.00	0.00	100.00	Sole Source	No
Thales	Thales Group	Syracuse 3 SATCOM Terminal	36.01	29.89	28.05	93.95	Sole Source	No
DCNS Group	DCNS Group	R91 Charles De Gaulle	31.43	30.31	29.19	90.93	Sole Source	Yes
CNIM	Constructions Navales et Industrielles de la Mediterranee	MAB	0.00	34.23	47.47	81.70	Sole Source	No
Thales	Thales Group	MARTHA NC3 Dev. and Prod.	26.76	26.76	26.76	80.29	Sole Source	No
Various	Various	A340-200 Services	16.34	31.65	31.65	79.64	Competitive	No
EADS	European Aeronautical Defense and Space Company NV	EC 145	0.00	25.86	52.22	78.09	Sole Source	No
DCNS Group	DCNS Group	R91 Charles De Gaulle Support	0.00	0.00	75.40	75.40	Sole Source	Yes
Thales	Thales Group	DR-4000	26.39	27.56	21.36	75.32	Sole Source	Yes
EADS	European Aeronautical Defense and Space Company NV	EC 145	71.13	1.38	1.37	73.88	Sole Source	No
Thales	Thales Group	SIC 21	23.82	24.46	25.10	73.37	Competitive	No

System Supplier	System Supplier Full Name	Item Name	Program 2006	Program 2007	Program 2008	Program TOTAL	Procurement Type	Legacy
Thales	Thales Group	RIFAN	18.67	26.17	28.01	72.85	Competitive	No
Thales	Thales Group	France TSC 2000 NGIFF	22.67	24.27	25.87	72.81	Multinational	No
EADS	European Aeronautical Defense and Space Company NV	EC135	0.00	28.82	43.79	72.61	Multinational	No
ThalesRaytheon	ThalesRaytheonSystems (TRS)	M3R	0.00	23.40	47.71	71.11	Multinational	No
Northrop Grumman	Northrop Grumman	APY-2 RSIP Upgrade Kit	59.98	4.52	4.52	69.02	Sole Source	No
EADS	European Aeronautical Defense and Space Company NV	AS.565SA	29.59	37.49	1.37	68.45	Sole Source	Yes
Nexter	Nexter	AMX-30 EBG	54.45	10.97	2.65	68.06	Sole Source	Yes
Nexter	Nexter	AMX-10P Upgrade	12.25	30.97	24.46	67.68	Sole Source	Yes
Thales	Thales Group	PR4G	21.44	22.46	23.48	67.39	Sole Source	Yes
EADS	European Aeronautical Defense and Space Company NV	SIR Command Post Production	22.21	23.82	19.27	65.31	Sole Source	Yes
Thales	Thales Group	France MOE SIC Terre	6.79	6.79	51.05	64.63	Sole Source	No
Volvo Group	Volvo Group	TRM 2000	23.99	21.17	18.35	63.50	Competitive	No
Socarenam	Socarenam	Coast Guard Patrol Craft	30.18	30.36	0.36	60.90	Sole Source	No
Moss S.A.S.	Moss S.A.S.	SCCOA-3	42.44	14.39	3.04	59.87	Sole Source	Yes
Nexter	Nexter	MUSJAS 3 (Adv. Aerial BONUS)	22.01	22.01	13.84	57.86	Sole Source	Yes
Thales	Thales Group	France SOCRATE	19.74	19.14	18.55	57.43	Sole Source	Yes
AUVERLAND	Societe Nouvelle des Automobiles Auverland (SNAA)	VBL M11	46.82	7.12	3.04	56.98	Sole Source	No
Nexter	Nexter	MUSJAS 3 (Adv. Aerial BONUS)	22.01	22.01	11.01	55.03	Sole Source	Yes
Thales	Thales Group	ARABEL C2	10.80	21.79	22.19	54.78	Sole Source	Yes
Dassault	Dassault Aviation	Mirage 2000 D	18.98	17.98	16.99	53.95	Sole Source	Yes
Conoship Intl	Conoship International B.V. (CI)	A 759 Dupuy De Lome	51.20	1.20	1.20	53.60	Multinational	Yes
MBDA	MBDA	ARF / French Anti-Radar Missile	21.41	16.06	16.06	53.53	Multinational	Yes
Thales	Thales Group	PR4G VS4-IP	8.80	17.62	26.59	53.00	Competitive	No
Alcatel-Lucent	Alcatel-Lucent	Polar Platform Metop-3	23.11	23.11	6.60	52.83	Sole Source	Yes

Source: Documental Solutions.

Figure 64   France—Total Procurement by Award Type

Figure 65   France—Legacy vs. New Procurement

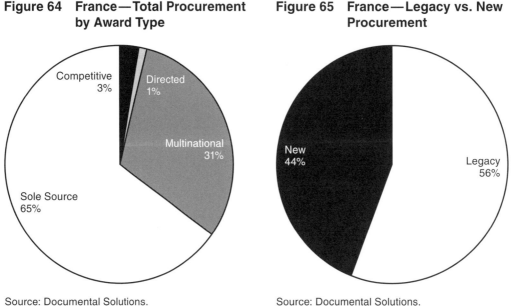

Source: Documental Solutions.

Source: Documental Solutions.

petitive award ($121 million). This suggests that France still prefers to procure its most complex and expensive systems from national sources or through cooperative development programs with other European countries (e.g., Eurofighter, Tiger, TTH90).

- **Overall Data Can Mask Differences Between Legacy/New Buying.** As discussed below, this overall data on total French buying in 2006-2008 may mask any distinctions between "legacy" programs (i.e., programs where the initial award for development and/or procurement were made somewhere in the past before 2006) and "new" programs started during 2006-2008 (which are more likely to show any meaningful shifts in procurement policy). Hence, we have separately reviewed the data on "legacy" and "new" programs below to capture any different trends that may exist.

- **A Large Share of Spending Is on Legacy Programs.** As shown on Figure 65, roughly 56 percent ($15.2 billion) of total procurement since 2006 was for legacy programs, reflecting the long development cycle of large programs and the long service life of major systems. (Interestingly, the French legacy share of spending is notably less than that of the United States, which had 77 percent legacy awards for major programs during the same period (see Chapter 3, Figure 32). The list of Top French Defense Programs (Table 29) is dominated by legacy programs initiated many years earlier (e.g., Rafael, ASMP, nuclear submarines and guided missile destroyers). The data also shows no new national programs worth more than $100 million started after 2004—indicating that economics is limiting significant new national program starts.

- **The existence of significant legacy systems also will likely cause any opening of the market to be gradual in nature.** Most of the sole source contracts relate

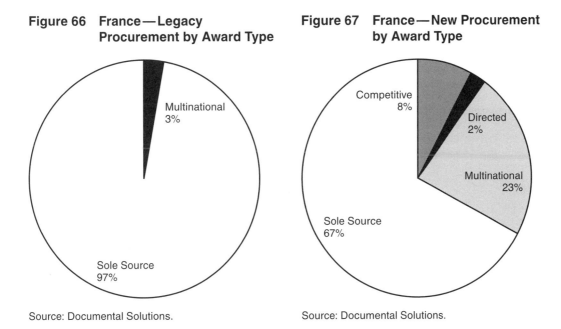

Figure 66 France—Legacy Procurement by Award Type

Multinational 3%

Sole Source 97%

Source: Documental Solutions.

Figure 67 France—New Procurement by Award Type

Competitive 8%

Directed 2%

Multinational 23%

Sole Source 67%

Source: Documental Solutions.

to legacy systems, which are likely to be fielded for years to come. In this platform area, it is less likely that the DGA will turn to new suppliers or open the market to competition (although, as in the United States and the UK, additional competition is possible in subsystems markets where technology refreshes can occur and new competitive procurements can be shaped). Indeed, France is considering entering into long-term support contracts for these legacy systems—an approach similar to that recently adopted by the UK (see Chapter 13). In these circumstances, competitive procurements are more likely to occur in major upgrades and new systems and products that are developed and fielded as legacy systems are replaced—a long-term exercise. This type of competition is likely in the short term in new ground systems like Scorpion (the French equivalent of the Future Combat Systems) or in UAV programs. It remains to be seen of course how much American participation will be permitted in these programs (i.e., whether all or most of the programs' elements will be restricted in significant ways to European participants).

- **Most Legacy Spending Is Sole Source or Directed and Goes to National Firms.** As Figure 66 shows, in this major program data set, approximately 97 percent of the legacy procurement awards by value were sole source; some 3 percent were multinational, and *none* were awarded through "open and competitive" procurement. The magnitude of sole source buying reflects the realities of large defense programs. After a major system has been awarded to a particular firm, the follow-on production buys, upgrades, modifications and maintenance on such legacy programs are often awarded to the same firm again (e.g., after an award is made for an aircraft developed and produced by one firm, it is much more likely to be awarded to that firm for future buys). Indeed, it would be uneconomic to change system level contractors midstream on large programs unless the incumbent is not performing (although government customers can and should compete the subsystems upgrades

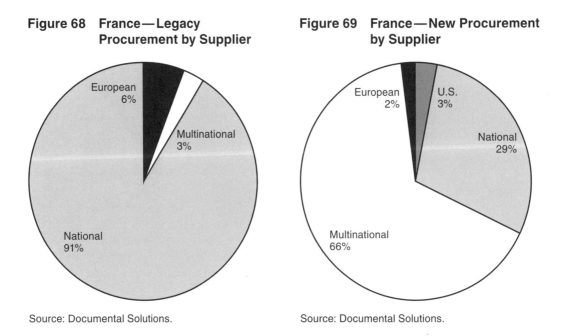

Figure 68   France—Legacy Procurement by Supplier

European 6%

Multinational 3%

National 91%

Source: Documental Solutions.

Figure 69   France—New Procurement by Supplier

European 2%

U.S. 3%

National 29%

Multinational 66%

Source: Documental Solutions.

and refreshes). Therefore, not surprisingly, the data (Figure 68) reflects that most of these legacy program sole source awards went to national firms—underscoring that France has continued to rely heavily on "national champions" such as EADS, Dassault and Nexter for its major acquisitions and has not opened most competition to non-French suppliers (European or American). It is noteworthy that there are virtually no sole source awards to other European suppliers.

- **New French Awards Show a Greater Emphasis on Cooperative Programs With a Small Amount of Open and Competitive Procurement.** In contrast, an assessment of new French procurement programs shows a marked change in buying habits—with significantly less reliance on sole source national awards and more focus on cooperative programs. As shown in Figure 67, approximately 67 percent of buying on new major contracts was sole source or directed, 8 percent was competitive, and the remaining 25 percent was multinational. While France still has the lowest level of competitive procurement of any country evaluated, that even 8 percent of new procurement was awarded competitively is a substantial improvement over the past (which saw little competitive procurement). Most competitive procurements of the last three years appear to be COTS solutions or in subsystem areas where France does not have a strong competitive advantage. In this regard, competitive programs were primarily in electronics, communication, command and control, and sensors—all areas where numerous off-the-shelf solutions were available.

- **New French Buying Is Heavily Multinational in Orientation With Some National Acquisitions.** As set forth on Figure 68, some 91 percent of legacy procurement was awarded to national companies, with multinational programs accounting for 6 percent and other European companies just 3 percent; U.S. companies did not win any major legacy contracts. However, as shown on Figure 69, new procurement is dominated by multinational programs (66 percent), with

Figure 70   France—Defense Market Share by Companies

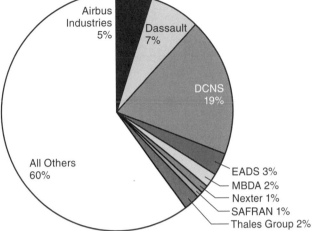

Source: Documental Solutions.

national companies accounting for 29 percent, U.S. companies 3 percent and other European companies 2 percent.

- **U.S. Firms Have a Miniscule Share of the French Defense Market.** No matter how the available program data is sorted, it is clear that U.S. companies have only a limited presence on major French defense programs. There are indications, however, that American firms can compete effectively in some circumstances:

    - **All Awards.** As shown on Figure 70, no American company ranked in the top ten for market share for *all awards*. Supporting data shows that General Electric had the largest contract award value among U.S. firms, but this amounted to just 0.2 percent of the total market.

    - **Legacy Awards.** As noted above, U.S. companies did not win any major legacy programs.

    - **New Awards.** U.S. firms received only 0.3 percent of all new procurement (competitive, sole source and cooperative) in recent years—a miniscule amount.

    - **New Competitive Awards.** U.S. companies won just one out of eight competitive contracts awarded for major programs, amounting to 25 percent of all competitive awards by value; this suggests that, in those instances when programs are competed, U.S. companies can in some circumstances win significant contracts.

- **U.S. Subsystems Sales Also Are Likely to Be Disadvantaged.** While there may be greater U.S. subsystem participation than this data shows (anecdotal evidence available to us suggests this), we lack the data to fully evaluate this part of the market. However, we do believe, as discussed elsewhere, that the trends toward buying European and avoiding ITAR products and technologies disfavor U.S. subsystem buying.

Fair and Transparent Procurement Process

In general, the French defense procurement system is viewed as relatively transparent and fair. France, like other EU Member States, is a party to the WTO Agreement on Government Procurement (AGP). However, its procurement of "warlike" goods is exempt from the AGP's coverage and, hence, only "non-warlike" goods are subject to the Agreement's disciplines.

The French government generally follows EC procurement regulations, which call for non-discrimination against foreign firms. In France, procurement regulations do not usually present barriers to entry for foreign firms. However, local political pressure and administrative procedures are often said to favor French companies. French government procurement comes under the jurisdiction of the Ministry for the Economy, Finance and Employment. The *"Commission Centrale des Marchés,"* or Central Procurement Board, has overall responsibility for monitoring compliance with procurement regulations.

The *Code des Marchés Publics*—the Public Procurement Code—is the cornerstone law governing French public procurements. Its revised version,[258] adopted in 2006, implements EC Directives in national law (i.e., Directives 2004/17/EC and 2004/18/EC on the procurement of goods, works and services). The Public Procurement Code applies to contracts in the field of defense (arms, munitions and war material). The Code promotes transparency and open competition in public procurement, and does not restrict foreign companies from bidding. A specific decree relating to defense procurement, the *Defence Specific Decree*, also states these general principles and gives a degree of flexibility for procurement covering specific needs and relating to the essential interests of the State, as defined under Article 296 of the Treaty Establishing the European Community (Article 296 EC Treaty).

For defense goods and services, France historically often invoked Article 296 EC Treaty to opt out of the EC public procurement disciplines. More recently, the French have adopted the voluntary EDA Code of Conduct on Defence Procurement.

In practice, both French and U.S. firms interviewed say that the process in competitive procurements is codified and reasonably open and transparent. American firms reported that requests for procurement are even being made available in English in some cases today.

Domestic Content Requirements

France does not have explicit "Buy French" domestic content laws. However, all firms interviewed noted the necessity of providing French content or value by either obtaining a domestic partner or teammates for programs. Simply put, the French, like most other European nations, are looking for French and European presence for jobs and more critically, to continue to build or enhance the domestic and European DTIB. This concern for maintaining jobs domestically is only underscored by the current global economic crisis. To illustrate, the French government is now requiring that French state funds applied to help sustain automobile manufacturers cannot reduce jobs located in France (even if those facilities are owned by German or other automotive firms).

Partnering or teaming with indigenous firms is a key driver in success. These partners not only provide in-country jobs and technology building—essential in France—but serve as local

---

[258] Decree 2006-975, JO 04.08.2006.

champions. Thus, the effect is much the same as having formal domestic content require-ments—albeit either more flexible or arbitrary, depending on one's perspective.

The increasing competition in French defense markets will likely put even more focus on domestic presence, content and partners as a discriminator. As French MoD bidding oppor-tunities become increasingly open to sources or teams that are not solely French, U.S. firms may find opportunities to bid via partnering or teaming with other French or European firms in order to provide more local content. On one level, this is beneficial to U.S. firms but on another it substitutes one type of barrier for another (albeit a more limited barrier that requires sharing the business with local partners rather than being completed excluded).

Offsets and *Juste Retour*

The DGA explicitly states that its established policy is not to require offsets in procure-ment. However, there appears to be in place an informal offset policy.[259] U.S. companies in France stated that they usually offer 100 percent *juste retour*—that is, some sort of job value relationship in the teaming or partnering for the program/product (e.g., domestic modifica-tions done to U.S. systems or products; co-production carried out domestically in many cases).

The U.S. Department of Commerce (DoC) annual report on offsets also indicates that effective offsets in France amounted to 84.6 percent of contract values from 1993 to 2006 (calculated from data submitted by the reporting U.S. firms of actual contracts and offset commitments).[260] A review of DoC offset reports over recent years shows the offset percent-age has remained remarkably stable. Thus, whether required or not, they do appear to be a major factor in defense trade with France.

Juste retour also continues to be an established practice in European multinational pro-grams in which France participates. Work share is usually proportional to national par-ticipation in a program. Programs including *juste retour* have included A400M, Eurocopter Tiger, and Multi-Role Armoured Vehicle (MRAV). Work share arrangements typically are negotiated in advance and included in the MOU among the participating governments.

Government Ownership

Traditionally, the French defense sector was largely government-owned, and the govern-ment was heavily involved in defining the state-owned companies' orientations. As recently as September 2003, Thomson SA, DCNS and GIAT Industries were still 100 percent gov-ernment-owned, and SNECMA Group was 99.7 percent government-owned.[261]

Over time, however, as described below, the French government has been gradually privatizing many firms. However, state ownership is still evident in the more traditional defense sectors: DCNS (Naval) remains 75 percent state-owned; and Nexter (former-GIAT,

[259] Offsets in Defense Trade, 10th Report to Congress, U.S. Department of Commerce (Jan. 2006), Appendix H, in Appendices, p. 69. Available at: http://www.bis.doc.gov/defenseindustrialbaseprograms/osies/offsets/offsetxappendicesreport.pdf.

[260] Offsets in Defense Trade, Twelfth Report to Congress, U.S. Department of Commerce (Dec. 2007), PDF p. 29 (report page 2-13) (Table 2-5). Available at: http://www.bis.doc.gov/defenseindustrialbaseprograms/osies/offsets/final-12th-offset-report-2007.pdf.

[261] Western European Industry Ownership Jigsaw, *Defence Systems Daily*, last updated Sept. 19, 2003.

ground vehicles and ammunition) and SNPE (nuclear) both remain essentially 100 percent state-owned.

When France began privatizing the defense sector, it retained control through the "*action spécifique*," the French counterpart of the "golden share."[262] The government used this type of golden share in the privatizations of Matra in 1988, Thomson-CSF in 1996, and Aérospatiale in 1999.[263] According to sources at the MoD/DGA, Thales may be the only remaining example of an *action spécifique* currently in use. The *action spécifique* is a strong tool to maintain government control over key matters. It affords the French government the right to:

- Veto acquisitions beyond a certain percentage (for Thales, acquisitions beyond each 10 percent of its capital are subject to authorization by the Ministry for the Economy, Finance and Employment);

- Veto the sale of certain specified assets (for Thales, listed assets include majority block of subsidiaries conducting defense activities); and

- Appoint a government representative to sit on the Board of Directors as an observer, without participating in votes. The observer's role is to report to the government on possible company action regarding sensitive activities. In the Thales case, the observer is a DGA civil servant.

Aerospatiale-Matra S.A. and EADS: The Move Toward Privatization

The gradual privatization trend is perhaps best illustrated in the creation of the European Aeronautic, Defense and Space Company (EADS), the largest aerospace and defense firm in Europe. As noted above, in 1999, Aérospatiale, a leading French defense and aerospace firm, was partially privatized and merged with Matra Hautes Technologies, another leading French firm. As part of the restructuring, the Lagardère Group purchased 33 percent of Aérospatiale-Matra shares, while 20 percent were sold on the stock exchange and the rest of the equity was retained by the French state. The French government retained its direct control over the firm through a golden share designed to "protect the essential interests of national security," the retention of a significant government ownership interest, and other mechanisms. Similar to the golden share the French state created in privatizing Thomson-CSF into Thales, the Aérospatiale-Matra golden share gave the government the rights to: name a non-voting member to the Aérospatiale Board; approve any new shareholding of 10 percent or more; approve any increase in an existing stake by 10 percent or more of the total capital; and block the sale of any part of the shares if it would threaten Aérospatiale-Matra's control in its ballistic missile, laser, nuclear, and armaments units.

Subsequently in 1999, Aérospatiale-Matra merged with leading German defense firm DaimlerChrysler Aerospace AG (DASA) and Spain's *Construcciones Aeronaticas* (CASA) to become EADS. Under the heavily negotiated and complex terms of EADS' creation, the French government retained a sizable stake (15 percent) in the merged entity (and the Spanish government a smaller stake (6.2 percent), and the charter of EADS afforded the French government various veto rights over major decisions such as mergers and acquisitions.

---

[262] The privatization law, Loi no. 86-793, of July 2, 1986, authorizes the use of "action spécifique" to protect national interests.

[263] J-P. Maulny, T. Taylor, B. Schmitt, F-E. Caillaud, *Industrial and Strategic Co-operation Models for Armament Companies in Europe* (2001), pp. 91-92. Available at: http://ec.europa.eu/enterprise/defence/defence_docs/rapp_iris_en.pdf.

A key issue during negotiations of EADS' creation was the degree of government owner-ship. At that time, DaimlerChrysler, a private firm with no government ownership, wanted EADS management free of potential governmental interference. However, this approach was not taken.

Today the equity shares in EADS remain complex, with the French (and Spanish) states maintaining significant shares through holding companies and the French state still holding a direct golden share. The following provides holdings as of December 31, 2007:

- *Sociedad Estatal de Participaciones Industriales* **(SEPI)** (5.49 percent equity) A holding company owned by the Spanish government

- **Daimler—Other Activities Segment**[264] (22.52 percent equity)

- **SOGEADE**—(27.53 percent) SOGEADE (*Société de gestion de l'aéronautique, de la défense et de l'espace*) is a French holding company owned 50 percent by **Lagardere SCA** and 50 percent by SOGEPA (*Societé de Gestion de Participations Aéronautiques*), a French government-owned holding company. This stake is managed by the Lagar-dere Group, but the French government retains a veto over EADS' strategic deci-sions, including investments worth more than €500 million and capital injections that would affect voting rights.

- **Public or 'Free Float'** (43.88 percent equity). This stake has increased from 27.35 percent at the time of the company's initial public offering in 2000.

- **French state (0.06 percent equity)** The French government's direct stake in EADS.

- **EADS N.V.** (0.52 percent equity) Treasury shares.

The 2004 French MoD Policy to Reduce Ownership

In 2004, Francois Lureau, the then-Chief Executive of DGA, articulated the shift in French policy on government ownership as follows:

> The government held the majority of shares but now prefers to exercise a strate-gic control through golden shares or share holders agreements at least for main security sensitive companies. As part of this process, the government intends to proceed with a controlled sale of its holdings in defense companies to allow them more freedom of action and promote European consolidation. The UK is already involved in half of the investments projects in France. The government owner-ship is no longer a policy in France.[265]

Hence, in general, the French government has been gradually moving away from the traditional model of protecting state interests through total government ownership and control and toward a private ownership-based model that allows foreign investment even in firms with sensitive capabilities. Today, the government ownership shares have changed in

---

[264] Daimler AG's Other Activities segment consists of its holding in EADS and, since Jan. 1, 2004, the Daimler Off-Highway business unit.

[265] François Lureau, then Chief Executive of DGA, French MoD, Speech to the Royal United Services Institute for Defense and Security Studies (RUSI), London, Nov. 19, 2004.

many cases; for example, today the state retains only a 27.29 percent interest in Thales (see Table 30).

French Government Ownership of Defense Firms Today

The following describes the situation today, based on a review of available data and interviews with market participants:

1. While the French government continues to own significant shares of leading French defense firms (see Table 30), its ownership shares are gradually declining and are expected to shrink further. The French government recently spun off one of its nuclear related businesses to private industry, for example. Such steps reflect recognition of the need to reduce government ownership to create more natural commercial market conditions among defense firms and to facilitate European defense industrial consolidation.

Table 30   French Government Ownership of Defense Companies (2007)

Company	Government Ownership Percent (%)	Golden Share (Y/N)	Other Owners
Nexter (GIAT)	100	Yes	None
DCNS	75	Yes	Thales Group (25%)
SAFRAN	35.90	Yes	Pratt & Whitney (1.7%); general public (35.9%)
Thales	27.29	Yes	Dassault Aviation (20.87%); Group Industriel Marcel Dassault (5.81%); Alcatel-Lucent (20.95%); Industrial Partners (9.5%); general public (37.9%)
EADS	0.6% Direct; 27.53% indirect via holding companies SOGEADE and SOGEPA	Yes	General public (43.88%); SOCEADE (27.53%-50% Lagardere/50% SOGEPA); SOGEPA (13.76%); Daimler—Other Activities (22.53%); SEPI (Spanish Governmentt holding company-5.49%); EADS NV treasry Shares (0.52%)
SNPE	100	Yes	None-but selling off some business units

Source: DACIS.

The French government's reduction of its ownership of defense firms is slow in nature—especially compared to other leading European nations that have shed ownership of defense firms. Sweden has almost totally privatized its defense industry in the course of a single decade, while Poland and Romania plan to sell the remainder of their state defense industries in the next 2 to 4 years (assuming, of course, that they can find buyers, a serious question). In contrast, the pace of French privatization, and in particular, the retention of the golden share, is slow and reflects the desire for some continued direct state hand in national security firms. This is similar to the UK's golden shares in BAE, Rolls-Royce and other firms, as discussed in Chapter 13. While the trend in France is toward decreased ownership, it is likely the government will maintain substantial positions in these leading firms for a considerable period of time; this study team was presented with no clear plan to totally divest these interests.

2. The French government still maintains golden shares or other comparable special rights (for example, through shareholder agreements) in leading French defense firms. As a number of European firms suggested, the existence of such rights very well may slow consolidation and limit the ability of these firms to fully participate in capital markets.

3. The French government has board positions in some of the defense companies in which it owns shares but, according to the companies involved, does not actively interfere in corporate decisions. The firms involved indicated uniformly that they are permitted to conduct their businesses on an arm's length commercial basis.

4. The French government generally does not get involved in management matters except in limited circumstances. Specifically, these typically include situations involving: 1) a prospect of foreign ownership that raises issues of stewardship (e.g., selling off key defense assets or closing facilities), which are of course subject to regulatory review; or 2) concerns over the impact of domestic mergers on security, continuity of program support and needed skills/employees. France would also be concerned over the impacts of job losses in communities where there is a potential closing of facilities or the potential for losing important technologies. There are instances where the State played explicit roles, such as in merging Sagem and Snecma to form SAFRAN (completed May 11, 2005), and orchestrating the 2007 acquisition of a 25 percent of DCNS by Thales. In 2006, the State imposed explicit conditions on the merging of the satellite businesses of Alcatel and Thales to ensure that strategic interests of the French government will always be met—if not, the government can impose actions to rescind the government's support of the combination.

5. The French government is gradually moving toward exercising control over defense industrial matters of concern to it through its role as a *buyer and regulator (rather than owner)*, including its research and development strategy and its acquisition policies and buying decisions.

While these developments are salutary in nature, there is no evidence the French government intends at this time to fully divest its shareholdings in defense firms or eliminate its golden shares. An evolution in this direction is possible but probably long-term in nature.

Foreign Direct Investment

According to the U.S. Commercial Service, France generally has one of the least restrictive investment regimes in terms of openness to foreign ownership, with only limited approvals needed in most sectors.[266] In practice, however, U.S. firms generally face hurdles to investment in France. The American Chamber of Commerce aptly summarizes the situation:

> While today's foreign investors face less interference than was once the case, more than a decade of reforms has not entirely overcome a traditional preference for state intervention and a sometimes reflexive opposition to foreign investment. In some cases, this can be seen in labor organization opposition to acquisitions

---

[266] Reference the U.S. Commercial Service: http://www.buyusa.gov/france/en/doingbusinessinfrance.html and the American Chamber of Commerce in France. See their website: http://www.amchamfrance.org/theme1.php?idcontenu=107&idpage=156&idmenu=108.

of French businesses by U.S. firms, often reflecting a perception that U.S. firms focus on short-term profits at the expense of employment. In other cases, French firms have stated a preference for working with French and European, rather than U.S., firms.[267]

This description applies to the defense sector as well, where there are substantial approval requirements for the foreign acquisition of French defense firms as well as general cultural and institutional barriers. Under French law, a foreign investor must obtain approval from the Ministry of Finance and the Ministry of Defense (which typically includes an agreement with the MoD). Buyers apply to the Ministry of Finance, which in turn triggers a review by the French MoD. In practice, prospective buyers must hold extensive discussions with MoD, which must be satisfied on numerous issues, including possible formal or informal commitments to maintain local capability and of how firms will deal with long-term security interests and the firms' know-how. MoD could require long-term commitments and "evergreen" clauses for areas of vital concern (that is, a clause allowing the government a long-term right to reverse or "undo" all or part of a company merger or acquisition of a business unit).

Recent French legislation revising the regulation of foreign direct investment also highlights the trend toward privatization and foreign ownership of defense firms.[268] In the case of foreign investment in areas of national defense and security, armament, and explosives, the foreign investor must obtain prior authorization from the Ministry of the Economy if the aggregate foreign ownership in the company will exceed one third of the total capital as a result of the transaction, or there is a change in structure of an existing foreign ownership block of more than one third of the capital. The provision reflects the fact that the origin of the foreign investor is an important consideration; foreign investors of a different origin may not trigger the same type of security review. Although the authorization is given by the Ministry of the Economy, the transaction is effectively reviewed and approved or rejected by the Ministry of Defense.

Finally, like the UK, France may require behavioral undertakings from a foreign party seeking to acquire an ownership interest in a company with sensitive activities. According to the DGA, once the authorization is issued, the Ministry of Defense will require behavioral undertakings in only 50 to 60 percent of the cases. These undertakings are formally provided by the foreign investor or foreign-controlled successor of the French company to the Ministry of the Economy. However, the undertaking includes the clauses required by the Ministry of Defense DGA. Typically, undertakings require maintenance of strategic capabilities in France, security of supply, and maintenance of key manufacturing and R&D activities in France. Such restrictions will target only core sensitive activities—after an assessment that letting such activities move abroad would leave a gap in the French and European capacity. Interestingly, these undertakings appear more focused on protecting against possible export restriction by the country of origin of the foreign owner rather than protection of strategic secrets. The DGA seems more concerned that if an activity is

---

[267] Reference American Chamber of Commerce in France. See their website: http://www.amchamfrance.org/theme1.php?idcontenu=107&idpage=156&idmenu=108.

[268] Décret No. 2003-196 of March 7, 2003, Regulating Foreign Investment Relations, J.O. No. 58, March 9, 2003, p. 4140, Arts. 1, 6, 7; Arrêté of March 7, 2003, Specifying certain rules of application of the Décret of March 7, 2003, J.O. No. 58, March 9, 2003, p. 4153. Where a company is already under 50 percent or more foreign ownership, no further governmental approval is necessary.

relocated abroad, a foreign country would be able to cut the supply line by enacting export-restrictive legislation. The undertakings are thus seen as measures to protect against dependence rather than devices to protect national security secrets.

In practice, there are few cases where foreign buyers have been denied the right to acquire French defense firms. According to DGA, there have been no denials in the last 5 years and only 2 in the last 10 years. Thirty cases were reviewed in 2006 and none were rejected, according to both DGA and the U.S. Foreign Commercial Service.[269] The DGA officials reported that about 50 percent of these buys were by U.S. investors.

> Nevertheless, there is limited foreign ownership of French defense or national security firms today. More specifically, a review of available data shows that there have been virtually no significant U.S. acquisition of defense firms in France over the years and virtually no "French footprints" for U.S. defense firms other than several with small organically grown presences in the subsystem area (e.g., Rockwell Collins).
>
> In contrast, through mergers and acquisitions, there is a greater degree of European ownership of French defense firms. More generally, analysts of the French industry interviewed by this study team noted the foreign ownership percentage in France remains low relative to other nations with large economies and sizable defense spending.

The bottom line is that France is liberalizing its foreign investment regime, including in the defense sector. Yet, overall foreign, and particularly U.S., ownership of defense companies remains low in France due to formal and informal restrictions and policies favoring national ownership as a means of ensuring security. A summary of recent U.S. acquisitions in the French defense, aerospace and homeland security industries is set forth on Table 30.

As Table 31 shows, most recent acquisitions have involved dual-use technology companies rather than purely defense companies. Moreover, these acquisitions tend to be relatively small and involve second- and third-tier subcontractors with specialized market niches. Although total U.S. equity in the French industry is difficult to calculate, the overall impression is U.S. ownership and presence remains very modest in comparison with the U.S. presence in other European countries.

Industrial Security

To protect information and sensitive activities, France relies on conditionality clauses attached to procurement contracts. These conditions are applicable whether the company involved in defense contracts is foreign owned or not. The clauses deal with standard security clearance and access restrictions.

There are no legal restrictions that prevent France from contracting in classified matters with foreign-owned firms. The *Defence Specific Decree* (of the *Code des Marchés Publics*, or Public Procurement Code, discussed above) underlines that, for highly classified con-

---

[269] See U.S. Foreign Commercial Service in France website (section on Openness to Foreign Investment). Available at: http://www.buyusa.gov/france/en/117.html.

Table 31   **France—U.S. Acquisitions of French Defense, Aerospace and Security Companies (Millions of Dollars–$)**

Date	Buyer	Seller	Business Line	Price	Revenue	Defense/ Dual Use
Jul 2008	United Technologies	Revima APU (49%)	Aircraft Maint	NA	NA	Dual Use
Apr 2008	General Electric Company	ULIS SA (15%)	Nuclear Energy	NA	60.00	Dual Use
Jan 2008	Gores Group LLC	SAGEM Communications (90%)	Telecom	552.00	1,870.00	Dual Use
Dec 2007	Hypercom Corp	Thales SA (E-transactions)	IT	152.00	222.00	Dual Use
Dec 2007	United Technologies	Initial Securite Holdings	Security	NA	NA	Dual Use
Oct 2007	Eaton Corporation	MGE UPS Systems	IT	612.00	245.00	Dual Use
Oct 2007	Apax Partners SA	Faceo Group	Facility Mgmt	NA	490.00	Dual Use
Sep 2007	Carlyle Group	Zodiac Marine	Shipbuilding	NA	NA	Defense
Sep 2007	FLIR Systems	Cedip Infrared Systems (67.8%)	Electro-Optics	57.10	25.10	Defense
Sep 2007	Westinghouse Electric	Astare	Nuclear Energy	NA	NA	Dual Use
Aug 2007	AMETEK, Inc.	Cameca	Precision Instruments	112.00	NA	Dual Use
Aug 2007	SPX Corporation	Johnson Controls European Diagnostics Div	Test Equipment	43.60	80.00	Dual Use
Jun 2007	Intercim, Inc.	Pertinence, SA	IT	NA	NA	Dual Use
May 2007	Anixter, Inc.	Eurofast SAS	Engineering Fasterners	27.00	18.00	Dual Use
Apr 2007	Mathworks, Inc.	PolySpace Technologies	IT Engineering	NA	NA	Dual Use
Feb 2007	United Technologies	Dosatron International	Pumping Systems	NA	NA	Dual Use
Jan 2007	Garmin, Ltd.	EME TecSat SA	GPS Products	NA	NA	Dual Use
Dec 2006	SeaMobile, Inc.	Geolink	Telecom	NA	NA	Dual Use
Nov 2006	Barnes Group, Inc.	Orflam Industries	Gas Springs	NA	NA	Dual Use
Jul 2006	Parker Hannifin, Inc.	Acofab SA & Adecem SARL	Electronics	NA	12.90	Dual Use
May 2006	Honeywell International	Gardner Groupe Europe	Security	256.00	260.00	Dual Use
Apr 2006	Comverse Technology	netcentrex SA	IT	164.00	50.00	Dual Use
Jan 2006	United Technologies	Delmo Delsecco $ Cie	Environmental Control	NA	30.00	Dual Use
Jan 2006	Measurement Specialities	ATEX	Instrumentation	3.20	1.80	Dual Use

Source: Defense Mergers and Acquisitions Data Base.

tracts, the MoD can derogate from the Code. In these very specific cases, a contract may be awarded without prior publication and without competition. However, for classified contracts security clearance requirements must be met in all cases.[270]

Ethics and Corruption

In general, France is perceived as having a low incidence of corruption. The World Bank's worldwide governance indicators show France at 90 percent for rule of law and control of corruption.[271] There is also no apparent evidence of illicit payments in connection with obtaining defense procurement contracts in France. For 2007, France is rated the 19th country in the world on Transparency International's Corruption Perception Index—for example, below the UK but above the United States—which is ranked 20th—and well above Italy, which is ranked 55th.[272]

However, France continues to have a mixed track record with respect to French firms making illegal payments in third-country defense markets. France is a signatory of the Convention on Combating Bribery of Foreign Public Officials in International Business Transactions (OECD Anti-Bribery Convention), and has enacted implementing legislation in 2000. The OECD Anti-Bribery Convention is enforced through both amendments to the French Tax Code and to the French Code of Criminal Procedure. Moreover, Transparency International's (TI) recent progress report found France to be a "strong performer" in enforcing the Convention and its anti-bribery laws—with 19 judicial investigations pending and 16 preliminary investigations.[273] French attitudes on enforcement in a related area were made clear in the aerospace industry last year when French authorities arrested some very senior EADS leaders—Noel Forgeard and Jean Paul Gut—with respect to insider trading charges.

Despite these salutary developments and a growing focus on these issues in France, there continue to be allegations that leading French firms, including defense firms, have engaged in these practices in global defense markets. France is rated worse than the United States and all other LOI countries except Italy in TI's Bribe Payers Index.[274] Available information reflects that the longstanding culture and practices by French firms in this area are difficult to change and that change is slow. TI also has reported various deficiencies in French enforcement efforts.

---

[270] *L'instruction générale interministérielle no. 1300/SGDN/SSD du 25 août 2003 sur la protection du secret de la défense nationale ; Arrêté du 18 avril 2005 relatif aux conditions de protection du secret et des informations concernant la défense nationale et la sûreté de l'Etat dans les contrats, JORF no.92 du 20 avril 2005.* Available at: http://www.ssi.gouv.fr/fr/reglementation/igi1300.pdf.

[271] See World Bank Governance Indicators, 1996-2007 (Country Data Report for France, 1996-2007). Available at: http://info.worldbank.org/governance/wgi/pdf/c76.pdf.

[272] Transparency International 2007 Corruption Perception Index, available at: http://www.transparency.org/policy_research/surveys_indices/cpi/2007/regional_highlights_factsheets.

[273] F. Heimann and G. Dell, *Progress Report 2008: Enforcement of the OECD Convention on Combating Bribery of Foreign Public Officials in International Business Transactions,* Transparency International (June 24, 2008), pp. 10, 21-22. Available at: http://www.transparency.org/news_room/in_focus/2008/oecd_report.

[274] Available at: http://www.transparency.org/policy_research/surveys_indices/bpi/bpi_2006.

Export Controls

France is a member of major multilateral export control regimes, including the Nuclear Suppliers Group, the Australia Group, the Missile Technology Control Regime, the Wassenaar Arrangement and the Chemical Weapons Convention. France is also a Member State of Organisation for Security and Co-operation in Europe (OSCE), and has approved the OSCE principles governing transfers of conventional arms and the 2000 OSCE document on Small Arms and Light Weapons.[275]

France, like other EU Member States, also is a signatory to the 1998 EU Code of Conduct on Arms Exports, which harmonized regulations across all Member States in the European Union, and established general principles for the transfer of armaments and military technology, and set up a system whereby each Member State must inform the others whenever an export license is denied. Under the Code, each State must also consult with the other Member States whenever it wishes to grant an export license that has been denied by another Member State for "essentially identical transactions," although the ultimate decision to deny or transfer a military item remains at the national discretion of each Member State.[276] The EC Transfers Directive recently adopted by the European Parliament is a further step in aligning the policies of EU countries regarding intra-Community transfers and simplifying procedures to permit such transfers among Member States and certified defense companies. The focus of this EC Directive is intra-Community transfers and, thus, the main beneficiaries of reduced barriers within the EU are European defense companies. It is not at all clear that U.S. firms will be eligible for similar treatment; this is a matter for national authorities to decide.

On a national level, the French arms export control regime and its implementation is relatively transparent. The MoD publishes an annual public report to the French Parliament on how its arms export laws are implemented, including levels of sales, major products exported and export country destinations. The issue for the United States is that U.S. policies on technology release and acceptable destination countries do not necessarily comport with French views and policies.

Some with an inside view suggest the key issue in such cases concerns the French interagency process for the export control/release. An interviewee told the study team the French decision-makers across the process "don't know what they don't know"—i.e., they lack, or do not use, a "systems" knowledge approach to how certain defense items can be integrated to produce threat systems or to advance the research, development, testing and engineering of potentially hostile nations. In many ways, they reported, the United States and France have similar export policies but differ in identifying how pieces of key technologies may be integrated and applied to create concern.

Concerns about the rigor of French export control laws was fueled by the discovery of French missiles and other weapons systems produced after 1991 in Iraqi arms stockpiles after the 2003 U.S. invasion. Iraq, of course, was under a UN arms embargo during that period, and the export of all categories of weapons to Iraq was specifically prohibited.

---

[275] The Organization for Security Co-operation in Europe (OSCE). Details on French membership and OSCE activities are available at: http://www.osce.org/about/13131.html.

[276] See http://www.eubusiness.com/Trade/european-code-of-conduct-on-arms-exports/.

ITAR as a Market Access Barrier

Historically, numerous defense products and systems developed and sold in France have ITAR-incorporated components. Today, while there is no official policy calling for exclusion of ITAR-controlled components or subsystems from French products and systems, there are clear tendencies in this direction. French officials are concerned about security of supply of ITAR products (the risk of licensing denials) and autonomy and flexibility. They say that French defense programs or product lines must not be put in a position where French decisions on how to deploy their products, or when they can sell to partners or allies, might be held hostage to "intergovernmental decisions."

Viewed in this context, ITAR restrictions are viewed increasingly unfavorably by French officials and some in French industry insofar as they afford the U.S. government some ability to control whether and when France deploys it products or when it may sell them to third parties. ITAR licensing requirements also are viewed as creating unwanted unpredictability and limiting the ability to export items on a timely basis. Some French firms interviewed for this study said they are feeling European market pressure to "design around" ITAR. Alternatively, some French firms are used to dealing with ITAR and see the United States as an important market; these firms are more willing to continue to deal with ITAR components where they are the best solutions, and these firms discussed concepts where they may in some cases create products in two configurations, one with and one without ITAR components.

The new French White Paper explicitly calls out ITAR relative to electronic components and cites the need for electronic components not to be subject to restrictions that limit French freedom of action. The White Paper states France will "instead support a European approach conducive to a European industrial base. The goal is to preclude situations of critical dependency which increasingly restrain our ability to export freely."[277] This is a relatively transparent reference to ITAR restrictions and makes clear a French preference for dependency on non-ITAR controlled substitutes (e.g., products and systems subject to European export controls that afford France flexibility and autonomy in the use and sale of such products and systems). Also, as noted above, in the French industrial strategy for Competitive Autonomy, the second, largest circle of sources is *European cooperative*. According to DGA officials, "European means European."

This policy thrust toward non-ITAR products and systems also is reflected in evolving commercial and defense acquisition practices in France, which plainly have implications for U.S. defense firms doing business in France. As the success of many U.S. firms in France has been in dual-use products or in commercial aerospace, these firms have needed to solve the re-export dilemma ITAR can pose. Firms report modifying elements of the products in Europe so they can meet needs, or developing two versions—one ITAR-controlled and one ITAR-free.

The bottom line is that ITAR has become a material competitive disadvantage for U.S. firms seeking to compete in France. Ironically, the new DGA competition policies may accentuate this dilemma. As U.S. firms (which understandably report "ITAR is their bible") increasingly must compete for work, rather than obtain sole source awards as in the past, they may face tough competition from other teams operating without ITAR restrictions.

---

[277] French White Paper (English summary), op. cit.

Intellectual Property Protection

France adheres to the major multilateral intellectual property (IP) regimes, including (i) the WTO Agreement on Trade-Related Aspects of Intellectual Property Rights, which provides core IP protection and enforcement rights (including for trade secrets); (ii) the Paris Convention for the Protection of Industrial Property, covering patents, trademarks and industrial designs; (iii) the Patent Cooperation Treaty, protecting patents; (iv) the Berne Convention, covering copyrights; (v) the Madrid Protocol, covering trademarks; and (vi) the World Intellectual Property Organization (WIPO).

According to the U.S. Commercial Service, "France is a traditionally strong defender of IP rights and has highly developed protection for IP."[278]

In the context of French defense procurement, we are not aware of any indications or concerns by U.S. firms that France has not recognized U.S. IP rights or allowed U.S. firms to protect their own background IP.

Technical Standards

France is a party to the WTO's Technical Barriers to Trade Agreement, which prohibits discrimination and seeks to ensure that regulations, standards, testing and certification procedures do not create obstacles to trade. However, every country has the right to adopt those regulatory standards it considers appropriate in areas concerning national security. Thus, France has the discretion to, and has put in place, its own specific technical standards for defense products that could in theory serve as a non-tariff barrier to competing foreign products.

France's long association with NATO also means that French military products are tied to NATO Standardization Agreements where these exist. As discussed in Chapter 5, however, there is some prospect of increased risk that an eventual EU set of standards being developed might become a disguised market access barrier—but there is no indication that this is a policy result sought by France today.

In the commercial area, however, France has developed technical product standards different from those of the United States, and "rigorous testing and approval procedures must sometimes be undertaken before goods can be sold in France, particularly those that entail risk. When EU-wide standards do not exist, specific French standards apply. The United States and the EU have negotiated mutual recognition agreements covering the testing and certification of certain specified regulated products."[279]

However, in the defense arena, we did not learn of any specific situations involving France where technical standards were used as non-tariff barriers to protect domestic producers and markets against foreign defense products.

---

[278] See "Doing Business in France: 2008 Country Commercial Guide for U.S. Companies," U.S. Commercial Service (2008), U.S. Department of Commerce, at p. 111. Available at: http://www.buyusainfo.net/docs/x_639864.pdf.

[279] "The French Investment Climate," (see section entitled Transparency of Regulatory System," on website of American Chamber of Commerce in France. Available at: http://www.amchamfrance.org/theme1.php?idcontenu=107&idpage=156&idmenu=108.

Chapter 8

Accessing the German Defense Market

Germany, more than any other country in Western Europe, has undergone enormous change over the last two decades and its defense market has evolved accordingly.

The end of the Cold War and German reunification led to the substantial downsizing and reorientation of a large German military force focused on territorial defense. From a force of 285,000 active (mainly conscripts) and 360,000 reservists, Germany has reduced its military to 250,000 active troops (mainly professional) and 300,000 reservists. The subsequent post-Cold War emphasis on the need for expeditionary war fighting capabilities has caused Germany to expand its concept of defense beyond its own borders and participate in North Atlantic Treaty Organization (NATO) and European Union (EU) expeditionary operations around the globe. While maintaining a strong U.S. bilateral relationship and link to NATO, Germany has fully supported the development of the European Security and Defense Policy (ESDP) and the gradual creation of an EU defense identify.

In 2006, Germany released a new defense strategy and defense transformation plan to address twenty-first century threats. However, domestic political and budgetary realities are likely to constrain its ability to meet the goals outlined in its recent White Paper. At this point, Germany's embrace of transformational thinking is more a matter of PowerPoints than it is a matter of strategic, operational or acquisition reality. Germany also continues to invest in expensive legacy defense systems that are designed for a territorial defense or are not otherwise clearly related to its expeditionary war fighting goals—the implication being that industrial policy and jobs rather than operational requirements do have a role in German defense acquisition.

Developed after World War II to provide the German military the full spectrum of defense capabilities, the German defense industry emerged as a world leader in a wide range of market sectors, including armored vehicles, submarines, electronics and optics. During the Cold War, Germany was able to sustain multiple prime contractors in various sectors on the back of German domestic requirements and exports to other NATO countries. With the end of the Cold War, however, Germany faced a set of serious challenges: the decline in demand for its defense products both at home and abroad (as Germany and other European nations cut their defense budgets) and the unique need to integrate East German forces and state-owned industries. As a result, the German defense industry was plagued throughout the 1990s by excessive fragmentation and overcapacity.

Since the mid-1990s, there has been considerable consolidation at the prime contractor level in most sectors (with land systems bringing up the rear). Similar consolidation has not yet affected the subcontractor tiers, where each of the remaining prime contractors maintains a separate network of domestic suppliers—although very small by U.S. standards. Moreover, German defense consolidation has not resulted in the same synergies and efficiencies experienced by the U.S. defense industry; the consolidated firms tend to maintain the facilities and product lines of each of the component companies to preserve employment levels. Thus, even today, the German defense industry has significant overcapacity except in the military aircraft market.

The German government's defense market policies pose significant market access challenges for U.S. defense firms. On the demand side, German acquisition policy is largely wedded to a traditional, status quo approach, with a primary reliance on sole source national buying for most national systems. In contrast to some of the other Western European countries examined, there is no apparent emerging pattern in Germany of seeking to subject any of its major systems (even on a European basis) to international competition. The German Ministry of Defense (MoD) is increasingly willing to consider solutions from firms in other European countries and has significant resources tied up in European cooperative programs. However, available data shows that Germany is simply not very open to U.S. prime level firms even on new competitive awards. In practice, German markets are largely closed to U.S. participation, with U.S. firms having a miniscule presence on all recent major German programs reviewed (4 percent by value overall).

The difficult environment for U.S. defense firms seeking to enter the German market reflects a number of additional underlying market access impediments. First, U.S. defense companies seeking to do business in Germany acknowledge the need to either team with a German prime contractor or otherwise have a strong in-country presence. U.S. firms that follow this model can generate sizable sales revenues, but mainly as first- or second-tier subcontractors. Second, U.S. International Traffic in Arms Regulations (ITAR) restrictions are a significant issue for both the German government customer and German companies doing business with American companies. A consistent theme among government and business representatives in Germany was concern over the ITAR, and associated costs, schedule delays and risks to third-country exports. German government and business representatives expressed that informal German policy and corporate strategy is to find ways around ITAR where possible by building or relying on ITAR-free equivalents of various systems and components.

On the "supply" side of the market, Germany issued a Defense Industrial Policy concurrent with the 2006 Defense White Paper, which reflects a tension between recognizing the growing globalization and Europeanization of the industry, on the one hand, and the need to maintain a broad scope, autonomous German national capability on the other hand. Germany has identified sixteen "strategic sectors" (each consisting of several capabilities) to be protected from foreign competition through the exercise of Article 296 of the Treaty Establishing the European Community (Article 296 EC Treaty). The list of defense industrial sectors in which Germany wishes to maintain system level national capabilities is striking in its breadth. Whereas France, Sweden and, to some extent, UK industrial policies today are choosing to maintain autonomy in only select areas, the German list of national autonomous areas covers most of its industry. While German officials concede that the list is too long, it is fair to conclude that a core objective of the German policy is to maintain strong domestic production capacity across a range of strategic capabilities.

One notable element of the new German Defense Industrial Policy is its increased focus on review of foreign acquisitions of its defense firms (especially those with "key defense technologies") and its increasingly protectionist view of this type of acquisition by U.S. firms. The German investment environment thus appears relatively closed to U.S. defense firms seeking acquisitions of German prime contractors, but relatively open to such acquisitions by firms from other European countries. There is little U.S. ownership today at systems or major subsystem levels juxtaposed against considerable European ownership at that level. Thus, U.S. ownership or investment—especially of more sensitive or system level assets—seems to have significant political implications inhibiting acquisitions above a certain level.

Finally, the distinct "European" shift in Germany's procurement policy is also reflected in Germany's relatively limited cooperative engagement in defense programs with the United States. U.S.-German defense industrial cooperation has a long and deep history going back to the beginning of the Cold War, when the United States was providing Germany with the bulk of its equipment under the Military Assistance Plan. Since the 1990s, however, U.S-German cooperative development programs have dwindled to a handful of missile systems, notably Medium Extended Air Defense Systems (MEADS) and Guided Multiple Launch Rocket System (MLRS). Germany today seems to prefer cooperative programs involving other European countries, such as Eurofighter, Eurocopter Tiger, and various naval ship programs.

The future of the U.S.-German defense industrial relationship depends on the broader context of U.S.-German relations and on how, within that context, Germany resolves its ambivalent attitude toward military power and its own defense budgets.

I. Market Background

A. From Cold War to Reunification: A Sea Change in Strategic Context and Military Strategy

As the front-line state on the NATO Central Front during the Cold War, the Federal Republic of Germany maintained the second largest military force in the NATO Alliance behind the United States. Germany's forces were optimized to fight an armored-mechanized war along the Inter-German Border. At the peak of its strength toward the end of the Cold War, the German military (*Bundeswehr*) included some 285,000 active troops backed by 359,000 reservists. The German Army (*Heer*) consisted of no fewer than three army corps, with seven armored (*Panzer*) divisions, four mechanized (*Panzergrenadier*) divisions, one alpine (*Gebirgs*) division, and one airborne (*Luftlande*) division.[280] These were supplemented by a Territorial Army of 26 independent brigades (8.66 division equivalents), manned by mobilized reservists in wartime.

Faced with the overt threat of Soviet aggression, Germany was steadfast in its role as the keystone of NATO's European defenses—despite periodic challenges from left-wing and pacifist groups within Germany. Germany typically invested about 3.6-3.7 percent of gross domestic product (GDP) for defense throughout the 1970s and '80s.[281] This robust spending level was difficult to maintain after the USSR's *Perestroika* led to a perceived reduction in the Soviet threat. As can be seen in Figure 71, by the end of the 1980s Germany was devoting only some 3 percent of GDP to defense, though the growth of the German economy allowed spending levels to remain fairly constant or even grow slightly through that period.

The collapse of the Soviet Union in 1989 and the reunification of Germany that followed in October 1990 created a profound shift in the 35-year German security status quo. In one moment, the *Bundeswehr* found its primary mission rendered irrelevant at the same time it

---

[280] Figures from the *IISS Military Balance, 1989-1990*. By way of comparison, the U.S. Army at this time consisted of 18 active divisions, the UK just six.

[281] Ibid.

confronted an entirely new set of problems—most notably the integration of the East German National People's Army (*Volksarmee*) into the consolidated armed forces of the reunited Germany. With a front-line strength of six divisions (plus five reserve divisions), 1800 main battle tanks and several hundred combat aircraft, the *Volksarmee* included 170,000 active troops and an additional 175,000 reservists. As most of the *Volksarmee's* Soviet-manufactured equipment was obsolescent or obsolete, as well as not interoperable with the *Budeswehr's* NATO-standard equipment, it was decided to discard most of it immediately as well as to demobilize most of its troops and retire most of its senior officers no later than 1994.[282]

This was a costly and complex process that involved closing (and decontaminating) superfluous bases in eastern Germany; demilitarizing and scrapping thousands of tanks, armored vehicles, artillery and aircraft; retraining and relocating demobilized troops; and pensioning off retired officers. The problem of integrating the *Volksarmee* into the *Bundeswehr* paralleled in microcosm the problem faced by Germany as a whole in integrating the former East Germany into a unified state. The cost of closing or selling the myriad state-owned industries, of bringing infrastructure up to Western standards, of providing the East German population with job training and the level of social welfare found in West Germany was immense—estimated by some at more than $70 billion per year.[283]

As a consequence of reunification, German defense spending increased from $55.5 billion to $58.5 billion (+4.7 percent) in 1990, in order to cover the initial costs of integration and downsizing of the *Volksarmee* (see Figure 71).[284] Thereafter, however, the German defense budget fell rapidly to just $40.8 billion in 1997. As a share of GDP, the German defense budget fell from 2.8 percent in 1990 to 1.5 percent in 1998. It remained at that level through 2002 before falling to 1.4 percent of GDP in 2003, and only 1.3 percent in 2006. Germany thus spends less proportionally than any other country in this study, including Italy.[285]

The collapse of German defense spending mirrored a collapse in the public consensus regarding defense. Absent the Soviet threat, most Germans favored reducing defense expenditures. According to one survey, almost a quarter of all Germans questioned the need for armed forces at all. Conscription became increasingly unpopular, and the term of service had to be reduced from 2 years to 18 months to 12 months, and finally, to a very short and ineffective 9 months.

Domestic economic factors also put pressures on the defense budget. On the one hand, there was the need to modernize and reintegrate eastern Germany, which proved more difficult and took much longer than expected (to some extent, the former East Germany still has not reached the level of economic prosperity of West Germany). This enormous challenge is in addition to long-term systemic problems such as ballooning pension and social welfare payments (by 2030, about 30 percent of the German population will be over age 65). The combination of circumstances—the need to pay for reunification and stimulate growth

---

[282] Only the most advanced East German equipment was integrated into the *Bundeswehr*, and then only for a limited time; most notable among these were several squadrons of MiG-29 Fulcrum fighter aircraft. Though the performance of these was comparable to the F-16 Falcon, lack of commonality with other Luftwaffe aircraft, as well as the high cost of maintaining them, led to their disposal after just a few years of service.

[283] Ozgur Ozdamar, "Germany," in K. DeRouen and U. Heo, eds., *Defense and Security: A Compendium of National Armed Forces and Security Policies*, ABC-Clio, 2005, p. 255. For catalog information on this publications, see: http://www.abc-clio.com/products/overview.aspx?productid=109845&viewid=1.

[284] SIPRI Defense Expenditures Database, constant 2005 dollars.

[285] Ibid.

Figure 71   Germany—Defense Expenditures, 1998-2007

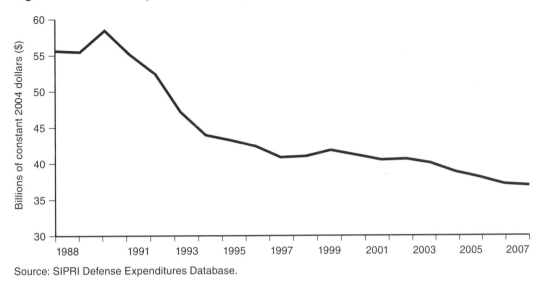

Source: SIPRI Defense Expenditures Database.

in eastern Germany as well as to meet the inflation and deficit targets of the Maastricht Treaty—created an environment unfavorable to defense spending.

Once the East German army was absorbed and disbanded, *Bundeswehr* underwent very little change through the subsequent decade. To be sure, it was increasingly recognized that, in light of current strategic requirements, German forces were too large and ill-suited for the kinds of missions on which it was being called (e.g., peacekeeping operations in Bosnia and Kosovo). Indeed, there was little in the way of large-scale training, and only a few formations were maintained at full strength. Nevertheless, there was a reluctance to make substantial cuts in force structure because of NATO force commitments and the political leverage the "force in being" gave Germany in NATO and EU security discussions.

The result was a predictable "hollowing out" of German military forces. While Germany successfully liquidated the assets of the *Volksarmee* and also reduced its own force structure to comply with the Treaty on Conventional Forces in Europe, it proportionally reduced its defense spending much more—canceling or delaying much-needed new equipment and upgrades to older systems. Operations and maintenance (O&M) costs for rapidly aging tanks, aircraft and other weapon systems consumed an increasing portion of the budget. To contain costs, few divisions were maintained at full strength (many were reduced to cadres); training and large-scale exercises were curtailed.

New Security Challenges, Budget Declines and a Changing German Force Structure

While the German military was in serious decline, it was facing an array of new operational challenges as the German government sought to establish its position in post-Cold War Europe. Despite considerable popular opposition and constitutional issues, the German military began participating actively in a host of United Nations, NATO and EU-sponsored peacekeeping, stabilization and humanitarian operations in the Balkans, Africa, and elsewhere. It soon became apparent that German forces were ill-trained and badly equipped to perform such expeditionary missions—lacking the ability to sustain forces "out of area" (i.e., beyond NATO territory).

At the same time, Germany and France became the leading exponents of the new ESDP, as fully discussed in Chapter 5.[286] As early as 1987, France and Germany had formed a "Franco-German Brigade" at Strasbourg to explore the challenges of multinational command outside the NATO framework. In 1992, German Chancellor Kohl and French President Mitterand announced the formation of a "Eurocorps." Inviting all members of the then-Western European Union (WEU) to participate, the Eurocorps had three potential missions: wartime operations under NATO command; peacemaking and peacekeeping operations under WEU control outside the NATO treaty area; and humanitarian operations worldwide. While Eurocorps has been superseded by the EU Battle Groups, but it is important to the German military as its most tangible contribution to the ESDP.[287]

The combination of over-commitment and underinvestment marked the 1990s as a period of drift and uncertainty in German defense strategy, as the military sought out new and relevant missions while trying to maintain its existing organization and force structure.

Once in office in 1999, the Schroeder government made reassessing the roles and capabilities of the *Bundeswehr* a high priority. In May 2003, the Schroeder government issued a "Defense Policy Guidance" that was subsequently supplemented by a "Directive on *Bundeswehr* Transformation" in October 2003. Together, the two documents attempted to lay out a new direction for German security policy and the restructuring of the *Bundeswehr* into a smaller, more agile force capable of conducting out-of-area operations and able to meet the challenges of the twenty-first century.[288]

The Defense Policy Guidelines called for the integration of the *Bundeswehr* for almost all missions into multinational coalitions operating with a clear mandate and within the framework of the United Nations (UN), NATO or the EU. The Directive on *Bundeswehr* Transformation pointed out the need for enhanced interoperability with coalition partners and of moving toward network-centric capabilities.

The plan called for a *Bundeswehr* of some 250,000 military and 75,000 civilian personnel.[289] Most of the military personnel would be long-term professionals. Universal conscription has been retained for all 18-year-old men, but the term of service will remain just nine months, and exemptions are extremely generous.

---

[286] ESDP was formally adopted by the EU in Cologne in 1999, during the German presidency of the Union.

[287] In 2008 the European Parliament voted with a large majority a resolution proposing: "to place Eurocorps as a standing force under EU command. With the Franco-German Brigade as its nucleus, the Eurocorps consists of up to 60,000 troops "pledged" from six "framework" nations (Germany, France, Spain, Belgium, Luxembourg and Poland) and seven other European nations—Austria, Greece, Turkey, the United Kingdom, Finland, Italy and the Netherlands. Although elements of the Eurocorps have deployed to Bosnia, Kosovo and Afghanistan, only its headquarters and staff are permanently constituted.

[288] See Col. Ralph Thiele, Commander, *Bundeswehr* Center for Analyses and Studies, "*Bundeswehr* Transformation— Towards 21st Century Transatlantic Partnership", Heritage Foundation/Konrad Adenauer Foundation Roundtable, Washington, DC, Oct. 31, 2003.

[289] German Federal Ministry of Defense, White Paper 2006 on German Security Policy and the Future of the *Bundeswehr* (White Paper) (Bonn) 2006, at p. 69.

Table 32   ***Bundeswehr* Force Structure, 1990 vs. 2010**

	1990	2010		1990	2010
Active Manpower	285,000	250,000			
Conscripts	200,000	25,000			
Reservists	359,000	300,000			
			Air Force		
Army			Fighter Wings	2	3
Corps HQ	3	1	Fighter-Bombers Wings	10	2
Panzer Divisions	7	2	Reconnaissance Wings	2	1
Panzergrenadier Divisions	4	1	Special Operations Wing	0	1
Mountain Divisions	1	0	Transport Wings	2	2
Airborne Divisions	1	1	**Navy**		
Special Operations Div	0	1	Long-Range Frigates	0	4
Helicopter Regiments	9	6	Logistic Support Ships	0	2

Source: David C. Isby, *Armies of NATO's Central Front, Jane's* (N.Y.) 1985; *White Paper,* op. cit.

The Schroeder government's transformed force, as revised by the Merkel government[290], has been divided into three elements: a 35,000 man Response Force; a 70,000 man Stabilization Force; and a 147,000 man Support Force.

- **The Response Force,** intended for "high-intensity, joint network-enabled operations and evacuation operations,"[291] consists entirely of long-term professionals, and is earmarked for various international commitments, including: 15,000 for the NATO Response Force; 18,000 for the European Headline Goals and the EU Battle Groups; 1,000 for the UN Standby Arrangement System, and 1,000 for humanitarian operations. A comparison of the "old" and "new" *Bundeswehr* is presented in Table 32.

- **The Stabilization Force** consists of one *Panzer* and one *Panzergrenadier* division, some elements of which are deployable as follow-on reinforcements for the Response Force while others are primarily responsible for territorial defense.

- **The Support Force** consists mainly of logistic units assigned either to the divisions or the newly organized Joint Support Command; most of the conscripts will be assigned to the Support Force and cannot be deployed outside of Germany.[292]

Army reserve forces are being reorganized to support the new structure and missions, but given their level of training and political sensitivities involving their use, it is unlikely that they would ever be deployed outside of Germany, being used, instead, to backfill any openings created by the deployment of the Response and Stabilization forces.

Significantly, the Defense Policy Guidance did not envisage a substantial increase in the defense budget, which would remain fairly constant between €24 and €25 billion ($30-32 billion), or somewhat less than 1.5 percent of GDP.

---

[290] Ibid. p. 80.

[291] Ibid. p. 80.

[292] Ibid. pp. 90-91.

Unfortunately, neither the Defense Policy Guidance nor the Directive on *Bundeswehr* Transformation had the authority of an official Defense Policy White Paper. The Schroeder government had difficulty achieving the consensus necessary for this significant step. Thus, not surprisingly, little was done to advance the objectives of either document before the Schroeder government stepped down in 2005.

Subsequently, Chancellor Angela Merkel's government continued the work of the Schroeder government, and published a formal *White Paper 2006 on German Security Policy and the Future of the* Bundeswehr[293] — the first such document issued by the German government in 12 years. Based mainly on the 2003 Policy Guidance, the White Paper represents an agreed vision of a comprehensive national security strategy that can form the basis for the transformation of the German military.

Among the key points of the White Paper:

- Germany faces a wide array of threats, including terrorism, proliferation of weapons of mass destruction, economic and cyber warfare, and an array of asymmetrical threats in addition to conventional attack on the German homeland.

- Germany's defense therefore can begin far from Germany, and defensive actions may require German intervention far outside the NATO area.

- *German forces* will operate only as part of a multinational coalition legitimately formed under the auspices of the UN, NATO or the EU; Germany neither accepts nor has the capability to engage in unilateral military operations.

- The Transatlantic relationship "remains the foundation of Germany and Europe's common security"; the NATO Alliance remains the cornerstone of German security policy, and "the bonds between Germany and the United States must be continually cultivated and deepened through mutual consultation and coordinated action."

- A primary security goal is strengthening "the European area of stability through the consolidation and development of European integration and the EU's active neighborhood policy." The White Paper thus points to the EU as an emerging center of gravity for European defense and security affairs, as Germany seeks the ability to "militarily plan and lead ESDP operations autonomously... to do this it should be able to draw on force structures of its own, at least to a limited extent."[294]

The White Paper also codified the idea of transforming the *Bundeswehr* into a smaller, lighter military focused primarily on low intensity expeditionary operations, consisting of a small, highly professional rapid reaction force; a larger and deployable sustainment force; and a logistic support force consisting mainly of conscripts and reservists.

Viewed in context, the principal role of the *Bundeswehr* remains the territorial defense of the Federal Republic. However, a host of additional missions have been added, including peacekeeping and peace enforcement; stabilization and reconstruction; and humanitarian assistance. As the German constitution limits the *Bundeswehr* strictly to "defensive" operations, the participation of the German military in combat operations in Kosovo and Afghanistan was extremely controversial and required a series of court rulings resulting in the doctrine that the defense of Germany may begin on the other side of the world — explicit

---

[293] Ibid.

[294] Ibid.

recognition of the interconnectedness of Germany in a globalized economy. Germany has also signed on to the equally controversial "obligation to protect"; i.e., the duty of countries to intervene in other countries to protect innocent people from genocide or death from neglect in cases of famine and other national disasters.

The Air Force and Navy are also being reorganized as part of the force transformation. With the introduction of the Eurofighter, the Luftwaffe will retire its remaining Tornado strike fighters and F-4F Phantoms, leaving it with just a single type of combat aircraft organized into six combat wings, one reconnaissance wing, and one special operations wing. The biggest change is a substantial increase in tactical and strategic airlift capability through the introduction of the A400M and A310 aerial refueling tankers, which will allow German military units to self-deploy out of area. The Navy in its turn is expanding it horizons beyond the Baltic Sea by acquiring long-range, multimission frigates and logistic support ships that will allow the Navy to support *Bundeswehr* and coalition operations outside the NATO operating area.

The Situation Today: Domestic Constraints on German Security Objectives

In sum, the new envisioned *Bundeswehr* has the potential to become a valuable contributor to Europe's common defense and the maintenance of international order. However, for this vision to be translated into reality, Germany will have to develop a political consensus on the use of force and apply additional resources. To date, there has been little political will to move in either of these directions, with security taking a back seat to the financial crisis and other economic, social and environmental objectives.

Politically, there does not seem to be much support for the active role outlined for the *Bundeswehr* in the White Paper. While Germany has continued to participate in a wide range of international peacekeeping, stabilization, and peace enforcement missions, the activities of its troops have been severely circumscribed by operational "caveats" defining what they may and may not do. This has been the cause of friction with Germany's International Security Assistance Force partners in Afghanistan, where German troops have been prohibited by their government from taking "offensive" action against Taliban and al-Qaeda forces, and have on several occasions been prevented from going to the aid of other coalition forces under attack in neighboring areas of operations. This has been a cause of some frustration within the German military, whose officers and increasingly professional enlisted soldiers are eager to demonstrate their willingness to fight proficiently in battle.[295] Overriding the caveats has been difficult, despite widespread criticism of German policy, because there is a strong domestic opposition to placing German troops in harm's way under any circumstances, which in turn places the credibility of the White Paper's strategic posture in doubt.

Finally, the White Paper does not address in any detail the resources needed to effect the kinds of transformation it outlines and there is little prospect that Germany would increase its defense spending—which is needed—to achieve its force transformation goals. Despite German statements over the years committing itself to real increases in defense spending

---

[295] See, for example, ISAF Video Tele Conference: Interview With Major General Bruno Kasdorf, Chief of Staff, ISAF Headquarters, Oct. 11, 2007 (available at: http://www.nato.int/isaf/docu/speech/2007/sp071011a.html) and "Germany's Non-Combat Caveats to Be Reviewed by NATO," DW-World.de, Nov. 28, 2007 (available at http://www.dw-world.de/dw/article/0,2144,2250071,00.html).

Figure 72   European Defense Expenditures as Percentage (%) of GDP

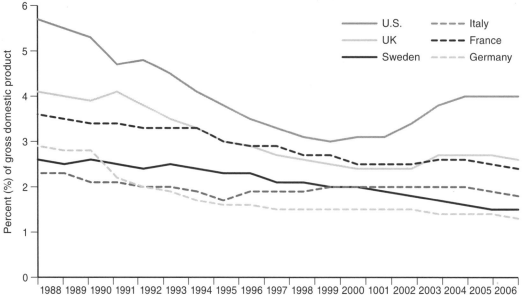

Source: SIPRI Defense Expenditures Database.

(both in absolute terms and as a share of GDP), in reality German defense spending has continued to decline. As shown on Figure 72, by way of context, the German defense budget fell from 2.8 percent of GDP in 1990 to 1.5 percent in 1998; the budget remained at that level through 2002, before falling to 1.4 percent of GDP in 2003, and to only 1.3 percent in 2006. Germany thus spends less proportionally than any other country in this study, including Italy.

In fact, Germany's ability to increase defense spending is seriously constrained by the explosive growth of its social welfare programs—particularly pensions (by 2025, more than 30 percent of the German population will be over age 65), sluggish economic growth, and debt limits imposed by the Maastricht Treaty.

Thus, as Germany struggles with the global financial crisis and resulting economic downturn, any near-term increases are unlikely, which in turn makes it difficult to see how Germany will be able to translate the defense transformation objectives laid out in the White Paper into operational and acquisition realities.

Also problematic for the future is Germany's chronic underinvestment in defense research and technology (R&T). All European countries tend to spend less of their defense budgets, proportionally, on R&T than does the United States. However, Germany is exceptional for how little of its budget is spent toward the development of new technologies and capabilities. In 1989, for example, Germany spent just $3.1 billion out of $51 billion (in 2005 dollars) on defense research, only about 6 percent. By 2002, this had fallen to only $0.75 billion of $40 billion, or barely 2 percent.[296] Several factors account for this. First, Germany

---

[296] See J. Bialos and S. Koehl, eds., *European Defense Research and Development: New Visions and Prospects for Cooperative Engagement*, Johns Hopkins-SAIS Center for Transatlantic Relations (Washington, D.C.), 2004.

has maintained an excessively large and aging force structure that consumes an increasing share of the budget in O&M costs. Second, O&M costs are being driven up by Germany's unprecedented overseas commitments, for which neither the budget nor the German military is properly structured. Third, the transition from a mainly conscripted force to a professional, volunteer military has been driving up personnel costs. With Germany committed to a number of large, multinational procurement programs such as A400M, Eurofighter, Eurocopter Tiger and Multi Role Armored Vehicle (MRAV)/Boxer, as well as to a number of prominent national programs such as the U-212 class submarines, the K-124 Corvette, the F-125 Frigate and the Puma infantry fighting vehicle, the defense budget is under severe pressure. The loser in this equation is the R&T budget; Germany apparently looks to the establishment of an integrated European defense R&T program under the aegis of the EDA as a means of at least partially ameliorating the shortfall.[297]

The U.S.-German Security Relationship: A Longstanding Anchor of NATO

Throughout the Cold War era, relations between the United States and Germany were generally close, whether Germany was ruled by the Social Democrats or the Christian Democrats. The prevalence of the Soviet threat had established a strategic consensus between the two countries that managed to weather a series of sporadic crises, including German opposition to the Vietnam War, the nuclear disarmament movement in the 1980s, and opposition to sanctions against Iraq in the 1990s. German-American relations were strengthened in the immediate post-Cold War period by U.S. support for German reunification.

But, under the Social Democratic government of Gerhard Schroeder, U.S.-German relations reached their nadir due to German opposition to the U.S. invasion of Iraq and antipathy to U.S. President George W. Bush. For its part, the United States objected to what it perceived as German obstructionism in dealing with Saddam Hussein, Germany's underinvestment in the common defense, and its failure to pull its weight in Afghanistan and elsewhere. Both sides recognized the situation had deteriorated, and the election of Angela Merkel as Chancellor created an opportunity to mend political fences.

However, beyond Iraq, there have been other gradually emerging differences in perspective between Germany and the United States—especially as Germany has developed a close relationship with France over the years. There has been some drift on issues such as America's role in the world, the emergence of the EU and ESDP as the focus for European security, and the use of force. Since the accession of Angela Merkel, relations have improved considerably but the underlying questions have not been resolved. Although Chancellor Merkel is much more devoted to the Transatlantic relationship than Schroeder was, the structure of her coalition tends to limit the steps she can take to improve relations.

It must be noted that even during the lowest point of U.S.-German relations in 2004-2005, the working relationship between the German and United States military forces remained close. In some ways, military-to-military relations have never been better, particularly as German and U.S. commanders work together in Afghanistan.

---

[297] See, e.g., German Defense Industries Committee, *Position Paper of the German Security and Defence Industry Regarding the European Defence Agency*, Document D 0037-E, Federation of German Industries, August 2006.

Figure 73   Total U.S. Trade Flow With Germany (Billions of Dollars – $)

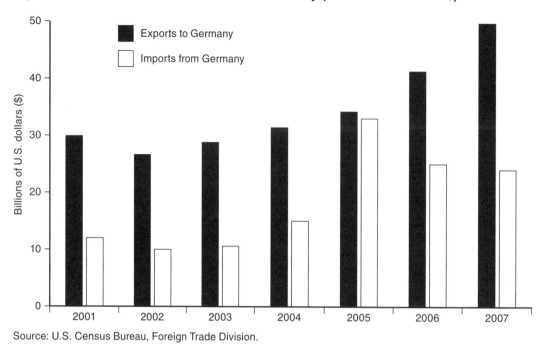

Source: U.S. Census Bureau, Foreign Trade Division.

Legal Frameworks for Defense Industrial Cooperation

U.S.-German armaments cooperation has longstanding legal underpinnings. Germany has the special benefit of several bilateral agreements with the United States to ease the flow and speed of defense trade and cooperation between the nations. Of particular note, the two nations are parties to a reciprocal defense procurement Memorandum of Understanding (MOU) regarding defense procurement, which provides, among other things, that Germany and U.S. defense suppliers, respectively, are treated in principle no less favorably in regard to procurement than domestic companies.[298]

U.S.-German Defense Trade and Industrial Cooperation

Germany is a major U.S. trading partner in the broader economy, with trade flows averaging about $150 billion per year (see Figure 73). The balance of trade is generally in Germany's favor, with U.S. imports from Germany nearly double German imports to the United States in recent years. Overall, the United States typically runs a trade deficit with Germany of about $45 billion.

Although Germany has long been a major customer for U.S. defense products, as well as a partner in a number of major cooperative development programs, defense trade with Germany is only a small fraction of overall U.S.-German trade. In the defense market, the United States consistently posts trade surpluses of $300-700 million per year (see Figure 74). While the United States exports a wide range of systems and subsystems to Germany,

---

[298] See 1991 amendment to MOU (noting that covered "procedures will follow the principles that foreign suppliers shall be treated the same as domestic suppliers."). Available at: http://www.acq.osd.mil/dpap/Docs/mou-germany.pdf.

Figure 74   U.S.-German Defense Trade (Billions of Dollars–$)

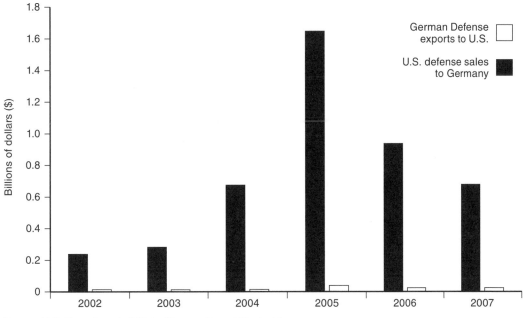

Source: U.S. Department of State, German Export Control Agency.

including radar, missiles, avionics and electronics, German exports to the United States tend to occupy distinct niches in which German companies have unique products (e.g., lightweight tank tracks, high-frequency signals intelligence) or a competitive advantage (precision optics).

The Historical Context

As noted, the *Bundeswehr* was rapidly reconstituted in the 1950s using U.S. equipment, including M47 and M48 main battle tanks, Fletcher and Charles F. Adams class destroyers, and above all, combat aircraft including the F-86 Sabre and F-84 Thunderjet. This experience gave the German military a strong preference for U.S. technology.

As the German defense industry matured, Germany became first a supplier of components for U.S. systems and then a co-producer of major systems, including guided missiles such as the AIM-9 Sidewinder. German participation in the Starfighter Consortium (discussed below) was a major effort for German aerospace and pointed the way toward further cooperation on a joint development program for a futuristic tank called MBT-70. The MBT-70 program eventually failed—both because it incorporated too many immature technologies and because, with very different perspectives on the role of the tank, Germany and the United States had difficulty harmonizing their requirements. The program was cancelled and each country then established independent national tank programs (Leopard II and M1 Abrams) that incorporated much of the technology developed through MBT-70.

In many ways, MBT-70 was the high point of U.S.-German defense industrial cooperation. As noted, Germany declined to participate in the F-16 Falcon Consortium in favor of developing the European Fighter Aircraft and the Panavia Tornado. Germany did buy several hundred F-4F Phantoms in 1973 as gap-fillers when the Tornado was delayed. However, that purchase marked the last major weapon system procured from the United States—with the exception of four battalions of Patriot air defense missiles.

Since the late 1970s, the primary bilateral defense cooperative programs involving joint ventures between U.S. and German firms have been more modest—mainly focused on the development of new guided missiles. These include:

- Medium Extended Air Defense System (MEADS)
- NATO Enhance Sea Sparrow Missile (ESSM)
- Rolling Airframe Missile (RAM)
- Guided MLRS (G-MLRS)
- AGM-88 Block-6 High Speed Anti-Radiation Missile (HARM) Precision Navigation Unit (PNU)

Past U.S.-German cooperative programs have been marked by a number of significant problems. MBT-70 suffered from overly ambitious goals and difficulties in requirements harmonization. RAM was plagued by serious technical problems and program delays, despite the missile's extensive use of non-developmental items. All of these programs were affected by funding turbulence on the European side, and lukewarm commitment by the United States.

There are now no "big ticket" U.S.-German cooperative programs such as F-35 Joint Strike Fighter—nor have there been since the late 1960s. Discussions concerning joint development of major systems including armored fighting vehicles, artillery and surveillance aircraft have foundered on key issues such as requirements harmonization, budgets, technology transfer, or work share arrangements.

U.S. German Defense Cooperation Today

Like a number of other countries studied, the DoD has signed a Declaration of Principles (DoP) with Germany. The DoPs are non-binding bilateral agreements on defense industrial cooperation. The U.S. signaled its willingness to enter into the DoPs on a nation's approach to the so-called "Five Pillars of Compatibility and Confidence"—that is, five factors that describe the willingness of the United States to engage in deepened defense industrial relationships with other countries: 1) export controls commonality and reciprocity; 2) industrial security commonality and reciprocity; 3) intelligence cooperation; 4) law enforcement cooperation; and 5) guaranteed reciprocity of access to defense markets. The DoP signing initiated a process of bilateral working groups designed to facilitate strong cooperation. To date, no firm agreements have been reached under the DoP.

U.S.-German defense industrial cooperation today remains not robust, but no worse than it has been for the past several decades. Despite tense geopolitical relations between 2003 and 2005 as Operation Iraqi Freedom proceeded, U.S.-German defense industrial cooperation did not suffer any severe disruptions. Instead, the established programs have continued. As indicated on Table 33, however, there have been only a few new programs initiated over many years.

Table 33   Ongoing U.S.-German Cooperative Programs

Program	Initiated	Description	U.S. Companies	German Companies	Status
AGM-88 High Speed Anti-Radiation Missile (HARM) Block 6 PNU	1998	Anti-radar Missile	Raytheon	Diehl-BGT MBDA-Deutschland	Production
AIM-9 Sidewinder	1960s	Air-to-Air Missile	Raytheon	Diehl-BGT	Production
EuroHawk	2005	High-Altitude Long Endurance UAV	Northrop Grumman	EuroHawk GmbH	Development
Guided MLRS	1998	Guided artillery rocket	Lockheed Martin	Euro Rocket System GmbH	Production
Medium Extended Air Defense System (MEADS)	1996	Ground-based air-and-missile defense	Lockheed Martin	EuroMEADS GmbH	Development
RIM-116 Rolling Airframe Missile (RAM)	1995	Shipboard air defense	Raytheon	RAM-System GmbH	Production
RIM-7PTC NATO Evolved Sea Sparrow (ESSM)	1996	Shipboard air defense	Raytheon	RAM-System Gmbh TDW Gesellschaft	Production

There also have been very few bottom-up joint ventures since 2000, when General Dynamics Land Systems and MTU formed Performance Diesels LLC to pursue the engine contract on the U.S. Army's abortive Crusader self-propelled gun. Two newer ventures include: the EuroHawk, a "Europeanized" version of the Global Hawk high-altitude long-endurance unmanned air vehicle (UAV) for intelligence, surveillance and reconnaissance (ISR); and a joint venture between Diehl and Raytheon Missile Systems GmbH, formed in 2004 to overhaul and upgrade older versions of the AIM-9 Sidewinder for export customers.

b. Bilateral Market Access Issues

Based on interviews with market participants, there is considerable dissatisfaction in the German industry and government regarding the U.S. procurement system and U.S. export controls. Both see the U.S. system as being inherently protectionist. The proof in the pudding, they say, is that most of their efforts to penetrate the U.S. market have failed. Therefore, they argue, the U.S. market is effectively closed except for some specialty products. They point to U.S. domestic content laws such as the Buy American Act and the Berry Amendment, which, even if generous exemptions are made for NATO Member States, reflect, in their view, an attitude of preference for U.S. systems.

In almost every meeting with German industrial and government representatives, the ITAR process was represented as slow, opaque and arbitrary. According to market participants, even when technical assistance agreements are issued, the delays imposed by the process make it difficult to rely upon U.S. companies as suppliers on time-critical projects. While German government representatives did not go so far as to support an "ITAR-free" procurement policy, many saw such a policy developing in a de facto manner as European firms develop work-arounds and other equivalents for technology denied by the United

States. They pointed in particular to how U.S. technology restrictions have resulted in the development of autonomous European-based industrial capabilities. Many suggested the security of supply and global license provisions of the new European Commission (EC) Defense Package had the potential to jump-start an ITAR-free initiative within Europe that would amount in fact to a European preference in defense procurement.

U.S. defense firms interviewed had very consistent views that were mirror images of those held by German government and industry representatives. They perceive, and report the following:

- At the prime contractor level, the German market is largely closed to U.S. companies—not because of any overt regulatory discrimination, but because of a relatively closed and non-competitive German procurement system. There is an unspoken German policy to maintain control over almost all aspects of defense procurement.

- At the first- and second-tier subcontractor level, the market is more open. The key to success, one company representative said, is to let the Germans lead or "carry the flag"; i.e., pick a German company as prime contractor and establish a long-term strategic relationship. At the same time, many companies found German bureaucracy and regulations tedious and time-consuming, though not usually employed in an overtly discriminating manner.

- At lower sub-tier levels, however, the market is largely closed to smaller companies because each German defense company has its own proprietary set of preferred suppliers.

Future Outlook

The future of the U.S.-German defense industrial relationship depends on the broader context of U.S.-German relations and on how, within that context, Germany resolves its ambivalent attitude toward military power and its own defense budgets. Despite issuing the White Paper, Germany has not been able to fully fund the defense transformation it outlined, which in turn will put added stress on the defense industry in the near future.

II. The German Defense Market: Supply and Demand Dynamics

The German Defense Industry

Like the German military, the German defense industry has undergone significant evolution since the end of the Cold War. Yet, in many ways, it remains unchanged as compared to several of its neighbors.

The Cold War Revitalization of Germany's Defense Industry

At the end of World War II, most of the established German armaments companies were either liquidated or converted to civilian production. When the German military was reestablished in the mid-1950s in response to the increasing Soviet threat, Germany was almost totally dependent on foreign military assistance from the United States and the other NATO Allies for major weapon systems, including tanks, artillery, aircraft and ships.

Gradually, the old firms—Krupp, Thyssen, Henschel, Krauss-Maffei, Messerschmidt, Dornier, Blohm & Voss, HDW—were brought back into the defense business, first as suppliers, then with licensed production of U.S. and other systems, and finally as standalone designers and developers of major weapon systems. By the 1960s, Germany was capable of developing and producing outstanding designs of small arms, ordnance, armored fighting vehicles, surface ships, submarines and helicopters, many of which were sold to other countries within NATO.

Land combat systems became the backbone of the German defense industry. With its Leopard I and II, Germany developed two of the best tanks in the world, in the same class with the U.S. M1 Abrams and the British Challenger II. The Leopard family of tanks enjoyed considerable export success, having been adopted by many NATO countries (Britain, France and Italy, each of which has its own national tank, being the principal exceptions) as well as by Sweden, Switzerland, Finland, Singapore, Austria and Chile. The Leopard II's 120mm smooth-bore gun was later adopted by the United States on the M1A1 version of the Abrams tank.

Germany also became a world leader in diesel-electric submarines, with the HDW and Thyssen shipyards between themselves competing for the majority of the (non-Soviet) global submarine market. Beginning with small, coastal submarines intended for operations in the Baltic Sea, and drawing heavily on late World War II U-boat technology, the two German shipyards developed a wide range of short- to medium-range submarines intended to meet the requirements of a broad customer base. Indeed, more than 58 examples of the HDW Type 209 have been sold to 13 countries. Intended exclusively for export and built in five different versions, the Type 209 is the most prolific non-Russian submarine built since World War II.

Germany also became a leader in small and medium surface combatants, and maintained its traditional leading role in defense electronics and especially optics. German firms later branched out into new specialized areas such as robotic underwater vehicles for mine countermeasures operations

The one area in which Germany did not attempt to re-assert its pre-war capability was modern combat aircraft. Throughout the 1950s, the Luftwaffe was equipped almost entirely with U.S. aircraft, with companies such as Messerschmidt and MBB sometimes producing components and subsystems under license. In the 1960s, Germany stepped forward by joining the Starfighter Consortium with Belgium, the Netherlands, Italy and Canada to produce the highly advanced F-104G Starfighter multirole fighter under license from Lockheed Corporation. Under the consortium, each of the participating countries produced various elements of the aircraft, which were then assembled and used by all. From an industrial perspective, the consortium was a tremendous success, producing 1,122 aircraft. However, the Starfighter was very controversial within Germany because of its high accident rate.

Nonetheless, the experience seems to have convinced Germany that maintaining an indigenous fighter aircraft development capability was beyond its resources. All subsequent German fighters were developed through multinational cooperative programs, including the Panavia Tornado and the Eurofighter Typhoon. The one major exception to the rule was the acquisition of the F-4F, a simplified version of the McDonnell Douglas Phantom, pro-

Table 34   Major German Defense Companies, Pre-1989

| Land Systems | | Naval Systems | | Aircraft and Missiles | |
Company	Sector	Company	Sector	Company	Sector
Porsche	Tanks, AFVs	HDW	Submarines	Dornier	Aircraft
Henschel	AFVs	Nordseewerke	Ships	Messerschmidt	Aircraft
KUKA	AFVs	Blohm & Voss	Ships	LFK GmbH	Missiles
MAK	AFVs	Rheinstahl	Ships	Diehl BGT	Missiles
Rheinmetall	Ordnance	Lurssen	Patrol Craft	MBB	Helicopters
Heckler & Koch	Ordnance	Thyssen	Submarines		
Krauss-Maffei	AFVs				
Wegmann	AFVs				

cured directly from the United States under the "Peace Rhine" program,[299] mainly because of delays in the Tornado program. It is also significant that, when the United States initiated the Multinational F-16 Consortium in the 1970s as a follow-on to the Starfighter Consortium, Germany declined to participate—having already decided to team with other European countries to develop European Fighter Aircraft (eventually the Eurofighter Typhoon).

By the 1980s, therefore, Germany had a large and diverse defense industry capable of designing and producing almost the full range of modern weapon systems. There were multiple German competitors in each market segment (see Table 34). These companies were supported by a large array of small second- and third-tier subcontractors, many family-owned and providing a very narrow range of products and services. This large and fragmented defense industrial landscape was sustainable through the 1980s for a number of reasons. Fundamentally, the *Bundeswehr* was a large, viable domestic customer and Germany had become a major export supplier to other NATO countries. Moreover, the German government took a highly proprietary and protectionist interest in the defense industry, typically favoring German-developed or co-produced systems, except when no other alternative was available. Politically as well, Germany needed to maintain a strong defense industry, together with its high wage employment base, to sustain support for its relatively high defense budget across the Cold War period. At its peak, the German defense industry employed more than 120,000 workers and generated approximately $6 billion in turnover.

Post-Cold War German Defense Industrial Consolidation and Downsizing

With the end of the Cold War, demand for all defense goods dropped significantly, particularly for systems such as main battle tanks, which had been the backbone of the German defense industry. For example, in the German military vehicle sector alone, employment declined from 44,000 to 10,000 between 1989 and 2000.[300] By the mid-1990s, consolidation

---

[299] The aircraft were assembled in St. Louis by McDonnell Douglas, with major subassemblies built by MBB and MTU in Germany.

[300] H. Baumann, "Consolidation of the Military Vehicle Market in Western Europe and the United States," *Background Paper on the SIPRI Yearbook—2003*, Stockholm International Peace Research Institute (SIPRI), Stockholm, 2003.

was inevitable. This occurred in two distinct waves: the aerospace industry followed by ground combat system suppliers.

The aerospace consolidation involved a two-stage process, wherein smaller German companies were first absorbed into larger ones. Notably, Dornier and MBB were absorbed into DaimlerChrysler Aerospace AG (DASA), which in its turn divested most of its defense holdings to the European multinational European Aeronautic Defense and Space (EADS) Company formed in July 2000 by the merger of Aerospatiale Matra SA (France), CASA (Spain) and DaimlerChrysler Aerospace AG (Germany).

Since the formation of EADS, most of the remaining German aerospace companies have been absorbed by it or one of its subsidiaries. For instance, the missile company LFK GmbH was first acquired by EADS in 2000, then sold to the EADS missile subsidiary MBDA in 2006. Similarly, helicopter manufacturer MBB was acquired by DASA and then transferred to the DASA-Aerospatiale joint venture Eurocopter in 1992, which became part of EADS in 2000. *Notably, in many of these cases, the former German companies remain largely autonomous within their multinational conglomerates.* MBB still exists as Eurocopter Deutschland GmbH within the structure of EADS Eurocopter, while LFK GmbH is still a distinct entity under the name MBDA Deutschland. Though ostensibly "multinational," these companies function more in a "multidomestic" manner—autonomous German companies under foreign ownership and management.

It is also important to note that EADS is not a "German" firm in ownership, but a multinational firm with shares held by the French State and Daimler directly and held by the French and Spanish states indirectly via holding companies.

Consolidation in naval shipbuilding took longer to accomplish, but was largely completed by 2004, when all of Germany's major shipyards (HDW, Nordseewerke, Blohm & Voss and Rheinstahl) were acquired by the ThyssenKrupp Group.

The consolidation in the land systems market has moved more slowly. In the early 1990s, there were seven distinct ground systems prime contractors in Germany. Today, there are just three: Rheinmetall Defense, Krauss-Maffei Wegmann (itself formed by the 1998 merger of Krauss-Maffei Wehrtechnik and Wegmann & Co.); and Diehl-BGT Defense. Rheinmetall Defense, which absorbed MAK, KUKA, and Henschel Wehrtechnik, specializes in light vehicles, small- to medium-caliber ordnance, and defense electronics, while Krauss-Maffei Wegmann builds main battle tanks and other heavy vehicles, large-caliber ordnance and air defense systems.[301] Diehl-BGT Defense, in contrast, is focused on guided munitions, electronics, unmanned air vehicles and other advanced technologies. That these businesses are privately held by family interests has complicated further consolidation.

Organizationally, at the prime contractor level, the German defense industry today appears to have consolidated in accordance with new market realities. In actuality, however, it is still plagued by overcapacity due to the unwillingness of the German government to allow the newly consolidated prime contractors to rationalize and streamline their operations by closing redundant plants, reducing workforce, and achieving synergy by closer internal integration.

---

[301] This division of labor resembles that which existed in the U.S. between General Dynamics Land Systems (GDLS) and United Defense before GDLS expanded into the light armored vehicle market.

In short, the old German defense industrial structure still largely survives underneath the veneer of the new, with the same basic problems unresolved. This extends to the second and third tiers, where similar consolidation has not taken place—in large part because each of the newly reorganized prime contactors has retained the existing fragmented supplier networks of its subsidiary companies.

The leading German defense companies are listed in Table 35. (As noted above, EADS is a European multinational firm with several subsidiaries located in Germany; EADS shares are not fully held by German sources.)

German Acquisition Policy: A Tension Between Transformational and Legacy Systems

German acquisition policy also has evolved over the years. The 2006 German White Paper spells out German acquisition priorities within the context of the new defense transformation plan, with much more emphasis on strategic mobility, deployability, and sustainability out of area. The requirement to participate in high-intensity coalition operations mandates the acquisition of network-centric capabilities, including: ISR platforms; secure tactical communications systems; broadband satellite communications capabilities; and interoperable data networks. The need to operate out of area for extended periods requires the acquisition of strategic air- and sea-lift capabilities, tactical transport vehicles, and additional transport helicopters.

While conceptually sound, many of the specific programs were already on the books—in effect, the White Paper primarily ratified existing German procurement priorities. These include such programs as the A400M transport, the Tiger multirole helicopter, the F-125 class frigates, and the Boxer/MRAV wheeled armored personnel carrier.

Also, Germany continues to face tension between its transformational goals and the continuation of legacy programs that reflect older territorial missions such as the new Lynx infantry fighting vehicle, the PzH.2000 self-propelled gun, the Eurofighter Typhoon, and the U-212 class of air-independent propulsion submarines. For example, the Eurofighter is the leading German defense program, accounting for more than $1 billion over the past three years.

In ground systems, as well, this tension exists. Germany is still pursuing Leopard II upgrades although it is unlikely any German tank regiment would ever deploy outside of Germany or meet any comparable threat. Germany also is developing the Puma Infantry Fighting Vehicle as a replacement for the aging Marder. A state-of-the-art tracked infantry fighting vehicle equal or superior to the Bradley Fighting Vehicle, Puma is still too large to be transported by air, even in an A400M, and funding for its development and production competes with the lighter, more transportable Boxer/MRAV wheeled armored personnel carrier, a vehicle much better suited to the types of expeditionary scenarios outlined in the White Paper.

A review of the relative distribution of Germany procurement funding relative to the requirements in the White Paper creates an impression that some programs may be less driven by operational need than by industrial policy; i.e., the need to maintain some capability in low demand areas such as tank manufacturing, submarine design and development, and light armored vehicles.

Table 35   Leading German Defense Companies, 2008

Name	Revenues (Million of Dollars–$)	Employment	Market Sectors
EADS*	4,079.7	41,000	Aircraft, Ground Combat, Electronics, Space
ThyssenKrupp Marine	2,860.0	9,300	Ships, submarines, electronics
Rheinmetall	2,587.8	18,800	Ground Combat Systems, Ordnance
Krauss-Maffei Wegmann	1,914.7	2,800	Ground Combat Systems
Diehl BGT Defense	972.1	1,800	Ground Combat, Electronics
MTU Aero Engines	500.0	6,000	Aircraft propulsion
Heckler & Koch	195.0	700	Small Arms

*Only in Germany; revenues estimated.
Souce: DACIS.

In all events, Germany's defense spending trajectory—likely to be exacerbated in the context of the current global financial crisis and recession—will probably force choices between transformation and legacy systems. Meeting the White Paper's procurement goals would have been possible had Germany increased or at least maintained its defense budgets at their 2004 level. Since the implementation of the new White Paper, however, German defense spending has actually decreased in real terms, from $38.8 billion to $36.9 billion in constant 2004 dollars.[302] As the German economy slows in response to the global financial crisis, it seems likely further reductions will ensue, with the inevitable program slippage and cuts in production. Reductions in German R&T funding (averaging less than $1 billion per annum[303]) also point to declining levels of innovation in future German defense systems.

Germany's Defense Industrial Policy: Issues of Nationalism and Realism

Germany's evolving policy on the sustainment of its defense industry reflects a tension between recognizing the growing globalization of the industry and the need to maintain a broad autonomous national capability. It also raises questions of realism: German notions of the wide range of national capabilities they need to maintain appear to be misaligned with budgetary realities.

These tensions are apparent in the 2006 German White Paper. On the one hand, the White Paper highlights the trend toward a European wide industry:

> A modern *Bundeswehr* requires an efficient and sustainable defence industry base. This will need to be defined increasingly in a European context, given the limited national resources and restrained national demand. Political, military and eco-

---

[302] SIPRI Defense Expenditures Database, Supra.

[303] SIPRI *Yearbook*, 2001, 2003.

nomic aspects make in-depth cooperation highly important for the EU Member States to meet the materiel requirements of their armed forces. For this reason, the development of a European armaments policy is a central goal in establishing and expanding the European Security and Defence Policy.[304]

On the other hand, the White Paper states that:

> Germany needs to maintain "indigenous defence technology capabilities in order to co-shape the European integration process in the armaments sector. These will guarantee cooperability and assure an influence in the development, procurement and operation of critical military systems. Only nations with a strong defence industry have the appropriate clout in Alliance decisions.

> The political leadership and industry must jointly define the strategic positioning of German defence technology in Europe. *The federal government will do its utmost in this regard to preserve a balanced mix of defence technology, including its high-technology areas, in Germany.* National consolidation, such as is taking place in the shipbuilding industry, is preparing Germany's defence technology enterprises to suitably position themselves for the restructuring process in Europe.[305] (Emphasis added.)

In 2007 Germany developed its own defense industrial policy, intended to provide guidance to industry in light of its limited budgetary resources, the ongoing consolidation of the defense industry across Europe, and the emergence of a nascent integrated European defense market in the context of the evolving European Union role in defense and security matters.

The industrial policy is unique in that it is not a governmental pronouncement, but a "Joint Declaration" of German MoD and the Defense Economics Committee of the Federal Ministry of German Industries. Foreshadowing its primary thrust, this document is referred to as a Joint Declaration on National Key Defense Technology Capabilities.[306] The Declaration is a reflection of intensive coordination and consultation between the MoD and the German defense industry and is designed to implement the 2006 White Paper's transformational strategy.

The Declaration, like the White Paper, also clearly reflects the tension between the Europeanization of the defense industry and the desire to maintain autonomous national assets. In a remarkably candid statement focused on the preservation of German defense industrial capabilities, the Declaration thus states:

> [A] strong and reliable national defence industry offering a great deal of technological expertise and adequate capacities is therefore a vital partner in security.... [T]he ongoing consolidation process within the European and [T]ransatlantic defence industries must be viewed from a particular, quite national angle.

---

[304] White Paper, Supra, p. 63.

[305] Ibid.

[306] "Joint Declaration of the Federal Ministry of Defense and the Defence Economics Committee in the Federal Ministry of German Industries on National Key Defence Technology Capabilities" ("Joint Declaration") (Unpublished) (Berlin, Nov. 20, 2007).

Table 36   Key Defense Technology Capabilities

Systems	
Space-Based Reconnaissance	Combat Aircraft
Transport Aircraft	Helicopters
Unmanned Air Vehicles	Air Defense Systems
Protected Wheeled Vehicles	Tracked Vehicles
Infantryman of the Future	Submarines
Autonomous Underwater Vehicles	Surface Combatants
Sea Mine Countermeasures	Modeling and Simulation
Bundeswehr IT Systems	

Subsystems	
Electronic Reconnaissance	Electronic Warfare
NBC Defense Components	Munitions Defense Components

Sources: Joint Declaration, op. cit., Annex. BWB.

Europe's governments have to provide suitable framework conditions for ensuring that a balance is struck in the consolidation of the industries in Europe. Even if the purely national assessment and evaluation of the development of the defence industries' strength and competitiveness will give way more and more to international considerations, the identification of indispensable key defence technology capabilities is of paramount interest to the Federal Republic of Germany as regards its industrial and security policy. In order to also meet the demands of its role as a security partner of equal rank in future, Germany needs to maintain a modern, competitive and strong defence industry. Only the preservation and improvement of defence technology capabilities and capacities at a qualitatively and quantitatively high level and geared toward the necessary and long-term capabilities for modern armed forces that are fit for the future will ensure that Germany has a say in European and [T]ransatlantic affairs and the capability to both shape developments and engage in cooperation.[307]

Thereafter, as shown in Table 36, the Declaration sets forth 14 "indispensable national key defence technology capabilities" for Germany to retain "at the system level." The Declaration notes that German industry today has only partial capabilities in three of these areas and must rely on cooperation with partners to achieve full system level capability. The Declaration also notes three "indispensable national key defence technology capabilities" to be sustained at the subsystem level."

What is striking about this list is the *breadth* of industrial sectors in which Germany wishes to maintain system level national capabilities. Whereas the French, Swedish and to some extent UK industrial policies call for maintaining autonomy in only select areas, the German list of national autonomous areas covers most of its industry. Restated, it is difficult to see sectors of the German defense industry not covered.

---

[307] Ibid.

National Autonomy vs. A European Approach: Irreconcilable Differences

On balance, the differences between the long-term German policy of promoting an integrated European defense policy, and the protectionist thrust of the German defense industrial policy, are hard to reconcile. These internal contradictions point to the inherent difficulties of subordinating national interests to European interests when faced by serious domestic repercussions such as job losses in high-paying industries. This is reflected in Germany's apparent unwillingness to draw distinctions and identify market areas that are non-strategic where Germany would be willing to source through international competition. Germany, under its succession of weak coalition governments, does not appear to have the political will to effectively reorganize the defense industry in a manner that would enhance efficiency and promote real competition.

Hence, it remains to be seen if Germany will effectively reorganize its defense industry in a manner that would enhance defense industrial efficiency and competition within Europe.

Finally, it should be recognized that the broad scope list of defense industrial capabilities Germany seeks to maintain also stands in sharp juxtaposition to its budgetary realities. The combination of large legacy programs and flat to declining spending will prevent Germany from maintaining autonomy in most of these areas.

In short, in the likely absence of strategic action by the German government—either a scaling back of areas of industrial autonomy or increased budgetary outlays, both of which are unrealistic, the German defense industry is likely to gradually continue to be hollowed out over time.

German Industrial Policy as a Negotiating Tool. Thus, this broad list reflects an inherent conflict in the German position. Despite Germany's apparent commitment to ESDP, European defense industrial consolidation, and the EC Defense Procurement Directive, Germany nevertheless seeks to maintain strategic sovereignty (i.e., autonomy) in a broad range of technological capabilities, including some where Germany does not, and never has had any significant capabilities (e.g., combat aircraft). Pressed on the matter, a number of German officials admitted that the list was too broad, but that it was a "bargaining position" for use in the EC and EDA with regard to the EC Defense Procurement Directive and the application of Article 296 EC Treaty exclusions from competition. They noted it didn't make sense to "give up" areas of national autonomy in advance and it was better to await negotiations within the EDA with European partners to do this and eliminate redundancies.

III. Evaluation of Market Access Metrics

Tariff Barriers

By and large, tariffs are not significant barriers between Germany and the United States. All of the countries studied are members of the World Trade Organization (WTO) and thus must provide most-favored nation and national treatment to imported goods from every other country included in the study. Although defense products are generally exempt from WTO rules governing tariffs and trade, reciprocal procurement MOUs between the United States and Germany generally provide duty-free treatment for imported defense products procured from the other country.

However, these MOUs do not apply to dual-use products and technologies such as general aerospace systems that have both military and civil applications. Thus, as more military programs rely on commercial off-the-shelf (COTS) technology, this would tend to put U.S. companies at a competitive disadvantage *vis-à-vis* European firms that get the benefit of the lower intra-European rates that apply under EU rules unless specific exemptions are negotiated on a bilateral basis.

Competition in Procurement

German Procurement Policy: A Status Quo Picture

In theory, Germany requires all defense procurement contracts to be awarded through open competition except in certain limited circumstances:

- National security considerations require the procurement from a domestic company;

- Requirements that can only be met by one company due to specialized capabilities or proprietary technology; or

- Industrial base reasons.

In policy and practice, however, the German MoD procurement agency, the *Bundesamt fur Wehrteknik und Beschaffung* (BWB) still tends to make the bulk of its awards on a sole source or directed competitive basis to national suppliers or to European consortia for European cooperative programs. According to market participants interviewed, Germany habitually invokes Article 296 EC Treaty in procuring a wide array of products, not all of them strictly defense-related.

Thus, unlike other Western European countries we reviewed, there is no indication that Germany has adopted any significant shifts in its procurement policy toward greater use of competition on major programs or other better buying habits. By all indications, the status quo largely prevails.

German Procurement Practice: Understanding the Data

In practice, as shown below, the available data continues to show substantial reliance on sole source national buying in Germany, as well as a sizable and growing reliance on Euro-

Table 37   Competition in Major German Defense Programs in Billions of Dollars ($)

Type	Number	Value	Percent (%) by Value
Competitive	28	1.95322	21.1
Multinational	7	2.66087	28.8
Sole Source	28	4.62319	50.0
Total	63	9.23728	100.0

Source: Documental Solutions.

pean buying (whether through competition or cooperative programs). This market reality does not augur well for market access by U.S. firms—indeed, U.S. firms have a minor market share in Germany today and limited prospects for the future under current German policy and practice.

- **German Buying of Major Weapons Systems: The Limited Role of Competition.** A review of the top 63 German defense programs by value[308] (see Table 38) shows that only one-fifth of these programs by value (21 percent or $1.95 billion) were awarded competitively (see Table 37). Roughly one-half were awarded on a sole source basis (50 percent or $4.62 billion), with the remaining 29 percent ($2.66 billion) awarded through European cooperative programs. (Note that in European cooperative programs work share is typically established through intergovernmental MOUs and contracts that are awarded through directed procurement without full and open competition.) Several other key points about overall German buying also are worth noting:

  - **Sole Source Awards Are Larger Than Competitive Awards.** The average award for a sole source contract was considerably larger ($165 million) than the average award for a competitive contract ($70 million). This suggests Germany's current preference is to procure its most complex and expensive systems from national sources or through cooperative development programs with other European countries (e.g., Eurofighter, Tiger, TTH90).

  - **Overall Data Can Mask Differences Between Legacy/New Buying.** As discussed below, this overall data on total German buying in 2006-2008 may mask any distinctions between "legacy programs" (i.e., programs where the initial award for development and/or procurement were made somewhere in the past before 2006) and "new" programs started during 2006-2008 (which are more likely to show any meaningful shifts in procurement policy). Hence, we have separately reviewed the data on "legacy" and "new" programs below to capture any different trends that may exist.

  - **Half of All Major Program Spending Is on Legacy Programs.** As shown on Figure 75, roughly half ($4.6 vs. $4.5 billion) of all spending in the last three years has been on legacy programs. This reflects the long development cycle of large programs and the long service life of major systems. The list of Top German Defense Programs (Table 37) shows that legacy German national programs and cooperative

---

[308] RDT&E and Procurement programs totaling more than $50 million for 2006-2008.

Table 38   Leading German Defense Programs, 2006-2008, over $50 Million (in Millions of Dollars−$)

Program	Description	Prme Contractor	Country	2006	2007	2008	Total	Award Type	Legacy
Eurofighter	Multi-Role Fighter	Eurofighter	EUR	801.51	116.14	53.70	971.35	Multinational	Yes
K-130	Corvette	ThyssenKrupp AG	GE	299.92	301.70	201.91	803.53	Sole Source	No
Tiger	Helicopter	EADS	EUR	226.53	232.71	238.88	698.12	Multinational	Yes
TTH90	Helicopter	NH Industries	EUR	67.31	291.44	296.95	655.71	Multinational	No
TAURUS	Air-to-Surface Missile	Taurus Systems	GE	68.26	259.22	266.01	593.49	Sole Source	Yes
SS Type 212	Submarine	ThyssenKrupp AG	GE	190.76	161.05	131.16	482.97	Sole Source	No
CH-53GA Mod	Helicopter	EADS	EUR	250.00	150.00	71.00	471.00	Sole Source	Yes
F-125	Frigate	ThyssenKrupp AG	GE	100.00	150.00	135.06	385.06	Sole Source	Yes
Puma IFV	Infantry Fighting Vehicle	PSM	GE	132.59	81.54	163.76	377.89	Sole Source	No
F InfoSys Heer	Command & Control	EADS	EUR	90.27	91.93	93.58	275.78	Competitive	No
SASPF	Command & Control	SAP AG	GE	86.43	87.92	62.41	236.75	Competitive	No
Tornado EW Upgrade	Strike Fighter	EADS	EUR	72.13	72.84	73.55	218.53	Sole Source	Yes
HERKULES	IT System	Siemens	GE	0.00	100.00	100.00	200.00	Competitive	No
Eurofighter GFE Engine	Jet Engine	Eurojet	EUR	157.18	22.78	10.53	190.49	Multinational	Yes
SATCOM Payload Production	Satellite Communications	EADS	EUR	0.00	74.58	75.29	149.87	Competitive	No
Fennek	Reconnaissance Vehicle	Krauss-Maffei	GE	48.26	50.69	45.86	144.81	Sole Source	Yes
Leopard 2A6	Main Battle Tank	Krauss-Maffei	GE	74.36	21.17	21.09	116.62	Sole Source	Yes
Duro III	Tactical Vehicle	General Dynamics	US	22.75	45.16	46.36	114.27	Competitive	No
Hope/Hosbo	Guided Bomb	Diehl	GE	42.96	53.66	10.77	107.39	Sole Source	No
P-3 CUP	Patrol Aircraft	Lockheed Martin	US	51.05	51.05	0.00	102.10	Sole Source	Yes
Euro Hawk SIGINT	Signals Intelligence	EADS	EUR	30.00	35.00	35.00	100.00	Competitive	No

Table 38 Leading German Defense Programs, 2006-2008, over $50 Million (in Millions of Dollars−$) (continued)

Program	Description	Prime Contractor	Country	2006	2007	2008	Total	Award Type	Legacy
IRIS-T	Air-to-Air Missile	Diehl	GE	34.85	28.23	35.15	98.24	Sole Souce	Yes
Bv206	Tactical Vehicle	BAE SYSTEMS	UK	31.29	32.88	31.49	95.66	Competitive	Yes
STR 2000 NGIFF	Combat ID System	EADS	EUR	31.40	32.14	31.53	95.07	Competitive	No
Meteor	Air-to-Air Missile	MBDA	EUR	26.76	26.76	26.76	80.29	Multinational	Yes
PzH 2000	Self-Propelled Gn	Krauss-Maffei	GE	23.94	23.86	23.79	71.59	Sole Source	Yes
AMRAAM	Air-to-Air Missile	Raytheon	US	32.20	25.01	14.08	71.30	Sole Source	Yes
Mungo	Tactical Vehicle	Krauss-Maffei	GE	22.89	23.26	23.86	70.00	Sole Source	No
PSB2	Bridgelaying Vehicle	MAN	GE	58.35	5.25	5.25	68.85	Sole Source	No
BIGSTAF	Communications System	Thales	FR	6.19	29.61	29.94	65.75	Competitive	No
SATCOM 1m Term	Satellite Communications	SES Global SA	EUR	20.35	21.23	24.13	65.72	Competitive	No
TRM 6021V/UHF Transceiver	Tactical Radio	Thales	GE	15.38	23.83	25.48	64.69	Competitive	No
SAR-Lupe	Radar Surveillance Satellite	OHB Technology	GE	43.72	10.72	5.36	59.80	Sole Source	Yes
SATCOM 2.4m Term	Satellite Communications	SES Global SA	EUR	13.57	19.50	20.09	53.16	Competitive	No
TETRAPOL Sys	Communication System	EADS	EUR	22.95	23.87	2.74	49.56	Competitive	No
P-3 CUP Services	Patrol Aircraft	EADS	EUR	15.32	15.32	15.32	45.95	Sole Source	Yes
EC135	Helicopter	EADS	EUR	2.18	34.25	2.79	39.23	Sole Source	Yes
Wiesel 2 CP	Tactical Vehicle	Rheinmetall	GE	23.25	13.14	2.42	38.81	Sole Source	Yes
K-130 Int Com	Communications System	EADS	EUR	10.54	16.25	11.64	38.43	Competitive	No
Land Com R&D	Tactical Radio	Rohde & Schwarz	GE	12.60	12.60	12.60	37.79	Sole Source	No
HEROS-1/2	Command & Control	ESG GmbH	GE	16.06	10.71	10.71	37.47	Sole Source	No
TPz-1	Tactical Vehicle	Rheinmetall	EUR	25.09	10.49	1.78	37.36	Sole Source	Yes

Program	Description	Prme Contractor	Country	2006	2007	2008	Total	Award Type	Legacy
MOLEM	Laser Rangefinder	Carl Zeiss GR	GE	12.12	12.62	11.28	36.02	Competitive	Yes
UH-Tiger (GFE Engine Set)	Helicopter Engine	MTR JV	GE	11.33	11.64	11.94	34.91	Multinational	Yes
TRS-3D/16	Radar	EADS	FR	15.26	16.14	2.21	33.61	Competitive	No
MU-90 Impact LWT	Torpedo	EUROTORP	EUR	10.11	10.22	10.33	30.66	Sole Source	No
Boxer	Armored Personnel Carrier	ARTEC	EUR	10.00	10.00	10.00	30.00	Multinational	Yes
Laser Com Ter	Laser Communications	Tesat Spacecom	GE	10.00	10.00	10.00	30.00	Sole Source	No
YAK	Tactical Vehicle	Rheinmetall	GE	9.14	9.58	10.02	28.74	Sole Source	No
Euro Hawk GS	Unmanned Air Vehicle	Raytheon	US	25.92	1.38	1.38	28.69	Sole Source	No
ALR-95	ELINT System	EDO	US	23.71	1.79	1.79	27.28	Competitive	No
K-130 Datalinks	Communications System	EADS	EUR	7.03	10.84	7.76	25.62	Competitive	No
K130 Corvette CMS	Corvette	ET Marinesysteme	GE	12.16	12.49	0.82	25.47	Competitive	No
ELCRODAT 4-2 Crypto Set	Communications	Rohde & Schwarz	GE	5.95	8.57	10.81	25.32	Sole Source	Yes
TACTICOS CMS	Combat Information System	Thales	FR	5.94	9.02	9.18	24.14	Competitive	No
NuKomBw	IT System	EADS	EUR	7.78	7.93	8.07	23.78	Competitive	No
RAT-31	Radar	Finmeccanica	IT	11.16	11.59	0.87	23.62	Competitive	No
SATCOM SCC	Satellite Communications	SES Global SA	EUR	1.05	11.17	10.29	22.50	Competitive	No
BREVEL	Unmanned Air Vehicle	Rheinmetall	GE	20.36	1.07	1.07	22.49	Competitive	No
GIADS	Radar	EADS	EUR	18.29	2.09	2.07	22.45	Competitive	No
SATCOM Services	Satellite Communications	MilSat Services	GE	0.00	5.25	15.74	20.99	Competitive	No
SECCOM	IT Sysem	EADS	EUR	6.73	6.85	6.97	20.55	Competitive	No
ANCS	Combat Information System	EADS	EUR	0.00	8.00	12.00	20.00	Competitive	No

Source: Documental Solutions.

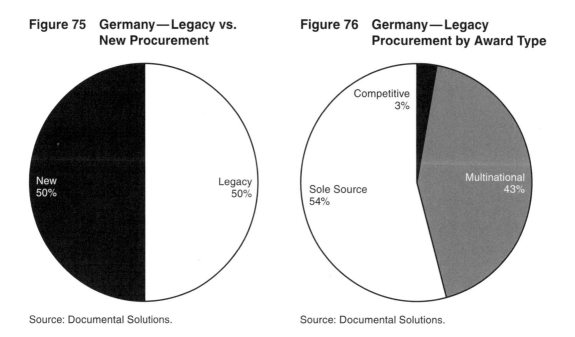

Figure 75   Germany—Legacy vs. New Procurement

Figure 76   Germany—Legacy Procurement by Award Type

Source: Documental Solutions.

Source: Documental Solutions.

programs such as Eurofighter Typhoon, Eurocopter Tiger, the Type 212 submarine—all started years ago—receive the largest amounts of funding.

- **Most Legacy Spending Is Sole Source or Directed.** As Figure 76 shows, approximately 54 percent of the legacy procurement awards by value were sole source basis; only 3 percent were awarded through "open and competitive" procurement while the remaining 43 percent were awarded through cooperative programs (i.e., which, as noted above, were neither competed nor open to foreign participation). The magnitude of sole source buying reflects the realities of large defense programs. After a major system has been awarded to a particular firm, the follow-on production buys, upgrades, modifications and maintenance on such legacy programs are often awarded to the same firm again (e.g., after an award is made for an aircraft developed and produced by one firm, it is much more likely to be awarded to that firm for future buys). Indeed, it would be uneconomic to change system level contractors midstream on large programs unless the incumbent is not performing (although government customers can and should compete the subsystems upgrades and refreshes). Therefore, not surprisingly, EADS/Airbus and Thyssen, the incumbent on numerous legacy programs, together received approximately 59 percent of all contracts awarded (by value) in the 2006-2008 period.

- **New German Awards Show Little Change; Sole Source Buying Still Dominates.** To assess whether Germany is changing its buying habits away from sole source national buying toward more competitive awards, we separately reviewed, on Figure 77, awards on "new" major programs in 2006-2008. Unlike in most other European countries, the resulting data on new programs showed only a modest positive change in buying habits. Specifically, approximately 46 percent of buying on new major contracts was sole source—with 14 percent of the purchasing done cooperatively with other European countries and 40 percent done competitively,

Figure 77   Germany—New Procurement by Award Type

Figure 78   Germany—Legacy Procurement by Supplier Country

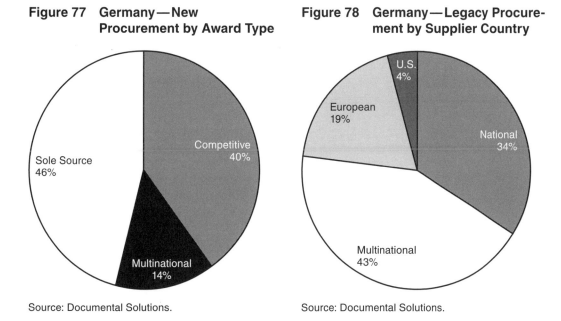

Source: Documental Solutions.

Source: Documental Solutions.

the lowest level of competition in new procurement of any European country other than France (where anecdotal evidence does show more competition and confirms a clear shift in policy toward better buying). The "new" and sizable sole source awards tend to be for either national programs in "strategically vital" industries such as shipbuilding or armored vehicles (K-130 Corvette, F-125 Frigate, Type 212 Submarine, Puma Infantry Fighting Vehicle) or for upgrades of existing systems (CH-53G modifications; P-3 Orion modifications; Tornado upgrades, etc.). In contrast, most of the competitive procurements of the last three years appear to come in areas that are either addressed by COTS solutions or in subsystem areas where Germany does not have a strong competitive advantage (e.g., competitive programs were primarily in electronics, communication, command and control, and sensors).

- **New German Buying Is Still Heavily National in Orientation With a Notable Amount of Inter-European Acquisitions.** As seen in Figure 78, legacy procurement was weighted almost equally between national companies (34 percent) and multinational programs (43 percent), with other European companies winning 19 percent and U.S. companies just 4 percent. Significantly, in New Procurements (Figure 79), the share of awards to national companies actually *increased* to 56 percent while the percentage of contracts covered by multinational programs fell to 17 percent. The percentage of contracts awarded to other European companies increased modestly to 23 percent while contracts to U.S. companies remained constant at 4 percent. Although the German defense market has become marginally more competitive, it would appear that this trend has served mainly to benefit German national companies.

- **U.S. Firms Have a Miniscule Share of the German Defense Market.** No matter how the available data on major program awards is sorted, it shows a remarkably limited presence for U.S. defense firms in Germany.

- **All Awards.** The data on market share (Figure 80) of firms for *all awards* (legacy and new) shows no American defense company ranked higher than 15th in total market share. General Dynamics received just 1.2 percent of the market, Lockheed Martin and Raytheon each accounted for 1.1 percent of the market, while then-EDO Corporation (now part of ITT) managed just 0.3 percent. German companies accounted for the overwhelming majority of prime contract awards by number and value.

- **Legacy Awards.** As shown on Figure 78, American firms received approximately 4 percent of all legacy awards, which are primarily sole source.

- **New Awards.** Notably, U.S. firms only received only 4 percent of all new German awards (competitive, sole source and cooperative, Figure 79) in recent years—a miniscule amount.

- **New Competitive Awards.** In order to see if overall award data masked trends on competitive programs, we again reviewed the competitive awards separately. However, there was no meaningful difference. The reality on new programs awarded competitively in Germany is that U.S. firms received only 9 percent of these contracts while national firms received 37 percent and firms from other European countries received 37 percent.

U.S. Subsystems Sales Also Likely Disadvantaged. While there may be greater U.S. subsystem participation than this data shows (anecdotal evidence suggests this), there is not enough data to fully evaluate this part of the market. However, the trend lines—toward buying European and avoiding ITAR products and technologies—appear to disfavor U.S. subsystem buying.

Market Fragmentation

As also shown in Figure 80, the German defense market remains highly fragmented despite ongoing consolidation. No fewer than 32 individual companies have prime contractor responsibility for the 63 top German programs. While three companies—EADS, Eurofighter and ThyssenKrupp—account for almost 55 percent of the total market by value, the remaining 45 percent is contested by 29 different companies, none of which has more than 7 percent market share. This degree of fragmentation at the prime level casts into doubt the long-term viability of the German defense industry absent real consolidation and reform.

Fair and Transparent Procurement Process

In general, the German defense procurement system is viewed as relatively transparent and fair. Germany, like other EU Member States, is a party to the WTO Agreement on Government Procurement (GPA). However, its procurement of "warlike" goods is exempt from the GPA's coverage and, hence, only "non-warlike" goods are subject to the Agreement's disciplines.

In Germany, requirements are generated by the various service offices, which turns them over to the BWB, the centralized procurement agency for the German MoD. Since January 2006, invitations to tender (Requests for Proposals) are posted on the federal government's central internet portal. BWB also posts both tenders and contract awards on the EDA's

Figure 79   Germany—New Procurement by Supplier Country

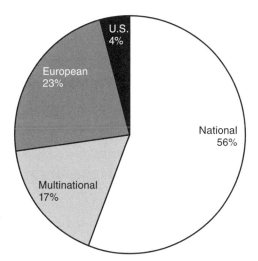

Source: Documental Solutions.

Figure 80   Germany—Defense Market Share by Companies

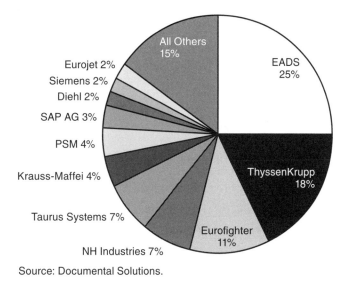

Source: Documental Solutions.

Electronic Bulletin Board, particularly for "hard defense articles"—weapons, munitions, aircraft, naval vessels and armored vehicles.

All pertinent standards are indicated on the tenders, and can be accessed through various government internet sites. Germany makes use of the new *European Handbook for Defense Procurement*, though not all the requisite standard documents are available.

Overall, U.S. companies had few complaints about the transparency of the procurement process. While they noted that there is an extensive array of informal "requirements" for doing defense business in Germany (e.g., offsets), these are well known and understood by all, and therefore do not create an uneven playing field.

Domestic Content Requirements

Germany does not have a formal domestic content law or regulation analogous to the U.S. Buy American Act. Even if it did, the law would not apply to the United States under the reciprocity terms of the U.S.-Germany reciprocal defense procurement MOU.

That said, U.S. firms seeking to sell into Germany must generally work with German partners in order to succeed. Through such informal understandings and offsets (see discussion below), Germany essentially imposes a *de facto* domestic content requirement as a bidding factor for foreign competitors. In the case of pure procurement contracts, Germany requires offsets to be in the form of co-production agreements, which essentially forces a certain percentage of every German defense product to be manufactured onshore.

Offsets and *Juste Retour*

Although it has no "official" offset policy,[309] Germany considers offsets to be a "sale argument" (i.e., a bid evaluation factor) to be addressed as an industrial balances issue by the Federal Office of Defense Technology and Procurement. In practice, Germany aims for at least 100 percent offsets against the face value of each contract awarded to a foreign company. Both direct and indirect offsets are permitted. However, since the stated objective of the offset program is to increase German company participation in defense projects, most companies opt for direct offsets in the form of German co-production.

According to the U.S. Department of Commerce (DoC), Germany has largely succeeded in meeting its informal offset goal in practice.[310] Specifically, the U.S. DoC annual report on offsets reflects offsets in Germany totaled roughly 100 percent of contract values in practice for U.S. firms over the period 1993-2006 (calculated from data submitted by the reporting U.S. defense firms of actual contracts and offset commitments).[311] A review of DoC offset reports over recent years shows the offset percentage has remained remarkably stable. Thus, whether required or not, they do appear to be a major factor in defense trade with Germany.

Germany also follows a firm policy of *juste retour* in defense programs, preferring to negotiate a work share proportional to its investment in a particular project.

Government Ownership

West Germany began privatizing state-owned industries in 1961 — most notably by its sale of Volkswagen to small private investors. By the 1970s, all industrial companies in Germany were in private hands, either publicly traded or family-owned. Through unification,

---

[309] *Offsets in Defense Trade*, Twelfth Report to Congress, U.S. Department of Commerce (Dec. 2007), PDF, Appendix F. Available at: http://www.bis.doc.gov/defenseindustrialbaseprograms/osies/offsets/final-12th-offset-report-2007.pdf.

[310] Ibid. The report indicates that Germany negotiated offsets worth $933 million on $933 million in contract awards to U.S. companies.

[311] *Offsets in Defense Trade*, Op. Cit., p. 2-13 (Table 2-5) (indicating that Germany negotiated offsets worth $933 million on $933 million in contract awards to U.S. companies).

The German Acquisition System Bottom Line: A Status Quo Story

In short, the German contract data is consistent with what we learned in interviews with market participants, and confirms several fundamental realities of the German acquisition system:

- **First, Germany's defense acquisitions remain very national in its orientation—even with respect to new buying.** In contrast to some of the other Western European countries examined, there is no apparent emerging pattern in Germany of seeking to subject any of its major systems (even on a European basis) to international competition. Germany remains largely wedded to national suppliers for its national acquisitions of systems except in limited instances where it acquires systems from the United States. While German officials noted that the actions of the EU and EDA are increasingly pressuring national procurement authorities to rely less on 296 and award contracts competitively ("peer pressure"), the available evidence shows little movement in this direction in Germany.

- **Second, the German MoD is increasingly willing to consider solutions from firms in other European countries and has significant resources tied up in European cooperative programs.**

- **Finally, Germany is simply not very open to U.S. firms even on competitive awards.** While some of these new competitive awards may have been technically open to U.S. firms, in practical terms most were effectively closed to U.S. firms. Indeed, interviews indicated that markets in a number of sectors (ground armored vehicles, command and control) are largely closed to U.S. participation—with awards generally made domestically and few systems not built by German firms.

the German government inherited some 45,000 state-owned companies, including many in the armaments industry. To dispose of these companies, the German government created the *Treuhandenstalt* (Trust Agency or THA), which became formal owner of all former East German state companies. THA was authorized to close or sell its properties, negotiating directly with West German and foreign investors to sell these companies, a process completed by 1994. THA's operations were criticized for their lack of transparency and apparent bias against non-German investors, as well as what was perceived as the unnecessary closure of profitable businesses. THA ended its operations some $130 billion in debt, having managed to gain only some $15 billion in sales.

In any event, today the entire German defense industry is neither government-owned nor controlled. However, the government exerts indirect influence over strategic decisions through its various roles as financier, purchaser and regulator of German defense firms, including its authority to review all foreign investments that would result in a more than 25 percent ownership share, and through the close relationship of leading industrialists with military and political authorities.

Foreign Direct Investment

In the broad economy, Germany has always encouraged foreign direct investment, with foreign investors receiving national treatment under German law. Any foreign company registered in Germany as a GmbH (limited liability company) or an AG (joint stock company) is treated in the same manner as a German company. There are, in general, no special nationality requirements with respect to directors or shareholders. Nor do investors need to register their investment intent with the German government *except* in cases involving mergers or acquisitions of defense or encryption-related companies.

According to the U.S. DoC Foreign Commercial Service,

> The investment-related problems foreign companies do face are generally the same as for domestic firms; for example, high marginal income tax rates and labor laws that impede hiring and dismissals. The German government has begun to address many of these problem areas through its reform programs. German courts have a good record in upholding the sanctity of contracts.[312]

Under the U.S.-German Treaty of Friendship, Commerce and Navigation, U.S. investors in Germany receive national treatment. The Treaty also allows the free movement of capital between the United States and Germany.

German law does allow restrictions on private direct investment flows in either direction for reasons of foreign policy, foreign exchange, or national security. Historically, according to the U.S. DoC, these have largely not been imposed in practice. To implement such restrictions, the federal government must first consult with the *Bundesbank* and the governments of the federal states.

In recent years, however, there is growing evidence of German limitations on foreign (especially U.S.) investment in German defense firms. In July 2004, a new law was implemented requiring foreign entities that seek to purchase more than 25 percent equity in German armament or cryptographic equipment companies to notify the Federal Ministry of Economics and Technology, which then has one month in which to veto the sale, which otherwise is considered to be approved. A draft law currently in review will broaden these rules and establish a procedure similar to the U.S. Committee on Foreign Investment in the United States. Advocacy by domestic companies, as well as industrial policy considerations, have occasionally delayed decision-making on defense investment.[313]

Also, the 2007 Joint Declaration on German defense industrial policy reflected a more robust review of foreign acquisitions of German defense firms that possess "key defence technology capabilities." As stated therein, "[k]ey defence technology capabilities reflect sensitive technological know-how that requires special protection. The Federal Ministry of Defense will make the national key defense technology capabilities the basis for the approval or rejection of bids by foreign investors to obtain shares in German defence enterprises or

---

[312] U.S. Commercial Service, *Doing Business in Germany: A Country Commercial Guide for U.S. Companies—2009*, U.S. Department of Commerce (Washington, D.C.)PDF, p. 59. Available at: http://www.buyusa.gov/germany/en/download.html.

[313] Ibid.

to take them over."[314] While the Joint Declaration goes on to note that foreign investment decisions will be made case by case and that the involvement of a "key defence technology capability does not mean… that an acquisition is automatically to be prohibited," it nevertheless conveys a relatively protectionist view toward these types of acquisitions.[315]

The recent practice tends to reflect this attitude. Table 39 lists U.S. acquisitions of German defense, aerospace, homeland security and other dual-use companies (selling defense and other products) since 2002. *Note that with just one exception (HDW), which was controversial, the purchases do not include major prime contractors or significant subsystem providers. Most are concentrated in the second and third tiers of subcontractors and suppliers, and the vast majority are in dual-use as distinct from pure defense technologies.*

The HDW transaction reflects the growth of domestic opposition to foreign, and especially U.S., acquisitions of sensitive or system level defense assets. The German reaction also may have been partly engendered by the fact that the buyer was a financial player (with some suggestion it was serving as a proxy for an undisclosed U.S. defense firm). Specifically, in 2002, One Equity Partners, an international investment group led by the U.S. company BankOne, first acquired a 75 percent stake in HDW AG shipyard, a leading designer and builder of diesel-electric submarines. One Equity subsequently acquired the remaining 25 percent later that year. Though the terms of the transaction were confidential, speculation in the press pointed to a sale price of $650-800 million (a gross exaggeration, according to company representatives). The sale was controversial in Germany because it would have marked the first time a major German defense company was owned outright by a U.S. company. One Equity Partners had to agree to maintain HDW as an independent German shipyard, to not take a dividend from the business for five years, and to not exert any influence over the operations of the shipyard. One Equity Partners also agreed to not to resell the company for at least two years. In January 2005, One Equity Partners sold its entire stake in HDW to ThyssenKrupp AG for $273 million. This transaction itself was a major impetus in the enactment of the 2004 legislation noted above.

Since the new law was enacted, the German MoD also confirmed at least one other case where U.S. firms seeking to buy the German defense firm Atlas Elektronik GmbH (then owned by BAE Systems) were informally advised by the German MoD that such an acquisition would not be welcome. German officials indicated that Atlas had important work and knowledge in areas such as combat management systems for surface ships and submarines the MoD did not want to be foreign controlled. In 2006, Atlas was subsequently jointly acquired by ThyssenKrupp Group and EADS. German officials did note this as *the only case* where approval was declined out of 15 cases since the 2004 law was put in effect. They also noted that foreign ownership would be allowed in a number of cases so long as security of supply arrangements could be put in place.

In contrast, Germany has allowed other *European* companies—even those with substantial European government ownership (e.g., EADS)—to merge with or acquire *major* German defense companies. As noted above, the multinational EADS and MBDA have absorbed most of Germany's aerospace companies. In practice, however, the resulting German subsidiaries are very much "stand alone" entities, tending to function like "multido-

---

[314] Joint Declaration, p. 4.
[315] Ibid.

Table 39   U.S. Acquisitions of German Defense/Aerospace Companies (Millions of Dollars−$)

Date	Company	Bought By	Price	Revenues	Notes
Sep 2008	Lingk & Sturzebrecher GmbH	Parker Hannifin Corp	NA	11.2	Carbon fibre gas cylinders & actuators
Sep 2008	RollelMetric	Trimble Navigation, Ltd	NA	NA	Aerial Imaging Systems
Apr 2008	Moeller Group	Eaton Corporation	2,430.0	1,600.0	Industrial Control Systems
Apr 2008	HighQ-IT GmbH	Perot Systems	23.6	NA	Manufacturing process controls
Jan 2008	JUWE Laborgeraete GmbH	Bruker BioScience Corp	NA	3.0	Engineering Analysis
Jan 2008	HIGHYAG Lasertechnologie	II-VI, inc.	NA	6.2	Laser technologies
Dec 2007	CoCreate Software GmbH	Parametric Technology	250.0	80.0	PLM and CAD modeling solutions
Oct 2007	Tyco Electronics Power Systems	Gores Group, LLC	100.0	NA	Power supply systems
Sep 2007	Secorex	Autoweb, Inc.	NA	NA	B2B information Systems
Sep 2007	TAO Technologies GmbH	GobeTel Communications	NA	NA	50% Stake; Unamanned Air Vehicles
Sep 2007	Ingenieurburo Breining	Trimble Navigation, Ltd	NA	NA	Geospatial Information Systems
Aug 2007	Phoenix X-Ray	General Electric Company	NA	NA	3D Tomography for Industrial Use
Aug 2007	Matra-Werke GmbH	SPX Corporation	NA	26.0	Heavy truck maintenance and repair
Jul 2007	GPS GmbH	Garmin Ltd	NA	NA	Distributer of GPS products
Jul 2007	Adaptif Photonics GmbH	Agilent Technologies, Ltd	NA	NA	Sensors and lasers
May 2007	Itellium Systems & Services	EDS Corporation	NA	174.6	Information Technology
Apr 2007	Lumburg Automation Comp	Belden, Inc.	NA	75.0	Factory automation systems
Apr 2007	Rectus AG	Parker Hannifin Corp	NA	115.0	Pneumatic couplers
Mar 2007	Hirschmann Automation	Belden, Inc	260.0	250.0	Ethernet solutions
Feb 2007	INPHO GmbH	Trimble Navigation	NA	NA	Photgrammetry solutions
Nov 2006	Boehringer Group	MAG Industrial Automatio	NA	184.0	Manufacturing solutions
Oct 2006	Scroth Safety Products	Armor Holdings, inc.	28.6	39.0	Vehicle suvivability systems
Oct 2006	ITEDO Software	Parametric Technology	17.0	NA	Technical illustration software

Date	Company	Bought By	Price	Revenues	Notes
Oct 2006	SEG GmbH	Woodward Governor Co.	45.0	60.0	Power control and distribubtion
Jul 2006	Draeger Aerospace	B/E Aerospace	80.0	NA	Aircraft oxygen systems
Jul 2006	Sintec Group	Kennametal, Incl	NA	NA	Adsvanced ceramic components
May 2006	DEPA GmbH	Rockwell Automation	NA	NA	Change management SW for Industry
Mar 2006	Magnet-Motor GmbH	L-3 Communications Corp	59.0	7.0	High tech electric motors
Feb 2006	Skyware Radio Systems	Andrew Corporation	9.0	12.0	Broadband SATCOM systems
Jan 2006	SAM Electronics GmbH	L-3 Communications	180.4	257.8	Maritime electronic systems
Dec 2005	Zentrum Mikroelektronik	Simtek Corporation	10.0	7.5	Specialized integrated circuits
Nov 2005	Poppenhager Grips	Intergraph Corporation	NA	NA	Geospatial Information Systems
Nov 2005	HL Planarteknik GmbH	Measurement Specialties	7.1	NA	MEMS-based sensors
Jun 2005	SPECTRO Betteligungs	AMETEK, Inc.	98.0	104.0	Atomic spectrographic systems
Jun 2005	TulLaser AG	Coherent, Inc.	27.1	28.9	Laser technologies
Mar 2005	Eagle-D GmbH	MTC Technologies	NA	NA	Military vehicle overhaul services
Mar 2005	Teldix GmbH	Rockwell Collins, Inc.	53.0	90.0	Military avionics
Sep 2004	Walterscheid Rorverbindungs	Eaton Corporation	48.0	52.0	Hydraulic systems
Sep 2004	RP Sicherheitssysteme	Verint Systems, inc.	11.9	NA	Onboard vehicle video security
Aug 2004	ESK Ceramics GmbH	Ceradyne, Inc.	142.0	90.0	Advanced Ceramics
Apr 2004	Triatron GmbH	Hewlett-Packard Co.	NA	465.0	IT services
Mar 2004	Diehl-Raytheon Missile Sys	Raytheon	NA	NA	JV between Diehl and Raytheon
Jan 2004	MTU Aero Engines GmbH	Kohlberg Kravis Roberts	1,727.0	2,450.0	Aircraft Engine Systems
Jan 2004	ZN Vision Technologies	Viisage Technology, Inc	29.8	NA	Biometric Identification Systems
Sep 2002	HDW AG Shipyard	One Equity Partners	NA	NA	Remaining 25% equity stake.
Mar 2002	HDW AG Shipyard	One Equity Partners	NA	NA	75% Equity Stake. Submarine builder

Source: Defense Mergers and Acquisitions.

mestic" companies managing the German portions of the parent company's multinational programs such as Eurofighter and Eurocopter Tiger.

The bottom line is that the German investment environment appears relatively closed to U.S. defense firms seeking acquisitions at the top tiers in the industry but relatively open to such acquisitions by firms from other European countries. There is little U.S. ownership today at systems or major subsystem levels juxtaposed against considerable European ownership at that level. Thus, U.S. ownership or investment—especially of more sensitive or system level assets—seems to have more political implications that inhibit acquisitions above a certain level. In cases where companies have been acquired by European owners (as, e.g., in the case of those companies absorbed by EADS), the main concern seems to be the retention of jobs and onshore industrial capabilities.

Ethics and Corruption

Germany has a generally strong reputation for an internal commitment to rule of law, ethics and corruption, with generally strong laws and enforcement mechanisms. The World Bank's worldwide governance indicators show Germany in the 94 percent range for both rule of law and control of corruption—among the highest scores of any major Western industrialized nation.[316] Germany is ranked 14th—somewhere in the middle—in the Transparency International (TI) 2008 Corruption Perception Index. By way of comparison, France is 19th, the United States ranks 18th, and Sweden is tied at 1st (with Denmark and New Zealand).[317]

According to the U.S. Department of State, the German "construction sector and public contracting, in conjunction with undue political party influence, represent particular areas of continued concern. Nevertheless, U.S. firms have not identified corruption as an impediment to investment. The German government has sought to reduce domestic and foreign corruption. Strict anti-corruption laws apply to domestic economic activity and the laws are enforced."[318] The German government has successfully prosecuted hundreds of domestic corruption cases over the years.

There continues, however, to be a mixed track record with respect to German firms' propensity to make illegal payments in third-country defense markets and the German government's apparent tolerance thereof. On the one hand, Germany is a signatory to the Convention on Combating Bribery of Foreign Public Officials in International Business Transactions (OECD Anti-Bribery Convention) and has enacted implementing legislation and repealed its pre-existing tax deduction for foreign payments. While deficiencies remain, legislation is pending in Germany to broaden the scope of its overseas anti-bribery prohibitions. Also, while Germany lacks a central coordination point for enforcing its anti-bribery laws, TI reports that Germany has initiated a sizable number of enforcement cases (includ-

---

[316] See World Bank Governance Indicators, 1996-2007 (Country Data Report for Germany, 1996-2007). Available at: http://info.worldbank.org/governance/wgi/pdf/c59.pdf.

[317] Transparency International's Corruption Perception Index. Available at: http://www.transparency.org/news_room/in_focus/2008/cpi2008/cpi_2008_table.

[318] *Doing Business in Germany*, op. cit.

ing 43 prosecutions and more than 88 pending investigations).[319] Among other cases, TI reported on an investigation of allegations of bribes paid by German firms in the German Frigate Consortium and MAN Ferrostaal to South African officials in relation to a defense contract in 1999. Germany also is rated 7th in TI's Bribe Payers Index of 30 major exporting nations—better than the United States (ranked 9th), France (15th) and a number of other Western European countries.[320]

Yet, despite these salutary developments, there continue to be allegations that leading German firms have engaged in these practices in global markets. Available information reflects that the longstanding culture and practices by German firms in this area are difficult to change and that change is slow. The ongoing corruption scandal involving Siemens AG, with significant charges and large fines, may bring new public awareness to the issue and enhance compliance with anti-bribery laws by German firms. The Siemens scandal involved senior managers establishing slush funds in shell companies used to pay bribes to foreign officials in order to secure orders. The illegal activity apparently began in 2002, and involved payments totaling up to $2 billion. In December 2008, Siemens agreed to pay a $1.34 billion fine to settle anti-bribery charges in both the United States and Germany. As part of the agreement, a former German finance minister was appointed to monitor the company's compliance with the U.S. consent decree.[321]

Export Controls

The German System

Germany is a member of major multilateral export control regimes, including the Nuclear Suppliers Group, the Australia Group, the Missile Technology Control Regime, the Wassernaar Arrangement and the Chemical Weapons Convention. Germany is also a Member State of Organization for Security and Co-operation in Europe (OSCE), and has approved the OSCE principles governing transfers of conventional arms and the 2000 OSCE document on Small Arms and Light Weapons.[322]

Germany, like other EU Member States, also is a signatory to the 1998 EU Code of Conduct on Arms Exports, which harmonized regulations across all Member States in the EU, and established general principles for the transfer of armaments and military technology, and set up a system whereby each Member State must inform the others whenever an export license is denied. Under the Code, each State must also consult with the other Member States whenever it wishes to grant an export license that has been denied by another Member State for "essentially identical transactions." However, the ultimate decision to deny or transfer a military item remains at the national discretion of each Member State. The recently adopted EC Transfers Directive is a further step in aligning the policies of EU countries regarding intra-Community transfers, providing reassurance for security of

[319] F. Heimann and G. Dell, *Progress Report 2008: Enforcement of the OECD Convention on Combating Bribery of Foreign Public Officials in International Business Transactions*, Transparency International (June 24, 2008), pp. 10, 22-23. Available at: http://www.transparency.org/news_room/in_focus/2008/oecd_report.

[320] Available at: http://www.transparency.org/policy_research/surveys_indices/bpi/bpi_2006.

[321] "Siemens settles bribery cases," *International Herald Tribune* (Dec. 15, 2008). Available at: http://www.iht.com/articles/2008/12/15/business/15siemens.php.

[322] Details on German membership and OSCE activities are available at: http://www.osce.org/about/13131.html.

supply, and simplifying procedures to permit such transfers among Member States and certified defense companies. The focus of this EC Directive is intra-Community transfers, and thus the main beneficiaries of reduced barriers within the EU are European defense firms. It is not clear that U.S. firms will be eligible for similar treatment; this is a matter for national governments to decide.

German export control policy is administered by the Ministry of Foreign Affairs, which issues export licenses for all military and dual-use items. Licenses include stringent end-user certification in conformance with the EU Code of Conduct on Arms Exports. Under the War Weapons Control Act (KWKG), exports to "third party" countries outside of the EU, NATO and "NATO-equivalent" countries (Australia, New Zealand, Switzerland and Japan) are severely restricted.

Each year the German federal government issues a *Report on Military Equipment Exports*, which details how many export licenses were granted, to whom, and for what particular items.

The Report does not cover actual deliveries, except for two particular categories of defense products—*Kriegswaffen* (literally, "War Weapons" or major end items) and small arms and ammunitions delivered to Third World countries. In general the value of licenses issued each year is many times greater than the value of the *Kriegswaffen* delivered (e.g., $650 million in licenses vs. $34 million in *Kriegswaffen* deliveries to the United States in 2007). Licenses are issued for all items on the Wassenaar munitions list, of which *Kriegswaffen* is only a small subset. Moreover, German export licenses are valid for just one year, and companies that have open-ended, multiyear contracts with the United States and other countries tend to file each year for the maximum value of their contract. The *Report* thus tends to overstate the value of German defense exports by an order of magnitude at least.

On the other hand, neither the German Ministry of Defense nor the Ministry of Trade require companies to report their actual deliveries, other than Kriegswaffen and small arms; discussions with German MoD representatives indicated they have no idea of the total value of actual defense deliveries. Attempts to draft regulations requiring German companies to report all deliveries of goods covered by the Wassenaar munitions list have so far been unsuccessful.[323]

Although a number of pacifist parties and organizations have protested that the German export control process lacks rigor and transparency, Germany's reputation in export controls is fairly good. It should be noted, however, that illegal German arms transfers to Iraq apparently occurred during the 1990s—indeed, right up to the outbreak of the Iraq War in 2003.

ITAR Attitudes and Behaviors

A consistent theme among market participants (private and government) in Germany was concern over the ITAR, and costs, schedule delays and risks to third-country exports. German government and business representatives expressed the desire to find ways around ITAR by building ITAR-free equivalents of various systems and components. One executive called it a "trend all over Germany to do without ITAR parts and components."

---

[323] This has significant implications for any discussion of defense trade flow and balance of trade, as discussed in Appendix I.

German government officials highlighted a number of problematic technical issues they have encountered in recent years and related lengthy delays; issues related to such matters as end-use certificates needed for re-transfers. They characterized some of these issues as a "bureaucratic nightmare" and increasingly see a movement in Europe to avoid ITAR reliance in order to eliminate "unmanageable risk" and administrative burdens.

German government officials have not, however, gone so far as to make ITAR-free an element of German procurement policy—primarily because it is impractical at the present time. They noted that it could cost more and take longer to develop ITAR-free solutions and that they ultimately could end up with less capability for their investment. But they did seek more efficient and timely licensing solutions.

Some German market participants believe ITAR policy is used as a protectionist rather than security policy at times. Some executives noted that U.S.-German joint ventures fare better than German firms seeking ITAR authorizations to compete against U.S. firms.

German attitudes toward the EC Defense Procurement Directive reflected their views on ITAR. German officials readily conceded the "security of supply" provisions could be used by a European procurement authority to discriminate against bidders relying on ITAR-controlled technology (i.e., on the ground that such ITAR products/systems are "insecure"). However, they saw no problem with this approach and believed that the United States had brought this on itself through unreasonable defense trade rules and policies.

Intellectual Property Protection

Germany adheres to the major multilateral intellectual property (IP) regimes, including (i) the WTO Agreement on Trade-Related Aspects of Intellectual Property Rights (TRIPS), which provides core IP protection and enforcement rights (including for trade secrets); (ii) the Paris Convention for the Protection of Industrial Property, covering patents, trademarks and industrial designs; (iii) the Patent Cooperation Treaty, protecting patents; (iv) the Berne Convention, covering copyrights; (v) the Madrid Protocol, covering trademarks; and (vi) the World Intellectual Property Organization (WIPO).

According to the U.S. Commercial Service, "[i]ntellectual property is well protected by German laws."[324] Germany also does not appear on the U.S. Trade Representative watch list for IP violations. In July 2008, the Bundestag adopted a new Act on Enforcement of Intellectual Property Rights (German IP Act), which implements an EC Enforcement Directive of the European Parliament and the Council on the Enforcement of Intellectual Property Rights. The EC Directive requires the Member States to harmonize the measures, remedies, and procedures to protect against infringements of IP rights and is designed in particular to combat piracy and counterfeiting. The German Act lives up to this mandate by providing virtually identical measures and remedies for infringements of patents, utility models, trademarks, copyrights, plant varieties, and semiconductor products by amending the respective acts.

Both the EC Directive and the German legislation introduce strong information rights to uncover infringements. In the recent German IP Act, the existing German Copyright

---

[324] Doing Business in Germany, Op.Cit., p. 64. Available at: http://www.buyusa.gov/germany/en/download.html.

Act was amended to grant information rights not only against infringers and users of their products, but against providers of services that facilitated the infringement.

U.S. defense companies have not raised with us during the course of our study any specific complaints regarding IP protection in the German defense market.

Technical Standards

Germany is a party to the WTO's Technical Barriers to Trade Agreement, which prohibits discrimination and seeks to ensure that regulations, standards, testing and certification procedures do not create obstacles to trade. However, every country has the right to adopt those regulatory standards it considers appropriate in areas concerning national security. Thus, Germany has the discretion to, and has put in place, its own specific technical standards for defense products that could in theory serve as a non-tariff barrier to competing foreign products.

Germany's long association with NATO also means that German military products are tied to NATO Standardization Agreements where these exist. As discussed in Chapter 5, however, there is some prospect of increased risk that an eventual EU set of standards might become disguised market access barriers—but there is no indication that this is a policy result sought by Germany.

According to the U.S. DoC Country Commercial Guide:

> Germany's regulations and bureaucratic procedures can be a difficult hurdle for companies wishing to enter the market and require close attention by U.S. exporters. Complex safety standards, not normally discriminatory but sometimes zealously applied, complicate access to the market for many U.S. products. U.S. suppliers are well advised to do their homework thoroughly and make sure they know precisely which standards apply to their product and that they obtain timely testing and certification.[325]

Subject to this general caveat, in the course of this study, we did not learn of any specific situations involving Germany where technical standards were used as non-tariff barriers to protect domestic producers and markets against foreign defense products.

---

[325] *Doing Business in Germany*, op. cit., Chap. 5.

Chapter 9

Accessing the Italian Defense Market

Italy has a strong and enduring relationship with the United States, dating to the end of World War II. Throughout the Cold War, the United States valued Italy as a barrier to Soviet expansion in the Mediterranean, and a valuable staging area for U.S. forces on the southern flank of the territory of the North Atlantic Treaty Organization (NATO). A strong member of NATO from its inception, Italy views the Alliance and close relations with the United States as the core of its security strategy. An original signatory of the Treaty of Rome in 1957, Italy has also seen the European Union (EU) as central to its foreign policies and has embraced the European Security and Defense Policy (ESDP) vision of more closely shared security plans and instruments.

Italy has deployed forces in support of both NATO and EU operations around the world with a high level of effort relative to its size and economy. The Italian government has done this despite anemic Italian defense budgets (about 1 percent of gross domestic product (GDP)) and hostile public opinion. Since September 11, Italy has also been a key U.S. partner in the operations against international terrorism (building on its own experiences in addressing this challenge in the 1980s).

Because of its NATO-centric strategy, Italy has tried to maintain interoperability with U.S. and other Allied forces. Over the decades, Italy has acquired a wide range of U.S. systems and subsystems, including aircraft, missiles, armored vehicles and C4ISR (command, control, communications, computers, intelligence, surveillance and reconnaissance) systems. Aside from selective U.S. buys, the Italian defense market in many ways remained closed until the 1990s. The Italian state owned most defense firms, and has always placed a high priority on its resources and contracts going to indigenous firms and their international partners. To that end, U.S. and other foreign suppliers were (and are) strongly encouraged to provide direct industrial returns in connection with work they perform for the Italian armed forces.

Since 1990, the Italian defense market and industry have changed significantly. The post-Cold War decline in defense budgets, both in Italy and across Europe, intensified European efforts at cross-border cooperation, as, e.g., in the Letter of Intent (LOI) process. Since then, Italy has relied mainly on international cooperative efforts for its major defense programs, reinforcing a trend that began in the late 1970s in areas such as combat aircraft. Whereas previously Italy often relied on U.S. foreign military sales (FMS) or licensed production of U.S. systems, in the last 15 years Italy has sought to have higher value added work performed in Italy, viewing this as essential to sustaining its industrial and technology base.

At the same time, as European industrial consolidation proceeded, Italy gradually relinquished significant state ownership of its large defense firms. Finmeccanica SpA (now some 30 percent state-owned) became a holding company for dozens of Italian businesses and emerged as the leading Italian defense firm. Finmeccanica also became a multidomestic firm, with key holdings in the United Kingdom (UK) and a growing presence in the United States (especially with the recent acquisition of leading defense electronics company, DRS Technologies, Inc.). Directly and indirectly, through its extensive business holdings and national and multinational program participation, Finmeccanica today receives about 70 percent of the Italian defense research and technology and procurement budget. Increasingly, all roads in the Italian defense market pass through Finmeccanica.

Italy has one of the more imperfect defense markets in Europe, marked by a relatively opaque, informal acquisition system; by limited, informal competition; and by acquisition decisions determined largely by political considerations, jobs and work share factors. Notwithstanding the strong geopolitical relationship between the United States and Italy and deep cooperation, U.S. firms face substantial market access challenges in Italy. In defense acquisitions, the Italian government prefers that U.S. companies team or partner with Italian firms; this approach also ensures that Italy's robust offset requirements are met. Consequently, direct U.S. presence on the ground is less visible in spite of the Italian preference for U.S. products generally. Other than one large competitive award to Boeing for aerial refueling tankers, much of Italy's buying from U.S. firms has been on a sole source basis, when Italy needs a developed capability. In contrast, when a U.S. firm seeks to access the market directly and compete, the challenges are significant. In the investment arena, Italy's business conditions—arcane bureaucracy, opaque procurement processes, rigid labor laws and the remaining government ownership of major defense firms—are such that U.S. companies have made very few investments in Italian defense businesses.

Italy's defense acquisition strategies, driven by its very limited and stagnant defense budget, have three primary goals: 1) NATO interoperability; 2) maintaining readiness and support for its deployment commitments; and 3) sustaining Italian jobs and technologies. Italian acquisition typically has few open competitions and many sole source awards, carried out as an exemption under Article 296 of the Treaty Establishing the European Community (Article 296 EC Treaty). From 2006-2008, only 15 percent of Italian defense contracts (by value) were competitively awarded, with the remaining 85 percent split roughly equally between sole source programs and multinational cooperative programs in which workshare is largely negotiated through intergovernmental Memorandums of Understanding (MOUs).

While Italy has not articulated a formal national industrial policy, its attitudes are reflected in a series of decisions that point to conflicting priorities. In fact, Italian procurement authorities are trying to optimize a calculus that may not be possible over the long term: ensuring national jobs and technology while promoting more competition and more efficiency, and balancing between U.S. and EU relationships and rules.

Italy supports a more robust ESDP as well as a growing role for the European Commission (EC) in regulating the European defense market. Italy generally supports the new EC Defense Package. An Italian government official reported that Italy supports the package overall because, despite the fact that "this needs to be tested—it is a No Man's Land right now," the EU needs to remove internal barriers. As for the future of the EU defense market, an Italian government official summarized it by saying "this is an irreversible process."

Italy still sees its military links to the United States as vital. In fact, Italy and the United States have a deep and broad security relationship, with significant cooperation in armaments and other areas—in effect, a "special relationship" second only to that between the United States and the UK. Italy views as essential the presence of its defense products in the U.S. market, and the U.S. defense products in Italy; above all, Italy wants to avoid any Fortress Europe-like situation.

Ultimately, what will emerge? From an Italian perspective, this depends on the course chosen by the United States: whether to take the opportunity to reduce its barriers to entry and begin discussing a multilateral framework that goes beyond the bilateral relationships established with some countries. Will there be a level playing field and the reciprocity of trade with European nations? Will the United States enable its allies and coalition partners to be real partners by increased disclosure and technology sharing with them? Italian officials made clear that U.S. International Traffic in Arms Regulations (ITAR) rules could hamper the U.S. ability to sustain its long-term place in Italian systems. "It is not a national policy [of Italy]—it is simply a genuine economic expedient for European firms to avoid ITAR products," said one senior Italian government official.

I. Market Background

A. Italy's Strategic Context and Military Strategy

Italy's defense policy reflects a long-term commitment to the Western alliance of democratic, market-based countries, dating to the defeat of Fascism in World War II and Italy's 1949 membership in the Atlantic Alliance.

A founding member of NATO, Italy has a strong commitment to the Alliance. NATO has been the foundation of Italy's bilateral and multilateral Transatlantic relationships; Italy shares NATO nuclear weapons. At the same time, Italy is a founding member of the EU, having signed the Treaty of Rome in 1957. It is fully anchored in the process of integration into the EU. Italy's commitment to both NATO and the EU form the two main pillars of the country's foreign and security policies.

Italy has the world's ninth largest defense budget and the fourth largest among NATO members (based on its 2007 budget of $33.1 billion, including military police and other paramilitary functions).[326] However, defense spending has never been particularly appealing as a political choice for any of the many governments that have held power in Italy. Hence, Italy's defense spending remains chronically low as a percentage of GDP (approximately 1 percent for 2008 as compared to some 2.5 percent for France and the UK). This reflects Italy's weak overall economic performance since the late 1980s: Italian GDP growth was 1.7 percent in 2007, 1.9 percent in 2006; 0.1 percent in 2005.[327] Anemic economic performance has proved a significant obstacle to any of its governments' attempts to increase defense investment spending.

During the 1990s, the receding Soviet threat led to cutbacks in defense spending and reductions in forces (from 360,000 to 190,000 men). Italy abandoned conscription in favor of a smaller (and more expensive) professional force, and began a gradual military transformation from territorial defense to expeditionary operations. However, the country's Cold War posture continues to exert significant influence on military organization. In particular, Italy's security strategy still retains some focus on territorial defense. Despite recent attempts to change its force structure, this legacy still in part determines the distribution and presence of non-deployable forces.

---

[326] 2007 ranking of NATO members is not available; Italy is the 4th largest NATO spender based on its 2006 budget about 1.8 percent of its 2006 GDP. See Stockholm International Peace Research Institute, available at: http://www.sipri.org/contents/milap/milex/mex_trends.html.

[327] U.S. Department of State website, Background note on Italy; available at: http://www.state.gov/r/pa/ei/bgn/4033.htm.

The main driver in Italian military policy in recent years has been the effort to reorganize its military as an expeditionary force for "operations other than war"—i.e., peacekeeping, peace enforcement, and support of stability operations in international environments. The traumatic experiences of the Balkans interventions was largely responsible for this shift in the strategic gravity of the Italian Armed Forces.

While most of the military operations Italy has participated in have been NATO-led, Italy equally supports the ESDP and the overall drive toward greater European defense integration. Italy's long-term strategy is viewed as "hedging its bets" by maintaining a close U.S. relationship and strong role identity with NATO while sustaining and building Italy's role in ESDP.

Post-September 11 Environment

Unlike the United States, Italy has long been a victim of organized terrorist organizations and has developed strong internal capabilities to address the threat. More recently, Italy has focused on the possibility of an internationally networked terrorist node inside Italy. In February 2005, the *Terrorist Monitor* reported that Italian security services investigations since 2001 indicate Italy has become a platform for al-Qaeda associated terrorist operations in Europe and Iraq. Milan appears to be the base of Italy's extremist network, which has connections to other Islamic radical groups in Europe, specifically in Spain and Germany. The Italian intelligence services are working in close coordination with the Spanish, German and Dutch counterterrorism authorities, and believe the majority of *jihadis* in their country are connected to *Ansar-al-Islam*.[328]

Italian intelligence and *Carabineri* (police and special military forces) have been actively engaged in both domestic and U.S./international cooperative efforts to help address these and other terrorism issues. But while the strategic importance of the U.S. and NATO counterterrorist operations is well understood within Italy, Italy has not significantly increased its defense budget since September 11 to directly address elevated terrorist threats. Overall defense spending remains feeble, characterized by low investments, inefficiencies (an excess of personnel, too much bureaucracy, etc.) and difficulties in maintaining operational readiness.

At the same time, a significant transformation of armed forces is underway; it includes streamlining and downsizing the force while professionalizing it and moving away from conscription. Unfortunately, this ongoing process is not accompanied by the necessary increase in resources.

Italian Military Forces Today

There are four branches in the Italian Military. The Italian Army (*Esercito Italiano*) is the ground defense force of the Italian Republic; in 2004 it became a professional all-volunteer force with more than 110,000 active duty personnel. In addition to the Navy (*Marina Militare*) and Air Force (*Aeronautica Militare*), the fourth major military arm is the *Carabinieri*—a 110,000-member force combining both police and special military units.[329] However, only

---

[328] The Terrorism Monitor, The Jamestown Foundation, *Italy: Europe's Emerging Platform for Islamic Extremism*, Feb. 24, 2005, available at: http://www.jamestown.org/single/?no_cache=1&tx_ttnews%5Btt_news%5D=27596http://www.jamestown.org/single/?no_cache=1&tx_ttnews%5Btt_news%5D=27596.

[329] More information on the Italian military and their operations may be found, in Italian, at http://www.difesa.it/. This site also provides links to the four military branches.

about 7.5 percent of the overall *Carabinieri* is available for deployment abroad and for military police roles; the bulk of force provides internal security as a regular police force.

At the G-8 Sea Islands Conference in 2004, the *Carabinieri* received a mandate to establish a Center of Excellence for Stability Police Units. This Center spearheads the development of training and doctrinal standards for civilian police units attached to international peacekeeping missions. Other than the *Carabinieri*, the *Guardia di Finanza* is a specialized police answering to the Treasury, with the role of fighting financial crimes, illegal drug trafficking, customs and borders control, money laundering, and cybercrime.

Italy is able to deploy up to 10,000 men simultaneously, with a total deployable force of about 30,000 men. There is no overall legal limit on the size of a deployment, but the Italian Parliament is responsible for financing the additional costs encountered during operations abroad, thus setting manpower ceilings for each mission. The annual additional funding appropriated for those missions is in the €1 billion range, but the *actual* costs may be almost double. In the current context of increased international operations, the external role of *Carabinieri* has increased, even though less than 11,000 of that 110,000-person force are deployable for operations abroad.

Italian Global Deployments

As shown on Figure 81, Italy participates in nearly all NATO cooperative activities and is a very active participant in numerous NATO, EU and United Nations (UN) operations around the world. Italy also hosts the NATO Defence College at Cecchignola, near Rome.

It is difficult politically for Italy to deploy into high-risk areas. First, the public has little tolerance for loss of life for the types of global deployments in which Italy has been involved—but of course the position of the public depends on the type and purpose of the mission being undertaken. Nevertheless, the Italian military has been participating in "high intensity" peacekeeping and peace enforcement in several settings, even when the Italian public was not entirely supportive.

- Starting with Operation Enduring Freedom in 2002, Italy has made an ongoing contribution to the operations in Afghanistan, with about 2,500 troops presently deployed as part of International Security Assistance Force (ISAF), the NATO force in Afghanistan. An infantry company from the 2nd *Alpini* Regiment provides security for ISAF headquarters; other Italian units provide support forces in engineering, nuclear biological chemical (NBC), logistics, staff elements, and military police.

- Italy participated in operations in Iraq from late summer 2003 until the end of 2006, when Italian military personnel were essentially withdrawn. The greatest single loss of life in Iraq for Italian forces came on November 12, 2003, in a suicide car bombing that left a dozen *Carabinieri*, five Army soldiers, two Italian civilians, and eight Iraqi civilians dead.

- Italy today has about 2,700 soldiers in the Balkans. Finally, in August 2006 Italy sent about 2,700 soldiers to Lebanon for the UN peacekeeping mission UNIFIL II (Emerging and Evolving European Engagement in Lebanon and the Middle East).[330]

---

[330] See "Italian Soldiers Leave for Lebanon," *Italian Evening Courier*, Aug. 30, 2006. Available in Italian at: http://www.corriere.it/Primo_Piano/Cronache/2006/08_Agosto/29/libano.shtml.

Figure 81   Italian International Missions—2008

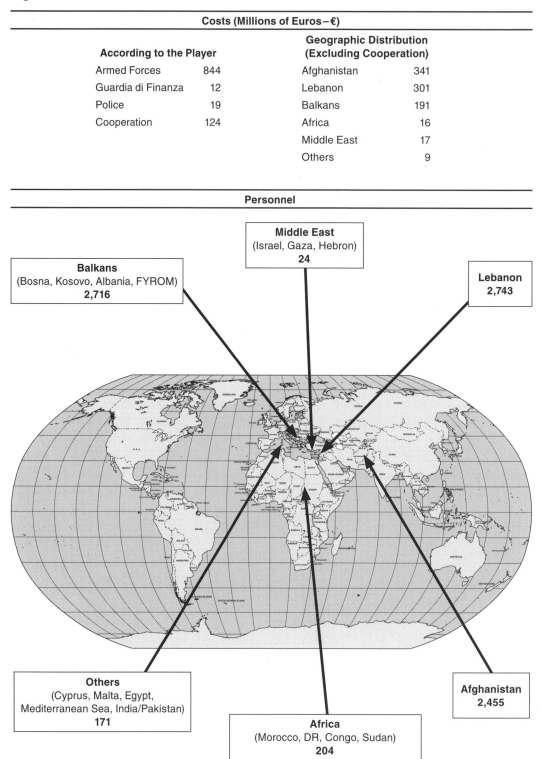

Costs (Millions of Euros–€)

According to the Player		Geographic Distribution (Excluding Cooperation)	
Armed Forces	844	Afghanistan	341
Guardia di Finanza	12	Lebanon	301
Police	19	Balkans	191
Cooperation	124	Africa	16
		Middle East	17
		Others	9

Personnel

Middle East
(Israel, Gaza, Hebron)
24

Balkans
(Bosna, Kosovo, Albania, FYROM)
2,716

Lebanon
2,743

Others
(Cyprus, Malta, Egypt,
Mediterranean Sea, India/Pakistan)
171

Africa
(Morocco, DR, Congo, Sudan)
204

Afghanistan
2,455

Sources: based on data from Law n. 45 (13-3-2008), Italian Ministry of Defense, and Instituto Affari Internazonale.

Figure 82   Italy—Ministry of Defense Budget, 2002-2008 (Billions of Dollars–$)

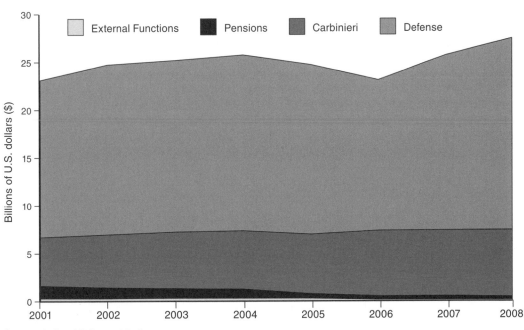

Source: Italian Ministry of Defense

Figure 83   Italy—Defense Spending by Function (Billions of Dollars–$)

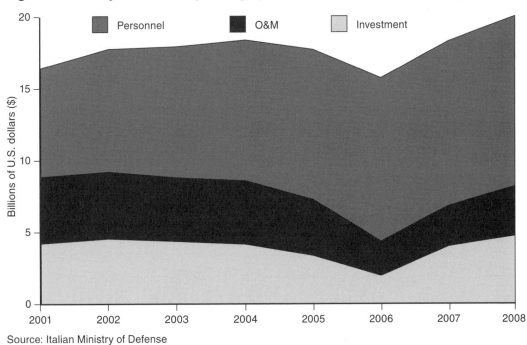

Source: Italian Ministry of Defense

Italian Defense Spending

From 2001 to 2008, the Italian total defense budget (excluding pensions, *Carabinieri* and some external functions) has ranged from $17.2 billion to $21 billion (see Figure 82). For 2008, this represents about 0.98 percent of Italian GDP—one of the lowest levels of spending among major European countries and roughly half the amount requested by NATO (i.e., about 2 percent of GDP). The personnel portion of that Italian budget has ranged from €5.8 billion to €9.1 billion (see Figure 83). By way of comparison, the 2007 French Defense Budget was about $50 billion, or nearly 2.5 percent of GDP (about 1.7 percent pensions and *Gendarmerie*), while the United States spends about 4 percent of its GDP on defense.

The gap between ambitions, international engagement and available Italian defense resources is more striking when considering Italy's participation in international missions. Increased operational expenses put more strain on defense budgets, as the additional funds voted by the Parliament on a yearly basis barely covers additional expenses. Moreover, the country faces continued systemic economic problems. Italy has one of the lowest growth rates of countries in Europe and is affected by a very large and expensive public bureaucracy. The prominence of public jobs and social spending makes jobs a particularly important consideration in *all* Italian government decisions, including military force downsizing and procurement.

B. Italy and the United States—A "Special Relationship"

The bilateral Italy-U.S. relationship has always been very strong, despite the historic presence in Italy of a strong communist party and a pacifist Catholic community. The strong U.S.-Italian relationship evolved particularly during the Cold War period. After World War II, the United States saw the value of southern partners and included Italy in the Atlantic Alliance in 1949 as a barrier to Soviet expansion.

The situation today is quite similar: the United States and Italy have evolved into a close relationship in recent years—often called a "special relationship." The U.S. Department of State describes the relationship as follows:

> Italy remains a strong and active [T]ransatlantic partner which, along with the United States, has sought to foster democratic ideals and international cooperation in areas of strife and civil conflict. Toward this end, the Italian government has cooperated with the United States in the formulation of defense, security, and peacekeeping policies.[331]

The elements of this renewed partnership are:

- Italy's support of the U.S. efforts in the operations against international terrorism through information exchange and expeditionary forces (Operation Enduring Freedom). The United States considers Italy a leading partner in the fight against terrorism.[332]

- A strong U.S. force presence (roughly 13,000 active duty in nine bases) in the Italian territory and regular guarantee to U.S. over-flight clearance. Under longstanding bilateral agreements flowing from NATO, the United States has important military

---

[331] U.S. Department of State (DoS) website, Background Note on Italy, op. cit.

[332] U.S. DoS website, op. cit.

facilities in Italy, including Vicenza (home of 173d Airborne Brigade) and Livorno (Army); Aviano (Air Force); and Sigonella, Naples and Gaeta, home port for the U.S. Navy Sixth Fleet.[333]

- Italy's role as the regional center for a number of U.S. government agencies in Europe, serving as a coordinating point.

- A historic Italian Ministry of Defense (MoD) preference for U.S. hardware and software and training, due to the ongoing desire and need for Transatlantic interoperability, particularly of interest as the United States and Italy are often in operations together.

As noted earlier, Italy has supported U.S security policies even when these actions were unpopular with its citizens. In 2007, there were large demonstrations of followers of the Communists, the Greens, part of the Democrats of the Left (DS), and of the Margherita—political parties in Italy—against a U.S. projected extension of a base near Vicenza.[334] Along with the need for refinancing the Italian troop deployment in Afghanistan, the Vicenza base extension provoked Prime Minister Romano Prodi's loss of a vote of confidence in the Italian Senate in February 2007. Prodi decided to maintain a left-to-center alliance, which retained the commitment for deployment in Afghanistan[335] and in January 2008, the Prodi government fell when one coalition partner withdrew support. Former Prime Minister Silvio Berlusconi was then returned to power (for his fourth term) after elections on April 13-14, 2008.[336]

Prime Minister Berlusconi is viewed as a pro-U.S., pro-NATO and generally pro-military leader. Berlusconi had a close relationship with the Bush White House in his previous terms as Prime Minister. While Prodi was viewed as leaning more toward the EU and multilateralism, Berlusconi may alter the tone or rules of engagement (while no doubt maintaining a strong balance with the EU). However, during the previous 5 years of Berlusconi's government (2001-2006), the budget for defense was regularly reduced; the overall defense budget reduction during those years was in the range of €3.5 billion from procurement and some €2.3 billion from operations and maintenance (O&M). During the following two years of Prodi's government, additional resources were given to defense. The 2009 budget proposed by Berlusconi government is cutting heavily again both the O&M and investment components, to a point where the effectiveness of the military forces are put into question even in the short term.

U.S.-Italian Trade and Defense Cooperation

Legal Framework for Cooperation

A key umbrella for the bilateral defense acquisition relationship has been the U.S.-Italian reciprocal Procurement MOU. This MOU provides in principle that U.S. firms are afforded access to Italian defense markets and are treated no less favorably than are domestic firms

---

[333] U.S. DoS website, op. cit.

[334] See article at: http://news.bbc.co.uk/2/hi/europe/6370671.stm.

[335] See article at: http://news.bbc.co.uk/1/hi/world/europe/6388455.stm.

[336] Berlusconi was sworn in as Prime Minister in May 2008. U.S. Department of State website, Background Note on Italy, op. cit.

(and provides reciprocal equal treatment in the United States for Italian firms). The United States and Italy recently signed an amendment to the MOU to address areas where Italy perceived the need for change; the amendment is currently in the ratification process and, when adopted, will serve as an umbrella agreement for further technical documents on specific elements.

Like several other countries studied, Italy and the U.S. Department of Defense (DoD) have also signed a Declaration of Principles (DoP). DoPs are non-binding bilateral agreements on defense industrial cooperation. The U.S. signaled its willingness to enter into the DoPs on the basis of a partner nation's approach to the so-called "Five Pillars of Compatibility and Confidence," that is, five factors that describe the willingness of the United States to engage in deepened defense industrial relationships with other countries: 1) export controls commonality and reciprocity; 2) industrial security commonality and reciprocity; 3) intelligence cooperation; 4) law enforcement cooperation; and 5) guaranteed reciprocity of access to defense markets. The DoP initiated a process of bilateral working groups designed to facilitate stronger cooperation, but so far no firm agreements have been reached under the DoP.

U.S.-Italian Cooperative Programs

Since interoperability of Italian forces with the U.S. forces is a key requirement for Italy, there has, not surprisingly, been a significant amount of cooperation in the past and it continues today.

The initial contracts between Italy and the United States were for production under license (e.g., production under license of the Lockheed F-104 Starfighter, as described in Chapter 8). This early licensed production was fundamental to the re-birth of Italian defense and aerospace industry after WWII.

From the Italian perspective, the nature and the quality of cooperation has improved over the decades. Two of the most significant cooperative programs underway today include:

- **Medium Extended Air Defense System (MEADS).** MEADS is a joint U.S., Italian and German cooperative program under the NATO umbrella. Designed to replace the Hawk and Patriot missile systems, MEADS will protect mobile forces and fixed installations against aircraft tactical ballistic and cruise missiles and unmanned aerial vehicles (UAVs). MEADS International, the company formed to develop MEADS, is made up of three original participating companies: MBDA (formerly Alenia Marconi Systems) in Italy, EADS in Germany, and Lockheed Martin in the United States. Funding for the research and development (R&D) is provided by the United States (58 percent), Germany (25 percent) and Italy (17 percent). Development work was allocated in accordance with national funding. The program has had a very long gestation with many ups and downs—including near-death phases. ITAR-related problems have figured prominently in the program. In December 2007, NATO MEADS Management Agency awarded MEADS International a contract to incorporate the PAC-3 missile segment enhancement as the baseline interceptor for the program.[337] Italy is unhappy with some aspects of the U.S. participation in MEADS. Italian officials reported to this study team that Italy

---

[337] MEADS details are from the UK Army Technology website: http://www.army-technology.com/projects/meads/.

is "forced to duplicate parts of the MEADS the United States refuses to release to Italy." This underscores Italian concerns on the U.S.'s technology release policy toward Italy, discussed in detail below.

- **F-35 Joint Strike Fighter.** Over the years, licensed production has been increasingly replaced by joint development or production programs, which more fully engage Italian industrial and technological capabilities. The most significant and strategic level of cooperation and technological transfer for Italy today has been the F-35 Joint Strike Fighter (JSF) program, intended to replace the F-16 Falcon, AV-8B Harrier and FA-18 Hornet strike fighters. In June 2002, Italy joined the JSF program in the System Development and Demonstration (SDD) phase, with an initial investment of just over $1 billion. In February 2007, Italy signed the Production, Sustainment, and Follow-on Development (PSFD) MOU, investing another $1 billion in the JSF program. These investments cover development only and do not include production and delivery of actual aircraft. Production aircraft must be ordered within the next three years and then paid for at a current cost of $48 to $65 million per copy, depending on which F-35 variant is purchased. Other than the United States, Italy is the only other nation expected to buy both the conventional takeoff-and-landing and the short-takeoff-and-landing variants of the F-35. Italy has upwards of a $6.5 billion work share in the JSF program overall.

In 2006, Washington and Rome finalized an agreement that gave Italy the only European JSF final-assembly line. Alenia Aeronautica, already a second-source supplier of F-35 wings, will execute the assembly work near Cameri, in the northern part of the country. Current planning calls for final assembly of all Italian (131) and Dutch (80) aircraft to take place there. In June 2006, *Aviation Week* reported:

> [T]he [JSF] final assembly deal is another bridge between the defense industries of Italy and the [United States]. Last year, a Lockheed Martin team was [also] chosen over incumbent U.S. contractor Sikorsky to supply an [Finmeccanica] AgustaWestland-designed helicopter to transport the president. "The U.S. administration has realized that Italian products are very, very competitive products," Giordo says [CEO, Alenia North America]. "During last year, the U.S. industry and U.S. administration realized that we can really contribute.[338]

Despite the criticality of the JSF program to the Italians, in October 2008 Italian budget constraints resulted in Italy announcing "… [Italy] will abandon its participation in the JSF IOT&E [initial operational test and evaluation] and, along with that, the purchase of the first test aircraft this year…The new [Italian] government has invoked the need to reduce expenditure. The Italian government has, however, reaffirmed its explicit support for the JSF program, and the Italian participation to the SDD phase."[339] This means that Italy cannot fund its initial aircraft buy and so cannot participate in the JSF initial testing—as it had planned to do. However, Italy is still very much committed to its role in the JSF program and the eventual purchase of the aircraft. These are the types of issues endemic to multinational programs.

---

[338] *Aviation Week*, June 19, 2006, http://www.aviationweek.com/aw/generic/story_generic.jsp?channel=aerospacedaily&id=news/JSFM06196.xml.

[339] Source: Dutch MoD release of Letter to Parliament, issued Oct. 7, 2008, available at: http://www.worldaffairsboard.com/military-aviation/47240-italy-pulls-out-jsfs-iot-e.html.

Figure 84   Italy-U.S. Defense Trade Flow (Billions of Dollars—$)

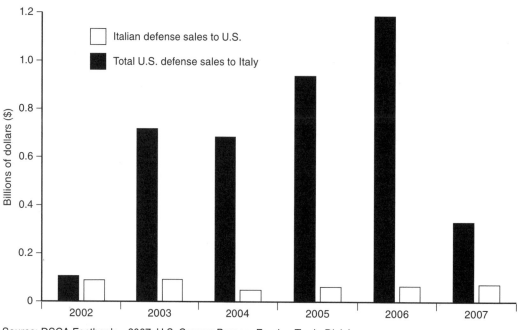

Source: DSCA Factbook—2007; U.S. Census Bureau, Foreign Trade Division.

Nevertheless, Italy remains unhappy with several aspects of the U.S. treatment of Italy on the JSF program, including the fact that the U.S. entered into a Framework Agreement with the UK on JSF but only signed a less broad in scope PSFD MOU with Italy. Italian officials remain unsatisfied with U.S. disclosure policy on JSF, which Italy believes directly limits their ability to merge the JSF into existing Italian forces and systems/subsystems.

U.S. Sales and Market Presence in Italy: Strong Legacy, Changing Model

Strong U.S. Legacy in Italian Defense Markets. As set forth on Figure 84, the data on U.S. defense trade with Italy reflects a fairly low level of U.S. defense sales to Italy from 2002-2007. Specifically, U.S. sales to Italy in the period ranged between about $300 million and $1.2 billion a year (except for 2002, in which sales were about $100 million). This period shows an increase in U.S. sales to Italy; these years may be higher than previous years due to U.S. exports in support of the conflicts in Iraqi and Afghanistan. Data provided separately by the U.S. Office of Defense Cooperation (ODC) in Italy (located in the U.S. Embassy) suggests that annual U.S. defense sales to Italy is somewhat lower, averaging between $400 million and $500 million annually.[340] The ODC estimates that the average total is upwards of $550 million if FMS training sales are included.

Based on the data we have, a good portion (estimated at about 50 percent) of the U.S. defense firms' annual sales in Italy are from U.S. FMS, with the remainder from direct

---

[340] As discussed in Appendix I, the differences in these defense trade figures reflects different methodologies and the relative lack of precision of any available data.

Table 40   U.S. Defense Systems and Programs In Italy

Systems/Platforms	Missiles/Smart Munitions	C4ISR Products
F-16A/B (34 in leasing agreement via FMS)	Delta II Launch System	Joint Tactical Radio System (JTRS)
CH-47 (Agusta Prime, Boeing platform)	JDAM	Night Vision Goggles
C-130J	Stinger	Airborne Early Warning & Control (AEW&C)
Predator/Reaper UAVs	Small Diameter Bomb	
Boeing KC-767 Tanker (4 aircraft)	TOW Missile	
	PAC-3 Missile Support	
	AIM-120 AMRAAM	
	AGM-65 Maverick	
	AGM-88 HARM	

commercial sales. The type of system or nature of the system/product being sold is typically the determinant of whether the U.S. sale is made through FMS or commercial channels.

This very modest level of U.S. sales to Italy under-represents the relative importance of U.S. products in Italy. For comparison, the United States averages about $450-500 million in defense sales a year to both Italy and France, *but the French annual defense budget is about twice the size of the Italian budget.* Thus, viewed as a percentage of the Italian defense budget, the U.S. presence in the Italian defense market has over the years been particularly significant, with the United States often providing key platforms and prime level contracts. As Italy is a close ally, leading U.S. platforms have been sold to Italy without many specific restrictions or limitations on the subsystems included.

As seen in Figure 84, Italy's sales of defense goods to the United States have been even more limited. During this period, Italy's sales to the United States are less than $100 million a year.[341] Italy's modest defense sales to the United States also understate the value of the Italian relationship to the United States as a coalition partner and program participant, as discussed earlier. Table 40 provides a representative list of the range of U.S. programs in which Italy is participating (in addition to the JSF program), as well as defense systems and products Italy has purchased, leased, or ordered.

Generally, the U.S. participation level in Italian subsystems markets has largely remained stable over time. It should be noted, however, that increased competition with Europeans and Italians with ITAR-free solutions is challenging the U.S. position in areas of less-critical technologies.

These U.S. system and product sales also bring a stream of follow-on logistics and FMS training business to the U.S. manufacturers. Today, even on some of the older U.S. systems, U.S. firms have revenue flow from ongoing modification or logistics support work.

---

[341] This data does not include sales of Italian firms based in the United States. Further, this trade data may not reflect all international cooperative sales, such as JSF related investments made by Italy (which may not necessarily be reflected in defense trade).

U.S. System and Product Presence, But Little U.S. Ownership in Italy

Given the list of U.S. products Italy has bought for its military, there is surprisingly little U.S. defense firm presence in Italy. This in part reflects the past practice of U.S. firms selling systems and products made in the United States. It also reflects the limited acquisitions made by U.S. firms of Italian defenses businesses, which is discussed in detail below. For a variety of reasons, including Italian MoD concerns about foreign ownership of this important source of security, jobs and technology, the Italian climate has not been attractive for U.S. investment in defense businesses. The very rigid labor market rules and demands, and the onerous Italian bureaucracy in general, also dissuade U.S. buyers.

Most U.S. defense firms work through Italian agents to help promote sales and provide ongoing contacts for any issues in program execution. Boeing and Lockheed are the two U.S. firms with the highest levels of defense activity in Italy today. While these U.S. firms have significant activities in Italy, they do not have subsidiaries or wholly owned companies.

- Boeing has the largest presence of a U.S. defense firm in Italy, with about 80 people in country, the majority of whom work at the Alenia Aeronavali facility in Naples doing aircraft modification work, including the KC-767.[342] Boeing also has a significant amount of activity there, with not only the past sales of Boeing products to Italy (JDAM, the KC-767 tanker, etc.) but with current programs such as business development on the CH-47F, AEW&C, and space launch services. Boeing is a teammate with Finmeccanica on Italy's new Network-Enabled Soldier program.

- Lockheed Martin also provides support for its products in Italy. It has a about $700 million support contract for the F-16 (34 leased of which 5 have been lost due to accidents), and has delivered C-130Js (22 sold) as well as other programs such as the PAC-3 missile. While Lockheed has agent support and a limited formal presence now, Lockheed's presence is expected to grow as it develops the Italian JSF final assembly line. Lockheed also actively bids in new system contract opportunities.

- Northrop Grumman had established a presence around the prospect of selling UAVs to Italy, but as of this writing, the sale did not proceed and their representative is no longer in Italy.

- In the aerospace area, Rockwell Collins has an office in Rome and GE has some technology work (as well as other commercial activities) in Florence and Milan.

A Changing Model for U.S. Sales. However, increasingly, the model for U.S defense sales in Italy has been shifting. U.S. systems and products face more competition, and must offer more Italian participation in the solution.

In the past, Italy has often not used competitive procurement in any meaningful sense of the term, transparency lacking in many of its contract awards. Italy has awarded about 85 percent by value of its contracts either as sole source or as part of a multinational program.

---

[342] "Boeing's three-year delay in delivering the first of four new aerial tankers to Italy is likely to cost Boeing a financial penalty, according to Bloomberg News. The company is negotiating with the Italian government over the size of that compensation, said the news service. Boeing had promised to provide the first tanker to Italy in November 2005, but that delivery is now set for this November [2008]. The second tanker's delivery is now projected to be 21 months late while the third and fourth planes are expected to be 16 and 12 months late." *Tacoma Washington News Tribune*, Aug. 14, 2008. Available at: http://blogs.thenewstribune.com/business/2008/08/14/italy_will_penalize_boeing_for_late_tank.

U.S. firms have at times benefited from those sole source awards, as Italy often did an informal early review and determined to buy a U.S. system to meet its needs.

Today, when a U.S. company bids on an Italian program, it must often compete against other global defense firms—all of which are working to offer Italy the best solution, price and Italian partnering/jobs offer. While the JSF is a very large-scale cooperative program and so perhaps a unique example, it is representative of the approach of incorporating Italian industry that the Italian government equally seeks for smaller systems or products. U.S. firms today have the best success in winning awards in Italy when they have a desirable, unique capability and can pull in local partners. In fact, for U.S. firms, the key formula to prevailing is to have both "a better widget" *and* to provide local jobs (through partnering) and technology. As one data point, the JSF program has the possibility of bringing nearly 10,000 jobs to Italy over the 40-year life of the program.

II. Italian Defense Market: Supply and Demand Side Dynamics

Evolution of Italian Defense Industry

Historically, the defense industry in Italy primarily consisted of state-owned defense and dual defense-commercial aerospace companies. But post-Cold War budget cuts and the gradual transformation of the military forces and systems have gradually led to a significant evolution of Italian defense industry. Force reductions, the changing nature of the threat, and the new transformational focus on network-centric and expeditionary warfare, all translate to less emphasis on traditional platforms than in the past. Italy is making gradual progress in this direction, but does not have all the pieces in place. Its doctrine and procurement priorities are still platform-driven and are beyond what is possible under planned budgets.

Over the years, budget cuts resulted in fewer programs and a smaller defense market; the internal Italian market could not sustain a significant level of investment across all Italian industry business areas, leaving industry with no choice but to seek more sales outside national boundaries. This drove Italy and its industry to participate in multinational programs and export sales to maintain a sufficient volume of sales to keep unit costs down and product lines viable.

Italian Cooperative Programs With European Partners

To compensate for declining budgets, Italy began entering into numerous joint or "cooperative" defense programs with other European governments in the 1990s. While there were some examples in the past (e.g., the Tornado program in the late 1970s), the post-Cold War decline in military budgets accelerated the trend toward cooperative development. At present, Italy is involved simultaneously in dozens of bilateral and multinational programs with European partners, primarily with France, the UK and Germany. Major programs include the Eurofighter Consortium (with Germany, Spain, UK) and the MEADS program (with the United States and Germany).

Table 41   Italy—Top Suppliers to Italian MoD (Millions of Dollars–$)

Company	2006	2007	2008	Total	Market Share (%)
Finmeccanica	1,278.38	1,150.35	1,011.51	3,326.03	29.4
Fincantieri	677.20	689.56	701.92	2,068.68	18.3
Fiat Group	478.47	487.21	495.95	1,461.63	12.9
Eurofighter	400.02	407.33	414.64	1,221.99	10.8
Dassault	326.62	211.04	256.70	794.36	7.0
Boeing	230.91	237.38	243.85	712.15	6.3
NH Industries	0.00	133.72	269.98	403.69	3.6
Fiat-Finmeccanica	117.46	73.79	143.71	334.96	3.0
Eurojet	78.45	79.88	81.31	239.64	2.1
Orizzonte Navale	12.00	33.64	155.91	201.55	1.8
MBDA	50.74	52.05	53.37	156.16	1.4
BAE Systems	43.21	45.39	37.40	126.01	1.1
SITAB	26.24	26.24	26.24	78.72	0.7
Diehl	14.82	30.02	30.81	75.64	0.7
Rolls Royce	14.62	29.70	30.59	74.91	0.7
Lockheed Martin	25.53	30.63	0.00	56.16	0.5
Total	**3,774.66**	**3,717.93**	**3,953.90**	**11,332.27**	**100.0**

Source: Documental Solutions Database.

Consolidating and Internationalizing

Consolidating into National Champions. The Italian defense industry has been radically restructured over the past decade. Some traditional companies were downsized or closed facilities, while a myriad of small and medium-sized companies were merged—many under Finmeccanica's control. In fact, consolidation in Italy brought many formerly separate Italian defense firms under the aegis of two national champions: Finmeccanica (aerospace and defense) and Fincantieri (shipbuilding). Further, in keeping with overall policy, the Italian government began privatizing both Finmeccanica and Fincantieri (as discussed in detail in III. Evaluation of Market Access Metrics, later in this chapter).

Figure 85   Italian Aerospace and Defense Companies (Billions of Dollars–$)

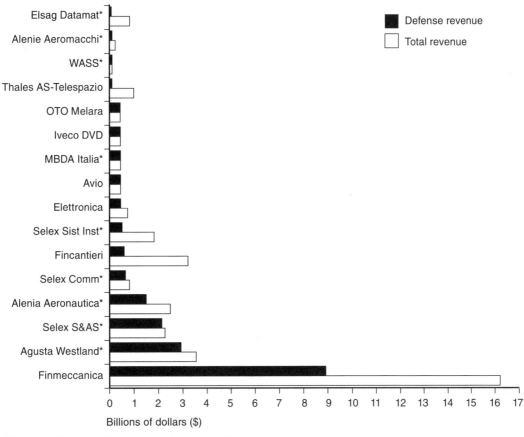

*Finmeccanica controlled company; included in Finmeccanica revenues
Source: *Itituto Affari Internazionali,* April 2008.

Italy's defense industrial capabilities are today very concentrated in a small number of firms, many of which are owned or controlled by Finmeccanica (see Figure 85). Not surprisingly, as shown on Table 41, the Italian MoD awards a large share of its work to these Italian firms. Finmeccanica and its affiliated firms, by its own account, now receives an estimated 70 percent of Italian defense research, development, testing and engineering and procurement spending. Hence, today Finmeccanica is the dominant actor, in industrial and technological terms, of the internal Italian market.[343]

---

[343] On Table 41, "Top Suppliers to Italian MoD," Finmeccanica does not appear to have a 70 percent share because of how the funding is distributed. The 70 percent is net of direct and indirect sales, i.e., some of the funding is via Italian multinational cooperative programs – e.g., Eurofighter – in which Finmeccanica receives the Italian funds through its participation on that program. Figure 85, however, does reflect the many Italian businesses within Finmeccanica's domain that receive such funds.

Figure 86   Finmeccanica International Links

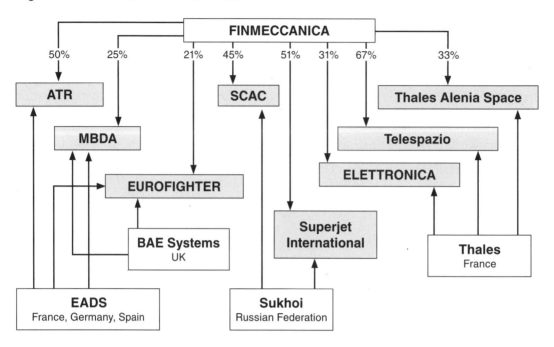

Source: *Istituto Affari Internazionale.*

Italian industry has inevitably had to become more export-oriented and increasingly moved into other European markets. Finmeccanica today is a multidomestic company, with the UK MoD as the second main customer and a widespread local presence in England. This is in large part due to Finmeccanica's acquisitions of the UK firms AgustaWestland (2004) and Selex (partial ownership in 2006 and full ownership in 2008).

Avio (propulsion) and Fincantieri (shipbuilding) are the only two Italian large defense companies outside Finmeccanica's ownership and control. That said, both have significant work agreements with Finmeccanica as the Italian leader for the production of joint programs. In addition to these larger players, there remain dozens of medium and mostly small private companies, often specialized in niche capabilities and depending on subcontract work assigned by the main players.

The state ownership of Finmeccanica, Fincantieri and other Italian firms facilitated the process of internal concentration and restructuring because the State could allow or encourage specific mergers and acquisitions. Nevertheless, some interviewed believe that Finmeccanica's dominant Italian position today could reduce the appeal of further consolidation within international alliances.

Internationalization

As all Italian defense firms gradually are losing their original national roots, they are becoming less reliant on Italy and its relatively small and stagnant market. Instead, they

Figure 87   Main Links Among Leading International Groups

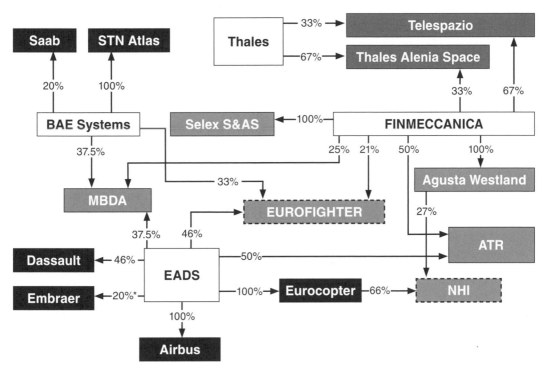

*With Thomson-CSF, Dassault and SNECMA.
Source: Istituto Affari Internazionale.

are exploiting a more multidomestic strategy, seeking entrance, contracts and industrial capabilities in the UK and the United States, in particular, as well as some less-developed Eastern markets.

The result of this process of internationalization is the buildup of more joint ventures (JVs) and alliances with European firms in light of the broad range of European joint programs. In recent years, the complex set of European JVs have led in time to complete European corporate consolidations (MBDA, etc.) in which Finmeccanica is a significant shareholder and strategic industrial partner (see Figures 86 and 87).

Italian Defense Acquisition—Key Drivers and Players

Italian security and military strategy sets the context for Italian defense acquisition. Specifically, Italian defense acquisition strategy is shaped by the following primary factors:

- Stagnant Italian national budgets with a low level of defense;

- Sustaining operational and deployment capabilities to meet commitments to the United States, NATO and the EU context; and

- Realistic desires to keep "a foot in both camps"—that is, to simultaneously maintain both its special closeness and technical ties with the United States and a central position in the EU.

Organizations and Players in Italian Defense Acquisition

In practice, multiple governmental entities are involved in Italian defense acquisition.

Segredifesa **(SG/DNA), a joint military and civilian organization reporting directly to the Chief of Defense Staff of Italy (CHOD),** is in charge of the defense procurement process, but the procurement decisions are finally decided by the Joint Staff, together with the individual Service's Staffs. Technically, Italy's CHOD is the final authority on all acquisition decisions. The most relevant procurement decisions, those having a significant international or economic impact, need the direct support of the Minister of Defense, who is often asked to convince the Prime Minister and the Treasury to support the funding for the program.

The Parliament has a role as it approves the defense budget and provides a mandatory, legally non-binding, approval of each procurement decision that involves the acquisition of hardware or the improvement of any defense capability. Participation in development programs, even on the scale of the JSF, does not technically require approval of Parliament. However, the defense staff will often seek approval if they believe the timing is propitious to get future procurement approvals.

Ministry of Economic Development—Some additional defense R&D funds, as well as some procurement funds, are provided for by this Italian domestic economic development department. This funding is allocated more on the basis of industrial and technological logic than of defense operational requirements. Development funds provided by the Italian Ministry of Economic Development (approximately $1.5 billion a year), must be placed into Italian industry; some of the funds for JSF are from this source. These additional funds have been instrumental to the start-up of new programs or upgrade of old capabilities, thus relieving in part the burden on the defense budget. A large portion of Eurofighter procurement comes from this budget.

Many Other Political Players—In Italy, the study team was told, everything is political. This is especially true in defense matters affecting national budgets and jobs, and where the State still holds an ownership share in key defense firms. Government representatives are a part of some company boards, although they often play an arm's-length role. As noted above, many decisions need the Minster of Defense, Prime Minister and Treasury support. To that end, decisions on programs involve a complex combination of political players and party interests, depending on the situation. For example, the Prime Minister's Political Advisor played a key role in facilitating the approval of the JSF MoU.[344]

Key Drivers of Italian MoD Acquisition Strategy

Inadequate defense budgets have driven the Italians toward buying mature "non-developmental" systems or joining multinational development programs. There are simply not enough funds for large national-only programs. While the Italian military has the goal to develop network-centric capabilities, and to more generally move in step with its NATO Allies, its budget often allows only slow progress toward the transformation and change the military wants to achieve.

---

[344] Once the MoU was approved, the Deputy Secretary General of Defense for Procurement signed it with the United States. Information on political aspects of decisions were obtained through study team interviews. For JSF MoU signing, see American Forces Press Service, June 24, 2002, at: http://www.defenselink.mil/news/newsarticle.aspx?id=43725.

Realistically, the key drivers for MoD acquisitions are:

- Maintain significant operational capabilities in the near and medium term to perform vital security missions;

- Maintain commonality and interoperability with the United States, NATO and European forces for smooth operations in deployment;

- Ensure security of supply for sources beyond Italian borders; and

- Provide for adequate local industrial and technological participation in defense program work, to sustain and build Italian technology and industrial capabilities.

Complex Italian Buying Preferences

When Italy plans new contracts or new systems, its preferences for sourcing vary and sometimes run at cross purposes. Government officials and market participants described the Italian preferences as follows:

Italian Military Preferences

1. Buy American—a preference for U.S. technology; seek strong U.S. and NATO interoperability. This is most true for the Italian Air Force and for some C4ISR capabilities, and less true for the Navy, which tends to prefer French and German solutions, and ground forces which often buy Italian.

2. Buy Italian or European.

Italian Political or National Government Preferences

1. Buy Italian

2. Buy European

3. Buy American

The relative priority of the United States and the EU in the list of preferences depends on the pro-U.S. vs. pro-EU leanings of the government and officials at a particular time. These preferences reflect the long-term close alignment of the Italian military with the U.S. military and desire for best technology on one hand and on the other, the natural need for government officials to have a wider view, which includes building Italian and European industry and technology.

Italian Industrial Policy: Optimizing a Calculus of Jobs, Competition, and the U.S. and EU Relationships

Italy lacks an explicit written policy or any coherent, across-the-board approach toward defense industrial policy, but it is shaping an *implicit* policy through its decisions. Overall,

Italy continues to juggle multiple competing priorities, living with very limited defense budgets and a peace-minded populace, while trying to sustain deployments and operations, support and build defense industrial capabilities, buy for value and utilize competition, and remain aligned with both the United States and the EU.

Technology/Jobs vs. Competition. First, as discussed earlier, Italy must strengthen and sustain its technology and industrial base by ensuring that sufficient contracts and jobs are awarded to Italian-based industry—including jobs requiring increasingly higher levels of technology.

To do this, Italy's contract awards and "competitions" for defense have several "unique" features. The long and somewhat behind-the-scenes way that such contract decisions are handled reflect, and add to the perception of, an overall lack of transparency in its acquisition processes. Italy's procurement process is discussed in full below. When Italy does allow competition for awards, it often proceeds as follows:

- **An informal up-front analysis to consider possible solutions.** A first phase of competition for new systems and concepts is done in a less formal manner, short of an official Request for Procurement type of announcement. This "off-line" competition is a sort of streamlined first assessment of existing products and systems that may prove suitable as a solution. Both government and industry officials in Italy reported to the study team that in most cases Italy simply does not have the budget to do otherwise; they simply cannot afford to carry multiple firms through a development phase of a program (a typical pattern in the United States).

- **Foreign firms must find Italian partners for "industrial return participation."** Italian work share is a key deciding factor in procurement decisions. Non-Italian firms need to line up with Italian partners and suppliers in offering even these informal solutions. For example, a U.S. firm with an existing solution needs to offer Italian elements on-board that system or offer specific technology or jobs to support or match the value done outside Italy. Firms must also offer efficient system solutions as they follow through with these "offsets."

- **A formal award is typically made on a sole source basis to one of the teams whose solution was reviewed informally.** Rarely will the Italian MoD fund developmental costs other than those for major weapons systems programs. Due to budget constraints, the MoD will increasingly opt for already developed solutions, where development was funded by a contractor or other agencies. The Italian MoD prefers firm, fixed-price contracts; depending on the situation, other types of contracts can possibly be negotiated.

- **Long delays and interruptions occur.** At the same time, Italian procurement decisions may drag on for months or be postponed and restarted due to Italian budget limitations or uncertainties over political support for the program in question. Further, although contracts often take longer to execute, sometimes two or more years from the date of bid acceptance, a price is typically considered firm until the contract is finalized. Firms trying to market solutions must have patience, expend capital and have Italian agents or representatives who know the political process.

Italy's Historic Reliance on EU Rules to Avoid Competition: Emerging Constraints

To make frequent sole source awards, or awards that appear to be made without clear or open solicitation, Italy has often invoked the Article 296 EC Treaty exemption.

As fully discussed in Chapter 5, Italy's use of Article 296 EC Treaty has received particular attention. In April 2008, the European Court of Justice (ECJ) ruled that Italy violated the EC Public Procurement Directive by following its common practice of granting sole source contracts for helicopters to AgustaWestland.[345] In this case, Italy awarded a contract to supply helicopters to meet the requirements of several military and civilian corps of the Italian government, including the Fire Brigade, Forestry Service, and Coast Guard.

Italy defended its sole source award to AgustaWestland under Article 296 EC Treaty, arguing that the helicopters were dual-use in nature and could be used for both military and civilian purposes. With the potential—but not the actuality—of military use, Italy asserted that it should be allowed to claim an exemption from the public tendering rules under Article 296 EC Treaty because of its alleged "essential interests" in security. Significantly, the ECJ squarely rejected this claim, ruling "[i]t is clear from the wording of [Article 296]… that the products in question must be intended for specifically military purposes. It follows that the purchase of equipment, the use of which for military purposes is hardly certain, must necessarily comply with the rules governing the award of public contracts. The supply of helicopters to military corps for the purpose of civilian use must comply with those same rules."[346]

This ruling garnered the attention of many Member States for its enforcement of the growing position asserted by the Commission that defense should not be exempt from EU competitive practices, as has often been the norm. Italy was of course particularly concerned. In interviews with this study team, Italian government officials said the ECJ findings on this case "put Italy on the spot" but that they "welcome a stricter discipline on the use of Article 296 across the EU." They said they do want to encourage a wider European-based market, as Italian firms could benefit from those opportunities as well.

Given the forces at work today, the general outlook for the future in Italy is of a market increasingly somewhat more open to competition on a case-by-case basis, but with competition still more informal and backroom in nature than traditional open and competitive public procurement processes.

Balancing the U.S. and an Evolving EU Defense Market

Moving Toward the EU Market. While sometimes expressing doubts and cautions, Italy supports EU efforts to build up ESDP and move toward an open European defense market. The Italian industrial and MoD procurement leadership recognize Italy's internal buying cannot sustain the current Italian defense industry—especially in legacy areas like ships. They understand that more rationalization is needed at the European level, and the days of true nationally fed "national champions" are ending.

---

[345] See Case C-337/05, Commission of the European Communities vs. Italian Republic (Judgment of the Court) (April 8, 2008) ("ECJ Italian Helicopter Ruling"). Available at: http://eur-lex.europa.eu/LexUriServ/LexUriServ.do?uri=OJ:C:2008:128:0002:0003:EN:PDF.

[346] Case C-337/05, ECJ Italian Helicopter Ruling, pp. 6-7.

However, national tendencies still exist and the internal market is still considered an essential element for further growth. Italian government and industry officials recognize that national programs are very inefficient and often not affordable. They also recognize that the current nation by nation markets, where each EU Member State has its own procurement rules and defense standards and specifications, causes a good deal of extra expense and added time—making European products more costly than equivalent U.S. products. This makes it particularly challenging for European multinational cooperative programs to achieve efficiencies, and for European systems to be competitive with U.S. systems in wider global markets.

For all these reasons, Italy supports increased European defense and armaments cooperation, including support for the program management agency OCCAR (Organization for Joint Armament Cooperation) and other bilateral and multinational acquisitions among European partner nations. Italy has also for some time recognized the need to develop a better regulatory environment for transnational cooperation and defense companies. In the past this led to the promotion of Italian participation in joint procurement managed by OCCAR, as well as the LOI process. More recently, it has led to increased joint activity with the European Defence Agency (EDA), in particularly in R&D and common capabilities.

Italy also generally supports the new EC Defense Package. An Italian government official indicated that Italy supports the package overall because the EU needs to remove internal barriers—despite the fact that "this needs to be tested—it is a No Man's Land right now." They also suggested the new EC Directives might also "remove some global barriers." Italy sees the need for consistent rules in all EU Member States governing defense markets in a wide range of areas (e.g., security of supply, information security, transfers, etc.).

Italian government officials also reported that Italy worked with like-minded Member States—France and Austria, for example—to make improvements to the EC Directives before they were recently approved by the European Parliament (as discussed in Chapter 5). When it comes to creating a truly European defense market, an Italian government official summed it up by saying "this is an irreversible process."

No Fortress Europe. The trend toward increased internationalization in Italian procurement is strong and will be further reinforced by the continuing reduction in resources and advancements in the process of transforming national players into veritable transnational or multinational defense companies.

In this regard, Italy apparently has a different view of the EU initiatives than does France. Whereas the French view implies an element of "European (i.e., European-Gaullist) preference," Italy does not seek to move in that direction. Rather, Italy still sees its armaments and industrial cooperation with the United States as vital to its security. Thus, the Italian government wished to avoid creation of a Fortress Europe situation. Italians suggest the EU effort to create an internal market for defense will reinforce the ongoing globalization of the defense market, and should not be seen as an obstacle to further Transatlantic developments.

According to Italian officials, however, the final result of this process will largely depend on the U.S. willingness, in their view, to establish a fair partnership, reducing barriers to entry and obstacles to the creation of a truly Transatlantic market. In their view, this will also require a multilateral framework that goes beyond the bilateral relationships the United States has established with some countries.

Italian officials warned the United States could create its own destiny in this setting. The basic question, they say, is a level playing field and the reciprocity of trade with European nations. The Italians seek to be treated as full partners with the United States and, in their view, this requires a greater degree of technology sharing (i.e., less restrictive ITAR and national disclosure policies toward Italy). They also indicated that the ITAR could hamper U.S. ability to continue its long-term place in Italian systems. "It is not a national policy [of Italy]—it is simply a genuine economic expedient for European firms to avoid ITAR products," said one senior Italian government official.

The Italian government's defense industrial policy guidance and direction for the future remains uncertain—in the absence of a formal policy stating what sectors should be considered strategic and, therefore, should be maintained locally.

That industry view may be best summarized by the remarks to the study team made by a senior Italian industry official:

> The Italian market was self-contained until just a few years ago. The industrial landscape has undergone an evolution, and at the same time there are evolving EU policies and the defense markets in Europe are opening up. Increasingly, the defense market will be expected to behave as other public markets behave. But local national firms will continue to take the large shares of the local market—they know the national military forces, the logistics, they are closest to the customer and will accept unique features of the local setting (military, political, etc.). This will always give them a better position.[347]

III. Evaluation of Market Access Metrics

Tariff Rates

By and large, tariffs are not significant barriers between Italy and the United States. All of the countries studied are members of the World Trade Organization (WTO) and thus must provide most-favored nation and national treatment to imported goods from every other country included in the study. Although defense products are generally exempt from WTO rules governing tariffs and trade, reciprocal procurement MOUs between the United States and Italy generally provide duty-free treatment for imported defense products procured from the other country.

However, the MOUs do not apply to dual-use products and technologies such as general aerospace systems that have both military and civil applications. Thus, as more military programs rely on commercial off-the-shelf technology, this would tend to put U.S. companies at a competitive disadvantage *vis-à-vis* European firms that get the benefit of the lower intra-European rates that apply under EU rules unless specific exemptions are negotiated on a bilateral basis.

---

[347] Interview with a senior VP of an Italian defense firm.

Competition in Procurement

Italian Procurement Policy: A Largely Ad Hoc Approach

Defense procurement is a significant part of the country's public procurement and is in theory subject to EU market rules that prescribe by law that public tenders above a certain threshold must be competed. In practice, however, Italy has long invoked the Article 296 EC Treaty exemption to these rules for defense acquisitions—asserting "essential security" grounds. This has the consequence of affording Italy considerable discretion in conducting its defense procurements.

In exercising its discretion, Italy does not appear to have a clear or explicit overall acquisition strategy (or, as discussed above, an overall defense industrial strategy). Rather, the MoD's decision whether to use competition in defense procurement appears to be relatively ad hoc in nature—decided on a program-by-program basis—and is driven by a mix of objectives, including, as noted above, a limited budget, the desire to stay in both camps (U.S. and European), developing technology and jobs, meeting its operational needs, and ensuring NATO force interoperability.

Despite Italian support for ongoing EU initiatives to open and integrate the European market, competition in defense procurement is not perceived in Italy as a positive thing per se. Hence, not surprisingly, the Italian procurement process has been largely based on sole-source contracts and contracts awarded in connection with European cooperative programs.

Moreover, as discussed above, when Italy does hold a competition, it is informal in nature and considerably different than those held in the United States. It tends to be a top-level review that happens very early in the decision-making process; the limited economic resources available do not allow Italy to carry two firms beyond the very early phase of programs (e.g., the equivalent of a Request for Information or set of written concept proposals). Therefore, Italy tends make selections earlier in the process—after initial drawings and designs and before prototypes are developed.

The Italian calculus of best value in decision-making, which is informal in nature, is also very different from an American style best value calculation. In this regard, there is a strong focus on Italian jobs and access to technology, which are viewed as crucial to Italy as cost, schedule and performance are to the United States.

Significantly, in contrast to France and Sweden, there is no clear change in policy in favor of increasing competition in Italian government defense acquisition. As discussed below, however, there is some indication of a growing use of competition in practice on new programs within the time period this study examined.

Italian Procurement Practice: Understanding the Data

In practice, as set forth below, the available data continues to show substantial reliance on both sole source national buying and cooperative programs in Italy. This market reality does not augur well for U.S. market access in the future.

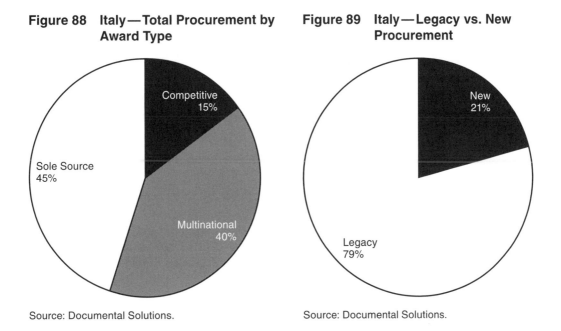

Figure 88   Italy—Total Procurement by Award Type

Competitive 15%

Sole Source 45%

Multinational 40%

Source: Documental Solutions.

Figure 89   Italy—Legacy vs. New Procurement

New 21%

Legacy 79%

Source: Documental Solutions.

- **Italian Buying of Major Weapons Systems: The Limited Role of Competition.** As shown in Figure 88, of the top 34 Italian defense programs by value,[348] only 15 percent ($1.5 billion) were awarded competitively; some 45 percent ($4.47 billion) were awarded on a sole source basis and 40 percent ($4.053 billion) were awarded through European cooperative programs (where work share is typically established through inter-governmental MOUs and contracts that are awarded through directed procurement without full and open competition). Several other key points about the overall Italian buying also are worth noting:

  - **Overall Data Can Mask Differences Between Legacy/New Buying.** As discussed below, this overall data on total Italian buying in 2006-2008 may mask any distinctions between "legacy programs" (i.e., programs where the initial award for development and/or procurement were made somewhere in the past before 2006) and "new" programs started during 2006-2008 (which are more likely to show any meaningful shifts in procurement policy). Hence, we have separately reviewed the data on "legacy" and "new" programs below to capture any different trends that may exist.

  - **A Large Share of Spending Is on Legacy Programs.** As shown on Figure 89, roughly 79 percent ($7.9 billion) of all contract awards during the period studied went to legacy programs, giving Italy the highest percentage of legacy systems of any country examined (although the United States' percentage of spending on legacy programs (77 percent) during the same period is not far behind). The list of Top Italian Defense Programs (Table 42) shows that legacy Italian national programs and cooperative programs such as Tornado, Eurofighter Typhoon, and the Cavour-class aircraft carrier receive the largest amounts of funding.

---

[348] RDT&E and Procurement programs totaling more than $50 million for 2006-2008.

Table 42   Leading Italian Defense Programs, 2006-2008 over $50 Million (Millions of Dollars – $)

Program Name	Type	Prime Contractor	2006	2007	2008	Total	Award Type	Legacy
Tornado	Strike Aircraft	Finmeccanica	50.07	600.78	901.18	1,552.03	Sole Source	Yes
Eurofighter	Fighter	Eurofighter	400.02	407.33	414.64	1,221.99	Multinational	Yes
KC-767A	Tanker	Boeing	230.91	237.38	243.85	712.15	Competitive	No
CV Cavour	Carrier	Fincantieri	326.62	168.09	169.05	663.76	Sole Source	Yes
Project Horizon	Destroyer	Fincantieri	96.14	239.22	240.64	576.00	Multinational	Yes
AMX ACL	Light Fighter	Finmeccanica	192.86	241.70	218.53	538.87	Sole Source	Yes
C-27J	Transport	Finmeccanica	155.30	273.28	42.97	471.54	Multinational	Yes
FREMM	Frigate	Orizzonte Navali	101.58	154.97	204.77	461.31	Multinational	No
VTLM	Armored Vehicle	Fiat Group	138.52	142.30	146.07	426.89	Competitive	No
TTH90	Transport Helicopter	NH Industries	0.00	133.72	269.98	403.69	Sole Source	Yes
Project Horizon	Firgate	Fincantieri	193.42	194.55	5.67	393.64	Multinational	Yes
Eurofighter GFE Engines	Fghter	Eurojet	78.45	79.88	81.31	239.64	Multinational	Yes
SAR-2000	Radar Satellite	Finmeccanica	40.15	81.42	80.29	201.86	Sole Source	Yes
Ariete	Main Battle Tank	Fiat Group	60.21	60.05	59.90	180.16	Sole Source	Yes
APACHE	Tactical Missile	MBDA	50.74	52.05	53.37	156.16	Multinational	Yes
Meteosat Sensors	Satellite	Finmeccanica	5.50	5.50	127.78	138.78	Multinational	Yes
SS Type 212	Attack Sub	Fincantieri	126.20	3.68	3.68	133.55	Sole Surce	No

Program Name	Type	Prime Contractor	2006	2007	2008	Total	Award Type	Legacy
PzH 2000	Self-Propelled Gun	Fiat-Finmeccanica	0.00	42.95	87.65	130.60	Competitive	No
AW101	Transport Helicopter	Finmeccanica	117.91	4.43	4.43	126.77	Sole Source	Yes
Bv206	Light Armored Vehicle	BAE SYSTEMS	43.21	45.39	37.40	126.01	Competitive	No
Dardo	Infantry Fighting Vehicle	Fiat-Finmeccanica	108.84	5.82	5.82	120.48	Sole Source	Yes
EMPAR	Shio-Based Radar	Finmeccanica	46.42	46.92	20.87	114.20	Multinational	Yes
COSMO-SkyMed Payload	Satellite	Finmeccanica	97.84	4.29	3.86	105.99	Multinational	Yes
FREMM	Frigate	Orizzonte Navali	0.00	0.00	99.01	99.01	Multinational	Yes
SRT-635	Tactical Radios	Finmeccanica	28.03	28.47	28.91	85.41	Sole Source	Yes
Centauro	Wheeled Armored Vehicle	Fiat-Finmeccanica	8.62	25.01	50.24	83.87	Sole Source	Yes
Sicral 1 SATCOM Services	Satcomm	SITAB Consortium	26.24	26.24	26.24	78.72	Competitive	No
AW 109	Transport helicopter	Finmeccanica	26.97	26.97	24.27	78.21	Sole Source	Yes
IRIS-T	Air-to-air missile	Diehl	14.82	30.02	30.81	75.64	Multinational	Yes
AMX GFE Engines	Light fighter	Rolls-Royce	14.62	29.70	30.59	74.91	Sole Source	Yes
HH-3F Upgrade	Helicopter	Finmeccanica	6.49	28.14	28.14	62.77	Sole Source	Yes
KC-130J Kit Upgrade	Tanker Aircraft	Lockheed Martin	25.53	30.63	0.00	56.16	Sole Source	Yes
Falcon 50	Transport	Dassault	54.11	0.00	0.00	54.11	Sole Source	Yes
Falcon 900EX	Transport	Dassault	54.11	0.00	0.00	54.11	Sole Source	Yes

Source: Documental Solutions.

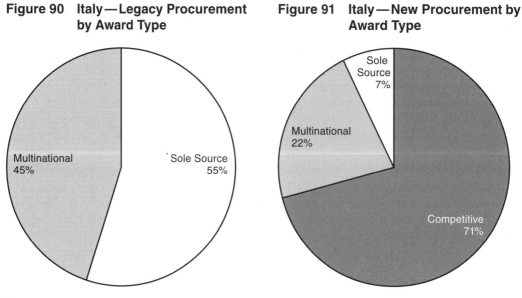

Figure 90   Italy—Legacy Procurement by Award Type

Source: Documental Solutions.

Figure 91   Italy—New Procurement by Award Type

Source: Documental Solutions.

- **Most Legacy Spending is Sole Source or Directed.** As Figure 90 shows, approximately 55 percent ($4.3 billion) of legacy procurement awards was sole source; some 45 percent were awarded through cooperative programs (i.e., which, as noted, were neither competed nor open to foreign participation). It should be recognized, of course, that most countries studied had high degrees of sole source awards on their legacy programs (e.g., 79 percent for the United States) and little competition (although most have more competition than does Italy). The magnitude of sole source buying reflects the realities of large defense programs. After a major system has been awarded to a particular firm, the follow-on production buys, upgrades, modifications and maintenance on such legacy programs are often awarded to the same firm again (e.g., after an award is made for an aircraft developed and produced by one firm, it is much more likely to be awarded to that firm for future buys). Indeed, it would be uneconomic to change system level contractors midstream on large programs unless the incumbent is not performing (although government customers can and should compete the subsystems upgrades and refreshes). Therefore, not surprisingly, Finmeccanica and its affiliates, the incumbents on numerous legacy programs, received approximately 70 percent of all contracts awarded (by value) in the 2006-2008 period.

- **New Italian Awards Show Some Change and More Use of Competition.** To assess whether Italy is changing its buying habits away from sole source national and European cooperative buying toward more competitive awards, "new" major programs were evaluated separately (see Figure 91). Significantly, the data did show a significant positive change in buying habits, with 71 percent ($1.5 billion) of new major contracts awarded competitively, 22 percent awarded for multinational programs and just 7 percent on a sole source basis. However, several cautionary points about new buying are worth noting:

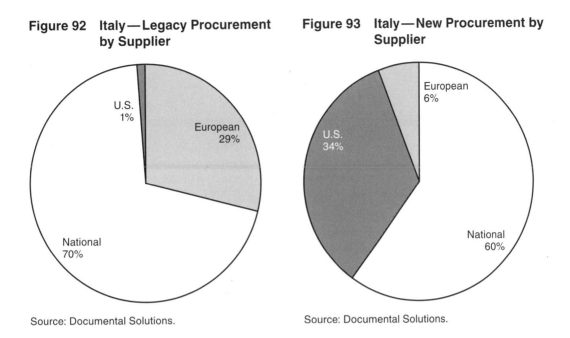

Figure 92   Italy—Legacy Procurement by Supplier

Source: Documental Solutions.

Figure 93   Italy—New Procurement by Supplier

Source: Documental Solutions.

- **Large Awards Can Skew Data.** Of the five new programs awarded competitively in the last three years, European firms won two ($204.7 million), Italian firms won two (totaling $557.5 million) and a U.S. firm (Boeing) won one award ($712 million) for the KC-767 aerial tanker. This large one-off program skews the data in favor of both competition and U.S. companies. Absent the tanker program, the division between competitive and non-competitive awards would have been 56 percent to 44 percent—a marked improvement, but not as significant as the total figures would suggest. Thus, the degree of change in buying habits must be viewed as tentative; it is too soon to make definitive statements about the extent of change.

- **U.S. Firms Face Robust Competition.** Today, it is not unusual for U.S. firms to compete against foreign (European, Israeli) firms for Italian contracts. For example, Boeing competed against ATR and Thales for maritime patrol aircrafts and against EADS/Airbus for the tankers. Lockheed Martin competed against Airbus on transport airplanes, and General Atomics competed against Israeli Aerospace Industries for drones.

- **Sole Source Buying Is Prevalent in Some Sectors.** Even among new awards, sole source national procurement remains the rule in some sectors, particularly the traditional sectors such as shipbuilding and land systems, where the degree of international integration at the industrial level is less advanced. Strategic assets are rarely subject to completely open bidding, restricting the process to invited ones. Open bidding also is much less prevalent when large international programs are concerned, even if a certain level of competition remains viable at the early stage of the process. These types of programs are often decided on a much more complex set of factors that include foreign policy or security considerations as well as *juste retour* principles.

Figure 94   Italy—Defense Market Share by Companies

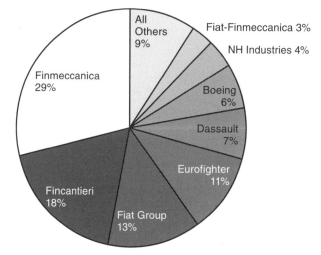

Source: Documental Solutions.

- **Competition Exists in Off-the-Shelf Products.** Some considerable competition happens in areas where either a domestic product is not immediately available (mostly off-the-shelf acquisitions) or in minor contracts where international consortia involving the Italian industry are not possible.

U.S. Firms Have a Modest Share of the Italian Defense Market. Historically, and still today, the largest share of the internal market goes to local firms. As shown in Figure 92, about 70 percent ($5.5 billon) of legacy procurement was awarded to Italian companies—mainly Finmeccanica and Fincantieri. Another 29 percent ($2.3 billion) was awarded to other European companies, while only about 1 percent ($56 million) was awarded to U.S. companies. Looking at new procurement only (Figure 93), we see only modest improvements: 60 percent ($1.2 billion) was awarded to Italian companies, 6 percent ($126 million) to European companies, and 34 percent ($712 million) to U.S. companies. But again, in light of the fact of the large Boeing contract, we caution against viewing the 34 percent U.S. market share as a meaningful observation. Excluding the Boeing tanker, Italian companies would have won 90 percent of all new procurement and other European companies just 10 percent, while the United States would not have won *any* programs at all.

The modest position of U.S. companies in the Italian market is also shown in Figure 94. Specifically, three Italian companies—Finmeccanica, Fincantieri and Fiat Group—have a 60 percent share of the Italian defense market; the multinational Eurofighter Consortium has 10.8 percent, French aircraft manufacturer Dassault 7 percent, and Boeing 6.3 percent. No other American company has more than a 0.5 percent share of the Italian market.

- **U.S. Subsystems Sales Also Are Likely Disadvantaged.** While there may be greater U.S. subsystem participation than this data shows (anecdotal evidence available to us suggests this), we lack the data to fully evaluate this part of the market. However, we do believe, as discussed elsewhere, that the trends toward buying European and avoiding ITAR products and technologies disfavor U.S. subsystem buying.

Fair and Transparent Procurement Process

Italy's procurement system is generally one of the least transparent and rule-based of any systems studied, and therefore poses challenges for U.S. firms seeking to enter the market.

Italy, like other EU Member States, is a party to the WTO Agreement on Government Procurement (GPA). However, its procurement of "warlike" goods is exempt from the GPA's coverage and, hence, only "non-warlike" goods are subject to the Agreement's disciplines.

In sectors other than defense, the Italian government generally follows EC procurement regulations, which call for non-discrimination against foreign firms. The overall Italian defense procurement process, however, is characterized by a certain degree of informality in approach that prevails over the strict following of written rules. There is no disciplined structure of precise procurement rules and processes that apply for all defense buys; there is a general lack of process clarity. An intricate understanding on how to work in the Italian system, and likely some support, is required to get access to opportunities and awards. These pose barriers to entry for foreign firms.

Further, local political pressure and administrative procedures are often said to favor Italian companies. While there is no formal restriction on a foreign firm's ability to compete (especially for European and U.S. firms), there are a number of cases where officials utilize private bidding or bidding by invitation; other firms are not able to compete.

However, there is an increasing practice of providing public notice of bidding opportunities and making the request for procurement available (in newspapers and on the internet), thereby making bidding opportunities increasingly more visible. Therefore, Italy's participation in European initiatives such as OCCAR and the EDA Electronic Bulletin Board System, the latter of which requires voluntary publication of bids on the EDA internet website, are gradually catalyzing change. Today, most Italian opportunities outside the scope of large international cooperative programs are published and more open for bidding.

Awards are published and it is possible to protest the fairness of the process in local courts both for formal and substantial errors. It also is possible to bring a challenge to the ECJ in certain cases (i.e., for abuse of the application of Article 296 EC Treaty). However, such challenges often are not successful; the Italian judicial process is very slow and cumbersome, the rulings can take a long time, and the entire matter can damage the reputation of the protestor with the customer.

Domestic Content

There is no Italian law requiring a minimal share of national content in defense assets; Italy does not have any law or rule similar to the U.S. Buy American Act. However, as discussed below, in practice, foreign firms are strongly encouraged to provide a significant local return of investment when they want to bid for defense contracts of any real value. (Note that large contracts by Italian standards may be much smaller than a U.S. view of a large contract.)

The role of Finmeccanica as a "natural" partner for foreign companies willing to operate in the Italian market has grown recently, parallel to the process of internationalization and globalization of defense markets. In light of its superior knowledge of the Italian environment and its direct links with the political and military leadership, this Italian industry leader has significant leverage *vis-à-vis* foreign firms and its own subcontractors given its size and dominance in the internal market.

As a practical matter, obtaining Finmeccanica's agreement to partner can be key to getting an award. Depending on the circumstances, the foreign partner can often retain a major role in the partnership; in turn, U.S. partnering can make Italian firms more competitive in Italy and elsewhere.

As a broad general trend, the relative degree of Italian-national content is slowly diminishing and the international dimension of the procurement programs is growing in light of customer preferences to acquire better capabilities at a relatively cheaper price. This is a natural result of the increase in multinational programs in the last 15 years, and the pressures toward the European market's overall globalization of defense industry.

Offsets and *Juste Retour*

There is no law requiring a direct or indirect offset of defense procurement, but there are informal guidelines that require the procurement agency to seek significant compensation, mostly in the form of technological transfer and industrialization within the same program. The Italian military and government do not want an *offset law*; they prefer flexible working relationships to be developed among partners to meet needs as each circumstance may offer.

The U.S. Department of Commerce (DoC) annual report on offsets also reflects that offsets in Italy totaled roughly 100 percent of contract values in practice over the period 1993-2006 (calculated from data submitted by the reporting U.S. firms of actual contracts and offset commitments).[349] A review of DoC offset reports over recent years shows the offset percentage has remained remarkably stable. Thus, whether required or not, they do appear to be a major factor in defense trade with Italy.

To provide for this "industrial return participation," the foreign bidder may use one of several options:

- Identify a domestic industrial partner to involve, often as a critical subcontractor or partner (e.g., Alenia Aeronavali in the conversion of Boeing tankers);

- Offer to provide the product to an Italian producer under license (e.g., U212 submarines built by Fincantieri under HDW license, PzH-2000 howitzer by OtoMelara under Rehinmethall license).

- Select Italian final assembler (e.g., JSF fabrication, assembly and check out in the future);

- Offer work to Italian firm as supplier or prime contractor of foreign products into a U.S. acquisition; or

- Offer other jobs, technology, or intellectual capital of interest to the Italian MoD or industry more broadly.

---

[349] Offsets in Defense Trade, Twelfth Report to Congress, U.S. Department of Commerce (Dec. 2007), PDF p. 29, report p. 13 (Table 2-5). Available at: http://www.bis.doc.gov/defenseindustrialbaseprograms/osies/offsets/final-12th-offset-report-2007.pdf.

In practice, the first option—industrial partnering—appears to be the one most typically used today.

Italian political decision-makers also evaluate the impact of the proposal specifically on the creation of local jobs. Thus, the industrial return is evaluated not only in purely economic terms (return on investment) or technological advancements, but also for the social impact, in particular in the few Italian districts operating in the aerospace and defense business (Turin, Varese, La Spezia, Naples, Foggia).

For example, the C-130J requirement for "offset" work in Italy was written formally into the contract language between Italy and Lockheed. Study interview sources reported Lockheed Martin was required to submit a specific offset plan to Italy—this included direct and indirect arrangements.

Today, Italy prefers direct work that is a normal part of the product being procured, or some similar level of work or technology to be augmented for compensation. There is a strong preference for industrial participation by local firms—i.e., a preference for direct rather than indirect offsets. The MoD is aware of the complexity of managing offsets and the additional costs that they impose, but nevertheless remains eager to maintain a certain level of operational sovereignty through local production and technological knowledge and transfer.

The emerging discipline of the European defense market is based on the *principle* that indirect offsets are a clear breach of market rules and should not be permitted, while direct offsets are an element of additional costs that have to be limited and eventually eliminated. On October 24, 2008, the EDA issued a new voluntary Code of Conduct on Offsets to evolve toward more transparent use of offsets to better shape the European industrial base while reducing reliance on them and eventually eliminating the need for them.[350]

Italy has also supported *juste retour* principles, and there are no indications the Italian government would like to end the practice. The concept of "*juste retour*" is generally applied to cooperative programs under MoUs and managed by international consortia. In the Eurofighter program, the work share for the Italian industry equals the cost share for the MoD acquisitions. This policy also applies in programs with Italian participation managed by OCCAR, where *juste retour* is sought as a balance within a plurality of contracts rather than directly on a specific program. The implementation of *juste retour* over the years has been instrumental in guaranteeing resources for the local industry. However, as Italian industry becomes bigger and stronger and more transnational and export-oriented, Italian leaders are increasingly aware of the obstacle *juste retour* poses to specialization, integration and project efficiency.

The position of the Italian defense industry on offsets and *juste retour* is ambiguous. The leading contractors are conscious that requiring offsets nationally implicitly means accepting the same logic from other countries when seeking export sales.

Today, however, these practices remain a key part of any competition in Italy. Firms competing for awards must provide some kind of offset; showing the ability to provide jobs in Italy as well as to transfer significant technology can be discriminators in the selection process.

---

[350] The EDA's first goal is to work toward transparency and a process of voluntary participation. Recognizing also the need to adjust national policies to this provision, National Armament Directors agreed to defer the application of the 100 percent ceiling until Oct. 15, 2010.

Table 43   Italy — Government Ownership and Control of Defense Companies

Company	Government Ownership Percent (%)	Golden Share	Other Owners
Finmeccanica S.p.A	33.98	Yes	Publicly traded on Milan stock exchange; Government appoints 9 of 13 directors
Fincantieri	83	Yes	Government shares held by Institute for Industrial Reconstruction (IRI); nine financial institutions hold remaining 17%
Avio S.p.A	5	Yes	Finmeccanica holds 15% share in Avio, has veto rights over strategic decisions
Eletronica S.p.A	11	No	Finmeccanica holds 31.3% equity share; Thales holds 33%.

Source: DACIS.

Government Ownership

As discussed above, looking back a decade or so, the Italian state owned much of its defense industry. Today, this has been notably reduced by the conscious design of the Italian government. Equally purposeful at this time, however, is the retention of shares in certain major Italian defense firms.

Today, as shown on Table 43, the Italian government is a partial owner of Finmeccanica (down from full ownership back in the 1990s) and near-full owner of Fincantieri.[351] The Italian government also has some minor ownership interests in other defense firms.

Moreover, the Italian government has golden shares with rights concerning strategic decisions, such as international alliances, entrance of major shareholders, and the sale of strategic assets. While Fincantieri today is 83 percent state-owned, there are discussions to consider reducing the government's ownership stake to 50 percent.

With its significant remaining equity interest and golden shares, the Italian government today has control over the Management and the Board of major Italian defense contractors. In practice, however, government officials and market participants interviewed stated that the government largely does not interfere in day-to-day commercial decision-making. The firms' managements are quite independent to make decisions.

The government's political control is more visible when the board seats and jobs are distributed. According to those interviewed, board members of these companies are appointed by political parties that may pay little attention to the management capability of those appointed. Occasionally, political authorities also exert pressure on board members regarding strategic decisions such as where to locate key production plants and create vital jobs, as well as on the hiring of politically affiliated supporters.

---

[351] Information available to the study team from DACIS suggests the Italian government ownership may have dropped to only 83 percent of Fincantieri, with 17 percent held by private equity groups.

At present, there is no indication that the Italian government plans to divest its remaining interest and role in defense firms. Undoubtedly, this will depend on a range of considerations, including Italy's financial position. There is apparent interest in reducing the government's stake in Fincantieri to 49-51 percent, thus enabling the firm to better finance its growth strategy and international partnership by raising capital from the market. Treasury's share of Finmeccanica also could be trimmed to 30 percent, the lowest legal limit at present. It is, however, very likely that the Italian government will maintain its golden shares for the foreseeable future.

Foreign Ownership

The Italian investment climate, both generally and with respect to the defense sector, is not very positive for foreign investors (with significant regional variations).

Generally, foreign investment in large Italian firms is difficult. In some "strategic" sectors, the Italian government often seeks and promotes an "Italian solution" to ownership. In the past few years, this has happened in the automotive, telecommunications, energy and airline sectors. For example, Alitalia's efforts to find a foreign investor were contentious for so long that even when the Air France investment was ultimately approved, it could not prevent the airline from failing. In any event, such a solution requires the participation of a prominent Italian partner in an alliance with a strong foreign company.

In general, there is a tendency to favor "informal" foreign direct investment, i.e., foreign firms partnering with an Italian firm via joint ventures or international industrial alliances (e.g., with Thales Alenia in the space sector, MDBA in missiles, and DCNS (Direction des Constructions Navales Services) in shipbuilding). By contrast, investment by passive financial investors is relatively easy and increasingly requested.

Where foreign-owned firms or joint ventures with foreign partners perform classified contracts, Italian authorities ensure security by "ring fencing" the classified information at the company. For example, this approach has been used with respect to some missile programs managed by MBDA and some space programs that are of direct interest to Italian authorities (Sicral MilSatCom).

Italy has no formal legal process for approving foreign acquisitions. The most significant cases are discussed at the Cabinet level, but reviews through informal channels are also very important, and government-to-government discussions also take place at the highest levels. Again, political and employment issues, as well as local constituency issues, will generally be important factors. The lack of transparency that often surrounds the approval process for foreign acquisitions is related to the intricacy of the process of "moral suasion" exercised by government officials.

Additionally, labor market laws are very rigid and the Italian bureaucracy complex and onerous. The judicial system also poses challenges for potential investors; firms cannot be sure whether cases will be adjudicated in a timely manner and cases against the Italian State (such as protests contractors might make in the United States against DoD decisions) are not well received in Italy.

These and other adverse factors have effectively deterred foreign investment in Italian defense firms. As a result, there is little foreign ownership of Italian defense firms today.

While one can point to foreign investment funds becoming increasingly large shareholders in Finmeccanica, the Italian government today retains its ownership share of more than 33 percent.

The most visible U.S. investment in an Italian defense firm is the Carlyle acquisition of Avio. Carlyle is a private equity firm with some other global defense holdings; Avio supplies rocket and naval and aircraft engines, gas turbines and parts. Italy decided to allow this deal to proceed. However, the government-sponsored solution required the U.S. investor to accept Finmeccanica as the leading industrial partner, with a 30 percent share, and also required that key Italian management be kept in place.

As Carlyle's target was not industrial integration but the financial returns of a well-performing company, the agreement was considered mutually beneficial. However, it probably would have proven more difficult if the acquisition bid had come from an industrial rather than a financial entity (such as a large U.S. defense firm). A different type of firm would probably not have accepted being the major shareholder with the Italian government still able to exercise strategic guidance. Political issues would have been more acute in a case connected with the direct state ownership of Italian defense industry. In the case of Avio this was not relevant, however, as the company was owned by Fiat.

Table 44 shows the very small values of U.S. acquisitions of defense firms in Italy since 2000 (excluding Carlyle/Avio transaction discussed above). Indeed, most of the firms acquired are not primarily defense firms. Rather, they are firms in aerospace, security, and information technology that have some minor defense work.[352]

In sum, as a result of all of the Italian government's policies and the overall investment climate, U.S. firms have not sought significant ownership of defense firms in Italy. Currently, for U.S. defense firms to participate in the Italian market as bidders, it is not critical to have a local subsidiary or local onshore presence; instead they must ensure that they provide for adequate work share in some form in Italy. The larger defense firms do, however, tend to establish a small office as an "antenna" to follow the market's evolution and be ready to catch opportunities as well as to have a better understanding of the political and industrial environment.

Ethics and Corruption

Italy has experienced ethics and corruption issues generally in its internal market. The World Bank's worldwide governance indicators show Italy at 60 percent for rule of law and 70 percent for control of corruption—below most other major Western industrialized nations.[353] Italy also is ranked 55th in the Transparency International (TI) 2008 Corruption Perception Index. By way of comparison, the United States is ranked 18th, France 19th, the UK 16th, and Sweden tied for first.[354]

---

[352] The Defense Mergers & Acquisitions database we utilized includes aerospace, defense, and homeland security firms, including information technology firms, telecommunications firms and others. A review of the acquisitions shows that very few of these firms primarily served defense markets, the subject of this study.

[353] See World Bank Governance Indicators, 1996-2007 (Country Data Report for Italy, 1996-2007). Available at: http://info.worldbank.org/governance/wgi/pdf/c110.pdf.

[354] Transparency International's Corruption Perception Index is on their website, available at: http://www.transparency.org/news_room/in_focus/2008/cpi2008/cpi_2008_table.

Table 44   U.S. Acquisitions of Italian Defense, Aerospace and Security Companies

Date	Company	Buyer	Price	Revenue	Comments	Defense/ Dual Use
Nov 2007	Synergy SpA	Garmin, Ltd	NA	NA	GPS applications	Dual Use
Sep 2007	Officine Maccaniche Industiali	Ingersoll-Rand Co. Ltd.	NA	NA	Compressed air equipment	Dual Use
Aug 2007	Arcotronics Italia SpA	Kemet Corp	23.9	207.0	Capcitors	Dual Use
Jan 2007	C-Map	Boeing Company	75.0	NA	Maritime Cartography Applications	Dual Use
May 2006	BCS Group	Twin Discs, Inc.	22.7	29.2	Marine systems	Dual Use
Apr 2006	Intercast Industries SpA	PPG Industries, Inc.	NA	NA	Resin optics	Dual Use
Dec 2005	AONet International Srl	MSGI Security Solutions	1.0	3.0	IT security	Dual Use
Dec 2004	Excelssa SpA	Media Services Group, Inc	1.6	10.2	Video surveillance (minority stake)	Dual Use
Jul 2004	BAI Srl, BAI Tecnica Srl	Oshkosh Truck Corp	18.7	37.4	Military trucks (75% stake)	Defense
Oct 2003	FiatAvio SpA	Carlyle Group	1,216.0	1,740.0	Aircraft and rocket engines (70% stake)	Dual Use
Feb 2003	Fiocco Engineering SpA	Aviation Innovations and Research	NA	NA	Advanced composite materials	Dual Use
Feb 2002	ITR SpA	Parker Hannifin Corp	68.0	147.0	Oil and gas technology	Dual Use
Dec 2001	Magnaghi Aerospace SpA	United Technologies	NA	20.0	Flight control actuators	Dual Use
Jun 2001	BEA Filtri SpA	ESCO Technologies, Inc.	NA	10.5	Filtration systems	Dual Use
Mar 2001	InfoSer SpA	Computer Sciences Corp	NA	14.0	IT services	Dual Use
Feb 2001	BAG SpA	Sequa Corp	NA	NA	Airbag systems	Dual Use
Feb 2001	SBC Eletronica SpA	Parker Hannifin Corp	NA	20.0	Servo drives	Dual Use
Oct 2000	Aeroquip-Vickers SpA	Moog, Inc.	10.0	20.0	Electric drives	Dual Use
Jun 2000	Finmeccanica SpA (units)	McDermott International	NA	NA	Power units	Dual Use
Jun 2000	Microset Srl	Moog, Inc.	1.1	NA	Electronic controls (33% stake)	Dual Use

Source: Defense Mergers and Acquisitions Database.

While there have been some issues in the defense industry in the past, in general the defense industry must be assessed separately from other Italian economic sectors. Business Monitor International's newly released *Italy Defence and Security Report Q108* judges the nation overall this way:

> As far as fundamentals are concerned, Italy has a medium-term stable political outlook.... This must be qualified by a continuing vulnerability to corruption at various levels within the political system, and an antagonistic relationship between the judiciary and the politicians. A further complicating factor is the question of bias in the media, with new legislation expected to tackle this thorny question.[355]

Further, the type of defense business environment that exists in Italy might suggest caution on this matter. While their paper did not expressly address Italy, representatives of Transparency International assert that settings in which single-source defense contracts are often used are "intuitively more prone to corruption." Specifically, TI states:

> [I]n a defense procurement environment in which the single-source method is permissible, and even common, individual officials making procurement decisions have great power over which companies are going to be given the most lucrative contracts.... It is not a great leap for officials to make these decisions based on what might benefit them... Further, there is a chance for procurement officials and companies to form ongoing corrupt relationships, in which contracts can be continually awarded in exchanges of personal gain. Competitive process necessarily includes multiple levels of oversight... with these layers of appraisal, corruption becomes much more difficult. If corruption is expected in a competitive procurement process, losing companies have the opportunity to call public and judicial attention to their concerns.[356]

To be clear, we found no recent specific allegations of bribery in connection with defense contracts awarded in Italy (the last case this study team could find was in the 1970s, involving Lockheed). However, the relative lack of transparency and competition in the Italian system create the prospects that such problems may exist. On the other hand, some dynamics suggest that this propensity will be mitigated in the future. In particular, the increase in EU oversight of defense markets generally and a more transparent and competitive procurement process in particular is likely to mitigate these types of concerns over time.

There continues, however, to be a mixed track record with respect to Italian firms' propensity to make illegal payments in third-country defense markets. On the one hand, Italy is a signatory to the Convention on Combating Bribery of Foreign Public Officials in International Business Transactions (OECD Anti-Bribery Convention) and has enacted implementing legislation.[357] Moreover, TI's recent progress report found that Italy has taken "significant enforcement actions with respect to anti-bribery laws—including prosecu-

---

[355] Business Monitor International (UK Market Risk assessment firm). Summary available at: http://www.business-monitor.com/defence/italy.html.

[356] R. Wilson, D. Scott and M. Pyman, *The Extent of Single Sourcing and Attendant Corruption—Risk in Defence Procurement: A First Look*, Transparency International (UK) presented at the conference 'Public procurement'; University of Nottingham, June 19-20, 2006. Available at: http://www.defenceagainstcorruption.org/index.php?option=com_docman&task=doc_download&gid=9.

[357] The Italian implementing legislation was the Law of 29 September, n. 300, published in Ordinary Supplement 176-L to the Official Journal of 25 October 2000 n. 250. See OECD website; available at: http://www.oecd.org/document/30/0,3343,en_2649_34859_2027102_1_1_1_1,00.html#italy.

Figure 95   Italy—Arms Export Sales, 1999-2006 (Billions of Euros—€)

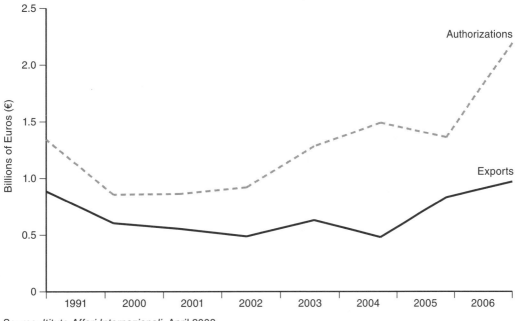

Source: *Itituto Affari Internazionali,* April 2008.

tions—although a number of deficiencies remain with respect to Italy's enforcement of its anti-bribery laws."[358]

Italy is, however, rated twentieth in the TI Bribe Payers Index of 30 major exporting nations—worse than the United States and all other Western European countries.[359] Available information reflects that the longstanding culture and practices by Italian firms in this area are difficult to change and that change is slow.

Export Controls

The Italian System

Italy is a major arms exporting country, with nearly $1.2 billion in arms sales in 2006; in recent years, the volume of Italian defense exports has been rising (see Figure 95). A member of major multilateral export control regimes, including the Nuclear Suppliers Group, the Australia Group, the Missile Technology Control Regime, the Wassernaar Arrangement and the Chemical Weapons Convention, Italy is also a member of the Organization for Security Cooperation in Europe (OSCE), and has approved the OSCE principles gov-

---

[358] F. Heimann and G. Dell, *Progress Report 2008: Enforcement of the OECD Convention on Combating Bribery of Foreign Public Officials in International Business Transactions,* Transparency International (June 24 2008), pp. 10, 21-22. Available at: http://www.transparency.org/news_room/in_focus/2008/oecd_report.

[359] Available at: http://www.transparency.org/policy_research/surveys_indices/bpi/bpi_2006.

erning transfers of conventional arms and the 2000 OSCE document on Small Arms and Light Weapons.[360]

Italy, like other EU Member States, also is a signatory to the 1998 EU Code of Conduct on Arms Exports, which harmonized regulations across all Member States in the European Union, and established general principles for the transfer of armaments and military technology, and set up a system whereby each Member State must inform the others whenever an export license is denied. Under the Code, each state must also consult with the other Member States whenever it wishes to grant an export license that has been denied by another Member State for "essentially identical transactions," although the ultimate decision to deny or transfer a military item remains at the national discretion of each Member State. The recently adopted EC Transfers Directive is a further step in aligning the policies of EU countries regarding intra-Community transfers, providing security of supply reassurances, and simplifying procedures to permit such transfers among Member States and certified defense companies. The focus of this EC Directive is intra-Community transfers, and thus the main beneficiaries of reduced barriers within the EU are European defense companies. It is not clear at all that U.S. firms will be eligible for similar treatment; this is a matter left to national governments.

Italian export controls over defense materials are legally very stringent and often considered a strong obstacle to domestic firms' exports. They are also an obstacle for international joint programs and industrialization, as the law does not readily distinguish between European and NATO Allies and other countries.

The management in Italy of export licenses is cumbersome, very time-consuming and is based on a "punitive" assumption against trade of weapons. Italy is trying to modify the export rules to make them more effective and streamlined in their application, and is in favor of a more liberal approach to intra-EU transfer of defense goods and reduced restrictions to Transatlantic trade. In an industry roundtable with small Italian defense and aerospace firms, the firms told the study team that the largest barrier to Italian businesses doing foreign work was the bureaucracy of Italy itself, particularly its export licensing regime. These firms were all hopeful that the EC Transfers Directive would be implemented and would simplify these matters in some way.

ITAR: A Concern Affecting the U.S.-Italian Relationship

An issue of particular concern to the Italian government and senior military leaders today is the perception that the United States is unwilling to grant what Italy sees as an "equitable" level of national disclosure and technology release to Italy. As one Italian government leader asserted, Italy has been the staunchest U.S. Ally and has supported U.S. operations even when not popular in Italy. However, in terms of technology release, Italy is treated "like any other friendly nation—like Botswana or Sierra Leone."

Italian military leaders equally express frustration with ITAR release and national disclosure policies. For example, with respect to the JSF, the United States has not supported Italy's request to make Italian unique modifications in order to integrate some of their existing Italian military systems/subsystems onto the aircraft (e.g., missile systems). This creates suspicions in Italy that the DoD is taking this position to protect its industry rather than for

---

[360] Details on Italian membership and OSCE activities are available at: http://www.osce.org/about/13131.html.

a legitimate security reason and, hence, is not playing fairly with allies. Further, Italian military leaders are frustrated that they can only play in unclassified aspects of JSF intellectual property (IP), and neither Italian military nor Italian industry are able to discuss certain matters with the United States. From an Italian perspective, this makes it particularly hard for Italy to execute this complex program.

Beyond JSF, Italian officials are concerned more generally with lack of access to higher level U.S. technologies. They view restrictive U.S. release policies as a problem for Italian security generally, including military interoperability and the evolution of Italian industry. In some cases, U.S. restrictions on certain critical elements have caused the need to find non-U.S. substitutes, and the Italians have had difficulty with such substitutions. The challenges of finding reasonable alternatives on programs have served to increase the incentives to develop some key capabilities locally.

Italian firms have similar concerns; several sources interviewed said that the "number one" complaint of Italian firms in dealing with U.S. products and firms is the onerous and uncertain technology transfer rules. Italian officials have become so frustrated, after numerous attempts to seek U.S. action to alleviate these concerns that they are now willing to "fight for a better technology transfer and disclosure policy."

In short, it is becoming clear that restrictive ITAR and national disclosure policies are limiting bilateral cooperation and imposing real costs on U.S. suppliers in several ways.

First, numerous Italian government officials and market participants reported that the U.S. reputation (and often, reality) for not sharing technology with Italy is increasingly costing the United States actual system and subsystem sales it could otherwise make. One example cited was of an Italian UAV research project that sought to use a small U.S. engine. However, the U.S. determined the engine technology was not releasable to Italy. As a result, the whole project with the United States was dropped. Another example, relayed by a senior Italian government official, concerns Italy's proposed sale of a single C27J to Lithuania. Italy had to seek U.S. permission for this sale as it contained an item with an ITAR-subject license. This license approval then took many months to obtain—for no clear reason. In fact, several officials discussed how the ITAR release process can frequently take one or two years to grant an approval, for seemingly benign items such as unclassified microprocessors.

Second, there is a growing Italian tendency to avoid ITAR-regulated components wherever possible on non-U.S. platforms. ITAR-free is considered particularly important in the space and missile sectors. This trend to "design around" or "source around" ITAR will likely continue over time and increasingly minimize the U.S. content in Italian systems. Today, more than ever, Italian officials and market participants indicated, there are alternative, non-ITAR controlled choices for the solutions the MoD is looking to buy. In these choices between U.S. products and other foreign products, the MoD is often more willing to accept less capable solutions that are less expensive and more open to international cooperation and technological transfer. Ironically, years of U.S. partnering with Italian firms and offsets have also helped to develop Italian choices, and other European choices are increasingly competitive.

Moreover, leading Italian firms like Finmeccanica are aware of the impact of U.S. restrictions and have a dual-track policy (with ITAR-free configurations used for export when possible). Hence, if Finmeccanica can eliminate ITAR-controlled articles without losing value, it will do it.

Although there is no official ITAR-free policy in Italy, there is a growing concern over restrictive U.S. technology release policies and a real and growing ITAR-free movement embraced by both Italian government customers and defense firms. The result, according to both government and industrial officials interviewed, is a clear trend toward limiting the U.S. content on non-U.S. systems—thus restricting U.S. control and making exporting as well as operations and maintenance of its systems easier for Italy.

Intellectual Property Protection

Italy adheres to the major multilateral IP regimes, including (i) the WTO Agreement on Trade-Related Aspects of Intellectual Property Rights (TRIPS), which provides core IP protection and enforcement rights (including for trade secrets); (ii) the Paris Convention for the Protection of Industrial Property, covering patents, trademarks and industrial designs; (iii) the Patent Cooperation Treaty, protecting patents; (iv) the Berne Convention, covering copyrights; (v) the Madrid Protocol, covering trademarks; and (vi) the World Intellectual Property Organization.

According to the U.S. DoC Foreign Commercial Service, Italy's protection of intellectual property in the general economy lags behind many other Western European countries and remains an area of concern for U.S. companies doing business in Italy.[361] To address this problem, Italy has enacted strong legislation aimed at curbing intellectual property rights infringement. However, many of the laws are not yet fully or effectively enforced. In particular, steep fines for the purchase of counterfeit goods and severe punishments for peer-to-peer file sharing are being challenged in the Italian courts.[362]

IP protection for defense goods and services in defense contracts is generally sought on a case-by-case basis. IP policy for defense products is focused primarily on the Italian government's desire to retain IP in Italy for international programs and for work performed with Italian defense resources. This is part of Italy's overall effort to maintain or enlarge the technological return of defense procurement, both for industrial reasons and for operational sovereignty. However, this can be a factor limiting the profitability of foreign competitors in Italy, as Italian firms seek to exploit the intellectual property of foreign firms.

Companies that bid on Italian procurements, however, can protect pre-existing background rights in articles and technology they already developed before the Italian procurement. The actual protection is specified in contracts on a case-by-case basis.

---

[361] See IPR Toolkit for Italy, at U.S. Commercial Service for Italy website. Available at: http://www.buyusa.gov/italy/en/iprtoolkitforitaly.html.

[362] Ibid.

Technical Standards

Italy is a party to the WTO's Technical Barriers to Trade Agreement, which prohibits discrimination and seeks to ensure that regulations, standards, testing and certification procedures do not create obstacles to trade. However, every country has the right to adopt those regulatory standards that it considers appropriate in areas concerning national security. Thus, Italy has the discretion to, and has put in place, its own specific technical standards for defense products that could in theory serve as a non-tariff barrier to competing foreign products.

Nevertheless, in the course of this study, we did not learn of any specific situations involving Italy where technical standards were used as non-tariff barriers to protect domestic producers and markets against foreign defense products.

Italy's long association with NATO means that Italian military products are tied to NATO Standardization Agreements (STANAGs) where these exist. Further, consistent with Italy's position in favor of enlarging this common experience to the EU-EDA sector, there is no evidence it has sought to use technical standards as a market access barrier. In the future, we expect Italy will increasingly shift to the standards being codified under the EU for defense markets. These are in part today based on STANAGs and are also expected to include recognized commercial standards. As discussed in Chapter 5, however, there is some prospect of increased risk that an eventual EU set of standards can become disguised market access barriers—but there is no indication that this is a policy result sought by Italy.

Chapter 10

Accessing the Polish Defense Market

Integration with the EU structure is the guaranty of our developing and prosperity, and the alliance with the USA in the frame of NATO—[it] is our security guaranty. Both options, European and Atlantic, should not rival each other, but they have to complement and harmonize. It is a Polish vital interest requirement. In the situation, when both sides of the Atlantic come to dissonances and misunderstandings, the task of Poland is to do its best to eliminate those negative tendencies.

—Kasimierz Marcinkiewicz, Prime Minister of Poland, 2005[363]

Formerly a major member of the Warsaw Pact military alliance, Poland since the fall of the Soviet Union has endeavored to fully integrate itself into the Western European family of nations and become a robust liberal democratic society. To a very large extent, Poland has succeeded in those objectives, but much work remains to be done—particularly with regard to creating strong civil institutions and suppressing a culture of endemic corruption that is a lasting legacy of communist rule.

Although now a full member of North Atlantic Treaty Organization (NATO) and the European Union (EU), Poland to some extent remains an outsider, not fully accepted by original members of these organizations—and in turn Poland does not fully understand or trust other members to have Poland's best interests at heart.[364] Although Poland is becoming fully integrated into the EU's economic regulatory regime and has been a significant beneficiary of the EU's development grants, Poles remain suspicious of the EU's tendency to interfere in their internal affairs. On the other hand, in March 2009 Poland stressed its connectivity to the EU by committing to join the Eurozone rapidly.[365] Poland made this overture toward the EU during the current financial crisis, and has sought financial support from the large Western European nations. However, Poland has not yet received the level of support for which it hoped. While the current circumstances tend to reinforce Polish distance and distrust, in the long term this crisis is likely to bring Poland closer to the EU.

Concurrent with the dynamic changes in its political and civil life, Poland has been moving to transform its military forces. Poland has abandoned the Soviet-style organization and equipment it inherited from the Warsaw Pact period in favor of a lighter, more agile force focused on expeditionary operations in support of NATO and EU low intensity operations. Within the context of limited budget resources, Poland has been attempting to modernize and professionalize its armed forces. The two main pillars to this plan are: 1) the replacement or modernization of Soviet-era equipment with NATO compatible systems; and 2) the replacement of most conscript troops with long-term professional volunteers. The dilemma is that Poland's efforts to boost its investment spending (procurement plus research and

---

[363] "Exposé of the Prime Ministry of Poland, 11 October 2005," quoted in COL Marek Tomaszycki, Polish Army, *Civil-Military Relations and Defense Reform in Poland*, U.S. Army War College Research Project, U.S. Army War College (Carlisle, PA), March 2006, p. 7.

[364] This perspective was repeatedly expressed in interviews with Polish military, government and industry representatives.

[365] "Poland on Monday renewed its commitment to bid for rapid accession to the eurozone amid signs the financial crisis has prompted European Union leaders to consider shortening the entry process." *Financial Times*, March 2, 2009, available at: http://www.ft.com/cms/s/0/c96f43ac-076d-11de-9294-000077b07658.html.

technology (R&T)) to higher levels to achieve the first element of the plan is being impeded by excessive personnel and operations and maintenance (O&M) costs.

Since the attacks of September 11, 2001, Poland has been a steadfast U.S. ally in the war on terrorism, providing combat units for the coalition forces in both Iraq and Afghanistan. U.S. forces have developed a close operational relationship with the Polish military. Polish special operations forces are particularly well respected for their professionalism and willingness to go in harm's way. Poland has also cooperated with U.S. intelligence services in gathering information on al-Qaeda and other terrorist organizations, and has agreed to establish bases for U.S. forces on its territory. In August 2008, Poland signed a Memorandum of Understanding with the United States whereby elements of a ballistic missile defense system will also be constructed in Poland for defense against potential Iranian missile attack.

Polish relations with the United States remain closer than with those of almost any other European country save Great Britain. This is due mainly to the Polish perception that the United States remains the ultimate guarantor of their political independence, particularly in light of an increasingly militaristic and aggressive Russia. While the United States is viewed as the cornerstone of NATO, Poland expresses little confidence in the ability or will of the EU to maintain Polish security.[366]

However, Poland is also beginning to feel taken for granted by the United States and to feel a certain inequality in the relationship. Poles feel that their support for the United States has an intrinsic value, which they would like to see recognized through the extension of certain rights and privileges already granted to more established U.S. Allies such as the UK and Australia. They also are dissatisfied with the level of U.S. Foreign Military Financing (FMF) military credits.

This developing situation has caused a division within Polish political circles between those who wish to maintain the present very close relationship with the United States, and those who would, without abandoning the U.S. alliance, move closer to the EU, particularly in defense industrial policy. Whether Poland will become a leading member of the EU's nascent defense and security structure is a key question, the answer to which depends in large part on U.S. policy toward Poland over the next 5 to 10 years.

Consistent with the strength of the overall U.S.-Polish bilateral relationship, Poland has become a major customer for U.S. military hardware—both to address immediate operational needs in Iraq and Afghanistan and to meet Poland's long-term military requirements and NATO interoperability goals. The most noteworthy by far has been the acquisition of 48 new F-16 fighters, together with a package of airborne weapons and logistics support, in a package worth upwards of $3 billion. Future missile and air defense systems deployed in Poland will ensure that Poland remains a major U.S. defense industry customer for the next decade or more. Over time, Poland also will likely emerge as a valued supplier of products and services to U.S. forces deployed in Poland.

Poland has also turned to its Western European neighbors for new equipment, including surplus Leopard II main battle tanks and reconditioned MiG-29 Fulcrum fighters from

---

[366] One should not underestimate also the sentimental regard in which Poland views the United States as being ultimately responsible for the demise of the Soviet Union and the liberation of Poland. Poland is one of the European states in which the United States as a country is held in very high regard.

Germany. European countries have also provided Poland with battlefield radars, command and control systems, and armored fighting vehicles.

Through this period of transition, the Polish defense industry has struggled to maintain its viability. Once entirely state-owned, most of its factories are obsolete and unprofitable. Poland has been systematically privatizing its defense industry, selling its assets to foreign companies including EADS, Pratt & Whitney, Sikorsky, Textron and Ericsson. Poland plans to sell its remaining state-owned defense companies within the next 18 to 24 months, assuming that buyers can be found.

There have been some concerns that the Polish military's penchant for state-of-the-art foreign military equipment has been starving the Polish defense industry of funding to modernize its plants and expand its technology base. Observers have noted that while there are Polish companies capable of upgrading existing Soviet designs to almost the same level of capability as their Western counterparts at only a fraction of the cost, the Polish military shows little interest in acquiring these systems. The long-term effect may be the gradual dissolution of an indigenous, broad-based Polish defense industry—to the ultimate detriment of Poland and Europe's defense industrial capabilities.[367]

Within this strategic and armaments context, Poland has reshaped and reformed both the demand and the supply elements of its defense market.

On the demand side of the ledger, Poland has benefited from a "clean slate" as it discarded its Soviet-era acquisition system. The Polish Ministry of National Defense (MoND) has implemented a wide-ranging reform of the defense procurement process based on Western European standards and processes. However, the Polish MoND's lack of experience and resources inhibits its ability to manage programs successfully.

Poland's new acquisition policy is based on a modern model of competitive and open procurement. Because Poland, like Romania, has discarded most of its Soviet-era armaments systems, Poland has fewer sole source purchases of legacy systems than any country in Western Europe. Hence, most Polish defense contracts on new programs are competitively awarded.

Moreover, the Polish market is not only competitive but also largely open to U.S. and other foreign companies due to the need to modernize Polish forces rapidly and bring them into compliance with NATO standards. With the Polish military's obvious preference for Western military systems and the Polish defense industry's limited ability to meet those needs through domestic production, Poland is more than willing to buy foreign systems—particularly if these are provided with attractive financing. Available data on Polish procurement awards reflects these realities, and show that U.S. and other European firms have won a significant share of competitive awards in Poland.

Despite this relatively open environment for U.S. firms, Poland does offer other challenges to potential defense market participants. Poland relies heavily on offsets—with among the highest offset rates in Europe on its defense contracts. The Offset Law, however, is perceived as onerous by foreign companies and may be counterproductive to its expressed objectives, since as structured it does not really facilitate technology transfer or result in "noble work" for Polish defense companies.

---

[367] See R. Johnson, "Maintaining a Base: Trouble in Poland's Defense Industry," *The Weekly Standard*, Jan. 17, 2008.

Moreover, corruption remains endemic throughout Polish society, although the situation is improving slowly and is much better than it was a decade ago. Although Poland is working hard to implement transparent procurement regulations and has enacted strict anti-corruption laws, defense trade is not immune from this problem. U.S. companies are for the most part not directly affected by corruption due to the stringency of the Foreign Corrupt Practices Act. However, Polish subcontractors and suppliers have difficulty complying with U.S. ethical standards.

I. Market Background

A. Warsaw Pact Heritage

Poland was a key member of the Warsaw Pact alliance, with substantial ground, air and naval forces fully integrated into the Soviet/Warsaw Pact command and control and logistic systems. For most of the Cold War period, Poland had the third largest military force in Europe, after the Soviet Union and West Germany, with more than 350,000 troops (750,000 at full mobilization).

At the time the Warsaw Pact alliance collapsed in 1989, Poland still had a very large Army whose formations were equipped, organized and trained along Soviet lines (although mostly with previous generation equipment). Operational plans focused on a rapid advance into Western Europe, supported if necessary by tactical nuclear weapons (for which Polish forces had excellent decontamination equipment). Poland thus had very large inventories of tanks, infantry fighting vehicles and artillery.

The Polish air force consisted of three Air Corps, each consisting of a fighter division, a fighter-bomber division, and a reconnaissance squadron. Each division consisted of 3 to 4 air regiments, each with 45 aircraft. At the end of the Cold War, its inventory was large if somewhat obsolescent, including various MiG variants and other aircraft. The Polish Navy was a coastal force optimized for operations on the Baltic Sea; it consisted mainly of corvettes, missile patrol boats, amphibious assault ships, and landing craft.

The Polish forces were far in excess of the Poland's requirements for territorial defense. In fact, as Polish government archives have revealed, the Polish military was sized to meet the needs of the Warsaw Pact's integrated operational plan that called for offensive operations to overrun Western Europe; almost no defensive planning was conducted between 1948 and 1989. The excessive size of the Polish military became an insurmountable burden after the collapse of the USSR and the abolition of the Warsaw Pact made such forces superfluous.

Effect of Integrated Warsaw Pact Production Planning

Under the Warsaw Pact treaty, Member States had very little autonomy. Force levels, organization, equipment and deployments were all determined by the Soviet general staff in accordance with a single integrated operational plan. The Soviet Union also controlled Polish defense industrial policy, setting out detailed plans for the production of various systems in factories laid out according to Soviet norms.

Typically, the USSR would pass down to the Warsaw Pact states responsibility for production of a particular MoND tank, aircraft or other system (MoNDel) when it was ready to transition to a newer model. Thus, production of the T-55 was given to Poland when Soviet forces transitioned to the T-62; Poland began manufacturing the T-72 when Soviet forces shifted to the T-80, and so forth. A certain amount of discretion was afforded to some countries to develop indigenous improvements to some systems, provided that a high degree of commonality was retained in elements such as propulsion, drive trains and armament. Poland produced several modified versions of Soviet combat vehicles.

The Soviet Union also imposed a "rational" division of labor among the Warsaw Pact states. The USSR usually retained control over the most sensitive technologies so that no one country had control of all the critical parts needed for any one system. Thus, with the breakup of the Warsaw Pact, it became difficult for Poland and other Warsaw Pact states to maintain their large inventories of Soviet-designed equipment, much of which became unusable in short order.

The legacy of Soviet control over defense production has had a lasting and deleterious effect on the Polish defense industry. Nothing resembling a competitive defense market was allowed to develop. Worse, nothing resembling an independent acquisition agency ever existed: the state was the customer, but also owned the means of production and therefore also set prices for raw materials, labor and finished products. The range of goods and services was not even set by the Polish government, but by the Soviet Ministry of Defense in Moscow.

The collapse of the Soviet system and the Warsaw Pact thus created a vacuum of power in which both the Polish government and the Polish defense industry had to discover, *ab initio*, a new way of doing business with each other. This process has not yet been completed, which in turn is responsible for many of the challenges still facing Polish industry today.

The Evolution of the Polish Defense Industry

Prior to World War II, Poland had a number of thriving and dynamic defense companies such as PZL and Radnor, producing a range of goods from tanks and ordnance to aircraft. A thoroughly Westernized country, Poland had a well-trained labor force and a cadre of well-educated scientists and engineers. Most of that was swept away during World War II. Nonetheless, between 1945 and 1948, a number of these companies were reestablished and a semblance of domestic defense production began, often using factories established by the Germans to build German weapons.

When the Soviet Union installed a communist government in Poland and integrated Poland into the Warsaw Pact, all the traditional Polish defense companies were nationalized and, as noted, retooled to produce Soviet-designed equipment using Soviet production processes.

Under the communist system, defense production was divided between the MoND and the Ministry of Industry. The former operated 19 manufacturing and repair factories, while the latter controlled no fewer than 80 "defense industry enterprises" covering a full range of products and services. The leading defense manufacturers included the Stalowa Wola Steel Works, the Kasprzak Radio Works, the Krasnik Ball-Bearing Plant, the Wifama Textile Machinery Combine, the Stomil Tire Plant, the Polish Aviation Combine (PZL), the Pronit firm, the Northern and Wisla Shipyards in Gdansk, the Luczik Works, the Staracho-wice Truck Factory, the Polish Optical Works, the Bumar-Labedy Engineering Equipment Combine, and the Olkusz Enamel Plant.

Most of these companies also manufactured civilian products from vehicles to electronics to clothing; only a few—including the shipyards, the Bumar-Labedy Engineering Equipment Combine, and the Salowa Wola Steel Works—were exclusively military companies. In 1988, the last year before the collapse of communism, state "defense industry enterprises" employed more than 236,000 people and accounted for about 3 percent of total industrial production under the Ministry of Industry. In 1992, after the collapse of the USSR, defense companies accounted for just 1 percent of industrial output—even though industrial output overall had fallen from 1988 levels.

It has been post-Soviet-era Polish government policy to divest all state holdings, including those in the defense sector. Privatization of the civilian sector has generally been accomplished, but at present, a number of defense companies are still wholly or partially owned by the government. Most of the smaller companies have been wrapped up into a large government-owned holding company, PHZ Bumar Sp. z.o.o., whose primary mandate is preparing these businesses for divestiture. Further details of the Polish government's privatization initiatives are set forth below in III. Evaluation of Market Access Metrics.

Polish Defense Exports Under Communism

Defense products accounted for roughly 6 percent of total Polish exports in the 1980s. The USSR was the largest single customer of the Polish defense industry, accounting for roughly 50 percent of total production during the communist era. The USSR also used arms exports as a diplomatic tool throughout the Cold War era. Since the Soviets rarely transferred their own first-line systems to client states, production of specialized export MoNDels was delegated to the various Warsaw Pact countries. Poland was a leading supplier of arms for export within this system, producing tanks, armored fighting vehicles, artillery and small arms. The value of these arms transfers is difficult if not impossible to calculate, since they were not commercial transactions; most of the equipment was either provided through grant aid by the Soviet Union or sold at a steep discount. According to a 1992 study by the Stockholm International Peace Research Institute (SIPRI), Poland ranked 20th in the world in defense exports, with sales totaling more than $1.6 billion. A listing of major Polish arms sales from 1994-2002 is set forth in Table 45.

The need to supply the Soviet military as well as provide defense systems for export to Soviet client states contributed to the large overcapacity of the Polish defense industry—which became an impediment to privatization in the post-communist era.

B. Post-Communist Developments

The overthrow of the communist-era government, the establishment of democracy in Poland, and the adoption of significant economic reforms led to an extended period of economic and political instability marked by high inflation and unemployment, rampant corruption in both the public and private sectors, and attempts by former communists to roll back reforms.

Table 45   Major Polish Arms Sales, 1994-2002

Recpient	System	Type	Year Sold	Years Delivered	Number Delivered	Comments
Angola	BMP-2	AFV	1994	1994-95	52	Ex Polish army
Cambodia	T-55AM2	MBT	1994	1994	50	Ex Polish army
Czech Republic	W-3 Sokol	Helicopter	1995	1996-97	11	Exchanged for 10 ex-Czech AF MiG-29s
Djibouti	An-28TD	Lt. Transport	1995	1995	1	
India	TS-11 Indra	Jet Trainer	1998	1998-99	13	Ex Polish air force
India	WZT-3	ARV	1999	1999	44	Deal worth $31.1M
Iran	T-72M	MBT	1993	1994-95	104	
Latvia	Mi-2 Hoplite	Helicopter	1994	1995-96	4	Ex-Polish army
Latvia	BRDM-2	AFV	1992	1992	2	Ex-Polish army
Lithuania	Mi-2 Hoplite	Helicopter	1996	1996	5	Ex-Polish air force
Lithuania	BRDM-2	AFV	1994	1995	11	Ex-Polish army; gift
Lithuania	MT-LB	AFV	2000	2000	10	Ex-Polish army; aid
Lithuania	P-37 Barlock	Radar	1996	1996	3	Ex-Polish air force
Lithuania	P-40 Knife Rest	Radar	1996	1996	2	Ex-Polish air force
Lithuania	PRV-11 Side Net	Radar	1996	1996	2	Ex-Polsh air force
Myanmar	Mi-2 Hoplite	Helicopter	1990	1990-92	22	
Russia	Ropuchka class	Landing Ship	1980	1992	1	Originally ordred by USSR
Sudan	T-55AM-2	MBT	1998	1999	20	Ex-Polish army. Export license originally granted to Yemen, but shipment diverted illegally to Sudan
Togo	BMP-2	AFV	1996	1997	20	Ex-Polish army
Uganda	Mi-21bis Fishbed N	Fighter	1999	1999	7	Ex-Polsh air force. Deal worth $8.5M—funds used for Polish Su-22 modernization
Uruguay	MT-LB	AFV	1998	1999	3	Ex-Polsh army; delivered via Czech Republic
Venezuela	M-26 Iskierka	Trainer	1997	1998	2	For National Guard
Venezuela	M-28 Skytruck	Lt. Transport	1995	1996-97	6	For Natonal Guard
Venezuela	M-28 Skytruck	Lt. Transport	1997	1999-2000	12	For National Guard. Deal Worth $20M
Venezuela	M-28 Skytruck	Lt. Transport	1999	2000-2001	12	
Yemen	Deba Class	Landing Craft	1999	2001	3	Deal Worth $50M, including Lublin class landing ship
Yemen	Lublin Class	Landing Ship	1999	2001	1	Included in deal for Deba Class

Source: Safeworld Arms and Security Programme, Arms Production, Exports and Decision-Making in Central and Eastern Europe (2001).

Figure 96   Polish Defense Manpower, 1988-2007 (Hundreds of Thousands)

Source: Polish Army Facts and Figures (in the Transition Period), Warsaw (MOND) 1991; Brief Information on the Armed Forces of the Republic of Poland, Warsaw (MON) 1996.

The guiding principle of the various Polish governments during this time was greater economic, political and military integration with Western Europe.[368] To further this objective, Poland joined with Hungary and Czechoslovakia (later the Czech and Slovak Republics) in 1991 to form the Visegrád Group for mutual assistance in reforming their economic and political systems. All the members of the Visegrád Group became members of NATO in 1997 and the EU in 2004; the group continues to be active today exploring areas of joint economic and military cooperation, including a common EU Battle Group earmarked for peacekeeping operations. The Visegrád Group also has established an Expert Working Group on Energy to explore ways of ensuring energy security in light of Russian use of oil and natural gas supplies as an economic weapon.

Gradually, democratic institutions and a free-market economy took root in Poland. The early and painful economic reforms also began to bear fruit. The currency stabilized and budget deficits were brought under control as the country moved toward membership in both NATO and the EU. During this time—from middle to late 1990s—both the military and the defense industry were left adrift. With the new government chronically short of cash and the need to transfer control of non-defense state industries to private hands while meeting ongoing budgetary obligations such as pensions, Poland drastically reduced the size of its military forces and sold off much of its surplus equipment at fire sale prices (see Figure 96). This had the net effect of glutting the market for such products as tanks, armored vehicles, artillery and aircraft—thus depressing demand for new production.

---

[368] Tomaszycki, op. cit., p. 2.

At the same time, the USSR (later the Russian Republic) suffered a financial collapse. Polish defense sales to Russia, which once accounted for half of defense industry revenues, dwindled to insignificance. The result was the precipitous collapse of most Polish state-owned defense companies, which hampered efforts at both conversion and privatization of the defense industry.

Planning for conversion had actually begun as early as 1987, when the Warsaw Pact developed a newer, more "defensive" posture under Soviet Union Communist Party General Secretary Mikhail Gorbachev's Glasnost policy. At that time, some 20 of the 80 defense enterprises were marked for closure or conversion to purely civilian production. Concurrently, the entire Polish defense industry supposedly made long-term plans for greatly reduced orders from 1991 to 1995. By 1990, the Polish defense procurement budget had been slashed by 84 percent as compared to 1988 levels, already causing massive underutilization and unemployment in the defense industry. At the same time, the Polish government reduced or simply abolished all of the defense industry's special privileges, including supply priority, low interest loans, state subsidies and tax exemptions.

These changes created major obstacles to the conversion and privatization of the defense industry. Reductions in defense procurement starved the industry of the capital needed to fund conversion, while uncertainty in defense planning made it difficult to attract private capital to acquire or convert existing plants. Some plants were so antiquated that they could not be converted or modernized in an economical manner.

In 1992, the Ministry of Industry proposed to restructure the defense industry as rapidly as possible by creating three classes of linked holding companies based on the degree of competitiveness of the enterprises being held. This plan, discussed in detail below, had varying degrees of success.

NATO Membership

In facilitate closer relations with the West, in 1994 Poland became a member of NATO's Partnership for Peace, preparing the groundwork for full membership in the Alliance. On July 8, 1997, Poland (along with Hungary and the Czech Republic) was invited to join NATO. Despite opposition from Russia, Poland formally joined the Alliance in 1999, thus further cementing Poland's growing ties to both the United States and Western Europe.

With NATO membership came the pressing requirement to modernize Poland's military forces and bring its equipment and training up to NATO standards. In effect, this meant either replacing or upgrading every major system in the Polish military inventory, from radios and small arms to armored fighting vehicles and aircraft. But with a total defense budget of barely $3 billion per year, Poland could hardly begin to address this task. In addition, under the Soviet system, Poland was discouraged from manufacturing state-of-the-art defense electronics, avionics and weapons guidance systems, making Poland utterly dependent upon Western technology for these critical components.

Fortunately, rapid integration of new Member States into the Alliance military structure was a high priority for NATO. Poland became a beneficiary of a series of subsidized loans, gifts and grants to accelerate its defense transformation. Among these were:

- **Central European Defense Loan (CEDL).** Intended to provide credit-worthy countries in Central Europe and the Balkans with upwards of $100 million in U.S.

Foreign Military Financing (FMF) funding to purchase NATO-standard equipment, Poland signed the CEDL agreement in 1998, the only country to qualify for the low-interest loans at that time. Poland made use of this and other FMF funds to acquire some $135 million in U.S. equipment in 1999-2000, the vast majority of which were committed to programs to meet NATO force goals and minimum military requirements.

- **NATO Security Investment Program (NATO-SIP).** Established to help finance the development and modernization of military infrastructure of the Member States, the NATO-SIP program made more than $650 million available to Poland, of which $380 million was used to modernize seven military airfields, five fuel and supply depots, and two naval bases; a further $10 million was used to upgrade military telecommunications networks.

- **Bilateral sales and grants in aid.** Poland was able to benefit from the drawdown and consolidation of other NATO forces to bolster its combat capabilities. For instance, Poland's original force of 12 MiG-29 Fulcrum fighters (received from the USSR in 1989-1990) were supplemented in 1995 by 10 Fulcrums transferred from the Czech Republic in exchange for an equal number of surplus light helicopters. In 2004, 22 more Fulcrums were effectively donated to Poland by Germany,[369] of which 14 were modernized and placed in service. Poland also acquired some 132 German army surplus Leopard 2 main battle tanks[370] to supplement its force of indigenously produced T-72Ms.

For strategic and cultural reasons, Poland has worked hard to live up to its NATO commitments, participating in a wide range of operations, including the coalition forces in Afghanistan, peacekeeping forces in Bosnia and Kosovo, and NATO Baltic Air Policing patrols in Lithuania. In addition, Polish forces have been part of the Multinational Forces in Iraq, as well as United Nations (UN) peacekeeping forces in Lebanon and the Golan Heights, and EU peacekeeping forces in Chad. Poland has also earmarked forces for various rotations of the NATO Response Force, as well as forming part of the EU's Visegrád Battle Group with Hungary and the Czech Republic.[371]

Meeting NATO capability and interoperability standards has been the driving force behind Polish defense modernization, as enunciated by Bronislaw Komarowski, then-Minister of National Defense, back in 2001:

Poland's participation as a member in defense planning since 1999 has been a major spur to reform, and the latest programme of reform is aimed at fulfilling Alliance objectives. At the time when Poland joined NATO, Alliance members adopted a new Strategic Concept and launched the Defense Capabilities Initiative. The resulting force goals, which are primarily concerned with the technical modernization of the armed forces, the organization of rapid reaction forces, and

---

[369] The aircraft were first brought up to NATO standard and then sold by Germany to Poland for the symbolic price of €1.

[370] Sold at scrap prices.

[371] It is significant that U.S. analysts never expressed any reservations concerning Poland's ability and willingness to contribute to the NATO Alliance, similar to those they expressed regarding the other Central European countries (Czech Republic and Hungary) that joined at the same time as Poland, due mainly to Poland's strong demographics and broad-based social support for the military and NATO. See J. Simon, "The New NATO Members: Will They Contribute?" *National Defense University Strategic Forum*, No. 160, April 1999.

improvement of operations, require substantial expenditure and development of better long-term financial planning framework, as well as a complete change of philosophy of military reform. *The Programme of Restructuring and Technical Modernization of the Armed Forces of the Republic of Poland 2001-2005* is based on such principles.[372]

With some modification to account for changing strategic circumstances, these principles guide Polish military reform and transformation today.

EU Membership and Its Effects

Entry into the EU was a major objective of Polish security policy from the early 1990s, driven partly by the desire to break free entirely from the orbit of Russia, but also partly by necessity. Poland knew that only through EU membership and closer integration into the European Community could it attract the investment capital it needed to become a prosperous, free-market democracy.[373]

Poland joined the EU on May 1, 2004, after several years of preparation to meet the requirements governing financial stability, transparency and civil institutions. Full integration is an ongoing process.[374] Poland has not yet reached the criteria of the Maastricht Treaty to adopt the single European currency in place of the zloty, but entry into the Eurozone is scheduled for 2012.

Poland has, in general, benefited greatly from its EU membership. It has been one of the largest recipients of EU development funds. For the period of 2007-2013, the EU has made a total of some €60 billion ($87.3 billion) for a variety of infrastructure and other projects. Poland, however, has had a relatively poor "absorption rate" of only 24.5 percent for EU funds to date—i.e., only about one-fourth of all EU funds remain in Poland, with the majority simply passing through to various foreign entities. It has been estimated that if Poland manages to absorb the available EU funds, annual gross domestic product (GDP) growth could average 7-8 percent.[375]

In any event, thanks to EU funding, Poland has managed to modernize much of its infrastructure. Per capita income is now roughly 51 percent of the EU average, and increasing rapidly, but rising wages are creating price pressures that must be kept under control if Poland is to meet the Maastricht targets by 2012. Entry into the EU has broken down most barriers to intra-European trade and investment. Foreign direct investment (FDI) reached €14 billion ($20.4 billion) in 2007, with 70 percent coming from within the EU.

On the defense and security front, however, Polish relations with the EU are not proceeding as smoothly due in part for Poland's preference to view NATO as the nexus for European security affairs. This puts Poland somewhat at odds with those pushing for a

---

[372] B. Komorowski, "Reforming Poland's Military," *NATO Review*, Web Edition, Vol. 49, No. 2, pp. 26-27.

[373] Tomaszycki, op. cit., p. 3 and footnote 2.

[374] There is a very strong sense of Polish national identity that bridles at the idea of surrendering sovereignty to a supra-national entity, particularly in light of Poland's domination by the Soviet Union from 1945-1989. There is significant belief that there is an inherent "Polish Way," and most Poles object to EU interference in what they see as properly internal affairs, such as laws governing morality, as well as more mundane things such as regulation of foodstuff and tax policies.

[375] "Poland At A Glance," Raytheon International briefing, June 2008.

more Eurocentric approach to European security and defense (e.g., Germany and France). Poland is firmly committed at this time to a "Euro-Atlantic" model of security, in which the United States and NATO are the guarantors of Polish security.

Poland has some doubts about the ability of the EU to provide that degree of security, particularly in light of a resurgent Russia. The EU's inability to take action against Russian use of oil and natural gas contracts as economic and political weapons against Poland and Ukraine fueled Polish questions about the seriousness of the EU's role in security matters.

The Polish government and the Polish defense industry also disagree with the direction in which the EU is moving with its new European Commission (EC) Defense Package, particularly the provisions restricting use of Article 296 of the Treaty Establishing the European Community (Article 296 EC Treaty) to shield programs from competitive procurement. In essence, Poland seeks to preserve its ability to be protectionist with its defense industry. Its officials are keenly aware of the weakness of its defense industries and the need to protect them through the period of transition to private ownership and control.

Poland also opposes any effort to restrict or eliminate the use of offsets in defense trade. Polish authorities view offsets as important to maintaining a reasonable balance of defense trade, as well as the only viable means at present of directing capital into uncompetitive state-owned defense enterprises—enterprises which the Poles are convinced can be competitive if they can only be nurtured through this period of weakness. It is clear that the new EU initiatives are steps toward reducing and eventually eliminating offsets—which the Poles (as well as other smaller members of the EU) are likely to work hard to resist.

Despite its reservations, Polish leadership is convinced that the EU will be playing an increasingly important role in European defense. Hence, Poland is intent on being an active participant—if for no other reason than to have a place at the table when decisions are being made. Poland has thus been one of the more forthcoming Member States with regard to participation in EU Battle Groups and peacekeeping operations. In fact, Poland tends to be much more interventionist than most of the older EU Member States, a fact that has not gone unnoticed in Poland.

Poland is also intent on participating in the development of any future integrated European defense market and defense strategy. Thus, one leading Polish diplomat expressed the opinion that the emergence of the European Defence Agency (EDA) is one of the most important developments of the last decade, one that Poland supports and in which it would like to play a greater role. Through the EDA, Poland could provide itself with a say in the formation of new EU standards and procurement decisions as well as ensuring itself a significant portion of work in future EU-directed programs.

EU membership has also had tangible benefits for the Polish defense industry through cooperative programs that take advantage of Poland's well-trained labor force and low labor rates. EADS has been a leading partner in the process, becoming either an outright owner or a major stakeholder in a number of Polish defense companies. For instance, CASA-EADS bought a 51 percent share in the aircraft factory PZL Warszawa-Okecie SA to build the C-295 transport aircraft for the Polish air force and other customers. EADS has also performed upgrades for the Mi-24 Hind helicopter, T-72 tank, and MiG-29 fighter in Poland, utilizing Polish subcontractors and facilities. Other EADS programs in Poland have included provision and servicing of the MICA air-to-air missile, support services for the International Space Station, development of a border control system, production of mobile

Table 46   Foreign Financial Assistance to the Polish Ministry of National Defense (Millions of Dollars – $)

Funding Source	2005	2006	2007
NATO SIP	85.7	130.8	109.6
U.S. FMF	79.8	30.0	30.0
U.S. IMET	2.5	2.0	2.0
U.S. CTFP	0.0	0.2	0.2
Total	167.9	163.0	141.7

Source: Ministry of National Defense, Budget Division.

hospitals, and development and integration of C4ISR (command, control, communications, computers, intelligence, surveillance and reconnaissance) systems for the Polish military.

Much of the economic benefit to the Polish defense industry comes through Poland's stringent offset requirements, which most companies fulfill by subcontracting much of the work to Polish companies. This in turn has led to spin-off opportunities to use the newly developed capabilities on other projects. For example, PZL-Polskie Zaklady Lotnicze (Polish Aviation Factory Ltd) has developed a thriving business as subcontractors to BAE Systems for Hawk trainer maintenance, to Boeing on B-757 maintenance and overhaul, and to AgustaWestland, Saab and Pratt & Whitney on their commercial and military systems.

C. Reconciling Defense Budgets With Strategic, Force Transformation and Acquisition Goals

The challenge for Poland is reconciling its limited defense budget with its ambitious strategic, force transformational, and acquisition needs as it reforms its force structure, organization, and equipment and personnel policies.

Military Expenditures

Poland consistently spends only between 1.7 and 2.0 percent of its defense budget on national defense. This is consistent with other NATO countries, however. Since Poland's economy has been growing at a rate of 5.5-6.5 percent, its actual expenditures have increased substantially since 2002, as shown in Figures 97 and 98. However, as these Figures reflect, the largest portions of the budgets have continued to go to O&M, personnel and pensions; investments, while modestly increasing, remain at a very low level.

In addition to national funds, the Polish MoND has access to considerable amounts of foreign funding, including the NATO-SIP, the U.S. FMF, the U.S. International Military Education and Training program (IMET), and the U.S. Counter-Terrorism Fellowship Program (CTFP). As shown in Table 46, these "off budget" funds, while still at modest levels, provide a significant supplement to the Polish defense budget, without which effective modernization would be impossible.

Figure 97   Polish Defense Expenditures by Function 2002-2007 (Percent–%)

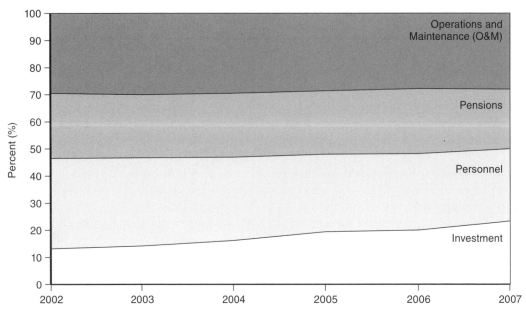

Source: Polish Ministry of National Defense, Budget Department.

**Figure 98   Polish Defense Expenditures by Function 2002-2007
(Billions of Dollars–$)**

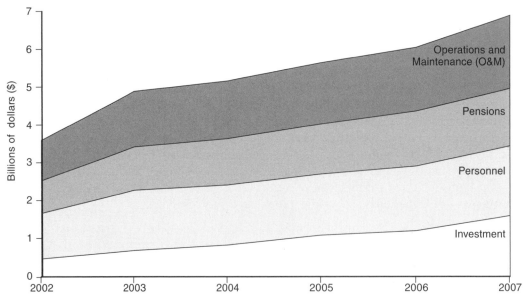

Source: Polish Ministry of National Defense, Budget Department.

In addition to these sources of revenue, the Polish MoND also has access to funds raised by the sale of state defense enterprises as well as R&T funding from the Ministry of Science and Technology and the Armed Forces Modernization Fund (although these sources of funding seldom exceed $80 million in a given year).

Strategic Posture

The National Security Strategy of the Republic of Poland, promulgated in 2003, defines the Polish national interest as:

> … independence, sovereignty, and the territorial integrity of the country, and the stability of its borders; democratic constitutional order, in particular all human rights and dignities, and the safety of the citizens of the Republic of Poland… and maintaining the national heritage and developing the national identity; stable and fair peace in Europe and throughout the world, based on the principles of democracy, human rights, law abidingness and solidarity.[376]

Poland's strategic posture is predicated first upon the collective security guarantees of the NATO Treaty, particularly Article 5, under which an external attack upon one member is seen as an attack on all. Poland relies implicitly on NATO to provide security from external attack, which in turn allows the Polish military to focus on the wide range of asymmetric threats that dominate strategic thinking since September 11.

Based on the "national interest" as defined in its National Security Strategy, Poland accepts that foreign intervention may at times be necessary, either to stabilize failed states, implement international agreements, or to maintain peace. Its participation in Operation Iraqi Freedom indicates Poland also accepts that preemptive action may be necessary to maintain peace when one country threatens the stability of its neighbors.

Polish forces thus fall into two categories: 1) heavy units intended primarily for territorial defense; and 2) light forces intended mainly for expeditionary operations. The latter include light infantry battalions, special operations forces, engineer and transportation units, air defense units, and chemical/biological defense units, supported by helicopter and tactical transport squadrons to provide intra-theater mobility. Polish forces lack strategic lift capabilities, and will depend on other states—the United States, NATO or EU—to move its forces from Poland to places such as Iraq and Afghanistan. This is not a particular weakness, as Poland intends always to fight as part of a coalition force.

As noted, Polish forces have worked well with U.S. forces in Iraq and Afghanistan—Polish special operations troops being particularly well regarded. Of late, some U.S. observers note what they consider deterioration in the quality of Polish forces, but this has been attributed, by both Polish and U.S. commentators, to the rotation of Iraq and Afghan veterans back to Poland to allow the transfer of lessons learned to the rest of the Polish armed forces.

The Polish focus on expeditionary operations at the expense of territorial defense may be re-evaluated in light of the Russian invasion of Georgia. The deployment of U.S. air defense missile batteries and the development of a ballistic missile defense system, while ostensibly directed against a nebulous Iranian threat, also provide some concrete reassurance against

---

[376] Ministry of National Defense, *National Security Strategy of the Republic of Poland* (2003).

a very real Russian threat. Given that the Swedish military is considering devoting more resources to territorial defense at the expense of expeditionary capability, there is some prospect that Poland could follow suit—investing more in tanks and infantry fighting vehicles, and less on tactical transports and trucks.

Force Structure and Organizational Reform

Within the constraints of its relatively meager budget, the Polish military has ambitious plans to modernize and professionalize its forces and make them fully equal to any others in NATO. There are two main pillars to this plan: 1) the replacement or modernization of Soviet-era equipment with NATO compatible systems; and 2) the replacement of most conscript troops with long-term professional volunteers. To achieve the first objective, Poland has plans to boost its "investment" spending (procurement plus R&T)—from 13.2 percent of the defense budget in 2002, to 23.3 percent today—to eventually more than 25 percent (considerably better than many Western European states).

Both objectives, however, have been impeded by excessive personnel and O&M costs. To reduce both, Poland cut total defense personnel by 54,000 troops and either scrapped, mothballed or sold some 7,000 items of obsolete or non-NATO compatible equipment, including aircraft, ships, tanks and armored vehicles. Estimated annual savings from both initiatives is on the order of $250 million, to be reinvested in new equipment as well as better pay and living conditions for the professional soldiers. Only through these measures has Poland been able to bring its personnel, pension and O&M costs under control and continue with its ongoing transformation program.[377]

The primary objective of Poland's military reform program is the creation of a small, agile professional force capable of meeting NATO force commitments and EU Headline Goals alike. Interoperability with U.S. and NATO forces is a primary objective of the Polish defense modernization plan.

In practice, Poland has emphasized out-of-area expeditionary operations with a focus on low intensity operations in a wide range of contingencies—from guerrilla warfare and counterinsurgency to counterterrorism to peacekeeping and humanitarian assistance. To that end, Poland's military structure has been revised and simplified to deal with the new strategic realities. These changes are summarized below:

- Military Districts: reduced from four to two

- Army Corps: reduced from two to one

- Army Divisions: reduced from eight to four

- Army personnel; reduced from 130,000 to 90,000

- Air Forces: reduced numbers of MiG-29 and Su-22 fighters replaced by F-16s

- Naval Forces: reduced from 56 warships and four submarines to 30 warships and five submarines

---

[377] Tomaszycki, op. cit., p. 14; also Komarowski, op. cit., pp. 2-3.

While reducing total force size, Poland has increased combat capabilities by retiring obsolete systems such as the T-55 MBT while retaining and upgrading modern systems such as the T-72M and the Leopard 2, as well as by fielding modern C4ISR systems.

Acquisition Priorities

As a small country with limited resources, Poland has had to stringently prioritize and phase its acquisition of new systems and the upgrading of older ones. The highest priority has been placed on NATO interoperability. Hence, Poland has put emphasis on procuring: a NATO-interoperable Headquarters Command Systems (Szafran-ZT); a digital signal system (Krokus 2000); army C4ISR and electronic warfare systems; an airspace management system; and a national air defense system.

Much like in the United States, each military service also has its own acquisition agenda:

- The Polish Army has as its main priorities a weapons of mass destruction defensive system; a chemical and biological decontamination system; an air defense artillery system; a wheeled armored personnel carrier; an anti-tank guided missile; upgrades of Soviet-era air defense systems (ZSU-23-4 and SA-6); and personal troop equipment.

- The Polish Air Force for its part is focused on creation of four national air defense centers, upgrading of airfields, and modernization of Soviet-era air defense missile systems such as the SA-4. The cornerstone of the air force modernization plan is the acquisition of some 48 F-16 multirole fighters under a potential $3 billion deal ($6 billion if offsets are counted).

- The Polish Navy, whose mission area is the Baltic Sea, is focused on modernizing its mine countermeasures ships and systems; anti-surface and anti-submarine warfare in a littoral environment; and support of amphibious operations. However, Polish national strategy also requires a blue water navy for power projection and logistic support of Polish expeditionary forces. The Navy thus also has both a support ship and a command ship on its list of priorities, but as the "junior" service it has the smallest budget and lowest priority for resources.

In addition to these "planned" acquisition priorities, they also need to respond to urgent operational requirements from deployed combat forces. Since the beginning of the wars in Iraq and Afghanistan, these have tended to "break into" the long-term modernization plan. Among the urgent acquisitions made to support ongoing operations have been high mobility multipurpose wheel vehicles (HMMWVs), mine-resistant vehicles and M113 armored personnel carriers. When possible, Poland tries to acquire these systems through grants in aid, rather than through purchase, because they siphon off resources from long-term modernization requirements.

II. Polish Defense Market: Supply and Demand Dynamics

Poland's defense "market" reforms have addressed several chronic problems: the procurement process itself, which lacks transparency and has been inefficient; the overcapacity and obsolescence of the defense industry, most particularly the remaining state-owned enterprises; and the suppression of the endemic corruption found throughout Polish society but which is especially troubling in the defense sector.

A. Acquisition (Demand) Reform

As noted earlier, under the communist system, the government was both the customer and the supplier—setting requirements, allocating the resources, and setting prices. With the transition to a free-market economy, it became necessary for the government to learn how to establish its own requirements, formulate requests for proposal, evaluate tenders, make awards, and manage programs in a cost-effective manner. For some time after the liberation, the old system continued in place simply because so many companies remained state-owned.

Gradually, because of the increasing volume of defense imports from the West, and the growing privatization of the Polish defense sector, it became necessary to establish a formal procurement agency based on Western standards of objectivity and transparency. Poland used a portion of its CEDL funds specifically to train a professional acquisition corps. Numerous military and MoND personnel were sent to the United States and Western Europe to study at the acquisition colleges and learn "best practices and procedures." During that time, Poland ran a very unsatisfactory ad hoc procurement system that was widely criticized for its inefficiency, corruption and lack of transparency.

Finally, in 2004, Poland put in place a modern, Western-style acquisition system. The system was codified in the Act of 29 January 2004 on Public Procurement Law, which is supplemented by Ministerial Decrees (covering, e.g., items on the list of affected armaments and the list of approved defense companies) and by Decisions of the Minister of National Defense on rules and procedures for implementing the new Public Procurement Law as it applies to defense procurement.

While the Polish procurement system is now based on Western European norms, it does not function well in practice, according to market participants. The challenges sound eerily reminiscent of problems that continue to plague the United States.

Specifically, Poland continues to suffer from a shortage of trained acquisition professionals. Each acquisition professional is managing a larger portfolio than is practical, and cannot provide the extent of oversight needed. Poland also lacks a well-established network of System Engineering and Technical Assistance contractors to its staff program offices. Indeed, for reasons associated with the endemic corruption of Polish society (see below), there is relatively little formal coordination between government and industry. This requires the Polish government to make decisions without the input of industry regarding what is available, practical and affordable.

A second major problem is poor coordination between military officers who set requirements, the civil servants who manage and staff the program offices, and the Ministry of Finance who funds the projects. Because the military has a difficult time expressing its real requirements to procurement officers, Requests for Procurement often do not accurately reflect the military needs. And given the limited communication between the industry and military, the military have only a vague idea regarding what industry can provide.[378]

---

[378] U.S. industrial representatives mirrored these observations and complaints but attributed the ongoing inefficiency and lack of transparency in the system not to malice or corruption, but simply to a lack of resources and personnel with sufficient experience to administer the system effectively.

B. Defense Industrial Reform

After the fall of communism, the Polish government sought to divest and privatize all the state defense enterprises as quickly as possible. However, this proved to be impractical given market conditions. Few of the companies had a competitive product or technology base, all lacked adequate capital either to upgrade or to convert to civilian production and, hence, few could attract either private capital or foreign investors.

A more realistic 1992 plan was designed to allow the most competitive elements of the defense industry to begin operating in the free market rapidly while maintaining government control over critical defense manufacturing capability. This plan did not succeed as well as hoped because of the defense industry's condition. With antiquated product lines based on Soviet-era designs, the industry could not: 1) find adequate export sales for its remaining product lines (by 2001, Poland was exporting only 13 percent of its defense production) or; 2) meet the pressing need to bring Polish military systems in line with NATO standards.

To facilitate the sector's transition, the government formed two large, state-owned holding companies, Bumar and Cenix (the latter of which was eventually absorbed by Bumar) to own and operate most of the companies in ordnance, armored vehicle and munitions — products that did not have any civilian market counterparts. Other sectors, including shipbuilding and aerospace, were gradually sold since most of their operations were already commercialized or dual-use. Bumar now controls and operates 17 individual companies, all of which are to be readied for privatization in the next two years.

There has been significant controversy over Bumar and its affiliated firms, however, due to rampant cronyism between its management and members of the Polish military. Thus, most of the Bumar holdings are not regarded as suitable for privatization at this time, and a new management team has been brought in to establish a new privatization plan.

Thus, today there are three types of companies constituting the Polish defense market:

- **State-Owned Defense Enterprises.** Bumar now controls and operates 17 individual companies with more than 13,000 employees. Mainly relics of the Soviet era, these companies have large, obsolescent factories and an even larger, underemployed workforce. They are dependent on Polish government contracts and/or offset work share for survival. Most do not have a competitive technology base or product line, reflected by the fact that exports account for only 13 percent of Poland's defense sales — and most of them not generated within Bumar. A leading Polish industrial representative characterized the Bumar marketing approach as "sitting around a table waiting for something to be tossed over the transom." Without work provided through offsets, Bumar probably would have to close its operations, according to market participants.

- **Formerly State-Owned Enterprises.** While some firms may still have majority government ownership or a significant equity stake (a de facto "golden share"), these companies were inherently more viable than the Bumar companies simply because they had product lines that could penetrate the civilian market. Among the more successful of these have been the Polish aviation companies and the Gdansk shipyards, most of whose work is actually either commercial or dual-use. The quality of these companies varies widely depending upon the sector and the nature of the workforce.

Some are quite modern and cost-effective; others work according to rigid trade union rules and have high costs. In the case of those companies still doing defense work, a number seem to rely on cronyism to win contracts, according to market participants; i.e., they use their contacts in the state-owned companies and in the military/MoND to obtain work share in various programs, either as subcontractors to the state companies or as offset partners with foreign prime contractors. Some are transitioning to a more open-market management style, but others will probably be left behind.

- **Commercial Start-Up Companies.** Founded privately after the fall of communism—frequently by scientists and engineers from state enterprises or universities and research institutes, these small to mid-sized companies develop niche technologies and capabilities (particularly in telecommunications and information technology). They are generally able to compete in the commercial and dual-use markets; relatively few are purely defense as the defense sector is so small. A number have entered into mentorship/strategic partnerships with U.S. and European technology companies, which use both their unique technology offerings as well as their on-shore presence to leverage their bids on Polish defense programs. Most of these companies will either thrive in their niche or be acquired by larger offshore companies as they mature. It is impossible to tell at this time how many will emerge to become major players in their own right.

These three types of companies exist in an environment shaped by an industrial policy that is "on paper" totally dedicated to free-market reforms. Under Polish policy, all companies must eventually sink or swim on their own merits although some may be protected until such time as they have either managed the transition to the free market or demonstrated their inability to compete. Both the Polish government and industry are convinced that, due to their trained workforce, low labor rates and relatively low taxes, Polish defense products should be able to compete on the European and world market, *if* (and it is a big *if*) they can develop systems up to NATO standards. So far, they have not been able to demonstrate that capability on a large scale, which suggests numerous Polish businesses will either consolidate or fold.

Some market analysts place the blame for this squarely on the shoulders of the Polish MoND, which has become so enamored of Western (particularly U.S.) equipment and the low-cost loans and grants available to pay for it, that it has systematically ignored and under-invested in Polish companies offering more effective (and sometimes cheaper) solutions than foreign solutions. Thus, Poland chose to acquire the U.S. Patriot PAC-3, paid for under FMF rather than indigenous designed surface-to-air missile systems mating Soviet radars and fire controls with U.S. missiles such as the AIM-120 AMRAAM or the RIM-7 Sea Sparrow. Similarly, Poland has one of the premier MiG-29 maintenance, overhaul, upgrade and repair facilities in the world, but has not attempted to transform it into a new F-16 logistics facility—preferring to rely on contractor support (free for the first three years of operation) provided by Lockheed Martin. As a result, according to some market participants we interviewed, Polish companies are losing out on opportunities to develop their own cutting-edge capabilities and products, and are reduced to "techno-serfs" of Western companies.[379]

The Polish government, for its part, is committed to improving the Polish technology base by investing 24 percent of the Polish defense budget in research and technology.[380] But

---

[379] See R. Johnson, op. cit.

[380] *Basic Information on the MoND Budget for 2007*, Ministry of National Defense (Warsaw). 2007.

when one considers that the total Polish defense budget (exclusive of grants in aid) is less than \$4 billion, that investment is not sufficient to jump-start the Polish defense industry.

C. Strategic Partnership With the United States

Poland feels a strong affinity with the United States, the roots of which go back at least to U.S. support for the Solidarity movement under the Reagan Administration in the 1980s. Whether one considers it historically accurate or not, the average Pole thinks the United States was primarily responsible for the collapse of the Soviet Union and the elimination of communism in Poland. This, combined with Poland's belief that the security of Europe is best ensured by a strong U.S. presence on and interest in the continent, has made strategic partnership with the United States a cornerstone of Polish security strategy. Not only did Poland support the United States diplomatically in the UN and other international forums, but it was also among the first countries to provide troops for service with the U.S.-led coalitions in Afghanistan and Iraq. The resurgence of Russia as an aggressive economic and military force, its use of oil and gas contracts in an attempt to blackmail Poland and Ukraine, and finally, its invasion of Georgia in August 2008, have all cemented a consensus among the Polish leadership that Poland must maintain close ties with the United States.

The most concrete manifestation of this strategic partnership has been Polish participation in the war in Iraq and Afghanistan. In contrast to many other European countries, Poland has placed no caveats upon the use of its forces in combat. Polish forces go where U.S. forces go, face the same dangers, and address the same missions. The cooperation between U.S. and Polish special operations forces has been especially fruitful—the Poles proving to be brave, well trained and enthusiastic.

However, at the beginning of their commitment, Polish forces were woefully unprepared to interoperate with U.S. forces, which required the United States to provide Poland with a wealth of equipment, including tactical radios, HMMWVs, mine-resistant vehicles, body armor, and weapons, in addition to providing most in-theater logistic support. Much of this was provided either as an outright grant in aid or at discounted prices through the FMF program. The net effect has been to boost the professionalism and combat readiness of a portion of the Polish military as well as providing a leavening of combat experience that has been taken back and integrated into the total force.

Poland, Bulgaria, Romania and several other countries are eager to have U.S. bases on their soil for a variety of reasons—ranging from the economic benefits of providing support for U.S. forces to the implicit promise of protection against Russian aggression. As U.S. strategic interests shifted from Western Europe into the Middle East and Central Asia, the need for a redeployment of U.S. forces in Europe became evident. Bases in Eastern Europe would put troops closer to active combat theaters and shorten lines of communication. The United States also felt that there would be fewer restrictions on training and other operations in Eastern Europe than at existing bases in Germany. Poland, for its part, used a large portion of its NATO-SIP funds to upgrade airbases and supply depots to NATO standard. These facilities could serve as the nucleus of a permanent U.S. presence in Poland, possibly as part of a ballistic missile defense system.

On the down side, operations in Iraq and Afghanistan have stressed the Polish defense budget and delayed modernization of the total force, particularly in regard to heavy weapons such as tanks and artillery. There has also been, of late, a certain latent hostility to the

U.S. due partly to the perception the relationship between the two countries is "unbalanced." Members of the Polish government and business community consistently expressed to the study team the view that the United States takes Poland for granted and does not appreciate Poland's commitment to the United States.

There was considerable resentment in Poland over the terms of the F-16 fighter sale (see below) as well as to the construction of a missile defense system in Poland. According to Polish government officials, the long and arduous negotiations concerning the U.S. missile defense agreement reflected Poland's desire to get the best possible deal and gain U.S. respect. Thus, after 18 months of negotiation, on August 18, 2008, Poland indicated it would sign the agreement with the United States on missile defense.[381]

On the other hand, a number of U.S. government and industry representatives have spoken of an outbreak of "Poland fatigue" in Washington. This reflects a feeling that the United States has done too much for Poland at the expense of other allies, and that the Poles have perhaps too exalted an opinion of themselves.

Recent Developments

Recent developments in the U.S.-Polish relationship tend to bear out these observations. On August 8, 2008, Russian forces entered the region of South Ossetia in the Republic of Georgia, ostensibly as peacekeepers, but obviously to occupy and eventually annex this province, the site of a long-standing separatist insurgency (itself sponsored and supported by Russia). Shortly thereafter, on August 20, 2008, the United States and Poland signed both an agreement on the emplacing of a ballistic missile defense system in Poland and a Declaration on Strategic Cooperation. According to the U.S. Department of State,

> The Declaration affirms the commitment of the United States to the security of Poland and of any U.S. facilities located on the territory of Poland. The Declaration underscores that both nations face a growing threat from the proliferation of weapons of mass destruction and associated delivery systems. Missile defenses, including the interceptor base in Poland, provide a necessary and critical capability that can be used to defend both our nations and other NATO Allies from long-range missile threats.

> The United States and Poland intend to enhance their security through political-military cooperation, information sharing, and defense industrial and research and technology cooperation. A Strategic Cooperation Consultative Group will serve as the primary mechanism for furthering the U.S.-Poland strategic relationship.[382]

The Declaration called for the United States to deploy a Patriot PAC-3 air-and-missile defense battery to Poland in 2009, with the possibility of upgrading or supplementing this with a more capable Theater-Area High Altitude Air Defense System battery in the future. It probably was not coincidental that all the issues dogging the U.S. missile defense agree-

---

[381] Available at: http://www.huffingtonpost.com/2008/08/14/us-poland-reach-agreement_n_119053.html.

[382] Office of the Spokesman, U.S. Department of State, "Press Release: Declaration of Strategic Cooperation Between the United States of America and the Republic of Poland," Aug. 20, 2008. Available at: http://poland.usembassy.gov/poland/official_texts_and_speeches/official-text-and-speeches-2008/declaration-on-strategic-cooperation-between-the-united-states-of-america-and-the-republic-of-poland-20-august-2008.html.

ment were resolved in the immediate aftermath of this Russian invasion. Strong declarations of support for Georgia and its immediate admission to NATO (together with Ukraine) emanating from the Polish government made clear the degree of alarm, even fear, the Russian invasion had caused.

At this writing, however, it should be noted that the Obama Administration is reviewing the 2008 arrangements and it remains to be seen whether the deployments will go forward as planned.[383]

U.S.-Poland Defense Trade and Industrial Cooperation

The United States and Poland do not have a legal framework in place for defense industrial cooperation. Unlike other Western European countries studied, the United States has neither a reciprocal procurement Memorandum of Understanding (MOU) nor a Declaration of Principles with Poland. However, in light of the close bilateral relationship that has evolved, the United States and Poland are also in the process of negotiating a reciprocal defense procurement MOU.[384] If executed, the MOU would exempt Polish defense exports to the United States from the Buy American Act and also would exempt U.S. companies from analogous Polish laws. Another core principle of such reciprocal procurement MOUs typically is the concept of national treatment for each other's defense firms (with the nature of the obligation varying from one agreement to another).

From an economic standpoint, defense trade with Poland is at the present time very much a one-way street financed by the United States. As seen in Figure 99, the United States has sold Poland, either through direct commercial sales or foreign military sales, more than $4.5 billion in military equipment since 2002. The bulk of that revenue, approximately $3.2 billion, is directly associated with the F-16 program, leaving about $1.3 billion in sales for all other programs and applications. These figures do not include outright donations of equipment or grants in aid with which equipment was actually purchased with *U.S.* funds.

In contrast, Polish defense sales to the United States are negligible. The most noteworthy contracts between the United States and Polish defense companies are in fact subcontracts related to the Polish F-16 sale, mandated as part of the project's offset requirements.[385]

While some representatives of the Polish government attributed this to protectionist policies of the United States, Polish industry representatives were more honest in their assessment: the United States buys little from Poland because Poland at this point has little to offer in the way of interesting products or technology. The emergence of a viable Polish defense export market is dependent on the revitalization of Polish industry, and not on any real or perceived market access barriers in the United States or elsewhere. In that light, the exemption from the Buy American Act and Balance of Payments Program contained in the

---

[383] *Foreign Policy*, March 3, 2009. Available at: http://thecable.foreignpolicy.com/posts/2009/03/03/us_missile_defense_policy_under_review_0.

[384] "Feasibility of a Reciprocal Defense Procurement Memorandum of Understanding With Poland," 73 Federal Register 33992 (June 16, 2008). Available at: http://edocket.access.gpo.gov/2008/pdf/E8-13458.pdf.

[385] According to the InfoBase Publishers' DACIS Contracts Database, in November 2002, Lockheed Martin awarded a $200 million subcontract to PZL-Milesc to act as in-country partner on the program. In July 2004, L-3 Communications, selected by U.S. Air Force Systems Command to provide training and simulation support to the Polish air force for the F-16, issued a subcontract to ETC-PZL Aerospace Industries for $6.6 million to assemble, test and support Link flight simulators being installed in Poland.

Figure 99   U.S. Defense Sales to Poland, 2002-2007 (Billions of Dollars–$)

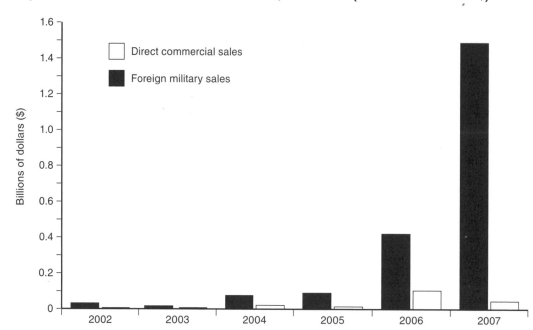

Source: U.S. Department of State, U.S. Department of Defense.

U.S.-Poland bilateral agreement has long-term implications but at present is mainly of symbolic value, signifying the closeness of the relationship between the two countries.

The new Declaration on Strategic Cooperation and the missile defense agreement—if implemented by the United States—have the potential to energize U.S.-Polish industrial cooperation in several ways. First, these arrangements can put Polish companies in line to provide logistics and maintenance services to U.S. forces deployed in Poland. Second, they can potentially lead to a meaningful industrial role for Poland in some elements of the design, development and deployment of a missile defense architecture in Europe. That, in turn, could lead to industrial partnerships between leading U.S. and Polish defense firms. However, much depends on how Poland shapes its industrial policy related to missile defense, and whether it continues to rely on its existing defense offsets policy to provide Polish companies with work, or focuses instead on obtaining greater technology transfer and doing "noble work" onshore.

The F-16 Fighter Deal and Its Fallout

In 2002, the U.S. and Poland negotiated the sale of 48 F-16 Block 52 multirole fighters to Poland at a cost of approximately $3.2 billion (including training and logistic support). This was by far the largest defense sale to Poland in history, intended both as the centerpiece of the Polish air force modernization and of a solidifying U.S.-Polish relationship in the aftermath of September 11. Poland had issued a requirement for a new multirole fighter to replace its aging MiG-29s in 2001. The Polish Parliament (Sjem) passed a law in June 2001 specifying a requirement for 16 second-hand and 44 new fighter aircraft to be acquired by 2006: the cost was not to exceed 0.5 percent of Poland's GDP per annum and an offset agreement had to be reached within 45 days of contract award.

This proved overly optimistic as a corruption scandal forced the dismissal of the assistant defense minister responsible for negotiating the sale. These circumstances, together with budget constraints, placed the multirole fighter program in jeopardy. However, the new Minister of Defense appointed in 2002 insisted the acquisition had to proceed due to the rapidly deteriorating state of Poland's existing inventory. An expert team from the MoND and the Ministry of Economy was formed to draft the outline of an acceptable contracting arrangement, and the Agency for Military Property was designated as the program management agency.

The urgency of the program was mitigated by the transfer of 22 refurbished MiG-29s from Germany for the symbolic price of €1. This meant Poland would have 32 MiG-29s in service, pending replacement by F-16. This allowed Poland to push back delivery for new fighters from 2006 to 2008 and use a more deliberate acquisition process.

A MoND study indicated the MiG-29s were, in the long run, too expensive for Poland to operate in the numbers needed to meet its operational requirements. But they did allow the number of new multirole fighters to be reduced from 60 (new and used) to just 48 new aircraft. The inter-ministerial commission then outlined an acquisition plan to cost $3.5 billion, but paid for outside of the normal defense budget, allowing defense expenditures to remain stable at 1.95 percent of GDP.

A tender commission consisting of a 23-person evaluation committee was formed to evaluate offers using a point system for criteria that included cost, operational suitability, tactical and technical requirements, and offsets. Among the competitors were the Saab JAS.39 Gripen, the Dassault Mirage 2000, and the Lockheed Martin F-16 Block 52. Based on the point system, the F-16 was declared the winner in December 2002. The Poles were particularly impressed with the performance and interoperability of the F-16. Ultimately, however, the deal was sealed on the basis of cost and financing arrangements. While the cost differential among the three bidders amounted to less than 10 percent, the creative offer by the United States of a low-interest, 15-year loan for the entire $3.8 billion program ultimately carried the day. Neither the British and Swedish governments backing the Gripen, nor the French government backing the Mirage 2000, could match such generous terms.

The U.S. financial package was novel in nature—designed to work around the limitations of existing U.S. rules. Specifically, the existing Export-Import Bank Program did not cover defense sales and the Defense Export Loan Guarantee (DELG) Program did not offer competitive financing. Thus, as an alternative, pursuant to Section 23 of the Arms Export Control Act, the Bush Administration extended a loan to Poland directly from the U.S. Treasury, which then allowed the Defense Security and Cooperation Agency (DSCA) to ensure 100 percent of the loan (rather than just 85 percent under DELG). Congress acquiesced to Poland's desire to defer payments to the out-years by authorizing a 13-year loan with principal payments deferred for eight years, at an interest rate of approximately 5 percent. Congress also authorized DSCA to reduce financing fees and to obtain a letter of credit from a commercial bank to serve as a performance bond, in order to allow Poland to meet the default subsidy requirements of the package. Finally, the deal allowed Poland to "buy down" its debt by accelerating up-front payments.

The final piece in the F-16 deal was the offset package. As discussed below, Polish law requires 100 percent offsets for every substantial foreign defense sale, with direct offsets at no less than 50 percent of the total offset commitment. For the F-16, this meant prime contractor Lockheed Martin would have to meet an offset requirement of some $3.8 billion; nearly $2 billion would have to be direct offsets to the Polish defense industry. This was some 28 times greater than the next largest offset package to date (a $212 million commitment by EADS for deliver of C-295M transport aircraft). Lockheed Martin submitted an offset package valued at $9.8 billion (although the actual cash value would be much lower, due to multipliers applied to calculate offset credits)—nominally three times the contract value. Neither the Gripen nor the Mirage 2000 teams could meet these terms.

In short, through the combination of an attractive financing package and offsets, the United States in effect made an offer on the F-16 that Poland "could not refuse."

On the face of things, Poland scored a remarkable triumph in its negotiations for the F-16—getting the aircraft on very attractive terms. Nonetheless, the F-16 deal has been controversial in Poland and has generated considerable ill will toward the U.S. defense industry. It is difficult for a U.S. observer to understand why. Lockheed and its subcontractors have been scrupulous in meeting not only the program's cost and schedule requirements, but the onerous and complex offset commitments. The offset requirements are a constant source of complaint among U.S. contractors involved in the program, largely due to the opacity of the credit formula and the extensive bookkeeping it requires.

Discussions with both Polish government and U.S. industry representatives suggest the Polish government oversold the benefits of the F-16 program to the Polish people. First, the government created the impression that the offset commitment of $9.8 billion would represent a real injection of $9.8 billion into the Polish economy (as opposed to the perhaps $2.5-3.5 billion realized after taking credit multipliers into account). Second, there was a perception this influx of cash would come either in the form of a lump sum, or at least front-end loaded into the program, as opposed to amortized over a ten-year period. As one Polish businessman put it, "We were told that the sky would open up and it would rain dollar bills." When this did not happen, there was widespread public disillusionment. Fortunately, this does not extend to the Polish government, which is very happy with the performance of Lockheed and its contractors, but it does point to the pitfalls of selling a program politically based on factors such as offsets.[386]

U.S.-Polish Areas of Contention

From the U.S. side of the ledger, offsets are the main item of contention with the Polish government. U.S. companies find the offset law too rigid, too complex to administer (particularly for smaller companies), and too draconian in its penalties. This is fully discussed in Section III below (section on offsets).

For the Poles, the situation is more complex. As noted above, Poland desires above all to be treated with respect as a valued strategic partner—hence the importance of (presently) symbolic gestures such as exemption from the Buy American Act. At the same time, Poland

---

[386] For an outstanding summary of the Polish F-16 decision, see B. Seguin, *Why did Poland Choose the F-16?* Occasional Paper Series No. 11, George C. Marshall European Center for Security Studies, June 2007. Available at: http://www.marshallcenter.org/mcpublicweb/en/component/content/article/43-cat-pubs-occ-papers/620-art-pubs-occ-papers-11.html?directory=19.

is keenly aware it is still a relatively poor country that depends on U.S. financial assistance to meet its defense commitments. Its officials nevertheless feel that Poland, as a valuable ally in the war on terror, deserves some degree of material recognition for its sacrifices (which, according to some Polish officials, amount to more than $600 million expended on operations in Iraq and Afghanistan). In return for this expenditure, which had taken funds from its planned defense modernization, Poland would like to see a substantial increase in its FMF allotment, certainly more than the relatively small $30 million it presently receives per annum.

U.S. officials, for their part, think the United States has been more than generous, having given Poland more than $220 million in grants since the mid-1990s. While Poland is a valuable ally, they believe the United States must consider *all* of its allies and commitments in the allocation of scarce military aid resources.[387] While constant complaints from Polish representatives contribute to the "Poland Fatigue" described earlier, any friction in the relationship was quickly covered over in the wake of the Russian invasion of Georgia.

Future Outlook

Although there will continue to be some frictions between the two countries, the United States and Poland seem on course to create a "special relationship" in Central Europe. This evolution reflects Poland's perception of the United States as the ultimate guarantor of its security, and the U.S. perception of Poland as a small, but utterly reliable, ally in the war on terror. The Russian invasion of Georgia served to focus the minds of both countries' leaders on the core strategic elements of the relationship, which are laid out in the Declaration of Strategic Cooperation, the missile defense agreement, and the pending reciprocal procurement MOU. With these in place, the United States will continue to draw closer to Poland, and Poland's defense industry will become more closely aligned with that of the United States, particularly if U.S. forces establish a permanent presence in Poland.

As for the United States, there is risk that Poland's strong ties to the United States could weaken if perceptions that the United States takes Poland for granted continue. Poland's alignment with the United States has cost it politically within the European Union. Nonetheless, Poland remains a part of that Union and increasingly views it as the key to its future economic prosperity. Although most Poles are presently in agreement that its security is best served through a Transatlantic focus, there is a small but vocal minority that wants closer integration with the nascent EU security system. Like the UK, Poland will likely keep one foot strongly in each camp given its interests.

---

[387] This was borne out in conversations with both U.S. and Polish officials, but it is clear that these are widely held views on both sides. See, e.g., B. Graham, "Poland Links Bid for U.S. Aid to Presence in Iraq," *The Washington Post*, Dec. 10, 2005, p. A-13.

III. Evaluation of Market Access Metrics

Access to the Polish defense market needs to be assessed in the context of a generally favorable trade and investment climate in Poland. Poland has largely made the economic and political transition to a Western democratic, market-based society and is becoming a fully integrated member of the EU. While it still suffers from excessive bureaucracy and red tape, a slow judicial system, and regulatory unpredictability, Poland has become a strong trade and investment partner for other Western countries, including the United States.

Tariff Barriers

By and large, tariffs are not significant barriers between Poland and the United States, although Poland is somewhat disadvantaged relative to other European countries studied.

Specifically, all of the countries studied are members of the World Trade Organization (WTO) and thus must provide most-favored nation and national treatment to imported goods from every other country included in the study. Although defense products are generally exempt from WTO rules governing tariffs and trade, the United States has entered into reciprocal procurement MOUs with most of its European Allies that generally provide duty-free treatment for imported defense products procured from the other country. Of the European countries studied, however, Poland (along with Romania) stands out as a country that has not yet entered into such an MOU with the United States. As noted above, however, the United States is in the process of entering into such an MOU.

Thus, for now at least, U.S.-Polish defense trade (like U.S.-Romanian defense trade) is somewhat more burdened than U.S. defense trade with the other European countries studied—although the applicable tariff rates are relatively low and not much of a trade impediment. Because of this distinction, Poland (together with Romania) has a lower score on tariff barriers than the other countries examined.

Moreover, in any event, these MOUs do not apply to dual-use products and technologies such as general aerospace systems that have both military and civil applications. Thus, as more military programs rely on commercial off-the-shelf technology, this would tend to put U.S. companies at a competitive disadvantage *vis-à-vis* European firms that get the benefit of the lower intra-European rates that apply under EU rules unless specific exemptions are negotiated on a bilateral basis.

Competition in Procurement

Polish Procurement Policy: Tabula Rasa

As noted, Poland has reformed its procurement system to comply with EU standards as it gradually discarded its legacy Soviet system. The Polish Public Procurement Law requires all "common use" goods to be awarded competitively, with very narrow exceptions. Armaments are exempt from the law, and are instead subject to rules and regulations established by the MoND. Thus, under Polish defense procurement rules and policies, most systems and products must be competitively sourced and are open to the United States and other Western European sources of supply.

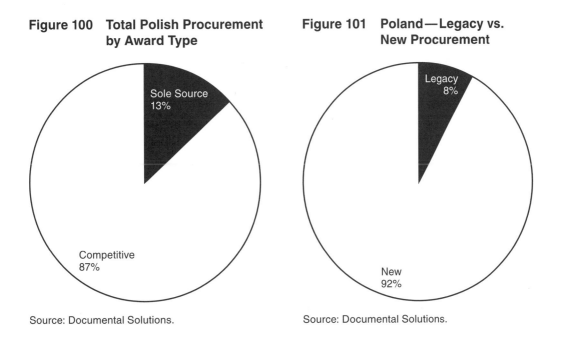

Figure 100   Total Polish Procurement by Award Type

Sole Source 13%

Competitive 87%

Source: Documental Solutions.

Figure 101   Poland—Legacy vs. New Procurement

Legacy 8%

New 92%

Source: Documental Solutions.

As Poland is seeking to modernize its armaments as rapidly as possible, its general policy is to entertain proposals from whatever source offers the best prices or financing (including offsets as discussed below). It should be recognized, however, that on major awards such as the military fighter aircraft, the competitive landscape is shaped by political considerations and the attractiveness of the financing and offset package offered.

Polish Procurement Practice: Understanding the Data

In practice, as shown below, the available data on Polish procurement awards in fact confirms that most Polish buying is on the basis of competitive awards of new systems with a modest amount of sole source legacy buying from primarily Polish state-owned suppliers. The Polish market also is very accessible to U.S. suppliers, which have a considerable market share.

- **Polish Acquisition of Major Weapons Systems: The Prevalence of Competition.** As set forth on Table 47, a review of major Polish defense programs for 2006-2008 (i.e., those valued at $10 million or more a year during 2006-2008) shows that 87 percent were awarded competitively ($3.86 billion). Only 13 percent ($582 million) were awarded on a sole source basis (see Figure 100).

- **Sole Source Awards Are Mostly Legacy and Mostly Awarded to Polish Suppliers.** Poland made 92 percent of its legacy awards on a sole source basis (see Figure 102). Not surprisingly, most sole source awards were made to government-owned Polish suppliers. These contracts were primarily to upgrade or maintain legacy systems on which they were the prime contractor and possibly the only available source of parts and technical expertise. Some of these awards also are designed to sustain these enterprises, which otherwise face a limited market for their products.

Table 47   Leading Polish Defense Programs, 2006-2008 (Millions of Dollars−$)

Program Name	Prime Contractor	Country	2006	2007	2008	Total	Award	Legacy
F-16 Falcon	Lockheed Martin	US	434.56	1,146.26	946.52	2,527.3	Competitive	No
Patria XC-360P AFV	Wojskowe Zaklady Mechaniczne	PO	224.76	242.53	254.57	721.9	Competitive	No
F-16 GFE Engines	United Technologies	U.S.	57.40	144.46	146.90	348.8	Competitive	No
PZL-130	EADS (PZL)	PO	99.09	43.65	33.99	176.7	Sole Source	Yes
W-3 Helicipter	Panstwowe Zaklady Lotnicze	PO	25.29	58.65	36.41	120.3	Sole Source	Yes
MEKO Type 100 Frigate	Stocznia M/Wojennej	PO	39.64	39.87	40.10	119.6	Sole Source	No
C.295M Transport	EADS	EU	4.7	4.7	64.3	73.6	Competitive	No
RAT-31DL Radar	Finmeccanica SpA	IT	24.06	13.78	3.06	40.9	Competitive	No
AIM-9X Sidewinder	Raytheon	US	0.35	33.79	0.57	34.7	Sole Source	No
Polish SW Defined Radio	Radnor SA	PO	0.00	18.36	15.24	33.6	Sole Source	No
TS-11F Trainer Mods	United Technologies	U.S.	2.04	5.11	22.39	29.5	Competitive	Yes
DB-110 Recon Pod	ITT	U.S.	0.00	5.86	17.83	23.7	Competitive	No
Honker Tactical Truck	International Truck Alliance	INT	7.26	7.49	7.72	22.5	Sole Source	Yes
BM21M MRL	Huta Stalowa Wola	PO	0.0	5.4	16.1	21.5	Sole Source	Yes
Tyoe 207 Submarine	Rheinstall	GE	6.24	5.76	5.28	17.3	Sole Source	No
High Capacity Data Radio	ITT	U.S.	0.38	2.95	12.70	16.0	Competitive	No
PERI-R 7A2 Weapons Sight	Carl Zeiss GR, Carl Zeiss AG	GE	5.60	5.74	4.18	15.5	Competitive	No
CBU-97 Sensor Fuzed Wpn	Textron Systems	U.S.	0.80	9.65	4.87	15.3	Sole Source	No
TACTICOS BM/C3I System	Thales Group	FR	12.15	0.49	0.49	13.1	Competitive	No
M3AR UHF/VHF Recever	Rohde & Schwarz	GE	4.53	5.52	2.84	12.9	Competitive	No
44SG Mk.II FLIR	FLIR Systems	U.S.	4.9	5.1	0.4	10.4	Competitive	No
RKS-8000 SW Def Radio	Radnor SA	PO	3.70	3.85	2.80	10.4	Sole Source	No
MSTAR Radar	DRS Technologies	U.S.	4.10	3.02	3.12	10.2	Competitive	No
Commander's Sight	PCO-Cenzin - Poland	PO	10.06	0.06	0.06	10.2	Sole Source	No
Griffon 2000 Hovercraft	Griffon Hovercraft	UK	10.06	0.06	0.06	10.2	Competitive	No
Patria XC-360P AFV	Patria Vehicles OY	FL	3.09	3.09	3.09	9.3	Competitive	No

Source: Documental Solutions.

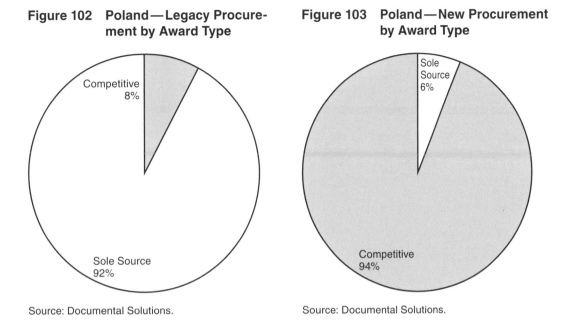

Figure 102   Poland—Legacy Procurement by Award Type

Competitive 8%

Sole Source 92%

Source: Documental Solutions.

Figure 103   Poland—New Procurement by Award Type

Sole Source 6%

Competitive 94%

Source: Documental Solutions.

- **Limited Spending on Legacy Systems.** However, as shown in Figure 101, only some 8 percent ($370 million) of all spending from 2006-2008 was for legacy programs (i.e., older platforms in existence prior to 2006); a very large 92 percent ($4,625) of all awards were for new systems. This reflects the rapid replacement of Soviet-era systems with new platforms. Poland, like Romania, therefore spends relatively little on sustaining its old systems and applies most of its resources on force modernization. Thus most of Poland's large, expensive programs are new procurements such as the F-16 Falcon, the Patria XC-360 APC and the MEKO 100 Frigate. This is in stark contrast to Western European countries studied, which typically spend the majority or more on legacy platforms that remain in service for many years.

- **New Polish Buys Are Even More Competitive.** As set forth on Figure 103, a separate analysis of "new" Polish acquisition (i.e., programs started in 2006-2008) shows even more competition—with more than 94 percent of all new awards ($3.8 billion) competed. Poland and Romania (in order) have the most competition in new buying of all the European countries studied. The remaining "new" sales were largely made sole source to state-owned enterprises.

- **New Competitive Buys Are Clearly Open to U.S. and European Firms.** Significantly, we believe that most, if not all, of the new Polish competitive awards were open to U.S. firms. Indeed, Figure 104 reflects that U.S. firms won 73 percent ($2.986 million), mostly as a result of "big ticket" programs such as the F-16 sale. Polish national firms won 22 percent ($895 million) while other European firms won 5 percent ($192 million). The degree of U.S. wins is substantially affected by the large F-16 program, which accounts for a significant amount of the 73 percent U.S. share. It remains to be seen if European firms will gain a larger share in time as other products are procured. Given Poland's strong ties with both the United

**Figure 104   Poland—New Competitive
Procurement by Supplier**

**Figure 105   Poland—U.S. Wins by
Award Type**

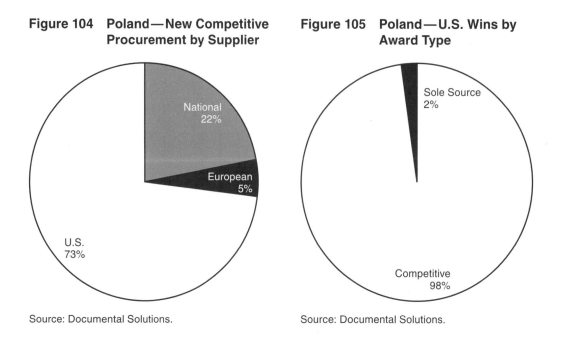

Source: Documental Solutions.   Source: Documental Solutions.

States and other European countries, one might expect somewhat more balance in its defense buying in the future.

- **Market Share Data Confirms a Sizable U.S. and European Participation.** Indeed, as shown on Figure 106, U.S. firms have captured roughly 67 percent of *all* Polish major program markets in the last three years (by value), with Polish firms accounting for 27 percent and firms from the rest of Europe combining for 6 percent. U.S. firms Lockheed Martin and United Technologies respectively had significant shares (57 percent and 8 percent respectively) of Polish program awards over recent years—both due to the large value of the F-16 sale. Thus, Poland plainly does not exhibit any aversion to buying foreign systems. To the contrary, Poland is seeking newer, advanced capabilities from Western nations. However, two things should be recognized. First, the degree of U.S. competitive success partly reflects the extent to which the United States has provided generous grants and financial assistance. Second, the Polish offset law does result in considerable subcontract work being directed toward Polish defense companies.

- **Polish Buys of U.S. Products Are Largely Through Competitive Awards.** Additionally, in contrast to Western Europe (where U.S. suppliers have traditionally received significant sole source awards), the United States participation is largely through competitive awards. As shown on Figure 105, approximately 98 percent of U.S. suppliers' awards in Poland were made competitively with only 2 percent made on a sole source basis.

- **Virtually No European Cooperative Engagement**. Finally, in contrast to Western European nations, Poland has no participation to date in European cooperative programs. This may change in the future as geopolitical and economic consider-

Figure 106 Poland—Defense Market Share by Company

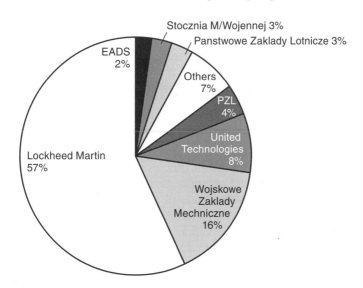

Source: Documental Solutions.

ations drive Poland toward this approach, which has become a major element of defense spending in Western Europe.

In sum, no matter how the data is evaluated, it shows a clear pattern of open and competitive awards—with U.S. firms bidding and winning on a sustained basis—albeit with significant financial aid that affords U.S. firms a competitive advantage.

Fair and Transparent Procurement Process

In general, the Polish defense procurement system is fair and transparent on paper but is still a work in progress in actuality.

Poland, like other EU Member States, is a party to the WTO Agreement on Government Procurement (GPA). However, its procurement of "warlike" goods is exempt from the GPA's coverage and, hence, only "non-warlike" goods are subject to the Agreement's disciplines. Poland also adopted the EU Public Procurement Law as a condition of its accession to the Union, but as is the case with most Member States, it deliberately exempted defense procurement from the regulation in order to maintain freedom of action in defense industrial policy.

The 2004 Polish Public Procurement Law explicitly excludes weapons system procurement from the obligation to follow the existing EC Public Procurement Directive (this preceded the new EC Defense Procurement Directive). Indeed, for defense goods and services, Poland has invoked Article 296 EC Treaty to opt out of the EU public procurement disciplines. In June 2006, Poland did adopt the voluntary EDA Code of Conduct on Defence Procurement and appears to be trying to comply with its tenets, according to market participants interviewed.

The Polish law does, however, distinguish between "common use items" (clothing, food, fuel, dual-use equipment, etc.), which must be procured under the EU regulations, and weapons systems, which are procured through a system established by powers granted to the MoND, particularly National Defense Decision 291. Under that decision, acquisition is executed by the MoND's Armed Forces Procurement Department for off-the-shelf items, and by the Armament Policy Department in the case of developmental items. There are six distinct ways of awarding military contracts under the new law:

- Tendering: If the object of the contract is generally available supplies or services of fixed quality standards and there are more than two competitive bidders.

- Negotiations with several contractors

  - When there is a need for consolidation or unification of equipment, but there are several contractors able to fill the order

  - For Research and Development (R&D) projects

  - For contracts not subject to the EDA Code of Conduct on Defence Procurement

- Negotiations with a single contractor

  - When there is only one viable provider of the product or service

  - In case of an emergency, time-critical requirement

  - When the value of the contract is less than €10,000

- Electronic auctions

- Foreign Military Sales

- NAMSA (NATO Maintenance and Supply Agency) contracts

The procurement system in practice therefore resembles that of most Western European countries, although in many ways it still does not function adequately.

However, as noted above, administration of the system is hampered by a shortage of trained acquisition program management personnel and a lack of adequate coordination between government and industry. Lacking experience in Western-style acquisition management, Polish program managers often tend to take a mechanistic approach to regulations, applying them "by the book" in cases where they should be waived or modified. According to market participants, this tends to create friction with industry and delays in delivering on various programs. Lack of coordination between the different government agencies involved in defense procurement adds confusion to the process and sometimes results in unrealistic requirements and expectations.

Further, this study team was told that in the case of those formerly owned state companies still doing defense work, a number seem to rely on cronyism to win contracts, according to market participants; i.e., they use their contacts in the state-owned companies and in the military/MoND to obtain work share in various programs, either as subcontractors to the state companies or as offset partners with foreign prime contractors. This suggests a climate is still in place in parts of industry that is not altogether in accord with competitive market principles.

In practice, both Polish and U.S. firms interviewed say that the government process in competitive procurements is codified and reasonably open and transparent. American firms reported that requests for procurement are even being made available in English in some cases today. The process itself is considered to be acceptably transparent. Defense budgets, acquisition plans and programs are public documents; procurement procedures are available through government websites; and tenders and contract awards are posted on the EDA's Electronic Bulletin Board.

Domestic Content Requirements

Poland does not have any law or regulation analogous to the Buy American Act nor does it normally include any explicit requirement for domestic content in its tenders. Regardless, Poland's rigorous offset law (discussed below) pushes foreign companies into assigning work share to domestic companies as the path of least resistance toward meeting offset obligations. This has the net effect of mandating a high degree of domestic content in many programs either through the manufacturing of components and subsystems, or in providing life cycle support once the system is deployed.

Offsets and *Juste Retour*

Offsets are perhaps the single most contentious element of the Polish defense acquisition process. Founded in the Offset Act of 10 September 1999 as Amended in January 2007, Poland requires a minimum of 100 percent offsets on all foreign military purchases worth more than €5 million over a period of three years; at least 50 percent of the total offset must be direct offsets for the Polish defense industry. Offset agreements must be signed between the foreign supplier and the Ministry of Economy within 60 days of the contract award, and the offset period cannot exceed ten years. Offsets are administered by the Ministry of Economy, and parties are prohibited from withdrawing from the offset agreement—even if the program is terminated at the discretion of the Polish government.

Offset credits are awarded on the basis of a formula embedded in the offset law. Generally, the nominal value of the offset transaction is multiplied by a factor ranging from 0.5 to 5.0, depending upon the nature of the arrangement and its perceived value to the defense industry, as determined by the Offset Office of the Ministry of Economy. Most work share arrangements are given a factor of 2-4, which makes work share the easiest and most economical way for most defense companies to meet their obligation. Other types of offset arrangements, particularly indirect offsets, often get bogged down in negotiations over the factor to be applied, which most companies therefore try to avoid.

The U.S. Department of Commerce (DoC) annual report on offsets confirms the significant role this practice plays in Poland. Indeed, offsets in Poland averaged 167.7 percent of contract values in practice over the period 1993-2006 (calculated from data submitted by the reporting U.S. firms of actual contracts and offset commitments).[388] Among defense

---

[388] Offsets in Defense Trade, Twelfth Report to Congress, U.S. Department of Commerce (Dec. 2007), PDF p. 29, report p. 2-13 (Table 2-5). Available at: http://www.bis.doc.gov/defenseindustrialbaseprograms/osies/offsets/final-12th-offset-report-2007.pdf.

purchasers, Poland also was one of the largest recipients of offset agreements (more than $6 billion in value over the same period).[389]

U.S. companies complain about the complexity of the bookkeeping needed to track offset credits, as well as the tendency of the Ministry of Economy to "lose" or miscalculate credits. However, the most contentious element of the Offset Law is the penalty for non-performance. Specifically, if a company fails to meet a specified offset commitment, it is liable for 100 percent of that commitment, not merely the balance of the commitment that remains unfulfilled. Thus, if a company has an offset commitment of $1 million, and it only performs $900,000 of that commitment, it must pay a penalty of $1 million—not merely the missing balance of $100,000 (as would be the case in most other countries).

Poland justifies its Offset Law as meeting the following objectives:

- Development of the Polish industry, especially the defense sector;

- Gaining access to new export markets or increasing current export potential;

- Transfer of new technologies;

- Development of research work in Polish universities and R&D centers;

- Creation of new jobs in Poland, particularly in areas of underemployment; and

- Creation of a knowledge-based economy.

Yet, even Polish government and industry representatives interviewed for this study noted that the Offset Law as presently constituted does not further most of these objectives. In particular, they say, it has failed to develop the Polish defense industry; it has not significantly bolstered Polish export potential, it has not fostered the transfer of new technologies or created many new jobs, or facilitated the creation of a knowledge-based economy. Rather, it has functioned mainly to force most foreign suppliers to direct most of their offset work to existing state-owned or controlled entities, which are in turn almost totally dependent on offset work for their continued viability. Thus, the Offset Law, instead of creating new jobs, merely keeps under-employed state workers at old ones; rather than transferring new technologies, it keeps the Polish defense industry locked into old ones. As some observers have noted, this form of offset keeps inefficient state-owned industries solvent at the price of strengthening their dependence on Western defense companies both for work and for the kinds of technology they can use.

In fact, government and industry representatives interviewed by the study team note that the main function of the Offset Law in practice is to serve as a *de facto* domestic content law. Ironically, however, the Offset Law does not in fact ensure that Polish industry obtains any new technology or performs any "noble" production or R&D in the process.

The offsets on the F-16 program illustrate these issues. Lockheed Martin partnered with PZL-Mielsc in a contract worth (initially) $200 million, and ETC-PZL is assisting L-3 Communications in setting up training facilities in Poland. For the most part, however, Polish industry is reduced to "design-to-print" contracts on the program that offer little opportunity for acquiring advanced technology or developing their own high-end products. U.S. defense industry representatives indicated more innovative and creative offset packages

---

[389] Ibid., PDF p. 39, report p. 4-3 (Table 4-1). As noted, the F-16 program accounts for most of these offset agreements.

that actually build up the Polish defense industry should be considered in future agreements (e.g., those related to the missile defense agreement and future cooperative programs).

Although Polish officials, even in the Offset Office, recognize the problems inherent in the current offset law, they cannot imagine how Polish defense companies could survive without it. Nor do they believe they could repeal or substantially alter it in the present political environment. In the long term, they realize that Poland needs to review and revise its offset laws to make them more "user friendly" and realign them in a manner that actually strengthens the Polish defense industry so that it can stand on its own feet as distinct from being reliant on offset work for its survival.

Government Ownership

As noted above, a considerable portion of the Polish defense industry is now privately held (with some firms having limited government ownership in some cases). The Polish government is attempting to liquidate, convert, or sell all of its remaining defense industries, which are listed in Table 48. To that end, as discussed above, most of them have been grouped under the Bumar holding company, which is supposed to prepare them for disposition in the next two years. Given controversies surrounding the management of Bumar, the failure of most of its companies to effectively transition either to dual-use or civilian production, and the lack of progress in modernization of plants and management, meeting this timetable does not seem likely.

How long the Polish government will continue to support this remnant of the communist era is uncertain; every year these companies remain in state control is a year when the revenues of their sale cannot be directed toward defense modernization. At the same time, the large number of (relatively) high-paid, unionized workers in these enterprises makes it politically difficult simply to let them fail. If, however, these firms do not manage to reform themselves, it will be difficult to attract foreign buyers. The exception to the rule is situations where the acquisition is structured as part of an offset package for a particularly lucrative procurement, as was the case when EADS-CASA bought a 51 percent stake in PZL- Warszawa as part of its C-295 transport contract.

Foreign Direct Investment

Poland generally has a favorable climate for foreign investment, and has attracted more than $120 billion in FDI since 1990 (including $19.2 billion in 2006). According to the U.S. DoC Foreign Commercial Service, the United States "is the fifth ranked foreign direct investor in Poland, with nearly 13 percent of FDI, and almost $15 billion invested since 1990."[390]

Within this generally favorable climate, the defense sector does pose challenges for potential Western investors—not because of Polish government policy but because of the general unattractiveness of the state-owned firms (aging, obsolete facilities, too many employees, unattractive capabilities, etc.). Indeed, Poland is actively soliciting foreign buyers for its state-owned defense enterprises, but has had trouble attracting investors to these

---

[390] *Doing Business In Poland: Country Commercial Guide 2008*, p. 6, U.S. Foreign Commercial Service, U.S. Department of Commerce. Available at: http://www.buyusainfo.net/docs/x_2387888.pdf.

Table 48   Current State-Owned or Controlled Defense Enterprises

Company	Government Share Percent (%)	Other Shareholders Percent (%)	Notes
EADS PZL Warszawa-Okecie SA	18	EADS Military Transport— 77.21%; PZL Employees—6%	Aircraft manufacturer
ETC-PZL Aerospace Industries Sp.z.o.o	35	Environmental Tectonics Corp	Aircraft simulators. Government share held through PZL Warszawa-Okiecie.
PZH Bumar Sp.z.o.o	100		Holding company for underperforming state-owned defense companies.
Zaklady Mechaniczne Bumar-Labedy SA			Tanks and armored vehicles
Zaklady Mealowe (ZM) "Mesko" SA			Missiles, munitions, and fuzes
Zakladay Mechaniczne Tarnow SA			Electro-mechanical and defense systems
Centrum Naukowo-produckcynie Elektroniki Profesionalnei Radwar SA			Defense electronics
Fabrika Broni Lucznik-Radom Sp.z.o.o			Defense electronics
Przemyslowo Centrm Optyki SA			Optical systems
Przedsielorstowo Handlowo-uslaowo Centrex Sp.z.o.o			
Przedsielorstowo Sprzetu Ochronnego Maskpol Sp.z.o.o			
WSK PZL-Warsawa-II SA			Aircraft systems
Zaklady Produkcii Specialnei W Plonach			
Zaklady Mealowe Krasnik Sp.z.o.o.			
Fadroma-serwise-remonty Sp.z.o.o.			
Buman Hoch-und-Teifban GmbH			
Bumar Bauunternehmen GmbH			
PZL Military Aircraft Works No.4 (WZL-4)	100		Aircraft engine maintenance and overhaul
PZL Swidnik SA	63	Sikorsky Aircraft	Helicopter manufacturer
Radmor SA	100		Radio and electronics manufacturer
WSK PZL-Rzeszow SA	15	Pratt & Whtiney	Aircraft and vehicle engine manufacturer

Source: InfoBase Publishers, DACIS Companies Database.

Table 49   Foreign Acquisitions of Polish Defense Enterprises (Millions of Dollars–$)

Date	Buyer	Bought	Price	Revenues	Notes
Sep 2007	Undisclosed Investor	PZL Swidnik SA	NA	32.0	Government sold 37% stake in state aircraft company
Jan 2007	Sikorsky Aircraft	PZL Mielec	83.0	NA	Formerly Polish Government heicopter manufacturer
Apr 2002	Pratt & Whtiney	WSK PZL Rzeszow SA	70.0	99.0	P&W bought 80% stake in Government-owned aero engine company
Oct 2001	EADS-CASA	PZL Warszawa Okecie SA	NA	NA	EADS-CASA bough a 51% stake in a Government-owned aircraf company as part of a deal to purchase eight C.295 transports from CASA
Sep 2000	Environmental Tectonics	PZL Aerospace Industries	1.5	NA	Bought 95% stake in Government-owned manufacturer of aircraft simulators
May 1996	Coltec Industries, Inc.	WSK PZL Krosno	NA	NA	Coltec Menasco bought a 73% share in a Government-owned producer of aircraft systems

Source: Defense Mergers and Acquisitions.

antiquated and under-producing companies. Foreign buyers do have to undergo review by the MoND, the Ministry of Industry, the Ministry of Economy, and the Ministry of Foreign Affairs, but in most cases this has been pro forma. Companies may have to pledge not to immediately shut down a particular plant, or not to terminate certain critical programs or production lines, and will have to agree to abide by the EU Code of Conduct and Best Practices with regard to armaments production and transfer, but the overwhelming majority of transactions are approved. These types of obligations can limit the potential buyers' ability to achieve efficiencies and deploy businesses to their best use.

In short, the combination of circumstances—the potential obligations buyers face and the limited technological attractiveness of many Polish firms—are likely to continue to deter foreign defense firms from making significant acquisitions.

Not surprisingly, as shown on Table 49, there have been only a small number of foreign acquisitions of Polish defense firms by both U.S. and European firms.

Ethics and Corruption

Poland, like most ex-communist countries, continues to face corruption problems although the situation is improving. The World Bank's worldwide governance indicators show Poland at 59 percent for rule of law and 61.4 percent for control of corruption.[391] For 2007, Poland is rated the 61st country in the world on the Transparency International (TI)

---

[391] See World Bank Governance Indicators, 1996-2007 (Country Data Report for Poland, 1996-2007). Available at: http://www.buyusainfo.net/docs/x_2387888.pdf.

Corruption Perception Index—on the same level with Cuba, Kuwait and Tunisia, but better than Bulgaria (64th) or Romania (69th).[392]

Nonetheless, the situation is much improved over what it was in the early 1990s. Indeed, Poland's anti-corruption campaign was a necessary prerequisite for its admission to the European Union. Anti-corruption laws are rigorous and apparently are applied vigorously and uniformly without regard to faction or party. The problem is simply that bribery is so ingrained it is impossible, overnight, to root out a common way of thinking. As one Polish employee of a U.S. defense company put it, "[w]e are a people who have been conditioned not to turn down an opportunity if one presents itself."

Interestingly, U.S. companies do not seem directly affected by the atmosphere of corruption due largely to widespread knowledge of the Foreign Corrupt Practices Act and the seriousness with which the United States enforces it. Since it is commonly known that U.S. companies will not pay bribes and kickbacks, most people do not ask. With the Polish suppliers and subcontractors of U.S. companies, however, it is a different matter. Also, foreign firms from countries with more ambiguous attitudes toward foreign corrupt practices are constantly approached. As for the Polish companies in U.S. supply chains, maintaining ethical practices is a constant struggle for U.S. prime contractors.

One effect of the anti-corruption campaign has been to erect artificial barriers between government and industry representatives, who are eager to avoid even the appearance of impropriety. Thus, there is less coordination between government and industry than is common in the United States (let alone Western Europe) for fear of being accused of collusion; this in turn creates unnecessary delays and misunderstanding in executing procurement decisions and managing existing projects.

Because Poland is not an active player in international arms markets, there is little evidence of Polish firms making bribes with respect to such sales. Poland is, however, a signatory of the Convention on Combating Bribery of Foreign Public Officials in International Business Transactions (OECD Anti-Bribery Convention), and has enacted implementing legislation. TI's recent progress report found, however, that Poland's statute needs revision to be effective (it does not confer liability on legal persons and does not clearly bar the tax deductibility of foreign bribes). There also is no visible enforcement of the Poland anti-bribery law; Poland has conducted no investigations to date of foreign bribery although there was a parliamentary inquiry into alleged bribery with respect to an internal Polish privatization.[393]

Export Controls

The Polish System

During the early 1990s, when Poland was rapidly liquidating its surplus armaments holdings and no formal export control agency was yet in place, Poland developed a reputation

---

[392] Transparency International 2007 Corruption Perception Index, available at: http://www.transparency.org/policy_research/surveys_indices/cpi/2007/regional_highlights_factsheets.

[393] F. Heimann and G. Dell, *Progress Report 2008: Enforcement of the OECD Convention on Combating Bribery of Foreign Public Officials in International Business Transactions*, Transparency International (June 24, 2008), pp. 10, 21-22. Available at: http://www.transparency.org/news_room/in_focus/2008/oecd_report.

for selling to dubious regimes or allowing arms shipments to be diverted to third parties. In one known example, twenty T-55AM main battle tanks acquired by Yemen were diverted to Sudan with the collusion of several Polish officials.

Since its admittance to the European Union, however, Poland has worked hard to clean house and abide by international norms on arms transfers. In preparation for joining the EU, Poland became a signatory to the EU Code of Conduct on Arms Exports, the EU Joint Action on Small Arms and Light Weapons, the OSCE Criteria on Conventional Arms Transfers, and the OSCE Document on Small Arms and Light Weapons.[394] Poland also is a member of major multilateral export control regimes, including the Nuclear Suppliers Group, the Australia Group, the Missile Technology Control Regime, the Wassenaar Arrangement and the Chemical Weapons Convention. The core principles embodied in these agreements have all been implemented in Polish national law.

The EC Transfers Directive recently adopted by the European Parliament is a further step in aligning the policies of EU countries regarding intra-Community transfers and simplifying procedures to permit such transfers among Member States and certified defense companies. The focus of this EC Directive is intra-Community transfers and, thus, the main beneficiaries of reduced barriers within the EU are European defense companies. It is not at all clear that U.S. firms will be eligible for similar treatment; this is a matter for national authorities to decide.

Under Polish law, export licenses for military and dual-use products and technology are issued by the Department of Economy and Labor Department of Export Control. Poland has stringent end-user certification requirements, particularly for small arms and munitions, which constitute its primary export commodities. Since 2001, there have been no major complaints or scandals involving Polish arms exports, which, considering the culture of corruption in the country as a whole, is a remarkable achievement.

In contrast to the consensus in most other European countries, Poland has no major complaints about U.S. technology transfer regulations, including U.S. International Traffic in Arms Regulations. This may be attributed to the fact that Poland exports relatively few defense products with U.S. components or subsystems and also has little cooperative engagement with U.S. firms in advanced technology areas. As Poland becomes more deeply involved in U.S. programs as a partner, as opposed to just a customer, and develops an advanced defense industrial base that can be competitive in global markets, this attitude may change and its reliance on U.S. systems and products may encounter more resistance.

Intellectual Property Protection

Poland adheres to the major multilateral intellectual property (IP) regimes, including: (i) the WTO Agreement on Trade-Related Aspects of Intellectual Property Rights (TRIPS), which provides core IP protection and enforcement rights (including for trade secrets); (ii) the Paris Convention for the Protection of Industrial Property, covering patents, trademarks and industrial designs; (iii) the Patent Cooperation Treaty, protecting patents; (iv) the Berne Convention, covering copyrights; (v) the Madrid Protocol, covering trademarks; and (vi) the World Intellectual Property Organization.

---

[394] Details on Polish membership and OSCE activities are available at: http://www.osce.org/about/13131.html.

Poland enacted a new Intellectual Property Law in June 2000, which replaced four previous laws covering different aspects of intellectual property (Inventive Activity; Trademarks; Integrated Circuit Patents; and the Patent Office). The new law regulates the protection of inventions by patents and utility models; Polish patent attorneys must represent foreign applicants. Polish law also is compliant with all EU regulations regarding intellectual properties.

Through its new law and other steps, Poland has taken major steps in improving its protection of intellectual property rights. As the U.S. Foreign Commerce Service notes, "Polish authorities have made significant progress in recent years, but the piracy of intellectual property remains a significant problem and Poland remains on the lower level of the U.S. Trade Representative 'Watch' List."[395] Indeed, software piracy remains an endemic problem in Poland as it does throughout Central and Eastern Europe. According to some sources, the piracy rate today approaches 50 percent, which is a considerable improvement over the 71 percent rate reported in 1996. Software piracy will continue to be a problem until the general culture of corruption in Poland abates through the building of robust civil institutions with a high level of social trust.

This study did not uncover any expressions of concern by U.S. defense companies that Poland has not recognized U.S. intellectual property rights or allowed U.S. firms to protect their own background intellectual property.

Technical Standards

Poland is a party to the WTO's Technical Barriers to Trade Agreement, which prohibits discrimination and seeks to ensure that regulations, standards, testing and certification procedures do not create obstacles to trade. However, every country has the right to adopt those regulatory standards it considers appropriate in areas concerning national security. Thus, Poland has the discretion to, and has put in place, its own specific technical standards for defense products that could in theory serve as a non-tariff barrier to competing foreign products.

Given Poland's desire for full NATO interoperability, Poland's military systems and products are closely tied to NATO Standardization Agreements where these exist and EU standards as well. As discussed in Chapter 5, there is some prospect of increased risk that an eventual EU set of standards might become disguised market access barriers—but there is no indication that this is a policy result sought by Poland.

Subject to this general caveat, in the course of this study, we did not learn of any specific situations involving Poland where technical standards were used as non-tariff barriers to protect domestic producers and markets against foreign defense products.

---

[395] *Doing Business In Poland: Country Commercial Guide 2008*, p. 30, U.S. Foreign Commercial Service, U.S. Department of Commerce. Available at: http://www.buyusainfo.net/docs/x_2387888.pdf.

Chapter 11

Accessing the Romanian Defense Market

All of the former communist countries of Central and Eastern Europe face difficult challenges making the transformation to liberal democratic government and free-market economics. While Romania has advanced at a slower pace than others, it has made considerable progress recently. One of the poorest countries in Europe,[396] Romania's development has been hindered not only by the usual problems of inefficient and undercapitalized state industries, endemic graft and corruption, and weak social institutions, but also by the unique legacy of political and financial mismanagement left by the regime of Nicolae Ceaucescu.

Economically and militarily, Ceaucescu pursued a policy of autonomy and centralized control. Ceaucescu's policies required Romania to maintain very large armed forces and to develop design and production capabilities for the full range of military systems, from small arms and ammunition to tanks and armored vehicles to combat aircraft and missiles. By the end of the communist era in 1989, Romania maintained a military force of some 300,000 men and an arms industry that employed more than 200,000 people—all with a population of just 23 million. To sustain this military establishment, Romania became Europe's fourth largest arms exporter—often providing weapons to rogue states and outlaw regimes unable to procure them elsewhere.

After Ceaucescu, a series of democratically elected governments attempted to implement free-market reforms, including large-scale privatization of state-owned industries. These reforms were generally successful over time (with fits and starts) but caused severe unemployment and social disruption. However, the defense industry was generally exempted from these reforms. Hence, the privatization of the defense sector has proceeded at a much slower rate; a large number of defense companies are still either owned or controlled by the Romanian government today.

To counteract unemployment and promote economic growth, the post-Ceaucescu government followed a policy of low interest and tax rates, which succeeded in attracting large amounts of foreign direct investment, but which also generated very high rates of inflation. Inflation peaked at 45 percent in 2000, but austerity programs and currency reform (the New Leu) have reduced inflation to a still high but manageable 6.9 percent. As a result of its low tax burden and investment-friendly environment, Romania has experienced economic growth averaging close to 5 percent since 2001.[397]

Unfortunately, however, this growth is slowing to a halt as the financial crisis has hit Romania particularly hard; its government credit position eroded and its ability to meet its financing needs grew imperiled. On March 25, 2009, Romania secured €20 billion in emergency loans to the International Monetary Fund (€12.95 billion), the European Union (€5 billion), the World Bank (€1 billion) and European Bank for Reconstruction and Devel-

---

[396] Per capita GDP $9,045 in 2006, according to the United Nations Development Program.

[397] Though inflation is apparently under control, Romania runs a high current accounts deficit, which could interfere with its plans to join the Eurozone.

opment (up to €1 billion over two years). The IMF has said this will aid Romania in preparing to enter the Eurozone.[398]

Since the overthrow of Ceaucescu, Romania has sought closer security and economic ties with the West, and in particular with the United States, which Romania views as the ultimate guarantor of peace and stability in Europe. Romania was the first country to sign onto the North Atlantic Treaty Organization (NATO) Partnership for Peace program in 1994, joined NATO itself in 2004, and has participated in NATO exercises and peacekeeping operations ever since, including operations in the Balkans. Romania was a member of the U.S.-led coalition in Iraq, sending some 850 troops to fight alongside U.S. forces. Similarly, Romania became a member of the EU in January 2007 — which required it to bring its laws into compliance with EU standards.

Romania's relationship with the United States is close, but is not on the same plane as the U.S. relationship with Poland. Romania at present has only a limited armaments relationship with the United States. There is no U.S.-Romanian reciprocal defense procurement Memorandum of Understanding (MOU) in place to provide national treatment or the equivalent in acquisitions, and no Declaration of Principles (DoP) fostering closer defense industrial cooperation. (The United States has had reciprocal defense procurement MOUs in place with all of the other countries studied except for Poland, which is being negotiated now.) While Romania would like to elevate its relationship with the United States to that level, the United States has not yet been ready to take these steps.

Romania's relationship with the EU is somewhat more ambivalent. Romania has clearly benefited from its membership in the EU (particularly access to European capital markets and EU development funds). Also, the Romanian government and military view the EU as the emerging center of gravity in European security affairs. However, there is widespread doubt about the ability of Brussels to provide real security for Romania, particularly against a resurgent Russia. Hence, there is a continuing preference for closer ties to NATO and the United States. Further, there is some resentment of European Commission (EC) directives and initiatives, which Romania tends to follow when it sees tangible advantages and treat less favorably whenever these seem to clash with Romanian preferences.

Since 2005, Romania has been attempting to modernize its armed forces and bring them up to NATO standards for capability and interoperability. Intended to develop a "modern, fully flexible, deployable, sustainable military structure capable of conducting a wide range of missions on both national territory and abroad,"[399] the Romanian armed forces transformation plan has three stages culminating in full integration into NATO and the EU.

However, Romania's economic and budgetary environment will make it challenging for Romania to execute its force transformation plan. While growing at a robust pace in recent years, growth and credit are extraordinarily challenged now. Even in the best economic times, Romania's economy is small in absolute terms with a total defense budget of just $3 billion (2.1 percent of gross domestic product (GDP)). With substantial portions of the defense budget dedicated to personnel costs (59 percent) and operations and maintenance

---

[398] BBC News, "Romania Gets IMF Emergency Loan," March 25, 2009. Available at: http://news.bbc.co.uk/2/hi/business/7962897.stm.

[399] "Romanian Defense Policy," Black Sea Defense and Aerospace Exhibition and Conference (BSDA)-2008, Romaero (Bucharest), 2008.

(O&M) costs (22 percent), only 19 percent (about $570 million) is available for "investment" (procurement plus research and technology).[400]

Despite this austere budgetary environment, Romania has an extremely ambitious long-term procurement plan, focused on six "Strategic Programs" equally divided among the Army, Navy and Air Force, pointing to a political compromise ensuring each Service its fair share of the acquisition budget. However, as all six programs are intended to run concurrently, the total annual cost of these six programs alone is likely to exceed the total Romanian defense budget by more than $1 billion per year. Thus, Romania will need to make hard choices as its plan moves forward.

Additionally, there is a strategic disconnect between Romania's long-term defense strategy (focused on expeditionary, out-of-area low intensity conflicts) and its strategic acquisition programs, which are focused on larger systems suited to conventional warfare. More investment is needed in areas like logistics infrastructure and strategic transport systems for Romania to reposition its forces for the low intensity missions it is likely to face in the future. The 2008 Russian invasion of Georgia is causing a reassessment of security needs throughout Central and Eastern Europe, which could lead to a shift in emphasis from expeditionary operations to territorial defense; if this happens, the six strategic programs may gain new relevance.

Within this strategic, budgetary and acquisition context, Romania has reshaped and reformed both the demand and the supply elements of its defense market.

On the demand side, Romania has benefited from a "clean slate," discarding its Soviet-era acquisition system and implementing wide-ranging reforms of the defense procurement process based on U.S. standards and processes (including personnel sent to the United States for training). However, Romanian Ministry of National Defence (MoND) lack of experience and resources has inhibited its ability to manage programs effectively.

Romania's new acquisition policy is based on a modern model of competitive and open procurement. Because Romania, like Poland, has discarded most of its legacy Soviet-era armaments systems, Romania makes fewer sole source purchases of legacy systems than any country in Western Europe. Most Romanian defense contracts are for new programs and are awarded through free and open competition. Moreover, the Romanian market is not only competitive but also largely open to U.S. and other foreign companies due to the need to modernize Romanian forces as quickly as possible and to bring them into compliance with NATO standards.

With its domestic defense industry unable to meet those requirements, Romania is not only willing, it actually has little choice but to buy equipment from other countries, preferably the United States. However, it prefers arrangements whereby systems are either co-produced or assembled in Romania. Available data reflects these realities and shows that U.S. and other European firms have won a significant share of competitive awards in Romania. The availability of attractive financing packages also has proven to give a significant competitive advantage to the United States.

Despite this relatively open environment for U.S. firms, Romania does offer other significant challenges to potential defense market participants. Like Poland, Romania relies heavily on offsets in defense contracts—with some of the highest offset rates in Europe.

---

[400] *Jane's Sentinel, Country Risk Assessment-Balkans, 2008.* Available at: http://www.janes.com/articles/indepth/balk.html.

Romania's offset policies are regarded by Western companies as complex and somewhat capricious in their application. Because they do not facilitate technology transfer or "noble work" for Romanian companies, they also are viewed as counterproductive in the long run for Romanian industry.

Corruption remains a pervasive problem in Romanian society, where bribery is common-place and accepted as a cost of doing business. Although the government has enacted many reforms to bring greater transparency to the public sector, the situation is only modestly better than it was five years ago. Hence, corruption and complex bureaucracy are key factors that limit the effectiveness of its reforms in the defense and other sectors of the economy.

Finally, Romania's relative attractiveness to foreign investors in recent years does not seem to extend to the defense industry—or at least the state-owned element of it. Privati-zation of the remaining state-owned defense companies is lagging badly behind the priva-tization of the civil and commercial sectors due mainly to the unwillingness of potential Western buyers to pay the prices sought by the Romanian government. Romania must either lower its expectations with regard to price or invest capital to make the companies more attractive to foreign buyers. It appears these companies will remain in state hands for the foreseeable future despite ambitious plans for divestiture.

I. Market Background

A. The Legacy of Ceaucescu

The effect of Ceaucescu's rule on the social and economic fabric of Romania cannot be overstated. Even today, 19 years after his overthrow and execution, it is impossible to escape visible reminders of his megalomania and systematic misrule. After coming to power in 1965, Ceaucescu broke with the Soviet Union over the 1968 invasion of Czechoslova-kia and withdrew from active participation in the Warsaw Pact. Ceaucescu developed an independent foreign policy that actively courted Western support through participation in European Community economic agreements. While this won him the label of "liberal reformer" in some Western circles, Ceaucescu's regime became more repressive and Stalin-ist over time.

In the 1970s, Ceaucescu adopted a policy of "systematization" requiring Romania to develop a high degree of autonomy in all sectors of its economy.[401] To pay for this develop-ment, Ceaucescu leveraged his position as a communist "maverick" to borrow more than $13 billion from Western governments and banks. Repaying the interest on these loans had a devastating effect on the Romanian economy. In the 1980s, Ceaucescu passed laws to prevent Romania from incurring foreign debt, which effectively meant plunging much of the population into deep poverty.[402] Together with the lack of social trust engendered by

---

[401] Marked by large-scale demolition of towns and villages, the forced resettlement of populations and construction of "model settlements" designed around Ceaucescu's own theories, the policy was punctuated by a series of gargantuan public works programs (the *Casa Poporului* or People's House in Bucharest is the most infamous) that were monu-ments to Ceaucescu's growing megalomania. Ceaucescu enforced his policies through intimidation by the secret police (*Securitate*), which had extensive networks of informants.

[402] The problem was exacerbated by Ceaucescu's 1966 law to increase the population and punish sterility. This boosted the population from 19 million in 1966 to 23.2 million in 1989, without a concomitant expansion of the economy. Romania's population has since declined to about 22 million, due to reductions in birthrate and substantial out-migration since the 1990s.

Ceaucescu's police state, the endemic corruption fostered by his economic mismanagement may prove to be the most lasting legacy of his misrule, affecting wide swaths of political and economic life.

Effect of Ceaucescu's Independent Defense Policies

Ceaucescu's foreign policy required a very large military to deter Soviet intervention and preserve his independence of action. A large military also became a matter of prestige, a sign of Romania's success that generated international respect. Thus, by 1989, the Romanian military numbered some 300,000 men under arms (475,000 at full mobilization). This force included more than 1,700 tanks, 500+ combat aircraft, 3,000 surface-to-air missiles, six corvettes and numerous smaller naval vessels. The army consisted of no fewer than two tank divisions, seven motorized rifle divisions, two mountain infantry brigades, and an airborne brigade.

This force was maintained by universal conscription (with the exception of the air force, where some two-thirds of personnel were long-term professionals), still generally organized and trained along Soviet lines. Political reliability ranked higher than did competence in the selection of officers, and overall tactical proficiency was rated low by Western analysts, though there were some exceptions, such as the air force.

The Shape of the Romanian Defense Industry

Ceaucescu's break with the Soviet Union meant Romania could no longer depend on its traditional source of armaments, and most especially for spare parts and technical support to keep its existing inventory in operation. Romania thus had to look to alternative sources of supply. Though some equipment was procured from Western sources (notably helicopters and light transport aircraft), Ceaucescu was determined to make Romania autonomous in armaments production. In April 1968, he publicly announced that development of a domestic arms industry was a national priority. By 1985, Romania met more than 70 percent of its armaments requirements from domestic sources. By the end of the communist era in 1989, the Romanian arms industry directly employed more than 200,000 people — almost 1 percent of the total population.[403]

At first, Romania's state armaments factories focused mainly on manufacturing those Soviet systems already licensed for production in Romania. These included the TAB-72, a modified version of the BTR-60 wheeled armored personnel carrier (APC); the TAB-77, a modified version of the BTR-70 APC; the TAB-C, a variant of the BRDM scout car; and the M77 main battle tank. Romania also began producing copies of obsolescent Soviet combat aircraft, including the MiG-15 and MiG-21 (Romania later received small numbers of MiG-23 and MiG-29 fighters from the USSR), and began producing indigenously designed trainers and light attack aircraft such as the IAR-93 Jurao. From the mid-1980s, the Romanian shipbuilding industry also designed and produced six light frigates, numerous torpedo boats, mine sweepers and riverine vessels (for the Danube flotilla).

Romania thus had a broad-spectrum defense industry capable of meeting most of its defense needs, and by the end of the communist era certainly had the ability to develop and

---

[403] S. Vaknin, "Romania's Private Defense," *Global Politician*, Feb. 2007. Available at: http://www.globalpolitician.com/22481-romania.

produce its own indigenous designs. However, the industry was hampered by an impoverished technology base—cut off from the latest in both Soviet and Western designs. Romanian designs were little more than refined versions of increasingly obsolete Soviet systems. In addition, the defense industry was plagued by the inefficiencies that characterized the entire Romanian economy under Ceaucescu: parts and materials were increasingly difficult to obtain, quality control was wildly uneven, and aging factories were overstaffed and had low productivity.

Romanian Defense Exports Under Ceaucescu

Both to sustain the outsized Romanian military establishment, and to pay off its massive foreign debt, Ceaucescu became Europe's fourth largest arms exporter (ninth globally), with exports averaging some $620 million per year by the mid-1980s (about 5-6 percent of total Romanian exports).[404] Aside from small arms, Romanian armaments were generally inferior to those available from other sources, which limited Romanian customers to countries unable or unwilling to buy weapons elsewhere. Key customers included Iraq, Libya, North Korea, Algeria, Angola and Ethiopia, as well as various guerrilla and separatist organizations supported by Ceaucescu.[405] However, as Romanian arms fell further behind the technology curve (and international tensions began to ease with the adoption of Glasnost in the USSR), export sales began to decline, falling to about $250 million per year by the end of the 1980s. The arms industry ceased to be a source of hard currency and became a drag on the Romanian economy.

B. Post-Communist Developments

After the fall of Ceaucescu in December 1989, the provisional National Salvation Front government attempted to implement multiparty democratic government and free-market economic reforms. Widespread social unrest, culminating in deadly riots in Bucharest in June 1990, resulted in the National Salvation Front and led to the development of several major political parties, including the Social Democratic Party, the Democratic Party, and the Alliance for Romania. There are also numerous minor parties, including the Conservative Party and the Hungarian Party.

Since 1990, there have been several peaceful, democratic transitions of government, with one of the major parties ruling either on its own or in coalition with minor parties. Although the major parties each have different constituencies and diverging domestic policies, there is a consensus among them on foreign policy and national security, which is founded on closer cooperation and integration with the West—the cornerstones of which are membership in NATO and the EU.

NATO Membership

Romania views NATO as the foundation of its security in post-communist Europe, as well as the framework around which it must structure its military transformation. To this

---

[404] Stockholm International Peace Research Institute (SIPRI) data.

[405] Romania also traded weapons to Middle Eastern countries in exchange for oil, to supplement the declining production of its Ploesti oil fields and to develop a source of oil independent of the USSR.

end, Romania became the first member of the NATO Partnership for Peace. As the Romanian Military Strategy stated in 2003:

> The system of partnership is currently the best way to prepare the Romanian Armed Forces for integration into a collective security environment. We will actively develop our military relations with the member states, using mainly the opportunities offered by the Partnership for Peace, the strategic partnership with USA and by the special partnerships developed with United Kingdom, Germany, France and Italy. Besides, we shall enhance bilateral cooperation with candidate countries for NATO membership and with the other states capable of supporting our efforts to join the North Atlantic Alliance. With bilateral and multilateral cooperation, our Armed Forces will participate in Combined Joint Task Force exercises and multinational peace support operations. First, we shall contribute with units nominated for peacekeeping, support and service support, and with officers who are experts in civil military relations.[406]

Romania made good on this commitment, participating in a host of NATO operations despite strong domestic opposition, including implementation force (IFOR) and stabilization force (SFOR) operations in Bosnia and NATO operations in Kosovo. Romania was one of the "Coalition of the Willing," providing troops for Operation Iraqi Freedom and the subsequent occupation of Iraq in 2003. At the peak of its involvement, Romania had more than 850 troops in Iraq,[407] including infantry, engineer, intelligence and medical units. Romania also contributed forces to Operation Enduring Freedom in Afghanistan and maintains a contingent of some 570 in that country under the command of the International Security Assistance Force (ISAF). More recently, Romania withdrew it 500 peacekeeping troops from Iraq at the end of 2008 while some additional military personnel will continue to work in an advisory capacity in Iraq through 2009.[408]

Because of Romania's cooperation with the United States in the war on terror, the United States became a forceful sponsor of full NATO membership for Romania at the 2002 Prague Summit—at which Romania was formally invited to join the Alliance. Romania moved rapidly to bring its command, control and communications systems into compliance with NATO standards, assisted by generous loans and grants from the United States and other NATO Allies. Having met the prerequisites, Romania was granted full membership in March 2004.[409]

Since then, Romania has been a full participant in NATO joint planning processes and has accepted NATO force commitments, which form the basis for Romania's long-term defense transformation plan. Recognition of Romania's place in the Alliance was signified by the hosting of the NATO Summit Meeting in Bucharest in April 2008.

---

[406] *Ministerul Aparari* (Ministry of National Defence), Military Strategy (Bucharest) 2003. Available at: http://english. mapn.ro.

[407] Equivalent to some 11,500 U.S. troops on a per capita basis.

[408] "Romanian minister says 500 troops to leave Iraq," AOL (Nov. 7 2008). Available at: http://www.aol.co.nz/celebrity/ story/Romanian-minister-says-500-troops-to-leave-Iraq/1253141/index.html

[409] Bulgaria, Estonia, Latvia, Lithuania and Slovakia also joined the Alliance at this time.

EU Membership and Its Effects

While integration into NATO was seen as essential to Romania's long-term security, integration into the EU was seen as necessary for its long-term economic growth and stability. Romania considers itself a European country, with a western outlook and its closest ties with its European neighbors. In the words of Teodor Melescanu, current Minister of Defense and a former Minister of Foreign Affairs,

> As a Central European country where institutions, political culture and economic life have been—except for the Cold War years—an intrinsic part of Western European democracy, Romania's desire to become a member of the EU (and other European and Euro-Atlantic institutions) is a natural one.[410]

After the fall of Ceaucescu, Romania immediately began taking steps for entry into the EU. This required extensive internal reform, particularly in areas of finance, transparency in government, and the suppression of corruption and organized crime. Romanian officials saw EU integration, and particularly the need to harmonize Romanian laws with EU regulations, as a critical tool for reforming Romanian society, the economy and the government.[411]

The EU accession process, however, was long and difficult, due to insufficient funds, a shortage of trained staff, lack of expertise in EU law and regulations, general government inexperience and inefficiency, an obsolete mindset, and a confused and over-stretched legal system.[412] Gradually, Romanian national law was brought into conformity with EU laws, as seen, for example, in the new Romanian copyright law of March 1996, modeled directly on the EU law and considered "one of the most modern [copyright] laws in Europe" because it was the first to include all relevant EC Directives.[413]

After a long process of internal reform, Romania (together with Bulgaria) was formally approved for EU membership on September 26, 2006, with accession on January 1, 2007. However, significant conditions were attached to the decision. The EU Report noted that both countries still fell short of Western standards in many areas, and economic assistance was conditional upon further progress in suppressing corruption and organized crime, improving the administration of justice, and improving food and aviation safety standards. Romanian and Bulgarian workers would also be restricted in their ability to work in other European countries, particularly Great Britain, Sweden and Ireland, which absorbed a massive inflow of workers from Central Europe during the 2004 expansion of the EU.

Membership in the EU has generally been beneficial to Romania. As noted, the need to harmonize Romanian and EU laws, regulations and standards has been an engine driving internal reforms. Access to EU development funds has assisted in the reconstruction of

---

[410] T. Melescanu, "The Accession to the European Union: the Fundamental Option for Romanian's Foreign Policy," *Romanian Journal of International Affairs*, Vol. 2 No. 4 (1996). M. Ram, "Romania's Reform Through European Integration: The Domestic Effects of European Union Law," Harvard Kennedy School of Government (Cambridge, MA). Available at: http://www.hks.harvard.edu/kokkalis/GSW1/GSW1/20 Ram.pdf.

[411] M. Ram, "Romania's Reform Through European Integration: The Domestic Effects of European Union Law," Harvard Kennedy School of Government (Cambridge, MA). Available at: http://www.hks.harvard.edu/kokkalis/GSW1/GSW1/20 Ram.pdf.

[412] Ibid.

[413] Ibid.

Romania's ravaged infrastructure, and membership in the EU's free trade zone has facilitated trade with other Member States. Romanians generally have a positive view of the EU, but there are several points of friction. Specifically, Romania's fiscal policies of low taxation and easy credit, which have made it a leading destination for foreign direct investment (FDI), have raised issues. With a skilled workforce, low labor rates and a 16 percent flat tax for individuals and corporations, Romania attracted some $12 billion in FDI during 2006, up some 600 percent since 2000. While effective in boosting the Romanian economy, this policy has put Romania at odds with other members of the EU—primarily high-tax-, high-labor-rate states like France and Germany, which are being placed at a competitive disadvantage (and which thus support efforts at "tax harmonization").

Romanian fiscal policies have also jeopardized Romania's objective of joining the Eurozone by 2010 due to failure to meet Maastricht Treaty convergence criteria. The Treaty requires Member States to limit inflation to 3 percent per year. At present, Romania's inflation rate is 6.5 percent, projected to fall to 5 percent in 2010, causing many analysts to believe that Romania's transition to the Euro will not occur before 2014 or thereabouts.

As noted at the outset, the recent financial crisis and Romania's need for emergency financing to maintain its solvency has created significant uncertainty over the future of its economy. Given these circumstances and Romanian desires to enter the Eurozone, the future of "easy credit" and low taxation in Romania remain to be seen.

Romanian officials interviewed concur with the view that the EU is emerging as the new center of gravity for European defense and security affairs. However, they do not see the EU coordinating effectively either with NATO or the Member States in this area. There is a strong belief among Romanian military officials that the EU simply lacks the resources and political will to provide effective defense for Romania against foreign threats (Russia not the least). Thus, they wish to maintain a strong NATO alliance and close bilateral relations with the United States. At the same time, they want a place at the table when the EU discusses defense and security policy, and thus have been active participants in two EU Battle Groups—the Balkans Battle Group (with Greece, Bulgaria, Cyprus and Romania) and the Italo-Romanian-Turkish Battle Group.

Romania has adopted the European Defence Agency (EDA) Code of Conduct on defense procurement. While Romania is not actively opposing the new EC Defense Package, Romanian officials are extremely skeptical of it. They fear that the new EC Defense Procurement Directive will inhibit Romania's ability to use Article 296 of the Treaty Establishing the European Community to protect its vulnerable defense companies. There are also fears that these and future EU initiatives will interfere with the Romanian Offset Law, which is seen as essential to balancing defense trade and providing work share for Romanian defense companies.

C. Reconciling Romania's Limited Defense Budget With its Strategic, Force Transformation and Acquisition Needs

Romania spends between 2.1 and 2.4 percent of its GDP on defense, which is greater than the NATO requirement of 2 percent and better than the European NATO average of 1.9 percent. However, the Romanian economy at this point is so small that this amounts only to some $3 billion per year, as shown in Figure 107. Given the IMF's very modest March 2009 projection for economic growth for Romania of -1 to -1.5 percent a year, the outlook

Figure 107   Romanian Defense Expenditure, 2002-2007 (Billions of Dollars–$)

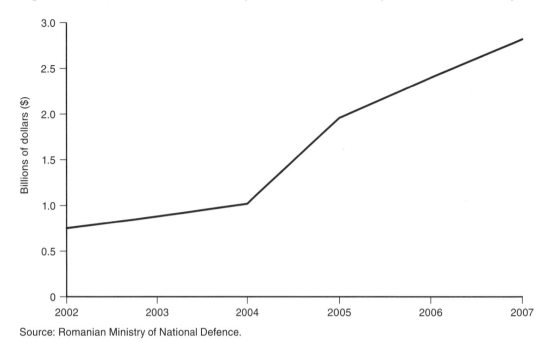

Source: Romanian Ministry of National Defence.

for increased budgets is relatively grim.[414] Higher budgets are likely only if Romania could return to the type of sustained economic growth it enjoyed in recent years—which is not likely in the short term.

Romania's dilemma is reconciling its limited defense budget with its extensive strategic, force transformation, and acquisition requirements.

Defense Budget Insufficiency and the Need for Foreign Military Assistance

It has been estimated that meeting Romania's immediate requirements for complete NATO interoperability—a strategic imperative—would require an expenditure of perhaps $4.5 billion per year for 3 to 5 years—as much as the total defense budget. The situation is much more difficult, however, because Romania has had to allocate about 59 percent of its defense budget to personnel expenditures, a result of the end of conscription, the need to provide support services and pensions for separated officers, and the need to raise salaries and living conditions for the new volunteer force. Once O&M expenditures are deducted, only about 19 percent of the budget is available for investment in new equipment—little more than $570 million per year.

---

[414] *China View*—Business, March 19, 2009. Available at: http://news.xinhuanet.com/english/2009-03/19/content_11032902. htm. The IMF's report said the Romanian budget deficit might be higher than 4 percent of the GDP, significantly above the 3 percent Maastricht Treaty threshold, according to Mihai Tanasescu, a former Finance Minister from Dec. 2000 to Dec. 2004.

Romania therefore is heavily dependent upon foreign military assistance and other forms of aid, such as donations of surplus military equipment, in order to make ends meet. As discussed further below, the United States has provided the bulk of military assistance to Romania, including $435 million in Foreign Military Sales (FMS) credits provided between 2002 and 2006. Germany also has provided assistance (donating several Gepard self-propelled air defense systems from surplus).

Yet, even with its U.S. and other foreign assistance, Romania will face hard choices as it moves forward with its strategic, military transformation, and acquisition plans.

Strategic Posture

According to Romania's 2005 Military Strategy, the main threats facing Europe are international terrorism, instability in critical resource areas, and low intensity conflicts creating humanitarian crises. Romania sees itself playing a positive role in cooperative security arrangements to enhance global stability, reducing the threat of major conflicts. At the same time, Romania recognizes it faces regional threats in its own back yard, be it renewed ethnic conflict in the Balkans or military aggression by Russia on the Black Sea. As the Military Strategy says, Romania "lies at the crossroads of four strategic evolutions win the following areas":

- Central Europe—a future pole of regional prosperity
- South-Eastern Europe—a source of instability
- Commonwealth of Independent States—currently undergoing an identity crisis
- Black Sea—an area of strategic importance for NATO's southern flank, as well as a transit for energy resources from Central Asia[415]

To meet the requirements for territorial and regional defense, Romania is focusing on airspace management and control, early warning against attacks by air or sea, rapid reaction forces to respond to sudden threats, and the ability to fight interoperably with NATO, EU and other allied forces in a major regional conflict. At the same time, Romania is developing the capability to project and sustain forces in out-of-area contingency operations, as part of a coalition of nations.

These divergent objectives drive divergent Romanian requirements for force transformation and equipment acquisition in the context of serious budget limitations, which, as noted above, will necessitate hard choices as Romania begins modernizing its forces.

Force Structure and Organizational Reform

According to the Romanian 2005 Military Strategy, force transformation is structured based on five strategic objectives:

- Development of a credible national defense capability;
- Fulfillment of Romania's commitment to NATO;
- Contribution to European Security and Defense Policy;

---

[415] Military Strategy, op. cit.

Figure 108   Romanian Armed Forces Troop Levels, 1989-2007

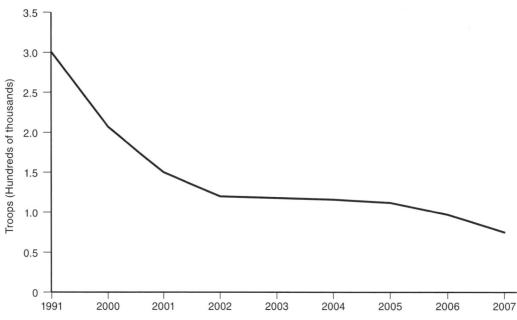

Source: Romanian Ministry of National Defence, IISS Military Balance.

- Projection of regional stability and security; and
- Participation in the fight against terrorism.[416]

To achieve these goals, Romania has adopted a 3-phase, 20-year defense transformation plan:

- Phase I (2005-2007): Complete basic restructuring of armed forces
- Phase II (2007-2015): Modernization to become fully NATO/EU-interoperable
- Phase III (2015-2025): Modernization to become fully NATO/EU-integrated

With the first phase just completed, Romania has achieved some significant accomplishments. The most noteworthy is a massive reduction in force and the transition from a conscript to an all-volunteer force. As noted, in 1989, the Romanian military had no fewer than 300,000 troops under arms (not counting reserves and paramilitary forces); by the end of 2008, the Romanian armed forces will have reached their end-state goal of a 75,000-man force. The reduction in troop strength was accomplished quite rapidly, as shown in Figure 108.

Romania's force modernization has had costs. Volunteer forces are inherently more expensive than conscripts, since the military must offer competitive pay and benefits, as well as a reasonable standard of living, in order to attract quality recruits. In addition, a smaller professional force does not need the large officer cadre of the previous conscript force. Surplus officers, as career professionals, had to be provided with retraining, job placement, new housing, and in some cases, pensions. This has caused a short-term bulge in Romania's military personnel budget, placing a strain on funds for procurement and operations.

---

[416] Military Strategy, op. cit.

Table 50   Romanian Army Organization, 2007

Units	Active	Territorial	Total
Corps Headquarters	1	2	3
Division Headquarters	2	0	2
Tank Brigades	1	1	2
Mechanized Brigades	3	6	9
Mountain Brigades	1	2	3
Airborne Brigades	1	0	1
Artillery Brigades	1	2	3
Air Defense Brigades	1	2	3
Logistic Brigades	1	0	1
Engineer Brigade	0	1	1
Total Brigades	**9**	**14**	**23**

Souce: IISS Military Balance.

Romania has also adopted a new, streamlined force structure intended to integrate into larger multinational coalitions. In place of the old 10-division army of the Ceaucescu era, the new Romanian army consists of independent brigades as shown in Table 50.

Romania's small, antiquated Air Force has only limited combat potential at present. Its nominal inventory includes some MiG-21 fighters, trainers and transport aircraft that were a Soviet-era legacy, a fleet of assault and transport helicopters (including the EADS Puma), and more recently systems from the United States, as described below.

The Romanian Army maintains a very large inventory that includes 1,258 main battle tanks, 84 assault guns, 177 infantry fighting vehicles, 1,585 armored personnel carriers, 1,238 artillery pieces and rocket launchers, 9 surface-to-surface missile launchers, and 64 surface-to-air missile launchers. Most of these weapons are more than 20 years old, built to obsolete Soviet designs, and require extensive modernization to meet NATO interoperability standards.

The Romanian Navy operates on both the Black Sea and the River Danube. Its command structure consists of one fleet headquarters (Black Sea) and one flotilla headquarters (Danube). Its present inventory consists of 3 frigates, 4 corvettes, 3 missile patrol boats, 12 motor torpedo boats, 38 patrol craft, 1 minelayer, 10 mine countermeasures ships, and 10 support vessels. Most of these date to the communist era and must be replaced over the next

5 to 8 years. Romania recently took possession of 3 ex-Royal Navy Type 22 Frigates at a cost of some $225 million.[417]

Acquisition Priorities

During the first phase of the Romanian defense modernization (the basic restructuring of the armed forces), Romania's major acquisitions focused on bringing command, control and communications systems into conformity with NATO standards; this included the re-equipping of all major unit headquarters, provision of new tactical radios, and revised logistical support systems. One cornerstone of the modernization is the new Air Sovereignty Operations Center (ASOC), which networked the Romania early warning system, the air traffic control system, the ground controlled intercept system, and the land-based air defense system to provide a single integrated air picture.

At the same time, Romania needed to meet urgent needs for its troops operating in Iraq and Afghanistan. To this end, the U.S. provided Romania with surplus C-130 transports, to allow Romanian forces to self-deploy to the combat areas, as well as additional C4ISR (command, control, communications, computers, intelligence, surveillance and reconnaissance) equipment, combat ID systems (to avoid fratricide) and force protection systems (body armor, improvised explosive device detection equipment, armored vehicles, etc.).

With the first phase of the modernization plan considered complete, Romania will now begin focusing on bringing its forces up to full interoperability with NATO and EU forces. In addition to continuing to modernize its C4ISR systems, Romania has identified six "strategic programs" that form the centerpiece of its long-term modernization plan:

- Modernized main battle tanks

- New armored personnel carriers

- Acquisition of up to 48 multirole combat aircraft

- New search-and-rescue helicopters

- Modernization of its three ex-British Type 22 Frigates

- Acquisition of four new multirole corvettes

In discussions with Romanian MoND and Ministry of Economy and Finance officials, it was clear that these six programs were determined by consensus of the armed services, none willing to be excluded from the modernization bandwagon. Thus, each service was allowed to place two of its priorities on the list of strategic programs, and it was determined that all the programs would be implemented concurrently.

Funding all of these priorities concurrently is not possible. Their combined cost is estimated to exceed $9 billion at a time when the entire Romanian defense budget is barely more than $4.5 billion, and the acquisition budget barely more than $550 million per year. Yet prioritizing the six programs, or better still, revisiting the list, has also become politically difficult. Hence, all six programs will be allowed to go forward until it becomes impossible

---

[417] This sale created a political controversy in Romania when it was revealed that the Netherlands had offered to sell similar frigates to Romania at a cost of some $40 million each. It is also alleged that Romania will have to spend an additional $250 million to fully modernize and equip these ships. See D. Leigh and R. Evans, "We Paid Three Times Too Much for UK Frigates, Romania Says," *The Guardian*, June 13, 2006.

to ignore the looming funding shortage. The first major test of the "strategic programs" concept will probably come in 2009, when Romania awards a contract for new multirole fighters (see below)—in the context of the ongoing financial crisis.

Complicating the problem still further is the need to support Romania's deployed forces and their immediate operational needs. While the final withdrawal of Romanian forces from Iraq may have lessened the burden, Romania still has troops supporting ISAF in Afghanistan and others in NATO, EU and United Nations (UN) peacekeeping missions around the globe.

II. Romanian Defense Market: Demand and Supply Dynamics and Reform

Acquisition and industrial reform, together with the military transformation plan discussed above, are considered three essential elements of an overall strategic transformation aiming at Romania's full integration into the Western European security system.

Romania's defense "demand" and "supply" side reform efforts are aimed at addressing several pressing problems simultaneously:

- Overcapacity and obsolescence in the defense industry, particularly in the remaining state-owned defense companies;

- Inefficiency and lack of transparency in the defense procurement process; and

- Endemic corruption, which still plagues the defense sector.

A. Acquisition System (Demand) Reform

Like most other Central European countries, Romania has had to develop an effective and modern defense acquisition system essentially from scratch—working on a largely clean slate on the "demand" side of its defense market.

Under the communist command economy, the government served in multiple roles: customer, producer, supplier and agency regulating the costs. After Ceaucescu withdrew from the Warsaw Pact command system, Romania, unlike the other Warsaw Pact countries, had full authority over what it produced and for whom. In contrast, the other members of the Pact had to produce to meet Soviet-defined plans. Romania was also able to develop a full range of design and production capabilities, which gave its military some degree of flexibility in setting requirements and specifications. On the other hand, defense planning under Ceaucescu could be arbitrary and capricious, as well as riddled with corruption and inefficiency from top to bottom.

For some years after the fall of Ceaucescu, the old system continued to operate—largely out of inertia. However, with the transition to a free-market economy and accession to the EU, it became necessary for the Romanian government to bring its defense procurement process into line with Western norms. It therefore had to learn how to formulate requirements, issue requests for proposals, evaluate tenders, make awards and manage programs in a transparent and cost-effective manner. In 1998, Romania adopted a procurement system based largely upon U.S. Department of Defense (DoD) Directive 5000.2—to the point of simply translating large sections of the regulations from English into Romanian. A number of senior Romanian defense officials were sent to the United States to be certified as defense acquisition professionals. Upon their return, they began training programs to develop a cadre of acquisition professionals to staff the new Romanian procurement system.

Under the new procurement system, the Armaments Department of the MoND is responsible for all defense acquisition, formulating requirements with assistance of the general staff and the different inspectorates (armor, artillery, infantry, air, naval, etc.). The Armaments Department then generates requests for proposal, conducts proposal evaluations, and makes contract awards. In theory, all major acquisitions are supposed to be competitive. However, as many programs are legacies of the communist era, work related to these existing systems is almost automatically directed to the state-owned or formerly state-owned enterprises that have responsibility for a particular system.

As fully discussed below in the analysis of market access metrics, awards for most new or substantially modified systems are made on both an open and a competitive basis. However, some major organizational and management challenges hamper Romania's ability to achieve its defense acquisition reform goals.

One problem is a lack of coordination between the Armaments Department and industry—mainly the result of recent legislation against corruption, which makes government officials fearful of contacts with industry that may create the appearance of impropriety. This, combined with a general lack of experience in the Romanian acquisition community, often results in requirements that are either unnecessary or unreasonable—leading to excessive cost and delay, and occasionally excluding otherwise qualified bidders.[418]

Even assuming a higher level of experience among the acquisition corps, there are simply too few professionals to manage all of the new programs being initiated by the Romanian military as it moves into Phase II of its modernization plan.

Several other major organizational and management dysfunctions affect the operations of the Romanian acquisition system. First, the MoND has no oversight over the defense industry and thus cannot coordinate its actions to facilitate research and development (R&D) or otherwise maximize efficiency. That task resides with the Ministry of Economy and Finance, which also has oversight of state-owned defense companies (a potential conflict of interest), and has little understanding of defense acquisition and military requirements in any case.

Second, the MoND has no equivalent to the Defense Contracts Audit Agency (DCAA) to audit and certifies the rates of actual and potential bidders over time. Instead, every bidder must be audited anew with each bid, creating a bottleneck in the acquisition process and multiplying paperwork.

Third, each new Romanian government has a tendency not to stand behind the procurement decisions of its predecessors. Because Romania has not adopted multiyear budgeting for major procurements, this creates turbulence at the beginning of each fiscal year—especially if an election is pending or has just resulted in a change of government. Thus, a company might have won a contract in the previous year that requires three years to complete. At the beginning of each year, it must have the budget for that program validated and approved. If a new government has or is about to come into office, officials at the Arma-

---

[418] One U.S. company related that it wanted to bid on a 4×4 tactical vehicle for Romanian forces in Iraq, but had to withdraw because the requirement, derived from a NATO Standard Agreement, required the vehicle to be amphibious. As it turned out, only one company produced an amphibious vehicle of that type.

ments Department tend to delay that approval pending a decision by the new government on whether to proceed.

On occasion, while not canceling a program outright, the new government might decide the old government had been too generous in its terms and insists on renegotiating the contract. This problem is exacerbated by the government's tendency to put all risk on the shoulders of the contractor. Should, for example, the cost of some raw material—steel, aluminum, petroleum, etc.—suddenly experience a price increase due to market forces, the MoND usually does not allow the contractor to raise his rates to compensate. Either the contract must be renegotiated—a long and tedious proposition—or the company must simply absorb the cost out of its profit. These practices create turbulence and uncertainty in major programs, which has a tendency to scare off potential bidders and raise costs to the Romanian government in the long term.

B. Defense Industrial Reform

With the fall of Ceaucescu, the Romanian defense industry underwent a startling collapse. According to the Romanian Ministry of Industry and Trade:

> Starting with 1990, following the structural changes in the world arms market and the politic economic and social transformation in Romania, this sector has entered an increasing decline. The drastic decrease of the demand on the world market and lack of local orders, the low level of technology automation and labour productivity, associated with an improper management were the main factors which have led to this situation. Privatization was started, with some performing companies sold to private local investors.[419]

Privatization of state-owned *civil and commercial* enterprises proceeded relatively smoothly in the 1990s. Under the Privatization Law of 1991, some 6,000 state-owned enterprises were to divest the contents of their portfolios in seven years. By 2000, almost all commercial state-owned enterprises had been totally or mostly privatized; by 2007, the Romanian government held no significant ownership interest in the commercial sector.[420]

Matters were very different in the *defense* sector, however. First, the state itself was both the owner and the main customer for the state-owned defense companies. Second, the products of these companies had only a limited and highly regulated market. Third, its products and facilities were obsolete and unprofitable, therefore unlikely to attract foreign capital. Finally, with more than 200,000 employees, the defense sector was too large and too important, both strategically and economically, to allow for an uncontrolled restructuring.

The Romanian government in effect performed a triage on its defense industry, determining which companies could immediately be privatized under the terms of the Privatization Law; which companies would need extensive restructuring before being divested; and which companies either (1) could not be made attractive for privatization in the near term or (2) would be held as "strategic assets."

---

[419] Statement of the Ministry of Industry and Resources, quoted in Vaknin, op. cit.

[420] J. Earle and A. Telegdy, "Privatization Methods and Productivity Effects in Romanian Industrial Enterprises," Upjohn Institute Staff Working Paper No. 02-81, W.E. Upjohn Institute for Employment Research (Kalamazoo, MI), April 2002. Available at: http://ideas.repec.org/a/eee/jcecon/v30y2002i4p657-682.html.

Thus, eleven defense companies were sold immediately to local investors in the early to mid-1990s. Twelve others, scheduled for later privatization, had non-core businesses closed or sold off, factories converted to commercial production, and excess personnel laid off to make them more attractive to investors; among these were producers of ammunition, vehicles, electronics, aerospace and ships. These remain under the control of the Romanian State Ownership Fund, as described under III. Evaluation of Market Access Metrics later in this chapter.

An additional remaining 15 companies, plus one research institute, were bundled into the Romanian National Company ROMARM S.A. (RomArm), described by several analysts as "an opaque and ubiquitous state holding group."[421] These tend to be the most unreconstructed, least efficient companies, which survive mainly through sole-source procurement and government-directed work share under the Romanian Offset Law (see below).

Romania today has some eleven private defense firms that together form the Romanian Business Association of the Military Technique Manufacturers (PATROMIL), a non-government trade organization for the promotion of the Romanian defense and aerospace industries. Among the more important of these are:

- Aerostar S.A., a manufacturer of aerobatic and trainer aircraft, aircraft components and upgrade and overhaul services for commercial and combat aircraft. Aerostar is a major maintenance contractor for the Romanian air force and several commercial carriers. Aerostar has a 60/30 joint venture with Thales Communications in Aerothom Electronics, a producer of defense and civil electronics systems. Aerostar is also minority partner in a 51/49 percent joint venture with Elbit Systems called S.C. AE Electronics S.A., which has had great success developing and marketing custom upgrades of MiG-21 fighters.

- Turbomecanica S.A., a manufacturer of aircraft engines, helicopter gearboxes, rotor heads and components, as well as a provider of helicopter maintenance, repair, overhaul and upgrade services.

- MFA Mizil, specializing in the maintenance, upgrade and repair of tanks and other armored fighting vehicles for the Romanian military and export customers.

- S.C. Roman S.A., a producer of military and commercial trucks.

At present, the Romanian defense industry is still oriented toward providing the needs of the Romanian military. According to PATROMIL figures provided in Table 51, the Romanian defense industry had sales revenues of about $125 million in 2005, of which only $36 million or 20 percent were from exports. At the same time, Romania imported approximately $155 million in defense goods, more than the total sales revenues of all domestic companies combined. As discussed above, Romania was able to import large dollar amounts of equipment in large part due to U.S. FMS credit sales and grants; the indigenous Romanian acquisition budget would not have covered these purchases.

At this point, Romanian defense exports are at a low dollar value, consisting mainly of small arms and ammunition and aircraft upgrades and overhauls. While the vast number of licensed transactions involve small arms and ammunition, aircraft upgrades provide much greater value added and account for almost half of all export revenues. Romania has been

---

[421] Vaknin, op. cit.

Table 51   Romanian Defense Market (Millions of Dollars—$)

	2003	2004	2005	Total
Total Market Size	184.0	202.8	244.3	631.1
Total Local Production	107.5	88.8	125.0	321.3
Total Local Production for Domestic Market	71.5	69.6	89.0	230.1
Total Exports	36.0	19.2	36.0	91.2
Total Imports	112.5	133.3	155.3	401.1
Total Imports from U.S.	10.1	35.7	38.1	83.9

Source: ROMARM S.A. and ROHMTEHNIC S.A.

extremely successful in that field due to its highly trained and technically proficient aerospace industry and low labor rates, which allow Romanian companies to offer quality work at a fraction of the costs in Western Europe. Servicing and upgrades of both military and commercial aircraft represent one of the few bright spots in the Romanian defense industry. As shown on Table 51, total Romanian exports had a one-year dip in 2004 but increased in 2005 to $36 million (as in 2003).

Recognizing that the survival of most Romanian companies depends on large infusions of foreign sales or investment capital, the Romanian government is encouraging Romanian defense companies to enter into strategic partnerships and joint ventures with foreign companies, a policy reinforced by the provisions of the Offset Law. Some of these joint ventures such as Aerothom Electronics and S.C. AE Electronics have been fairly successful. Others, such as the General Electric/Turbomecanica joint venture GE/Turbomecanica S.A., have yet to be proven.[422]

There is a general consensus that Romania must do more to make its defense industry attractive to foreign investors, much of which hinges on the success and direction of Romania's defense modernization plan and its integration into the European defense system.

C. U.S.-Romania Defense Trade and Industrial Cooperation

Legal Framework for U.S.-Romanian Cooperation: The 2005 Defense Cooperation Agreement

In December 2005, then-Secretary of State Condoleezza Rice meet in Bucharest with Romanian President Traian Basescu, and signed a bilateral defense cooperation agreement that allowed for the joint use of Romanian military facilities by U.S. troops. In May 2007, the Parliament of Romania ratified the agreement by a wide margin—despite some very vocal opposition to the basing arrangement. The first proof of principle exercise took place at Mihail Kogalniceanu Air Base from August to October 2007.

---

[422] Though the presence of a qualified GE engine overhaul and maintenance facility in Romania could prove highly lucrative if Lockheed Martin's F-16 wins the upcoming Romanian Multirole Fighter Competition.

Figure 109   U.S.-Romania Defense Trade, 2002-2006 (Millions of Dollars–$)

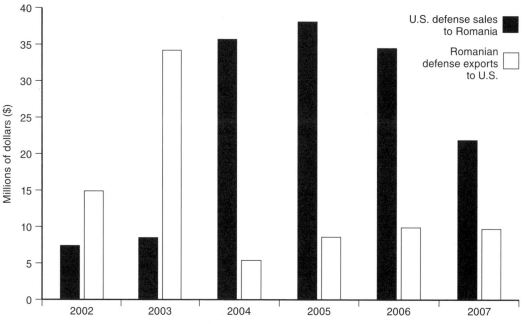

Source: U.S. Department of State; U.S. Department of Defense; Romanian Defense Exports Agency.

At this point, the United States does not have any plans for permanent basing of U.S. combat forces in Romania. Nonetheless, several bases in Romania are being upgraded to U.S. standards. Also, Romania's strategic position near the Black Sea has suddenly achieved new salience after Russia's invasion of Georgia, an event that has also changed Romania's position regarding ballistic missile defenses on its soil. In 2003, Romania strongly denied talking to the United States about such a program, and political opposition was strong. But after the signing of the missile defense agreement with Poland, many in Romania are reconsidering the strategic and economic advantages of participation in any U.S. or NATO-sponsored program.

Significantly, the United States has not yet entered into reciprocal defense procurement MOU with Romania (like the one recently signed with Poland and in force in other European countries) or a DoP on deepened industrial cooperation. According to its officials, Romania greatly desires such agreements. It recognizes that the reciprocal defense procurement MOU would give it preferential treatment in the U.S. market, including exemption from the Buy American Act. There is no indication at this time that the United States is seeking to negotiate such an agreement, given the ongoing problems with Romania's compliance with EU and international norms regarding transparency, corruption and organized crime.

The U.S. and Romania began defense cooperation as early as the mid-1990s, but the process was greatly accelerated by the attacks of September 11 and Romania's emergence as one of the key U.S. Allies in the war on terrorism and the occupation of Iraq. It includes significant U.S. military assistance as well as developing U.S. sales to Romania of a variety of systems.

As reflected in Figure 109, U.S. defense sales to Romania have been somewhat episodic, but grew notably in 2003-2004, during the early period of the Iraqi conflict. Eager for any show of support from Europe, the United States provided Romania with the funds and equipment it needed to deploy and support forces in both Iraq and Afghanistan. Much of this was provided through the FMS program—Romania received $135 million from FMS from 2002-2006—as well as from transfers of surplus military equipment. The United States provided training for Romanian officers and technicians to increase professionalism in the Romanian forces, including specialized counterterrorism training for Romanian special forces. The United State also helped Romania establish a Romanian Non-Commissioned Officers Academy to elevate the professionalism of the non-commissioner officer (NCO) corps, and paid to train several hundred Romanian officers and NCOs at military institutions in the United States.

Direct commercial sales by U.S. companies from 2002-2006 totaled about $130 million—slightly less than FMS contracts. Lockheed Martin (LMT) has by far been the most successful company in this regard, mainly through sales of the FPS-117 and TPS-79 ground-based air surveillance radars. Romania bought additional radar systems from Lockheed Martin in 2007 and 2008, and contracted with Lockheed to provide system integration and logistic support for its air surveillance system. LMT has also provided maintenance, repair, overhaul and upgrade services for C-130 aircraft donated by the United States.

Perhaps most significantly, in December 2006, Romania selected the Lockheed Martin Alenia Tactical Transport Systems (LMATTS) C-27J Spartan tactical transport aircraft over the similar EADS C.295. The contract for seven aircraft is worth some $293 million over five years. LMATTS is a joint venture between Lockheed Martin and Alenia Aerospace formed in 1996 to develop an improved version of the G.222 transport to meet the U.S. Joint Cargo Aircraft requirement. As is normally the case in such deals, much of the work will be performed in Romania by Romanian companies to meet offset requirements.

The U.S. relationship with Romania deepened and matured as U.S. and Romanian officials worked closely together on issues related to terrorism, Iraq and Afghanistan. As early as 2003, there were rumors of discussions concerning the basing of U.S. forces in Romania, a development welcomed by some Romanians but strongly opposed by others.[423]

Although the United States remains Romania's most important military supplier, Romania has also been developing defense industrial ties with European nations and other countries, both to meet its domestic requirements and to bolster its defense technology base. The deepest relationship has been with the Israeli firms IAI and Elbit, which together with the Romanian companies Aerostar S.A. and SC A.E. Electronics, developed the MiG-21 Lancer upgrade for the Romanian air force and export customers. In addition, Elbit has also worked with Romanian companies on Mi-8 helicopter upgrades and the MiG-29 Fulcrum "Sniper" upgrade.

Romania has close ties to EADS-Eurocopter through a series of Ceaucescu-era helicopter production licenses that spawned a thriving upgrade market. Romania also relies on Thales for much of its command, control and communications equipment. At the subsystem level, the Romanian military has a broad supplier base that includes European, American, Russian, Ukrainian and Israeli companies.

---

[423] See, e.g., T. Fuller, "Romania Dangles Use of a Sea Base to Woo U.S.," *International Herald Tribune*, June 18, 2003.

Modernizing Romanian Defense Forces: The U.S. Role

U.S. defense firms have significantly participated in the Romanian defense modernization plan (although the size of most contracts has been small compared to our trade with other countries). Among the U.S. companies presently active in Romania are:

- AAI Corporation: Shadow 600 Tactical Unmanned Air Vehicle (TUAV)

- Honeywell (legacy Allied Signal): IAR-99 Soim trainer/light attack aircraft avionics

- Harris Corporation: MLI-84M Infantry Fighting Vehicle Upgrade Program; STAR-Radio tactical communications system

- ITT Corporation: Technical Ground Assistance System for Air Navigation

- Lockheed Martin Corporation: Gapfiller Radar Program; National Air Command and Control System

- Mason: IAR-99 Soim trainer/light attack aircraft subsystems

- Northrop Grumman Park Air Systems: Technical Ground Assistance System for Air Navigation

- Northrop Grumman: Consulting services for MoND

- Trimble: IAR-99 Soim trainer/light attack aircraft navigation system

- BoozAllen & Hamilton: Preliminary study of SCOMAR

- General Dynamics Land Systems (via Canadian Commercial Corp, partnered with BAE OMC So. Africa): Mine Resistant Ambush Protected (MRAP) Vehicles

Other U.S. companies, including GE, have ongoing joint ventures with Romanian companies. Despite this evolving trade, only one U.S. company—Lockheed Martin—has a permanent presence in Romania through its local business office (but has no local production facilities); other firms deem the market too small and manage their Romanian portfolios through offices in Warsaw, Berlin or Rome. Lockheed Martin has become a major participant in the Romanian defense market based on sales of its FPS-117 radar system and its integration of the ASOC and the national air command and control system. If Lockheed manages to win the upcoming Romanian fighter competition with the F-16 Falcon, its footprint and that of its suppliers will grow exponentially.

The Romanian Fighter Competition and Its Fallout

Romania's fleet of MiG-21 Lancer aircraft is approaching the end of its fatigue life, and the Romanian air force has identified the acquisition of some 48 new multirole fighters as one of its "strategic programs." Romania began investigating the possibility of acquiring new fighters back in 2003, but became serious only in the last quarter of 2007 when Defense Minister Teodor Melescanu indicated that Romania would select its next fighter through a competitive procurement involving five aircraft:

- Lockheed Martin F-16 Block 52 Fighting Falcon

- Eurofighter Typhoon

- Saab JAS.39 Gripen

- Dassault Rafael

- Boeing FA-18E Hornet

The estimated cost of the 48 aircraft is between $4 and 4.5 billion, including training and logistics support. The aircraft must achieve operational capability with the Romanian air force no later than 2011, at which time the Lancers must be withdrawn from service.

At present, the competition, focused primarily on cost and performance, seems to have been narrowed down to three aircraft: the F-16, the Eurofighter and the Gripen. Commonality might have played a role in this process, given that the F-16, the Gripen and the Typhoon are all in use by Romania's close neighbors and allies. The aircraft apparently eliminated from the competition, the FA-18 and the Rafael, have no similar user base in Central and Eastern Europe. Given the severe economic crisis in Romania, it remains to be seen if Romania will move forward with the program, defer its decision or cancel it entirely. The prospect of such a large buy was already causing consternation even prior to the crisis. In July 2008, the Romanian Secretary of State for Defense Policy, Corneliu Dobritoiu, stated "[w]e aren't so rich as to be able to buy everything our armed forces might need." He indicated that perhaps half of the fighter budget might be spent on other priorities such as helicopters, APCs and unmanned aerial vehicles.[424] The matter has exposed divisions between the Atlanticist President Traian Basescu, and the more Eurocentric Prime Minister Calin Popescu Tariceanu. Whether the Georgia situation will cause Romania to look more toward territorial defense as opposed to expeditionary operations remains to be seen.

In any event, Romania certainly cannot afford to buy 48 multirole fighters without significant offset and financing arrangements. Given the cost of the program, price and financing arrangements will be the key to winning, as was the case with the Polish fighter competition won by Lockheed Martin. Romania will be looking for an offset package at least as lucrative as that offered by Lockheed for the Polish program, and financing support as well. According to market participants, Lockheed ultimately won the Polish contract not only because of its $9 billion offset commitment, but because the U.S. government offered very creative financing arrangements for Poland including low interest rates, deferred payments, and a loan buydown option. Taken with the offset program, the financing arrangements allowed Poland to acquire F-16s with relatively little money out of pocket—a major consideration for small countries with equally small procurement budgets.

However, it is unclear whether the global credit crisis will constrain the ability of the U.S. government to offer financing terms as generous as those offered to Poland—which no other government was able to match. Still, the prospect of a strong Lockheed offer (with a U.S. financial package) is prompting some of the other competitors to look at more ingenious incentives. Italy, backing the Eurofighter team, has proposed buying the Romanian company Avioane Craiova, and turning it into a Typhoon logistics center, at which the Romanian aircraft would be assembled and serviced; it left open as well the possibility of the Romanian logistics facility servicing Typhoons from other countries.[425] Lockheed Martin could potentially match that kind of offer. Moreover, its engine supplier, General Electric, already has a joint venture in Romania for the overhaul and repair of jet engines.

---

[424] T. Escritt, "Defense Options Put Romania in the Hotseat," *Financial Times*, July 2, 2008.

[425] "Italy Pitches Romanian Eurofighter Offset," *Defense News*, Nov. 5 2007.

Should Lockheed Martin win, the American footprint in Romania will grow considerably as will U.S. investments in Romanian defense companies through the offset requirements. A U.S. win therefore will strengthen considerably the depth and breadth of U.S.-Romania defense industrial cooperation and opens the door for much closer political and strategic cooperation as well.

Areas of Contention

At present, there are relatively few areas of contention between Romania and the United States. The illegal sale of small arms and ammunition to embargoed countries and organizations, which had been a major problem in the 1990s, has been largely addressed by the adoption of EU and international codes of conduct and the implementation of a rigorous export control regime (see below).

Romania remains strongly pro-American in sentiment and Atlanticist in outlook, but there is considerable pressure brought upon the relationship due to domestic Romanian political concerns. If one party is pro-American, the opposition tends to reflexively adopt a pro-European stance. Under the circumstances, minor disagreements can get blown way out of proportion.

Future Outlook

Despite considerable challenges—from an inefficient and antiquated defense industry to weak social institutions to corruption—Romania is definitely moving toward a place in the community of European countries while simultaneously maintaining close relations with the United States. The potential for these relations to grow deeper and broader in the near term hinges on several variables. First, at a macro level, the prospect of a re-emergent, militarily threatening Russia may convince Romania that only a closer relationship with the United States can ensure its security and independence. Second, a key driver is whether the United States entry wins the fighter competition. Finally, there is the question whether Romania decides it wants to participate fully in a European missile defense system; these will help shape the extent of bilateral cooperation.

It should be recognized that Romania's increasingly close integration into the EU creates a natural pressure from other European countries to present a united front, including giving preference to European solutions in defense procurement. Romanian government officials reported they are frequently "encouraged" in EU meetings to give preference to European solutions, especially for "big ticket" items, such as aircraft, radars, armored vehicles, etc. Romanians, however, are independent-minded and can be expected to carefully weigh their own interests before moving one way or the other. The 2006 selection of the Lockheed Martin-Alenia C-27J Spartan tactical transport over the EADS G.222 provides one example of Romanian independence from the EU (albeit the C-27J is based on an Italian design). The outcome of the Romanian Multirole Fighter competition could be yet another.

III. Evaluation of Market Access Metrics

Tariff Barriers

By and large, tariffs are not significant barriers between Romania and the United States although Romania is somewhat disadvantaged relative to other European countries studied.

Specifically, all of the countries studied are members of the World Trade Organization (WTO) and thus must provide most-favored nation and national treatment to imported goods from every other country included in the study.[426] Although defense products are generally exempt from WTO rules governing tariffs and trade, the United States has entered into reciprocal defense procurement MOUs with most of its European Allies that generally provide duty-free treatment for imported defense products procured from the other country. Of the European countries studied, however, Romania stands out (along with Poland) as a country that has not yet entered into such an MOU with the United States.

Thus, U.S.-Romanian defense trade (like U.S.-Polish defense trade) is somewhat more burdened than U.S. defense trade with the other European countries studied—although the applicable tariff rates are relatively low and not much of a trade impediment. Because of this distinction, Romania (like Poland) has a lower score on tariff barriers than do the other countries examined.

Moreover, in any event, these MOUs do not apply to dual-use products and technologies such as general aerospace systems that have both military and civil applications. Thus, as more military programs rely on commercial off-the-shelf technology, this would tend to put U.S. companies at a competitive disadvantage *vis-à-vis* European firms that get the benefit of the lower intra-European rates that apply under EU rules unless specific exemptions are negotiated on a bilateral basis.

Competition in Procurement

Romanian Procurement Policy: Writing on a Clean Slate

As noted above, Romania essentially adopted the core elements of the U.S. acquisition system when it discarded its legacy Soviet system. Under Romanian defense procurement law and policy, most systems and products must be competitively procured and are open to the United States and other international sources of supply. As Romania is seeking to rapidly modernize its armaments, its policy is to entertain proposed solutions from whatever source may offer the best prices or financing (including offsets as discussed below).

Romanian Procurement Practice: Understanding the Data

In practice, as shown below, the available data on Romanian procurement awards confirms that most Romanian buying is based on competitive awards of new systems, with a

---

[426] Romania's Most-Favored Nation (MFN) status has undergone several major changes. In 1988, Ceaucescu repudiated the MFN agreement between Romania and the United States, resulting in prohibitive U.S. tariffs on Romanian imports. In 1993, the U.S. Congress restored Romania's MFN status in a new bilateral trade agreement. In 1994, tariffs on Romanian goods dropped to zero with the inclusion of Romania in the Generalized System of Preferences. There were then no tariffs on U.S. exports to Romania.

Table 52   Romania—Defense Programs, 2006-2008 (Millions of Dollars—$)

Program	Type	Prime Conractor	Country	2006	2007	2008	Total	Award Type	Legacy
BAC 1-11	Transport	BAE SYSTEMS	UK	0.10	0.09	0.07	0.27	Sole Souce	Yes
L-39ZA	Trainer	Aero Vodochody	CZ	0.08	0.07	0.06	0.22	Sole Source	Yes
ATROM	SP Artillery	Aerostar S.A.	RO	0.06	0.06	19.82	19.94	Sole Source	Yes
An-30	Transport	Antonov	RU	0.35	0.30	0.25	0.90	Sole Source	Yes
An-26	Traqnsport	Antonov	RU	0.29	0.25	0.21	0.74	Sole Source	Yes
An-24	Transport	Antonov	RU	0.10	0.08	0.07	0.25	Sole Source	Yes
ARO 24	Tac Vehicle	ARO SA	RO	3.09	3.20	3.30	9.60	Sole Source	Yes
ARO Dragon 1/2/3	Tac Vehicle	ARO SA	RO	3.09	3.20	3.30	9.60	Sole Source	Yes
IAR-99	Trainer Acft	Avioane SA	RO	0.66	32.59	20.64	53.89	Sole Source	Yes
SA.330L Naval Upgrade	Helicopter	IAR SA	RO	0.00	38.16	38.16	76.32	Sole source	Yes
SA.330L	Helicopter	IAR SA	RO	0.99	0.85	0.71	2.55	Sole Source	Yes
T-55	MBT	Kharkiv Morozov	UK	0.73	0.65	0.56	1.94	Sole Source	Yes
T-72	MBT	Kharkiv Morozov	UK	0.17	0.15	0.13	0.44	Sole Source	Yes
M1974 (2S1)	SP Artillery	Romania/Veh/Ind'ty	RU	0.01	0.00	0.00	0.01	Sole Source	Yes
MIG-21	Fighter	RSK-MIG	RU	0.85	0.72	0.60	2.17	Sole Source	Yes
R-27	Missile	Russia/Msl/Ind'ty	RU	0.35	0.30	0.25	0.89	Sole Source	Yes
R-73	Missile	Russia/Msl/Ind'ty	RU	0.31	0.30	0.28	0.89	Sole Source	Yes
BRDM2	AFV	Russia/Veh/Ind'ty	RU	0.07	0.06	0.05	0.17	Sole Source	Yes
SU-100	Assault Gun	Russia/Veh/Ind'ty	RU	0.03	0.03	0.02	0.08	Sole Source	Yes
R-862	Radar	Yaroslavl Radio	RU	0.01	0.01	0.00	0.02	Sole Soure	Yes
Romania NMCC	C2 System	Northrop Grumman	US	0.32	0.32	0.32	0.96	Competitive	Np
Romania Destroyer ICS Upgrade	Ship	Aeromaritime Grp	NG	0.08	0.08	0.08	0.23	Competitive	No

Program	Type	Prime Conractor	Country	2006	2007	2008	Total	Award Type	Legacy
RAT-31DL	Radar	Finmeccanica	IT	12.03	12.47	0.87	25.37	Competitive	No
Romania FICIS	Comms Syst	Finmeccanica	IT	2.87	2.87	2.87	8.62	Competitive	No
44SG Mk II	IR Sensor	FLIR Systems	U.S.	0.30	0.30	0.30	0.91	Competitive	No
Piranha IIIC	AFV	General Dynamics	U.S.	0.00	67.70	1.86	69.56	Competitive	No
RF-5800 Software Defined Radios	Radio	Harris	U.S.	0.73	0.70	0.68	2.11	Competitive	No
TPS-117/TPS-77	Radar	Lockheed Martin	U.S.	5.03	4.92	4.82	14.76	Competitive	No
FPS-117(V) and/or Variants	Radar	Lockheed Martin	U.S.	0.72	2.68	2.64	6.04	Competitive	No
Romania AF Infrastructure C2	C2 System	Northrop Grumman	U.S.	0.10	0.10	0.10	0.30	Competitive	No
Romania Frigate ICS	C3I System	Rohde & Schwarz	GE	0.16	0.16	0.16	0.47	Competitive	No
Saur B33 8×8	AFV	Romania/Veh/Ind'ty	RO	12.08	41.75	1.47	55.30	Competitive	No
B33 8×8	AFV	Romania/Veh/Ind'ty	RO	13.69	13.35	13.01	40.04	Competitive	No
Romania SIAAB	C2 System	Systematic	DK	10.58	10.78	10.97	32.33	Competitive	No
C-Flex Combat System	C2 System	Terma A/S	NO	13.90	6.04	0.33	20.27	Competitive	No
Panther Radios	Radio	Thales	FR	4.19	5.59	5.70	15.48	Competitive	No
TPS-73 MMSR	Radar	Lockheed Martin	US	34.44	35.70	36.95	107.09	Competitive	No
Zimbru 2000	AFV	Romania/Veh/Ind'ty	RO	20.99	18.89	0.00	39.88	Competitve	No
LAROM C2	C2 System	Aerostar S.A.	RO	0.02	1.10	0.51	1.63	Sole Source	No
Type 996	Radar	BAE SYSTEMS	UK	0.87	0.87	0.87	2.61	Sole Source	No
AH-1RO	Attack Helo	IAR SA	RO	0.03	0.02	0.02	0.07	Sole Source	No
Gepard	SPAAG	Krauss-Maffei	GE	22.45	26.43	1.33	50.21	Sole Source	No
C-130 Hercules	Transport	Lockheed Martin	US	0.28	0.26	0.23	0.77	Sole Source	No
GFE Actf Engine set for C-130B	Engine	Rolls-Royce	UK	0.03	0.02	0.02	0.07	Sole Source	No
Type 1007	Radar	Smiths	UK	0.09	0.09	0.09	0.28	Sole Source	No

Source; Documental Solutions.

Figure 110   Romania—Procurement Programs by Award Type

Figure 111   Romania Legacy vs. New Procurement

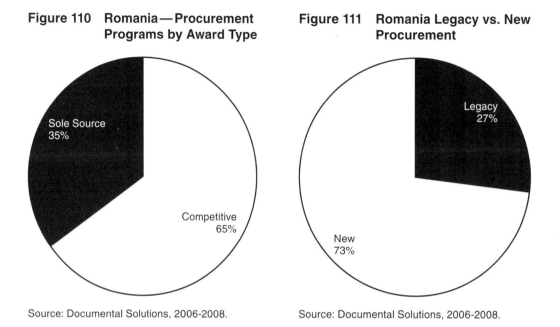

Sole Source
35%

Competitive
65%

Legacy
27%

New
73%

Source: Documental Solutions, 2006-2008.

Source: Documental Solutions, 2006-2008.

modest amount of sole source legacy buying from primarily Romanian suppliers. The Romanian market also is very accessible to U.S. suppliers, which have a considerable market share.

- **Romanian Buying of Major Weapons Systems: The Prevalence of Competition.** As set forth on Table 52 and Figure 110, from 2006-2008, some 65 percent of all Romanian defense contracts were awarded competitively ($429.7 million) and only 35 percent ($236.5 million) were awarded on a sole source basis.

- **Sole Source Buying Mostly Romanian.** Almost all Romanian sole source contracts in this period were for legacy systems, awarded mainly to government-owned defense enterprises that were the original prime contractors and, hence, the only available source of parts and technical expertise. Some of these awards also are intended to sustain these enterprises that otherwise face a limited market for their products.

- **Limited Romanian Spending on Legacy Systems.** As shown in Figure 111, only some 27 percent ($181 million) of Romanian defense procurement is directed toward legacy programs; 73 percent ($495 million) was for new systems, reflecting Romania's ongoing wholesale replacement of Ceaucescu-era equipment. Therefore, Romania, like Poland, spends considerably less on sustaining these old systems and applies most of its resources on systems and products to modernize its force. Not surprisingly, the largest Romanian programs are new buys—e.g., the TPS-73 radar, Pirhana IIIC and Saur B33 armored personnel carriers, Zimbru 2000 tactical vehicle and the Romania SIAAB command and control system. This is in stark contrast to Western European countries studied, which typically spend more on legacy platforms that remain in service for many years.

- **New Romanian Buys Are Even More Competitive.** As set forth on Figure 112, a separate analysis of "new" Romanian buying (i.e., awards on new programs started in 2006-2008) shows that some 89 percent of all contracts ($440 million)

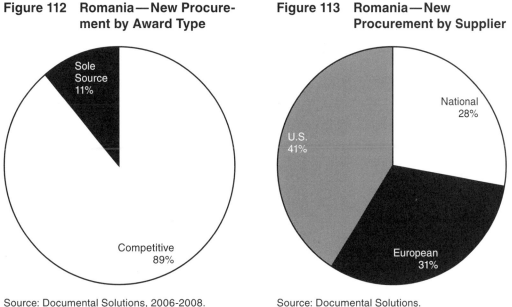

Figure 112   Romania—New Procurement by Award Type

Sole Source 11%

Competitive 89%

Source: Documental Solutions, 2006-2008.

Figure 113   Romania—New Procurement by Supplier

National 28%

U.S. 41%

European 31%

Source: Documental Solutions.

were awarded through free and open competition, while just 11 percent ($56 million) were sole source. Together with Poland, Romania has the highest percentage of competitive procurement of all countries studied. This is in stark contrast to Romanian legacy procurement, all of which has been awarded on a sole source basis. Indeed, of new programs awarded to national companies, 98 percent were awarded competitively.

- **New Competitive Buys Are Clearly Open to U.S. and European Firms.** Most, if not all, of the new Romanian competitive awards were open to U.S. firms. Indeed, Figure 113 shows that U.S. firms won 41 percent of new competitive buys ($202 million) while European companies won 31 percent ($155 million) and national companies only 28 percent ($137 million). This suggests a rather evenhanded approach in which Romania is open to both European and U.S. defense products. As Romania is seeking to acquire newer Western technology and meet NATO requirements, it often has little choice but to open itself to U.S. and other European sources, or other global sources (e.g., Israel), in supplying new products.

- **Market Share Data Confirms a Sizable U.S. Participation.** As shown on Figure 114, from 2006-2008, U.S. firms captured roughly 30 percent of the all major Romanian programs by value, with Romanian firms accounting for 46 percent and other European countries combined some 25 percent. U.S. firms Lockheed Martin and General Dynamics won 19 percent and 10 percent, respectively, of all major programs in that period. However, it should be recognized that the U.S. competitive success partly reflects the extent to which the United States has provided generous grants and financial assistance. Also, the considerable market share of Romanian firms in part reflects the effect of the Romanian offset law, which does result in considerable subcontract work being directed toward Romanian defense companies.

Figure 114   Romania—Defense Market Share by Company

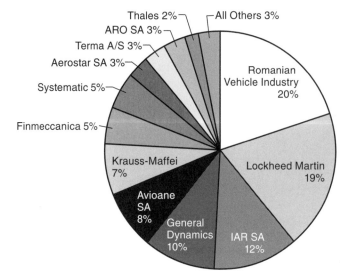

Source: Documental Solutions.

- **Romanian Buying From U.S. Firms Is Largely Through Competitive Awards.** Additionally, in contrast to Western Europe (where U.S. suppliers have traditionally received significant sole source awards), U.S. participation in the Romanian defense market is almost entirely through competitive awards. As shown on Figure 115, approximately 99.5 percent of U.S. suppliers' awards in Romania were made competitively, with only 0.5 percent made on a sole source basis.

- **Virtually No European Cooperative Engagement.** Finally, in contrast to Western European nations, Romania has no participation to date in European cooperative programs. Of course, Romania only joined NATO in 2004 and has had little opportunity or funds to join into major European cooperative programs—many of which have been underway for some years. This may change in the future as geopolitical and economic considerations drive Romania toward this approach, which has become a major element of defense spending in Western Europe.

In sum, no matter how the data is evaluated, Romania shows a clear pattern of open and competitive awards—with U.S. defense sales to Romania increasing since 2002 (Figure 108), and U.S. firms bidding and winning on a sustained basis since 2006 (Table 51).

Fair and Transparent Procurement Process

In general, the Romanian defense procurement system is fair and transparent on paper but in reality is still very much a work in progress.

Romania, like other EU Member States, is a party to the WTO Agreement on Government Procurement (AGP). However, its procurement of "warlike" goods is exempt from the AGP's coverage and, hence, only "non-warlike" goods are subject to the Agreement's disciplines.

Figure 115   Romania—U.S. Wins by Award Type

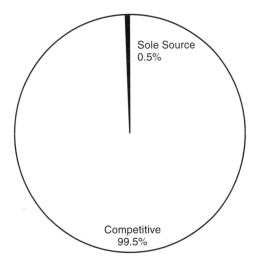

Sole Source
0.5%

Competitive
99.5%

Source: Documental Solutions.

Romania also adopted the EC Public Procurement Directive as a condition of its accession to the Union, but as is the case with most Member States, it deliberately exempted defense procurement from the regulation, to maintain freedom of action in defense industrial policy.

As noted above, the Romanian military and the Ministry of National Defence are largely based on U.S. regulations and procedures; Romania has implemented a wide-ranging reform of the defense procurement process, based on the DoD Directive 5000.2, *Operation of the Defense Acquisition System*, and has sent personnel to the United States for training as acquisition managers.

On paper, the Romanian system thus conforms to both U.S. and EU standards for fairness, openness and transparency. In practice, according to market participants, rules generally are applied fairly, but sometimes inappropriately or in too literal a manner due mainly to inexperience and a lack of resources in the defense acquisition system. Romanian authorities often compile requirements and tenders in a simplistic, mechanical fashion without regard to what industry can provide. U.S. companies have reported that this has on occasion inadvertently excluded U.S. products from consideration.[427] U.S. companies did not attribute this to a deliberate exclusionary policy, but primarily to inexperience and an unwillingness to consult with industry before drafting specifications for new systems (which they attributed to a fear of the appearance of collusion between the government and industry). Further, while U.S. firms complained about the slow Romanian bureaucracy, they admitted it was

---

[427] For example, Romania procured a light armored vehicle for use in Iraq, but included among the specifications a requirement for amphibious operation, even though there is no operational need for amphibious capability in Iraq, because that capability was incorporated into a NATO standard. U.S. companies had several viable candidates for the program that were subsequently excluded because they lacked amphibious capability; in fact, only one (European) vehicle met that specification, and thus won the competition by default, despite being inferior in several other areas, as well as more expensive.

equally slow for everyone, and they have not experienced regulations being applied in a discriminatory or exclusionary manner.

U.S. company representatives also raised concerns about the inability of the Romanian defense procurement system to manage multiyear procurements, and the frequent unwillingness of new governments to stand by contractual arrangements made by the previous government, leading to lengthy and costly renegotiations. The Romanian government prefers that firms assume all risks, and thus does not generally include escalation clauses in its contracts, making companies liable for cost fluctuations in raw materials, labor, etc. Romania lacks anything resembling the DCAA, and thus rates are reviewed from scratch for every contract award; repeated audits are costly and time-consuming, causing much frustration among suppliers.

That said, both U.S. government and industry representatives indicate the process for competitive procurements is codified and reasonably open and transparent. Budgets, programs, and procurement plans are all available as public documents through government websites; tenders and contracts are posted on government sites and the MoND increasingly uses the EDA Electronic Bulletin Board. Most expect the Romanian procurement system to become more transparent and efficient as the Romanian procurement agencies become more expert and better resourced.

Domestic Content Requirements

Romania does not have any explicit domestic content laws or regulations. In theory, the Romanian government is indifferent to the source of its defense equipment. In practice, it recognizes that the survival of the Romanian defense industry during the period of transition depends on its ability to generate work share from foreign companies. Thus, Romania's stringent Offset Law (see below) effectively serves the purpose of a domestic content law by funneling work from foreign suppliers to Romanian defense companies.

Offsets and *Juste Retour*

The Romanian Offset Law of 2003, modeled on the Polish Offset Act of 1999, requires all foreign military purchases of more than €5 million over a three-year period to include a minimum of 80 percent offsets, of which at least half must be direct offsets to the Romanian defense industry. It also mandates that all foreign companies wishing to bid on Romanian defense tenders must already have some previous investment in Romania (not necessarily in the defense sector). This "pre-offset" requirement is a kind of "anti-carpet bagging" feature, intended to ensure that companies bidding on Romanian defense programs have a long-term commitment to development in Romania. However, it does represent a barrier to market entry, the significance of which varies with the size and nature of the companies trying to enter. Large companies find it to be inconvenient and inefficient—they can meet the requirement by pushing work toward a Romanian company or by setting up a joint venture or Romanian subsidiary. Smaller companies can find it financially prohibitive, particularly if they are pushing niche products for which there is not much of a market outside of the military.

Offsets are administered by the Offset Office of the Ministry of Economy and Finance, which negotiates the terms of each offset arrangement. Offset credits are determined by a formula that multiplies the face value of an offset transaction by a factor ranging from 0.5 to 5.0, as determined by the Offset Office. The factors are heavily weighted in favor of direct offsets and work share arrangements, many of which are directed toward RomArm, the state-owned defense holding company. Thus the Offset Law serves as a de facto domestic content law, since the path of least resistance for most foreign defense companies is to subcontract to or team with a local Romanian company, regardless of qualifications.

According to the U.S. Department of Commerce, Romanian offsets have averaged 87.1 percent of contract face value since 1998. Given the way in which the multiplier formula is applied, the actual face value of offsets commitments is probably substantially higher—perhaps two or three times the nominal contract value.

Indirect offsets in the form of investments in Romanian companies (defense and non-defense) is not favored by American companies because of the difficulty in performing due diligence in the absence of financial transparency. Because this approach effectively reduces the Romanian partner to a "build to print" shop, it also defeats the ostensible purpose of the Offset Law, which is to create meaningful partnerships with foreign companies, promote technology transfer, and improve the skill set of the Romanian defense industry by engaging in "noble work" with high value added.

On the other hand, several U.S. companies have found ingenious ways of utilizing Romanian companies that result in value added on both sides. In one example, a Romanian company approached the U.S. company with a concept for an electronic device needed by the Romanian army. The U.S. company had a proprietary component, but the Romanian company had done all the necessary design work. The U.S. company obtained an export license to sell the component to the Romanian company, obtaining offset credits for the full face value of the Romanian company's contract with the Romanian army.

In a second example, a company negotiated an offset deal to install an environmental facility for the Romanian government based on the catalogue price of systems in the company's commercial sector. Because margins in the commercial sector are much higher than in the defense sector, the company got leverage for its offset commitment roughly equivalent to what could be obtained by a work share agreement (i.e., the company got credit for the list price of the system, which actually cost the company only 25 percent of list). In addition, the company also negotiated an agreement to operate the facility through a Romanian subsidiary, thus garnering more offset credits and ensuring positive cash flow from the project in later years. This kind of arrangement was possible only because the company had a substantial commercial business that was willing to cooperate with its defense business to make the arrangement work. For most "pure" defense companies, this kind of arrangement is simply too complex.

U.S. companies raise concerns mainly about the complexity of the Offset Law formula for calculating credits, which is not particularly transparent; and also about the amount of bookkeeping needed to keep track of the credit account. On the other hand, it affects all companies equally and thus is not a discriminatory factor against the United States alone.

Table 53   State Ownership and Control of Romanian Defense Companies

Company	Government Percent (%)	Golden Share	Other Owners	Notes
Aerostar SA	0.00	Yes	IAROM (65%); SIF Moldova (11%); PAS Aerostar (5%); Others (19%)	Maker of trainer aircraft and aerospace components. Privatized in 2000
Aerotherm Electronics	0.00	Yes	Aerostar SA (60%); Thales Communications (30%); Others (10%)	JV of Aerostar and Thales; golden share via Aerostar
Avioane Craiova SA	19.07	Yes	Aerovodochody 80.93%	Aero Vodochody acquired majority stake in Julu 2008
Eurocopter Romania	49.00	Yes	EADS Eurocopter (51%)	Government stake via IAR Brasov
IAR Brasov	64.80	Yes	Publicly held (35.2%)	Majority stake held by Romanian State Ownership Fund
Romaero SA	27.00	Yes	Britain-Norman Group (73%)	Majority stake sold off in 1999
ROMARM SA	100.00	Yes	None	Has 16 subsidiary companies, including one R&D center. Main producer of tanks, armored vehicles, air defense systems and ordnance
SC AE Electronics SA	0.00	Yes	Elbit Systems, Ltd. (51%)	JV of Aerostar and Elbit for aircraft overhaul
Turbomecanica SA	0.00	No	Employees Assn Turboact (62.54%); others37.46%	Aircraft engine manufacturing and overhaul

Source: DACIS Database.

Government Ownership

As discussed above, the Romanian government still owns or controls large segments of the Romanian defense industry. Despite concerted efforts at privatization, there are just eleven privately held defense companies in Romania. Fifteen state-owned companies and one R&D center, remain under the control of the RomArm holding company. A number of other companies are partially government-owned.

To date, the rate at which the remaining state-owned defense enterprises are being divested has been much slower than originally anticipated. And, for the future, these firms probably will be difficult to divest. Several factors account for this, including the limited market appeal of most Romanian products, the inefficient and antiquated nature of the firms' facilities, and the unwillingness of the State Ownership Fund and the Treasury to accept terms and conditions being offered by prospective commercial buyers. In one recent transaction, the Romanian Authority for State Assets Recovery rejected an offer by Euro-

Table 54   Recent Foreign Mergers and Acquisitions (Millions of Dollars–$)

Date	Company	Buyer	Country	Price	Revenues	Notes
July 2008	Avioane Craiove	Aero Vodochody	CZ	26	NA	80.93% Stake; Romanian government holds remaining shares.
May 2004	Elettra Communications SA	Finmeccanica	IT	6.20	NA	51% Stake in JV with ROARM and its subsidiaries (49%)
April 2002	GEAE/ Turbomeccanica SA	General Electric Co.	U.S.	NA	NA	50% Stake in JV with Turbomeccanica SA of Romania
Feb 1999	Romaero SA	Brittain Norman	UK	21	NA	B-N acquired 73% stake from government

Source: InfoBase Publishers, Defense Mergers and Acquisitions Database.

copter SAS (a division of EADS) to buy the government's 64.9 percent share in IAR Brasov, a state-owned helicopter company with which Eurocopter and its predecessors have had a working relationship dating to the 1970s—despite the fact that Eurocopter was the only bidder. Specific reasons for the rejection included inadequate contribution of cash for working capital, inadequate environmental investments and a lower than expected price. A previous attempt by Eurocopter to buy Brasov in 2000 was also rejected.[428]

Moreover, even after divestiture, the Romanian government frequently retains "golden shares" in otherwise privately held firms that gives it control over strategic decisions affecting the company's management. The use of golden shares reflects an apparent government policy to retain control over the strategic direction of certain defense companies in critical sectors such as aerospace, but not in others such as electronics or small arms. Since Romanian companies frequently engage in joint ventures, both with each other and with foreign companies, this also has resulted in the government having a golden share in the joint venture (e.g., where the formerly state-owned company happens to be the majority shareholder in the joint venture).

The current state of government ownership of defense firms is shown in Table 53.

Foreign Direct Investment

According to the U.S. Commercial Service,[429] Romania has become an attractive destination for foreign direct investment as a result of the government's policies of low taxation and easy financing terms. Of course, this situation is in flux due to the financial crisis. Yet, even in the better environment of recent years, Romania has had difficulty attracting foreign investment in the defense sector for a number of reasons: the relatively poor quality and value of Romanian defense companies, many of which are wholly or partly state-owned; the

---

[428] InfoBase Publishers' Defense Mergers and Acquisitions Database.

[429] U.S. Commercial Service, *Doing Business in Romania: 2008 Country Commercial Guide for U.S. Companies*, U.S. Department of Commerce (Washington, D.C.), 2008, pp. 82-87. Available at: http://www.buyusa.gov/romania/en/doing_business_in_romania.html.

fact that the Romanian government has been a difficult negotiating partner when foreign companies are offering to buy; and the difficulties in conducting meaningful due diligence. All companies wishing to invest in Romanian defense industries must undergo governmental review for financial soundness, ethics and suitability. When the company being bought is owned by the government, the State Ownership Fund has at times set excessive or unreasonable conditions on the sale with regard to price, levels of investment, workforce guarantees, etc. While there have been a few foreign acquisitions in Romania (see Table 54), others have foundered because of these preconditions. These include the 1999 attempt by Textron to buy helicopter company IAI-Brasov, which was also the target of two failed takeover attempts by Eurocopter.

Ethics and Corruption

Systemic internal corruption is one of the lasting legacies of the Ceaucescu era. As the Romanian economy collapsed due to his policies, people took to bribery, kickbacks, and black marketeering just to survive. These tactics were practiced even by those running the system, so that corruption became an accepted part of life. This did not end when Ceaucescu fell. In the chaos of the transition to democracy, the old ways endured because they were effective in helping people get by.

As a condition for acceptance into the EU, Romania was required to suppress corruption, improve transparency in government, and crack down on organized crime. Since the mid-1990s, a succession of Romanian governments has implemented anti-corruption acts and embarked on a number of highly visible prosecutions for corruption. Yet corruption remains a serious problem.

Thus, today the World Bank's worldwide governance indicators show Romania in the 50 percent range for both rule of law and control of corruption—low scores.[430] Romania also ranks 69th on Transparency International's 2007 Corruption Perceptions Index, one of the worst records in Europe—worse than Poland and Bulgaria and almost on the same level as Serbia and Georgia.[431] Although Romania has brought its laws and regulations governing corruption and transparency into line with EU law, the problem remains significant and will only abate over time as a new culture grounded in the rule of law emerges.

Because attitudes toward corruption have become embedded in Romanian culture, change in Romania requires nothing short of a change of the culture itself. This is likely to come only as Romania modernizes its overall system of governance and becomes fully integrated into the greater global economy and Western political system, which does not accept corruption as a way of life. Thus, effectively addressing corruption is going to take considerable time to accomplish—perhaps an entire generation. That said, the situation is significantly better than it was a decade ago, which highlights how truly bad it was.

---

[430] See World Bank Governance Indicators, 1996-2007 (Country Data Report for Romania, 1996-2007). Available at: http://info.worldbank.org/governance/wgi/pdf/c.186.pdf.

[431] Transparency International's Corruption Perception Index. Available at: http://www.transparency.org/news_room/in_focus/2008/cpi2008/cpi_2008_table.

The head of the Romanian division of Transparency International recently aptly summed the situation up. "In everyday Romanian life," he said, "bribes have long been necessary as a second wage. They are not thought of as corruption which should be acted on."[432]

U.S. companies doing business in Romania do not report corruption as a serious problem for them since everyone with whom they do business understands that they will not violate the Foreign Corrupt Practices Act. Thus, U.S. firms are apparently not approached for bribes or kickbacks to any significant extent, according to interviews conducted. Other Western countries, with more ambiguous policies, have a greater problem working in Romania. U.S. companies indicated that they frequently have problems making their Romanian subcontractors and suppliers conform to U.S. codes of conduct.

Corruption creates several other problems for U.S. companies. The lack of transparency in financial records, for instance, makes it very difficult to conduct due diligence on many Romanian companies, which in turn discourages U.S. firms from using investment in otherwise attractive Romanian businesses as a way of fulfilling offset obligations. Providing local work share to domestic firms remains the safest and easiest approach, even if it yields smaller economic rewards for all sides.

With respect to illicit payments in third-country markets, Romania is not a signatory to the OECD Convention on Combating Bribery of Foreign Public Officials in International Business Transactions but is a party to numerous other agreements such as the UN Convention Against Corruption and the Council of Europe Civil Law Convention on Corruption and Criminal Law Convention on Corruption. There also is little data available on Romanian companies having any involvement in illicit bribery in third-country markets. The lack of data probably has more to do with the relatively small size of Romania's exports rather than any type of commitment to ethical conduct.

Export Controls

The Romanian System

During the early 1990s, Romania had an unhappy reputation as an arms supplier to various unsavory regimes, separatist movements and terrorist organizations, particularly with regard to small arms and infantry weapons. However, Romania has today very much shed this unfortunate legacy and has a working export control system in place.

In preparation for joining the EU, Romania became a signatory to the EU Code of Conduct, the Council of the European Union Joint Action on Small Arms and Light Weapons, the Organization for Security and Co-operation in Europe (OSCE) Criteria on Conventional Arms Transfers, and the OSCE 2000 Document on Small Arms and Light Weapons.[433] Romania also is a member of major multilateral export control regimes, including the Nuclear Suppliers Group, the Australia Group, the Missile Technology Control Regime, the Wassenaar Arrangement on Export Controls for Conventional Arms and Dual-Use

---

[432] A. Müller, "Romania: A Wealth of Poverty," Café Babel, *European Current Affairs Magazine* (Jan. 18, 2007). Available at: http://www.transparency.org/news_room/corruption_news/ti_in_the_news/2007.

[433] OSCE Criteria on Conventional Arms Transfers is available at: http://www.sipri.org/contents/expcon/oscecat. html. OSCE Document on Small Arms and Light Weapons is available at: http://www.osce.org/fsc/13281.html.

Goods and Technologies and the Chemical Weapons Convention. The core principles embodied in these agreements have all been implemented in Romanian national law.

The EC Transfers Directive recently adopted by the European Parliament is a further step in aligning the policies of EU countries regarding intra-Community transfers and simplifying procedures to permit such transfers among Member States and certified defense companies. The focus of this Directive is intra-Community transfers of defense-related products and, thus, the main beneficiaries of reduced barriers within the EU are European defense companies. It is not at all clear that U.S. firms will be eligible for similar treatment; this is a matter for national authorities to decide.

Under Romanian law, all military and dual-use products and technology must receive export licenses from ANCEX, the Romanian National Agency for Export Controls. An independent agency of the Ministry of Foreign Affairs, ANCEX maintains extensive databases on all arms companies doing business in Romania, tracking all of their production by serial numbers. Whenever military or dual-use materials are exported, the defense company must apply for a license that details the items being exported, the number of items, the cost, and the end user, which are used to ensure that shipments are not diverted to proscribed countries and organizations, or resold once in the hands of the authorized customer.

The Romanian system is very detailed and rigorous on the front end because Romania lacks the diplomatic personnel and contacts to effectively monitor shipments on the receiving end. According to Romanian officials, there have been no identified egregious violations or serious complaints about Romanian exports since 2005.

ITAR Attitudes and Behaviors

Romanian authorities had little to say regarding U.S. export control laws, due mainly to Romania's position as a net importer of U.S. defense products with little by way of exports or co-development/production with the United States. This may change if Romania should at some point develop a competitive defense export market, but at this time issues related to the U.S. International Traffic in Arms Regulations (ITAR) and other export regulations have little relevance to the question of access to the Romania defense market.

Intellectual Property Protection

Romania adheres to the major multilateral intellectual property (IP) regimes, including: (i) the WTO Agreement on Trade-Related Aspects of Intellectual Property Rights, which provides core IP protection and enforcement rights (including for trade secrets); (ii) the Paris Convention for the Protection of Industrial Property, covering patents, trademarks and industrial designs; (iii) the Patent Cooperation Treaty, protecting patents; (iv) the Berne Convention, covering copyrights; (v) the Madrid Protocol, covering trademarks; and (vi) the World Intellectual Property Organization.

However, Romania remains on the U.S. Trade Representative watch list for IP rights due to weak and ineffectual enforcement. The U.S. Commercial Service notes while "flagrant trade of retail pirated goods largely has been eliminated… personal use of pirated products and software remains high."[434] The U.S. government is working closely with Romania to

---

[434] 2008 Country Commercial Guide for Romania, op. cit.

reduce IP violations by holding seminars for law enforcement on cybercrime, by creating a new task force in the Romanian Ministry of Justice to prosecute IP rights enforcement, and by facilitating closer coordination between governmental and non-governmental entities responsible for monitoring IP rights violations.[435]

Despite such reports of lax enforcement, U.S. defense companies have not raised with us during the course of our study any specific complaints regarding IP protection in the Romanian defense market or any concerns over the ability of U.S. firms to protect their own background IP.

Technical Standards

Romania is a party to the WTO's Technical Barriers to Trade Agreement, which prohibits discrimination and seeks to ensure that regulations, standards, testing and certification procedures do not create obstacles to trade. However, every country has the right to adopt those regulatory standards it considers appropriate in areas concerning national security. But given Romania's desire for full NATO interoperability, Romania's military systems and products are closely tied to NATO Standard Agreements where these exist. As discussed in Chapter 3, however, there is some prospect of increased risk that an eventual EU set of standards might become disguised market access barriers—but there is no indication that this is a policy result sought by Romania.

Subject to this general caveat, this study did not reveal any specific situations involving Romania where technical standards were used as non-tariff barriers to protect domestic producers and markets against foreign defense products.

---

[435] U.S. Department of State, Bureau of European and Eurasian Affairs, "U.S. Government Assistance to and Cooperative Activities with Central and Eastern Europe," II. Country Assessment—Romania (Washington, D.C.), January 2007. Available at: http://www.state.gov/p/eur/rls/rpt/92682.htm.

Chapter 12

Accessing the Swedish Defense Market

Due to its strategic policy of neutrality and official non-alignment during World War II and the Cold War Period, Sweden developed broad indigenous capabilities to address its national security concerns and unique operational requirements. Despite its small population and limited financial resources, Sweden developed and produced world-class tactical aircraft, ordnance, ships and combat vehicles. Although officially non-aligned, Swedish soldiers, submarines, and aircraft were fielded to deter an invasion from the east and depended on the use of U.S. technology and hardware to field a strong navy and air force and equip its armed forces. Not surprisingly, a strong partnership developed between Sweden and the U.S. military and the countries' defense companies. That strong partnership continues, to the degree that some European Union (EU) countries today complain that Sweden is too much in the U.S. orbit and is not Eurocentric enough.

The collapse of the Soviet Union and changing face of Europe allowed Sweden to reconsider its strategic defense policies. Less concerned about territorial defense, Sweden undertook a defense transformation in the 1990s that embraced a collective security as part of the EU and Transatlantic family of nations and prioritized network-centric capabilities and participation in expeditionary operations in support of multinational initiatives. As a result, Swedish armed forces were greatly reduced and armored/mechanized units demobilized, while small, strategically mobile forces were trained for multinational peacekeeping missions.

Under the new strategy, Sweden no longer attempts to maintain autonomy in all areas of military production, but designs, develops and produces only those systems and capabilities they cannot acquire elsewhere. Such systems and capabilities are narrowly focused on unique aspects of Swedish national strategy or the Swedish operating environment—i.e., aircraft, tracked vehicles, corvettes and submarines, and ordnance able to operate effectively in the Baltic Sea, Gulf of Finland, and arctic regions of Lapland. All other procurements are to be acquired at "best value" through open, international competition, using whenever possible commercial or off-the-shelf technologies to reduce costs.

Consequently, Swedish defense acquisition policy supports market access by U.S. firms and other foreign competitors. Core elements of this policy that are relevant here include: (1) an open and competitive procurement process, with a significant degree of competition on new major program awards; (2) a transparent and fair procurement process; (3) the absence of formal domestic content rules; (4) strong protection for intellectual properties; (5) an extremely low level of graft and corruption; (6) strong export controls and end-user certification; and (7) a fair and reasonable regulatory regime. Of all the metrics of market access we examined, Sweden only scores poorly on offsets, which are relatively high on Swedish programs (although they can be accomplished flexibly through a variety of mechanisms).

On the "supply side" of the market, Sweden has taken steps to enhance market access. Sweden has privatized, and to a large extent, internationalized its defense industry. Only one major purely Swedish defense company, Volvo Aero Corporation, remains, and much of its work is in the commercial sector. Therefore, it may be more accurate to speak of "the defense industry in Sweden" rather than "the Swedish defense industry." Foreign ownership of Swedish defense companies has been permitted by the Swedish government in numerous cases as long as security of supply can be ensured. Through various investment approval procedures and manufacturing licenses, Sweden ensures that significant defense production capabilities remain onshore, and that foreign-owned Swedish defense companies continue to have access to the most advanced technologies available. Thus, the internationalizing of Sweden's defense industry reflects Sweden's commitment to a collective security policy that links Swedish strategic goals with those of the Nordic countries, the EU and the United States.

While Sweden should be, and generally is, very favorably disposed toward defense industrial cooperation with the United States, there are several contentious issues that, if not resolved, could cause a weakening of that relationship and Sweden to move closer to the emerging European integrated defense market. Foremost among these are U.S. technology transfer policies and export control regulations, perceived by Swedish defense and industry officials as protectionist, used to block Swedish firms from participating in major U.S. programs (except through a U.S. partner), and conversely, to keep cutting-edge technology out of Swedish military systems that could compete with U.S. systems in foreign markets.

I. Market Background

A. Sweden's Changing Strategic Context and Military Strategy

During the Cold War, Sweden continued its World War II strategic policy of neutrality and official non-alignment—a defense posture that reflects Sweden's size and geographic location. To be credible and maintain the capability for independence in foreign affairs, Sweden had to backstop its official neutrality with substantial armed forces capable of repulsing an attack by both North Atlantic Treaty Organization (NATO) and the Warsaw Pact. Because NATO posed no real threat to Sweden, however, Swedish forces were designed and deployed primarily to counter Soviet military power. Thus, despite its neutrality, Sweden served very effectively to anchor NATO's northern flank until the collapse of the Soviet Union.

Sweden developed extensive indigenous defense capabilities during this time in support of its non-alignment policy. Uncertainties about security of supply, together with unique operational requirements (i.e., arctic conditions, the need to fly from austere, dispersed air strips and highways) demanded that Sweden develop a strong domestic defense industry. Sweden not only became self-sufficient in tactical aircraft, ordnance, ships and combat vehicles but also became a world leader in these fields.

With the collapse of the Soviet Union, the primary threat to Swedish national security receded, allowing Sweden to re-think its entire strategic posture. No longer poised between two superpower blocs, Sweden abandoned official neutrality and sought closer integration with Western Europe by joining the EU in 1995 (though Sweden has not yet integrated its currency into the Eurozone), and by becoming a NATO partner in the Euro-Atlantic Partnership Council.

Further, the collapse of the USSR provided the Swedish military a "strategic pause," during which Sweden could re-evaluate its defense strategy and recast Swedish forces to meet future challenges. In a remarkable show of political unity and will, all major parties in the Swedish Parliament agreed in the early 1990s to a substantial cut in defense forces, including drastic reductions in the size of the territorial army, demobilization of most armored and mechanized units, and an overall reduction in military personnel.[436]

The threat to Sweden's security interests continued to diminish throughout the Post-Cold War period as the former Soviet states and Eastern European countries focused inward on creating independent democracies.[437]

Defense Transformation of the 1990s

During the middle 1990s, the Swedish military undertook a stringent "capabilities inventory" in which all systems were rated as either suitable for future service, suitable with upgrades and modification, or unsuitable. This evaluation was conducted on the assumption that in the future, Swedish defense policy would be focused less on territorial defense of Sweden against foreign invaders, and more on expeditionary operations in support of multinational initiatives.[438] Moreover, Sweden assumed that future operations would require "network-centric capabilities" to be interoperable with coalition forces. While the defense budget was left at close to existing levels, the large reduction in personnel and operations and maintenance (O&M) expenses freed significant funds for investment in defense transformation.

Sweden's defense transformation envisaged a small, highly professional, expeditionary-oriented force that would participate mainly in low intensity peacekeeping and reconstruction efforts. Sweden would retain a residual territorial defense force to deter potential aggression from points east. An emphasis on network-centric capabilities would allow Sweden greater synergy in addressing conventional threats such as ships, submarines, aircraft and tank/mechanized forces. Thus, the focus was on remote sensors, unmanned aerial vehicles (UAVs), precision strike systems and creating real-time sensor-to-shooter links. As one Swedish general put it, "We aim for the time when a Swedish UAV controlled by a Swedish army unit can pass targeting information to a Swedish patrol boat that will launch a missile at a target with terminal guidance provided by a Swedish fighter."[439] Sweden's goal is to flatten service divisions in favor of organization by function and capabilities as part of the sensor-to-shooter kill chain.

Post-September 11—Increased Cooperative Engagement

In the Post-September 11 environment, the original Swedish vision of defense transformation has undergone some changes. Sweden had traditionally maintained a strong homeland security capability due to the potential for Soviet infiltration and sabotage operations. In addition, Sweden had been part of the European campaign against left-wing terrorist organizations in the 1970s and '80s, which provided Sweden with the infrastructure and

---

[436] See J. Bialos and S. Koehl, *European Defense Research and Development: New Visions and Prospects for Cooperation,* Johns Hopkins University-SAIS Center for Transatlantic Relations (Washington, D.C.), 2004, pp. 147-162. See also Office of the Supreme Commander, Swedish Armed Forces, *Swedish Armed Forces Strategy for Research and Technology, R&T Strategy—2002,* (Stockholm) 2002; and The Norwegian Atlantic Committee, *Nordic Security: the Military Balance, 2001-2002,* (Oslo) 2002, pp. 40-44.

[437] Poland and the Baltic States joined NATO. Finland joined the European Union and cooperates in Nordic Security arrangements.

[438] As discussed below, the 2008 Soviet invasion and occupation of Georgia has altered some thinking and disrupted implementation of the new Swedish defense plan, which has been delayed.

[439] Based on study team discussions with the Swedish military commander.

specialized capabilities to deal with a variety of terrorist scenarios. Since September 11, Sweden has intensified its own internal security measures and established closer coordination with intelligence services in Europe and the United States.

Sweden was one of the first countries to volunteer forces for stabilization and reconstruction operations in Afghanistan. Immediate operational needs for Swedish forces deployed in Afghanistan have changed priorities to practical areas such as secure tactical radios, high-mobility tactical trucks, better body armor, explosive ordnance disposal systems and the like. These, together with the need to supply and sustain deployed forces, have eaten into the budget for high-end network-centric systems.

In more recent years Sweden's defense security and procurement strategy has been shaped by necessity. Increasingly, Sweden has been looking for ways to increase its collaboration with its neighbors and other countries with mutual security interests, to protect its own national security and maintain the viability of its defense industrial base.[440]

The Nordic Cooperation Group

One salient aspect of Sweden's defense posture in the last decade—even as it increasingly aligned with the EU and NATO—has been the formation of the Nordic Cooperation Group, a mutual defense agreement among Sweden, Norway, Denmark, Finland and the Baltic States. Since its inception in the late 1990s, the main objective of the Nordic Armaments Cooperation and the Nordic Coordinated Arrangement for Military Peace Support has been to share development and procurement costs on complex systems, and to provide for cooperative defense and burden sharing. The centerpiece of the emerging Nordic Cooperation Strategy, however, is the EU Nordic Battle Group, one of 15 EU Battle Groups formed under the European Security and Defense Policy. By all accounts, this 1,500-man force, consisting of troops from Sweden, Norway, Finland, Denmark and Ireland, is perhaps the best-trained and most combat-ready force yet deployed by the EU.[441]

More recently, the Swedish, Finnish and Norwegian defense commanders submitted a joint report to their respective governments that covers cooperation among their land, naval and air forces to procure equipment, conduct joint exercises and training, and share intelligence and tangible assets.[442] Steps to harmonize Nordic requirements for fighting units and the procurement of defense equipment systems continue to make progress, and Russia's incursions into Georgia appear to have accelerated these efforts.[443]

The New Swedish Security Strategy: "Defence in Use" Report— Policy Proposals for More "Usable" Armed Forces

In June 2008, the Swedish Defence Commission, appointed by the government and consisting of one member from each party in Parliament, proposed steps to increase the opera-

---

[440] See Security in Cooperation (Ds2007:46), Report of Swedish Defence Commission. Summary available at:. http://www.sweden.gov.se/sb/d/8182/a/93944.

[441] Because of issues with the Irish government, the Nordic Battle Group was unable to deploy in support of EU forces in Chad. This does not, however, detract from the significance of the Battle Group as a milestone in Nordic cooperation.

[442] "Nordic Supportive Defence Structures," HKV2008-06-16, 23 200:63137(June 16, 2008). Available at: http://www.mil.se/upload/dokumentfiler/NORDSUP.pdf.

[443] See "Nordic States Respond to Threat from Russia," *Defense News*, Sept. 1, 2008, Vol. 23, No. 33, p. 26; "Russian Invasion Grabs Nordic Attention," *Defense News*, Sept. 22, 2008, Vol. 23, No. 36, pp. 20, 22.

tional effectiveness of the Swedish Armed Forces.[444] The report proposes increased military cooperation with:

- Nordic countries, including Baltic surveillance activities and pooling of equipment, for example, for Strategic Airlift Capability;

- NATO, including in NATO's air situation picture and in NATO's international operations;

- The EU, specifying support for a stronger European Defence Agency (EDA) and peacekeeping operations; and

- The United Nations (UN), increasing the number of forces available for international operations.

The proposed strategy calls for a reduction in tanks, heavy combat vehicles, and combat aircraft; a phaseout of parts of the present ground-base air defense; and elimination of certain standing units. In line with Sweden's defense transformation goals, budget resources will be shifted from support and administrative activities to operational efforts, including the training and deployment of smaller units that are flexible, mobile and ready to deploy in support of national, UN, EU and NATO operations. The collaboration with NATO, and with the United States bilaterally, is viewed as essential for the development of Sweden's military capabilities, as well as for interoperability requirements. Although Sweden envisions increasing Nordic cooperation, perhaps eventually even to the degree of common forces, procurements and deployments, Swedish strategists are under no illusion that the Nordic countries can operate as a self-sufficient group.

Today, closer integration of Sweden into the NATO Alliance seems practically inevitable given Swedish Defense Minister Sten Tolgfors' statement in February 2008 that "NATO membership is a natural for the Moderates in the long run."[445] Ministry of Defence (MoD) sources have said full membership is not part of the mandate of the present coalition government, and Sweden may wait until Finland applies for membership before taking the decisive step. The fundamental underpinnings of Swedish defense policy, coupled with Russia's recent intervention in Georgia, however, all point in this direction.[446]

Russia and the "Nord Stream" Challenge—A Real Time Shift in Strategy?

Russia's more assertive posture under Vladimir Putin and Dmitry Medvedev is factoring into Sweden's strategic thinking, particularly after the late summer 2008 Russian invasion of Georgia.[447] The planned "Nord Stream" pipeline in the Baltic raises potential military implications. If Russian forces are assigned to protect the pipeline and riser platforms, Swedish officials are concerned that the Russian presence could lead to political friction with the Nordic and Baltic States. Indeed, the new Security Strategy and military transformation is on hold while Sweden works out just how much of its force it wants to put into expeditionary

---

[444] *Försvar i användning* (Ds2008:48). Available at: http:// www.regeringen.se/sb/d/108/a/107264.

[445] "Sweden's Defense Minister Says Joining NATO Would Be Natural," *International Herald Tribune*, Feb. 16, 2008.

[446] "Russian Invasion Grabs Nordic Attention," op.cit.

[447] In Swedish warfighting exercises, the presumed adversary is described as *"Stormakt Röd"* (Great Power Red), a transparent euphemism for Russia. Sweden's equipment, training and doctrine have always been directed mainly against Russia, in accordance with the Swedish military maxim, *"Fienden kommer alltid österifrån"* ("The enemy always comes from the east").

warfare, and how much into territorial defense. If Sweden decides that Russia is the more pressing threat, then more forces will be directed into naval and air forces; there may be a revitalization of Swedish heavy forces as well. At the very least, ground forces in Lapland will be reinforced and modernized.[448]

To address these new security concerns, Swedish officials recognize that Sweden may need to invest in new systems for its Navy and Coast Guard.[449] Russian activities could also serve as the impetus for increased cooperation among Sweden, Denmark, Norway, Finland and the Baltic States. Currently, these countries are conducting some joint exercises, using English as the command language.

Military Spending and Operational Commitments Today: Squeezing the Budget

The reduced threat after the Cold War resulted in a continual decrease in defense spending by Sweden as a percentage of gross domestic product (GDP) just as it did in many other European nations (although the growth of the Swedish GDP has offset at least part of that reduction). Nevertheless, since the mid-1990s, Sweden has very actively met its commitments to NATO—more so than some full members—including participation in NATO exercises and deployment of Swedish forces in support of NATO commitments in Afghanistan, Bosnia, Kosovo and elsewhere (in addition to maintaining its traditional role as a provider of UN peacekeeping forces).[450]

Sweden's increasing participation in multinational operations thus can be seen as one aspect of this strategy of closer integration and multilateral defense. However, funding these operations has put a strain on Swedish defense budgets. With 15 rapid response units as well as specialists included in various EU, UN and NATO deployments, the cost of Sweden's participation in international operations has almost doubled from 2004 to 2008 (SEK 1.1 billion to almost SEK 2.0 billion, or $170 to $309 million at 2008 exchange rates).[451] Increasing O&M expenditures for expeditionary operations has coincided with a decline in the total defense budget by some 20 percent since 2002, putting pressure on both procure-

---

[448] As mentioned above, the ongoing Soviet invasion and occupation of Georgia has disrupted implementation of the new Swedish defense plan, which has been delayed. According to Minister of Defense Sten Tolgfors, the speed with which Russia was able to mass a substantial force against Georgia pointed to the need for a larger and more heavily equipped active force for Sweden's territorial defense, in order to buy time for mobilization of reserves, perhaps at the expense of additional expeditionary units. See "Georgia Conflict Delays Swedish Defense Plan," *The Local*, Sept. 9, 2008, at: www.thelocal.se/14216/20080909.

[449] Discussions with Swedish defense officials. In the 2007 Swedish defense budget, enlargement of the Navy was rationalized by the need to support deployed forces in expeditionary situations (see "2007 Budget Proposal Cuts Swedish Gripen Force, Looks to Buy Strategic Lift," *Defense Industry Daily*, May 4, 2006, at: http://www.defenseindustrydaily.com/2007-budget-proposal-cuts-swedish-gripen-force-looks-to-buy-strategic-lift-02223/. However, given budget constraints, logistic support ships may be deferred in favor of more corvettes and submarines to provide security in the Baltic and Gulf of Finland. This is just one of many choices that must be made in light of the changing strategic situation *vis-à-vis* Russia.

[450] According to Swedish sources, the Swedish military is currently deployed in Lebanon, Bosnia, Afghanistan and Kosovo. Swedish forces were earmarked to support French peacekeepers in Chad, but were not deployed because of disagreements within the EU. It is presently reported that Sweden is sending military observers to Georgia to monitor the ongoing Soviet occupation of South Ossetia. See "Georgia Conflict Delays Swedish Defense Plan," *The Local*, Sept. 9, 2008, at: www.thelocal.se/14216/20080909.

[451] See Ministry of Defence, *Budget Bill 2007-Fact Sheet on the Government's Budget Bill for 2007*, Oct. 16, 2006; and *Budget 2008—Fact Sheet on the Budget Bill for 2008*, Sept. 20, 2007; confirmed through interviews with Swedish MoD representatives.

Figure 116   **Sweden—Defense Budgets, 2004-2008 (Billions of Dollars–$)**

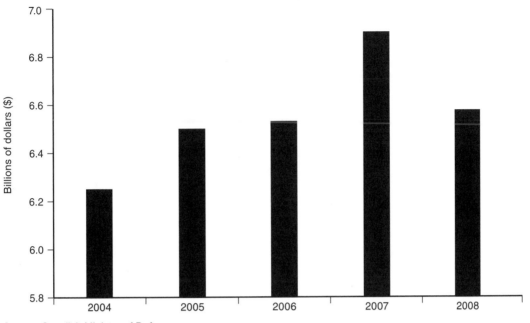

Source: Swedish Ministry of Defense.

ments and research and development (R&D). This has had the effect of slowing the pace of Swedish defense transformation.

Moreover, O&M funds, mainly spent to support expeditionary operations, constitute a larger percentage of the defense budget each year. Consequently, more spending is on equipment and training for flexible, rapid deployment forces and less on sophisticated, state-of-the-art systems that U.S. suppliers have traditionally been most successful in selling to Sweden.

Finally, budget cuts and the reduction in armed forces (from a million fully mobilized troops in the 1980s to 320,000 that could be mobilized today) has caused grumbling that northern Sweden is exposed and the country's best fighting units are abroad.[452]

The Swedish Defense Budget: A Sustained Decline

Military spending in Sweden has slowly been reduced in real terms since 2000. The government's defense budget has been held to about $6 billion (see Figure 116). There was a one-year budget spike in 2007, as the Swedish air force began long-lead procurement for the new Gripen C/D variant, and invested in upgrades to the existing JAS.39A/B. Other investments that year included C-130 upgrades, new transport helicopters, and a tactical UAV system. Further, Sweden had to increase its operations budget to cover its participation in International Security Assistance Force, which was underfunded.

---

[452] "Tight Budgets Force Sweden to Shift Forces South," *Defense News,* June 16, 2008, pp. 20, 28; also "Georgia Conflict Delays Swedish Defense Plan," op. cit. The Swedish military today consists of some 18,000 regulars plus 37,000 militia, for a total of just 55,000 active duty troops, backed by 262,000 reservists. But as Defense Minister Tolgfors noted, Sweden would need about one year to bring just 10,000 reservists to full combat readiness.

In real terms, from 2000 to 2007, nearly $1.4 billion in cuts have been made in defense allocations.[453] The reduction has been felt most strongly in the maintenance and support of existing material, training and cooperation. In contrast, the share earmarked for international operations, as noted above, has increased significantly.

In fact, defense as a proportion of GDP allocated to the armed forces in Sweden is only half what it was in the 1970s. From 1975 through 1982, military spending accounted for 3 percent or more of Swedish GDP, but by the year 2000 defense was only was 2.1 percent of GDP, by 2005 1.52 percent, and by 2007 only 1.48 percent.[454]

Sweden's armed forces face a budgetary shortfall of $128 million for 2009. Although new military planning directives call for more Swedish troop participation in international missions, the Swedish government has said that no additional funds would be provided to the approximate $6.2 billion 2009 defense budget.[455] Russia's invasion of Georgia, however, has convinced a number of Swedish leaders that Sweden's commitment to support international missions must be balanced by funding strong core operating units to protect Sweden's regional interests.[456] Disappointed that the EU Nordic Battle Group has remained idle, some government legislators argue that the funds spent to keep the Battle Group mission ready (about $150 million) would be better spent on home defense.[457] Determining the proper balance between funding of international missions and core operating units will undoubtedly be a topic of debate for future defense budgets.

One Defense Minister, Mikael Odenberg, has already resigned in protest against government defense cuts, stating that slashing defense procurement spending across the board cannot be done without impacting the capability of the armed forces to perform operations.[458] Despite the protest, the Swedish armed forces had an operating deficit of $160 million on a budget of approximately $5.9 billion for the year 2008. Current Defense Minister Sten Tolgfors has expressed similar concerns that there is just not enough funding to ensure adequate training of personnel.

B. The Swedish-American Relationship—Strong Ties Over Many Decades

Sweden has been able to field a strong navy and air force, equip its army, and develop intelligence in cooperation with the United States and by using U.S. technology and hardware. This relationship has been beneficial to both the United States and Sweden over many decades. As noted above, the United States and the rest of NATO benefited from Sweden's ability to protect Europe's northern flank against a Soviet threat during the Cold War period.

Although Sweden was officially neutral during the Cold War, this did not inhibit their significant defense industrial cooperation with the United States, particularly in aircraft systems and components, missiles and radar electronics. Through the 1960s, Sweden made

---

[453] "The Swedish Armed Forces in Figures," at: www.mil.se and *"Försvarsmaktens Anslagstilldelning"* at: www.mil.se and *"Budgetunderlag"* at: www.mil.se.

[454] "Armed Forces Proportion of GNP," Swedish Armed Forces Website. Available at: http://www.mil.se/en/About-the-Armed-Forces/The-Swedish-Armed-Forces-in-figures/Armed-forces-proportion-of--GNP/.

[455] "Sweden: Funds Short of '09 Needs," *Defense News*, Vol. 23, No. 46, Nov. 17, 2008.

[456] "Sweden Reassesses Defense Strategy," *Defense News*, Vol. 23, No. 46, Sept. 22, 2008.

[457] "Sweden Plans Changes on a Tight Defense Budget," *Defense News*, Vol. 23, No. 46, Nov. 17, 2008.

[458] "Swedish Defense Minister Resigns Over Cuts," The Local, Sept. 5, 2007. Available at: http:// www.thelocal.se/8395/20070905/.

many Foreign Military Sales (FMS) purchases of U.S. weapons systems, such as the AIM-4 Falcon and AIM-9 Sidewinder air-to-air missiles, while Swedish fighter aircraft such as the Saab 37 Viggen included a high percentage of U.S. content, including engines, avionics and aircraft systems.

By the 1970s, to maintain a viable defense industry, Sweden needed to increase exports to amortize the cost of producing new systems for the Swedish military. At times, this placed Sweden in competition with the United States for international markets. Questions as to the reliability of the United States as a defense trading partner came to the fore when Sweden was prohibited from selling its Viggen aircraft to India because the United States denied re-export approval for the U.S.-origin engines on the Viggen fighters.[459] Despite this incident (as well as significant disagreements on U.S. foreign policy), relations with the United States remained cordial and cooperative.

After the Soviet Union imploded, the security rationale for the close cooperation between Sweden and the United States changed. Although the threat of an invasion of Swedish territory greatly diminished, maintaining the Transatlantic relationship was nevertheless vital to Sweden as their systems were so reliant on U.S. technology

In more recent times, despite Swedish opposition to the Iraq War, Swedish relations with the United States on strategic and defense industrial levels have remained very good. Sweden has provided intelligence support and other forms of cooperation in both counter-terrorism and homeland security. Indeed, Sweden would like to play an even more active role in U.S. homeland security programs, where Sweden believes it has much to offer in the way of defensive technology. Moreover, U.S. and Swedish forces have recently engaged in a variety of cooperative efforts, including continuing military exercises. In one recent operation, the Swedish Gotland submarine was involved in shallow water operations outside of San Diego.[460] Sweden also supplies radar and other items to U.S. and UK troops fighting in Afghanistan and in Iraq, while Swedish equipment, both purchased directly and built under license in the United States, is used by the Army, Marine Corps, Coast Guard and Department of Homeland Security.

Indeed, Sweden's long-standing commitment to its Transatlantic relationship with the United States has led a number of European countries to view Sweden as being too much in the U.S. sphere of influence and not sufficiently Eurocentric.[461]

The Legal Framework for Continuing Cooperation

U.S. and Swedish armaments cooperation has long-standing legal underpinnings. The two countries are parties to a reciprocal reciprocal defense procurement Memorandum of Understanding (MOU) dating back to 1987. One of the most robust MOUs between the United States and its allies, the U.S.-Swedish agreement states in the most definitive terms that Swedish and U.S. defense suppliers, respectively, are provided so-called "national treat-

---

[459] Specifically, in 1978, the United States refused to provide an export license for the Volvo Flygmotor RM8 afterburning turbofan, a military derivative of the Pratt & Whitney JT8 commercial aircraft engine. India instead acquired the SEPECAT Jaguar.

[460] "Sweden Current Capabilities," Nuclear Threat Initiative Website. Available at: http://www.nti.org/db/submarines/sweden/index.html.

[461] In a number of interviews, Swedish industry leaders and government officials discussed this perception of Sweden held by other European countries.

Figure 117   U.S.-Sweden Total Balance of Trade (Billions of Dollars–$)

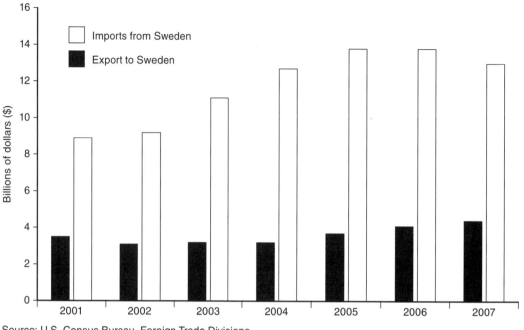

Source: U.S. Census Bureau, Foreign Trade Divisions.

ment"—i.e., treatment no less favorable in regards to procurements than what domestic companies receive. As the 2003 amendment states, "[b]arriers to procurement or coproduction at the prime and subcontract levels of an item of defense equipment that has been produced in the other country *shall be removed, insofar as laws and regulations permit, such that each country shall accord to industries in the other country treatment no less favorable in relation to procurement than is accorded to industries of its own country.*" (Emphasis added.) The 2003 amendment to the MOU also addresses security of supply, an issue of great concern to Sweden, and implements reciprocal systems under which each country can establish priority designations to ensure timely performance and delivery under defense contracts performed for the other country. A 2007 Memorandum of Agreement on Cooperation in Science and Technology for Homeland/Civil Security Matters provides a legal framework for homeland security matters.

Sweden is also a designated country benefiting from the Defense Trade Security Initiative (DTSI), established to streamline licensing within NATO and among a few other countries for government programs and commercial sales to foreign governments, international cooperative programs and commercial ventures. DTSI benefits reinforced Sweden's strategy to maintain interoperability with those countries with which it shares mutual security interests.

In 2003, Sweden, like a number of other Western European countries, signed a Declaration of Principles (DoP) with the United States that focused on enhancing defense industrial collaboration. Pursuant to the DoP, Sweden and the United States established an Export Control Working Group. This Group meets regularly to collaborate on export control issues, including re-export authorization requirements. The Swedish Inspectorate of Strategic Products (ISP) also meets regularly with its U.S. counterparts, the Bureau of Industry and Security (BIS) and the Directorate of Defense Trade Controls (DDTC), to address licensing and other concerns. Further, regular meetings of the DoP-based Market Access Working Group also facilitate access to each country's defense markets.

U.S.-Swedish Defense Trade and Cooperation: An Extensive Partnership

Over many decades, the United States has been an important supplier of defense technology to Sweden. Swedish officials indicated that this is in part because Sweden has perceived U.S. technology as superior to European technology, and because of the close working relationships that have existed between Swedish and U.S. defense companies. For example, the JAS.39 Gripen multirole fighter has greater than 50 percent U.S. content by value—if one includes all of the weapons systems and technologies it incorporates.

Many U.S. companies in the broader economy have successfully established operations in Sweden, to the degree that U.S. companies in Sweden employ more workers than any other foreign-owned companies operating in Sweden.[462] This is not true, however, in the defense sector, where U.S. firms have relatively minimal operations in Sweden.

In the broader economy, as shown on Figure 117, the United States habitually runs a trade deficit with Sweden, importing a wide range of products from furniture to automobiles to consumer electronics to pickled herring, while the United States exports to Sweden a wide range of consumer goods, agricultural products and raw materials. In the defense sector, however, as shown on Figure 118, the United States has typically run a fairly significant trade surplus, albeit the total volume of trade is relatively small. The United States typically buys niche systems from Sweden in such areas as littoral naval combat, mine countermeasures, and infantry anti-tank weapons while Sweden has acquired a broad range of technologies and capabilities from the United States.

These charts, however, tend to understate the depth of U.S. cooperation with Sweden. For many years, the Swedish model of defense industrial cooperation with the United States typically began with a direct sale, commercial or FMS, of a system or subsystem. Once the Swedes were satisfied with that system or product performance, they would manufacture the system under license—at which point the U.S. licensing firm would receive long-term royalties. To cite an example, in the 1950s, the Swedes bought AIM-4 Falcon air-to-air missiles from Ford Aerospace (later Hughes, later Raytheon), which they put on their Lansen fighters. A few years later, Sweden obtained a production license and Bofors began producing the missiles. Sometimes this process works at one level removed. For example, the Swedes armed their Viggen fighter with the BAE Skyflash missile, which in turn, was a British-built derivative of the AIM-7 Sparrow. Consequently, when the Swedes began licensed production of Skyflash, it was still U.S. technology, once removed.

Historically, this licensing of U.S. programs for production has been a central feature in Swedish defense programs and created a legacy of close connections between Swedish and

---

[462] *Doing Business in Sweden: 2008 Country Commercial Guide for U.S. Companies*, U.S. Foreign Commercial Service, U.S. Department of Commerce. Available at: http://www.buyusainfo.net/docs/x_3958211.pdf.

Figure 118   U.S.-Sweden Defense Trade Balance (Millions of Dollars – $)

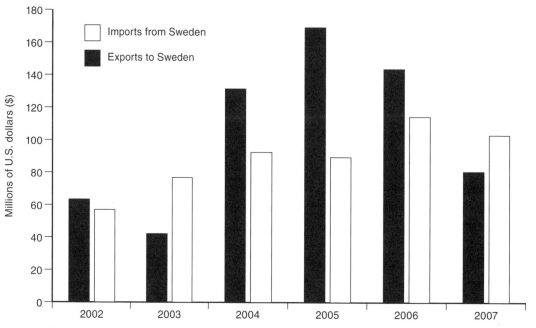

Source: U.S. and Swedish Export Control Reports, 2002-2007; SIPRI Databases.

U.S. firms. It also helped develop and sustain Sweden's production capabilities, and to some extent as a secondary effect of U.S. weapons development programs, Swedish technology. Because Sweden has become so intimately familiar with U.S. technologies, some of these have been integrated into the Swedish defense technology base. Swedish engineers naturally prefer to employ technologies with which they are familiar. Thus, U.S. or U.S.-derived technology has been the default in many of its defense programs.

Today there is a declining number of major platforms being procured by Sweden. Consequently, there is just not enough business for the large U.S. defense firms to justify the expense of a presence in Sweden. Moreover, Swedish defense spending is increasingly on equipment and training for flexible, rapid deployment forces; Sweden is spending less on the sophisticated, state-of-the-art systems U.S. suppliers have traditionally been most successful in selling to Sweden.

As a result, some U.S. defense firms that once had a physical presence in Sweden, such as Raytheon, no longer maintain offices there. Because Sweden does not require an onshore presence, U.S. defense companies also can easily service Swedish customers from offices in Brussels or London. Currently, General Electric is present in Sweden to service its jet engines, and FLIR Systems has a Swedish subsidiary to supply thermal imaging products.

Even without physical operating locations in Sweden, U.S. firms remain key suppliers for the Swedish defense industry. For example, the new generation Gripen NG fighter has more than 50 percent U.S. content by value (up from the roughly 33 percent of the original

Gripen A/B) and numerous other Swedish systems rely on U.S. components and technology. Among U.S. businesses providing components for the Gripen are:

- General Electric Engines in a partnership with Volvo Aero
- BAE Flight Control Systems (formerly Lockheed Martin Flight Control Systems — U.S. business, UK ownership)
- Lockheed Martin Flight Simulators
- United Technologies Sundstrand (Electrical Generator, Auxiliary Power Unit)
- Honeywell (Inertial Navigation System, Air Data Computer)
- Kaiser (Head-Up Display System)
- Signal Technology Corp. (Electronic Warfare System Components)
- Electrodynamics, Inc. (Crash-Survivable Memory Unit)
- Meggitt Aircraft Braking Systems (Wheels and Brakes) (U.S. business, UK ownership)
- Rockwell Collins (Radio Communications, Avionics)[463]

On the reverse side of the ledger, the U.S. military makes relatively little use of Swedish systems or technologies except in niche areas where the United States either lacks capabilities or does not have a competitive advantage. Thus, for example, Sweden has been a major supplier to the U.S. Marine Corps of anti-armor weapons, camouflage systems, and other niche systems. Saab and the U.S. Army began cooperating in the 1980s when the U.S. Army acquired the anti-armor weapon, AT-4. The U.S. Army also procured the follow-on system, AT-4CS, in 2004. Swedish and U.S. defense industries have cooperated on aim point, the red dot sighting technology, first procured by the U.S. Army in 1997. The U.S. Special Forces have acquired the Carl Gustaf System (MAAWS, or Multi-Role Anti-Armor Anti-Personnel Weapon System) and naval gun systems. Notably the 40mm anti-aircraft gun produced by BAE Systems Bofors, also used by U.S. land forces, has been used by the U.S. Navy (USN) since WWII. The USN also utilizes hydraulic cranes provided by MacGregor. Since 2005, BAE Systems Bofors has been delivering the 57mm MK 110 naval gun for the U.S. Coast Guard Deep Water Program; the same weapon has also been selected by USN for the Littoral Combat Ship (LCS) and the DD(X) Destroyer.

More recently, the strong ties have continued. Ericsson is providing wireless technology and services for the U.S. Department of Defense (DoD) next generation narrow band satellite communications system. Also, numerous Saab Group companies are supplying the U.S. Armed Forces, including: Saab Avitronics (countermeasures to the U.S. Navy and Air Force); Saab Barracuda LLC (camouflage and signature management systems); Saab Microwave Systems (Sea Giraffe AMB radar selected for the USN LCS); and Saab Training USA (live training systems). BAE Systems Hägglunds delivers all terrain vehicles, and BAE Systems Bofors and Raytheon Missile Systems are currently working on development of Excaliber smart ammunition in a collaborative project between Sweden and the United States. Finally, SWE-DISH Satellite Systems (recently acquired by DataPath, a U.S. firm) supplies mobile satellite communications equipment to SOCOM and other parts of the U.S. DoD, and Dockstavarvet and Swedish Defence Materiel Administration (FMV) have licensed

---

[463] *Jane's All the World's Aircraft-2007*, Jane's Information Group, 2007; InfoBase Publishers, DACIS Database.

production rights for its rigid inflatable boats to SAFE Boats International of Seattle, which produces a Riverine Command Boat based on Sweden's CB-90 for the U.S. Marine Corps. SAFE Boats also produces Dockstavarvet-designed small craft for the U.S. Coast Guard (USCG), the Department of Homeland Security, and various police forces throughout the United States.

In most cases, Swedish companies have licensed production to a U.S. partner to meet security of supply concerns, reduce political opposition to foreign procurement, and mitigate the difficulties of dealing with the very complex U.S. acquisition system. In the case of ordnance, Bofors has had a strategic partnership with Alliant TechSystems (ATK) to manufacture the AT-4, but the AT-4CS, a newer product, is produced in Sweden. The BAE Systems Bofors 57mm gun system and Mk110, chosen for the USN LCS system and DD1000 and the USCG Deep Water, are manufactured under license in Kentucky. Raytheon manufactures the Bofors/Raytheon jointly developed Excalibur in its U.S. plant, and Dockstavarvet's riverine boats are produced by SAFE Boats in Seattle, Washington, under a license agreement.

Swedish government and industry representatives expressed the belief that a U.S. partner is essential for any Swedish company attempting to penetrate the U.S. market. The current industrial practice also reflects this view. Although the Saab Group has had success with its own Saab Barracuda camouflage operations in North Carolina and Saab Training Operations in Florida, Saab recently entered into a partnership with Sensis Corporation to grow its radar business in the United States. Also, Saab Avitronics partners with BAE Systems in Texas to deliver countermeasures to the U.S. Navy and Air Force.

II. The Swedish Defense Market: Supply and Demand Dynamics

The degree of continued access to the Swedish defense market by U.S. firms will depend upon several factors, including evolving threat scenarios, the treatment of important bilateral technology transfer issues and, more broadly, how Sweden operates in the ongoing balance between the United States and the EU as driving forces in defense markets.

One reality is clear, however. Although Sweden still has the third largest defense sector in the EU, it cannot sustain its defense industry by domestic sales alone. Neither can it afford to develop full-spectrum military or industrial capabilities in high-end systems such as aircraft, armored vehicles and combat vessels. Sweden must participate in cooperative programs and seek sufficient foreign sales of defense goods to help sustain its industry.

Evolution of the Swedish Defense Industry: From Neutrality-Driven Independence to Internationalization

As noted above, during the Cold War uncertainties about security of supply, together with unique operational requirements (i.e., arctic conditions, the need to fly from austere, dispersed air strips and highways) demanded that Sweden develop a strong indigenous defense industry. Through companies such as Saab, Volvo, Kockums, Hägglunds and Bofors, Sweden became not only self-sufficient but also a world leader in tactical aircraft, ordnance, ships and combat vehicles, though its official neutrality and highly ethical export policies limited the number of potential customers for its products.

In its pursuit of strategic independence, Sweden tried to be self-sufficient even in supplying all first-tier systems. This included: the manufacturing of corvettes and submarines by Kockums; tanks and land vehicles by Hägglunds; mortar systems by Bofors; aircraft engines by Volvo Aero under license from GE; radars, electronics and control systems by Ericsson; and aircraft by Saab. Consequently, Swedish companies designed and developed specifically Swedish solutions.

As noted above, by the 1970s, the rising cost of developing and producing world-class weapon systems made it difficult for Sweden to maintain complete independence. To sustain a viable defense industry, Sweden has had an ongoing need to increase exports to amortize the cost of producing new systems for the Swedish military.

Downsizing, Privatizing and Internationalizing in the Late 1990s and Beyond

During the post-Cold War period, the Swedish defense industry had to adapt to government budget cuts, downsizing of Swedish forces, and restructuring of Swedish capabilities to participate in international operations that require flexibility, interoperability and quick deployment of small forces. Beginning in 1997 (and now complete) the Swedish government sold all state-owned interests in the Swedish defense industry. With the merger of Celsius and Saab, virtually all of Sweden's aircraft, robotic and avionics manufacturing fell under the ownership of the Saab Group. With its acquisition of Ericsson Microwave Systems from LM Ericsson Telephone Co. in 2006, Saab has added sophisticated radars and sensors to its defense portfolio and is the preeminent Swedish defense company.

Supply Side Dynamics: Swedish Industry Today

Swedish Industry—Adapting to Sweden's Shift Toward Security Cooperation With European Partners

The severe reduction in the size of the Swedish armed forces means that not as many platforms are required as in the past. Moreover, the transformation of Sweden's forces to network-centric and expeditionary warfare has also deemphasized the need for platforms of the past that were used to counter the threat posed by the Soviet Union.[464] In the last 15 years Sweden has gradually moved to a more cooperative rather than autonomous posture in defense, including its membership in the Nordic Cooperation Council, its participation in a number of NATO-sponsored efforts (including the Partnership for Peace program and the Euro-Atlantic Partnership Council), and its collaborative efforts with other individual countries, including on armaments programs.

Consequently, Swedish industry has had to adapt to the government's strategy of mutual cooperation—and rely increasingly on collaborative armaments projects to spread the cost of financing the procurement of equipment. Cooperating with other countries ensures mutual dependence for the supply of components, subsystems and complete systems, and of key importance, offers export sales opportunities for Swedish defense companies. In 2007,

---

[464] As noted above, this assumption is now undergoing review within the Swedish MoD. However, the review, whatever its outcome, is not expected to affect Sweden's new defense industrial policy of: 1) procuring its needs on the international market; 2) using cooperative development where a capability does not already exist; and 3) developing only those systems and capabilities it cannot procure either commercially or from other countries.

Table 55   Sweden-Leading Defense Companies (Millions of Swedish Krone)

Company Name	Defense Revenues (SEKM)	Total Revenues	Main Business Areas
Saab	16,635	21,063	Aircraft; Missile Systems; C4I; Communications; Electronic Warfare; Radar; Homeland Security
BAE Systems Hagglunds	1,905	1,925	Combat and Tracked Vehicles; Turrets and Weapon Stations
BAE Systems Bofors	1,296	1,319	Artillery and Heavy Ordnance
Kockums	1,165	1,194	Surface Ships; Submarines; Stealth Technology
Nammo Sweden	579	713	Ammunition-All Calibres
Volvo Aero	566	4,526	Aircraft and Aerospace Engines
Eurenco Bofors	252	207	Propellants and Explosives

Source: Association of Swedish Defence Industries.

for example, 65 percent of the Saab Group's sales were exports, and during 2006, 53 percent of all Swedish military products were exported.[465]

Principal Swedish Defense Firms

As set forth on Table 55 (revenues in Swedish kronor), Saab dominates the Swedish defense market. Among Swedish companies, only Saab is listed among the "Defense Top 100." Ranked at number 20 in 2007 (up from number 23 in 2006), Saab saw its defense sales rise 25 percent from $2.41 billion to $3.23 billion, due mainly to sales of the JAS.39 Gripen. The only other major Swedish-owned defense/aerospace company is Volvo Aero AB, with 2007 revenues of about $1.05 billion. However, the vast majority of Volvo's revenue comes from commercial, not military, sales.

Saab. Saab is the largest defense contractor in the Nordic countries, with approximately 13,600 employees—the large majority located in Sweden. Saab has subsidiaries in Denmark, Finland, Australia, South Africa and the United States. Approximately 80 percent of Saab's total sales were defense sales. About 30 percent of Saab's military sales were into the U.S. market. BAE Systems plc. owns 20 percent of Saab. Investor AB, controlled by the Wallenberg family, owns 38 percent and is the largest shareholder in Saab.

Volvo Aero. Volvo Aero's total revenues were about one-fifth the size of Saab's, and only 13 percent of those revenues were from military sales. Only 7 percent of Volvo Aero's 2,300-plus employees work in the defense sector. Volvo Aero has subsidiaries in the United States

---

[465] *Strategic Export Controls in 2006: Military Equipment and Dual-Use Products*, Government Offices of Sweden, Government Communication 2006/07:114. Confirmed in discussions with Swedish defense export control officials.

and Norway. It is the only major Swedish defense firm that is not at least partially foreign-owned. Volvo Aero has a major partnership with GE to modify and produce the engines for the JAS.39 Gripen.

The other major Swedish defense firms, including **BAE Systems Bofors**, **BAE Systems Hägglunds** and **Kockums**, are 100 percent foreign-owned. Although the Swedish defense industry is no longer autonomous, these companies—and Swedish security—can utilize the leverage provided by the global reach of the industrial groups to which they now belong. The companies still operate as viable parts of Sweden's industrial base, while benefiting from synergies in technical innovations, marketing, distribution, and Transatlantic and EU links provided by major defense firms like BAE Systems.

Increasing Foreign Ownership of Swedish Firms

Sweden has been highly receptive to foreign investment in and ownership of its defense companies, as discussed under III. Evaluation of Market Access Metrics later in this chapter, and as reflected on Table 57. This openness is a direct result of budget cuts and a conscious government policy to pursue cooperation and participate in international operations. Specifically:

- The development of Swedish surface ships and submarines still takes place at Kockums, but Kockums is now owned by the German company HDW, a part of the ThyssenKrupp Group;

- Ammunition and gunpowder is now manufactured by the Norwegian-owned Nammo Sweden, owned 50 percent by Nammo Norway and 50 percent by Patria Oyj of Finland, and EURENCO Bofors, which is owned by the Swedish/Finnish/French-owned EURENCO; and

- BAE Systems Inc. has acquired significant operations in Sweden. Through the acquisition of Bofors by United Defense (subsequently itself acquired by BAE North America), BAE Systems owns Sweden's artillery manufacturing. Through its purchase of Hägglunds, it also owns the combat and tracked vehicle production capabilities in Sweden. Even Saab is 20 percent owned by BAE Systems plc.

The Swedish government's decision to permit foreign ownership of Sweden's defense industrial base reflects the reality that Sweden simply could not sustain the requisite level of investment across all Swedish business areas. Indeed, for example, foreign ownership has helped Kockums sustain its manufacturing capabilities. Even with this influx of foreign investment, however, a number of Swedish programs are threatened by current budget cuts. For example, two programs vital to Kockums' ship-building production, maintaining the Visby Stealth Corvette and the diesel submarine Gotland, are vulnerable.

Demand Side: Re-Shaping Swedish Acquisition and Defense Industrial Strategy Acquisition Priorities: Refocusing on Expeditionary Strategy

The restructuring of the Swedish Armed Forces toward smaller, more flexible operational units, as well as the continual implementation of a network-based defense, caused Sweden to change its strategy for the acquisition of defense equipment. Pursuant to its 1990s Defense Transformation Plan, Sweden conducted a series of "warfighting experiments" between 2005 and 2007 intended to develop and test specific network-centric capabilities, culminating in an end-to-end demonstration in 2006-2007.[466] From the results of these tests, the Swedish military established materiel requirements, including: systems to be discarded, systems to be retained and upgraded, and new systems to be acquired.

Today, Sweden's procurement decisions, administered by the Swedish Defence Materiel Administration (FMV), continue to be shaped by Sweden's new expeditionary strategy. To a fair degree, the need to fund urgent operational requirements has displaced long-term development and procurement.

Sweden's New Acquisition Policy—From Self-Reliance to Competition and Limited Internal Development

Specifically, over time Sweden has shifted from an independent procurement strategy that focused largely on self-reliance on national sources of supply (often on a sole source basis) to increased use of cooperative solutions and "best value" buying through a competitive process that assigns national development the lowest priority.

For many decades, the Swedish FMV provided funding on a directed basis to key Swedish firms such as Saab, Hägglunds, Kockums and Bofors to develop national security solutions for Sweden's particular circumstances. Sweden's changing defense strategy and declining budgets have led to a significant shift, however, which is formally reflected in Sweden's 2008 draft "Defense in Use" report. This report essentially codifies the new Swedish acquisition policies that have evolved over time. Specifically, FMV has an established procurement policy with a clear set of priorities as follows:

- **Upgrade Existing Systems.** If feasible, upgrade existing equipment instead of making costly new acquisitions.

- **Acquire "Best Value" Off-the-Shelf Developed Solutions.** If the procurement of new systems is necessary, seek competitive bids to buy developed products available in the marketplace.

- **Cooperative Development.** Where developed solutions are not available, seek to undertake cooperative development programs with countries having mutual security interests where cost-effective.

- **National Programs in Limited Circumstances.** Investment in new Swedish national development programs should be a last choice, and to be utilized only where:

  - Proven products cannot be obtained cost-efficiently in the marketplace; or

  - Sweden has a leading technology that makes Sweden an attractive partner in cooperative arrangements.

- **Public/Private Partnerships.** FMV will also look to private and public partnerships to offer procurement opportunities.

Today, FMV weighs two important factors in making procurements of essential supplies for the Swedish Armed Forces: 1) cost-effectiveness; and 2) opportunities for international cooperation.[467] Although FMV factors in a long-term strategy to keep Sweden's industrial

---

[466] Koehl & Bialos, *European Defense Research and Development*, op. cit.

[467] See *Försvar i användning* (Ds2008:48). Confirmed by discussions with officials at MoD and FMV.

base viable and to ensure the reliability of technology transfer and security of supply, FMV makes purchases today based on "best value." FMV's strategy to utilize commercially available technologies to the greatest extent possible is required by Swedish regulations—public agencies must coordinate their research, technology, development and procurement of systems and material.

A notable exception to Sweden's new policy concerns legacy systems. Given the importance of the Gripen program to the Swedish industrial base, it is an easy decision to continue investment in an updated fighter. Given budget constraints, however, a decision to fund Kockums to develop a new submarine is a more difficult one. If a new submarine is not funded, Swedish officials have indicated that Sweden risks losing the expertise and motivation of its naval submarine defense sector personnel.

Maintaining Gripen's Viability

Because Sweden cannot afford the costs of a thriving defense infrastructure on its own, Sweden must create export opportunities to sustain its military and industrial base. The JAS.39 Gripen is the most significant export product for Sweden, with many Swedish companies involved in providing components and services. Sweden is campaigning hard to sell the Gripen to other Nordic countries. Much rides on Sweden's success because Nordic sales would ensure that Swedish industry has sufficient orders to develop leading technologies and stay in the race to sell fighter jets to third countries. Further, existing Nordic cooperation arrangements would be strengthened through various offset arrangements that encourage coordinated manufacturing, assembly, maintenance and training. This would effectively create an integrated regional defense market within the structure of the emerging European defense market, giving the relatively small Nordic countries leverage to compete within Europe against larger defense firms.

Efforts toward Nordic collaboration, however, received a serious blow recently with Norway's announcement that it would replace its aging F-16 fighters with the U.S. F-35 Joint Strike Fighter rather than the Gripen NG. The decision, according to Saab, eliminates an anticipated $7 billion worth of negotiated agreements and partnerships between Swedish and Norwegian firms on 156 projects over the next 10 to 15 years.[468] Perhaps more costly to collaborative efforts, however, is Sweden's perception that the competition for the procurement was unfairly evaluated. Among other things, Saab claims that Norway's conclusion that the Gripen did not meet Norway's operational demands was based "on an incomplete, or even faulty, analysis."[469] Companies learn to take the loss of bids in stride, but a public disagreement about the reasonableness and fairness of how a bid is evaluated erodes trust and will probably delay efforts to integrate the Nordic defense markets—despite official statements to the contrary.

An Expected Decrease in Research and Technology

Instead of using its budget to fund the Swedish industrial base to develop Sweden's own new systems, Sweden will now invest R&D in only those core capabilities in which it has a

---

[468] "Gripen Rejection Hurts Norwegian Firms," *Defense News*, Dec. 8, 2008, Vol. 23, No. 47.

[469] "Saab Slams Norway's Gripen Rejection," *The Local*, Dec. 10, 2008 (available at: http://www.thelocal.se/16252/2008/ 210/); "Saab Comments on Norwegian Evaluation," Dec. 10, 2008 (available at: http:// www.air-attack.com/news/article/3466.

competitive advantage or cannot acquire elsewhere; everything else will be procured through open competition.[470] FMV today invests approximately 10 percent of the defense budget in R&D and 25 percent for procurement. It is expected that the research and technology (R&T) percentage will decrease even further with the implementation of Sweden's new acquisition strategy. The new focus will be on procuring existing international solutions.

Evolving Policies and Practices: Sweden's Increasing Collaborative Engagement

The NH-90 Program: Collaborating With the Nordic Cooperation Group. Under the Nordic Cooperation Group's agreement, Sweden, Finland and Denmark held a joint Nordic Helicopter procurement (won by the multinational NH-90) and have begun joint procurement of ground-based surveillance radars and other equipment. The Nordic Helicopter program was marred by disagreements about requirements harmonization, funding, work share and other issues. While the Nordic Cooperation Group member countries share a common history and many common interests, they also have a number of unique requirements and preferences that pose potential problems. Differences in procurement practices and cultures threatened to derail the project but eventually an agreement was forged, and cooperation continued beyond the acquisition of the airframes. Thus, Norway and Sweden have implemented a joint logistics system and training program for the NH-90, and the countries have also cooperated in offset arrangements, with Norway having the primary maintenance role and Finland the key assembly responsibilities. Transfers of defense hardware, technology and services among the Nordic countries have been simplified by new regulations that permit and ease intra-Nordic transfers, although U.S. re-export authorization must still be obtained for those items controlled under the U.S. International Traffic in Arms Regulations (ITAR).

Wider European Collaboration. Today, FMV seeks to acquire equipment and systems harmonized to meet the requirements and needs of various partners engaged in international collaborations, with a focus on interoperability. The Swedish military has accepted that it is impossible for Sweden to be self-sufficient in most major systems. Hence, consistent with this strategy change, FMV officials have indicated that approximately 20 percent of all FMV's procurements are collaborative and 30-40 percent of all R&D funded by FMV is collaborative—which is rather high within Europe. For example:

- *Splitterskyddad Enhets Plattform* (SEP) Modular Combat Vehicle is a collaborative effort between the UK, France and Sweden;

- NH-90 Nordic Helicopter is a collaboration between the Nordic countries;

- A collaborative missile program is with the UK; and

- Sweden and Norway cooperate on a number of activities.

The collaboration with Norway, of course, would have increased significantly if Norway had chosen to purchase the next generation Gripen instead of the JSF. Sweden and Norway might have conducted joint exercises. It was anticipated that the collaboration may even have extended to land systems, with the countries using each other's test ranges for exercises and training. In time, such a collaborative relationship may still emerge, but Norway's

---

[470] Bialos and Koehl, op. cit.; *R&T Strategy—2002*, op. cit.; *Försvar i användning*, op.cit. Confirmed in discussions with MoD and FMV officials.

choice of the JSF—as detailed above—will certainly slow collaborative efforts between the two countries.

Cooperation in LOI 6 and EU Initiatives. Finally, Sweden's 2008 draft "Defense in Use" report confirms Sweden's commitment to European defense cooperation. As a participant in arrangements agreed to by the so-called LOI 6 (France, Germany, Italy, Spain, Sweden and UK), Sweden has a forum to influence decisions on issues that must be addressed to create a true European defense market. Sweden also participates in the European Defence Agency (EDA) and promotes its mission to create an internationally competitive European market for military equipment. Although Swedish officials believe it will take time for EDA to become truly integrated because EU countries are protecting so many legacy systems, officials indicate that Sweden is among those countries that want to work within EDA instead of bilaterally or within small groups of countries. A number of Swedish officials pointed out that not so many years ago few believed EDA would come into existence. Today, Sweden is more optimistic about EDA's future and believes it can be successful by focusing first on a few programs and low intensity operations (peacekeeping, etc.).

Sweden as a Street Smart Buyer. Despite its commitment to a new acquisition strategy, Sweden views the defense sector, particularly in Europe, as one of the last highly regulated markets with a dysfunctional structure. Sweden is in favor of liberalizing and opening defense markets to: 1) more competition and open procurement; and 2) less or no offsets. However, given imperfect markets in the rest of Europe, Swedish officials have indicated that Sweden must be a "street smart" buyer during the transition period. Sweden will therefore continue to fund development work by some Swedish companies in strategic areas while the transition to an open market occurs in Europe.

III. Evaluation of Market Access Metrics

Generally, Sweden is regarded as an attractive country in which to invest or trade. The country is consistently ranked by the U.S. Department of Commerce (DoC) and other bodies among the most competitive, corruption-free and technologically advanced economies in the world.[471]

Tariff Barriers

By and large, tariffs are not significant barriers between Sweden and the United States. All of the countries studied are members of the World Trade Organization (WTO) and thus must provide most-favored nation and national treatment to imported goods from every other country included in the study. Although defense products are generally exempt from WTO rules governing tariffs and trade, the reciprocal defense procurement MOUs between the United States and Sweden afford each country duty-free treatment for imported defense products procured from the other country. However, the MOUs do not apply to dual-use products and technologies such as general aerospace systems that have both military and civil applications. Thus, as more military programs rely on commercial off-the-shelf (COTS) technology, this would tend to put U.S. companies at a competitive disadvantage *vis-à-vis* European firms, which get the benefit of the lower intra-European rates that apply under EU rules (unless specific exemptions are negotiated on a bilateral basis).

---

[471] See U.S. Department of Commerce Report, *Doing Business in Sweden*, op. cit. Available at: http://www.buyusainfo. net/docs/x_3958211.pdf.

**Figure 119   Sweden—Total Procure-
ment by Award Type**

**Figure 120   Sweden—Legacy vs.
New Procurement**

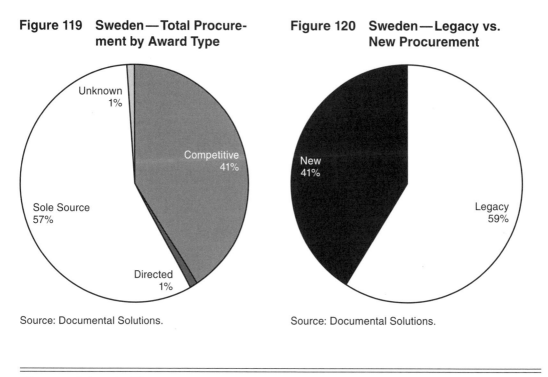

Source: Documental Solutions.   Source: Documental Solutions.

Competition in Procurement

Sweden's new acquisition policy is clearly shifting from a legacy of sole source acquisitions awarded to national firms to competition on a "best value" basis open to international sources, cooperative development where off-the-shelf solutions are not available, national development only when necessary (i.e., where cost-effective solutions are not otherwise available), and continued sole source procurement for legacy systems and add-ons.

Available data on actual Swedish awards on major defense programs during the 2006-2008 period shows both the continued importance of sole source buying from national firms on legacy programs and the prevalence of open and competitive buying on new programs. Swedish buying patterns also show an apparent shift toward buying European on competitive programs.

All Major MoD Defense Program Awards. A review of all major Swedish MoD program awards (i.e., awards exceeding $10 million during 2006-2008) shows that 58 percent ($1.5 billion) were sole source or directed; 41 percent ($1.1 billion) were competitive; and 1 percent (one award of $22 million) was made in an unknown manner (see Figure 119). This data is largely consistent with information provided to us by Swedish government officials.

- **Most Spending Is on Legacy Programs.** As shown on Figure 120, 59 percent of total Swedish procurement was spent on legacy programs (i.e., programs *where the initial* award for development and/or procurement were made at some point in the past). This reflects that large programs, which take years to bring to fruition, are recipients of most Swedish funding. The list of leading Swedish defense programs (Table 56) shows that legacy Swedish national programs such as the JAS.39 Gripen and the CV.90 armored personnel carrier receive the most funding.

Figure 121 **Sweden—Legacy Procurement by Award Type**

Figure 122 **Sweden—New Procurement by Award Type**

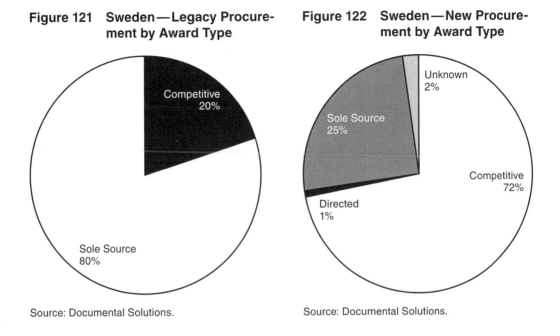

Source: Documental Solutions.

Source: Documental Solutions.

Figure 123 **Sweden—Defense Market Share by Company**

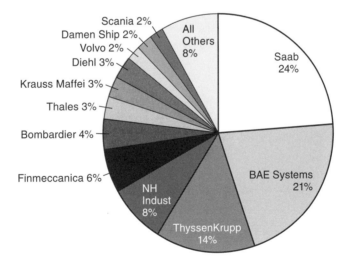

Source: Documental Solutions.

- **Most Legacy Spending Is Sole Source.** As Figure 121 shows, approximately 80 percent of legacy awards were sole source, with the remaining 20 percent awarded competitively. This data is fairly comparable to that of the United States and other Western European nations, where legacy buying is predominately done via sole source awards. The magnitude of sole source buying reflects the realities of large defense programs. After a major system has been awarded to a particular firm, the

Table 56   Sweden—Leading Defense Programs (Millions of Constant 2008 Dollars—$)

Prime Contractor	System Name	Program 2006	Program 2007	Program 2008	Program TOTAL	Procurement Type	New vs. Legacy
BAE SYSTEMS	CV 90	81.53	81.12	80.70	281.90	Sole Source	Legacy
NH Industries	TTH90	0.00	55.73	151.34	207.07	Competitive	New
ThyssenKrupp AG	K35 Karlstad	90.95	91.48	2.14	184.57	Sole Source	Legacy
Saab Group	JAS 39B Gripen	140.33	12.17	12.10	164.60	Sole Source	Legacy
Saab Group	JAS 39A Gripen	48.08	47.46	46.84	142.37	Sole Source	Legacy
BAE SYSTEMS	MUSJAS 3 (Adv. Aerial BONUS)	44.02	44.02	24.85	112.89	Sole Source	Legacy
Finmeccanica	HKP15TIS/IFT	44.50	66.75	0.00	111.26	Competitive	Legacy
ThyssenKrupp AG	MCMV Landsort Upgrade	34.46	34.46	34.46	103.38	Competitive	Legacy
Bombardier	DHC-8-Q300	0.00	92.82	1.80	94.62	Competitive	New
BAE SYSTEMS	RG-32M	29.40	30.96	32.52	92.88	Competitive	New
Saab Group	Giraffe Eagle	45.80	28.32	10.09	84.21	Sole Source	Legacy
Terma A/S	Modular Recon Pod	25.94	27.97	30.01	83.92	Competitive	New
Krauss-Maffei	Strv-122	27.10	26.99	26.89	80.98	Competitive	Legacy
ThyssenKrupp AG	K34 Nykoping	76.06	1.78	1.78	79.63	Sole Source	New
Diehl	IRIS-T	15.01	30.22	31.00	76.23	Competitive	New
Saab Group	S-100D ASC	0.00	15.32	38.29	53.60	Sole Source	New
Finmeccanica	Sweden HF 2000	20.70	21.52	10.42	52.63	Competitive	New
Damen Shipyards	KBV Class	0.00	20.51	30.88	51.39	Sole Source	New
Scania	Scania Family	25.18	12.83	13.06	51.06	Sole Source	Legacy
Saab Group	Giraffe AMB	4.24	4.39	4.54	50.38	Sole Source	Legacy
Saab Group	SPK-39	31.53	6.73	6.73	44.99	Sole Source	Legacy
MBDA	Meteor	12.85	12.85	12.85	38.54	Competitive	New

Prime Contractor	System Name	Program 2006	Program 2007	Program 2008	Program TOTAL	Procurement Type	New vs. Legacy
BAE SYSTEMS	SEP Development	0.00	17.36	17.38	34.73	Competitive	New
Saab Group	JAS 39C/D Gripen Upgrade	0.00	0.00	30.00	30.00	Sole Source	New
Saab Group	SLB Phase 1 (Sweden)	10.50	10.50	5.25	26.24	Sole Source	Legacy
EADS	IMCMS	0.00	7.89	15.93	23.83	Competitive	New
Unidentified	Communicationd Intercept System	8.67	4.84	8.98	22.49	Unkknown	New
Patria	Pasi	7.46	7.46	7.46	22.39	Competitive	New
Volvo/GE	GFE Acft Engine set for JAS 39B	17.43	1.51	1.50	20.44	Sole Source	Legacy
Boeing	C-130 AMP Sweden	5.11	15.11	0.00	20.22	Competitive	New
Volvo Group	Volvo FL6	6.49	6.65	6.80	19.94	Sole Source	Legacy
BAE SYSTEMS	Bv206S	4.11	7.70	8.06	19.87	Sole Source	Legacy
EDO	CRS-3701	6.79	5.83	5.99	18.60	Competitive	New
Volvo/GE	GFE Acft Engine set for JAS 39A	5.97	5.89	5.82	17.68	Sole Source	Legacy
Saab Group	Saab 105 Services	5.00	6.00	6.00	17.00	Sole Source	Legacy
Saab Group	ARTHUR	2.60	6.60	6.60	15.80	Sole Source	Legacy
Raytheon	AIM-120C	5.37	5.51	4.52	15.40	Competitive	Legacy
Saab Group	LedsystT	5.11	5.11	5.11	15.32	Directed	New
Griffon Hovercraft	Griffon 8000 TD(M) Class	5.03	10.09	0.09	15.21	Sole Source	New
Saab Group	RBS23 Missile Control Center	6.49	6.60	0.56	13.66	Sole Source	New
Rockwell Collins	Sweden TDRS	4.92	4.32	4.11	13.35	Sole Source	New
Thales	Sweden TS9000	4.37	4.07	3.77	12.20	Compettiive	New
BAE SYSTEMS	Archer SPA	2.38	4.70	4.70	11.79	Sole Source	New
ThalesRaytheon	Gerfaut	3.38	3.26	3.14	9.78	Competitive	New

Source: Documental Solutions.

Figure 124   Sweden—Competitive Awards by Supplier

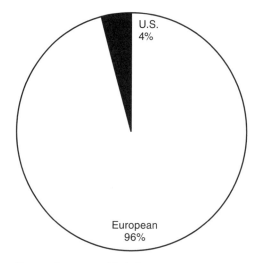

Source: Documental Solutions.

follow-on buys and upgrades are often awarded to the same firm again (e.g., after an award is made for an aircraft developed and produced by one firm, it is much more likely to be awarded to that firm for future buys). Indeed, it would be uneconomic to change contractors midstream on large programs unless the incumbent is not performing. Thus, today the original prime contractor—years later—typically remains the incumbent and is awarded the production and follow-on work (additional buys, upgrades and maintenance) largely on a sole source basis. *Thus, not surprisingly, as shown on Figure 123, three firms hold 60 percent of the Swedish major program market during 2006-2008: Saab, the incumbent on numerous legacy Swedish programs, with about 25 percent, BAE (Bofors, Hägglunds) with 21 percent and Thyssen-Krupp (Kockums) with 14 percent.*

- **Buying Habits Change Slowly.** The predominance of legacy programs in Sweden's procurement spending and the continuing role of national champions highlights that defense acquisition buying habits change slowly. Indeed, the changes are largely reflected on *new* programs (i.e., programs newly started in 2006-2008).

- **New Buys Are Largely Competitive**. As reflected in Figure 122, 72 percent of the new contracts value was awarded competitively while only 25 percent was sole source; 1 percent was directed procurement, and 2 percent was awarded in an unknown manner. While the sample of new programs is much smaller than the sample of legacy programs, it nevertheless appears to demonstrate the trend of future Swedish procurement.

- **New Buys Were Open to U.S. and European Firms But Awards Went Overwhelmingly to European Firms.** Most new Swedish defense competitions appeared open to U.S. firms. Interestingly, however, the award data shows that 96 percent of *all* competitive contracts from 2006-2008 were awarded to European bidders *outside* of Sweden, with only 4 percent to U.S. firms and no awards to Swedish firms. The willingness of Sweden to accept solutions from other European countries is notable and confirms its openness. See Figure 124. This data strongly suggests, however, a growing *European* focus in its competitive buying. In contrast, on *new* programs not competed, not surprisingly, Swedish firms received more than $90 million in sole source awards.

- **Limited Participation in European Cooperative Programs.** In contrast to other Western European nations, Sweden to date has not become a partner in any major European multinational program. Sweden's cooperative efforts, such as the Nordic Helicopter program, have instead focused on collective buying of major systems and not on the development of new systems in a cooperative program. Major challenges on such non-developmental programs are thus limited to requirements harmonization and "industrial participation" with the winning contractor.

- **Buying to Meet Needs.** Swedish officials also have stated, and both domestic and foreign firms confirm, that FMV procures to meet military needs and not to protect Sweden's industrial base. Consequently, non-Swedish defense firms have competed successfully under open competitions, and international firms do not need a Swedish presence or to partner with a Swedish company to be successful, although partnering can help navigate the Swedish procurement system.

- **Subsystem Level Buying.** We do not have specific data on subsystem level buying. However, based on anecdotal information, we believe the Swedish subsystem market also is reasonably competitive as even prime contractors in sole source programs strive to provide best value in both cost and technology.

* * *

In sum, the data indicates Sweden's newly articulated policy of competitive bidding with international participation is being implemented in practice. However, the prevalence of legacy programs with long-term incumbents in Swedish buying creates somewhat of a lag between Sweden's new policy and the results. Further, the new competitive awards reflect an apparent Eurocentric policy in buying decisions, a striking contrast to the legacy of success in Sweden of U.S. firms.

Fair and Transparent Procurement Process

Sweden is a signatory to the WTO Government Procurement Agreement (GPA), which establishes core principles for ensuring fair, transparent and non-discriminatory conditions in public procurement. Procurements by both the Swedish Armed Forces and FMV are subject to the GPA's standards. Specifically, under the GPA, tender notices must be made publicly available to ensure that a procurement is open and that foreign and domestic suppliers have an equal opportunity to compete for government contracts. Procedural rules that govern the submission, receipt and opening of tenders must be transparent and ensure fairness in the procurement process. Also, private bidders must be able to challenge procurement decisions and obtain remedial action if decisions do not comply with the rules of the GPA.

Sweden's Act on Public Procurement implements these WTO principles. FMV thus must follow the rules provided in the Act, which applies to all Swedish public sector organizations (although Swedish officials stated that certain military procurements may not be subject to these disciplines based on national security exceptions). Under the Act, FMV's procurements must be competitive and decided in an objective manner.

Although FMV is widely thought of as open, transparent and professional, the downsizing of Sweden's defense activities has led to outsourcing of some procurement responsibilities. Sometimes, for example, major domestic contractors serve in a role similar to that of a lead systems integrator in the United States and/or a support contractor for a program office. On some procurements, the domestic contractor may formulate the RFP and evaluate the bidders for the system or subsystem. Then, even if the platform is procured from outside of Sweden, the Swedish contractor may do the integration. Even in these scenarios, however, all bidders know that the Swedish contractor is the support provider or systems integrator—reducing the prospects of conflict of interest and limiting the potential for bias in the selection of winning bids.

Domestic Content

There are no Swedish laws requiring domestic content. Further, foreign defense firms are not required to be established or have a presence in Sweden in order to bid on defense contracts. There also is no requirement (officially or informally) to partner with a domestic contractor to bid on a contract. Of course, such a partnership may prove helpful in navigating procurement requirements and contacting agencies. In addition, as noted above, prime contractors on Swedish programs are encouraged to seek best value solutions at the subsystem and component level. Additionally, the new Swedish defense procurement policy stresses the need to buy COTS or non-developmental solutions (with concomitant international sourcing), while its national R&D strategy focuses only on areas in which Swedish industry has a comparative advantage. Thus, the domestic content of most Swedish defense systems will tend to fall over time.

Offsets and *Juste Retour*

Domestically, Sweden imposes offset obligations, or what the Swedes prefer to call "industrial participation" obligations, on acquisitions of SEK 100 million ($16.75 million) or more.[472] Under such circumstances, FMV may impose certain maintenance obligations, for example, or require that bidders use a specific type of electronics. In this way, offsets are used by FMV to gain know-how and maintain the competency of Swedish industry in certain areas. Offsets can be approved up to the value of the delivery. Multipliers to increase the value of a transaction are generally not applied, although exceptions can be made for R&D projects and programs that result in indirect offset benefits not related to goods and services sold under a specific project or program. However, both government officials and company representatives have confirmed that offsets are used to develop or maintain military and security competence, and not to provide employment or random industrial devel-

---

[472] *Guidelines for Establishing and Implementing Industrial Participation in Connection with Procurement of Weapon Systems and Defence-Related Items from Foreign Suppliers*, Swedish Defence Materiel Administration, June 10, 2002, FMV Analys 01840:27303/02.

opment. Formal offsets do not seem to apply in cooperative programs, where work share agreements are typically included in the MOUs with partner countries.

According to the U.S. DoC, offset payments by U.S. companies selling defense products to Sweden averaged 103.9 percent of contracts over the period 1993-2006.[473] These figures are calculated from actual data submitted by the reporting U.S. defense firms of actual contracts and offset commitments. A review of DoC offset reports over recent years shows that the offset percentage has remained remarkably stable. Thus, Sweden's offset requirements are relatively high among its European peers. This use of large offsets probably reflects that Sweden, as a small country, cannot expect foreign firms to have a meaningful onshore presence (it would not be economical). Also, in numerous market areas, it similarly would not make sense for the foreign firm to partner with a Swedish firm (e.g., due to lack of a capable Swedish competitor). In these circumstances, Sweden can accomplish through offsets what other larger countries can do more directly through informal requirements for partnering or onshore presence.

Swedish officials have indicated that they would like to see procurements shift toward open competition without offsets, which would tend to work in favor of Swedish defense exports. However, Sweden has not been averse to leveraging offsets in attempts to win new markets, sometimes through indirect methods. For example, to win a place in the Norwegian Fighter Competition for the JAS.39 NG Gripen, Sweden invested heavily in Norwegian technology companies and has made work share offers as part of its pre-proposal package. Åke Svensson, the CEO of Saab, for example, stated before Norway's decision to buy the JSF: "We can guarantee our industrial cooperation in excess of 100 percent of the order value."[474] Subsequent to Norway's rejection of the Gripen NG, Saab has indicated that 95 percent of the anticipated work share and partnership agreements with Norwegian companies will be cancelled.[475]

Government Ownership

The Swedish government began privatizing state-owned domestic defense firms in 1997. This process has been completed, and the Swedish government no longer holds equity or other means of influence in any Swedish defense company.

Foreign Direct Investment

A foreign company making an acquisition of Swedish defense assets needs approval from the Swedish Inspectorate of Strategic Products (ISP) to operate as a manufacturing facility in Sweden.[476] ISP thus has an opportunity to impose certain conditions on the manufacturing license it issues. The ISP generally seeks the advice of the Export Control Council, composed of members from all parliamentary parties, on the most significant foreign acqui-

---

[473] Offsets in Defense Trade, Twelfth Report to Congress, U.S. Department of Commerce (Dec. 2007), PDF p. 29 (report page 2-13) (Table 2-5). Available at: http://www.bis.doc.gov/defenseindustrialbaseprograms/osies/offsets/final-12th-offset-report-2007.pdf.

[474] "Norway Rules Out F-16 Upgrades," *Defense News*, May 5, 2008, p. 28.

[475] "Gripen Rejection Hurts Norwegian Firms," Defense News, Dec. 8, 2008, Vol. 23, No. 47.

[476] *Strategic Export Control in 2006: Military Equipment and Dual-Use Products*, Government Offices of Sweden, Government Communication 2006/07:114.

Table 57. Foreign Ownership of Major Swedish Defense Firms

Company	Ownership Percent (%)	Country	Notes
Saab AB	BAE Systems, Inc.–20	UK	Sweden's largest defense company
BAE Systems Bofors	BAE Systems, Inc.–100	U.S./UK	Supplies artillery and heavy ordnance
BAE Systems Hagglunds AB	BAE Systems, Inc.–100	U.S./UK	Manufacturer of combat and tracked vehicles
Kockums AB	HDW (ThyssenKrupp Group)–100	GE	Naval surface ships and submarines
EURENCO Bofors AB	EURENCO–100	SE/FR/FL	Propellants, explosives and ammunition
Nammo Sweden AB	Nammo–50; Patria Oyj–50	NO/FL	Ammunition

Source: "The Swedish Security and Defence Industry 2006-2007," op. cit.

sitions of Swedish defense companies, such as the German company HDW's acquisition of Kockums and BAE Systems Inc.'s acquisition of Bofors and Hägglunds. To operate as a defense manufacturer in Sweden, a foreign-owned defense company has to have a Swedish CEO, the company has to be registered in Sweden, and the CEO has to live in Sweden. If the company has contracts with FMV, the company must also provide informal assurances about security of supply, upgrading capabilities, and maintenance capabilities. The government agencies, particularly in more significant acquisitions, are involved in negotiations regarding potential shutdowns, employment layoffs, moving production lines offshore, and other similar issues. FMV must also approve and execute each cooperative agreement or licensing agreement entered into by Swedish companies.

ISP also administers FMS programs with the United States, although FMV handles the actual negotiations with its U.S. counterpart. However, all agreements and licenses entered into by FMV and the Swedish Armed Forces must be approved by ISP. ISP imposes special restrictions on accessing and protecting classified information. Generally, classified information is ring-fenced at the program level and only cleared personnel with a "need to know" will be given access. ISP meets annually with its U.S. counterparts at the State Department's Directorate of Defense Trade Controls (DDTC) and Commerce Department's Bureau of Industry and Security, and also participates in periodic meetings of Swedish and U.S. defense companies at the Swedish Embassy in the United States. FMV has a permanent representative at the Swedish Embassy in Washington who works on licensing and other issues.

As noted above, during the last decade, the Swedish defense industry has undergone an extensive restructuring, resulting in substantial foreign ownership of Swedish defense firms. Today, as shown on Table 57, most of the Swedish defense industry is in fact either wholly or partially foreign-owned. Among the leading Swedish defense firms, only Volvo Aero has no foreign ownership (although the bulk of its work is actually commercial today). The remaining Swedish defense companies are either small niche players or manufacturers of dual-use technology that derive most of their revenues from the commercial side of the ledger.

Ethics and Corruption

Sweden is viewed as one of the least corrupt markets in the world. The World Bank's worldwide governance indicators show Sweden at almost 98 percent for rule of law and more than 98 percent for control of corruption.[477] There is also no apparent evidence of illicit payments in connection with obtaining defense procurement contracts in Sweden. In 2007, for example, Sweden was ranked tied for second (with a score of 9.3 out of 10) as the least corrupt country in the Corrupt Perceptions Index published by Transparency International.[478] Sweden also ranks the second highest on Transparency International "Bribe Payers Index" of propensity of firms in that country to engage in illicit payments in third countries.[479]

Sweden has ratified the 1997 OECD Convention on Combating Bribery of Foreign Public Officials in International Business Transactions and has comprehensive laws on corruption. The Organisation for Economic Co-operation and Development (OECD) has noted that Sweden has long enjoyed a reputation for having little corruption. In its latest "Follow-Up Report on the Implementation of the Phase 2 Recommendations," the OECD noted that Sweden participates in a project to develop integrity pacts concerning arms exports.[480] Sweden has also held seminars on corruption in the international defense industry and on integrity measures that should be adopted.

Sweden has taken other steps in practice to deter illicit foreign payments. In determining whether or not to approve an export license application, ISP, for example, specifically considers whether any applicant has been involved in bribery. ISP holds regular meetings with Swedish arms manufacturers to obtain information about attempted bribes. These efforts to combat corruption have been reflected in Sweden's high ranking as among the least corrupt markets in the world. Despite these efforts, Swedish companies have on occasion become entangled in corruption cases regarding sales to third countries. In the 1980s, for example, Bofors was investigated for its sale of howitzers in India that involved illicit kickbacks and re-exports. More recently, questions have also been raised about alleged bribery payments in the Czech Republic in connection with the recent sales efforts involving the Gripen fighter. As Sweden competes more aggressively in the foreign export market, including in countries with dubious ethics previously precluded by Sweden's restrictive export policies, there is a risk that similar problems may reemerge until such time as Swedish companies gain more experience in dealing with foreign corrupt practices.

Export Controls

Sweden has implemented a robust export control regime. Sweden is a Member State of all the major multilateral export regimes, including the Nuclear Suppliers Group, the Australia Group, the Missile Technology Control Regime, the Wassenaar Arrangement on Export

---

[477] See World Bank Governance Indicators, 1996-2007 (Country Data Report for Sweden, 1996-2007). Available at: http://info.worldbank.org/governance/wgi/pdf/c206.pdf.

[478] Transparency International, 2007 Transparency Corruptions Perception Index (CPI). Available at: http://www.transparency.org/policy_research/surveys_indices/cpi.

[479] Available at: http://www.transparency.org/policy_research/surveys_indices/bpi/bpi_2006.

[480] OECD Directorate for Financial and Enterprise Affairs, Working Group on Bribery in International Business, *Sweden: Phase 2 Follow-Up Report on the Implementation of Phase 2 Recommendations*, Oct. 9, 2007, p. 3. Available at: http://www.oecd.org/dataoecd/3/43/39905457.pdf.

Controls for Conventional Arms and Dual-Use Goods and Technologies, and the Chemical Weapons Convention. Sweden is also a Member State of Organization for Security and Co-operation in Europe (OSCE), and has approved the OSCE principles governing transfers of conventional arms and the 2000 OSCE Document on Small Arms and Light Weapons.[481] Sweden, like other EU members, is also a signatory to the 1998 EU Code of Conduct on Arms Exports, which harmonized regulations across all Member States in the EU; and established general principles for the transfer of armaments and military technology; and set up a system whereby each Member State must inform the others whenever an export license is denied. Under the Code, each State must also consult with the other Member States whenever it wishes to grant an export license that has been denied by another Member State for "essentially identical transactions," although the ultimate decision to deny or transfer a military item remains at the national discretion of each Member State. This Code of Conduct on Arms Exports became elevated into an EU Common Position in December 2008.

Further, the European Commission (EC) Transfers Directive recently adopted by the European Parliament is yet another step in aligning the policies of EU countries regarding intra-Community transfers and simplifying procedures to permit such transfers among Member States and certified defense companies. The focus of this Directive is intra-Community transfers of defense-related products and, thus, the main beneficiaries of reduced barriers within the EU are European defense companies. It is not at all clear that U.S. firms will be eligible for similar treatment; this is a matter for national authorities to decide.

In Sweden, the export of military equipment is governed by the Military Equipment Act of 1993 (MEC), which prohibits all exports of military equipment as a general policy. Exports of military equipment are permitted only under an authorized license. The list of items prohibited from being exported without proper authorization is published in the MEC. Military equipment is divided into two categories: 1) military equipment utilized for combat; and 2) other military equipment. The distinction between the two categories is based upon whether the equipment has a destructive effect or not. Sweden has not implemented any "deemed export" rules, but certain high-level technology transfers are controlled. For example, production technology is generally controlled, but specifications and R&D technology are not.

The agency that implements and administers MEC is the ISP. As noted above, ISP also approves licenses to authorize companies to manufacture military equipment, as well as licenses to authorize all types of defense industry cooperation with foreign partners. In addition, ISP authorizes the transfer of manufacturing rights and agreements for the joint manufacture of military equipment. Finally, ISP, along with Swedish Customs, carries out inspections and audits to ensure that Swedish defense companies are complying with export control obligations.

ITAR Concerns Affecting U.S.-Swedish Relations

Because Swedish systems have often contained a high percentage of U.S.-origin parts and components, re-export restrictions imposed by the ITAR is a constant issue confronting ISP and Swedish defense firms. The requirement to obtain re-export authorization from the U.S. Department of State's DDTC prior to the transfer or sale of a Swedish product

---

[481] OSCE Criteria on Conventional Arms Transfers. Available at: http://www.sipri.org/contents/expcon/oscecat.html. OSCE Document on Small Arms and Light Weapons is available at: http://www.osce.org/fsc/13281.html.

containing U.S.-origin components to a third party is an irritation that is not only inconvenient, but it inevitably leads to delays. Thus, at least at the component level, purchasers may choose non-ITAR items to avoid U.S. re-export restrictions. In this way, ITAR restrictions serve as a trade barrier for U.S. companies, particularly lower-tier companies that are not selling sophisticated systems or subsystems. Swedish officials stress, however, that neither the government nor Swedish companies follow an "ITAR-free" policy. Ultimately, advanced technology and capabilities decide which systems will be purchased, and ITAR issues will not prohibit the Swedish government from purchasing advanced U.S. equipment.

Swedish companies confirmed that while they are not trying to design out ITAR components, ITAR restrictions are a factor in choosing suppliers. If given a choice in a competitive environment, the non-ITAR component will be chosen to avoid re-export issues, they stated. One Swedish firm gave as an example a case where it had to wait six months to obtain re-export authorization for an ITAR-controlled cooling fan used in a computer. To avoid a repeat of such a delay, the fan was replaced with a non-U.S. product. More ominous for U.S. manufacturers, the frustration caused by the delay is etched in the minds of those engineers who are doing future design work for that company—going forward, ITAR-controlled components will probably be avoided as much as possible.

Program managers and customers at Swedish companies also indicated that it just takes too long to obtain required licenses and agreements—whether Manufacturing License Agreements, Technical Assistance Agreements, or DSP-5 Export Licenses. They also find it difficult to maintain an open dialogue with their U.S. government contact, whether it is someone at DDTC or DoD. All Swedish companies and government officials agreed that U.S. export controls should focus on the technology flow, not on hardware down to the details of nuts and bolts. They also expressed concern that sometimes the U.S. government chooses to control different performance parameters going forward, thereby making certain items ITAR-controlled that were previously uncontrolled, and forcing Swedish companies to change their equipment and integration. Nevertheless, in most cases U.S. suppliers will continue to be the supplier of choice for systems and subsystems because in the final analysis Sweden will purchase the best product available.

Intellectual Property Protection

Sweden adheres to the major multilateral intellectual property (IP) regimes, including (i) the WTO Agreement on Trade-Related Aspects of Intellectual Property Rights, which provides core IP protection and enforcement rights (including for trade secrets); (ii) the Paris Convention for the Protection of Industrial Property, covering patents, trademarks and industrial designs; (iii) the Patent Cooperation Treaty, protecting patents; (iv) the Berne Convention, covering copyrights; (v) the Madrid Protocol, covering trademarks; and (vi) the World Intellectual Property Organization.

Generally, Sweden is known to have reasonable laws to protect intellectual rights and enforces such laws. According to the U.S. Department of Commerce's Foreign Commercial Service, "[t]he Swedish legal system provides adequate protection to all property rights, including intellectual property."[482] The Foreign Commercial Service does indicate, how-

---

[482] *Doing Business in Sweden: 2008 Country Commercial Guide for U.S. Companies*, U.S. Foreign Commercial Service, U.S. Department of Commerce, pp. 18-19. Available at: http://www.buyusainfo.net/docs/x_3958211.pdf.

ever, that Sweden's legal and enforcement framework "requires vast improvement related to Internet piracy." Swedish authorities have had some success in prosecuting illegal file-sharing, and existing laws are being strengthened to make it easier for enforcement officials to prosecute infringers.

We are not aware of any concerns expressed by U.S. firms that IP rights have not been protected in working with the Swedish defense procurement process.

Technical Standards

Sweden is a party to the WTO's Technical Barriers to Trade Agreement, which prohibits discrimination and seeks to ensure that regulations, standards, testing and certification procedures do not create obstacles to trade, though every country has the right to adopt those technical standards it considers appropriate in areas concerning national security. Thus, Sweden has the discretion to put in place its own specific technical standards for defense products that could in theory serve as a non-tariff barrier to competing foreign products.

The U.S.-Sweden reciprocal defense procurement MOU does afford Swedish and U.S. suppliers some protection against arbitrary discrimination on the basis of regulatory standards. An Annex to the MOU provides specific procedures to ensure that defense articles and services meet mutual government quality assurances. A purchasing government has the option to request that the other government independently test and provide a certification of conformity for defense articles produced by suppliers of the selling country.

U.S. companies did not identify any specific regulatory standards-based issues that interfered with or raised concerns in their effort to conduct business in the Swedish defense market.

Chapter 13

Accessing the UK Defense Market

The fulcrum of Transatlantic and European alliances, the United Kingdom (UK) is always balancing its truly "special" relationship with the United States, its role as a leading member of North Atlantic Treaty Organization (NATO), and its commitment to the European Union (EU) and the development of a stronger EU role in global affairs. For more than a century, the United States and UK have shared enduring interests and generally congruent views of foreign policy and national security strategy, and have been each other's most reliable ally.

The UK has one of the most professional, proficient and technologically advanced armed forces in the world, and is one of the few countries in Europe with a commitment to maintaining the capability to conduct high-intensity expeditionary operations. As home to the world's second largest defense industry, the UK accounts for 5 percent of the worldwide defense market.[483] The robustness of the UK defense industry is rooted in strong national traditions of industrial development, free trade and the desire to sustain a strong defense.

Like other NATO members, the UK's defense spending declined after the Cold War from about 5 percent of gross domestic product (GDP)—at its height—to about 2.5 percent of GDP in recent times. The UK and France (also at about 2.5 percent of GDP) have the highest relative level of national defense spending among European countries. While the overall UK defense budget saw some growth from 2002-2005, it has seen no real growth since 2005 and in 2007 was about $68 billion. The so-called "defence investment accounts," the rough equal of U.S. Research, Development, Testing and Engineering (RDT&E) and Procurement, have seen no real growth since 2004 and in fact have experienced a marginal decline. At the same time, the sizable UK military operations in Iraq, Afghanistan and other foreign locations have generated significant costs, squeezing the operational accounts yet further.

The budget reductions since the Cold War ended were part of a larger series of UK military strategy reviews and realignments of the British Armed Forces. Today British force levels are approximately 40 percent lower than during the Cold War and have been reoriented more toward expeditionary operations to address dispersed global conflicts and peacekeeping operations.

Within the context of an evolving post-Cold War security environment and changing force requirements, the UK has over the years adopted and implemented one of the most open market defense industrial policies in Europe. On the demand side, the UK has made competition the centerpiece of its defense procurement strategy and in practice made major awards to U.S. and other foreign suppliers. On the supply side, after privatizing its defense industry, the UK has allowed significant foreign investment in UK defense firms by both U.S. and other European suppliers. The LOI Framework Agreement, discussed in Chapter 5, created conditions that eased "security of supply" anxieties about European defense industrial consolidation and gave the UK government assurances that strategic assets would be sustained.

---

[483] U.S. Department of Commerce Foreign Commercial Service reports on the UK; available at: http://www.buyusa.gov/uk/en/ukresearch.html#_section2.

In recent years, the UK has begun to shift its defense industrial and procurement strategy in several significant ways:

- Through a series of defense industrial policy pronouncements, the UK has signaled that it would enter into long-term sole source sustainment contracts for some existing platforms and capabilities—indicating a shift from the open competition policy of the past. While competition will remain the main default position for new systems and other new purchases, and likely for major capability upgrades, a single firm will be held accountable for support—with contracts extending for possibly two decades. This is notable as legacy systems do account for a significant percentage of UK spending.

- The new UK policy defines the UK defense industry "in terms of *where the technology is created, where the skills and the intellectual property reside, where jobs are created and sustained, and where investment is made.*"[484] The combination of this "move onshore" approach and the UK's informal Industrial Participation policy is, in effect, an offset requirement with a velvet glove. This means that U.S. and other foreign firms seeking to compete in the UK market—especially at the prime level—need to develop a domestic presence and/or substantially partner in the UK to compete.

- Finally, with its focus on operational sovereignty, the UK, like other European governments, is signaling its concern over reliance on U.S. International Traffic in Arms Regulations (ITAR)-controlled capabilities and the risk of that dependence for its own exports as well as its ability to effectively manage its own capabilities in the context of real-time operations. The UK has had sustained concerns over its treatment by the United States with respect to both technology release and disclosure policy. Overall, the UK feels that such a close and special relationship warrants increased sharing and disclosure as well as streamlined processes for release.

I. Market Background

A. The UK Strategic Context and Military Strategy

The United Kingdom's deep foundational relationship to NATO, and its very close—"special"—relationship with the United States have for decades formed the core of its foreign and security policies. The UK is also a permanent member of the United Nations Security Council, and one of the 12 founding members of the EU at its launch with the 1992 Maastricht Treaty. All of these roles place the UK at the center of the Transatlantic and European alliances.

Today the UK has the world's second largest defense sector, accounting for 5 percent of the global defense market.[485] The UK is also the second largest spender on military science, engineering and technology.[486] The robust UK defense industry arose from a strong national tradition of industrial development, free trade, and the need for a small but economically powerful island-state to sustain a strong defense.

---

[484] UK Ministry of Defence (MoD), *Defense Industrial Strategy*, Dec. 2005, available at http://merlin.ndu.edu/whitepapers/UnitedKingdom-2005.pdf.

[485] U.S. Department of Commerce Foreign Commercial Service reports on the UK; available at: http://www.buyusa.gov/uk/en/ukresearch.html#_section2.

[486] T. Radford, Science Editor, *The Guardian*, "Military dominates UK science, says report," Jan. 20, 2005, available at: http://www.guardian.co.uk/uk/2005/jan/20/highereducation.science.

The UK has one of the most technologically advanced and best trained armed forces in the world. The UK, like the United States and France, is one of the few nations in the world to operate a "blue-water navy."[487] The British Armed Forces have long been recognized among the world's strongest and have a well-known legacy of global engagement, particularly in the past wide-ranging colonial operations. The United Kingdom is one of the five major nuclear powers; its deterrent is force, based on the Vanguard class ballistic missile submarine and the Trident II D5 missile system.[488]

After World War II, Britain's declining economic and political fortunes, together with changing public and government attitudes, resulted in a contraction of the UK Armed Forces' global role. A 1957 Defence White Paper abolished conscription and dramatically reduced the size of the military. By the late 1970s, Britain had withdrawn most all of its previously deployed forces "East of Suez."[489]

Subsequently, the British Armed Forces were reconfigured to address Cold War threats, with substantial forces committed to NATO in Europe and elsewhere. By 1985, continental Europe had become Britain's main overseas commitment, with some 73,000 personnel stationed in Germany and other Western European countries.[490] The Royal Navy in particular focused on anti-submarine warfare in the GIUK Gap[491] and the North Sea.

At the end of the Cold War, the UK's defense spending declined from some 5 percent of GDP to approximately 2.5 percent today. With a receding threat and reduced budget, the UK has performed a series of strategy reviews and realignments of its military strategy and of the British Armed Forces. The Conservative government led the "Options for Change" review in 1990-1991, seeking to benefit from a perceived post-Cold War "peace dividend."[492] All three services made considerable reductions in manpower, equipment and infrastructure. Although the Soviet Union threat had receded, some reduced British presence in Germany was retained for some time.

Another milestone review was published in July 1998: the Strategic Defence Review (SDR)—described as "foreign-policy-led." Shortcomings revealed during the First Gulf War had already prompted renewed efforts to enhance joint operational cohesion and efficiency among the British services by establishing a Permanent Joint Headquarters in 1996. In the White Paper that published findings of the 1998 SDR, expeditionary warfare and tri-service integration were the central focus as the UK sought ways to improve efficiency and reduce expenditure by consolidating resources. Based on these reviews, several actions were taken to reduce military forces and the nuclear arsenal through, among other things, increased jointness. Most of the Armed Forces' helicopters were collected under a single command and a Joint Force Harrier was established in 2000, containing the Navy and

---

[487] Blue-water navy is a colloquialism often used to describe Navies capable of operating in deep waters of open oceans.

[488] Information on ballistic missile submarines is available at: http://www.royal-navy.mod.uk/server/show/nav.2420.

[489] An in-depth history of the British military and its deployments may be found at many websites, including: http://en.wikipedia.org/wiki/United_Kingdom.

[490] Source: UK Defense Analytical Services and Advice, available at: http://www.dasa.mod.uk/natstats/ukds/1998/ukds1998.pdf.

[491] The Greenland-Iceland-UK Gap, through which submarines of the Soviet Northern Fleet would have to transit to attack NATO convoys from the United States.

[492] "Changes in the size and structure of British Armed Forces were unveiled from July 1990 to July 1991" under what is termed "Options for Change." This resulted in a Defence White Paper published as Cmnd 1559-1, July 9, 1991, A. Furst, V. Heise and S. Miller, *Europe and Naval Arms Control in the Gorbachev Era*, Oxford University Press, 1992.

RAF's fleet of Harrier Jump Jets. A Joint Rapid Reaction Force was formed in 1999, with significant tri-service resources at its disposal.[493] Gradually, the UK began to rebuild its capability for expeditionary warfare within the confines of its constrained defense budget.

Post-September 11—A New Defence Strategy for "Security in a Changing World"

The UK has extensive experience with counterterrorism operations both at home (Northern Ireland) and abroad (e.g., British colonial insurgencies), but after September 11, the threat of international terrorism was given new prominence. Following September 11, then-Secretary of State for Defence Geoffrey Hoon announced a new review of Britain's defense posture. The result was the SDR "New Chapter" of July 2002, which updated the SDR of 1998,[494] a partial review that focused only on the posture and plans; it focused on whether the UK had the right concepts, forces and capabilities to meet the challenges posed by international terrorism and asymmetric threats.

In December 2003, the MoD published a full future strategic capabilities review: the Defence White Paper "Delivering Security in a Changing World,"[495] which enhanced the vision of "mobility" and "expeditionary warfare" first articulated in the SDR. But the White Paper went further, setting out the MoD's complete analysis of the future security environment and the UK's strategic priorities in light of this assessment. This House of Commons Library Summary outlines key points:

> [T]he White Paper identifies international terrorism, the proliferation of weapons of mass destruction and failing states as the main threats to the UK's national security...the UK's strategic priorities have been defined into eighteen military tasks across a wider geographical area... these cover standing commitments, including defence of the UK homeland and military assistance to the civil authorities, defence of the UK's Overseas Territories, and contingent operations overseas.... [I]t is expected that multiple, concurrent, small to medium-scale peace enforcement or peacekeeping operations will become the overriding norm. The ability to undertake large-scale intervention operations, such as Iraq in 2003, will remain important.... As a norm, and without causing overstretch, the Armed Forces must be capable of conducting three simultaneous and enduring operations of small to medium-scale.[496]

The first major restructuring to implement the White Paper was set forth in the report *Delivering Security in a Changing World: Future Capabilities*, released in July 2004.[497] This aimed to rebalance the Military into more rapidly deployable light and medium forces,

---

[493] UK Secretary of State for Defence, White Paper, available at: http://www.premier-ministre.gouv.fr/IMG/pdf/sdr1998_complete.pdf.

[494] SDR New Chapter July 2002 is available at: the UK MoD web site at: http://www.mod.uk/DefenceInternet/About-Defence/CorporatePublications/PolicyStrategyandPlanning/StrategicDefenceReviewANewChaptercm5566.htm.

[495] The MoD White Paper is available at: the MoD web site at: http://www.mod.uk/NR/rdonlyres/051AF365-0A97-4550-99C0-4D87D7C95DED/0/cm6041I_whitepaper2003.pdf.

[496] UK House of Commons Library, Research Paper 04/71, Sept. 17, 2004, available at: http://www.parliament.uk/commons/lib/research/rp2004/rp04-071.pdf.

[497] UK MoD, *Delivering Security in a Changing World: Future Capabilities.* Available at: http://www.mod.uk/NR/rdonlyres/147C7A19-8554-4DAE-9F88-6FBAD2D973F9/0/cm6269_future_capabilities.pdf.

Figure 125   **Defense Expenditure as Percent (%) of GDP 1985-1995**[498]

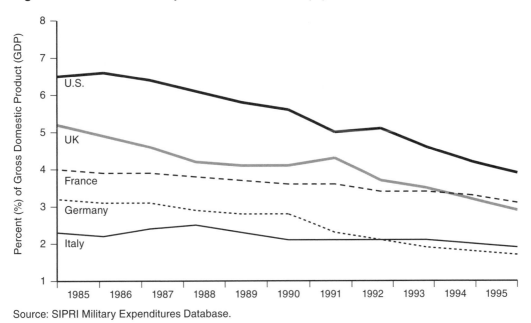

Source: SIPRI Military Expenditures Database.

capable of dealing with "concurrent and enduring" small and medium-scale operations. The strategy underscores a network-centric focus and emphasizes capabilities in intelligence surveillance and reconnaissance, theater operational entry, precision attack, and joint land and air operations. The strategy defined forces and associated major weapon systems in each area, and proposed revisions to the size and focus of forces, equipment and acquisition priorities to address both these smaller and more traditional large-scale operations. A consistent theme in the White Paper and Future Capabilities report was the plan to operate with the United States or NATO:

> [T]he full spectrum of capabilities is not required [to be held by the UK] for large scale operations, as the most demanding operations could only conceivably be undertaken alongside the U.S., either as a NATO operation or a U.S. led coalition, where we have choices as to what to contribute.[499]

UK Defense Spending and Military Forces Today

The UK budget decline from 1985 to 1995 was similar to that of the United States, and a sharper decline than that of France (reflected in Figure 125.) Thereafter, British defense spending increased from 2002-2005 but saw only marginal growth from 2005 to 2008 (see Table 58).

---

[498] B. Ardy, *NATO Military Expenditure in the Post Cold War Era*, 1996, Centre for European Research, Thames Valley University.

[499] Ibid, p. 2.

Figure 126   UK Defense Budgets, 2002-2007 (Billions of Dollars – $)

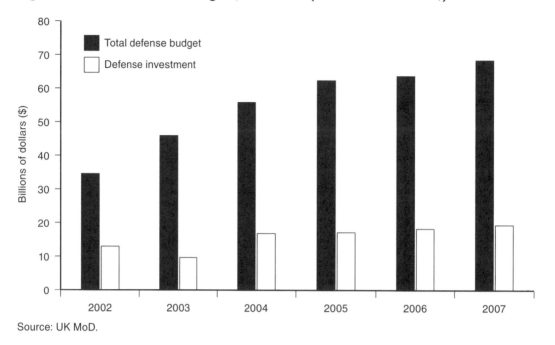

Source: UK MoD.

Table 58   UK Defense Spending (Millions of Pounds Sterling – £)[500]

	2005-2006	2006-2007	2007-2008
Total Defense Spending	33,164	34,045	37,407

Source: UK Ministry of Defense.

Further, the UK's Defence Investment accounts (which are analogous to the U.S. RDT&E and Procurement accounts) show no growth. As the top line of the budget increased, the investment spending represents an increasingly smaller proportion of the total defense budget. The investment account dipped in 2003 and has remained essentially stagnant across the period from 2004-2007, reflected in Figure 126 (in $ billions).

One of the reasons for the stagnant growth in Defence Investment is the reality of cost overruns on large programs. These are treated as "defense inflation" and absorb some of the planned budget as their time line moves to the right. Another reason is that the UK MoD is bearing a higher cost today for the support aspects of its peacekeeping operations, which are consuming a larger share of the budget (see Table 59). According to UK government officials interviewed by this study team, the direct costs of operations have typically come directly from the Treasury, not from the UK MoD budget. However, costs for replacement, rearming, supply backfills and other costs due to operations are borne by the MoD.

The MoD is likely to increasingly bear the costs of ongoing operations in the future. In this regard, in early 2009, in light of the global financial crisis and recession, Prime Min-

[500] UK MoD Statistics available at UK MoD DASA at: http://www.dasa.mod.uk/.

Figure 127   UK—Total Force Levels (Hundreds of Thousands)

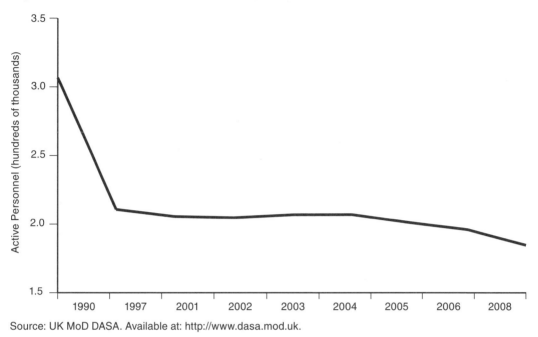

Source: UK MoD DASA. Available at: http://www.dasa.mod.uk.

Table 59   UK—Costs of Peacekeeping Operations, 2005-2008 (Millions of Pounds Sterling—£)

	2005-2006	2006-2007	2007-2008	Total
Bosnia/Kosovo	63	56	26	145
Afghanistan	199	738	1,504	2,441
Iraq	958	956	1,457	3,371
Totals	**1,220**	**1,750**	**2,987**	**5,957**

Source: UK MOD Annual Report and Accounts.

ister Gordon Brown's government decided that any unexpected costs of operations in Iraq and Afghanistan, not already budgeted for in the Treasury reserve account for operations, would be paid in full out of the core MoD defense budget. Thus, the cost of operations will increasingly constrain spending on other core MoD functions, including procurement.

The Armed Forces have been significantly reduced in size since the end of the Cold War—essentially a 40 percent reduction—the result of the several strategic reviews and restructurings outlined earlier. As shown on Figures 127 and 128, the UK end strength fell from 305,800 troops in 1990 to 184,710 in 2008. The SDR and related MoD policies reasoned that the reductions could be implemented without risk to national security due to three factors: 1) a more network-centric, precision-driven force with leading-edge technology is more effective despite a smaller force; 2) jointness among the Services and resulting

Figure 128   UK—Total Forces by Service, 2008

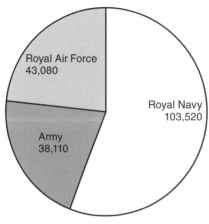

Source: UK MoD DASA, Ibid.

efficiencies; and 3) the changing nature of the threat—i.e., from preparing for a large Soviet land invasion in Central Europe to addressing a range of lower intensity risks (instability on NATO's borders, insurgency, terrorism).

UK Military Global Deployments

As these personnel reductions occurred over the last 15 years, the British Armed Forces ironically took on an increasingly international role. The UK often provides a major national contingent for peacekeeping missions under the auspices of the United Nations (UN) or NATO, and other multinational operations. The UK is organized so that nearly all of its Armed Forces and capabilities can be assigned to NATO as needed during crises. The UK also provides key system capabilities to NATO and makes major contributions to all NATO operations.[501]

Today, British forces are working with the United States in operations around the world. British and American militaries have a longstanding track record of training and operating together, and of shared strategies and systems. The most loyal ally of the United States during the conflict in Iraq, the UK contributed 45,000 troops to the 2003 U.S.-led invasion and maintained some 7,000 to 8,000 troops until 2007.[502] While the UK has drawn down its presence—at this writing there are some 4,000 troops in Iraq[503]—Prime Minister Brown has said they will all leave by September 2009.[504]

Over the past six years, the UK has also worked with the United States and NATO to improve security conditions in Afghanistan. With nearly 8,000 UK troops deployed to that

---

[501] UK Delegation to NATO, website available at: http://uknato.fco.gov.uk/en/our-offices-in-nato/our-role.

[502] "UK to halve its Iraq force to 2,500 troops" (News Agencies), Oct. 9, 2007, at: http://chinadaily.com.cn/world/2007-10/09/content_6160095.htm.

[503] UK Embassy to the U.S. (quoting Ambassador). Available at: http://ukinusa.fco.gov.uk/en/our-offices-in-the-us/ourambassador. Also see "UK says troops on track to end Iraq mission next year," Reuters News Alert, Oct. 28, 2008. Available at: http://www.alertnet.org/thenews/newsdesk/LS606783.htm.

[504] Scotsman.com, March 9, 2009. Available at: http://news.scotsman.com/iraq/Thousands-of-UK-troops-to.5050621.jp.

country, the UK government has also spent more than $650 million in military support to Afghanistan and more than $70 million in security sector reform, including $20 million for training of the Afghan National Army and $8 million to support the Afghan National Police Forces.[505]

Despite the specific goal of the SDR to avoid "overstretch," the reduced size of the Armed Forces has resulted in some problem of "overstretch" in recent years. This is challenging the military's ability to sustain its overseas commitments along with other commitments (e.g., acquisition, pensions) within its budget. As reported by the BBC:[506]

> [B]ritain's armed forces are struggling to maintain comparability and more importantly interoperability with their American counterparts. At the same time the level of operational deployments overseas has risen sharply.... Sustaining this deployment rate has been a challenge for the services... during Operation Telic, the invasion of Iraq, the British army had almost 60 percent of its personnel engaged in, or preparing for, operations.... This means that, while the present situation can be maintained, any further defence deployments of any size will only be able to be made at considerable risk either to that mission or to one of the other ongoing missions.

Representatives of the U.S. military underscored the point to this study team: the British military is challenged in keeping up with the demands of their expeditionary concepts and missions.

B. The U.S.-UK: a Very "Special" Relationship[507]

> [T]he United Kingdom and the United States have an incomparable relationship. Our shared language, shared values of freedom and democracy, and shared political and judicial systems are the bedrock of the "special relationship."[508]
>
> —*Nigel Sheinwald, British Ambassador to the United States*

> [T]he United States and the United Kingdom are often described as having a special relationship. This relationship is the natural outcome of our common history and culture, our shared support of the rule of law, our mutual belief in democracy, freedom and tolerance, and our commitment to free trade and open markets.
>
> —*U.S. Department of Commerce, Foreign Commercial Service*[509]

---

[505] Ibid. Quotes from Embassy discussion on Afghanistan, available at: http://ukinusa.fco.gov.uk/en/working-with-usa/conflict-prevention/afghanistan/.

[506] Dr. Andrew Dorman, Senior Lecturer at King's College, London, *Overstretch: Modern Army's Weakness*, Report by BBC News, June 15, 2005, available at: http://news.bbc.co.uk/1/hi/uk/4097828.stm.

[507] A Special Relationship is a colloquial term often used "to describe the exceptionally close political, diplomatic, cultural and historical relations, notably between the U.S. and UK, following its use in a 1946 speech by Winston Churchill." Quote from http://en.wikipedia.org/wiki/Special_Relationship.

[508] Op. cit. Available at: http://ukinusa.fco.gov.uk/en/our-offices-in-the-us/ourambassador/.

[509] U.S. Department of Commerce Foreign Commercial Service reports on the UK; available at: http://www.buyusa.gov/uk/en/uk_commercial_guide.html.

The United States and the UK have one of the strongest relationships in the history of nations, covering the full spectrum of security, economic and other policy areas; the scope and depth of U.S.-UK cooperation on sensitive matters is unrivalled. At the heart of this special relationship are enduring congruent interests, strong trade, common views on foreign policy, and cooperation on nearly all national matters. These historic relations, formed from the early days of the United States, were strengthened by the U.S. entry into World War II in Europe and in subsequent closely coordinated strategies and operations during the Cold War and after September 11. The level of bilateral investment between the two countries is strong and growing: the UK is the U.S.'s largest European export market with exports of $92.5 billion in 2006 (half in services); more than 40,000 U.S. firms export to the UK. The total bilateral trade in goods and services increased 8 percent to $184 billion in 2006. In addition, record numbers of people from the United States and the United Kingdom visit the other country."[510]

Both through bilateral accords and the core position of the two countries in NATO, the G-8 and the UN, the United States and the UK collaborate on a wide range of global challenges and initiatives. Traditionally, the United States and UK stand together in these multilateral settings, and as discussed earlier, in undertaking military operations around the world.

The relationship between the governments has also withstood trials on national security and military deployments. The British people tend to be more cautious than their government regarding military intervention by British forces. A clear recent example of the "government vs. the popular choice" was the Blair government's support of the invasion and occupation in Iraq. The British government had to endure consistently hostile public opinion against the war.

Despite the UK's public outpouring of disagreement with the Blair government on Iraq, and even some display of public resentment against U.S. military personnel inside the UK reported to this interview team, the U.S.-UK relations in military and national security matters remain extraordinarily close.

U.S.-UK Defense Trade and Industrial Cooperation—An Extraordinary Level of Interaction

Because of their longstanding security relationship and record of operational cooperation, the United States and Great Britain have extensive defense trade relationships, including a higher level of trade in defense goods and services with each other than with any other country. They often buy and sell weapon systems and other defense products higher on the "defense value chain" from each other, and have a consistently higher level of technology sharing.

Legal Frameworks for Defense Industrial Cooperation

The United States has broader and deeper mechanisms for cooperation and mutual support in defense with the UK than with almost any nation, excepting Canada.

The UK benefits from several U.S. bilateral agreements to ease the flow and speed of defense trade and cooperation. First, the two countries have signed a Reciprocal Defense Pro-

---

[510] U.S. Department of Commerce, Ibid.

curement Memorandum of Understanding (MOU) stipulating that UK and U.S. defense suppliers be afforded equal treatment with domestic defense companies. The latest amendment to the MOU (2004) addresses the flow of technical information and security of supply—reciprocal systems under which each country can establish priority designations to ensure timely performance and delivery under defense contracts performed for the other country.

On February 5, 2000, then-Secretary of Defense William Cohen and then-UK Secretary of State for Defence Geoffrey Hoon, signed the Declaration of Principles (DoP) for Defence Equipment and Industrial Cooperation.[511] The DoP was designed to further deepen our relationship and maintain close U.S.-UK ties even as the UK was expanding its security relations within Europe. More specifically, the DoP sought to improve armaments cooperation and defense trade by removing administrative obstacles and establishing principles for improved cooperation in key areas such as security of supply, export procedures, industrial security, foreign investment, research and development (R&D), and mutual market access. Annexes to the MOU are used to implement the DoP between the two nations.

U.S. Cooperative Programs: The JSF Partnership

In 2001, the United States and UK formed a substantial partnership on the F-35 Joint Strike Fighter (JSF) program.[512] As stated in a press release announcing the MOU for the program:

> [J]SF represents a commitment to develop a mutual security environment that will truly enhance future coalition operations—one that will require the United States, the United Kingdom, and their allies not only to fight together, but also to work together to develop weapons systems and equipment that are fully interoperable.[513]

The UK committed $2 billion toward the system development and demonstration (SDD) phase of the program—the largest contribution of any U.S. partner; Italy pledged $1 billion and the Netherlands $800 million to SDD). The UK is also funding additional development needed to integrate the JSF into the British forces. Like the U.S. Marine Corps, the Royal Navy and Royal Air Force plan to procure a short take-off vertical landing variant, which will replace the Current Joint Force Harrier and Sea Harriers FRAS.1 in the strike fighter role.[514]

This large investment and early commitment afforded the UK an unprecedented role in the program, including participation in the down select process that chose the Lockheed Martin aircraft.[515] Indeed, other participating nations have at times expressed dismay that they did not have the MOU status of the UK (see discussion in Chapter 9 on Italy for example). But the UK's expectations for a "two-way street" on the program have not always been fully satisfied.

---

[511] Available at: http://ukinusa.fco.gov.uk/en/defence/defence-materiel/defence-equipment/Trade/declaration.

[512] See also DoD Press Release Jan. 17, 2001("[J]SF represents a commitment to develop a mutual security environment that will truly enhance future coalition operations—one that will require the United States, the United Kingdom, and their allies not only to fight together, but also to work together to develop weapons systems and equipment that are fully interoperable.") Available at: http://www.fas.org/man/dod-101/sys/ac/docs/man-ac-jsf-010117.htm.

[513] DoD Press Release Jan. 17, 2001. Available at: http://www.fas.org/man/dod-101/sys/ac/docs/man-ac-jsf-010117.htm.

[514] There is a heated ongoing debate on the number of JSFs the UK may buy given current budget constraints, and whether it will replace all current Joint Force Harriers. See the *Telegraph*, Feb. 26, 2009. Available at: http://www.telegraph.co.uk/news/newstopics/politics/defence/4448256/Harrier-dispute-between-Navy-and-RAF-chiefs-sees-Army-marriage-counsellor-called-in.html.

[515] For more details, see JSF Program office website. Available at: http://www.jsf.mil/program/prog_intl.htm.

U.S. Export Licensing and Disclosure Policy: A Serious Issue in U.S.-UK Relations

The UK has long had broad concerns and outright frustration over U.S. export control policy. This includes both the procedural aspects of export controls—long delays and resulting implications for UK programs—and what the UK views as overly restrictive release policies (i.e., the limited extent, in their view, to which the United States is willing to share defense technology). These broader issues, and the recently signed U.S.-UK treaty on the subject (which is pending ratification in the U.S. Senate), are fully discussed under III. Evaluation of Market Access Metrics later in this chapter.

Today, the UK, like any other country, must apply separately for each export license when the UK government or its firms seek to purchase U.S. defense technologies or services. These licenses often can take weeks or months to be approved, and the time lines not only cause delay but create uncertainties when planning and developing complex systems.

These issues came to a head on the JSF program, where the United States and its partners recognized at an early stage the need for streamlining technology export release and disclosure to the foreign partners. Ultimately, the State Department issued a global project authorization (ITAR GPA), a special broad license allowing very quick turnaround times for export licenses for relatively low technology items used on JSF.

However, neither the ITAR GPA nor similar steps addressed the serious technology transfer problems inherent in the program. First, only 3 of the eligible 46 companies used ever used the ITAR GPA. As a Government Accountability Office (GAO) report noted, program participants said "many companies have chosen to use the traditional license process instead of the ITAR GPA to avoid the extra costs and administrative burdens associated with" the special compliance requirements for using the ITAR GPA.[516] The ITAR GPA was limited in other ways: it applied only to the system development and demonstration phase of the program and would need to be reauthorized for the production base and contained numerous provisos that limited its use on higher-end technologies. Accordingly, most firms have applied for licenses on a case-by-case basis, which has caused delays to the program.

Moreover, the U.S. Department of Defense (DoD) faced enormous challenges in determining whether to disclose certain technologies to its allies, including both process issues (there are numerous DoD components involved in the process) and substantive issues. From the outset, the UK and other allies complained that they were effectively precluded from participating in higher value "noble work" on the program.

As the GAO reported in July 2003 on the JSF export licensing process: "managing these transfers and partner expectations while avoiding delays has been a key challenge and [GAO has] recommended industrial planning tools be… used to anticipate time frames for national disclosure and technology transfer decisions."[517] The problems in technology release and disclosure policy were left unresolved for a sustained period, and the UK and other partners remained very frustrated. As one commentator noted, "tension between the [U.S. and UK] allies over information sharing bubbled to the surface in 2005 when the United Kingdom threatened to drop out of the international Joint Strike Fighter program because the

---

[516] Government Accountability Office, "Joint Strike Fighter: Management of the Technology Transfer Process," GAO-06-364 (March 14, 2006). Available at: http://www.gao.gov/htext/d06364.html.

[517] Ibid.

Figure 129   UK-U.S Total Trade Balance (Billions of Dollars – $)

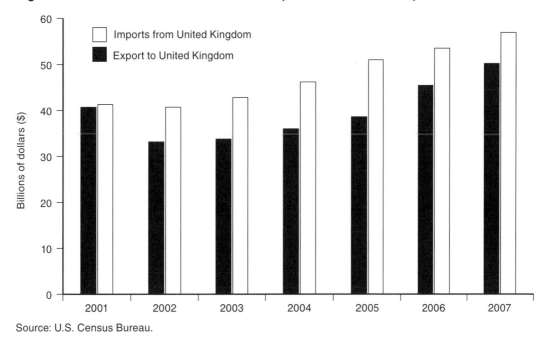

Source: U.S. Census Bureau.

Defense Department would not share computer codes and other critical information used in the design of the fighter airplane."[518]

The central British concern was their desire for operational sovereignty. The UK did not seek, or need, to produce or own intellectual property (IP) for every part of the JSF. But the UK asserted the need to make deliberate and independent decisions on a capability—especially in an operational context. In their view, the UK armed forces must be able to operate independently and without continually seeking permission—or worse, struggling to get permission—for the latest software updates, threat information, etc. The UK has its own operational approach, and seeks to act autonomously in operations, even when operating systems they acquire from or develop with the United States.

In August 2006, the U.S. and UK finally reached a technology transfer agreement for the F-35, which became the model for other F-35 partners. In December 2007, the U.S. and UK signed the JSF Production, Sustainment & Follow On Development MOU.[519]

But technology licensing on JSF remains a sore spot to this day and highlights an underlying reality of the longstanding U.S. policy of keeping defense strategy and armament cooperation largely divorced from technology transfer policy. JSF is only the latest of a series of cooperative programs on which the United States and its allies have faced intractable technology transfer issues.

---

[518] By B. Wagner, "U.S.-UK Defense Technology Pact Likely to Draw Fire," *National Defense*, publication of the National Defense Industrial Association, Sept. 2007. Available at: http://www.nationaldefensemagazine.org/archive/2007/September/Pages/U2510.S2510.-U2510.K2510.Def2510.aspx.

[519] *Defense Industry Daily*, Sept. 22, 2008, http://www.defenseindustrydaily.com/us-uk-treaty-aims-to-ease-itar-export-control-burdens-04371/.

Table 60   U.S. Defense Exports to the UK (Direct and Foreign Commercial Sales (Millions of Dollars–$)

	2002	2003	2004	2005	2006	2007
Commercial Sales	18.9	59.4	588.7	1,840.0	2,331.4	1,473.9
FMS Delivers	385.6	350.1	452.9	383.7	294.5	429.6
Total	**404.5**	**409.5**	**1,041.6**	**2,223.7**	**2,625.9**	**1,903.5**

Source: U.S. DoD Security Cooperation Historical Facts Book.

Thus, as discussed under III. Evaluation of Market Access Metrics later in this chapter, despite the Defense Trade Security Initiative (DTSI) and its bilateral agreements, the UK has long pressed for a special mechanism to greatly reduce and streamline U.S. controls on export of U.S. products and technologies to the UK.

U.S. Defense Sales and Market Presence Reflect Close National Ties

The UK is the world's fifth largest economy and the fifth largest export market for the United States.[520] The U.S. and UK enjoy one of the most open trade and economic relationships with each other of any two nations, the extent of which is shown in Figure 129.

Given the close U.S.-UK relationship, U.S. firms have had more defense market success in the UK—measured in sales revenues and ownership of defense assets—than they have in any other European nation. This reflects both the UK's longstanding open market policies with respect to U.S. participation in the UK defense sector and its commitment to military interoperability and commonality with the United States.

Specifically, our data shows that since 2002, the United States has had a higher level of sales of defense articles to the UK than to any other nation in Europe, rising from about $400 million in 2002-2003 to a peak of about $2.6 billion in 2006 and then somewhat down in 2007, to about $1.9 billion in 2007 (Table 60). If dual-use articles were included in the statistics, the extent of UK-U.S. defense trade would undoubtedly be higher. By way of comparison, the United States sales to France grew similarly but at a lower level: from about $225 million in 2002 to reach about $400-$500 million a year in 2005-2007. France is the European nation with the budget size closest to that of the UK. U.S. sales to Germany, which has a lower defense budget, ranged from $700 million to $1.6 billion in 2004-2007.

Direct commercial sales between U.S. companies and the UK government account for some 80 percent of all U.S. defense exports to Britain. Although UK exports to the United States are only a fraction of U.S. sales to Britain, both the magnitude and proportion of British sales rose from 2004-2006, likely reflecting the surge for Iraq and Afghanistan, as shown in Figure 130 (sales peaked in 2006 and fell somewhat in 2007.)

---

[520] Data on the overall UK economy and exports/imports is from the U.S. Department of Commerce Foreign Commercial Service, website on the UK; available at: http://www.buyusa.gov/uk/en/uk_economy_business.html.

Figure 130   UK-U.S. Defense Trade (Billions of Dollars–$)

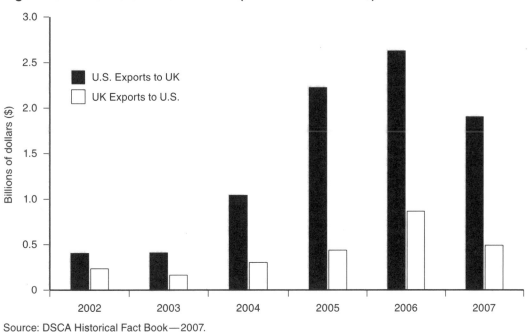

Source: DSCA Historical Fact Book—2007.

U.S. Defense Systems and Products in the UK

Not surprisingly given the close national relationships, the UK has over decades procured numerous U.S. platforms/systems and products down the value chain, as well as logistics and support services. Table 61 outlines major U.S. products and systems acquired by the UK in the last 10 years. This reflects the high value system/product levels that many major U.S. firms provide in the UK, mostly by direct commercial sale. This list does not represent the full range and scale of U.S. sales in the UK; there also are considerable sales of subsystems and components not captured by these data.

U.S. Firms—Increasing Role and Presence Since 2005

U.S. and other foreign-owned defense firms with subsidiaries in the UK report they are treated as UK firms. *Representatives of firms interviewed by this study team repeatedly say that the critical point is that the definition of a "UK defense firm" is changing*—the company headquarters and full shareholder base no longer needs to be in the UK for the firm to be treated as a UK firm. They attribute this shift in part to the clarity of goals and policies enunciated first in the 2002 Defence Industrial Policy and more subsequently in more detail in the UK Defence Industrial Strategy (DIS), both discussed in detail below.

The UK imposes conditions, evident but which may not need to be written, for U.S. and other foreign firms that seek to capture UK sales for complex systems or subsystems high on the value chain. First, these foreign firms need to have an adequately robust domestic presence in the UK. Increasingly, gaining market position up the value chain—notably to be what the UK terms a Tier 1 (prime contractor) or even a Tier 2 (complex subsystem) supplier—means having a credible domestic presence in terms of key skills and capabilities, with

Table 61   Products and Services of U.S. Defense Firms in UK

U.S. Company	Program	Status
Boeing	C-17A Globemaster III	Complete
	CH-47 Chinook Life Cycle Support	Ongoing
	Future Rapid Effects System (FRES)	Ongoing
	Integration subcontractor to Thales	
Lockheed Martin	Joint Strike Fighter Program Partner	Ongoing
	C-130J Hercules Support	Ongoing
	Teamed with Marshall UK	
	Merlin Shipboard Helicopter Upgrade	Ongoing
	Land Environment Air Picture	Ongoing
General Dynamics	FRES Utility Vehicle (Pirhana V)	Ongoing
	Digitization Battlespace Land BBL-CIP	Ongoing
	Bowman	Ongoing
	Defense Information Infrastructure	Ongoing
	Subcontractor to EDS	
	Chemical-Biological-Nuclear Protection	Ongoing
Raytheon	Coalition Warrior DCGS Integration	Demo
	AIM-120 AMRAAM	Sustainment
	Successor IFF	Ongoing
	Paveway Laser-Guided Bomb	Ongoing
	Airborne Standoff Radar (ASTOR)	Ongoing
Northrop Grumman	Bowman (Subcontractor)	Ongoing
	E-3 AWACS Support	Ongoing
L-3 Communications	Nimrod MR.4A Upgrade (Prime)	Ongoing
	LEAPP (Subcontractor to Lockheed Martin)	Ongoing
General Atomics	MQ-9A Reaper UAV	Ongoing
EDS Corporation	UK Defense Information Infrastructure, Increment 2b Prime Contractor	Ongoing

Source: InfoBase Publishers, DACIS Programs Database.

a sufficiently robust UK bench to take on the contracts for which they bid—not just a "proposal capture" team that will go home after the award or a sales office. As one senior U.S. VP in a London Headquarters said, "You have to have a 25-year plan; you can't just fly folks in." Second, as discussed below, there are other conditions—U.S. firms must partner with local businesses and provide a "subtle" but real domestic work share and create jobs, technology or IP benefits to the UK—in order to bid credibly for most programs of any value.

As a result, given the relative size and scope of the UK market, the major U.S. defense firms have made conscious efforts to come onshore and expand their UK footprint as they acquire businesses and skills to provide the "bench strength" and meet work share requirements. All "Big 5" U.S. defense prime contractors now have a formal UK corporate structure and an increasing but still modest on-the-ground presence:

- **Boeing UK**—Boeing has had a unit in the UK for about six years. Today Boeing has about about 600 employees, about half working on defense and half on commercial products. The UK is the "largest spend" location for Boeing outside the United States. Boeing has substantially enhanced its presence through several key awards, including serving as a subcontractor to Thales on the Future Rapid Effect System (FRES) Systems Integration and entering into a 30-plus year partnership arrangement with the UK MoD for Chinook Through Life Customer Support program.

- **General Dynamics UK Limited**—Headquartered in South East Wales, General Dynamics (GD) UK is "the fourth largest UK defense company and the third largest defense prime contractor in the UK… [has] approximately 1,700 staff at eight separate UK facilities."[521] GD UK's website also emphasizes charitable contributions and GD's role in building technology and innovation in the UK.

- **Lockheed Martin UK Company**—Lockheed Martin created a subsidiary in the UK in July 1999 with about 30 employees—consolidating its various UK businesses under a single entity. As of 2008, Lockheed had about 1,750 employees. However, Lockheed is not performing manufacturing in the UK. Lockheed is a part of the Atomic Weapons Establishment, a Joint Venture with two other UK firms, to manage and oversee the UK's nuclear stockpile (discussed below).

- **Northrop Grumman UK**—The firm has approximately 700 employees in the UK. The award of the large AWACS (airborne warning and control systems) maintenance support contract is a key aspect of its UK activity. Northrop has not to date succeeded in system sales in the UK.

- **Raytheon Systems Limited (UK subsidiary)**—Raytheon operates sites in England, Scotland, Wales and Northern Ireland (Derry, a software facility) with about 1,330 employees in total.

Although still not large in absolute terms, the U.S. defense primes have a considerably larger on-the-ground presence in the UK than in other European defense markets (see Table 62).[522] Of course, the sustained presence and growth of U.S. firms in the UK is highly dependent on continued opportunities and an acceptable "win ratio." Some U.S. firms stated they also can use a UK base as an operating location to sell into the Mideast and Europe, but it is not yet clear how well this has paid off.

---

[521] Quote from GD UK website: http://www.generaldynamics.uk.com/about-gduk/economic-benefits-to-the-uk.

[522] Table 62 includes firms like EDS, which, although not classically a "defense prime," does work for the UK MoD.

Table 62   U.S. Company Footprints in UK (Millions of Dollars–$)

Company	UK Employees 2003	UK Employees 2008	UK Revenues 2003	UK Revenues 2008
Lockheed Martin	1,000	1,700	329	667.5
Boeing*	425	600	2,400	900.0
Raytheon	1,591	1,400	431	420.0
EDS Corporation	2,500	2,500	255	300.0
General Dynamics	600	1,600	111	450.0
Totals	**6,116**	**7,800**	**3,525**	**2,737.5**

*Boeing revenues for 2003 include commercial sales. Defense accounts for 50% of Northrop Grumman 2008 revenue. Defense represents about 50% of Raytheon revenues. Boeing revenues for 2008 are defense only. EDS 2008 employment and revenues from DACIS.
Source: UK Ministry of Defence; InfoBase Publishers, Companies Database.

As shown on Table 63, however, the leading European defense firms, Thales, which acquired Racal, a leading UK defense firm, Finmeccanica (which includes AgustaWestlands), and EADS, have UK operations that considerably exceed the UK presence of major U.S. defense firms in size and scope of activities. These three European firms alone account for roughly 33,000 employees—which considerably exceeds the approximately 22,400 total presence of all known U.S. defense firms in the UK.[523]

Table 63   European Defense Company Footprint in United Kingdom (Millions of Pounds Sterling–£)

Company	Country	2007 UK Revenues	2007 UK Employees
Thales UK	FR	1,300	8,500
EADS	EUR	1,500	14,500
Finmeccanica	IT	1,800	9,700

Source: UK Ministry of Defense.

Why have U.S. firms decided to build up their UK presence? While UK policy clearly incentivizes this approach (i.e., U.S. firms can be treated as domestic firms if they follow this model), U.S. firms make this judgment purely on a business basis. Outside the United States, the UK is one of the largest and most accessible defense markets in the world. It is a challenging calculus to balance the costs of establishing, bidding and operating in the UK *vis-à-vis* successful market share results. The cost of doing business in the UK is high and it is

---

[523] Data on total U.S. defense related employee presence in the UK, set forth on Table 25 in Chapter 4, was provided by the British Embassy to the United States. In some cases the number of employees per firm listed in Table 25 vary from the number of employees reported to this study team by U.S. company representatives in the UK. The actual numbers of employees at any given time are naturally always changing as programs change and other corporate changes occur.

very costly to bring U.S. employees to the UK by creating incentives to have them locate and hire locally. The payoff for this extension into the UK must come in terms of value returned to shareholders; there is a constant need to defend the UK location "back home."

A Changing Model for U.S. Sales

U.S. firms must weigh and balance several factors in bidding and establishing a presence to address UK opportunities. While U.S. technology and system interoperability is attractive to the UK, ITAR frustrations are causing strain. At the same time, the UK is motivated by a desire for greater cooperation with various European nations, notably France. When the UK holds a competition, increasingly strong European firms and teams today can offer attractive alternatives to U.S. solutions—witness the strength of Thales UK and the increasing role of Finmeccanica. At the same time, the U.S. firms must offer sufficient value in the UK—jobs, technology development, IP, etc.. In the UK, as in the United States and the rest of Europe, there is also a shift away from platforms toward network-centric and capability-based acquisitions. This changes the nature of bidding opportunities—more often, pieces of larger system-of-systems are competed, and the solutions must interface broadly. New platforms are generally being acquired in a cooperative program, e.g., the JSF is a cooperative development program. The United States is winning some new system/platform awards and new positions as a Tier 1 prime to the UK (e.g., General Dynamics won the FRES Utility Vehicle lead designer contract in May 2008). But the U.S. firms now have to compete on UK and European turf and by their rules. Thus, a solution invented and produced in the United States will have a harder time succeeding than in past decades.

II. UK Defense Market: Supply and Demand Dynamics

With the world's second largest defense sector, the UK accounts for 5 percent of the global defense market. Its closely related aerospace industry is also the second largest in the world, enjoying a turnover of $39.6 billion in 2006—about 13 percent of the worldwide aerospace market. As of 2005, the UK Aerospace and defense industry employed more than 114,000 people in the UK and more than 40,000 overseas.[524]

The UK also has historically been one of the most open defense markets in Europe and has shown a willingness to acquire important defense products and services from overseas suppliers while allowing extensive foreign ownership of the UK defense industrial base. According to the UK's 2005 Defence Industrial Strategy, "In 2004-05 some 5 per cent of UK equipment spending was directed at imports; fourteen per cent was spent with foreign-owned companies located in the UK; and 13 percent in cooperative European programs (compared to U.S. spending of two per cent on imports and seven per cent with foreignowned U.S. companies)."[525] This reflects foreign participation in roughly 32 percent of its defense equipment spending, with the remainder (68 percent) apparently domestic in orientation.

---

[524] K. Hayward, *The UK Defence Industrial Strategy*, A Royal Aeronautical Society Position Paper, Nov. 2005. Mr. Hayward is the Head of Research.

[525] UK Defence Industrial Strategy (DIS), Dec. 2005, p. 29. Available at: http://www.mod.uk/nr/rdonlyres/f530ed6c-f80c-4f24-8438-0b587cc4bf4d/0/def_industrial_strategy_wp_cm6697.pdf.

Evolution of the UK Defense Industry

Britain's robust, world-class defense industry has its roots in a tradition of industrialization and free trade that the UK has pursued for decades. However, during much of the Cold War period, the British defense industry was largely state-owned and supported. While the British government's general economic policies shifted toward a more open market in the 1950s and 1960s, many major industrial and public service firms, including defense, remained government controlled.

After 1979, the dramatic privatization policies of Prime Minister Margaret Thatcher's Conservative government also began to affect defense businesses. Michael Bell, then-Deputy Under-Secretary of State for Defence Procurement, said "[i]n the eyes of the government, there was no overpowering reason why defence equipment and services had to be provided by nationalised organisations."[526] Thus, in the 1980s, major British defense firms were privatized, years ahead of their peers elsewhere in Europe. The British government still owns a small stake and has "golden share" rights in select firms, as detailed below.

The UK privatization program treated Defense companies somewhat differently from other nationalized industries, with the government retaining a stake in these firms for a period of time. Most shares of the defense firms were sold or floated on the stock market, some as a whole and others in pieces. At the time, the government retained some shares, including a golden share in some key companies, to protect the national interest. But the UK increasingly sought to treat the industry under the rubric of "the market rules," reinforced by the MoD's adoption of new procurement policies of full competition.

Moving to a "Full Competitive Model"

In the 1980s, the UK instituted fairly radical reforms to require full competition and more open sourcing of defense equipment. Known as the Levene Reforms (after Peter Levene, then-Chief of Defense Procurement), these were intended to encourage the defense industry to adopt better management practices and reduce costs. These, in concert with the post-Cold War UK "Options for Change" review and subsequent strategic reviews discussed above, led to demand for reductions and policy changes that had dramatic effects on the industry. The Levene Reforms, under the Conservative leadership, moved the MoD to an increasingly full and open competitive model. The UK MoD wanted "value for money," and encouraged defense firms to behave more in the model of firms in the larger commercial market; the theory was that this would help achieve cost-efficiencies. This meant full competitive forces and fixed-price contracts. Michael Bell, then-Deputy Under-Secretary of State for Defence Procurement, MoD, reflected:

> The move to competitive, usually fixed price, contracts means that companies have to assess very carefully the costs they are likely to incur. They should be able to make a reasonable profit, but if all other factors are equal, the… company which can do the job the most economically stands a better chance of being awarded the contract…. [Firms had] to become more competitive as a result of increased exposure to market forces, defence enterprises have had to restructure. From the government's perspective, privatisation has enabled us to pursue our policy of opening up defence procurement as fully as possible to competitive pressures.

---

[526] M. Bell, *Privatization in NACC Countries, Defence Industry Experiences and Policies and Related Experiences in Other Fields*, NATO Colloquia, 1994, available at: http://www.nato.int/docu/colloq/1994/eco9419.txt.

These reforms did make firms "feel competitive pressures" and work to rationalize. However, the push toward all-out competition with firm fixed prices became very difficult for defense firms, particularly in development programs and new defense system R&D where it was difficult to project costs accurately in advance. Firms interviewed for this study reflected on this period of what they perceived as overzealous competition—competition to a fault, not adequately balanced by the need for best value and life cycle cost considerations. Programs were experiencing cost overruns and the MoD was dissatisfied with performance.[527]

Smart Acquisition and Focus on Best Value

The 1998 SDR introduced key acquisition and industrial policy changes that would begin to shift these dynamics. Some of the critical changes in UK acquisition policy included:

- Launching the Smart Procurement Initiative and later Smart Acquisition, to transform processes and organizations to make acquisition faster, cheaper and better and to emphasize the MoD's concern for through-life customer support.

- Creating a unified Equipment Capability Customer organization, for setting capability requirements and priorities for procurement.

- Creating the Defence Procurement Agency (subsumed into the current Defense Equipment and Support Organization (DE&S)) and combining three Service Logistics Commands into a Defence Logistics Organisation.

Subsequently, in December 2001, the UK MoD issued Policy Paper Number 4, entitled "Defense Acquisition."[528] The Smart Acquisition and the related initiatives embodied therein were comparable in nearly every way to the U.S. DoD acquisition reforms. The UK variants included:

- A whole-life approach, applying "through-life" costing techniques;

- A better, more open relationship with industry;

- More investment during early project phases and trade-offs between system performance, through-life costs and time; and

- New procurement approaches, including incremental acquisition and a streamlined process for project approvals.[529]

To industry, the principles of Smart Acquisition were an appealing change: the UK MoD would take a more balanced view of risk, backing off the "full commercial enterprise" approach the industry struggled with in the 1990s. The new policies were a turning point toward a better value concept of acquisition, and form the basis for UK acquisition policies, with some continued evolution, today.

---

[527] British American Security Information Council, Occasional Paper (March 2006). ("Radical reforms to improve value for money in defence procurement have come and gone (e.g. the Levene Reforms of the 1980s and the launch of the Defence Procurement Agency in 1999), with little real impact on delays and cost overruns. Smart Procurement became Smart Acquisition in 1999, but the Public Accounts Committee concluded in 2005 that, *"Smart Acquisition is at risk of becoming the latest in a long line of failed attempts to improve defence procurement.")*. Available at: http://www.basicint.org/pubs/Papers/BP50.htm.

[528] UK MoD Policy Papers No. 4, Defense Acquisition, Dec. 2001, available at: http://www.mod.uk/NR/rdonlyres/1B07C74B-F841-4E78-9A13-F4A0E0796061/0/polpaper4_def_acquisition.pdf.

[529] Smart Acquisition Program, U.S. Embassy, at: http://www.usembassy.org.uk/odc/Smart_Acquisition.pdf.

Defense Industrial Consolidation in the UK

A second, and related, major result of UK policy and budget changes of the 1990s was the large-scale UK defense industrial consolidation that ensued. As described in the 2005 DIS, the European consolidation process more generally resulted in "several large European companies—namely BAE Systems, EADS, Thales and Finmeccanica. Within the UK, consolidation has been taken further than in wider Europe and the industrial structure is now relatively mature and stable, although further rationalisation within this construct is possible."[530]

As further described in a forthcoming book on the UK defense industry:

[T]he 1990s saw a number of medium sized defence contractors (such as Racal, Ferranti and Alvis) and divisions of diversified engineering firms (such as Dowty and GKN's armoured vehicles division) exit the market through divestment of their defence businesses or merger often acquired by UK firms who had decided to concentrate in defense and aerospace. The most significant transaction for the competitive landscape of the UK defence market was the 1999 acquisition of GEC Marconi by British Aerospace that led to the creation of BAE Systems. During the 1990s, UK government defence industrial and procurement policy had sought to sustain the GEC Marconi-British Aerospace duopoly as a means of maintaining a level of credible competition in the UK defence market. The formation of BAE Systems created a firm that had a central role on almost all major UK defence programmes from nuclear submarines to fast jet combat aircraft and (with its acquisition of Alvis Vickers) armoured fighting vehicles.[531]

The consolidation in the UK also affected the U.S. market. The merger in 1999 of two British firms with substantial U.S. assets—BAE and GEC (the Marconi Electronic Systems (MES) defense business of General Electric Company PLC, not related to General Electric Corporation)—stands out as a prime example where the UK consolidation posed competition issues for the United States. The merger created a set of complex competitive conflicts on leading defense programs: the Future Scout and Cavalry System (FSCS/Tracer) program (a land vehicle) and the F-35 Joint Strike Fighter (JSF) Program. In cases such as this one, the U.S. DoD and U.S. antitrust authorities worked closely with the British authorities (both the UK MoD and Office of Unfair Trading) to develop a novel set of mitigations needed to allow this transaction to proceed.

Move to European Cooperative and Collaborative Programs

The large UK defense programs today reflect a long-term trend toward international and cooperative programs, especially for large, complex platform systems.[532] In the last 15 or so years, the UK has increasingly pursued new programs through partnerships and shared

---

[530] DIS, op. cit., p. 26. Available at: http://www.mod.uk/nr/rdonlyres/f530ed6c-f80c-4f24-8438-0b587cc4bf4d/0/def_industrial_strategy_wp_cm6697.pdf.

[531] A. James and P. Hall, "Industry structure, procurement and innovation in the UK defence sector," in A. James (ed.) (2009) *The dynamics of innovation in the defence sector: economics, technology and the new security environment*, Cheltenham (UK): Edward Elgar (to be published in 2009).

[532] The trend began in the mid 1960s with a series of Anglo French cooperative programs, including the Jaguar ground attack helicopter and a family of helicopters including Lynx and Puma. Ibid., James 2009.

development, or by buying already developed off-the-shelf capabilities that could be adapted to UK needs.

The UK is spending about 8 percent of its major program budgets (greater than $50 million for 2006-08) on cooperative programs (excluding the JSF), but this percentage varies by the year and specific program activities in that year. The JSF is the only notable UK-U.S. cooperative program; the bulk of the UK's cooperative programs are with EU partners, as follows:

- **A400M Cargo Transport**—Managed by OCCAR (Organization for Joint Armament Cooperation), and cooperative with Spain, France, Turkey, Germany, Belgium and Luxembourg;

- **Eurofighter Typhoon**—a consortium for the Typhoon Multirole agile fighter with Germany, Italy, Spain, Austria and Saudi Arabia as buyers (representing a about 5 percent share of the UK defense procurement spending);

- **Eurojet**—consortium supplying jet aircraft engines for Eurofighter; its shareholders are Avio (Italy), ITP (Spain), MTU Aero Engines (Germany) and Rolls-Royce (UK);

- **Boxer/MRAV**—managed by OCCAR, a wheeled all terrain utility vehicle being developed with Germany and the Netherlands (demonstration unit); and

- **AirTanker "Leasing"**—In a novel form of a cooperative program, in March 2007, the British MoD signed a 27-year, private-finance-initiative contract with the Air-Tanker industry consortium for 14 Airbus A330-200s to meet the RAF's Future Strategic Tanker Aircraft requirement. AirTanker will own and support the tankers, providing air refueling and air transport services to the RAF. AirTanker is led by EADS, and includes Cobham, EADS, Rolls-Royce, Thales UK, and VT Group—it is about 50 percent British by value. The MoD selected the consortium in February 2005 (over a BAE-Boeing team offering a KC-767 tanker), but it took until 2008 to get the private financing assembled.[533]

The UK also has collaborative technology work with some other European nations, such as in future radar technology.

UK Defense Industry Today: Internationalizing and Shifting to Cooperative Programs

[The B]ritish aerospace [and defense] industry is a global player: a host to companies such as Thales, Lockheed Martin, Raytheon, EADS and Finmeccanica, as well as the home base for a significant part of European and U.S. industry—BAE Systems, Rolls-Royce, Smiths, and Cobham. So what happens in the UK will have some impact globally on the world defence aerospace industry.

—*Keith Hayward, Head of Research, Royal Aeronautical Society*[534]

[533] Global Security, available at: http://www.globalsecurity.org/military/library/news/2008/03/mil-080327-eads01.htm.

[534] K. Hayward, op. cit.

The UK and pan-European consolidation has created a significantly different supplier base for the UK MoD today. The larger indigenous British firms are more concentrated—many in BAE—and the mix of important suppliers for the UK MoD is more international in scope—with several "multidomestic firms"—than many of its peer European nations employ. UK market participants believe this cross-border interdependence among firms will lead to more interdependence among customers in the market. MBDA, formed through a consolidation of European missile joint ventures serving multiple European customers, is such an example.

More broadly, senior UK MoD leaders told this study team that the UK MoD and industry recognizes the trend toward increasing interdependence in the defense market. The large U.S., UK and continental European multinational defense firms are seeking global reach and market breadth.

The UK DIS 2005 gives a recent portrait of the UK industry.[535] While BAE remains the largest supplier, half of the top firms are not UK-owned (see Table 64). It should be noted that this data set is not limited to defense systems but includes "non-warlike" products and services such as telecommunications.

Major UK Defense Firms

The leading UK defense companies are as follows:

- **BAE Systems,** by far the largest UK-based defense firm, is a "multidomestic" global defense and aerospace company delivering a full range of products and services for air, land and naval forces, advanced electronics, information technology solutions and support services for customers in 100 countries. With 97,500 employees worldwide, BAE's sales exceeded £15.7 billion (U.S. $31.4 billion) in 2007. It is the third largest global defense company and sixth largest U.S. defense company.[536] Significantly, BAE Systems considers itself a "multidomestic" defense firm, with six "home" markets: Australia, Saudi Arabia, South Africa, Sweden, UK and the United States. The UK government retains a golden share in BAE that reflects its strategic interest in this company, as fully discussed below.

- **Rolls-Royce** plc, is a leading provider of power systems for land, sea and air in four global markets—civil aerospace, defense, marine and energy. Its customer base includes 600 airlines, 4,000 aircraft and helicopter operators, 160 armed forces, and 2,000 marine customers including 70 navies. Rolls-Royce employs 38,000 people in manufacturing and service in 50 countries. Its annual sales total £7.4 billion (about $11.8 billion), of which 53 percent are for services.[537] The UK government retains a golden share that reflects its strategic interest in this company, as fully discussed below.

- **QinetiQ,** formed from the partial privatization of the UK Defence Evaluation and Research Agency, provides research, technical advice, technology solutions and services to customers in core markets of defense and security. The firm had revenue of about £1.2 billion 2007 (about $2.1 billion). In addition to many UK operating locations, QinetiQ has five operating locations in the United States as well as

---

[535] UK MoD DIS 2005, op. cit., p. 30.

[536] Facts from BAE Systems website. Available at: http://www.baesystems.com/AboutUs/FactSheet/index.htm.

[537] Data drawn from Rolls-Royce website. Available at: http://www.rolls-royce.com/about/.

Table 64   UK MoD's Top 10 Direct Suppliers in 2004-2005 (Pounds Sterling – £)

Sales	Company
Up to 1 Billion	BAE Systems
500-700 Million	QinetiQ
	General Dynamics
300-500 Million	MBDA UK
	Rolls Royce
	Westland Helicopter
	(Finmeccanica Group)
	BT plc
200-300 Million	SERCO
	EDS Defense
	Fujitsu Services

Source: UK Defence Industrial Strategy 2005.

operating locations in Australia and Belgium.[538] This company is also subject to a golden share. In August 2008 the UK government sold its 19.3 percent direct share in this company, thereby completing the privatization process of the UK defense industries started in 1979.

- **Babcock** is a global engineering services firm with nine operating divisions. Babcock Defence Services delivers engineering, integrated support services (e.g., maintenance) and training of military personnel. Babcock is the largest supplier of facilities management to the MoD and a leading provider of support services to all British Armed Forces (with a particularly strong role in operating ship/submarine facilities and providing support services for the Royal Navy). The firm's 2007 Revenue exceeded $2 billion.[539]

- **VT Group** is a leading defense and support services company, providing engineering and other services to governments and large organizations around the world. Primarily based in the UK, with more than 14,000 employees, the VT Group has doubled in size over the past five years. VT has several units in the United States as well. VT's 2007 revenue was about £1.2 billion (about $2.7 billion). BAE and VT together have a joint venture called BVT Surface Fleet, which is the design and manufacturing lead, integrator and through life customer support lead for UK surface warships and support vessels. VT Group has 7,000 employees in three locations supporting this function.[540]

---

[538] Data drawn from QinetiQ website at: http://www.qinetiq.com/.

[539] Data drawn from Babcock website at: http://www.babcock.co.uk/dm/spaw2/uploads/files/Babcock_ARA2008.pdf.

[540] Data drawn from VT Group website at: http://www.vtplc.com/Display.aspx?&MasterId=ccc5b0d0-4dd1-405e-b36f-b269008b86e4&NavigationId=814.

Table 65   UK—Largest Defense Companies

World Ranking	Company	2007 Defense Revenue (Millions of Dollars—$)	Defense Revenue (Percent—%)
3	BAE Systems	29,800	95
16	Rolls Royce	4,400	29
32	QinetiQ	2,100	80
38	Babcock International Group	1,700	58
40	VT Group	1,700	70
48	Cobham	1,200	57
55	GKN Group	883	12
64	Meggitt	666	38
70	Ultra Electronics	619	38
82	Chemring	500	95

Source: Defense News Top 100.

Figure 131   UK—Defense Market Share by Company [545]

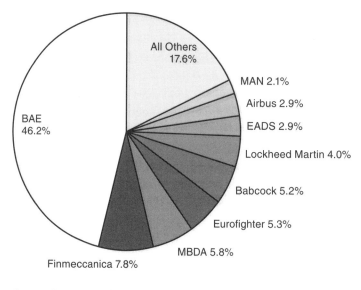

Source: Documental Solutions.

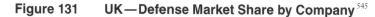

[541] This data may to a modest extent overstate the concentration in shares; it must be noted that there are scores of small enterprises whose data are not included in this Table (unless they are a downstream participant in one of these major programs). It is also important to note this data does not represent the market shares related to the full range of MoD spending, which would include spending for more widely available commercial products and services (e.g., telecommunications, petroleum, base infrastructure support, civil engineering services, etc.). These "non-warlike" items or services are generally not part of the Major Programs database we utilized.

- **Cobham** is a UK-based aerospace and defense equipment and service supplier. Its primary products are a suite of end-to-end avionics, network-centric technologies (notably in communications), and aviation mission systems and services. It has 13,500 employees across five continents and customers in more than 100 countries. Annual revenues approach $2 billion in 2007. Cobham is also multidomestic, with about 35 locations in the United States; among its U.S. holdings are the former Atlantic Microwave and M/A Com.[542]

- **Meggitt Group** designs and manufactures precision-engineered components and systems for aerospace and defense. In addition to aerospace, its sensors are sold in the medical, mainstream industrial, test engineering and transportation markets. The group employs more than 5,000 people in 30 operating companies within the market segments of aerospace, defense systems and electronics.[543] U.S. operating holdings include Avica U.S. and Dunlop Aerospace.

- **Ultra Electronics** is a group of specialist businesses designing, manufacturing and supporting electronic and electromechanical systems, subsystems and products for defense, security and aerospace applications worldwide. Ultra employs 3,000 people in the UK and North America, and focuses on high-integrity sensing, control, communication and display systems with an emphasis on integrated Information Technology solutions. Its 2007 defense revenue exceeded $600 million. In addition to its many UK businesses, Ultra has acquired several businesses in the United States and Canada.

- **Chemring** is a specialized manufacturer of decoy countermeasures and energetic materials for the global defense, security and safety markets. The Group employs more than 3,000 people at 21 operations in the UK, United States, France, Germany, Italy, Norway, Spain and Australia. Its revenue in 2006 was about £254 million (about $500 million) with sales to more than 70 countries.[544]

UK Defense Firms—More Scale and More Concentration

The scaling up of UK defense firms has resulted in firms with significant critical mass and much greater global reach. While Rolls-Royce has long been an important global player for jet engines, other British firms have gained strong new market positions in the last 20 years, particularly BAE. The Defense News Top 100 for 2008, which compares defense sales of all firms and ranks them worldwide, placed 10 UK firms in the Top 100, as shown in Table 65:[545]

The consolidation in the UK left BAE holding many of the previously independent UK businesses as well as numerous businesses in the United States. The lineage of BAE reflects so many acquisitions of so many businesses that the BAE Systems corporate website has three separate pages of organizational maps to reflect them. To list just a few of these, BAE now comprises former businesses of British Aerospace, GEC-Marconi, Alvis, GKN

---

[542] Cobham website. Available at: http://www.cobham.com/about-cobham/.

[543] Meggitt website. Available at: http://www.meggitt.com.

[544] Chemring website. Available at: http://www.chemring.co.uk/chg/ir/kfd/.

[545] Defense News Top 100 2008. Available at: http://www.defensenews.com/static/features/top100/charts/top100_08.php?c=FEA&s=T1C.

Table 66   UK DIS Key Prime Contractors—C4ISTAR Market

BAE Systems	Ultra Electronics
Thales	BT
EADS	EDS
General Dynamics	Fujitsu
Lockheed Martin	LogicaCMG
Northrop Grumman	QinetiQ
Raytheon	VT Communications

Source: Defence Industrial Strategy 2005.

Armored Vehicles, Vickers, Alvo, Royal Ordnance, and many former smaller British aircraft firms as well as Tracor, Cordant, United Defense, LMT Sanders, LMT Controls, and many others with both British and U.S. origins.[546] Notably missing from the list are significant buys from other European nations—e.g., French, Italian or German businesses (although the BAE Group has acquired significant businesses in Sweden from Bofors and Hägglunds and owns a sizable stake in Saab).

BAE also owned or has acquired many legacy programs and products in the UK for which they must provide support; this gives BAE an ongoing revenue stream from sales long ago. Given all the above, today BAE garners a about 46 percent share of the UK MoD resources spent on defense systems and related defense products and services. Figure 131 shows this and other relative market shares of leading defense firms in UK MoD Major Program spending (greater than $50 million) from 2006-2008.

BAE: A "Legacy" National Champion. As the data reflects, BAE Systems is, in some respects, still a "national champion" in the UK. It is an essential part of the UK national security: BAE has breadth, scale and wide reach inside the UK (and the United States) at the system level and at lower levels of the value chain, and it holds many key technologies. A recent report commissioned by BAE Systems found that in 2006, BAE Systems directly employed 35,000 people in the UK, added £2.4 billion to the UK GDP, recorded exports of £4.1 billion, paid nearly £500 million in taxes and channeled spending of nearly £900 million into R&D activities. According to the report, when the indirect and induced benefits of BAE Systems' activities were included, more than 105,000 people were employed as a result of its activities; more than £790 million in taxes were paid and BAE's contribution to the UK GDP was more than £5.8 billion.[547]

UK Major Programs: A More Balanced Future Supplier Base. However, the UK MoD's acquisition and industrial strategy (detailed below) has a much more sophisticated and relatively open market approach and it is not founded on preferential awards to a sole national champion. Outside of BAE, as the data reflects, a large remaining share of the UK major programs is divided among foreign firms and multinational consortia sales. Further, as discussed in detail below, the UK MoD is encouraging the presence and bidding of reli-

---

[546] Full BAE lineage charts available at: http://production.investis.com/heritage/baelineage/.

[547] Available at: http://www.baesystems.com/Newsroom/NewsReleases/2008/autoGen_10832143114.html.

able foreign-owned businesses in offering competitions and best value awards. Hence, 10 years in the future, one might see the BAE share shrink as its legacy sales wind down.

As one example of the UK MoD's openness to the "best sources," the DIS outlines a number of key firms viewed as participating primes in the UK C4ISTAR (Command, Control, Communications, Computers, Intelligence, Target Acquisition and Reconnaissance) market (see Table 66).[548] Notably, a number of these firms are foreign (especially U.S. firms).

Reshaping the UK Defense Market: The Acquisition and Industrial Strategy Today

In October 2002, the UK MoD issued an Industrial Policy to complement the Defense Acquisition Policy and Smart Acquisition initiatives. The Industrial Policy provided industry with a key change it sought: balancing risk between the MoD and industry and moderation of MoD's stance on competition. As the 2002 Defence Industrial Strategy declared:

> [O]pen and fair competition remains the bedrock of our procurement policy.... *But we will not use the competitive process beyond the point where it can offer long-term advantage....* We will seek to provide a more appropriate risk-reward ratio for programmes with high technological risk; and we are committed to public/private partnerships to deliver benefits in the provision of defence services... the MoD seeks to achieve *best value for money*... the solution that meets the requirement at the lowest *through-life* cost.[549] (Emphasis added.)

Subsequently, in 2005, the UK MoD released a new Defence Industrial Strategy White Paper (DIS 2005) that has been the subject of significant public discussion. DIS 2005 was written in the context of: industry concerns about the balance between risk-return under the existing MoD policies following a series of high-profile program disputes; growing MoD concerns about the limits on UK operational sovereignty imposed by dependence on foreign technologies in some areas; and a recognition that structural change in the UK defense industrial base was making competition increasingly impractical in some sectors if critical capabilities were to be retained.

The aims of the 2005 DIS are summarized as follows:

> Our Defence Industrial Strategy takes forward our Defence Industrial Policy, published in 2002, by providing greater transparency of our future defense requirements and, for the first time, setting out those industrial capabilities we need in the UK to ensure that we can continue to operate our equipment in the way we choose... to maintain appropriate sovereignty and thereby protect our national security... [it] explains more clearly how procurement decisions are made, and to assist industry in planning for the future commits government to greater transparency of our forward plans, noting that as in any business, these change over time.[550]

---

[548] UK MoD DIS, op. cit.

[549] UK MoD Policy Papers No. 5, Defense Industrial Policy, Oct. 2002, available at: http://www.mod.uk/NR/rdonlyres/25726BCE-8DD6-4273-BE8D-6960738BEE0A/0/polpaper5_defence_industrial.pdf.

[550] UK MoD DIS 2005, op. cit.

To achieve these goals, the 2005 DIS had two main thrusts: 1) providing a strategic view of future defense capability requirements by sector (both for new projects and the support and upgrade of equipment already in-service); and 2) articulating which industrial capabilities the MoD sought to retain in the UK for national security reasons. The DIS was designed to communicate the MoD's overall view to industry as clearly as possible while recognizing that plans change as the strategic or financial environment changes.

More specifically, the Defence Industrial Strategy sets out six "guiding principles" vital for firms to understand and engage with in order to participate in the UK market:

- **Appropriate sovereignty**—UK will maintain an appropriate degree of sovereignty over industrial skills, capacities, capabilities and technology to ensure operational independence against the range of operations that the UK will seek to conduct; ensures the UK of the delivery of ongoing contracts and the ability to respond to Urgent Operational Requirements.

- **Through-life capability management**—recognizes the importance of support, sustainability and the incremental enhancement of capabilities through technology insertions. This is a radical change for future procurement, emphasizing long-term through-life partnerships with industry to sustain existing platforms while requiring (or encouraging) competition for periodic upgrades and refreshing of subsystems in these platforms.

- **Maintaining key industrial capabilities and skills**—identifies key industrial capabilities for UK national security and those that may not necessarily be sustained by the UK, along with export market opportunities.

- **The importance of systems engineering**—highlights that the ability to understand and manage the complexities, challenges and costs for design, manufacture and upgrade of systems remains a general requirement if the UK is to sustain "intelligent customers and intelligent suppliers."

- **Value for defence**—balances best value buying from international sources with maintenance of domestic industry. The DIS continues to recognize that long-term best value for money is central to MoD's acquisition policy, and that exploiting the internationalization of the defense supply chain provides cost savings and other advantages. At the same time, the DIS sees benefits that flow from a healthy, competitive and dynamic *national* industry (e.g., amortizing overheads associated with export sales, and mitigating risks of being subject to monopoly power, should the UK have to look primarily overseas for some requirements).

- **Change on both sides**—establishes that industry and government need to change as a result of the DIS. MoD must set out more clearly its future plans and the improvement in performance it expects from the supply side.

Defining Key Defense Industrial Capabilities

The DIS set out for the first time to identify the industrial capabilities the UK should retain onshore. On the basis of its "guiding principles," the DIS analyzed the future prospects for a number of key industrial sectors in the UK, for acquisition and for support and upgrade. The DIS then set forth the industrial capabilities the MoD seeks to retain onshore for each of the following sectors (with some areas specifically called out as open for global competition):

- **Submarines and Surface Ships:** UK must retain the capabilities to design complex ships and submarines, and their nuclear steam plants, from concept to point of build; and the skills to manage the build, integration, test, support and upgrade of maritime platforms (and some complex systems and subsystems on board) through-life. The UK identified a number of specific key maritime system capabilities and technologies to retain onshore.

- **Armored Fighting Vehicles (AFVs):** There are "compelling advantages" to maintaining the UK AFV systems engineering, domain and design knowledge for through-life management. MoD must be an intelligent customer for new AFVs and their integration into networks. UK must have the ability to integrate critical subsystems and repair and overhaul AFVs onshore.

- **Helicopters:** UK must sustain AgustaWestland's systems engineering capability and some other firms' subsystem capability to maintain the UK's ability to support and upgrade the current UK helicopter fleet. The UK will look to global competition for future helicopter requirements (including support).

- **General Munitions:** The MoD will retain onshore the Design Authority role, its underpinning capability for munitions manufacture, and the ability to develop munitions for specific purposes to match UK doctrine.

- **Complex Weapons:** UK spending on complex weapons will fall by 40 percent over the years to 2010, raising significant questions about the sustainability of the sector. The UK would be prepared to source torpedoes from overseas while retaining certain support capabilities. The MoD will maintain the ability to design, develop, assemble, support and upgrade other complex weapons. The fragility of this sector means open international competition could put the sustainment of key industrial capabilities at risk.

- **C4ISTAR:** Generally this is a global industry with a large number of suppliers. However, national security requires the MoD to maintain certain industrial capabilities for high-grade cryptography and the continued ability to understand, integrate, ensure and modify mission critical systems.

- **CBRN Force Protection:** MoD requirements for CBRN (chemical, biological, radiological, nuclear) protection of forces may be met through a healthy competitive industrial marketplace.

- **Technology Strategy:** To support the industrial capabilities identified across the sectoral analysis there are a number of areas, set forth in the MoD's Defence Technology Strategy,[551] in which the UK must sustain existing technological strengths or should, resources permitting, consider developing its expertise. These are set out in the MoD's Defence Technology Strategy.

---

[551] DIS, para. xxxv, p. 10, and *Defence Technology Strategy*, Ministry of Defence, Oct. 2006 (available at: http://www.science.mod.uk/modwww/content/dts_complete.pdf).

Table 67   Progress of Long-Term Partnering Arrangements (September 2008)

Area/Defense Firm	Progress (Examples)
Maritime	
Partnering Agreement (June 2008) with BVT Surface Fleet, a joint venture of BAE and VT Group	Working on Agreement of surface ship design and build core workload required to sustain high-end skills
	Achieved:
	I. Alternative Contracting Arrangements
	II. Implementation of a united MOD submarine program management organization
Fixed Wing Aircraft	Long Term Partnering Agreement in development
Helicopters	
Strategic Partnering Arrangement (June 2006) and Business Transformation Incentivization Agreement with Agusta Westland	Launched Future Lynx contract to ensure crucial design, engineering and knowledge base will be retained at AugustaWestland
	Secured support for arrangements for MOD's current fleet from AugustaWestland
Armored Fighting Vehicles	
Partnering Agreement (December 2005) with BAE Land Systems	Transform BAE Land Systems for better through-life management
	I. Deliver capability for demonstrably better value; improve fleet reliability/availability
	II. Ensure UK has access to relevant IP rights for current and future AFV fleets
Complex Weapons	
Partnering Agreement (June 2008) with Team CW (MBDA, QinetiQ, Roxel and Thales UK)	Should lead to majority of current and future UK Complex Weapons being included in Long Term Partnering Agreement

Sustaining Key Capabilities: The Shift From Competition to Strategic Partnering

Significantly, in order to sustain key industrial capabilities, the DIS announced the MoD's decision to enter strategic partnering arrangements in maritime, armored vehicles, fixed-wing aircraft and helicopter sectors. Progress on this effort is set forth on Table 67. The aim of the strategic partnering arrangements is to guarantee security of supply to the MoD and to use target cost incentive fee contracts to provide incentives to industry to improve its performance in exchange for financial returns.

Partnerships for Procurements

The partnership model for procurement is the next stage in the UK MoD's strategy for an altered relationship with industry. The arrangement for the building of the new UK aircraft carrier is the highest profile example of how this new strategy will work. The carrier will be built by an alliance that includes BAE Systems, VT Group, Babcock and Thales UK. In return for industry co-operation, the government will guarantee a steady stream of work for up to 15 years. Other alliance agreements are under discussion: one covers support services for the surface warship fleet and another covers support services for submarines. The full implementation and success of this strategy remains to be seen. But in large scale, mature systems areas with limited demand and a desire to retain skills—such as aircraft carriers—there may not be many alternative strategies.

Future Implementation and Implications of DIS 2005

The 2005 DIS reflected a number of basic shifts in direction.

- Fundamentally, the 2005 DIS shifts UK procurement policy from total reliance on open competition to include greater reliance on partnerships and sole source sustainment arrangements for existing platforms.

- The DIS created a long list of "key industrial capabilities" it sought to sustain at home—despite budgetary constraints that made such sustainment questionable.

According to UK sources interviewed for this study, the UK industry tended to view the 2005 DIS as a life insurance policy of sorts. UK firms read the DIS to suggest that since the UK MoD wanted to keep the skills and capabilities outlined alive and in the UK, there would be less need for full-out competition and perhaps more work reserved for onshore firms. Further, the DIS implied broad funding and sustainment for many capability areas (and the programs and contracts therein, old and new). The question raised, however, was how the UK MoD would achieve such a wide range of objectives in light of its budgetary limitations.

The DoD also raised concerns directly with UK MoD over the new policy's consistency with the U.S.-UK Reciprocal Defense Procurement MOU and the suggestions of less reliance on competition.

According to UK government officials we interviewed, the DIS was misconstrued in several respects by the UK defense industry and other observers:

- First, it was not intended to be protectionist in nature. For example, the UK need not rely on UK-based firms to maintain operational sovereignty over a capability. A foreign firm with a UK operation could satisfy that need. Moreover, more generally, foreign firms with a UK presence were viewed as domestic in nature and would be so treated.

- Second, the DIS was not intended to suggest broad availability of additional funding for all the identified sectors. In retrospect, the DIS created too broad a set of capabilities for sustainment relative to available funding.

Since issuing the DIS, MoD has sent clarifications to industry and the U.S. government through words and actions. The UK has allowed an increased foreign ownership presence by holding competitions and making awards of important work to foreign firms in the UK. Moreover, there have also been changes on the broader political and economic climate. Tony Blair has left office and his successor Gordon Brown has faced significant political and economic challenges. Further, the resignation of Defence Procurement Minister Lord Paul Drayson in November 2007 was greeted with dismay by many observers since Lord Drayson was both architect and champion of the DIS process.

While the DIS approach has been broadly welcomed, it has failed to address two key issues—the eventual cost of programs and their timing. This means the widespread implementation of the DIS process has for some time been in doubt, with many in industry and government raising the question of whether it is possible to sustain a government-industry partnership over the long term without increased defense equipment spending.

To make matters worse, cuts or delays to major programs as a result of defense budget planning rounds have somewhat undermined the credibility of the entire DIS vision in the eyes of industry.[552] Further, as noted above, any unforeseen operational expenses will now come out of the core MoD budget—to the detriment of other core functions. A DIS 2 (a revised DIS) has been expected since December 2007, but has never been released and may be evolving into a dead issue.

The Financial Times reported on November 17, 2008, "[B]ritain's leading defense contractors have decided to stop pressing the government to publish the second phase of its strategy for the industry because of the lack of funding for major equipment programmes and indecision over which skills to support."[553] The article called this a "major shift by the sector...."[554]

The UK's ongoing overall economic crisis only exacerbates the defense budget crisis; there is now considerable uncertainty surrounding the future implementation of the Defence Industrial Strategy.[555] According to a February 2009 report, the UK defense industry still seeks a "DIS 2" but recognizes that given the current UK and global economic crisis, and the large number of unresolved defense budget issues, a DIS 2 will certainly not be done at this time.

The UK Balancing Act—Managing EU and U.S. Relationships

The UK DIS did not state explicit preferences for suppliers by nationality—or continent. The DIS made clear the capabilities that the UK wishes to retain onshore, some of which at core must be nationally held, but it did not exclude foreign owners or foreign suppliers for many of its defense sectors. Unlike the French *Livre Blanc*, released in June 2008 (and discussed in Chapter 7), the DIS did not explicitly call out its intent to place an integrated European defense market as a top objective in buying.

The DIS recognizes the potential of the U.S. market but also observes that the U.S. market poses high barriers and creates conflicts with UK interests—issues that each UK company's leadership has to address. As the DIS notes:

---

[552] S. Pfeifer, "Defence industry ends strategy plea," *Financial Times*, Nov. 17, 2008, 20:10.

[553] Ibid.

[554] Ibid.

[555] UK Defence Forum Viewpoint, Feb. 27, 2009. Available at: http://ukdf.blogspot.com/2009/02/give-us-defence-industrial-staregy-but.html.

[B]ritish companies such as BAE Systems, Rolls-Royce, Smiths Group, VT and QinetiQ have bought U.S. companies to overcome the high entry barriers and secure progressive access to the market. However, a continuing commitment to the UK market combined with the constraints on accessing and operating in the U.S. market, forces difficult boardroom decisions for UK companies on where to locate core capability and investment."[556]

At the same time, the DIS does not view the European market as a panacea. Not surprisingly, the DIS outlines a pragmatic view of the evolution of the EU defense market, recognizing the continued fragmentation of the European market and its legacy of national buying. The UK looks forward to a more open and competitive European market, but does not foresee that market replacing the United States in terms of attractiveness for UK firms.

[I]n practice, the European market remains fragmented although it is hoped that the European Defence Agency (EDA) will begin to make a difference in terms of supporting the more effective harmonisation of military requirements and promoting a more open defence equipment market. Progress is being made in opening project procurements to European competition and addressing security of supply concerns…. However, at current spending levels the market cannot offer the same scale and scope as the U.S. market.[557]

It should be recognized, however, that the British government and industry representatives interviewed for this study observed real, albeit slow, evolution of the European defense market and believed the new EC Defense Procurement Directive is certain to be implemented and will have salutary effects over the long term (discussed fully in Chapter 5).

Nevertheless, UK MoD officials were clear in remarks to the study team: the UK does not support moves toward a "Fortress Europe." The UK does not want the pending shift to an integrated EU defense market (e.g., the EC Defense Package) to freeze the United States out of the UK or broader European markets. Further, UK MoD officials repeatedly stated that the UK continues to see reliance and interdependence with the U.S. as a key to the UK strategy. The UK also does not want ITAR issues to become an excuse to eliminate the U.S. firms as unreliable for security of supply agreements.

More broadly, a fundamental question is whether the UK will continue to side so clearly with the United States on security matters as it has done during the last few years. Some are arguing that Gordon Brown can now afford to lean more toward the EU and away from the United States when it is useful to the UK. As one observer noted:

Prime Minister Brown can afford to *not* worry about Europe as he reassesses the relationship with Washington. His European counterparts [Sarkozy and Merkel] by and large have good working relations of their own with the United States. Britain has lost some of its usefulness to the United States, too … without UK leadership, the other Atlanticist EU countries, mostly new member-states in Central Europe, would have come under tremendous pressure from Germany and France to form a united EU front against the United States… EU members

---

[556] Ibid., p. 26.

[557] UK MoD DIS, op. cit., p. 26.

are far more pragmatic and less ideologically driven in decisions on their relations with the U.S. than they were in 2003. As U.S.-European ties become less confrontational, there is less need for the UK to play its balancing role within Europe.[558]

The attitude of the Labour government toward further integration with the EU is mixed and depends on the Prime Minister and the situation at a given point. However, the Conservative Party plainly favors less centralized EU governance and competency, and a Tory return to power may well work to slow UK moves toward the EU.[559]

As for defense market implications, regardless of which major UK political party wins the next election, a new UK DIS, if one is ever issued, may well pay more attention to the emerging European defense market than does the DIS issued in 2005. However, it would likely still be a very moderate reading of EU defense market realities. All sources predict the UK will remain a moderating force toward initiatives for a further enlargement of the EU's role in defense markets.

III. Evaluation of Market Access Metrics

The United Kingdom has an excellent investment climate and is a strong trading partner. Britain is consistently ranked by the U.S. Department of Commerce and other bodies among the most competitive, corruption-free and technologically advanced economies in the world.[560]

Tariff Barriers

By and large, tariffs are not significant barriers between the United Kingdom and the United States. All of the countries studied are members of the WTO and thus must provide most-favored nation and national treatment to imported goods from every other country included in the study. Although defense products are generally exempt from WTO rules governing tariffs and trade, the reciprocal defense procurement MOUs between the United States and the United Kingdom afford each country with duty-free treatment for imported defense products procured from the other country. However, the MOUs do not apply to dual-use products and technologies such as general aerospace systems that have both military and civil applications. Thus, as more military programs rely on commercial off-the-shelf technology, this would tend to put U.S. companies at a competitive disadvantage *vis-à-vis* European firms that get the benefit of the lower intra-European rates that apply under EU rules unless specific exemptions are negotiated on a bilateral basis.

---

[558] T. Valasek, Centre for European Reform, August 2007, available at: http://centreforeuropeanreform.blogspot.com/2007/08/europe-in-us-uk-special-relationship.html. Still it should be noted that during the current global economic crisis, the United States and Europe have been at odds on certain actions and the UK is again being cast as the moderator.

[559] Positions expressed at the UK Conservative Party website, available at: http://www.conservatives.com/Policy/Where_we_stand/Foreign_Affairs_and_Europe.aspx.

[560] Data on the overall UK economy and exports/imports is from the U.S. Department of Commerce Foreign Commercial Service, website on the UK; available at: http://www.buyusa.gov/uk/en/uk_economy_business.html.

Competition in Procurement

[W]e will continue to use market forces where we can to determine better value for money, but defence is not a perfect market place. We will therefore adopt procurement approaches that consider the nature of the market in the relevant sector and provide flexibility to respond to structural changes, so as to sustain key sovereign capabilities and ensure long term value for money," and "there are occasions when competition may not be able to deliver the best long term value for money or sustain key UK defence industrial capabilities. We will not pursue competition beyond the point where it can offer long term advantage or where the cost of running a competition is demonstrably disproportionate to the benefits....[561]

— UK Defence Industrial Strategy 2005

UK Procurement Policy: A Shifting Approach

As noted above, DIS 2005 marked a real shift in acquisition policy away from the past policy of full and open competition and the adversarial industry-government relationship that dominated UK defense procurement policy since the 1980s. The new emphasis is on a more balanced approach between competition and long-term partnership arrangements—which has prompted concerns that the DIS will result in reducing free and open competition and shifting toward domestic monopolies.

A Tension Between Stability and Competition. As senior leaders of the UK MoD stated, the challenge for the UK MoD is to maintain a constructive tension between, on the one hand, stability for firms and, on the other hand, competition and the value for money it can produce. Their goal is to sustain needed UK skills and provide stability to firms, particularly those in mature sectors with limited demand, while at the same time retaining the stimulus of competition. To do this, they have turned to a more measured and case by case approach to competition.

The DIS identified alternatives to competitive procurement, and created an initiative for more use of partnering arrangements in select instances (implemented with incentives for firms' performance). As the DIS 2005 stated, "[w]e will consider alternative approaches to competition in the procurement situations set out below....

- One supplier has the capacity and capability to deliver the requirement and is chosen because it is the sole source of supply, or it is chosen on the basis of consistently high performance compared to other suppliers, or it is the only suitable supplier to sustain sovereign capabilities....

- No single supplier has the capacity and capability to deliver the requirement and... an inclusive and willing group or groups of suppliers might be formed....

---

[561] UK MoD DIS, op. cit., p. 48-49.

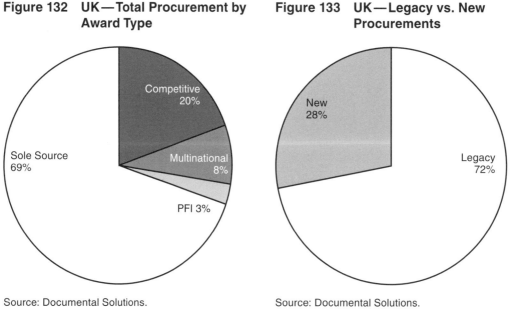

Figure 132   UK—Total Procurement by Award Type

Figure 133   UK—Legacy vs. New Procurements

Source: Documental Solutions.   Source: Documental Solutions.

- The through life support of a capability requires the engagement of the equipment Design Authority and/or other systems engineering capability."[562]

The Continued Role of Competition. The focus of attention on strategic partnering has somewhat masked the fact, however, that competition remains a critical element of UK procurement policy. The DIS states repeatedly that open and fair competition will remain a fundamental component of UK procurement policy to deliver affordable defense capability at better overall value for money.

UK Procurement Practice: Understanding the Data

In practice, the available data continues to show substantial competition in UK procurement tempered by the reality that legacy systems awarded years ago are now sole source programs—with ongoing production and sustainment contracts largely not being competed.

- **Total MoD Buying Is Largely Competitive.** Generally, MoD statistics for 2003-2004 show that roughly 75 percent by value of *all* UK MoD contracts were awarded competitively. This data, set forth in DIS 2005, reflects all manner of MoD contracts, however, including commercial goods as well as services (telecommunications, fuel, clothing, computers, etc.).

- **UK MoD Buying on Major Defense Program Buying Is Predominantly Sole Source.** A more targeted look at major UK defense programs (RDT&E and procurement programs exceeding $50 million) during 2006-2008 shows the continued importance of sole source buying on legacy programs and some degree of competitive buying. As shown in Figure 132, when one considers only major defense system procurement, the awards were 20 percent competitive and 69.5 percent made on a

---

[562] UK MoD DIS, op. cit., p. 49.

Table 68   UK—Major Defense Programs (Millions of Dollars—$)

Program	Description	Prime Contractor	Country	2006	2007	2008	Total	Award Type	Legacy
SSN Astute Class	Nuclear Attack Submarine	BAE SYSTEMS	UK	942.51	1,275.40	1,377.90	3,595.80	Sole Source	Yes
DDG Type 45	Destroyer	BAE SYSTEMS	UK	912.73	1,116.74	1,122.69	3,152.15	Sole Source	Yes
Bay Class	Amphibious Assault Ship	Swan Hunter	UK	1,584.36	530.81	462.08	2,577.25	Sole Source	Yes
AW101	Helicopter	Finmeccanica	IT	604.98	604.98	664.66	1,874.62	Sole Source	Yes
Eurofighter	Multi-Role Fighter	Eurofighter	EUR	1,189.63	129.78	67.35	1,386.76	Multinational	Yes
UK Nuclear Sub Refueling	Nuclear Submarines	Babcock Group	UK	394.73	401.03	394.73	1,190.49	Sole Source	Yes
CV Queen Elizabeth	Aircraft Carrier	BAE SYSTEMS	UK	262.40	262.40	596.14	1,120.93	Competitive	No
A400M	Transport Aircraft	Airbus	EUR	342.59	342.59	68.52	753.69	Multinational	No
Harrrier GR.9A Upgrade	Attack Aircraft	BAE SYSTEMS	UK	239.36	239.36	185.84	664.56	Sole Source	Yes
UK RN Merlin Upgrade	Shipboard Helicopter	Lockheed Martin	U.S.	15.32	255.25	357.35	627.92	Sole Source	Yes
Tornado Services	Attack Aircraft	BAE SYSTEMS	UK	0.00	306.30	306.30	612.60	Sole Source	Yes
Future Lynx	Helicopter	Finmeccanica	IT	160.25	255.75	153.65	569.65	Sole Source	Yes
Hawk	Trainer	BAE SYSTEMS	UK	178.68	111.56	261.97	552.20	Sole Source	Yes
UK Support Veh	Tactical Vehicle	MAN	GE	0.00	271.07	272.39	543.46	Competitive	No
WAH-64D Apache	Attack Helicopter	MBDA	EUR	106.31	134.37	290.07	530.75	Sole Source	Yes
ALARM	Anti-Radiation Missile	MBDA	EUR	136.11	175.24	179.64	490.99	Sole Source	Yes
Submarine Support Contract	Submarine Support	Rolls-Royce	UK	0.00	206.20	206.20	412.40	Competitive	No
UK FALCON Incrmnt A-C	Communications	BAE SYSTEMS	UK	125.26	132.44	137.63	395.33	Competitive	No
SKIOS	Helicopter	Finmeccanica	IT	91.89	112.31	190.00	394.20	Sole Source	No
Cougar Mastiff	MRAP	Force Protection	U.S.	91.12	98.83	184.16	374.11	Competitive	No
Nimrod	Patrol Aircraft	BAE SYSTEMS	UK	128.75	128.75	75.23	332.73	Sole Source	Yes
White Fleet	Tactical Vehicle Support	VT Group plc	UK	110.61	110.61	110.61	331.83	PFI	No
VC.10 TriStar	Tanker Aircraft	BAE SYSTEMS	UK	93.41	99.51	103.51	296.43	Sole Source	Yes
BOWMAN	Tactical Communications	General Dynamics	U.S.	107.06	107.06	80.29	294.41	Competitive	No
Skynet 5 SATCOM Services	Satellite Communications	EADS	EUR	36.74	110.21	146.94	293.88	PFI	No

Table 68   UK—Major Defense Programs (Millions of Dollars—$) (conitnued)

Program	Description	Prime Contractor	Country	2006	2007	2008	Total	Award Type	Legacy
ASRAAM	Air-to-air Missile	MBDA	EUR	90.96	93.16	94.29	278.41	Sole Source	Yes
ASTOR Sentinel R1	ASTOR Surveillance Acft	Raytheon	U.S.	90.96	93.16	94.29	278.41	Competitive	Yes
Eurofighter (GFE Engine Set)	Jet Engines	Eurojet	EUR	233.30	25.45	13.21	271.95	Multinational	Yes
LEAPP C2 Production	Command & Control	Lockheed Martin	U.S.	0.00	89.06	162.51	251.57	Competitive	No
CLV SDW/STA	Command Vehicle	BAE SYSTEMS	UK	13.13	131.17	100.79	245.09	Competitive	No
UK DII increment 2b	Information System	EDS	U.S.	0.00	58.09	184.44	242.53	Competitive	No
S-92	Helicopter	United Tech Corp	U.S.	214.48	6.13	6.13	226.74	Competitive	No
Skynet 5 Mil. Comm Payload	Satellite Communications	EADS	EUR	171.36	33.79	6.27	211.42	Competitive	No
UK HC2/3 TLS	Helicopter Support	Boeing	U.S.	61.26	71.47	71.47	204.20	Sole Source	Yes
Point Class PFI	Light Frigate	AWSR Shipping	UK	65.92	65.92	65.92	197.75	PFI	No
UK C-130 Services	Transport Aircraft	Marshall Group	UK	0.00	97.00	97.00	193.99	Competitive	Yes
DBL-CIP	Command & Control	General Dynamics	U.S.	100.43	74.56	17.06	192.05	Competitive	No
BOWMAN	Communications	ITT	U.S.	57.17	75.41	53.98	186.57	Competitive	No
E-3 AWACS	Airborne Early Warning Acft	Northrop Grumman	U.S.	61.26	61.26	61.26	183.78	Sole Source	Yes
C-17A	Transport Aircraft	Boeing	U.S.	0.00	183.02	0.00	183.02	Sole Source	Yes
FV430 MK3 Upgrade	Armored Personnel Carrier	BAE SYSTEMS	UK	41.13	85.69	51.41	178.23	Sole Source	Yes
C-130J Hercules	Transport Aircraft	Lockheed Martin	U.S.	30.18	72.93	74.83	177.94	Sole Source	Yes
Challenger	Main Battle Tank	BAE SYSTEMS	UK	57.92	56.75	55.58	170.26	Sole Source	Yes
Terrier CEV	Combat Engineer Vehicle	BAE SYSTEMS	UK	17.35	59.40	78.96	155.71	Sole Source	Yes
Skynet 4 SATCOM Services	Satellite Communications	EADS	EUR	110.21	36.74	0.00	146.94	Sole Source	Yes
Meteor	Air-to-Air Missile	MBDA	EUR	44.96	44.96	44.96	134.89	Sole Source	Yes
Titan AVLB	Bridgelayer Vehicle	BAE SYSTEMS	UK	44.39	45.60	33.69	123.68	Sole Source	Yes
Trojan breacher	Engineer Vehicle	BAE SYSTEMS	UK	44.39	45.60	33.69	123.68	Sole Source	Yes
LPH Ocean	Amphibious Assault Ship	Babcock Group	UK	0.00	34.80	84.30	119.10	Sole Source	Yes
Harrier T.12 Upgrade	Trainer Aircraft	BAE SYSTEMS	UK	9.74	97.40	0.00	107.14	Sole Source	Yes
Hellfire	Anti-Tank Missile	MBDA	EUR	44.17	40.61	19.65	104.42	Sole Source	Yes

Program	Description	Prime Contractor	Country	2006	2007	2008	Total	Award Type	Legacy
Pinzgauer Vector	Tactical Vehicle	BAE SYSTEMS	UK	7.08	79.63	6.83	93.55	Competitive	No
Sea King ASaC Mk 7 Mod	Helicopter	Thales	FR	0.00	60.61	30.30	90.91	Sole Source	Yes
King Air	Transport Aircraft	Hawker Beechcraft	UK	0.00	35.03	53.05	88.08	Sole Source	Yes
HEMTT	Tactical Vehicle	Oshkosh	U.S.	54.30	14.52	13.48	82.31	Sole Source	Yes
SSBN Vanguard	Ballistic Missile Submarine	BAE SYSTEMS	UK	25.88	24.96	24.03	74.88	Sole Source	Yes
VC-10 TriStar Services	Tanker Aircraft Services	Marshall Group	UK	0.00	25.53	48.00	73.53	Sole Source	Yes
Paveway	Laser Guided Bomb	Raytheon	U.S.	12.15	24.29	36.52	72.96	Sole Source	Yes
TIALD	Reconnaissance Pod	Finmeccanica	IT	23.26	24.17	25.09	72.52	Sole Source	Yes
Gas Turbine Support	Engines	Rolls-Royce	UK	23.48	23.48	23.48	70.45	Sole Source	Yes
UK Cormorant	Communications	EADS	EUR	33.50	33.78	2.03	69.31	Competitive	No
Eurofighter Services	Multi-Role Fighter Support	QinetiQ	UK	0.00	34.07	34.07	68.14	Competitive	No
Bowman Training	Communications Support	Finmeccanica	IT	22.46	22.46	22.46	67.39	Competitive	No
AS-90 Support	Tactical Vehicle	BAE SYSTEMS	UK	21.81	21.81	21.81	65.42	Sole Source	Yes
TARDIS	Tornado Upgrade	BAE SYSTEMS	UK	52.02	6.57	6.57	65.16	Sole Source	Yes
S-1850	Radar	Thales	FR	16.13	16.69	31.69	64.50	Competitive	No
MWMIK	Gun Turret	Babcock Group	UK	0.00	0.00	63.48	63.48	Competitive	No
UK S-92 SAR Services	Helicopter	CHC Helicopter	UK	20.42	20.42	20.42	61.26	Competitive	No
AMRAAM	Air-to-Air Missile	Raytheon	U.S.	19.68	20.21	20.73	60.62	Sole Source	Yes
SINCGARS	Tactical Communications	ITT	U.S.	19.68	21.93	16.70	58.31	Sole Source	Yes
BOWMAN	Tactical Communicatons''	Northrop Grumman	U.S.	36.76	9.52	9.52	55.79	Competitive	No
Commander	Radar	BAE SYSTEMS	UK	2.66	2.66	47.32	52.64	Competitive	Yes
UK DHFCS	Communications	VT Group plc	UK	10.50	15.74	26.24	52.48	Competitive	Yes
Land Rover	Tactical Vehicle	Ford Motor Co.	U.S.	16.94	17.45	17.95	52.35	Sole Source	Yes
Panther CLV	Command Vehicle	BAE SYSTEMS	UK	3.72	32.14	16.19	52.05	Sole Source	Yes
LEAPP AP1 - EADS	Air Defense	EADS	EUR	27.00	25.00	0.00	52.00	Competitive	No
LEAPP AP1 - LM	Air Defense	Lockheed Martin	U.S.	27.00	25.00	0.00	52.00	Competitive	No

Source: Documental Solutions.

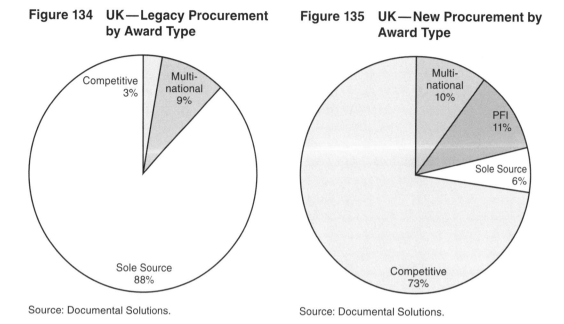

Figure 134   UK—Legacy Procurement by Award Type

Competitive 3%
Multi-national 9%
Sole Source 88%

Source: Documental Solutions.

Figure 135   UK—New Procurement by Award Type

Multi-national 10%
PFI 11%
Sole Source 6%
Competitive 73%

Source: Documental Solutions.

sole source basis. The remainder of awards went to multinational buys (including the AirTanker publicly funded initiative). As discussed below, however, this overall data is somewhat misleading, and understates the degree of competition, because the data set of all major awards is predominantly composed of follow-on awards for legacy programs.

- **Most UK Spending Is on Legacy Programs.** As shown on Figure 133, some 72 percent ($21.6 billion) of all spending in the last three years has gone toward legacy programs (i.e., programs *where the initial* award for development and/or procurement was made at some point in the past). This is not surprising and reflects that large development and production programs, which take years to bring to fruition, are recipients of most MoD funding. The list of Top UK Defense Programs (Table 68) shows that legacy UK national programs and cooperative programs such as the Eurofighter and the Astute class nuclear submarines—started years ago—receive the largest amounts of funding.

- **Nearly All Legacy Spending Is Sole Source or Directed.** As Figure 134 shows, approximately 88 percent of legacy awards were sole source, with only 3 percent awarded through "open and competitive" procurement and another 9 percent directed through multinational programs. The magnitude of sole source buying reflects the realities of large defense programs. After a major system has been awarded to a particular firm, follow-on production, modifications, upgrades and maintenance contracts are often awarded to the same firm again (e.g., after an award is made for an aircraft developed and produced by one firm, it is much more likely to be awarded to that firm for future buys). Indeed, it would be uneconomic to change contractors midstream on large programs unless the incumbent is not performing (although subsystem upgrades and some maintenance work can be awarded competitively). Thus, not surprisingly, as shown on Table 68, BAE Systems, the incumbent

Figure 136   UK—New Procurement by Supplier

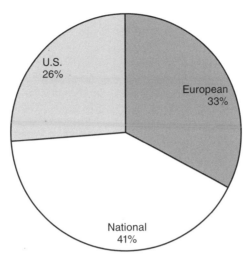

Source: Documental Solutions.

on numerous legacy programs, received approximately 46 percent of all contracts awarded (by value) in the 2006-2008 period.

Further, all of the UK's long-term partnering arrangements have been let on a non-competitive basis. This accounts for some of the sole source awards and market share gained by BAE and some other UK firms in Table 67.

- **Buying Habits Change Slowly; New Buys Are Largely Competitive.** The predominance of legacy programs in the UK's procurement spending and the continuing role of national champions highlights that defense acquisition buying trends change slowly. Indeed, any changes will largely be reflected on *new* programs (i.e., programs that are newly started in 2006-2008 and did not have incumbent contractors). To take this into account, we have separately evaluated new programs (i.e., excluding legacy major programs from the analysis). *As shown on Figure 135, 73 percent of all new UK major defense procurement contracts were awarded competitively, with 10 percent going to multinational programs, 11 percent to privately financed initiatives (PFIs), and 6 percent sole source.* This is consistent with the historical MoD reality that most major weapons systems have been awarded on a competitive basis in recent years *at some phase* of the program. The new sole source and PFI contracts—together just 17 percent of new programs—largely reflect the new UK emphasis on partnering arrangements. While the sample of new programs is much smaller than the sample of legacy programs, it nevertheless appears to reflect a tendency in the new buying and the likely future buying habits in the UK (see Figure 135).

- **New Competitive Buys Were Open to U.S. and European Firms.** Most of new UK MoD competitive awards were open to U.S. firms, with 26 percent of all competitive awards by value awarded to U.S. companies (see Figure 136). Indeed, as shown on Figure 137, Lockheed Martin (4.2 percent), General Dynamics (1.8 percent) and Boeing (1.5 percent) are winning modest, but nevertheless, material amounts of new UK program awards over recent years. While 41 percent were

Figure 137   UK—Defense Market Share by Company

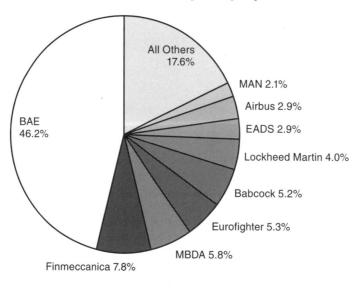

Source: Documental Solutions.

awarded to UK firms, what is also notable is that 29 percent were awarded to firms from Western Europe—reflecting a UK willingness to accept solutions from European firms (several of which have a sizable UK presence).

- **Cooperative Engagement is Modest in Percentage Terms But Sizable in Real Terms.** Significantly, as shown on Figure 132, the data shows that the UK MoD spends a modest portion of its resources (8 percent) on major cooperative programs (legacy and new) but a fair amount in dollar terms ($2.4 billion). This percentage is among the lowest of any of the Western European nations studied. Rather than reflect lack of cooperation, it reflects the large size of the UK's defense budget relative to most other European countries.

C. The Competitive Implications of Partnering

While competition appears to be the MoD's preferred acquisition strategy, there are occasions when it may not be able to deliver the best long-term value for money or sustain key UK defense industrial capabilities. Britain's ability to run competitions, particularly for support services, may be limited if the scale of long-term investment required in facilities is too high for any single company to undertake without the confidence of a return, or if there is only one supplier with access to key IP. In such circumstances, the MoD believes that a long-term, sole-source partnering award may be the only viable option.

Thus, in the UK, there is a general expectation that the percentage of defense contracts let competitively will decline in the future because of the shift to long-term partnering arrangements.[563] The increasing complexities of systems integration work and the reduction in the number of Tier 1 Prime Contractors who are capable of managing the largest system and platform programs also may lead to that decline. Some companies have expressed concerns about the consequences of long-term partnering arrangements for the nature of competition in the UK market.

Among other things, there have been concerns that the prime contractor in a long-term partnering arrangement may pursue vertical integration strategies that favor their own internal sources of subsystems and components over competition in the supply chain. For instance, with respect to legacy AFV platforms, affected firms consider it important that the partnering agreement with BAE Systems should not restrict competition, especially with respect to major system integration and subsystem activities. Suppliers believe that such partnering agreements should not become rigid monopolies and that they should be transparent to the supply chain. Other firms have expressed concerns that firms in long-term partnering arrangements may use their positions as a barrier to entry onto a new program. For instance, some firms stated that arrangements for the legacy AFV fleet (i.e., the BAE Systems-MoD Partnering Agreement) should not influence the decision on how the FRES program is awarded.

The MoD has responded to such concerns by noting that in long-term partnering arrangements, MoD plans to place a responsibility on primes to compete requirements at a subprime level wherever possible and will expect full transparency of the value of work being offered across the supply chain. MoD is also seeking to find ways of introducing competition at various stages of the long-term partnering arrangement relationships. For example, if a contractor fails to meet agreed performance criteria, there may be opportunities to introduce competition at various points.

Thus, when viewed in total, there is still a fair degree of competition in the UK defense market—it remains the mainstay, in policy and in practice, of the UK MoD's procurement program. However, one can anticipate somewhat less competition in the future in light of the new emphasis, under the DIS and in practice, on long-term partnering arrangements.

Fair and Transparent Procurement Process

In general, the UK has one of the most open, fair and reasonable procurement systems in the world. The UK, like other EU Member States, is a party to the WTO Agreement on Government Procurement (although its defense procurement, as distinct from the procurement of "non-warlike" goods, are exempt from its coverage).

The UK MoD conducts procurements of non-warlike goods and services in accordance with the EU Procurement Regulations. Requirements are advertised using the MoD Defence Contracts Bulletin and the EDA Electronic Contracts Bulletin. The UK MoD is not governed by specific UK national legislation in the procurement of "warlike goods"

---

[563] There may have already been some reduction in the total number of contracts let competitively due to these long-term partnering agreements and other changes in MoD Strategy under the DIS. However, the UK MoD data available does not separate program and support contracts from more general commercial contracts so the percentages are not easily discerned from official MoD data. Official MoD contracting values and percentages of contract competition are available at: http://www.dasa.mod.uk/natstats/ukds/2007/c1/table116.html.

(that is, goods and services defined within the Article 296 of the Treaty Establishing the European Community (Article 296 EC Treaty) national security exemption) and today has no equivalent of the U.S. Federal Acquisition Regulations.

Rather, the UK MoD publishes its contracting policies and processes so all bidders can have access. Today these are called out in the MoD's Defense Contract Conditions (DEF-CONs). (Although DEFCONs are flowed down to suppliers much like the Federal Acquisition Regulation (FAR) and Defense Federal Acquisition Regulation Supplement (DFARS) clauses contained in U.S. DoD contracts, their content is not necessarily similar to comparable FAR and DFARS clauses.)

These Guidelines are being updated at this time. New Guidelines for Industry are being prepared by the Defence Commercial Policy Group at UK Defense Equipment and Support Organization (DE&S), Abbey Wood. As the UK MoD has indicated:

> [t]hese [Guidelines] will progressively supersede DEFCON Guides and General Notices to Defence Contractors (GNDCs). These guidelines are intended to provide defence contractors with reasonably brief but clear statements of MoD policy and procedures on various aspects of contracting. Contractors are reminded that the guidelines are not contractual documents and are issued for information purposes only.[564]

Finally, it should be recognized that the UK develops its defense procurement regulations within the larger context of the EU procurement regulations and with the UK understanding that Article 296 EC Treaty applies to "all warlike goods"—allowing it considerable flexibility in practice. However, this will change with the EC Defense Procurement Directive, with which the UK will need to comply (presumably through newly issued UK Defence Procurement Regulations).

Transparent Goals and Process Implementation

The DIS is a straightforward presentation of the UK MoD needs, industrial goals and priorities, detailed by each industrial sector. This in itself is an extraordinary action in terms of offering transparent policy and industrial and acquisition strategy information to the widest possible audience. This level of clarity and transparency in defense industrial strategy for the complete range of sectors is not available from the U.S. DoD or from any other European nation examined in this study. The French *Livre Blanc* is closest but does not offer nearly the industrial detail of the UKDIS.

In fact, the reason for creating and publishing the Defence Industrial Strategy was to increase transparency in the procurement process. The MoD emphasizes that *it is vital that potential bidders have confidence that competitions are fair and transparent*. Further, it benefits the MoD to receive competitive bids that are acceptable against all their criteria. It has long been MoD policy that, where wider national interests are relevant to the outcome of a competition, these will be declared and explained to potential bidders as far as foreseeable. This allows industry to frame their bids accordingly and to take account of any factors outside their control at the outset.

---

[564] MoD Contracts Bulletin at: http://www.contracts.mod.uk/selltomod/guidelines.shtml.

The DIS took this a stage further by listing the "wider factors" the UK may also wish to take into account in making procurement decisions—i.e., potential MoD selection criteria in future programs. These will be declared and explained to potential bidders at the earliest opportunity in the bidding process, although there is no indication in the DIS as to the relative weight of these wider factors in awards. The wider factors are:

- **Security of Supply.** DIS 2005 states that the MoD recognizes it needs to be realistic about security of supply advantages, recognizing that increasing mutual reliance on security of supply is inevitable for all nations. The weight to be put on security of supply is a question of judgment case by case, taking into account the risks involved (including any mitigation provided through collaborative agreements such as the six-nation European Letter of Intent and the U.S./UK DoP Security of Supply Arrangement) and the cost implications. According to the DIS 2005, in some cases, the capability is so significant to overall military effectiveness that the MoD will wish to retain it onshore at least partly for that reason: security of supply, in terms of both physical and intellectual resources, is often a critical factor in deciding which capabilities must be sovereign. In most other cases, however, the DIS states that MoD will need to balance the risk against any additional cost for onshore supply on a case-by-case basis, taking into account value for money and affordability.

- **Industrial Participation (Offsets).** The MoD's Industrial Participation (or offset) policy can encourage technology transfer and ensure investment in particular industrial capabilities within the UK. Where this contributes to developing or maintaining sovereign capabilities, industrial participation may be a key factor in its own right; where the benefit is of broader industrial benefit, it may help discriminate between two otherwise similar proportioned bids.

- **Industrial Capabilities.** The DIS recognizes that there are some industrial capabilities that do not meet strict defense criteria for sustainment but may be desirable to retain in the UK due to their high economic value.

- **Key Technologies.** In some cases, key underpinning technologies may be important to maintain for national security reasons. These key technologies are identified in Part B of the DIS 2005 and also in the MoD's Defence Technology Strategy.

- **Export Potential.** An assessment of export potential, and the benefits that may accrue to MoD and more widely, is made at the key decision points in the MoD program.

- **Foreign and Security Policy Interests.** The DIS notes that the consequences of large projects and collaborative ventures for bilateral relationships and interoperability may also be taken into account.

- **Wider MoD Policy.** Legal, environmental and other considerations may also need to be taken into account in procurement decisions.

Implementation

The UK MoD has been hampered by budget constraints from implementing the 2005 DIS as it was envisioned. However, the spirit of this transparency has been implemented. The MoD has extensive websites offering documentation on its policies, budgets, manning and programs. The UK is participating in web-based portals and the EDA electronic bulletin board, as well as in the Official Journal of the EU. MoD acquisition teams are required to advertise through the Defence Contracts Bulletin portal all "warlike" and "non-warlike" requirements for goods, services or works valued from £40,000 and above, and may voluntarily advertise the above requirements valued at between £20,000 and £40,000 in MoD Defence Contracts Bulletin (published online) and Supply2.gov.uk.

Domestic Content Requirements

Buy National Requirements

The UK has no formal buy national laws analogous to the U.S. Buy American laws or the Berry Amendment that govern certain products and limit foreign sources.

In some quarters, DIS 2005 and its emphasis on "appropriate sovereignty" has been misinterpreted as a shift toward a "buy British" policy and a move toward procurement independence and total reliance on UK sources, but this is inaccurate. Rather, it highlights Ministry of Defence concerns about assured access to the IP and proprietary information necessary to ensure *operational independence* for UK forces.

"Appropriate sovereignty"—what MoD officials described as the policy—differs between technologies and projects. When operational sovereignty is a key concern, the MoD is likely to demand UK-based design authority for the program. In other circumstances, the UK has been willing to procure some defense equipment on the open market.

Distinguishing Appropriate Sovereignty and Domestic Sourcing

The DIS notes that:

> [A]s we look to non-British sources of supply, whether at the prime or subsystems level, we need to continue to recognise the extent to which this may constrain the choices we can make about how we use our Armed Forces—in other words, *how we maintain our sovereignty and national security.*[565]

The DIS explains its policy for assessing where there may be a continuing need for clear national sovereignty and therefore an assured UK source:

> [I]n many, even high priority areas, we can, and do, rely on overseas sources, and have made progress in recent years in developing increased assurances of security of supply, but there are critical areas where not maintaining assured access to onshore industrial capabilities would compromise this operational independence and hence our national security. The extent to which we feel comfortable sourcing defence equipment from overseas is also a function, amongst other things, of our ability to negotiate with other nations arrangements to share the technologies required to support such capabilities through-life and adjust them to our national requirements as necessary. Such national security considerations are also relevant where we need to retain sovereignty due to the extreme secu-

---

[565] UK MoD DIS, op. cit., para v., p. 6.

rity sensitivity of the technology concerned or for legal reasons; where specific UK capabilities give us important strategic influence, in military, diplomatic or industrial terms; and in some cases, where retention is necessary to maintain realistic global competition—in other words, where we are not prepared to risk dependency on an overseas monopoly which could in time frustrate our ability to maintain our freedom of military action.[566]

The DIS sets out the selection criteria used to identify those aspects of the industrial base that the UK considers essential to retain onshore in order to deliver the capability required by the Armed Forces:

- Strategic assurance (capabilities that provide technologies or equipment important to safeguard the state, e.g., nuclear deterrent);

- Defense capability (where the MoD requires particular assurance of continued and consistent equipment performance); and

- Strategic influence (in military, diplomatic or industrial terms), as well as recognizing potential technology benefits attached to those that have wider value.

There is an important distinction between "operational sovereignty" and domestic sourcing. Contrary to what some in the UK industry believe, maintenance of operational sovereignty, as discussed above, does not require the use of UK-owned suppliers. For example, a foreign-owned firm with presence in the UK can in various circumstances facilitate the maintenance of "operational" sovereignty. The MoD officials interviewed for this study reported that the true "UK sovereign" capabilities—i.e., capabilities that must remain UK-owned as well as located—would be limited to a few areas such as core nuclear and intelligence capabilities (such as cryptological capabilities). The DIS emphasizes that, even where the MoD wishes an industrial capability to be sustained in the UK for strategic reasons, this will not necessarily preclude global competition in that sector for some projects.

No Law, But Real Requirements

Despite the lack of any legal or policy-driven "Buy National" requirement, foreign firms seeking to win sizable defense contract awards in the UK must address the question of jobs, technology and general work share in the UK economy. Foreign firms have alternative means to achieve these subtle or "informal" demands. For example, they can:

- Acquire industrial presence in the UK through mergers and acquisitions;

- Partner with UK firms for major elements of the system;

- Use the UK supply chain as part of the product;

- Create new jobs, technology or IP for the UK by other contracts or investments; or

- Engage in some combination of such methods.

---

[566] UK MoD DIS, op. cit.

Offsets and *Juste Retour*

"The UK has one of the most benign offset policies in the world," reported one UK government official in a study interview. While benign may be defined differently by others, in this case it signifies the British view that their policy is not rigidly defined in a law and allows flexibility in arrangements to meet the requirement. Indeed, the UK government is willing to negotiate terms across programs and techniques to meet the requirements (jobs, technology, etc.).

However, the fact remains that offsets—habitually called "Industrial Participation" in the UK—are required. Specifically, "Industrial Participation," explicitly referenced in the DIS, is a Ministry of Defence policy that aims to stimulate work and business opportunities in the UK. These opportunities result from undertakings by offshore companies to place defense work in the UK in connection with contracts to supply equipment or services to the UK armed forces.

The UK MoD has consistently represented that it would prefer to operate without the need for Industrial Participation. The Industrial Participation policy is based on the UK view that British companies attempting to export directly from the UK frequently face barriers to trade in the form of protectionist measures or stringent offset regimes in other nations. Industrial Participation is a flexible response to these barriers. In the view of the MoD, it encourages offshore companies to use the UK's defense industry without some of the negative effects sometimes found in more restrictive offset policies.

The Industrial Participation component of the UK government is not in MoD. Rather, the Defense Export Services Organization (DESO) is a part of the UK Trade and Investment Group, a dual-hatted organization answering to both the Department for Business, Enterprise and Regulatory Reform (BERR) and the Foreign Office. The Industrial Participation Unit of DESO is responsible for implementing the MoD's Industrial Participation policy.[567]

Offshore firms can structure arrangements that cover either: direct Industrial Participation (i.e., work carried out by UK-based companies on the MoD program to which the Industrial Participation proposal relates); or Indirect Industrial Participation (i.e., other defense work won by UK-based companies from the offshore company as a result of the Industrial Participation commitment).[568] In general, a foreign firm can receive credit for an Industrial Participation agreement that results in the following types of work:

- Products/services purchased from a new UK supplier;

- New products/services from an existing UK supplier;

- Purchase orders/contracts for existing products/services from a UK supplier that has been the subject of re-competition or re-evaluation; or

---

[567] DESO's Industrial Participation Unit is responsible for: 1) working with teams of the UK MoD Defence Equipment and Support acquisition organizations to identify when Industrial Participation is applicable; obtaining and assessing Industrial Participation proposals from offshore companies looking to work on MoD programs; negotiating Industrial Participation agreements with offshore companies; providing input to Business Cases in accordance with Defence Industrial Strategy; and monitoring agreements to a successful conclusion.

[568] Work must be defense or defense-related to be credited against an offshore company's Industrial Participation commitment. Commercial equipment provided as part of a defense system may be admissible for Industrial Participation purposes. The work must be carried out in the UK. It is recognized, however, that a foreign firm will still get credit where it contracts with a UK company that in turn then subcontracts part of this work offshore for its own commercial reasons provided that the offshoring is not excessive and has not been directed by other parties.

- Provision of technology at least commensurate with the equipment forming the MoD procurement contract to which the Industrial Participation commitment relates.

Industrial Participation also can be credited in a variety of other flexible circumstances involving: the transfer of defense technology (covering work resulting from the transfer or subsequent exports generated by it); R&D (where the UK contractor receiving the IP is able to use it for its own research purposes); and marketing assistance (where free-of-charge assistance to a UK firm was instrumental in such firm winning orders to third parties).

In sum, the UK's policy is an offset requirement in a "velvet glove"—very flexible in nature and aimed at a negotiated approach that reflects a spirit of cooperation and a "win-win" for both the UK and the foreign or offshore firm bidding. However, as the details above suggest, the UK Industrial Participation policy is a carefully reviewed and managed construct—it is not ephemeral or to be ignored. After negotiations are done and a deal is made, the offshore firm's commitment is tracked and managed until it is met.

UK "Industrial Participation" Requirements in Practice

The U.S. Department of Commerce (DoC) annual report on offsets confirms that the Industrial Participation or offsets in the UK totaled roughly 82 percent of contract values in practice for U.S. firms over the period 1993-2006 (calculated from data submitted by the reporting U.S. defense firms of actual contracts and offset commitments).[569] A review of DoC offset reports over recent years shows that the offset percentage has remained remarkably stable. Thus, offsets, whether technically required or not, do appear to be a major factor in defense trade with the UK.

Juste Retour

The UK has participated in numerous European programs where *juste retour* principles have been invoked. At the same time, the UK has been a longstanding critic of *juste retour* and has sought (through OCCAR and other routes) to move European cooperative programs away from the *juste retour* approach.

Government Ownership

A History of State-Owned Industries and UK Privatization

During the 1980s, the UK government privatized large segments of its defense industry, including leading companies such as British Aerospace (now BAE Systems) and Rolls-Royce. This was much earlier than other European nations, many of which did not begin privatizing until the late 1990s or beyond. The reduction of government control and authorization of foreign ownership were progressive, with increasingly liberal rules over time.

---

[569] Offsets in Defense Trade, Twelfth Report to Congress, U.S. Department of Commerce (Dec. 2007), PDF p. 29 (report page 2-13) (Table 2-5). Available at: http://www.bis.doc.gov/defenseindustrialbaseprograms/osies/offsets/final-12th-offset-report-2007.pdf.

Table 69   UK-Government Ownership (Percent – %) and Control of Defense Companies

Company	UK Government Ownership	Golden Share
BAE Systems plc	0	Yes
QinetiQ Group plc	0	Yes
Rolls Royce plc	0	Yes
British Nuclear Fuels Group	100	Yes
Royal Dockyards	0	Yes

Source: InfoBase Publishers, DACIS Company Database.

Specifically:

- In 1981, British Aerospace became incorporated as a public limited company and at that time half of the shares were sold to the general public. In 1985 the government sold its remaining ordinary shares in British Aerospace.

- Rolls-Royce was similar; it became a public limited company in 1985 and was floated on the stock market in May 1987.

- Royal Ordnance was also floated on the Stock Market. However, this was impractical within the timescale involved and it instead was sold as a package by way of a private sale to the highest bidder.

- ROF Leeds, which made tanks, was sold separately to Vickers in July 1986, so that the business could be reshaped to meet future requirements. A number of companies submitted bids for the rest of the company. The number of bids was reduced in stages and eventually the company was sold to British Aerospace in July 1986.

- The shipyards of British Shipbuilders were sold off separately by various means, including management buy-outs, during the mid-1980s.[570]

Since that time, the UK government has gone further, including privatization of the larger part of the UK's defense research establishments to form QinetiQ. In August 2008, the UK government sold its final holding of 19.3 percent in QinetiQ.

UK Golden Shares Provisions

The UK government continues to retain ownership of golden shares in a few key firms that affords it special rights (see Table 69). As outlined in a February 2008 GAO report, through golden shares, the UK has various rights such as: UK citizenship requirements for the companies' boards of directors; control over the percentages of foreign-owned shares; and approval requirements for the dissolution or disposal of any strategic assets. This share

---

[570] Details of the history of UK defense privatization are drawn from M. Bell, NATO Colloquium, 1994. op. cit.

does not, however, give the government control over the companies' routine business activities, investment decisions, or appointments.[571]

BAE and Rolls-Royce Foreign Ownership Restrictions: A History of Gradual Relaxation

The original terms of the privatization of British Aerospace and Rolls-Royce afforded the UK government broad golden share rights in order to preclude foreign ownership and control of these firms; these rights subsequently were curtailed over time.

Originally, golden shares gave the government the power to veto certain changes to the fundamental rules of each company set forth in their Articles of Association; allowed the government to restrict the proportion of shares owned by non-UK interests; and to stipulate that the company boards have a majority of UK directors. These shares did not then, and do not today, afford the UK government a say in the management, development and profitability of the business.

The limit on total foreign share holding was gradually increased from 15 percent in 1981 to 29.5 percent in 1989 to no more than 49.5 percent in 1998. In April 2002, the government announced that this restriction would be entirely removed from the Articles of Association of both companies. In the case of BAE Systems, the government agreed in lieu thereof: "to remove the provision allowing the appointment of a Government Director; to change the current requirements that all Executive Directors are British to a requirement that a simple majority of the Board, including the Chief Executive and any Executive Chairman, are British; and to remove the aggregate foreign shareholding limit."[572] In the case of Rolls-Royce, the government agreed "to change the current requirement that 75 percent of the Board are British to a requirement that a simple majority, including the Chief Executive and any Executive Chairman, are British; to allow the appointment of a non-British non-Executive Chairman; and to remove the aggregate foreign shareholding limit."[573] However, the existing 15 percent limit on individual foreign shareholding was retained in both firms to prevent outright control by a single foreign individual or organization.

UK Foreign Ownership Share Restrictions Today

While today total foreign share ownership in BAE Systems and Rolls-Royce is now above 50 percent, the restriction on *individual* foreign ownership remains in place. When Boeing at various times showed interest in acquiring BAE Systems, the MoD considered waiving the ownership restriction for such a strategic foreign investor. However, it will take such action only on a case-by-case basis and with appropriate safeguards in place.

According to the GAO report, the use of golden shares has been successfully challenged in the European Court of Justice, which ruled in 2002 and 2003 that the use of such shares is acceptable only in specific circumstances and with strict conditions. However, the UK continues to use golden shares on the grounds of national security, and does not intend to dispose of these shares in certain strategic areas. In most cases, golden shares (officially

---

[571] GAO Report, *FOREIGN INVESTMENT: Laws and Policies Regulating Foreign Investment in 10 Countries*, GAO-08-320 (pp. 101-102). Available at: http://www.gao.gov/new.items/d08320.pdf.

[572] House of Commons Written Answer, 26 March 2002, Column 804W.

[573] Ibid.

called Special Shares) are maintained for companies related to the "national deterrent" (i.e., the UK nuclear force). Notably the government owns 100 percent of British Nuclear Group, which provides fuel for military and commercial reactors.

Golden Shares in Place Today

Specifically, company-specific limitations and UK government holdings in golden shares at this writing include the following:[574]

- BAE Systems limits individual foreign ownership of voting stocks to 15 percent.

- Rolls-Royce limits individual foreign ownership of voting stocks to 15 percent. The British government's consent is required for the disposal of the company's nuclear business or the group as a whole.

- British Energy requires the consent of the government to allow a purchase of more than 15 percent of its issued shares.

- The government holds a golden share in QinetiQ. Its Articles of Association grant the UK government various rights, including the ability to impose certain restrictions and oversee major company decisions.

- The government holds a golden share in Rosyth Royal Dockyard Limited, Davenport Royal Dockyard Limited, and BAES (Marine) Limited.

Each company's Articles of Association grants the government various rights, including the ability to impose certain restrictions and oversee major company decisions. While the UK sold its Navy yards to companies to manage and operate, the UK MoD retains this golden share. Babcock International owns the UK shipbuilding and refitting yard at Rosyth and runs the Navy's submarine base at Faslane on the Clyde and also purchased the Navy yard Devonport in 2007. Since that buy, Babcock not only has control over support work on Britain's submarines but also an 80 percent share of the support market for surface ships.[575]

One special case to note is the UK Atomics Weapons Establishment (AWE), a sub-element of British Nuclear Fuels (BNFL) that as of December 18, 2008, has two-thirds ownership by U.S. firms. AWE's responsibility includes designing, manufacturing and decommissioning nuclear warheads for Trident, the fleet of nuclear submarines that is the UK's sole nuclear deterrent.[576] AWE has been jointly owned by the government, through its stake in BNFL, Serco, the British support services group, and Lockheed Martin, the U.S. firm that works on the nuclear deterrent.

The AWE has been managed and operated for some time for the UK MoD through a contractor-operated arrangement: AWE Management Limited (AWE ML). AWE ML is formed of three equal shareholders: BNFL, Serco, and Lockheed Martin. This AWE contract is set to run until March 2025.[577]

---

[574] GAO-08-320. op. cit.

[575] S. Pfeifer, "BAE dives into battle for Devonport dockyard," *The Telegraph* (Dec. 18, 2006). Available at: http://www.telegraph.co.uk/finance/migrationtemp/2952528/BAE-dives-into-battle-for-Devonport-dockyard.html.

[576] It should be noted that the technology for the Trident warheads originated in the United States.

[577] AWE website. Available at: http://www.awe.co.uk/aboutus/the_company_eb1b2.aspx.

The UK government's stake in AWE was put up for sale last year after ministers decided to break up BNFL, the state-owned group that included AWE. The UK signaled as early as 2001 its intent to break up BNFL and sell pieces and at least partially privatize others. Jacobs, an engineering company with headquarters in Pasadena, California, announced on December 18, 2008, that it had bought the UK government's holding in AWE. With Jacobs buying the UK State's one-third share, AWE now will be two-thirds owned by U.S. companies.

Foreign Direct Investment

As discussed above, the UK has one of the broadest trade relationships with the United States of any nation, and more generally, is one of the most open industrial markets in the world, with an environment conducive to foreign investment. As the U.S. Department of Commerce observed:

> [T]he U.S. and the UK are the largest foreign investors in each other's country. In 2006, U.S. direct investment in the UK grew 12.5 percent to reach $364 billion in 2006. In fact, 40 percent of overseas direct investment in the UK is from the United States. UK direct investment in the U.S. totaled $303 billion in 2006, a 2 percent increase over the previous year.[578]

This open attitude has extended to the UK defense industry in a way that is notable relative to most other European countries. In some respects, the UK has one of the least restrictive foreign ownership regimes: it has permitted Finmeccanica, a leading Italian defense firm, to purchase AgustaWestland, and also has permitted Thales, a leading French firm, to acquire Racal and other businesses; both of the buyers also have some foreign government ownership. British acceptance of growing foreign ownership in its defense industry is a core part of the UK government's defense industrial policy and was at the heart of its *Defence Industrial Policy* paper published in October 2002.

The 2002 Policy paper stressed the UK government's view that the UK defense industry includes all defense suppliers that create value, employment, technology or intellectual assets in the UK—regardless of whether they are UK or foreign-owned. As it stated:

> One result of the defence industry's internationalization has been to blur the definition of what comprises the UK defence industry. An increasing number of companies with foreign parentage now have British boards and workforces.... Foreign-owned companies that set up in the UK can bring benefit in creating technology, employment and intellectual assets in this country.... *The UK defence industry should therefore be defined in terms of where the technology is created, where the skills and the intellectual property reside, where the jobs are created and sustained, and where the investment is made.*"[579] (Emphasis added.)

The Ministry of Defence has also stated that restructuring should be led by industry and that government should not dictate the pattern of merger, acquisition and joint venture

---

[578] U.S. Department of Commerce, Ibid. Quotes from website at: http://www.buyusa.gov/uk/en/uk_commercial_guide.html.

[579] UK MoD DIS, p. 9, paragraph 11.

activity. Instead, the UK government views itself as a facilitator of European restructuring, with the MoD empowered to manage individual mergers to protect value for money, competition and national security.[580]

However, the UK's openness to foreign ownership remains limited for a few key firms—i.e., those in which the UK holds golden shares, as discussed above. The UK will review on a case-by-case basis whether to waive that limitation for "the right buyer" and what conditions if any to put in place.

More broadly, the 2002 Defence Industrial Policy explains the MoD's thinking with respect to foreign acquisition decisions. As it states:

> There are a very small number of capabilities which for *national security* reasons we would place a high priority on retaining in the UK industrial base. Examples exist in the fields of nuclear technology, defence against biological, chemical and radiological warfare, and some counterterrorist capabilities.[581]

Transparent and Reasonable Standards and Processes for Buyers

UK merger regulations under the Enterprise Act (2002) provide the UK government with powers to intervene in a merger on the grounds of national security.[582] Under UK law, there is no general requirement to notify mergers to the UK competition authorities. However, guidance published by the UK Department of Trade and Industry (now BERR, as discussed earlier) recommends that: "If you consider the UK's essential security interests may be affected by the deal then you are advised to contact the Ministry of Defence."[583] The Secretary of State for Trade and Industry has formal responsibility for public interest cases (including national security).

The European Community Dimension

Under the EC Merger Regulation (ECMR), the European Commission (EC) has exclusive competence over mergers with a Community dimension. However, Article 296 EC Treaty allows Member States to opt out of EC merger reviews of defense firms to protect their essential security interests and instead conduct national competition reviews of the defense aspects of the merger.[584] The non-military aspects of the merger would remain with

---

[580] "European Perspectives on Competition in Aerospace & Defence Markets," presentation by Mr David Gould, Deputy Chief Executive, UK Defence Procurement Agency, at the conference on *The Defense Industry A Decade After The Last Supper: Taking Stock of Consolidation and Competition in Defense Markets*, Nov. 3-4, 2003, Johns Hopkins University, Washington, D.C.

[581] UK MoD Policy Papers No. 5, Defence Industrial Policy, 2002. Available at: http://www.berr.gov.uk/files/file10008.pdf.

[582] The Enterprise Act (2002) came into force on June 20, 2003, and replaced the merger control regime contained in the Fair Trading Act (1973). In practice, the treatment of national security mergers remains very much the same.

[583] *The EC Merger Regulation Guidance Notes*, Competition Policy Directorate, Department of Trade and Industry, Nov. 1998.

[584] Member States may also exercise a residual power under Article 21(3) of the ECMR to take "appropriate measures to protect legitimate interests other than those taken into consideration by this Regulation." Article 21(3) says public (or national) security shall be regarded as a legitimate interest. In most instances, Article 21 (3) has provided the legal basis for UK government review of mergers with a national security dimension. For example, Article 21 (3) was cited by the UK government to review the acquisition of Racal Electronics by Thomson-CSF, the formation of MBDA and the acquisition of Astrium by EADS.

the EC to consider. In practice, the UK government (like other EU Member States) has used Article 296 EC Treaty and its predecessor Article 223 European Community Treaty very sparingly with respect to defense mergers.

Specifically, when British Aerospace acquired the UK nuclear submarine maker VSEL in 1994, the UK government instructed British Aerospace not to notify the acquisition of VSEL's military activities to the EC—arguing that it was a matter of UK security covered by Article 223. In 1996, the UK and French governments jointly instructed British Aerospace and Lagardere not to notify the EC of the military aspects of their proposed guided weapons joint venture. Subsequently, in 1999, British Aerospace was instructed by the UK government not to notify the Commission of the military aspects of its acquisition of GEC Marconi.

Powers Under the Enterprise Act (2002)

The 2002 Enterprise Act also affords the government (through the Secretary of State for Trade and Industry) the authority to intervene in a range of mergers with a national security dimension.[585] In the reviews of most mergers, the Office of Fair Trading (OFT)[586] makes a report to the Secretary of State for Trade and Industry that, among other things, makes recommendations on the degree to which relevant public interests are affected. Where a merger raises national security concerns, the OFT relies heavily on representations made by the Ministry of Defence. The Defence Procurement Agency has a mergers and acquisitions adviser within its Industry Group who is responsible for MoD advice on defense industry mergers and acquisitions. In cases where U.S. technology or programs are important to the company's UK business, the MoD consults with the U.S. DoD.

For public interest (including national security) cases, the Secretary of State for Trade and Industry decides whether to clear a merger or refer the merger to the Competition Commission because it may be against the public interest.[587] Where a case is referred on public interest grounds, the Secretary of State will also decide on remedies (if any) following receipt of the Competition Commission report and seek undertakings (i.e., commitments) on key issues from the acquiring party in lieu of reference. In public interest cases, the Secretary of State may accept undertakings by the company concerned in lieu of a reference

---

[585] The Enterprise Act authorizes intervention in a range of situations: 1) to protect legitimate (including national security) interests under Article 21(3) of the ECMR; 2) in mergers that may raise one or more public interest (including national interest) considerations; and 3) in an exceptional category of mergers that can be referred on public interest consideration grounds only ("special merger situation"). These are mergers involving a government contractor (past or present) who holds confidential material related to defence—so triggering the consideration of national security—but who does not meet the normal qualifying thresholds relating to turnover or the share of supply. The provisions of the Enterprise Act also hold that, in normal circumstances, mergers can be considered by the UK competition authorities only if the turnover in the UK of the enterprise being taken over exceeds £70m or the merger creates or increases a 25 percent share in a market for goods or services in the UK or a substantial part of it.

[586] The OFT is an organization independent of government that is the principal body that investigates the competition aspects of mergers in the UK.

[587] The Competition Commission is an independent public body established by the Competition Act 1998. The Commission conducts in-depth inquiries into mergers, markets and the regulation of the major regulated industries. Every inquiry is undertaken in response to a reference made to it by another authority: usually by the Office of Fair Trading (OFT) but in certain circumstances the Secretary of State.

Table 70   UK—Foreign Acquisitions of British Defense/Aerospace Companies

Date	Company	Buyer	Price	Revenues	Notes	Defense/Dual Use
Oct 2008	SEOS Ltd.	Rockwell Collins, inc.	NA	NA	Deal Pending. Flight Simulators	Defense
Aug 2008	Filtronic plc	Teledyne Technologies	24.30	28.70	Defense electronics	Defense
June 2008	Brookhouse Holdings Ltd	Kaman Corporation	85.10	54.90	Composite aerostructures	Dual Use
Feb 2008	Pentland Systems Ltd	Curtis Wright Corporation	NA	NA	Ruggedize receivers	Dual Use
Jan 2008	Metals UK Group	A.M. Castle & Co	NA	72	Specialty metals	Dual Use
Jan 2008	SG Brown Ltd	Teledyne Technologies	57.70	23.90	Inertial systems	Dual Use
Nov 2007	Umeco plc	AMETEK, Inc.	73	57	Aircraft MROU service	Dual Use
Nov 2007	Firth Rixon Ltd	Oak Hill Capital Partners	1,960	1,040	Forgings, casting and specialty metals	Dual Use
Nov 2007	Logistic Business Systems	Parametric Technology	NA	NA	Integrated Logistic Support solutions	Dual Use
July 2007	Caledonian Alloys Group	Precision Castparts Corp	208.10	NA	Nickel superalloy and titanium parts	Dual Use
July 2007	Security Support Solutions	O'Gara Group, inc.	NA	NA	Armored vehicles	Defense
July 2007	Rentokil Initial Security	United Technologies	1,160	580	Integrated security systems	Dual Use
June 2007	Reactor Sites Mgmt Co.	EnergySolutions	NA	NA	Nuclear reactor management	Dual Use
June 2007	Thales Optronics	GSI Group	NA	NA	Beryllium mirrors and structures	Dual Use
May 2007	Smiths Aerospace	General Electric Co.	4,800	2,400	Aerospace subsystems	Dual Use
May 2007	McKechnie Aerospace	JLL Partners	855	258	Aerospace engineering & subsystems	Dual Use
May 2007	St. Bernhard Composites	Oak Hill Capital Partners	NA	NA	Composite aerostructures	Dual Use
Jan 2007	Kemfast Aerospace	Haas TCM	NA	NA	Aerospace chemicals	Dual Use
Dec 2006	Page Group, Ltd.	United Technologies	NA	43	Cockpit lighting and controls	Dual Use
Sep 2006	Radstone Technology plc	General Electric Co.	165	103.80	Ruggedized COTS computers	Dual Use
July 2006	TRL Electronics	L-3 Communications	171.40	40.20	Electronic Countermeasures (ECM)	Defense
June 2006	Nautronix Holdings plc	L-3 Communications	69	NA	Mine countermeasure and ASW	Defense
Apr 2006	Precision Antennas Ltd	Andrew Corp	26	46	SATCOM antennas	Dual Use
Apr 2006	BAE Aerostructures	Spirit Aerosystems, Inc.	203.50	367	Aircraft structural components	Dual Use

Date	Company	Buyer	Price	Revenues	Notes	Defense/Dual Use
Mar 2006	Wallop Defense Systems	Esterline Corporation	70.50	NA	Flares and countermeasuers	Defense
Mar 2006	G3 Systems Ltd	IAP Worldwide Services	NA	NA	Defense logistic & engineering services	Defense
Jan 2006	Adv. System Architectures	L-3 Communications	59.50	10	Multi-sensor fusion technology	Defense
Jan 2006	HNT Vehicles Ltd	Lockheed Martin Corp	23.60	NA	High mobility tactical vehicles	Defense
Dec 2005	Darchem Holdings Ltd	Esterline Corporation	121.70	70	Thermally engineered aerospace comp.	Dual use
Nov 2005	Cobham plc Fluid & Air	Eaton Corporation	270	210	Hydraulic and pneumatic systems	Dual use
Nov 2005	NP Aerospace	Carlyle Group	53.40	NA	Aerospace moldings	Dual use
Oct 2005	INSYS Group Ltd	Lockheed Martin Corp	180	47	Combat communication systems	Defense
Apr 2005	Automotive Technik	Stewart and Stevenson	47.20	NA	Light tactical vehicles	Defense
Feb 2005	STASYS Ltd	Lockheed Martin Corp	180	32	Defense interoperability solutions	Defense
Jan 2005	I2 Ltd	ChoicePoint, Inc.	90.20	NA	Visusalization technology for military	Defense
Dec 2004	Havensec Ltd	Global Marine Ltd	NA	NA	Private security company	Dual Use
Aug 2004	Coda Octopus Ltd	Coda Octopus Group, Inc	NA	NA	Underwater systems	Dual Use
Aug 2004	Babtle Group Ltd	Jacobs Engineering, inc.	169.30	300	Defense logistics	Defense
Jun 2004	Primagraphics Holdings	Curtis-Wright Corporation	21	12.50	Radar processing and display systems	Defense
Apr 2004	Thales Acoustics UK	J.F. Lehman & Co.	25.80	NA	Defense communications	Defense
Mar 2004	AF Aerospace Ltd	Airdrome Holdings, Ltd	NA	NA	Aerospace components	Dual Use
Jan 2004	Hymatic Group Ltd	Honeywell International	NA	40	Aerospace controls	Dual Use
Jun 2003	Emblem Group Ltd	EDO Corporation	29.20	25.20	Specialized aerospace products	Dual Use
Jun 2003	Weston Group	Esterline Technologies	94.50	51.50	Aircraft engine sensors	Dual Use
Feb 2003	Qinetiq	Carlyle Group	265	NA	30% Equity Stake	Dual Use
Jan 2003	Airtechnology Holdings	AMETEK, inc.	NA	46.50	Aerospace environmental control sys.	Dual Use
Apr 2002	Spirent Aerospace Sol	Curtis Wright Corporation	59.50	62.20	Aerospace sensors and controls	Dual Use

Source: Defense Mergers and Acquisitions (DM&A) Database.

to the Competition Commission following receipt of advice from the OFT. Again, it is the MoD, through the OFT, that proposes those undertakings.[588]

Increasing Foreign Ownership in the UK

In 2005, the DIS estimated that around 25 percent of the UK's defense industrial base was foreign-owned; since then, that percentage has continued to grow.[589] As discussed above, U.S. firms are cautiously expanding their UK presence through acquisitions and organic growth. U.S. firms have been slow to adopt this "onshore" approach in light of the past success of selling U.S. products in the UK without a UK presence, and the cost of establishing a permanent presence in the UK. The reality today is that conditions are changing. The policy of allowing foreign ownership, coupled with the policies of required Industrial Participation and the need to have on-the-ground presence in the UK to gain significant contract work, means that foreign firms have increasingly used acquisitions as a way to gain and increase market positions in the UK.

Still—despite the openness of the UK to foreign acquisitions—U.S. acquisitions of UK defense businesses have tended to be small to date. As Table 70 reflects, with only 4 exceptions (and one of those a financial buyer), all such U.S. buys have been less than $300 million. Most of the acquisitions on the Table are not pure defense firms, but include significant commercial aerospace, homeland security and related IT businesses.

> **GE/Smiths**—In the largest buy of a defense-related property by a U.S. firm to date, GE in 2007 acquired Smiths Aerospace for about $4.8 billion. The acquired firm, now called GE Aviation, is a leading global supplier to builders and operators of military and civil aircraft, engines and land vehicles, from large transports to fighters, unmanned aerial vehicles to armored vehicles, and from helicopters to regional and business jets. The company is a major first-tier supplier to both Boeing Commercial and Airbus, and to prominent regional and business jet manufacturers. It also holds important positions on current and future military systems, including F-22, F/A-18E/F, F-16 Block 60, Eurofighter Typhoon and F-35 Joint Strike Fighter programs and key transport and special mission aircraft.

Beyond U.S. buyers, other European nations have increased their stake in the UK through larger acquisitions. Thales, a leading French-owned multidomestic company, has acquired several holdings there, most notably Racal Electronics (in 2001 for £1.3 million). Today, Thales has more than 8,500 employees in the UK, in 26 major locations (60 altogether) that include manufacturing operations. Thales' UK sales, which typically exceed $2 billion annually, include about one-third to the British military, one-third to export, and one-third to other UK customers.[590] The Italian firm Finmeccanica acquired AgustaWestland in 2004, culminating an incremental process that originated in a joint venture. Agusta and Westland collaborated for more than 20 years on the development and production of

---

[588] By and large, undertakings in lieu of reference to the Competition Commission are likely to be preferred by the acquiring company not least because of the length of time a full Competition Commission enquiry takes—and the real prospect that the Competition Commission may find against the acquirer (on public interest grounds) and veto the transaction.

[589] UK MoD DIS, op. cit, para 3.38, p. 30.

[590] Data from Thales UK website at: http://www.thalesuk.com/bgan/files/documents/ThalesUK.pdf.

the 16-ton multirole EH101. In 2001, Finmeccanica S.p.A. of Italy and GKN plc of the UK signed the agreement for the formation of AgustaWestland, a 50-50 joint venture company. In December 2004, Finmeccanica acquired GKN's 50 percent stake in AgustaWestland to gain full ownership.[591]

Ethics and Corruption

The UK has a generally strong reputation for commitment to rule of law and ethics, with some of the most mature laws in the world and generally strong enforcement mechanisms. The World Bank's worldwide governance indicators show the UK in the 90 percent range or more for rule of law and control of corruption—among the highest scores of any major Western industrialized nations.[592] The UK also is ranked 16th in Transparency International's 2008 Corruption Perception Index. By way of comparison, France is 19th and Sweden is tied for first (with Denmark and New Zealand).[593]

Less salutary is the UK's stance toward foreign corrupt practices, which has been the subject of highly publicized debate in recent years. The UK is a signatory to the OECD Convention on Combating Bribery of Foreign Public Officials in International Business Transactions (OECD Anti-Bribery Convention). Part 12 of the UK's Anti-Terrorism, Crime and Security Act 2001 includes provisions to make it clear that existing UK law on bribery and corruption applied to bribery and corruption of foreign public officials and to bribery and corruption committed outside the UK by British nationals and companies. This law, which came into force in February 2002, effectively prohibits UK companies and nationals from committing acts of bribery overseas. UK registered companies and UK nationals can be prosecuted in the UK for an act of bribery committed wholly overseas.

Unfortunately, Organisation for Economic Co-operation and Development (OECD) reviews have found deficiencies in UK corruption legislation that remain uncorrected. Moreover, the UK has failed to bring any prosecutions of illicit payments despite numerous UK investigations.[594] Allegations also continue that UK firms participate in foreign corrupt payments. However, the UK is rated 6th in Transparency International's Bribe Payers Index of 30 major exporting nations—suggesting that it is better than most Western industrialized nations but by no means perfect.[595]

Recently, the UK government was subjected to intense criticism following the decision by the UK Serious Fraud Office (SFO) to discontinue the investigation into BAE Systems concerning payments made in relation to the longstanding and very large Al Yamamah defense contract with Saudi Arabia. The SFO said the decision was taken following representations to the Attorney General and the SFO concerning "the need to safeguard national and international security. It has been necessary to balance the need to maintain the rule of

---

[591] Details from AgustaWestland website at: http://www.agustawestland.com/company03.php.

[592] See World Bank Governance Indicators, 1996-2007 (Country Data Report for United Kingdom, 1996-2007). Available at: http://info.worldbank.org/governance/wgi/pdf/c80.pdf.

[593] Transparency International's Corruption Perception Index is on their website, available at: http://www.transparency.org/news_room/in_focus/2008/cpi2008/cpi_2008_table.

[594] F. Heimann and G. Dell, "Progress Report 2008: Enforcement of the OECD Convention on Combating Bribery of Foreign Public Officials in International Business Transactions," Transparency International (June 24, 2008), at 10, 21-22. Available at: http://www.transparency.org/news_room/in_focus/2008/oecd_report.

[595] Available at: http://www.transparency.org/policy_research/surveys_indices/bpi/bpi_2006.

law against the wider public interest. No weight has been given to commercial interests or to national economic interest."[596] The UK government argued that continuing the investigation would cause serious damage to UK/Saudi security, intelligence and diplomatic cooperation and, as a result, would likely have adverse consequences for UK national security objectives in the Middle East.

The allegations of illegal payments by BAE date back to the 1980s and the $85 billion Al Yamamah deal to supply Saudi Arabia with Tornado military aircraft and other equipment. The OECD asked the UK government to explain its decision. Subsequently, in October 2008, following an OECD inquiry into UK anti-bribery practices, the OECD anti-bribery group warned that companies doing business with the UK risk legal and reputational damage because of lax anti-bribery law and enforcement.[597]

Transparency International's recent progress report on the OECD Anti-Bribery Convention is also very critical of the UK, finding that "[t]he UK's termination of the investigation of Al Yamamah-related bribery allegations against BAE Systems (BAE) in December 2006 was a damaging setback for the Convention. The assertion that national security concerns overrode the obligation to enforce the Convention created a dangerous precedent that other governments could readily follow. The termination of the BAE investigation compounded prior concerns about lack of UK commitment..." to the OECD Convention.[598]

From a U.S. perspective, the allegations of BAE's involvement in foreign corrupt practices have given some pause to the U.S. government during its recent reviews of BAE acquisitions of U.S. defense firms. DoD, aware of the Al Yamamah situation in the late 1990s, sought assurances from BAE that it would comply with the U.S. Foreign Corrupt Practices Act (FCPA) during its acquisition of Lockheed AES. The issue subsequently arose during the 2007 BAE/Armor Holdings acquisition after the Al Yamamah situation was publicly disclosed. Various members of Congress and the press raised questions about the U.S. selling a key defense asset to a firm with a long record of illicit payments, and allegations that a U.S. bank facilitated the payments made matters worse. Ultimately, the U.S. government recognized that processes for reviewing foreign investments on national security grounds (under the Exon-Florio Act) was not the place for a full investigation of this matter. Rather, the U.S. government allowed the acquisition to proceed while at the same time the U.S. Department of Justice initiated its own investigation of the matter (apparently still pending).

Export Controls

The UK System

The UK is a member of major multilateral export control regimes, including the Nuclear Suppliers Group, the Australia Group, the Missile Technology Control Regime, the Wassenaar Arrangement on Export Controls for Conventional Arms and Dual-Use Goods and

---

[596] UK Serious Fraud Office, Dec. 14, 2006, Statement at: http://www.sfo.gov.uk/news/prout/pr_497.asp?id=497.

[597] M. Peel, "Warning over UK's overseas bribes culture," *Financial Times*, Oct. 17, 2008.

[598] F. Heimann and G. Dell, "Progress Report 2008: Enforcement of the OECD Convention on Combating Bribery of Foreign Public Officials in International Business Transactions," Transparency International (June 24, 2008), at 10, 21-22. Available at: http://www.transparency.org/news_room/in_focus/2008/oecd_report.

Technologies and the Chemical Weapons Convention. The UK is also a Member State of the Organization for Security and Co-operation in Europe (OSCE), and the UK has approved the OSCE principles governing transfers of conventional arms and the 2000 OSCE Document on Small Arms and Light Weapons.[599]

The UK, like other EU members, is also a signatory to the 1998 EU Code of Conduct on Arms Exports, which harmonized regulations across all Member States in the EU, established general principles for the transfer of armaments and military technology, and set up a system whereby each Member State must inform the others whenever an export license is denied. Under the Code, each State must also consult with the other Member States whenever it wishes to grant an export license that has been denied by another Member State for "essentially identical transactions," although the ultimate decision to deny or transfer a military item remains at the national discretion of each Member State. This Code of Conduct on Arms Exports was elevated into an EU Common Position in December 2008.

Further, the EC Transfers Directive recently adopted by the European Parliament is a further step in aligning the policies of EU countries regarding intra-Community transfers and simplifying procedures to permit such transfers among Member States and certified defense companies. The focus of this Directive is intra-Community transfers of defense-related products and, thus, the main beneficiaries of reduced barriers within the EU are European defense companies. It is not at all clear that U.S. firms will be eligible for similar treatment; this is a matter for national authorities to decide.

On a national level, the UK export control regime and its implementation are considered transparent and robust. Of particular interest to U.S. firms is UK export licensing policy, as notably reflected in the 2002 UK Export Control Act. This law establishes controls not only on goods but also on technology transfer and on trafficking and brokering activity. These provisions can cover negotiations held in the UK with any party from a third country, including discussions at trade shows.[600] The UK Department for Business, Enterprise and Regulatory Reform (BERR) has oversight of this area in its Export Control Organisation. The BERR has an extensive and clear website complete with full information on export control, current and past lists of controlled items (including items controlled for defense and security reasons), and the process of export control.[601] It has links to current legislation and even has explicit guidelines on potential concern areas, such as exports to Iran.

ITAR Attitudes and Behaviors: Declining Trust in the United States

A significant issue for U.S. defense firms seeking to access the UK market is the growing level of frustration and concern in the UK with the ITAR—as highlighted by the technology release and procedural issues discussed above with respect to the JSF program.

Beyond the frustration of the JSF program, the UK has more broadly faced a mounting issue of the delays and uncertainties posed by U.S. export licensing and their adverse implications for development and delivery schedules. "UK and EU trust in the United States has slid way down," said one UK government official interviewed for this study. As he noted, "the nations or firms spend millions or even billions of dollars on a program but cannot be

---

[599] OSCE Document on Small Arms and Light Weapons. Available at: http://www.osce.org/fsc/13281.html.

[600] Information on UK Export regimes was provided by the U.S. Embassy, DoC Foreign Commercial Service.

[601] Available at: http://www.berr.gov.uk/whatwedo/europeandtrade/strategic-export-control/index.html.

guaranteed an export license. How can we say we have security of supply with the United States?" Like elsewhere in Europe, UK firms and government representatives report that waiting for U.S. export licensing is creating unacceptable risk in their product and system development and delivery schedules.

Thus, despite the DTSI and its bilateral agreements, the UK has long pressed for a special mechanism to greatly reduce and streamline U.S. controls on export of U.S. products and technologies to the UK. The UK seeks to put itself on a new and unique footing with the United States in defense trade—one the UK feels it merits on the basis of the "special relationship," and the United States has been receptive to these overtures. Indeed, as European countries moved closer to each other through the LOI process in the late 1990s, the United States pursued special ITAR waivers for the UK and Australia to cement those relationships for the future.

Subsequently, when the ITAR waivers failed to receive Congressional authorization, the Bush Administration then shifted its approach. Specifically, in June 2007, President Bush and then-British Prime Minister Blair signed the U.S.-UK Defense Trade Cooperation Treaty days before Blair left office in an attempt to address longstanding issues with respect to U.S. defense export controls.[602] The treaty would allow the UK government and a community of trusted customers to access certain U.S. technologies and products without applying for export licenses, and put those approvals needed on a "fast-track." The concept was to create a "secure circle" consisting of U.S. and UK governments and trusted defense companies. The idea was not a new one: it was essentially an effort to turn the ITAR exemptions negotiated with the UK in 2000-2001 into a treaty and expand them in various ways.

Despite the UK's "special relationship" with the United States, the treaty faced criticism and the Bush Administration did not appear to put the full support of the White House behind it. The U.S.-UK Treaty was submitted to the Senate for ratification in September 2007. However, the Senate would not consider the Treaty until implementing arrangements were negotiated and conforming amendments to the ITAR were submitted. Unfortunately, these matters took considerable time; internal deliberations by DoD on what products/technologies would be exempt also were time-consuming. The proposed ITAR amendment was not submitted to the Senate until August 2008.

In late September 2008, the Senate Committee on Foreign Relations deferred consideration of the Treaty until 2009—indicating it lacked the time to properly examine it during this Congress. As the Committee noted in its letter notifying the Administration of this decision, the Committee believed its questions on the implementation and enforcement of the treaty, and its relationship to existing law, had not been resolved in a timely manner. "[T]he information provided by the Administration to date, much of which has only been received in the last several weeks, is insufficient to resolve Members' concerns," the letter stated. The Committee also chastised the Administration for "delays" in submitting draft amendments to the ITAR and "shifting approaches to implementation" that precluded a comprehensive Committee consideration in the short period left in the session. Ironically, according to Bush Administration officials, some of the internal U.S. government delays related to Justice Department concerns over proceeding with a treaty that would have afforded special benefits to BAE Systems at a time when the company was under investigation for violations of the FCPA arising out of the Al Yamamah contract.

---

[602] B. Wagner, NDIA, Ibid. Note the United States was also working on an equivalent U.S.-Australian treaty.

Needless to say, the British were not happy about this development. As Gerald Howarth, the UK shadow defence procurement minister, noted, "[w]e've been pressing for this for two years and it's a pretty poor show that Congress has failed to accord more support to its number one ally.... The British government has been hugely supportive of the U.S. government."[603] In recognizing the obvious, Derek Marshall, of the Society of British Aerospace Companies, said the organization was hopeful "momentum created by the negotiations will not be lost."[604]

Whether the treaty will be considered and ratified in 2009 remains to be seen. While the Foreign Relations Committee suggested the treaty will be considered in the next Congress, whether this happens remains to be seen. While the decision to defer consideration focused largely procedural and timing issues, some believe the concerns of one or more members and their staffs run deeper and are more substantive in nature.[605] Moreover, there also are concerns in the business community that the treaty's limitations, together with obligations for its use by the "trusted community" of covered firms, have rendered it of limited utility.

Intellectual Property Protection

The UK adheres to the major multilateral intellectual property (IP) regimes, including (i) the WTO Agreement on Trade-Related Aspects of Intellectual Property Rights, which provides core IP protection and enforcement rights (including for trade secrets); (ii) the Paris Convention for the Protection of Industrial Property, covering patents, trademarks and industrial designs; (iii) the Patent Cooperation Treaty, protecting patents; (iv) the Berne Convention, covering copyrights; (v) the Madrid Protocol, covering trademarks; and (vi) the World Intellectual Property Organization.

Generally, the UK is known to have strong laws to protect intellectual rights and enforces these rights vigorously. According to the U.S. DoC Foreign Commercial Service, the "UK legal system provides a high level of IP rights protection. Enforcement mechanisms are comparable to those available in the United States."[606] The UK also does not appear on the U.S. Trade Representative watch list for IP violations.

U.S. defense companies have not raised with us during the course of our study any specific complaints regarding IP protection in the UK defense market.

Technical Standards

The UK is a party to the WTO's Technical Barriers to Trade Agreement, which prohibits discrimination and seeks to ensure that regulations, standards, testing and certification

---

[603] S. Pfeifer in London and D. Sevastopulo in Washington, "Defence treaty delay to hit UK," *Financial Times*, Sept. 22, 2008. Available at: http://www.ft.com/cms/s/0/2af58b4a-883e-11dd-b114-0000779fd18c.html?nclick_check=1.

[604] S. Pfeifer in London and D. Sevastopulo in Washington, *Financial Times*, Ibid.

[605] Oct. 3, 2008, http://www.janes.com/news/defence/jdw/jdw081003_3_n.shtml ("Formal ratification is not expected to come earlier than 2009. Discussing the likelihood of U.S. approval of both treaties, Suchan [former Deputy Secretary of State from 2003 to 2007] warned of the [failure of] previous effort to negotiate Canada-style licence waivers for the U.S. and Australia, initiated by former U.S. President Bill Clinton in early 2000.")

[606] U.S. Commercial Service, *Doing Business in the United Kingdom: 2008 Country Commercial Guide for U.S. Companies*, U.S. Department of Commerce (Washington, D.C.), 2008, p. 21. Available at: http://www.buyusa.gov/uk/en/uk_commercial_guide.html.

procedures do not create obstacles to trade. However, every country has the right to adopt those regulatory standards it considers appropriate in areas concerning national security. Thus, the UK has the discretion to, and has put in place, its own specific technical standards for defense products that could in theory serve as a non-tariff barrier to competing foreign products.

The U.S.-UK reciprocal defense procurement MOU does afford the UK and U.S. suppliers some protection against arbitrary discrimination on the basis of regulatory standards. An Annex to the MOU provides specific procedures to ensure that defense articles and services meet mutual government quality assurances. A purchasing government has the option to request that the other government independently test and provide a certification of conformity for defense articles produced by suppliers of the selling country.

UK's long association with NATO means that UK military products are tied to NATO Standard Agreements where these exist. As discussed in Chapter 5, however, there is some potential risk that an eventual EU set of standards might become disguised market access barriers—but there is no indication that this is a policy result sought by the UK.

In the course of this study, we did not learn of any specific situations involving the UK where regulatory standards were used as non-tariff barriers to protect domestic producers and markets against foreign defense products.

Chapter 14

Accessing the U.S. Defense Market

Since 1990, the U.S. defense marketplace has experienced two distinct "security eras": First, there was the post-Cold War era marked by declining threat perceptions, large defense reductions, few new major acquisition programs, and a resulting large-scale defense industry consolidation. Second, there was a subsequent "reawakening," from the late 1990s to the present, characterized by a focus on defense transformation, network-centric warfare and growing asymmetric threats, large defense budget increases in the post-September 11 era, and a high operational tempo driven by U.S. operations in Iraq and Afghanistan.

Today, the equation is changing again, with a new emerging focus by the Obama Administration on shifting the balance of our defense investments toward the types of irregular warfare we have been fighting in Iraq and Afghanistan while maintaining strategic superiority in conventional forces as a hedge against high-intensity but less likely threats.

This new focus on institutionalizing our efforts for irregular warfare (through changes in doctrine, training, equipage, personnel and organizational structures) comes in the context of a changing defense procurement market. A series of Obama Administration statements signal an emerging set of defense market priorities, including affordability in a time of great budgetary stress and steps to address a procurement system perceived to be broken (e.g., including more competition and the development of more "rapid to field" capabilities). While innovation to provide solutions to our security challenges remains the objective, there is a new focus on achieving practical 70 percent solutions.

Throughout these dynamic eras, foreign companies have tried to participate in the U.S. defense market. When the entire range of market access issues is viewed together, the resulting mosaic is one of a very large and attractive market that nevertheless has been a difficult market for foreign defense firms to penetrate. Foreign participation in the U.S. defense market at the prime contractor (system) level has always been and remains very limited even today, while the situation at the subcontractor (subsystem) level is slightly better.

The U.S. market is characterized by significant competition and a transparent procurement system. Historically, however, foreign competitors have often been excluded through both formal and informal means for a variety of reasons. These include national security (especially the risk of accessing sensitive information and control of vital security assets by a foreign-owned entity), security of supply (i.e., the risk inherent in relying on a foreign supplier whose host government could choose to restrict supply in a time of exigency), industrial base and employment considerations, a view of U.S. indigenous technologies and solutions as inherently superior, and a simple aversion to foreign solutions (the "Not Invented Here" syndrome).[607]

Other major obstacles to foreign market penetration include the sheer complexity of the U.S. system (an issue especially for medium and small firms), the availability of domestic

---

[607] As Edward N. Luttwak pointed out years ago, the U.S. military maintains a large defense R&D establishment whose rationale is to develop new systems, not to acquire off-the-shelf solutions from foreign sources that do not further the bureaucratic agenda of the laboratories and R&D commands. See Edward N. Luttwak, *The Pentagon and the Art of War*, Simon & Schuster (New York) 1985. The situation has not changed markedly since that time.

sources of supply in most defense market areas (which puts a premium on foreign offerings that are truly "better widgets"), and the difficulties of collaboration due to the U.S. International Traffic in Arms Regulations (ITAR) and national disclosure policies governing classified information. Of these, the restrictions on the transfer of technology and technical information stand out as key obstacles to foreign participation in many program areas: by declining to release certain information on technologies, the acquisition community can effectively preclude foreign participation.

Nevertheless, in the context of the wartime "bull market" in defense acquisition, foreign companies *have* seen significant growth in U.S. sales and market penetration since 2003. Some of this growth reflects the sheer magnitude of market opportunities, the high demand for certain products provided in real time for operational needs in a wartime environment, and the fact that European suppliers have some offerings suitable for the new types of demands of the U.S. military (particularly in tactical systems, special operations and other ground combat systems). Some of this growth also reflects the ability of European companies to climb the learning curve of the complex U.S. defense market, utilizing a range of strategies suitable to their circumstances, including acquisitions (particularly for firms in the United Kingdom (UK)), partnering with U.S. firms and developing a U.S. presence through organically grown onshore facilities. Finally, some of the growth does reflect changing U.S. attitudes—illustrated by recent program awards to prime level teams that included major foreign defense firms as major participants (including most notably the U.S. Air Force selection of a Northrop Grumman/EADS team over a Boeing competitor for the tanker program).[608]

Changes in U.S. government policy have affected the pace and scope of foreign participation in the U.S. defense market. In the Clinton era, the focus on improving coalition warfighting capabilities and encouraging competition in consolidating defense markets drove a conscious policy effort to promote Transatlantic defense cooperation and industrial linkages. This resulted in export control reforms, increased European acquisitions of U.S. defense firms, and other market opening measures. After the September 11 attacks, a "circle the wagons" mentality took hold in the United States that for a time aggravated the "not invented here" tendencies in the defense acquisition community. This included a distinct lack of Congressional and Administration support for foreign acquisitions of defense firms (except by British companies) and continued rigidity in export control processes. Only later, during the second Bush term did a strategy emerge of increased cooperation with our allies which in turn translated to greater U.S. willingness, on an *ad hoc* basis, to approve foreign defense acquisitions and make program decisions favorable to foreign suppliers. At present, the prospects for European firms in the U.S. defense market look more appealing than previously due to signs of increased openness, including the willingness to allow European participation in some key programs and to allow foreign firms to "buy" into the U.S. market through acquisitions, collaborative arrangements and the establishment of greenfield manufacturing operations.

To be sure, significant challenges exist in the United States for European suppliers (especially for firms not from the UK), including institutional, cultural and security-driven impediments, as well as ITAR restrictions and the sheer complexity of the U.S. market and the costs of entry. However, the size and scope of U.S. spending and range of opportuni-

---

[608] While the GAO upheld a protest on the tanker source selection award, the ruling was based on technical issues related to the source selection process and had nothing to do with foreign supplier involvement.

ties, signs of increasing customer willingness to consider foreign sources, and increasing willingness of the United States to allow foreign firms to buy into our market, is gradually creating a more appealing environment for European firms.

Whether this upward trend continues depends in good measure on policies and decisions the Obama Administration will make regarding the market barrier issues identified by this study. However, the newly emerging Obama Administration priorities for the defense market—affordability, competition and continued innovation—suggest a shift in incentives that will tend to favor market access for foreign suppliers. As fully discussed in Chapter 6, market access is one means of facilitating competition and the innovation and affordability; it can offer existing off-the-shelf, 70 percent solutions that may be attractive to U.S. Department of Defense (DoD) customers in this new era.

I. Market Background: Demand Changes—A Story of Two Eras

Demand for defense systems and products evolves with the changes in the security environment. This is certainly true in the United States, where we really have seen two distinct but overlapping periods: 1) the post-Cold War era of large budget declines and a receding Soviet threat, fewer new programs and more emphasis on affordability; and 2) the post-September 11 era of budget increases, the emergence of a range of asymmetric threats (from terrorism to cyber warfare), and the need for significant innovation to provide real-time solutions to these challenges. While September 11 can be viewed as a watershed moment that certainly accelerated the second trend, the emergence of asymmetric threats and the need for defense "transformation" in order to respond actually began in the late 1990s.

A. The Post-Cold War Budget Drawdown and Its Consequences: Fewer Programs and an Affordability Focus

The dramatic decline in U.S. Defense Research and Development (R&D) and Procurement budgets from FY1991 through FY1997 reflected in Figure 138 speaks for itself. These budget dollars directly reflect a large portion of demand as experienced by defense firms. From a high of nearly $520.4 billion (in 2008 dollars) in 1987, the U.S. defense budget fell to just $345 billion in 1998 before beginning to again recover.[609] It has been widely noted that the overall budget reduction was 51 percent in research, development, testing and engineering (RDT&E) and procurement authority. However, procurement alone, so important to defense companies' revenue flow, was cut by some 70 percent from the mid-1980s high to the 1998 low. To sustain technology development for future systems, the Clinton Administration reduced RDT&E proportionally less than procurement. Nevertheless, former Deputy Secretary of Defense John Deutsch characterized the scale of decline in RDT&E as "a 40 percent drop, in real terms."[610]

---

[609] National Defense Budget Estimates for FY 2009, Office of Under Secretary of Defense (Comptroller), March 2008, pp. 62-67 (Table 6-1) (in 2003 constant dollars).

[610] John Deutch, Ph.D., former Under Secretary and Deputy Secretary of Defense, as well as Director of CIA. He characterizes the decline as a "more than 40 percent drop, in real terms, of DoD investment expenditures." See "Consolidation of the U.S. Defense Industrial Base," *Acquisition Review Quarterly*, Fall 2001, p. 137. Available at: http://www.dau.mil/pubs/arq/2001arq/Deutch.pdf.

Figure 138   U.S. Defense Procurement and R&D, 1991-2009

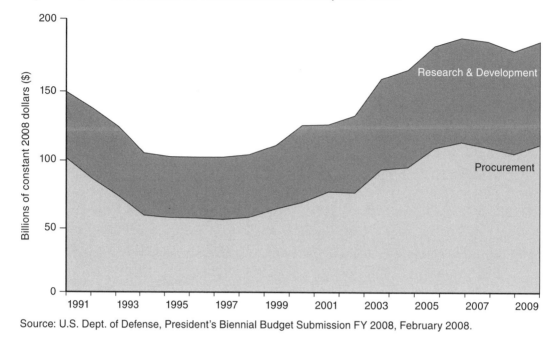

Source: U.S. Dept. of Defense, President's Biennial Budget Submission FY 2008, February 2008.

The 1990s budget decline was viewed differently from previous spending cycles, even from the Post-Vietnam War downward cycle. A 1990s Defense Science Board noted that the budget drawdown reflected a number of core factors:

1. A less clearly perceived or defined national security threat than before or during the Cold War;

2. The U.S. government's drive to balance the U.S. budget, and hence an unwillingness to achieve higher levels of defense spending via deficits;

3. The increasing complexity, and therefore increasing costs, to develop and produce defense systems in the 1990s (when compared to the 1970s).[611]

In light of these dynamics, DoD restructured its acquisition priorities in the 1990s. The result was fewer new large programs (see Table 71), an increased focus on affordability generally and an emphasis on modification and life extension programs for existing platforms in particular (with electronics added through upgrades). For example, Cost as an Independent Variable (CAIV) was an initiative to trade specific performance features or objectives against cost—to allow company and DoD program decision-makers better insight into cost for performance output. As part of its acquisition reforms (discussed below), the DoD undertook steps toward a price-based acquisition strategy and reduced use of fully open, cost-based contracting, with its attendant requirements for extensive documentation and oversight.

In a January 1999 speech to the Air War College, then-Under Secretary of Defense for Acquisition and Technology Jacques Gansler said "At the end of the Cold War, we stopped

---

[611] Report of the Defense Science Board Task Force on Vertical Integration and Supplier Decisions, May 1997, pp. 7-8. Available at: http://www.dtic.mil/cgi-bin/GetTRDoc?AD=ADA324688&Location=U2&doc=GetTRDoc.pdf.

Table 71   Major Program Starts, 1991-1999

Army	Navy	Air Force
Future Combat System	Virginia Class SSN	FA-22 Raptor
RAH-66 Comanche	DDG-51 Destroyer	Global Hawk
Crusader SP Artillery	San Antonio Class LSD	AEHF Communications
MEADS/PAC-3	FA-18E/F Super Hornet	Wibe-Band Gapfiller
Stryker IAV		SBIRS-Hi
		SBIRS-Lo

Source: U.S. Dept. of Defense, President's Biennial Budget Submissions; DACIS Programs Database.

modernizing—allowing our procurement account to plummet by around 70 percent (only recently allowing it to start creeping back up). Thus today we are spending tens of billions of dollars annually to maintain our aging and overworked equipment."[612] Then-Deputy Secretary of Defense John Hamre chartered the Defense Systems Affordability Council; as Operations and Maintenance costs continued to grow as a portion of the total DoD budget, one of its goals was a program to reduce Total Ownership (weapon system life cycle) costs by an established percentage each fiscal year.

New Acquisition Processes and Practices

The 1990s budget decline also promoted changes in DoD acquisition processes and programs, which reflected a decade of previous studies and research, including the Packard Commission's report.[613] The reforms were aimed at expanding the commonality between the commercial and defense industries, and minimizing the highly unique and specialized defense product and process features that have created an essentially separate industry from the rest of the economy. The shift from military specifications (MIL-SPECs) to commercial off-the shelf (COTS) purchasing was one element of these reforms.

The reforms aimed to bring the best management and technical processes of the larger commercial industry into the defense industry acquisition processes and organizations. To that end, wide-ranging acquisition reforms were adopted, from altering pricing and contracting concepts, to changing the system development model from stepwise phases to "evolutionary" and spiral concepts, to encouraging demonstrations of commercial processes and practices in defense programs.

---

[612] Jacques S. Gansler, Ph.D., Under Secretary of Defense for Acquisition, Technology and Logistics, remarks to the Air War College, Jan. 13, 1999.

[613] President's Blue Ribbon Commission on Defense Management, also known as the Packard Commission, final report June 1986. David Packard was Chairman. Paul Kaminski, later Under Secretary of Defense (Acquisition) under Secretary of Defense William Perry, was a technical advisor to this Commission. See also Jacques S. Gansler, Ph.D., *Defense Conversion*, MIT Press, 1995. This book was written prior to Dr. Gansler's appointment as Under Secretary of Defense for Acquisition, Technology and Logistics, which occurred in late 1997.

Changing Risk Management Models

Consistent with the concept of more commercial-like management, the DoD made significant internal manpower reductions, particularly in the number of people working in acquisition program offices and technical activities that provided engineering and technical support for acquisition programs.

At the heart of more commercial-like management concepts was an altered risk and responsibility model. Many programs contractually began employing a concept that placed increasing responsibility and risk on the prime contractor for things that the DoD used to control. One example of this is the Total System Performance Responsibility (TSPR) concept, which contractually assigns to the system prime contractor overall system performance and management responsibility. Another related concept was Lead System Integrator (LSI). In this model, where a complex system, or system of systems, is being developed, a prime contractor is afforded the lead role in defining and managing the multiple large-scale development efforts performed, at least in part, by numerous other firms.

The War on Terrorism, Defense Budget Increases and Defense Transformation

At the dawn of the twenty-first century, the primary drivers of the "Last Supper" defense industrial policy—the end of the Cold War, the perception of reduced security threats, and the resulting large defense budget declines and focus on affordability—became increasingly irrelevant due to significant changes in the security environment. At first, gradually, and after September 11, on a more accelerated basis, the heightened focus on the war against terrorism and full panoply of other emerging security threats has created new dynamics in defense markets that warrant consideration.

On the demand side of the market, there have been four dominant trends:

- Enhanced focus on the emerging range of low intensity and asymmetric threats, including terrorism, insurgency, failed states, weapons of mass destruction and cyber war (among others);

- High tempo of military operations for ongoing U.S. operations in Iraq and Afghanistan;

- Significant and sustained increase in the U.S. defense budget rivaling that of the Reagan buildup (including large supplemental funding to support our ongoing operations); and

- Evolving thrust toward military transformation and network-centric warfare.

While many observers view September 11 as a watershed event that created a very different security environment and resulting changes in U.S. budgets, strategy and military capabilities, in fact many of these developments originated in the late 1990s. As terrible as the September 11 attacks were, they did not alter what had already become a fundamental element of bipartisan post-Cold War security planning: that the United States and its coalition partners had to have the capabilities to defend against a wide range of security threats and must transform our forces accordingly. The full range of potential military threats has been identified, in relatively similar terms, in the last several Quadrennial Defense Reviews (QDRs)—the major defense planning document for the DoD. As the 1997 QDR highlighted, "of particular concern is the spread of nuclear, biological, and chemical weapons

(NBC) and their means of delivery; information warfare capabilities; advanced conventional weapons; stealth capabilities; unmanned aerial vehicles, and capabilities to access, or deny access to, space."

The QDR also noted "[i]ncreasingly capable and violent terrorists will continue to directly threaten the lives of American citizens and try to undermine U.S. policies and alliances" and that the "U.S. homeland is not free from external threats."[614] September 11 did, however, underscore that these threats were very real, not mere theories of Pentagon planners or of the intelligence community, and had a material effect on the scope and pace of our efforts to enhance the security of the United States and its allies against them.

As the security environment and nature of the threats we face have changed, the United States has shifted its national strategy, budgets, military requirements and acquisition programs to acquire the capabilities needed to address these threats—although some would argue, as discussed below, that the United States has not shifted enough. While much could be and has been written about these changes (the shift, for example, to "pre-emption" strategy), there are in particular two critical changes in U.S. security strategy relevant to defense markets: the increased focus on a "capabilities-based' paradigm for force planning; and the shift toward military "transformation" and, in particular, network-centric warfare.

B. The Capabilities-Based Paradigm

The Bush QDR 2001 eliminated the traditional two-front major theater of war (MTW) "threat-based" construct that was the centerpiece of U.S. force planning for more than a decade and replaced it with a new "capabilities-based" security paradigm. The MTW concept grew out of early post-Cold War DoD studies that developed what then-Chairman of the Joint Chiefs of Staff General Colin Powell called the "Base Force." This concept was used to refer to the minimum force structure necessary for the United States to meet the national security objectives defined by U.S. policy makers, including the capability to conduct two major theater wars simultaneously.[615] As the decade wore on, the MTW was maintained during the 1997 QDR and other DoD reviews but was subject to growing criticism that it was simply a force-sizing tool, not a viable strategy, and "a means to justify Cold War based force structure and as a roadblock to implementing transformation strategies that would enable the military to prepare for the threats of the 2010-2020 time frame."[616]

The 2001 QDR nevertheless was the first DoD planning document to move to the new "capabilities-based" approach, which reflects the view that the United States cannot know with confidence what nation, combination of nations, or non-state actors will pose threats to vital U.S. interests years from now. Under this approach, it no longer made sense to develop our force structure and armaments requirements against the goal of simultaneously fighting, defeating and occupying two major regional adversaries. It would be possible, however, to anticipate the capabilities an adversary (or range of adversaries) might employ. In contrast to a "threat-based" approach, the capabilities-based model focuses on identifying how an adversary might fight—what capabilities they might use—rather than precisely

---

[614] Report of the Quadrennial Defense Review (May 1997), U.S. Department of Defense, Section II ("The Global Security Environment"), p. 2. Available at: http://www.fas.org/man/docs/qdr/sec2.html.

[615] J. Brake, "Quadrennial Defense Review (QDR): Background, Process, and Issues," Congressional Research Service (Jan. 8, 2001).

[616] Ibid., p. 2.

who, where and when, and on identifying capabilities that the U.S. will likely need to deter and defeat adversaries. It also focuses on opportunistically developing capabilities, such as remote sensing and global precision strike, to overcome potential adversaries' capabilities.[617] Significantly, by eliminating the need to maintain a second occupation force, the new model in theory would allow DoD to free up resources for other uses, including future investment.[618] In practice, however, the Army has not eliminated any divisions, as events in Iraq and elsewhere have largely relegated this prospect to the back burner.[619]

Pentagon Officials as Diversified "Portfolio" Managers

In a sense, under the "capabilities-based" approach, senior DoD decision-makers are like equity portfolio managers in the investment world: they need to mitigate overall investment (security) risk and achieve overall returns (security benefits) by maintaining a "diversified" portfolio of equities (development and procurement programs). The DoD leadership has the difficult job of allocating scarce resources among a wide range of acquisition programs in order to defend against the range of capabilities that potential adversaries might develop.

While there has been increased recognition that "capabilities" planning is only one part of the equation (we also need to look at operational needs, regional threats and the like), it undoubtedly will be a mainstay of planning for years to come in an uncertain world.

Defense Transformation: A Lost Focus

The concept of "transformation" also became the organizing principle or "mantra" for applying the "capabilities-based" approach and allocating scarce defense resources in order to address the broad range of potential twenty-first century challenges we face. Unfortunately, this term, which became the centerpiece of defense planning, has been so often used and misused in recent years that its meaning is somewhat uncertain and obscure and it has lost its focus. But in short, "transformation" is used as a synonym for both:

- a *process* of institutional change for our overall defense establishment; and

- the development and fielding of a desired set of capabilities—the advanced, technologically leveraged forces of the future with the requisite set of *substantive capabilities* to deliver "effects" that address a wide range of potential twenty-first century security risks (i.e., forces that are more network-centric, rapid and mobile, with greater reliance on precision munitions and stealth, and more easily deployable and sustainable).

---

[617] The new construct does retain some theater-based elements. It places emphasis on deterrence in four key theaters, the ability to swiftly defeat two adversaries at the same time, while preserving the option for one major offensive to occupy an aggressor's capital and replace the regime. "Prepared Testimony on the FY2003 Defense Budget Request" by Deputy Secretary of Defense Paul Wolfowitz, U.S. Senate Appropriations Committee, Subcommittee on Defense (Feb. 27, 2002), p. 3. Available at: http://www.defenselink.mil/speeches/speech.aspx?speechid=194.

[618] Ibid., p. 3.

[619] For a critique of "capabilities-based planning," see F. Kagan, *Finding the Target: The Transformation of American Military Policy*, Encounter Books, 2006. According to Kagan, it is difficult, if not impossible, to transform military forces or develop requirements for weapon systems and force structure without having some specific adversary or set of adversaries in mind, comparing the failure of U.S. defense transformation from the mid-1990s, with the successful defense transformation of the mid-1980s.

Information Dominance and Sensor to Shooter Connectivity

At the heart of the vision of military transformation was "information dominance," that is, the capability to "collect, process, and disseminate an uninterrupted flow of information while exploiting or denying an adversary's ability to do the same."[620] One goal is to translate information superiority into a competitive advantage through "superior knowledge and decisions."[621] The idea is for joint forces (and allies) to make better decisions "implemented faster than an opponent can react, or in a non-combat situation, at a tempo that allows the force to shape the situation or react to changes and accomplish its mission."[622]

The Drive for Real-Time Innovative Solutions

Finally, the idea of transformation really had a core underlying concept—the need to innovate in order to develop and sustain a future, transformational force that inevitably must evolve on an ongoing basis as agile enemies adjust their approaches. Significantly, this requires a defense industry capable of real-time experimentation, technological innovation, and fielding of new capabilities.

The Transformation Track Record: Limited Success and Implementation

Much has been written and said about transformation.[623] When viewed in a historical context, military "transformation" to date has tended to be slow and incremental rather than radical or revolutionary. Significantly, DoD has largely failed to cut significant force structure or DoD infrastructures and has, for the most part, not cut or curtailed significant legacy acquisition programs.[624] Indeed, a considerable portion of the funding has been used for large legacy programs on the books prior to September 11—with the bulk of our spending still on a small number of large platforms. An ultimate irony is that the budget increases of recent years have essentially allowed DoD to put off difficult choices—*allowing DoD to increase funding for legacy programs while investing some modest additional funds for the future.*

The relatively slow pace of transformation reflects a number of factors. Certainly, there has been institutional resistance to change—to adjusting to new missions and eliminating major programs. Also, the pace in part reflects that true transformation is largely an intellectual process—a different way of looking at war and of using available technologies in radically different combinations. The U.S. military, on the other hand, originally tended to view transformation as technology driven; i.e., that the emergence of new technologies will lead to new capabilities, which will then change the way war is waged. This "bottom-up" approach to transformation tends to lack focus and discipline, resulting in some wasted motion. Transformation also was slowed by the need of senior DoD leaders to focus on the

---

[620] *Joint Vision 2020*, Joint Chiefs of Staff, U.S. Government Printing Office (June 2000). Available at: http://www.fs.fed.us/fire/doctrine/genesis_and_evolution/source_materials/joint_vision_2020.pdf

[621] *Joint Vision 2020*. See also *Joint Vision 2010*, Joint Chiefs of Staff, U.S. Government Printing Office (May 1997). Available at: http://www.dtic.mil/jv2010/jv2010.pdf.

[622] Ibid.

[623] See, for example, Kagan, op. cit; M. Boot, *War Made New: Technology, Warfare and the Course of History*, Gotham Books (New York) 2006; R.D. Kaplan, *Imperial Grunts: The American Military on the Ground*, Random House (New York) 2005; M. van Creveld, *The Changing Face of War: Combat from the Marne to Iraq*, Presidio Press, 2008.

[624] Two significant exceptions were the Army's RAH-66 Comanche scout helicopter, and the Crusader Mobile Gun System—both legacy programs too narrowly focused on Cold War capabilities. That the Army, of all the services, was under the most severe budget pressure due to ongoing wartime operations meant it did not have the luxury of pursuing expensive legacy programs and meeting its immediate operational needs.

ongoing wars in Iraq and Afghanistan, as well as (paradoxically) large wartime budgets that allowed DoD to defer hard choices. In some ways, the necessity of dealing with these wars, such as addressing counterinsurgency, has illustrated the need for change in ways not anticipated and advanced some changes in operations, doctrine, training, and equipage. Further, some needed acquisition solutions have been fast-forwarded due to the wars; e.g., the Army's rapid fielding of the Joint Network Node improved C4ISR (command, control, communications, computers, intelligence, surveillance and reconnaissance) connectivity for ground forces. However, these war-driven responses were too often forced by clear necessity or top-down direction rather than by deep cultural changes, and it is unclear if they will endure.

There is some truth to the statement of Bush Administration officials that "transformation" is a "state of mind" and "a journey not an end state."[625] However, for transformation to have long-term significance it must be translated into the hard realities of force structures, acquisition programs and budgets. Thus far, the results in this regard have been limited.

In truth, however, there always has been a "transformation," in a broad sense, of military forces in response to changing threats and the utilization of breakthrough innovations—it is the normal process of military history and really is nothing new. More specifically, since the end of the Cold War, there has been a tangible, albeit gradual "transformation" underway in U.S. force structure, personnel, readiness and weaponry—while at a slower pace than desirable and hindered by budgetary, industrial, political and institutional realities. During the first Bush and then the Clinton Administration, U.S. government laboratories, universities and industry have generated breakthrough or disruptive technologies that have changed the face of our military forces during the last decade. These innovations, which largely occurred during an era of defense industrial consolidation, are in large part a product of the continued and sizable U.S. investments in defense and dual-use technology (both in the defense RDT&E budget, other government budgets and private spending) during an era when other governments worldwide have invested at lower rates. These changes reflect changing threats and embrace the ongoing information revolution and the enormous pace of technological progress. These new technologies often have been funded as scientific experiments and have gradually become accepted and integrated into our forces as they were developed, tested and proven effective, and as military operational doctrine was adjusted to incorporate their use.

What *is* new is the reliance, in contrast to earlier epochs, on the global economy and civilian sector for innovation. Today the DoD and U.S. government fund only a small share of the R&D carried out in the United States. Moreover, commercially developed technology, rather than DoD-funded innovation, has been a significant source of the technologies that have become a key part of our threat—and solution—set.

While examples abound, the key innovations over the last two decades that enable our current qualitative edge on the battlefield include:

- Information technology, storage, movement and processing speed, and exploiting advances that have enabled linking operations and communications;
- Global positioning system and its use in precision munitions;
- Unmanned aerial vehicles;

---

[625] "Aerospace and Transformation: The Mutual Implications," Remarks of Under Secretary of Defense (AT&L) E.C. "Pete" Aldridge, Jr., American Institute of Aeronautics and Astronautics, p. 6 (April 24, 2002).

- Electro-optic capabilities used in cutting-edge night vision equipment;

- Ground moving target indicator radar used in the Joint Surveillance Target Attack Radar System (known as JSTARS);

- Synthetic aperture radar;

- Visual imaging systems used in the Global Hawk;

- Computer networks and real-time data for targeting and surveillance; and

- Missile defense systems advances.

Toward a New Paradigm: A Focus on Low Intensity Warfare

At this writing, President Obama and Defense Secretary Robert Gates, in the context of a stressful fiscal environment, are taking steps to reset the agenda for U.S. defense strategy based on our experiences in Afghanistan and Iraq and the threats we are likely to face. The Pentagon thus recently announced that the 2010 budget will rebalance our RDT&E and procurement spending, with more emphasis on irregular conflict and less on conventional warfare. As Secretary Gates stated in declaring the changes, "we must re-balance this department's programs in order to institutionalize and finance the wars we are in today and the scenarios we are most likely to face in the years ahead, while providing a hedge against other risks and contingencies."[626]

The Secretary noted that "our struggles to put the Defense bureaucracies on a war footing these past few years have revealed underlying flaws in the priorities, cultural preferences and reward structures of America's Defense establishment—a set of institutions largely arranged to prepare for conflicts against other modern navies, armies and air forces." Programs for counterinsurgency, stabilization and reconstruction and other missions relevant to the types of irregular warfare we are facing in theater in Iraq and Afghanistan have been developed ad hoc and funded outside the base budget, he said.[627] While Secretary Gates seeks to continue to sustain significant funding for conventional forces as a hedge, he noted that "[o]ur conventional modernization goals should be tied to prospective capabilities of known future adversaries, not by what might be technologically feasible for a potential adversary given unlimited time and resources."[628]

In short, the Secretary seeks to adopt an appropriate and sustainable force mix for the range of twenty-first century threats, with a central focus on low intensity missions—the wars we are likely to fight—and strong strategic deterrent capability as a hedge against high-level threats. Since the bulk of our RDT&E and procurement spending has been on conventional forces, some of which are less relevant today, this requires re-aligning our defense investment portfolio toward irregular threats.

Hence, Secretary Gates announced far-reaching plans to eliminate, cut or realign some major programs while accelerating or initiating others are consistent with this strategic shift. Program cuts and reductions included the F-22 Raptor fighter, the Marine One Presidential

---

[626] "DoD News Briefing with Secretary Gates From the Pentagon," News Transcript of April 6, 2009, Press Conference, U.S. Department of Defense, at p. 1. Available at: http://www.defenselink.mil/transcripts/transcript. aspx?transcriptid=4396.

[627] Ibid., p. 2.

[628] Ibid., p. 3.

helicopter, cuts in major surface combatants given the "healthy margin of dominance" at sea enjoyed by our existing fleet, and the elimination of the family of combat vehicles in the Future Combat Systems program, the leading Army modernization program. At the same time, the Secretary sought additional funding for: intelligence, surveillance and reconnaissance (including fielding and sustaining of a sizable fleet of unmanned aerial vehicles now funded largely through supplemental funding only); an increase in helicopter capabilities, a capability that is critical in Afghanistan; increased special forces personnel; an increased fleet of smaller, littoral combat ships, in theater missile defense; and the acceleration of the F-35 Joint Strike Fighters (JSF) program (as our existing fleet of aging tactical fighters are retired).

The changes do not suggest that efforts at jointness and network-centric warfare central to transformation are to be abandoned. Rather, they are part of a new set of priorities focused on the wars we are likely to fight in the future. The changes do suggest, however, more of a focus on unmanned rather than manned platforms and less focus on large conventional platforms overall. The changes also do require additional innovation to provide solutions to core challenges involved in irregular warfare.

The question for the future, as discussed below, is whether today's defense industrial structure can produce the types of innovation on a sustained basis warranted by the dynamic security challenges we face and how the change in demand will affect the platform-centric business model of large defense firms.

II. U.S. Defense Market: Supply and Demand Dynamics

A. Supply Side: The Phases of Defense Industrial Consolidation

On July 22, 1993, then-Deputy Secretary of Defense William Perry held a now-famous dinner meeting with leading U.S. defense industry executives that came to be known as the "Last Supper." Secretary Perry reflected the DoD policy response to the large planned budget declines and their expected effects on industry. He advised the executive attendees that:

- Given notable defense budget declines, the industry must consolidate;

- DoD would not interfere with consolidation, but firms must comply with antitrust law;

- DoD would not pay for unneeded overhead, so firms must eliminate excess facilities and promote efficiencies.

The industry responded to this call for action, and the 1990s defense budget declines and other dynamics clearly resulted in significant defense industrial consolidation. "What were 51 separate U.S. defense business units in 1980 became 5 large defense-focused firms by 1997—and those 5 firms became 4 by 2001.... The early to mid-1990s saw the merging of industry giants, and soon a repositioning of smaller and mid-size firms."[629] Industry consolidations occur in phases, or "waves," as some analysts call them, and the defense industry consolidation is not an exception.

[629] Suzanne Patrick, Deputy Under Secretary of Defense (Industrial Policy), remarks at an American Institute of Aeronautics and Astronautics Conference, Feb. 2002.

Figure 139   U.S. Defense Industrial Consolidation, 1980-2006

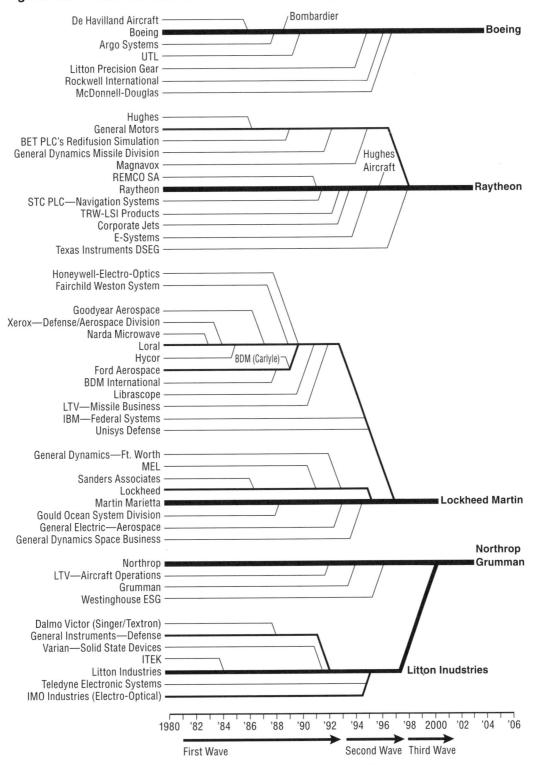

Source: Defense Science Board, May 1997; updated: DM&A, September 2008.

First Phase, 1983-1993: Multi-Industry Conglomerates Divest

The first phase was generally characterized by many multi-industry conglomerates divesting their defense businesses before the Last Supper.[630] Most multi-industry conglomerates still holding defense businesses divested them in 1993-1994 (e.g., General Electric) leaving fewer, more defense-focused or "pure play" firms in the industry supporting DoD.[631]

Second Phase, 1993-1997: Horizontal Combinations, Broader Product Lines, and Increased Vertical Holdings

The Last Supper was the primary stimulus for the second phase of consolidation, which saw rapid-fire mergers and acquisitions among large firms already focused in defense and closely related aerospace markets. In many cases, the consolidation resulted in firms obtaining new product breadth or diversity outside product areas previously owned. This phase of consolidation generally saw the increasing formation of large defense firms with much greater size and scale and a broader diversity of products (i.e., which were no longer specialized around one or two DoD customer or mission areas). Other firms, and some in the DoD customer base, were concerned about dealing with firms of this size and scale, with a wide range of vertical capabilities and impressive breadth of skills.

Third/Early Fourth Phase, 1998-2008: Further Repositioning, Subsystem Consolidation, and Dealing With Debt

By 1998, most of the large-scale prime level consolidation had occurred. The U.S. government's decision in 1998 to oppose the Lockheed Martin proposed acquisition of Northrop Grumman signaled that further prime level mergers would be difficult in light of the consolidated nature of the top level of the industry. Moreover, many attractive businesses had already been acquired. Nonetheless, in 2001, Northrop Grumman acquired Litton Industries and thus emerged with greater scale, breadth and enhanced system-integration capabilities—as a principal competitor to Raytheon in defense electronics.

This phase saw firms making increasingly targeted acquisitions and divestitures for portfolio shaping. Some firms wanted to shed certain businesses that had been acquired coincident with their target product businesses, or for cash flow to ease strained balance sheets. Financial vulnerabilities or continued lack of growth in certain markets made some businesses become available that had to this point resisted, or been seen as unattractive for, selling or merging.

Thus, while the consolidation of industry has continued, it has had several distinct features:

- Targeted acquisitions by system integrators in order to broaden their portfolios and position themselves in high-growth areas such as network-centric warfare and information technology (which also gives them an edge in maintaining their role as an integrator);

---

[630] General Dynamics was an exceptional defense firm that began divesting major businesses during this first wave; GD shed its Missile Business to Hughes in 1992 and some of its electronics businesses in 1993.

[631] Texas Instruments was a notable exception, not selling its Defense Systems and Electronics Group to Raytheon until early 1997.

- Divestitures by prime level firms in order to ease cash flow and address financial vulnerabilities that arose as the market capitalizations of major defense firms sharply declined;

- Consolidation of subsystem suppliers and emergence of large, defense-only subsystem providers; and

- Integration of traditional defense "hardware" firms with the growing defense service firms, which provide a range of support services.

The dynamics of the marketplace also have changed, resulting in fewer and fewer firms inevitably engaged in co-option, that is competition and cooperation with the same firms at the same time on different, or in some cases, the same program.

B. The Defense Industry Today

As a consequence of this evolutionary process, the U.S. defense industry's structure today is very different from that of 1990, and nearly unrecognizable from 1980. Figure 139 shows most of the top tier defense firms that emerged from the consolidation by the end of 2006.[632] The Top Five U.S. defense firms had defense revenue exceeding $135 billion in 2007 and own a very large portion of the high value added, complex defense system/subsystem product and engineering capabilities in the industry.[633] For nearly every type of major system or product, three to four of these firms have the depth and breadth in product, skills and resource scale to be a system integrator, with all the engineering, management and other challenges involved in developing and implementing complex architectures.

The Super Primes. Five years ago, a DoD Report to Congress highlighted the dramatic top-tier concentration. "By the end of 2001, the five largest defense firms received the same percentage of DoD prime contracts as the Top 10 suppliers received in 1985.... Lockheed Martin, Boeing, Raytheon, General Dynamics, and Northrop Grumman, the largest five in 2001, are as dominant in the market on a relative basis, as the largest ten in 1985. (Emphasis added.)]"[634] In 2003, the top five U.S. firms had defense revenues ranging from roughly $10-$23 billion; by 2007 this had increased to a level of $20-38 billion.[635] The relative degree of defense revenues and types of defense sales (systems, products and services) reflects the strategic choices these firms have made.

- With the exception of Boeing, with its parallel strength in commercial aerospace, the five largest firms are largely concentrated in defense, with 77-93 percent of their revenues coming from defense sales (see Figure 140).

- While these firms are focusing on systems integration and platforms, a considerable portion of their revenues is from the sales of subsystems and other sub-tier products and services. Each of these firms has some degree of vertical integration, with significant presences in subsystem markets.

---

[632] Figure 139 does not reflect the large consolidation into General Dynamics or BAE Systems North America.

[633] The 2007 Top 5 U.S.-owned defense firms were Lockheed Martin, Boeing, Northrop Grumman, General Dynamics and Raytheon. Raytheon is number six by revenue if UK-owned BAE is included in the list. *Defense News Top 100*, based on 2007 revenue, Available at: http://www.defensenews.com/static/features/top100/charts/top100_08.php?c=FEA&s=T1C.

[634] The DoD Industrial Capabilities Annual Report to Congress, March 2003, p. 5.

[635] *Defense News Top 100*, 2007. op. cit.

Figure 140   Leading U.S. Defense Companies

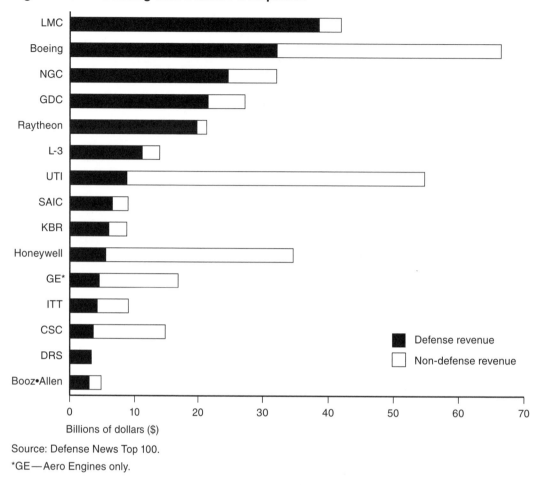

Source: Defense News Top 100.

*GE—Aero Engines only.

By way of comparison, the U.S. super primes have broader scope and larger size than all of the European defense firms other than BAE Systems—the third largest defense firm in the world by revenue, at nearly $30 billion in 2007, and with large U.S. holdings.

The Defense Sub-Tier

Below the super primes are a range of defense subsystem, product, and service providers that are varied in size and scope. The primes and these firms also draw from the broader commercial sector in meeting technology and other needs. As shown in Figure 141, the defense revenues of the leading continental European firms (EADS, Finmeccanica, and Thales) are considerably smaller than the revenues of the U.S. firms and are more comparable in defense revenue to U.S. subsystem firms.

The "Big Six" Subsystem Suppliers

Below the primes, the next group of U.S. defense firms (by revenue) had defense revenue between $2.8 and $3.8 billion in 2002; in 2007 those figures had increased to $4.5-11.2 bil-

Figure 141   Top Five European and U.S. Defense Companies Compared

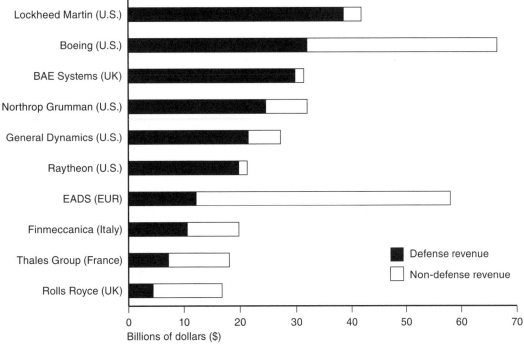

Source: Defense News Top 100.

lion (compare Figures 140 and 142).[636] The U.S. firms in this group differ significantly from the top-tier firms and from each other in products and focus.

As shown on Figure 140, L-3 Communications is a large subsystem or component supplier, with a predominant focus on defense (89 percent for L-3). Science Applications International Corporation (SAIC), a provider of defense engineering, technical and other services, also has a predominant defense focus, with about 73 percent of its revenue from defense. Interestingly, however, the other subsystem firms, shown on Figure 142, have a broader business focus beyond defense, with considerable offerings in aerospace, information technology, communications and related fields. Thus, while some conglomerates have departed the defense business as part of the "exodus" of commercial firms from the defense market years ago, others have not; there remains a group of significant "mixed" firms such as EDS (9 percent), Honeywell (16 percent), United Technologies (16 percent), General Electric (27 percent after its recent Smiths' acquisition), Harris (40 percent), Booz Allen (47 percent), Rockwell (50 percent), and ITT (46 percent). Among them, General Electric and Honeywell (16 percent) are larger, multi-industry firms with only some business units supporting defense, while KBR is a logistics company with its roots in the oil industry.

The sustained presence in defense of these dual-use firms largely reflects several things. First, their products and services are based on a technology or knowledge base common between defense and civilian product areas such as aerospace, making this multi-industry

---

[636] Figure 141 includes Boeing again, already discussed as one of the Top Tier prime contractors. While Boeing is reflected in this table due to it commercial-defense mix, it is obviously not only a subsystem or second-tier supplier.

Figure 142   Mixed Companies in the U.S. Defense Market

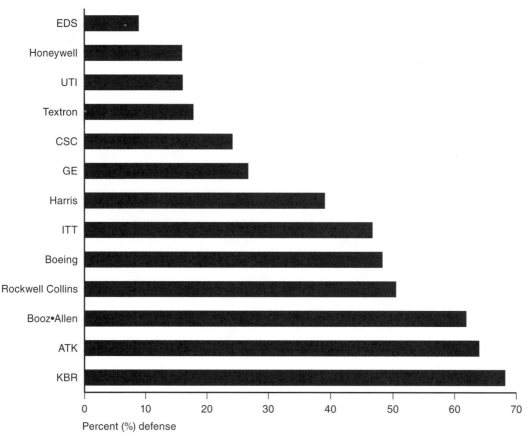

Source: Defense News Top 100.

model still attractive. Second, in some cases, these firms' presence in defense reflects the increasing reliance of the defense industry on COTS technology, especially for communications and electronics.

Some of the large second-tier firms have emerged as, or are aspiring to be, "subsystem" integrators. As the primes have increasingly focused on systems architecture and engineering, these second-tier firms have emerged to fill the void and integrate subsystem capabilities in certain areas. For example, in avionics, Rockwell and Honeywell are subsystem integrators that can provide overall avionics suites to primes. Similarly, in engines, Pratt & Whittney and GE can offer a panoply of engine-related capabilities and services—in many cases trying to extend commercial concepts such as "power by the hour" into the defense world. While it might sound far-fetched today, it is not far off that DoD may "lease" aircraft, tactical vehicles or even night vision systems and communications equipment from a defense firm for a period of time and return it when the lease is complete (for servicing and overhaul). The UK is already engaged in these types of efforts.

The last decade has seen the emergence of large professional and technical services companies supporting DoD in the areas of information dominance, information technology generally, and various analytical and system engineering capabilities (see Table 72). SAIC is

Table 72   Professional and Technical Services Companies in the Defense Market

Company	Business Areas	Company	Business Areas
Accenture Public Services	Management Consulting	Jacobs Engineering	System Engineering Testing & Evaluation
ACS Government Solutions	Information Technology		
Alion Sciences	Program Management Training System Engineering	Keane Federal Systems	Information Technology
		Parsons Infrastructure and Technologies	System Engineering Facilities Management Environmental Services
Bearing Point	Management Consulting		
Booz•Allen & Hamilton	Management Consulting System Engineering	Perot Systems	Information Technology
		Qualcomm Wireless Solutions	Information Technology Logistic Services
Ciber Custom Solutions	Information Technology		
Computer Sciences Corporation	System Engineering Information Technology Management Consulting Homeland Security	Science Applications International Corp.	System Engineering Software Development Information Technology Management Consulting
Day & Zimmerman	Logistics Facilities Management Logistic Services Environmental Services	SANZ, Inc.	Electronic Data Storage
		SRA International	System Engineering Information Technology
		URS, Inc.	System Engineering
EDS Corporation	System Engineering Information Technology	VT Services, Inc.	Training Education Services Information Technology
Intergraph Security	Software Development Information Technology Geospatial Information Systems		

Source: InfoBase Publishers, DACIS Companies Database.

the largest of these firms ($6.5 billion in defense revenues), but the list also includes Computer Sciences Corporation ($3.6 billion), Booz•Allen ($3 billion), and EDS ($2 billion). These and a number of smaller companies predominantly or solely provide engineering, technical knowledge and related services. The evolution of these firms began in the late 1970s but seriously accelerated during the Clinton Administration, when the Department dramatically increased its outsourcing of a wide range of services once performed in-house. Outsourcing was further expanded and accelerated under the Bush Administration, as part of its transformation and streamlining. The emergence of so many services firms likely reflects three trends: 1) increased DoD outsourcing; 2) consolidation in services firms; and 3) the economic trends toward knowledge and services as the commodity of value (in lieu of only physical products). Some of these services providers, e.g., Booz•Allen, Aerospace Corp, etc., may also be helping DoD bridge the experience gap resulting from a decade with exceptional losses of experienced employees to retirement.

The Lack of a Clear and Coherent Defense Industrial Policy

Over the Bush Administration's two terms in office, DoD did not articulate or execute any clear or coherent defense industrial strategy. As the defense industry has consolidated, grown and changed, DoD has not publicly signaled or internally established a clear policy basis for its decisions affecting the industry. Indeed, the last QDR was noteworthy for the lack of consideration of these issues or any significant consultations with industry. There have been few speeches laying out the Department's vision of the defense industry it would like to see, the role of competition in defense markets, its tolerance for sectors that might be consolidated, organizational conflicts of interests or anything else of this nature. The "Last Supper" in the early 1990s ushered in a period of industry consolidation, and the disapproval of the Lockheed/Northrop transaction in the late 1990s was accompanied by statements from senior leaders that further top-level consolidation would be more difficult.

Since that time, however, DoD has not given any top-level guidance. The only real signals in real years were the disapproval of the proposed General Dynamics acquisition of Newport News—a merger to monopoly, and later, the DoD's acceptance of the United Space Alliance, suggesting that a single joint venture source was acceptable in this high-cost, low-volume product area. Needless to say, these two decisions sent mixed signals.

The consequence of this policy vacuum has been a series of ad hoc approaches undertaken by various DoD components in the context of market areas and programs that run the gamut. In some areas, DoD has established "national teams" and eschewed competition and in others it has taken a different approach. There is no consistent approach to structuring acquisition strategies so as to take into account the implications for the defense industry.

Lack of DoD-wide Coherent Approach to the Transatlantic Defense Market: Supply and Demand

Similarly, there has not been an established policy on the Transatlantic defense market. On the demand side, there has been no effort to promote Transatlantic defense market cooperation except on an ad hoc basis in areas of Administration priority (such as missile defense). There has been no concerted approach to identify cooperative opportunities, such as the dormant International Cooperative Opportunities Group (ICOG) established in the mid-1990s.[637] Other than the F-35 Joint Strike Fighter, there have been few significant cooperative development programs in the past decade, though missile defense offers a number of promising opportunities moving into the future; the UK, Japan, Germany, Italy, and Israel are already involved in a number of ongoing missile defense programs and initiatives. As shown on Table 73, most cooperative programs are legacies of previous generations and,

---

[637] ICOG consisted of the National Armaments Directors (NADs) of the United States, UK, Germany, Italy and France. These nations' NADs met periodically to define common requirements and assess the potential for cooperative development.

Table 73   Ongoing U.S. International Cooperative Programs (Millions of Fiscal Year 2009 dollars – $)

Program	Partners	Funding ($)	Status	Description
FA-35 Joint Strike Fighter	UK, NO, IS, IT, CA, NE, TU, AS	9,000	Development	Multi-role stealth fighter
MEADS	GE, IT	251	Development	Medium-range air defense
RIM-116 RAM	GE	106	Production	Shipboard Air Defense
AIM-7 ESSM	GE	125	Production	Shipboard Air Defense
AGM-88 Blk.6	GE	32	Production	Production
Guilded MLRS	GE, FR, IT, UK	166	Production	GPS-guided rocket
Missile Defense	UK, JA, IS, NATO	79	Development	Broad-based program
Def. technology Analysis	NATO RTO	11	Development	Evaluates foreign technology
Multifunctional Information Distribution System (MIDS)	FR, GE, IT SP	53	Production	Link 16 Terminal; U.S. efforts now focused on JTRS w/o foreign participation
Total		**9,823**		

Source: U.S. Dept. of Defense, President's Biennial Budget Submission, FY 2009.

aside from JSF, do not account for a significant percentage of U.S. procurement or R&D spending.

Moreover, from start to finish, the Bush Administration did not articulate any consistent view on the merits of supplier globalization among our close allies.

The Clinton Administration adopted a concerted policy of encouraging Transatlantic defense industrial cooperation—mergers, acquisitions and other collaborative ventures—to promote competition in consolidating defense markets and enhance coalition war-fighting capabilities. They believed a more open, competitive Transatlantic defense market could lessen incentives for defense firms to proliferate to other defense markets. This paradigm included sharing more technology with these close friends in exchange for their agreement to "level up" their practices in sharing technology with third countries and other areas.

Focused on wars in Iraq and Afghanistan and worried about missile defense, the Bush Administration largely ignored this agenda; it did not articulate any view about the future of the defense industry, let alone the degree of foreign competition or cooperation. As discussed in detail below, the Bush Administration's *actions* on supplier globalization, as distinct from its *rhetoric*, were more mixed. On the one hand, it continued low-level dialogues with key North Atlantic Treaty Organization (NATO) Allies and signed non-binding Declarations of Principle with most of them. Moreover, in 2008 the Bush Administration approved the purchase of DRS Technologies by the Italian defense company Finmeccanica SpA. It also made decisions on several weapon programs that seemed to signal increased openness to foreign participation, and the Pentagon also fought against additional protectionist measures introduced by Congress.

But the Bush Administration also took several steps that undermined prospects for closer Transatlantic collaboration. Through a series of policies and practices, ranging from immigration to export controls to foreign investment, the Bush Administration created the impression that the United States was distancing itself from globalization rather than embracing it. Moreover, the Bush Administration failed to implement the regulatory "hard wiring" in the export control process for real supplier globalization. Despite an early commitment to reform, it failed to make meaningful changes to either export licensing processes or a technology release policy that was highly restrictive (even with close allies).

Fundamentally, there was not a clear focus on these issues at the most senior levels of DoD leadership, and decision-making was largely ad hoc. While the Finmeccanica/DRS approval is constructive, it does not substitute for a coherent policy.

Today's Demand Side Realities

Today, the Obama Administration is faced with several defense market realities that mark the start of a new era: 1) a worsening budget context and focus on affordability; 2) a sense that the defense acquisition system is broken and is producing systems that are too expensive and take too long to field; and 3) a new emphasis on limiting outsourcing (called "insourcing") and avoiding conflicts of interests while ensuring competition.

The Worsening Budget Context: Affordability and Cost Control as an Overriding Priority

A series of factors—the rising and very large federal deficit, the growth of domestic entitlements as a percentage of the budget, competing domestic needs (infrastructure and the like) and the ongoing financial crisis—confirm the obvious: after years of living in a "rich man's" defense world, our defense spending will be stressed.

Even assuming that the U.S. budgetary commitment to our national security writ large (the defense core budget with the former supplemental appropriations now coming "inside" the real budget, and other civilian national security spending) can be sustained at current levels, several other key factors specific to national security spending make the budget problem that much more challenging and will require real choices. These include: the need to bolster our civilian national security capabilities (including the size of the foreign service, foreign assistance levels and our capabilities for stabilization and reconstruction); the fact that a significant amount of "core" defense activities has migrated to the supplemental budgets and will need to be maintained even as our operations in Iraq wind down; and the escalating and fixed nature of many DoD expenditures, including personnel and health care. A recent Defense Business Board transition presentation notes that overall defense healthcare spending, at $93 billion (with $488 billion in unfunded liability in 2007), has grown $25.1 billion from FY 2000 to FY 2008 (a 144 percent increase, a rate faster than DoD discretionary spending). It concludes that these expenses are "eating up" the Defense budget and "represent an existential threat to the Department."

Accordingly, it is clear that affordability and the control of growing defense costs should and will be key defense priorities in its own right—a prerequisite to advancing the five top programmatic priorities set forth below.

DoD's Acquisition System—A System in Crisis

Year after year, the Government Accountability Office (GAO) has found that major U.S. weapons systems programs have exceeded projected costs by significant amounts, are considerably behind schedule and produce capabilities that perform not as well as promised. According to the Defense Business Board, the total acquisition budget for all major defense acquisition programs has more than doubled in the past seven years—from $783 billion to $1,702 billion. The reasons for this are multiple and include changing requirements, pressing forward on programs even where the technology is immature, and the lack of experienced program oversight and managerial expertise. There is a pressing need to address these underlying challenges while producing more affordable, rapidly fielded, and technologically superior weaponry.

Indeed, in May 2009, the Congress passed, and the President signed, the Weapon Systems Acquisition Reform Act of 2009. This new legislation is designed to address DoD's perceived inability to effectively control costs on and efficiently manage its acquisition programs. The key thrusts of reform efforts are cost control and speed—obtaining "faster to field" capabilities.

The new focus on affordability and faster to field inevitably has implications on a program basis for technical performance. There is, after all, a relationship between the cost of developing a capability, the speed of its development and the parameters of its performance. In years past, there has been an emphasis on robust capabilities—with cost as less significant in the best value equation. As Secretary Gates has stated, DoD "will pursue greater quantities of systems that represent the '75 percent' solution instead of small quantities of '99 percent' exquisite systems." In other words, the new focus invariably means seeking realistic and doable solutions to problems (i.e., not the Cadillac) in order to ensure timely fielding and avoiding excessive spending.[638]

A Focus on Ensuring Competition, Limiting Outsourcing, and Avoiding Conflicts

The new focus also includes a desire for more competition in defense procurement—reflected in new Obama Administration memoranda, statements of Secretary Gates and comments by nominees for office. Secretary Gates articulated the need for "increased competition" and the use of prototypes.[639]

Moreover, while of less relevance from a market access standpoint, there is an increased focus on expanding the acquisition personnel in the government to ensure better oversight and limiting the outsourcing of acquisition management and other key DoD positions. Secretary Gates announced in April 2009 a desire to lower the number of support-service contractors to pre-2001 levels and hire as many as 13,000 new civil servants.[640] This has significant implications for the defense services sector, which is beyond the scope of this study.

---

[638] Prepared Testimony of Secretary of Defense Robert Gates, Senate Armed Services Committee (Jan. 27, 2009), p. 11. Available at: http://armed-services.senate.gov/statemnt/2009/January/Gates%2001-27-09.pdf.

[639] Ibid.

[640] "DoD News Briefing With Secretary Gates From The Pentagon," News Transcript of April 6, 2009, Press Conference, U.S. Department of Defense, pg. 5. Available at: http://www.defenselink.mil/transcripts/transcript.aspx?transcriptid=4396.

Finally, there are a number of proposals to develop more comprehensive and rigorous rules on organizational conflict of interest to address the growing industrial consolidation between defense service suppliers and hardware providers. The thrust of these proposals is to limit the ability of firms to provide support services on a program through one of its business units while simultaneously bidding on providing systems or subsystems on the program.

Facilitating the Evolution of a Defense Industry Capable of Meeting Twenty-First Century Needs

> Given the emerging new thrusts on the "demand" side of the market—an emphasis on affordability and more rapid fielding in the context of a shift toward investment in solutions to irregular warfare challenges, the Obama Administration needs to develop an appropriate and coherent defense industrial strategy. In facilitating the transformation of the industry to meet this new demand, the Administration inevitably must address a fundamental disconnect between emerging needs for defense innovation and the evolving structure of the industry that must supply these needs.
>
> Available evidence suggests that the defense industry, which consolidated around twentieth-century needs, is not well structured to meet the needs of the twenty-first century. The inherent structure of the industry, including the autonomy of primes over the supplier base, together with anecdotal evidence of market behaviors, suggests that the industry has difficulty producing the types of innovative and affordable solutions needed for twenty-first century war fighting.

On the one hand, the significant innovation needed is nothing less than breathtaking—to provide mature new technologies and capabilities to address these new security challenges. We have agile enemies that can adjust their approaches rapidly and require us to rapidly change our responses. On the other hand, the United States has a relatively consolidated twentieth-century defense industry, with a small group of consolidated and vertically integrated super-prime defense firms that account for an increasing portion of the defense market. As noted above, these firms receive the lion's share of the DoD RTD&E budget and, through acquisition reform (TSPR, LSI, etc.), have been afforded the broad authority to manage the supplier base.

A recent Defense Science Board study addressed these issues and found that the desired industry of the future would include: at least two healthy suppliers in mature market areas and more in areas where innovation is critical and demand high; independent architecture firms; the funding of numerous small, mid-sized and commercial firms to demonstrate new ideas, and the adoption of structural solutions (beyond firewalls) to address growing conflicts of interest.[641]

---

[641] "Creating an Effective National Security Industrial Base for the 21st Century: An Action Plan to Address the Coming Crisis," Report of the Defense Science Board Task Force on Defense Industrial Structure for Transformation (July 2008). Available at: http://www.acq.osd.mil/dsb/reports/2008-07-DIST.pdf.

> ## Emerging Market Realities and Market Access:
> ## A New Set of Incentives
>
> In all events, the thrusts of all of these emerging market tendencies is to create a context more, rather than less, favorable to market access for foreign suppliers. As discussed in Chapter 6, a policy emphasis on affordability and faster to field, together with a renewed emphasis on facilitating coalition warfare, would tend to create incentives for DoD to allow increased market access for foreign suppliers in the future.

U.S.-European Defense Cooperation and Trade

While Europe is one of the United States' largest and most important trading partners, with which it habitually runs trade deficits, U.S. defense trade with European countries amounts to only a small fraction of total trade—with U.S. maintaining a very large trade surplus, as is shown in Figures 143 to 145.

European Firms' Entry to U.S. Markets: Obstacles and Strategies

As European defense budgets declined in the post-Cold War era, European defense firms, large and small, has increasingly sought access to the large and lucrative European defense market.

The value of European sales to the United States have always been relatively small in both absolute and relative terms (as a percentage of U.S. R&D and procurement, as discussed in Chapter 4. For reasons discussed below, there has been very limited foreign participation in U.S. defense programs and few sales by foreign firms at the system or major subsystem level. Indeed, recent studies show that "[t]he Department procures very few defense items and components from foreign suppliers. In Fiscal Year 2006, the Department awarded contracts to foreign suppliers for defense items and components totaling approximately $1.9 billion, less than one percent of all DoD contracts; and only about 2.4 percent of all DoD contracts for defense items and components."[642] This data reflects direct "prime" purchases by the DoD and does not offer a full accounting of foreign content at the sub-tier or component level, where those levels do not have direct contracts with the DoD. Hence, these percentages may understate foreign participation in the U.S. defense market. However, counting foreign subsystem participation probably would not change the percentages very much. Thus, it is ironic that Congress has in recent years become very focused on Buy American issues and has sought to enact additional protectionist legislation.

---

[642] *Foreign Sources of Supply (FY 2006 Report): Annual Report of United States Defense Industrial Base Capabilities and Acquisitions of Defense Items and Components Outside the United States* (Washington, D.C.: Office of the Deputy Under Secretary of Defense, Industrial Policy, Nov. 2007), p. 1. Available at: http://www.acq.osd.mil/ip/docs/812_report_fy06.pdf). See also *Defense Trade Data*, (Washington, D.C.: Government Accountability Office, Jan. 27, 2006), GAO-06-319R ("[T]he percentage of DOD purchases of defense articles and services from foreign companies as compared to all DOD purchases of defense articles and services, decreased from 2.4 percent in fiscal year 2000 to 1.7 percent in 2004.") Available at: http://www.gao.gov/new.items/d06319r.pdf.

Figure 143   U.S. Defense Exports To Study Countries (Billions of Dollars–$)

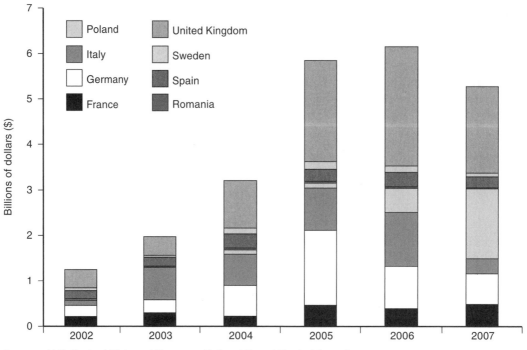

Sources: U.S. Dept. of State and European National Export Control Agencies.

Figure 144   U.S. Defense Imports From Study Countries (Billions of Dollars–$)

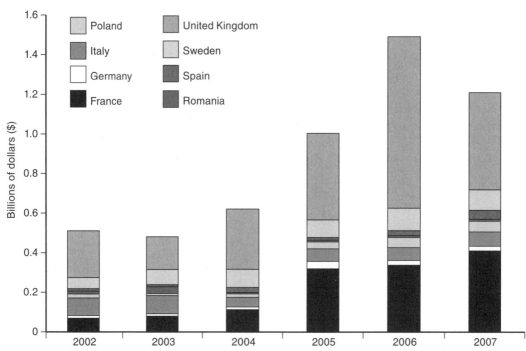

Sources: U.S. Dept. of State and European National Export Control Agencies.

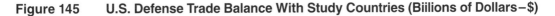

Figure 145   U.S. Defense Trade Balance With Study Countries (Billions of Dollars–$)

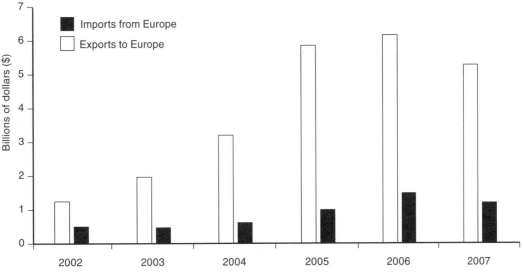

Sources: U.S. Dept. of State and European National Export Control Agencies.

Notwithstanding the absence of a coherent U.S. policy on Transatlantic cooperation and data showing limited sales, there has been significant growth of foreign defense sales in the United States over recent years during this defense "bull market." As fully discussed in Chapter 4, a number of European firms have penetrated the U.S. market in recent years in various ways and European firms have growing footprints in, and sales to, the United States.

Market Penetration Realities and Obstacles

The numerous interviews we conducted with European firms from various countries provided a series of very consistent and powerful insights into both the market impediments and realities that firms face and the strategies they utilize.

The following describes a range of impediments that appear most significant (and are discussed in detail in the market access metrics below). Some of these challenges are driven by legitimate U.S. security requirements while others reflect U.S. DoD procurement policies or practices and cultural perceptions discussed below.

The Need for a Better Widget: Developed Niche Subsystem Capabilities

European firms consistently report that, based on their experience, they must have a better product than is currently available in the United States for successful market penetration. Having "distinctive" capabilities or "daylight in capability" between their offering and those of American firms was, in their view, a threshold prerequisite for competing in the U.S. market. There are repeated stories of market penetration failures by European firms where they did not have this edge. Firms also reported situations where they initially made sales (especially in support of the recent U.S. operations) of products unavailable in the United States but were later unable to sell these products as American vendors ramped up their own capability.

Firms that have succeeded identified small niches requiring high technology, such as in electronics, weapons technology, robotics, underwater and land vehicles, and then the companies have focused on innovation. Typically, European firms have succeeded where they already have a developed niche subsystem capabilities not available in the United States at the same quality or capability level. The experience is that the foreign products must be better on technical performance than the comparable U.S. products. It helps, but is not necessarily required, for the product to be more affordable as well. This strategy is somewhat ironic and creates business asymmetry in that foreign firms that are primes in Europe and elsewhere—offering complex systems and services—essentially are reduced to operating as subsystem providers in the United States.

The Complexity of the U.S. Defense Procurement System and Sizable Investment Needed to Penetrate

The U.S. defense market, with its many components, poses a significant knowledge barrier to non-U.S. companies. A firm seeking sales must often have contact with and prove a product's capabilities to multiple defense communities, including, among others, the user community, the requirements community, the acquisition community, and the prime contractor in the case of subsystems. The foreign firm also will need to pay to have the product tested and demonstrated as well (possibly on multiple occasions for multiple audiences, with variations made to satisfy particular customer tastes). This effort can be very time-consuming and cause unwarranted delays. For example, one company reported it took six months and approvals by eight different organizations before a product could be used in-theater in Iraq. By contrast, it took the UK bureaucracy only 14 days to approve the same product for use in Afghanistan.

A number of European companies indicated that a Washington presence of some type is required to penetrate the government bureaucracy and demonstrate the capabilities of company products. Upfront resources have to be spent to comprehend the complex procurement process, and this is a recurring expense because the process must be monitored continuously. Firms need to hire or retain as consultants specialized personnel (former acquisition officials that can assist in identifying opportunities, preparing bids and interfacing with the acquisition community, ITAR experts, executives, and others) in order to compete effectively. Many foreign companies (especially small and medium ones) believe this is not worth the effort unless they can afford the potentially sizable expense associated with penetrating the market. One executive gave an example of a foreign business with $50 million in revenue. To cite executives of one European company, potential sales of $5 million in the United States were not worth pursuing in light of the high costs involved; the minimum potential market had to be at least $15 million.

Table 74 provides some examples of foreign niche products sold in the United States.

U.S. Bias ("Not Invented Here" Syndrome)

Firms also stated that biases against the use of foreign products still shape the mindset of numerous U.S. acquisition officials—even in situations where a DoD component has specified that it wants to purchase a foreign product. Foreign firms have also found that U.S. competitors try to play on these existing biases, and in some situations requirements and

Table 74   European Niche Products in U.S. Service

Defense Product	Country	Defense Product	Country
Canon-Launched Guided Projectile	Sweden	Multi-Spectral Camouflage Netting	Sweden
Ceramic Armor	Israel	Overhead Weapons Station	Israel
HF Direction-Finding Systems	German	Recoilless Rifles	Sweden
Infantry Anti-Tank Rocket	Sweden	Small Arms	Belgium, Germany, Italy
Light Scout/Utility Helicopter	France	Underwater Robotic Vehicles	Norway, Germany
Lightweight Tank Tracks	Germany	Vectored Thrust Turbofan Engines	United Kingdom
Mine Resistant Vehicles	South Africa, Israel		

acquisition authorities may be seeking to favor their favored domestic vendors in how they shape requirements and programs. They do note, however, that there appears to be less of this tendency than there was 5 to 10 years ago. Firms also indicated that the end-user community is generally less focused on the supplier's locale and more on the capability, while cultural resistance is more apt to come from the acquisition community.

Different DoD Components Have Different Degrees of Openness

Firms reported that there were distinct differences in attitudes to foreign participation in different parts of the acquisition community. In general, the Marine Corps was viewed as the most accessible and the Army the least with the other services somewhere in between.

ITAR and Classified Information

As discussed in detail below, European firms pointed out that it is not possible for foreign firms to obtain access to classified U.S. requirements (unless they have cleared U.S. subsidiaries) and that it can be time-consuming and difficult to obtain access to unclassified, ITAR-controlled specifications on a timely basis. Without obtaining this information in real time, European firms cannot bid on the program. Numerous firms reported finding themselves in these situations.

Development Programs, and Space and Intelligence Markets, Largely Closed

Most European firms interviewed believed they would have enormous difficulty winning a development program in the United States—an observation supported by the data (see Chapter 4). There are some market areas, including defense space, intelligence, electronic warfare, and the like, that are largely closed to European firms (except in some cases UK firms).

Unique American Standards

Some firms indicated the uniqueness of some U.S. standards and that the need to tailor their products to them can be a challenge. The situation has improved considerably since the armed services began moving away from military specifications (MIL-SPECs) and military standards (MIL-STDs) considerations in favor of commercial standards for off-the-shelf products. However, many unique standards still prevail in weapon systems performance, human factors and safety standards. Thus, even in cases where the United States has purchased a "non-developmental item" from a European source (e.g., the M249 Squad Automatic Weapon, the M120 120mm mortar), significant changes were mandated to conform to U.S. standards. This adds to the cost of the system and usually requires foreign suppliers to find a U.S. partner capable of interpreting and implementing the relevant standards.

Nationality Matters

Firms recognize that UK firms are treated generally better than firms from other countries, especially given the vicissitudes of geopolitics. Thus, at times, French firms have not felt welcome in the U.S. market (for example, during the recent Iraq war) in light of the French position on the war. In fact, the degree to which the United States has congruent policies and practices with the particular European country is viewed as a considerable factor relevant to market access.

Currency Values

The recent high value of the pound and the euro versus the dollar has added to the challenge of selling European products into the U.S. market and has encouraged some foreign suppliers to move to U.S. production in order to provide best value solutions. European companies are also attracted by relatively flexible U.S. labor laws and the high productivity of U.S. workers. The migration of European companies to the United States can thus be expected to continue even if exchange rates fluctuate to Europe's advantage.

Market Penetration Strategies

European firms have deployed a range of market penetration strategies discussed below. The following were consistent observations about these strategies made by market participants:

Direct Sales From Abroad: A Default Position of Limited Utility

While foreign firms would prefer to sell products developed and produced abroad into the U.S. market, in fact this is very difficult except in limited situations where the product is not available in the United States and is a subsystem. This approach is largely unavailable for prime level offerings. Sales from abroad pose a series of challenges. Customers are more likely to review reliance on offshore suppliers as creating program risk (both quality control and security of supply—that is, the risk of unavailability or cut-off during times of great need or exigency). Even in the case of a direct sale of a foreign subsystem (which is more plausible), the U.S. customer will generally insist that proprietary foreign source code, for example, be available in the United States—either licensed to a U.S. supplier or domestically maintained under some kind of an escrow arrangement.

Partnering

Most firms indicated that the most effective path to gain U.S. market entry is to partner with a well-known U.S. company that has existing market presence in the business area, contacts at relevant government agencies, and the expertise to comply with ITAR and industrial security rules. While partnering is viewed as valuable at all levels (systems, subsystems and components), it is essential at the prime level where market participants believe the DoD will not rely on foreign primes without the involvement of U.S. partners. The partnering has taken various forms, ranging from program-specific collaborations and joint ventures to product line joint ventures. Of course, all of the firms point out that partnering can be challenging, given the firms' different cultures, technologies and business incentives; concerns over protecting proprietary technology and the management of the partnership abound.

U.S. Presence and U.S. Content

A number of foreign defense firms have either purchased U.S. defense firms or opened greenfield operations here and grown them organically. In particular, the large UK firms have made significant U.S. acquisitions (including of prime level capabilities) in light of U.S. policies reflecting greater receptivity to such acquisitions. Defense firms from other countries, facing generally less receptivity over the years, have tended to grow their own subsidiaries organically or make smaller, less sensitive and less splashy acquisitions (typically at the subsystem level). One French industry leader termed it a strategy of "a small string of pearls" deals executed singly and properly before moving to make more buys—they do not want to move so fast they cannot integrate them. Firms reported they recognized there was some limitation on their ability to sell directly from abroad and that, at some point, as quantities grew, they were better off bringing their capabilities on shore.

In all events, foreign defense firms have increasingly offered U.S. content with respect to U.S. defense programs in which they participate. This means increasingly U.S. production in connection with program offerings. In most cases, the foreign firms have not been directed to do this but have made the calculation that such domestic content is much more palatable to the customer or even an essential door opener. At times, some foreign firms have shifted to U.S. content in order to reduce costs (in light of increasing European costs in recent years).

III. Factors for Evaluation

Tariff Barriers

By and large, tariffs are not significant barriers between the United States and the defense markets studied. All of the countries studied are members of the WTO and thus must provide most-favored nation and national treatment to imported goods from every other country included in the study. Although defense products are generally exempt from WTO rules governing tariffs and trade, reciprocal defense procurement Memorandums of Understanding (MOUs) between the United States and each country studied (other than Romania) generally provide duty-free treatment for imported defense products procured from the other country. However, the MOUs do not apply to dual-use products and tech-

Table 75   Competition in U.S. Defense Contract Awards, Fiscal Year 2006

	Number of Actions	Value (Thousands of Dollars–$)	Percent (%) of Total Number	Percent (%) of Total Awards Value
Competitive	1,208,124	184,181,227	32.8	62.4
Not Available for Competition	2,276,555	18,209,297	61.8	6.2
Follow-on	6,264	6,359,435	0.2	2.2
Not Competed	190,358	86,225,837	5.2	29.2
Total	**3,681,301**	**$294,975,796**	**100.0%**	**100.0%**

Source: U.S. Department of Defense, Summary of Procurement Awards—Oct., 2005-Sept., 2006.

nologies such as general aerospace systems that have both military and civil applications. Thus, as more military programs rely on COTS technology, this would tend to put U.S. companies at a competitive disadvantage *vis-à-vis* European firms that get the benefit of the lower intra-European rates that apply under European Union rules unless specific exemptions are negotiated on a bilateral basis.

Competition in Procurement

The clear thrust of U.S. law, policy and practice is to maintain competition for contracts in defense contracts—it is the norm, not the exception. However, DoD has to a large degree precluded foreign participation in the competitive process, especially at the prime level. Thus, the U.S. market has been competitive but not that "open." However, this is changing and an increasing number of programs are now open to foreign competition.

Subject to certain exceptions discussed below, it is a fundamental principle of U.S. law and regulation that there must be full and open competition for defense contract awards unless one of a number of exceptions is invoked.[643] The "default" position is to incorporate effective competition into the acquisition of weapons systems wherever practicable, and to work to stimulate competition in the industry where possible. In practice, many of the thousands of defense contracts awarded each year, including weapons systems, are competitively awarded (i.e., with competition at some point in the program's history).

Available data confirms this reality of "competitive but not that open" procurements in the U.S. defense market.

- **Total DoD Buying (Defense and Commercial).** Overall, DoD statistics for 2006, the last year for which data is available, show that roughly 62 percent by value of *all* DoD prime contracts were awarded competitively. As shown on Table 75 above, of the 38 percent awarded non-competitively, roughly 2.2 percent was follow-on work; 6.2 percent was not available for competition for statutory reasons; and 29

---

[643] See *Federal Acquisition Regulations* (FAR), Part 6 (Competition Requirements), prescribing "policies and procedures to promote full and open competition in the acquisition process and to provide for full and open competition, full and open competition after exclusion of sources, other than full and open competition, and competition advocates." Available at: http://www.arnet.gov/far/current/html/FARTOCP06.html#wp280339.

Figure 146   U.S.—Total Procurement by Award Type

Figure 147   U.S.—Legacy vs. New Procurement

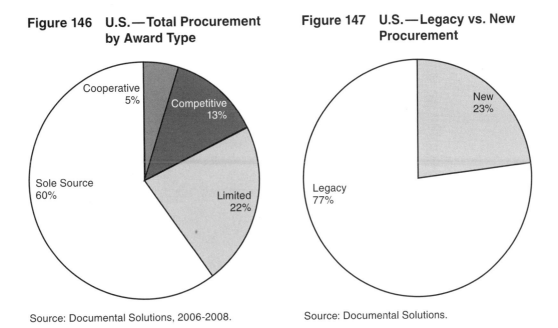

Source: Documental Solutions, 2006-2008.

Source: Documental Solutions.

percent was awarded sole source either because of a unique product, industrial base considerations, or national security reasons.[644] This data reflects all manner of DoD prime contracts, however, including commercial "non-warlike" goods and services (telecommunications, fuel, clothing, computer systems, etc.). This data also does not include R&D spending (i.e., this does not mean they may not be competed, but simply that this is not reflected in this set of data).

- **DoD Buying Patterns on Major Weapons Systems.** A more targeted look at 232 major U.S. RDT&E and Procurement programs (i.e., programs worth more than $100 million) during 2006-2008 also shows both the prevalence of competition and the limitations on foreign participation in such competitive awards. The list of 232 major U.S. programs reviewed are set forth on Table 76.

- **A Large Portion (60 percent) of Major DoD Program Awards Were Sole Source, and the Vast Majority (82 percent) Open Only to U.S. Firms.** As shown on Figure 146, only 13 percent ($34.4 billion) of major program awards in 2006-2008 were made through "open and competitive" procurement. Another 22 percent ($60.3 billion) were offered through "limited" competition (i.e., not open to foreign participation); 5 percent ($15 billion) involved international cooperative programs, and the remaining 60 percent ($163 billion) were awarded sole source.

- **Most Spending Is on Legacy Programs.** As shown on Figure 147, however, some 77 percent ($202 billon) of procurement in the last three years has been for legacy programs. This is not surprising and reflects that large development and production programs, which take years to bring to fruition, are recipients of most DoD fund-

---

Figure 148   U.S.—Legacy Procurement by Award Type

Figure 149   U.S.—New Procurement by Award Type

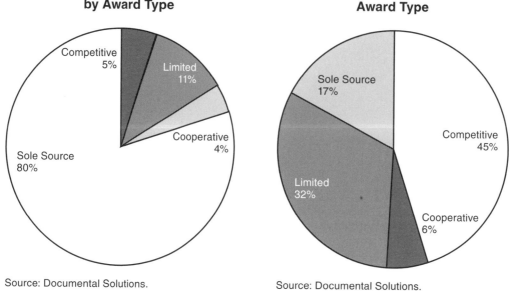

Source: Documental Solutions.

Source: Documental Solutions.

ing. The list of Top Defense Programs (Table 76) shows that the C-17, Joint Strike Fighter, F-22 and C-130 programs—some started more than 30 years ago—are receiving the largest amounts of funding.

- **Most Legacy Spending Is Sole Source.** Not surprisingly, as shown in Figure 148, approximately 80 percent of legacy awards were sole source. This reflects the realities of large defense programs, where most of these programs were competitively awarded to a prime contractor (in some cases after multiple competitive phases and down-selects) years ago. Thus, the original prime contractor remains as the incumbent and is awarded both production and follow-on work largely on a sole source basis. Indeed, it would be uneconomical to change contractors midstream on large programs unless the incumbent is not performing.

- **A High Percentage of Spending Flows to a Small Number of Large Defense Firms.** Also not surprisingly, a large share of all U.S. major prime contract awards is going to a very few prime level defense firms. As shown on Figure 150, Boeing, Northrop Grumman and Lockheed gained about 57 percent of all major program awards. If General Dynamics' awards (some 12 percent of the market) are included, the DoD is awarding 69 percent of its major program contracts to just four firms. This concentration of spending reflects demand and supply realities: 1) the fact that most of the awards (77 percent) are made on legacy programs—largely on a sole source basis to incumbent contractors; and 2) the fact that the defense industry consolidated down to a smaller number of large primes in light of declining demand in the post-Cold War era.

- **New Buys Are Largely Competitive.** In contrast, the data on "new" major programs (i.e., programs initiated in 2006-2008) shows that 86 percent ($53 billion) were awarded competitively *in some manner* (although as discussed below, a good

Figure 150   United States—Defense Market Share by Company

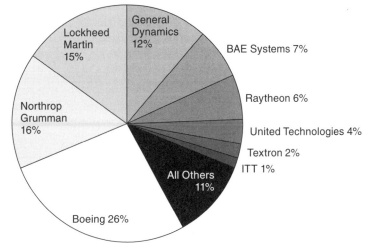

Source: Documental Solutions.

portion of these awards are competed only domestically) (see Figure 149). This is consistent with DoD's historical practice of awarding virtually every major weapons system in recent years through competition *at some phase* of the program. In some cases, the competition occurs at multiple points in the program, as, e.g., with the F-35 Joint Strike Fighter: in 1996, the Air Force selected two teams from a number competing for the Concept Demonstrator phase of the program, and then in 2001 down-selected to a single team for the System Development and Demonstration Phase of the program (which precedes production).

- **Much New Procurement Is C4ISR and War-Driven.** Much of the new procurement is related to C4ISR—such programs as Digital Modular Radios, GEMS, CSEL, Smart-T, and Integrated Tactical Wireless Network. A considerable portion of the new procurement also is for immediate operational needs for Iraq and Afghanistan, including Mine Resistant Ambush Protected vehicles.

- **The Openness of New Procurements to Foreign Competition Is Mixed.** Although 87 percent of new procurements were, as noted above, competed in some manner, only 45 percent were open to foreign competition. In contrast, approximately 32 percent of new buys were awarded through "limited" rather than "open" competition (i.e., where foreign participation is excluded). Thus, between this area of limited competition and the sole source buying on new programs, approximately 52 percent of program dollars were not truly accessible by foreign competitors. The remaining 6 percent were awarded on cooperative programs—also with some foreign participation. How one views this data is a matter of perspective. From a historical perspective, the fact that 45 percent of new procurements are open to foreign competition is somewhat remarkable given a legacy of relatively closed markets. On the other hand, there remains a significant portion of the market off-limits (some of which, of course, is for legitimate security-related reasons).

- **European Firms Won a Significant Share of New Awards in a Wartime Market.** As shown on Figure 151, European firms won 28 percent of new major awards.

Figure 151   United States—New Procurement by Supplier

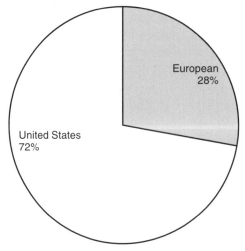

Source: Documental Solutions.

This data is in sharp contrast to traditional data showing foreign firms with 1-2 percent of total U.S. RDT&E and procurement, as discussed in Chapter 4. The difference is that this data focuses on only new awards and in a select set of market areas. The increased European participation in part reflects wartime exigencies. European companies were able to win a significant proportion of new procurement awards when they possessed a non-developmental solution to a pressing operational need. Whether their success will continue after accelerated wartime procurement processes are suspended remains uncertain. There is some anecdotal evidence suggesting that initial awards to foreign firms with developed solutions are shifted to U.S. suppliers once they catch up and develop reasonable substitutes.

- **Little Cooperative Engagement.** The data also shows a small percentage of U.S. buying—5 percent—is on cooperative programs, including most notably the F-35 Joint Strike Fighter and the Standard Missile.

- **Subcontract Buying Is Also Competitive.** While little data is available on the degree of competition in subcontract awards, it is well known that there is a fair degree of competition there as well, where the prime elects to compete the work or team with sub-tier partners rather than keep it in-house (i.e., make vs. buy). DoD policies, while not always easy to enforce, are intended to dissuade non-competitive vertical sub-tier solutions in favor of best value, competed solutions even where the prime holds a capable business unit in-house.

Foreign Exclusions: How and Why?

How are foreign firms excluded from participation in competitions (i.e., on what basis are they "limited" and not "full and open")? As noted above, under the Federal Acquisition Regulation (FAR) system, program managers in the DoD components must conduct full and open competition on programs unless one of a number of exceptions are satisfied. These exceptions effectively provide managers with the discretionary authority to exclude foreign participation in acquisition programs on a range of grounds.

In fact, the current procurement rules encourage the consideration of foreign participation and make it more difficult than in the past to avoid open and competitive bidding on defense contracts; specific written justifications are required to limit sources. Nevertheless, contracting authorities still have relatively broad authority to avoid a competitive procurement or exclude foreign firms from participating on a number of grounds:

- **National Security:** Authority to depart from full and open competition where disclosure of the government's needs would "compromise the national security."[645]

- **Industrial Base and Mobilization:** Exemption from free and open competition and exclusion of foreign suppliers is permitted to preserve a critical industrial capability, keep vital suppliers in business, prevent the loss of supplier and employee skills, and maintain balanced and secure supply in the interests of industrial readiness or response under the Defense Industrial Preparedness Program.[646]

- **Lack of Comparable Alternatives:** Only one responsible source, and no other, can supply services to meet agency requirements.[647]

- **Unusual or Compelling Urgency:** An agency's need for the services or supplies is of such compelling urgency that the government would be severely harmed unless the agency is permitted to limit the number of sources from which it solicits bids or proposals.[648]

- **International Agreement:** Full and open competition can be waived, and certain foreign suppliers excluded, according to the terms of international cooperative development agreements.[649]

- **Statutory Set-Asides:** Foreign suppliers can be excluded from procurements set aside for designated types of enterprises, including small business, minority-owned business, prison industries, and various non-profit organizations. Set-asides typically account for 10-15 percent of all U.S. defense procurement.[650]

- **Public Interest:** An agency head may waive the requirement for competition when he makes a written finding that it is in the public interest to do so—a "catch-all" regulation covering any circumstances not covered by those above.[651]

The only country exempt from these exclusions is Canada, which by statute is considered part of the U.S. defense industrial base. As Canada does not produce much significant defense equipment, mainly components and subsystems, its participation is not controversial. Indeed, Canada long ago made this conscious policy choice. In the so-called Hyde Park Agreement signed in the 1950s, Canada essentially gave up any idea of manufacturing large

---

[645] FAR 6.302-6. Available at: http://www.arnet.gov/far/current/html/Subpart%206_3.html#wp1086841.

[646] FAR 6.302-3. Available at: http://www.arnet.gov/far/current/html/Subpart%206_3.html#wp1086841.

[647] FAR 6.302-1. Available at: http://www.arnet.gov/far/current/html/Subpart%206_3.html#wp1086841.

[648] FAR 6.302-2 Available at: http://www.arnet.gov/far/current/html/Subpart%206_3.html#wp1086841.

[649] FAR 6.302-5. Available at: http://www.arnet.gov/far/current/html/FARTOCP06.html#wp280339.

[650] FAR 6.302-5. Available at: http://www.arnet.gov/far/current/html/FARTOCP06.html#wp280339.

[651] FAR 6.302-7. Available at: http://www.arnet.gov/far/current/html/FARTOCP06.html#wp280339.

Table 76   Top U.S. Defense Programs, 2006-2008 (Millions of Dollars—$)

Prime Contractor	System Name	Type	2006	2007	2008	Total	Award Type	Legacy	Supplier
Boeing	C-17 Globemaster III	Transport Acft	4,252.46	3,841.22	5,161.81	13,255.49	Limited	Yes	U.S.
Lockheed Martin	F-22 Raptor	Fighter	4,783.24	3,636.57	3,289.83	11,709.64	Limited	Yes	U.S.
Boeing	F-35 Joint Strike Fighter	Multi-Role Acft	2,965.35	3,156.95	2,212.21	8,334.51	Cooperative	Yes	U.S.
Lockheed Martin	C-130 Hercules	Transport Acft	2,645.89	2,679.25	2,735.47	8,060.61	Sole Source	Yes	U.S.
General Dynamics	SSN-774 Virginia Class	Submarine	2,277.75	2,565.52	2,847.40	7,690.66	Sole Source	Yes	U.S.
Northrop Grumman	DDG-51 Arleigh Burke Class	Destroyer	2,532.93	2,604.49	2,524.30	7,661.71	Sole Source	Yes	U.S.
Boeing	Future Combat Systems	Ground Systems	1,854.34	2,538.44	2,732.34	7,125.12	Sole Source	No	U.S.
Boeing	Ballistic Missile Defense System	Missile Defense	1,876.38	2,283.95	2,239.10	6,399.43	Sole Source	Yes	U.S.
United Technologies	UH-60 Blackhawk	Helicopter	1,490.11	2,067.76	2,486.18	6,044.05	Sole Source	Yes	U.S.
Northrop Grumman	DDG 1000 Zumwalt Class	Destroyer	1,367.73	2,249.94	1,486.00	5,103.67	Limited	No	U.S.
Boeing	F/A-18 Hornet	Multi-Role Acft	304.74	2,385.34	2,388.97	5,079.05	Sole Source	Yes	U.S.
BAE Systems	M2/3 Bradley Fighting Vehicle	Ground Vehicle	408.14	1,434.82	2,983.46	4,826.42	Sole Source	Yes	U.S.
General Dynamics	Stryker Interim Armored Vehicle	Ground Vehicle	1,247.18	1,650.76	1,718.39	4,616.33	Competitive	No	U.S.
Boeing	AH-64D Apache Longbow	Helicopter	713.37	1,218.47	2,572.74	4,504.58	Sole Source	Yes	U.S.
General Dynamics	M1 Abrams MBT	Ground Vehicle	1,189.93	1,347.47	1,849.88	4,387.28	Sole Source	Yes	U.S.
Boeing	LPD-17 San Antonio Class	Amphibious Ship	1,347.86	1,259.18	1,478.59	4,085.62	Limited	No	U.S.
Navistar	MaxxPro MRAP	Ground Vehicle	0.00	714.22	3,007.08	3,721.30	Competitive	No	U.S.
Boeing	V-22 Osprey	Tilt-Rotor	1,158.61	1,154.78	1,347.24	3,660.63	Sole Source	Yes	U.S.
AM General	HMMWV	Ground Vehicle	1,164.51	834.38	1,539.46	3,538.35	Sole Source	Yes	U.S.
Boeing	Minuteman	ICBM	1,065.78	1,373.40	1,066.89	3,506.07	Sole Source	Yes	U.S.
Lockheed Martin	P-8 Multimission Maritime Aircraft	Patrol Aircraft	885.24	975.45	838.28	2,698.98	Limited	No	U.S.
Boeing	Airborne Laser	Missile Defense	881.28	1,017.20	588.69	2,487.16	Sole Source	No	U.S.
Northrop Grumman	T-AKE-1 Lewis & Clark Class	Support Ship	799.25	882.80	783.96	2,466.01	Sole Source	Yes	U.S.
Northrop Grumman	B-2 Spirit	Bomber	681.06	784.01	997.63	2,462.70	Sole Source	Yes	U.S.
BAE Systems	Family of Medium Tactical Vehicles	Trucks	447.49	460.92	1,543.26	2,451.68	Sole Source	Yes	U.S.
Raytheon	Standard Missile	Missile	718.10	987.00	728.22	2,433.32	Cooperative	Yes	U.S.

Prime Contractor	System Name	Type	2006	2007	2008	Total	Award Type	Legacy	Supplier
Lockheed Martin	VH-71 Marine One Helicopter	Helicopter	797.00	600.00	1,000.00	2,397.00	Competitive	No	European
Lockheed Martin	Patriot PAC-3	Missile	827.08	760.98	759.92	2,347.97	Sole Source	Yes	U.S.
Northrop Grumman	E-2C Hawkeye	AEW Aircraft	750.84	636.13	946.67	2,333.65	Sole Source	Yes	U.S.
Northrop Grumman	CVN Overhaul/refueling	Aircraft Carrier	700.00	768.00	802.00	2,270.00	Sole Source	Yes	U.S.
BAE Systems	RG-31 MRAP	Ground Vehicle	60.74	518.83	1,677.17	2,256.74	Competitive	No	European
Northrop Grumman	CVN-77 Class	Aircraft Carrier	562.59	561.66	1,118.88	2,243.13	Sole Source	Yes	U.S.
ITT	SINCGARS	Tactical Radio	606.50	848.59	725.94	2,181.03	Competitive	Yes	U.S.
Boeing	E-3 AWACS	AEW Aircraft	620.64	727.81	780.76	2,129.20	Sole Source	Yes	U.S.
General Dynamics	SSBN-726 Ohio Class SSBN	Submarine	1,190.79	650.67	280.34	2,121.80	Sole Source	Yes	U.S.
BAE Systems	Caiman MRAP	Ground Vehicle	0.00	443.04	1,604.18	2,047.21	Competitive	No	European
Northrop Grumman	CVN 78 Ford Class	Aircraft Carrier	669.55	618.90	688.06	1,976.51	Sole Source	Yes	U.S.
Oshkosh	Medium Tactical Vehicle Replacement	Ground Vehicle	587.33	612.51	743.91	1,943.75	Sole Source	Yes	U.S.
Boeing	E-4 NEACP	C2 Aircraft	442.09	682.03	682.03	1,806.15	Sole Source	Yes	U.S.
Lockheed Martin	SPY-1 Aegis Radar	Radar	635.91	547.68	578.92	1,762.51	Sole Source	Yes	U.S.
Force Protection	Cougar	Ground Vehicle	135.09	557.22	1,053.38	1,745.69	Competitive	No	U.S.
Hawker Beechcraft	T-6A/B Texan II	Trainer Aircraft	444.45	591.02	688.05	1,723.52	Competitive	Yes	U.S.
Integrated Coast Guard Systems	Deepwater	Coast Guard	608.62	542.92	565.88	1,717.43	Sole Source	Yes	U.S.
United Technologies Corp	CH-53 Sea Stallion	Helicopter	705.23	593.11	418.69	1,717.03	Sole Source	Yes	U.S.
Boeing	JDAM	Guided Bomb	813.05	416.01	475.06	1,704.12	Sole Source	Yes	U.S.
General Dynamics	WIN-T	C4I	606.88	488.32	603.58	1,698.78	Limited	Yes	U.S.
Lockheed Martin	THAADS	Missile Defense	751.11	446.53	482.84	1,680.48	Limited	Yes	U.S.
General Dynamics	SSN-688 Los Angeles Class	Submarine	710.53	510.93	440.62	1,662.08	Sole Source	Yes	U.S.
Textron	M1117 Armored Security Vehicle	Ground Vehicle	462.90	519.06	652.73	1,634.69	Competitive	No	U.S.
United Technologies Corp	F-22 (GFE Engine Set)	Jet Engines	577.58	520.01	483.67	1,581.26	Limited	No	U.S.
Northrop Grumman	CREW Counter-IED	Counter-IED	437.37	554.93	452.80	1,445.09	Competitive	No	U.S.

Source: Documental Solutions.

systems and in return sought open access to the U.S. defense market for components and to be treated as part of the U.S. industrial base.

Of course, these exceptions are quite reasonable when invoked in appropriate circumstances. The exception for sole source work on legacy programs is eminently logical; it would make no sense to seek bids on old programs where an award was competitively bid years ago unless the prime contractor is failing to deliver. Similarly, the national security exclusion has very legitimate uses—such as protecting a unique U.S. capability whose underlying principles would be compromised if released to foreign companies. Although the rules make clear that the fact that a program is classified or requires access to classified data to bid or perform is not a sufficient basis for obviating competition,[652] security considerations nevertheless can still be a legitimate factor in precluding *foreign sources* from participating in certain sensitive areas (e.g., as system integrators on stealthy vehicles).

While the United States retains the legal basis to take many extraordinary actions in time of war or other emergency, such as excluding foreign sources on "industrial base and mobilization" grounds, industrial mobilization has in fact not been included in strategic planning or spending since the end of the Cold War. In the context of twenty-first century warfare, the entire notion of requiring domestic production to ensure wartime industrial ramp-up is antiquated: the short duration of modern wars and the complexity of modern weapon systems make the rapid expansion of production for anything other than munitions extremely difficult.

In addition, in a global industrial economy, maintaining several domestic sources can be both costly and unnecessary from both a security of supply standpoint (because, as discussed above, foreign sourcing does not necessarily imply vulnerability) or to ensure competition. In the past, the industrial base exclusion has been used where a DoD component sought to maintain two competitive sources in order to maintain competition (for example, in missile programs like Sparrow or Sidewinder or in certain ship programs). In today's globalizing economy, it may make more sense to allow a foreign producer to provide the competition rather than require the maintenance of a second source.

Informal Exclusion Authority

Defense acquisition executives also effectively have the informal ability, if not the authority, to preclude foreign participation without use of these formal legal exceptions. In fact, over the years, a number of major defense programs, through a variety of means (the specific terms of the request for procurement, informal guidance, etc.), have effectively barred foreign participation at the prime level even though they did not seek justification under government contracting rules for these informal decisions. According to DoD officials, the stated reasons of program offices for these decisions were often not well developed or vague and in fact probably reflect, in some cases, an outright hostility to foreign participation, and in others an undifferentiated mix of reasons (industrial base, national security, etc.).

The exclusion of foreign participants is accomplished in a variety of ways:

- There can be various types of requirements in Requests for Procurement (RFPs)— such as "NOFORN" (no foreign personnel allowed) or the need for a facility security clearance (which foreign firms could not have unless they have a cleared U.S. subsidiary).

---

[652] FAR 6.302-6. Available at: http://www.arnet.gov/far/current/html/FARTOCP06.html#wp280339.

- Several firms noted situations where an "industry day" event concerning a program was designated "U.S. Eyes Only" even though the matters covered were not classified and, in their view, there was no legitimate basis for closed-door treatment. In several cases, they reported being able to get the designation changed after making complaints on the lack of legitimate basis.

- Foreign firms also are at times effectively excluded through very short timelines between RFP release and proposal submission. This is generally not a problem for U.S. companies, whose business development departments maintain close contacts with sponsoring agencies and thus know the general content of an RFP weeks in advance. For foreign companies, the situation is very different. Most cannot maintain a continuous presence at U.S. military development centers. For example, on one large development program, the U.S. lead integrator called for proposals in 30 days. Given the ITAR lead times involved in putting licenses in place, that effectively precluded them from competing.

In sum, there is some credible history of situations where contracting officers and acquisition decision authorities using the discretionary authority available to them to deny foreign firms access to the U.S. procurement system (both through legitimate use of the rules and otherwise). These informal exclusions are probably the most significant barrier to the U.S. market. They are less legal or regulatory in nature than institutional, cultural and decentralized—making them more difficult to address. While there is some sense among those interviewed that they are encountering less of this type of conduct now as compared to five and ten years ago, it nevertheless is still present.

It must be underscored that, in some of these situations, there are very legitimate national security or security of supply considerations that do warrant limiting foreign participation, although the need for these preclusions is less today and the burden should be on the service seeking the exception. Yet, the fact remains that in some cases, it is institutional and cultural biases that inhibit reliance on foreign sources where security considerations do not necessarily warrant the exclusion.

DoD Actions to Encourage Foreign Participation: A Mixed Record

DoD has over the years taken action to encourage foreign participation in U.S. defense procurement in other ways, including rule changes, educational efforts and the like. At various times DoD procedures for major weapons programs have required that program managers, in developing an acquisition strategy, consider foreign sources of supply that can meet a program's needs (consistent with possible information security and technology transfer restrictions).[653] The procedures also require the approval of the Under Secretary of Defense for Acquisition, Technology and Logistics to restrict foreign competition for a program "due to industrial base considerations."[654] The dilemma is that while good rules and education efforts are useful, it is difficult to ensure their use by an acquisition community overburdened in recent years by a plethora of acquisition reform initiatives and various re-invention efforts.

---

[653] DoD 5000.2-R, Mandatory Procedures for Major Defense Acquisition Programs (MDAPS) and Major Automated Information System (MAIS) Acquisition Programs ("Mandatory Procedures" Manual, C2.9.1.4-Potential Sources (June 10, 2001), *Defense Acquisition Deskbook.*

[654] See Mandatory Procedures Manual, C2.9.2.1 (International Cooperative Strategy).

Further, the DoD has developed a series of programs designed to obtain the best foreign ideas and products for consideration and testing for use in our military. These include the Foreign Comparative Testing (FCT) Program (budgeted for $35 million in 2009), under which foreign defense products are tested against comparable U.S. equipment and made available for procurement if they prove to be superior in either performance or cost. The products involved tend to be in specialized "niches" and the dollar value of individual contracts rather small. Among the equipment procured recently through FCT are:

- Engine air particle separators for CH-47 helicopters (Canada)
- Laser marksmanship training system (South Korea)
- Shipboard GPS anti-jam antenna (UK)
- Deployable moving target training system (Germany)
- Non-dud 40mm training grenades (Germany)
- Eye-safe laser rangefinder for M1A1 tank (Germany)
- Airborne video display recorder (France)
- MEMS inertial measurement units (UK)
- Wireless Local Area Net monitoring system (New Zealand)
- Automatic chemical agent detector (UK)
- Buffalo Mine Protected Vehicle (South Africa)
- Lightweight road wheels for Expeditionary Fighting Vehicle (UK)
- Semi-rigid ammunition containers (Belgium)[655]

The concept of the program is to fund the testing and evaluation of mature equipment and technologies, developed by coalition partners, that meet U.S. war fighter needs. The concept of the program is "Test to Procure"; that is, if items test successfully, an acquisition program of record is expected to procure it. But foreign firms reported that a firm may expend extensive efforts to have a product participate in the program and successfully pass the tests, but nevertheless find no market for its product—with no interest from U.S. customers, no follow-through and even no feedback on their product once the testing program is complete. Some firms reported to this study group that their products were successfully tested and "that was the end of the story." It was as if their product fell into a black hole, they said.

Changing U.S. Procurement Attitudes

Recent anecdotal evidence suggests changing attitudes in the U.S. acquisition community, driven by basic economics and a desire for best value solutions. Specifically:

- In January 2005, the U.S. Navy awarded the prestigious Marine One Presidential helicopter contract (approximately $6.1 billion) to a Lockheed Martin-headed team that included AgustaWestland, a UK firm owned by Finmeccanica, a leading Italian

---

[655] Department of Defense, Office of the Deputy Under Secretary of Defense (Advanced Systems and Concepts), *Review of the Foreign Comparative Testing Program, FY 2005-FY 2006*, April 2007. Available at: http://www.acq.osd. mil/cto/pubs_files/FCT_Annual_Review_FY05-06.pdf.

defense firm. AgustaWestland is the manufacturer of the EH-101 (VH-71) helicopter in cooperation with Bell Helicopter Textron.

- In June 2006, the U.S. Army selected the UH-145 military helicopter produced by EADS, a leading European aerospace and defense firm, as its next-generation Light Utility Helicopter (LUH). The LUH requirement is for up to 352 aircraft with a potential total program life-cycle value of $3 billion.

- Finally, most recently in March 2008, the U.S. Air Force awarded its lucrative aerial refueling tanker contract (a $35 billion initial contract with the potential for much more—179 aircraft over 30 years) to a Northrop Grumman Corporation-led consortium. Significantly, the aircraft will be provided by EADS, a major consortium partner, largely through its U.S. subsidiary. Subsequently, Boeing, the losing bidder, successfully protested the contract award with the GAO. At this writing, after deferring the next steps beyond the 2008 Presidential election, DoD announced plans to re-compete the award on a best value basis in 2009.

On one level, these selections, made under best value criteria, appear to reflect that the individual DoD components are willing to seriously consider foreign firms for participation in its programs where they can provide significant advantage to the Pentagon. These contracts thus suggest the salutary prospect that a Transatlantic defense market could evolve, with Transatlantic teams bidding against each other and the winner selected solely on the basis of best value rather than nationality or where the jobs will go.

Of course, the significance of these decisions for the Transatlantic defense relationship must be tempered on several grounds. First, this changing attitude is not universal and there is no coherent, across-the-board attitude to encourage foreign participation. These decisions only are ad hoc judgments by particular DoD components. Second, the winning teams in these awards recognized that a significant portion of the value of the program must be provided in the United States. Thus, in all three cases, substantial content is U.S.-based, with EADS opening manufacturing facilities in the LUH and tanker cases. Third, the reality is that in all three programs the foreign participant is only providing essentially a commercial aircraft and not a defense system as such. The defense-related work on Marine One (with many sensitive systems and subsystems) and the tanker will all be done by U.S. firms at U.S. facilities. Thus, these are not cases where the Pentagon is truly willing to rely on a foreign defense system as such for these major needs and it remains to be seen if it would ever do so.

Whatever the relative merits of these awards for the Transatlantic market, the handling of the tanker award in particular has a number of implications. First, the protest decision, while technical in nature, is wrongly being viewed as a protectionist political decision in Europe—with potential repercussions for U.S. interests there. Second, the tanker decision could inspire a new round of protectionism at home that could result in more restrictive congressionally mandated Buy American legislation for defense programs (see discussion below).

On balance, foreigners entering the U.S. market, especially at the prime level, encounter significant challenges due to procurement policies and practices that result in significant exclusions of foreign sources. There is little indication to date that the DoD components are designing acquisition strategies in major weapons systems that are designed to encourage foreign industrial participation—at best there are salutary ad hoc decisions. Moreover, the "not invented here" syndrome plainly prevails in some corners of the U.S. acquisition system.

Sub-Tier Market Impediments

At the subsystem level, the situation is harder to discern as data is more difficult to obtain, but we believe, based on interviews and anecdotal evidence, that the market is probably more open. As DoD has increasingly devolved responsibility to the prime contractor, it has stepped out of the role of making sub-tier selections and has delegated this authority to the prime. Hence, it is up to prime suppliers to determine, through "make or buy" decisions, whether to utilize in-house capabilities for a particular subcontract item, another domestic vendor, or a foreign supplier. With the pressure on the prime to focus on "best value" and its need to consider foreign products that are more affordable or capable, one would imagine primes would be more open to foreign participation. However, primes recognize the difficulties in dealing with foreign contractors, including the problems associated with necessary ITAR licenses. Hence, they often tend to seek only foreign sources and to be willing to deal with the complex ITAR and other issues involved only where domestic sources are unavailable or are uneconomic.

Fair and Transparent Procurement Process

In general, the United States has one of the most open, fair and reasonable procurement systems in the world.

The United States is a party to international regimes establishing procurement disciplines. It is an original signatory of the WTO Agreement on Government Procurement. U.S. defense procurements by DoD, the Department of Homeland Security and the Coast Guard are subject to the transparency and non-discrimination disciplines set forth therein. However, a broad range of products procured by these agencies have been declared exempt based on national security grounds.

The U.S. Federal Acquisition Regulations set forth the governing rules on federal procurement. They incorporate a series of core requirements and procedures to ensure transparency, fairness and disciplined decision-making, including:

- Broad public notice of most contractual opportunities (with several publications disseminating this information in practice);

- Written solicitations that must include all information needed to bid, including product specifications, quantity, the criteria by which the award will be made, delivery schedule, etc.;

- Awards made in accordance with criteria set forth in the request for procurement, and rules on integrity to ensure impartial selection of sources in accordance with such criteria and without political influence; and

- A detailed protest system so that industry can challenge award determinations.

The United States is famously open in offering defense product and buying information for public consumption—there is a sense of a "taxpayer's right to know" about defense spending. U.S. defense program buying offices and all its many contractors have extensive websites, for example, and there are dozens of other public information sources on everything from defense leaders to specific performance and other technical features of U.S. military systems. Even the secretive National Reconnaissance Office has a public website. However, post-September 11, there was rethinking on this level of openness and some retrenchment resulted. The public information today on U.S. government and closely related national security industry sites is more circumspect, and the information displayed is a result of more deliberate decision-making than in the past.

Complexity and Scope as Market Access Impediments

While the procurement rules and process are relatively transparent, the U.S. system is large and complex in nature. A consistent theme from virtually all foreign firms interviewed was that the sheer scope and complexity of the U.S. defense market was itself a material barrier to access, especially with small and medium firms that lack the resources needed to understand and penetrate the market. In this regard, interviewees point out the lengthy and detailed nature of the U.S. procurement process, with the need to advocate their offerings with a wide-ranging set of managers up and down the hierarchy, inside and outside of the DoD, and possibly other government agencies and the Congress as well as prime contractors. Inside the DoD, for example, they need to understand the interests of, among others: the requirements community, the acquisition community, and the user community.

Domestic Content

The United States has long had a series of domestic content requirements in place that have created the impression of a closed market notwithstanding the fact that Presidential waiver authority and executive branch interpretations over the years have limited the impact of these statutes in practice. Efforts in recent years by Congress to expand these protections in the defense arena have sent strong protectionist signals and made it difficult for U.S. firms to maintain globalized supply chains even for commercial products.

Specifically, the Buy American Act and Berry Amendment have been mainstays of federal procurement for many years. The Buy American Act,[656] a depression era law originally passed in 1933, mandates preference for the purchase of domestically produced goods over foreign goods in U.S. government procurement subject to certain exceptions. The Buy American Act requires that more than 50 percent of the cost of the components that make up an end product must be mined, produced or manufactured in the United States.

For certain government procurements, however, the requirement may be waived if a product is not available domestically or is available only at a price that would harm the public interest. The President also has the authority to waive the Buy American Act within the terms of a reciprocal agreement or in response to reciprocal treatment of U.S. producers by foreign countries. Thus, all members of NATO, as well as selected countries with which the United States has reciprocal defense procurement agreements, are exempt from Buy American provisions for purposes of defense trade. Parties to the North American Free Trade Agreement and the U.S.-Canada Free Trade Agreement are also exempt from the Buy American Act. Even the Buy American provisions under the recent domestic economic stimulus package, which requires the use of U.S.-origin iron, steel and manufactured goods in funded projects, permit a waiver of the requirements if they are inconsistent with U.S. obligations under international agreements such as those described above.

---

[656] 41 U.S.C. § 10a-10d.

Similarly, the Berry Amendment,[657] originally passed by Congress in 1941 to protect the U.S. industrial base in time of war and expanded over the years, prohibits DoD from procuring products containing specialty metals mined or produced outside of the United States. Foreign suppliers to DoD were required to use U.S.-origin specialty steels even in components incorporated into larger assemblies, and had to spend time tracing the U.S. origin or face substantial fines. Recently, a 2007 Amendment eases the burden on foreign suppliers by permitting exceptions to U.S.-origin specialty metal requirements for certain COTS products. Nevertheless, the specialty metals restrictions are still in place for commercial items that are not purchased in large quantities without modification, as well as for items procured under contracts that were entered into prior to the 2007 Amendment.

In practice, these provisions were flexibly interpreted and, by and large, allowed DoD to source foreign items where appropriate. The President has the authority to waive the Buy American Act for countries that have entered into reciprocal trade agreements, and in fact the President has done so over the years. Moreover, the DoD has entered into reciprocal procurement MOUs with most NATO countries and other U.S. Allies that also waive Buy American. Similarly, the Berry Amendment was relatively flexibly interpreted over the years.

There also are a number of specific statutory restrictions that preclude DoD from procuring certain specific products or systems from foreign sources (such as shipbuilding, certain textile products, tents, tarpaulins, hand or measuring tools, anchor chain, buses, chemical weapons antidotes, certain valves). Aside from the requirement for use of U.S. yards on shipbuilding programs, these restrictions complicate, but do not outright prohibit, foreign participation in many types of defense programs. However, they are powerful symbols contributing to the perception by our allies that the U.S. defense market is not open to their industries. Indeed, this legislation is constantly raised by foreign governments and companies as evidence of U.S. protectionism. Further, the existence of these restrictions contributes to an ongoing attitude among some DoD acquisitions personnel that they should or may discount or not consider foreign sources. The restrictions imply that foreign sources are not trustworthy in time of exigency.

As discussed above, the reality has been that the limited accessibility of the U.S. defense market to foreign participation (especially at the prime level) is by and large not through these laws and rules, which afford DoD a measure of flexibility. Rather, the limited access is instead a result of longstanding institutional and acquisition practices by DoD buyers.

Thus, more "informal" or implicit domestic content "requirements" very much come into play where a European firm wants to bid as prime or major subcontractor in U.S. programs of size or importance. European firms, especially at the prime level, have come to realize that—despite the waiver of Buy American rules—they are likely to have a better chance of accessing the U.S. market if they have a domestic presence and their offering includes significant domestic participation. Hence, most of the key foreign offerings made at the prime level in recent years have involved significant domestic content—whether through their own subsidiary or teaming with another party. While such content is not mandated, the informal reality is that without a significant degree of domestic content, a foreign bid is unlikely to win a prime level contract (even on a teamed basis). The combination of security, program risk, political need for indigenous U.S. industry participation, and other issues leads to this reality.

---

[657] 10 U.S.C. § 2533a.

Customers do not often ask expressly for domestic work share but the desire for it is signaled in one way or another. These informal requirements come from "guidance" typically provided by someone in the program or budget chain—e.g., from program managers in DoD or industry, or from members of Congress or their staffs. Whatever the source, it is done on an ad hoc program-specific basis without a legal basis in most cases.

Thus, if the foreign firm wants to have a better chance to win an award, certain work needs to be done on shore. As this is done outside of formal solicitations or competitive selection processes, the data on these demands is not available to study although we have learned of such situations through interviews and our own experience. We believe that in most situations, foreign suppliers receive no explicit direction but are savvy enough to understand the steps they must take for acceptance of their bids and make the decision to move or establish work onshore to maximize their prospect of winning the award.

Continuing Congressional pressure raises the prospect of more stringent rules in the future—especially as we face a deep recession—and potential adverse consequences for the Transatlantic relationship. Congressional activity in this area grew beginning in 2001 when controversy arose over the procurement of black berets by the U.S. Army. DoD granted Berry Amendment waivers so the Department could purchase these berets from a foreign source—notably from China. Subsequently, September 11 fueled a "circle the wagons" environment in Congress.

The net result was significant congressional controversy and a series of legislative efforts, some successful, to make U.S. foreign sourcing rules yet more restrictive:[658]

- Congress made the Berry Amendment a permanent piece of legislation (rather than part of annual appropriations bills);

- Congressman Duncan Hunter, among others, proposed a variety of measures to expand Buy American and Berry Amendment coverage, including:

  - Tightening the waiver authority given the Secretary of Defense; requiring DoD and defense contractors to purchase U.S. made machine tools and specialty metals;

  - Raising the domestic content threshold in the Buy American law and broadening the items covered by the Berry Amendment; and

  - Creating a list of technologies and components critical to national defense and requiring that future items be 100 percent domestic in origin.

While most of the more onerous proposals were not enacted into law, the enormous Congressional scrutiny on these issues in recent years has created pressures (which undoubtedly will worsen during difficult economic times) for yet greater restrictions. Trade associations and major U.S. manufacturers, working with the Bush Administration, have had to expend considerable energy fighting further restrictions on their ability to compete.

These pressures are likely to grow in reaction to a series of recent DoD procurement decisions discussed above that made major prime level contract awards to teams that included significant foreign participation.

---

[658] See V. Grasso, "The Berry Amendment; Requiring Defense Procurement to Come From Domestic Sources," (Washington, D.C.: Congressional Research Report for Congress, April 21, 2005) for a useful review of Congressional activity in this area. Available at: http://digital.library.unt.edu/govdocs/crs/permalink/meta-crs-7513:1.

Offsets and *Juste Retour*

The United States does not require offsets, direct or indirect, in connection with the award of defense procurement contracts. This factor, prevalent in Europe, is really not a key impediment in U.S. defense markets. As discussed above, the real impediments relate to the U.S. relative lack of willingness to allow open competition on its large systems and the need for foreign firms to offer *significant local content* where they are allowed to compete. *Juste retour* also is certainly not a U.S. policy, although the United States has entered into programs in the past with its allies where this principal has been utilized. As reflected in the F-35 Joint Strike Fighter program, the United States would like cooperative efforts to move away from this inefficient practice.

Government Ownership

The United States has a long tradition of private ownership of defense firms. Today, most of the U.S. defense industry is private in character, with no government ownership or control. There also is no real interest or debate in changing that model. Indeed, to the contrary, a major thrust of U.S. policy in recent years—the so-called revolution in "business affairs"—has been to make changes in the defense procurement system that facilitate putting defense firms on a commercial footing and encourage them to adopt commercial practices. This focus began in the 1990s in order to promote affordability as defense budgets declined, gained new impetus as the post-consolidation frailties of defense firms became apparent in the late 1990s, and became an element of the Rumsfeld era defense transformation. Thus, across a dynamic era with a changing security environment, the focus has stayed on integrating commercial practices into the defense industry.

Arsenals, Munitions Plants, Depots and Laboratories: Exceptions to the Rule

Despite the long history of private ownership and control, the U.S. government continues to own several sizable segments of the defense industry: namely, arsenals and ordnance plants, depots and maintenance facilities, and government laboratories.

Public Arsenals and Munitions Plants. The U.S. Army's Army Materiel Command owns a number of Army arsenals and ammunition plants. The former serve as depots for Army ordnance and supplies, as well as manufacturing plants for cannon barrels and other heavy ordnance, and as engineering development centers for Army weapons. The Army also owns 21 Army and Joint Munitions Centers, each of which produces one or more types of ammunition ranging from artillery shells to aerial bombs to missile warheads. Most of these ammunitions plants are Government-Owned/Contractor-Operated (GOCO) facilities, in which the government owns the physical plant but contracts for its operation and maintenance with a private company. This arrangement allows the government to maintain control of a strategic asset while relieving it of the cost of maintaining an expensive and seasonal workforce. In return, the contractor is largely relieved of the environmental and safety liabilities associated with munitions production. These include plants that produce arms and ammunition, cannon and gun mounts, various propellants and explosives, and bombs. While some of these are GOCO facilities, others are not; the U.S. Army still operates some itself.

Depots and Maintenance Facilities. Each of the U.S. Services continues to own and operate large depots and other maintenance facilities for repairing and maintaining combat equipment. There has been considerable rationalization and outsourcing by depots, especially those managed by the Air Force in recent years. Moreover, newer platforms are increasingly purchased under total support agreements, which make primes responsible for lifecycle maintenance. Further, in many cases the organic depot managers hire companies to assist in performing workload. Nevertheless, there are statutory limits enacted by Congress that precludes each service from outsourcing more than 50 percent of the maintenance work on weapons systems.

Laboratories and Extensive Test Facilities. Finally, various DoD entities, including each of the U.S. Services, maintain a set of laboratories with different objectives and strategies. These laboratories perform missions that are to some extent technology-oriented (e.g., nanotechnology) but also with some portion focused on the missions of their respective Service. For example, the Navy laboratories naturally have a wide range of surface and subsurface marine technology programs while the Army labs have leadership in armor and night vision technology. Some R&D efforts are performed by DoD and other government organizations organically, but much of their budgets also fund university and private R&D work. Likewise the Services own a number of test ranges and test facilities for all types of systems they procure and deploy. Some efforts have been made to restructure and downsize these laboratories and test facilities to a more concentrated and DoD-shared model; this appears to be a work-in-progress.

Logic and empirical studies indicate that the United States should consider privatizing and further rationalizing more of these facilities and operations:

- The arsenals and munitions plants have run at significant underutilization of capacity and studies have suggested their rightsizing would produce significant savings—several billions over time according to objective estimates.[659]

- The DoD retains organic depot maintenance capabilities that may be more efficient if they were fully private rather than public activities.

- The government retains laboratories that overlap with private sector, university and federally funded R&D center activities. Indeed, the UK recently privatized a significant portion of the Defense Engineering and Research Agency, recognizing that putting these capabilities on a commercial footing can encourage both innovation and efficiency. Known as QinetiQ Group, the privatized entity now is a self-sustaining defense firm specializing in defense and commercial R&D activities. The UK did, however, retain government ownership of more sensitive laboratory activities, such as in the nuclear field. The United States might draw applicable lessons from this experience.

Of course, the dilemma facing the United States, like that facing Europeans, is that closing, privatizing or downsizing these governmental facilities undoubtedly would result in painful job loss as well as one time closure costs. Hence, political and institutional realities—including significant cultural resistance to change—make this difficult, and privatization of these functions is likely to be gradual and evolutionary in nature.

---

[659] See W.M. Hix, E.M. Pint, J. Bondanella, B. Held, M. Hynes, D. Johnson, A. Pregler, M. Stollenwerk, and J. Sollinger, *Rethinking Governance of the Army's Arsenals and Ammunition Plants*, The Rand Corporation (2003). Available at: http://www.rand.org/pubs/monograph_reports/MR1651/MR1651.pref.pdf.

Foreign Investment

President Bush signed into law the Foreign Investment and National Security Act of 2007 (hereafter called the 2007 Act), which in large measure codified and made mandatory many of the measures adopted in practice by the Bush Administration to strengthen the U.S. government review of foreign acquisitions on national security grounds since the controversy surrounding the 2006 Dubai Ports case. The case involved the purchase of a U.S. port operator by a Middle Eastern firm—Dubai Ports World—from the United Arab Emirates. While the Committee on Foreign Investment in the United States (CFIUS), the interagency group that reviews foreign acquisitions on national security grounds, initially approved the deal, the transaction led to an uproar in Congress and subsequently was withdrawn even though the President spoke publicly in support of the deal and the integrity of the CFIUS process.

Enhanced Restrictions in the Post-Dubai Ports Era

In the aftermath of the Dubai Ports case, the Bush Administration overhauled the CFIUS process—intensifying the level of scrutiny on reviews in 2006 and 2007 so as to ensure that further transactions would not create domestic controversy.

The 2007 Act codified these changes. Specifically, the new law:

- Expands national security reviews of foreign acquisitions to encompass transactions involving homeland security and critical infrastructure;

- Mandates investigations where U.S. firms are being sold to foreign-government controlled buyers;

- Adds additional U.S. government agencies as players in the Exon-Florio process; and

- Strengthens the review process, and strengthens Congressional notification.

The Expansion of CFIUS Reviews: The New Focus on Critical Infrastructure

A fundamental major change has been the expansion of the CFIUS review process. In the past, CFIUS has largely focused on two issues (technology transfer concerns and the uniqueness of the asset being sold. Now, CFIUS reviews have been expanded (informally at first and formally through the 2007 Act) to cover critical infrastructure cases.

- **Transactions as Technology Transfers.** CFIUS views foreign acquisitions as, in effect, transfers of technology (whether military or dual-use) from the U.S. business to the foreign buyer and analyzes whether such technology transfers are potentially adverse to U.S. interests (i.e., whether the transaction could facilitate the "diversion" of key technology to U.S. adversaries directly or indirectly).[660] The 2007 Act reinforces this focus, adding as a statutory factor in considering national security the potential for transshipment or diversions of technologies with military applications, including an analysis of national export control laws and regulations.[661]

---

[660] 50 U.S.C. App. 2170(f).

[661] H.R. 556 § 4 (amending 50 U.S.C. App. 2170(f).

- **Uniqueness of Target's Capability.** CFIUS has analyzed the uniqueness of the U.S. business being acquired (e.g., is it a sole source supplier and does it possess "critical" technology or capability) to ascertain whether the acquisition would raise "security of supply" issues. In other words, what risk exists to national security if the acquirer would let the business wither, and could military demand for its capabilities be met by other secure sources of supply. The 2007 Act reinforces this focus by adding as a statutory consideration the potential national security-related effects of the transaction on "United States critical technologies."[662]

- **A New Focus on Critical Infrastructure.** Since September 11, consistent with the broad interpretation of "national security" under existing law, CFIUS has in practice expanded its examination of the U.S. business being acquired to focus on a third area: the potentially averse impact of the purchase on homeland security. Under this rubric, CFIUS has examined in a series of cases where a foreign buyer could potentially disrupt the U.S. critical infrastructure (e.g., by putting malicious codes into software in U.S. computers or control systems at factories or electronic voting machines). The examinations have included a focus on physical protection of assets and screening of key assets from foreign access (to address risks of industrial espionage and sabotage, and the like). The 2007 Act codifies this focus and specifies that "homeland security" and "critical infrastructure" are part of "national security" and thus confirms the recent CFIUS practice. The 2007 Act also confirms that "critical infrastructure" is broad in scope; it is defined to mean virtual or physical systems and assets "so vital" to the United States that the incapacity or destruction of such systems or assets would have a debilitating impact on national security.[663] This could encompass such businesses as varied as telecommunications, information technology, or power plants.

Risk Aversion as the Bush Administration's Policy Preference

Quite a number of these legal changes are constructive, ensuring a more thorough and robust review of cases involving security risks and engendering more Congressional and public confidence in the process. On balance, however, the Dubai Ports case made CFIUS something of a lightning rod for the Bush Administration, with a much greater focus on the politics of cases. While mundane foreign investments in benign sectors generally are approved with a minimum of review, any review involving businesses touching on defense, space and critical infrastructure—categories defined in an increasingly broad manner—will undergo considerably more scrutiny.

---

[662] H.R. 556 §4 (amending 50 U.S.C. App. 2170(f)).

[663] H.R. 556 § 2.

> Risk aversion was the fundamental touchstone of the U.S. government review of foreign acquisitions during the Bush Administration. The question in individual cases is whether the "driver" of decisions was domestic political risk (like Dubai Ports) or legitimate national security risks.
>
> The Clinton Administration tended to see policy benefits in the globalization of the supplier base with close allies in defense and related areas (e.g., improved force interoperability and greater competition in consolidating defense markets) and balanced these benefits with security risks. In contrast, the Bush Administration focuses more on security risk and did not embrace or heavily weight cooperative benefits.

From top to bottom, the CFIUS process has become permeated with such a risk-averse posture, which is manifest in a number of ways:

- The more active engagement of senior level political appointees at departments and agencies in each case—and the 2007 Act's requirement that the CFIUS Chairperson and the head of the "lead agency" involved must certify to Congress that "there are no unresolved national security concerns with the transaction"—also tend to lead to more restrictive outcomes.

- The various U.S. government departments and agencies, by stepping up their scrutiny, have involved considerably more people in the process, many of whom had little prior background in these cases, and put them under stringent time lines driven by the statutory deadlines. Hence, they understandably tend to take more conservative positions.

- The intelligence and law enforcement agencies and agency components have more direct roles in the process and considerably more influence, and tend to focus on conjectural or theoretical risks. In particular, the Department of Homeland Security and the Justice Department, and through Justice, the Federal Bureau of Investigation, have considerably more clout than in the past. This increases the scrutiny on issues like potential industrial espionage and sabotage risks.

- In practice, while the Treasury Department remains the Chair of CFIUS, its role has subtly changed from that of a true "balancer" of U.S. interests at stake in a transaction to that of a "facilitator" to ensure that each department and agencies' equities are addressed. With the growing clout of the security and intelligence agencies, Treasury has largely been reduced to ensuring that their interests are accounted for and facilitating this outcome.

- CFIUS has negotiated an increased number of so-called mitigation agreements with transaction parties, which are designed to address national security risks, and has increasingly used onerous clauses in such agreements. This practice reflects the increasingly "least common denominator" nature of the CFIUS process, where Treasury lacks the clout to push back against agencies seeking unreasonable conditions. The result is mitigation agreements with a "kitchen sink" full of more onerous requirements that meet the individual demands of each CFIUS department or agency and allow Treasury to obtain their clearance on the transaction (as CFIUS operates by consensus and any one agency can force a case to full investigation or object to a mitigation agreement). One example of these clauses is the so-called "evergreen" provision now codified into law as well as liquidated damages clauses and other investment "chilling" measures. In 2006, the Bush Administration apparently only allowed Alcatel to acquire Lucent Technologies after attaching a stipulation that gives the Committee the authority to unwind the transaction in the future if the combined companies ever breach security commitments made to the U.S. government.[664]

The Cumulative Effect: Less Weight to Business Incentives and Legal Rules as Risk Mitigation Devices. The results of these process dynamics has been for CFIUS to give considerably greater weight to security considerations and less weight to countervailing considerations such as business incentives and the deterrent effect of law.

- **Focus on Access to Infrastructure and Capability to Harm Security.** The security agencies tend to value highly "security" risks even if somewhat conjectural in nature. For example, in situations where there is some risk that domestic infrastructure could be vulnerable to manipulation by a foreign owner (e.g., where the foreign owner has a degree of access that would allow the insertion of malevolent software code), this access will be highly weighted even if there is no evidence that the foreign owner intends to act harmfully and nothing in its track record to evidence such a propensity.

- **Discounting Business Incentives.** A powerful incentive for a foreign owner to avoid intentional or unintentional actions to damage U.S. infrastructure would be the prospect that such actions would substantially damage the business it purchased. Thus, for example, while Lenovo, after buying IBM's PC business could in theory put malevolent bugs in the software of machines it sells to the State Department, such an action would virtually destroy its business and substantially devalue its investment. While acquisitions of very small companies by very untrustworthy buyers might raise these risks, it is hard to imagine a large reputable foreign buyer intentionally engaging in this type of conduct. Yet, this type of practical business incentive is routinely given little weight by the security agencies in practice.

- **Limited Value of Export Controls and Other Laws.** Finally, there is a tendency, long in place but exacerbated recently, for security agencies to give limited credence to export controls and other laws as a means of mitigating security risks. For example, a foreign buyer of a U.S. firm with export controlled data cannot export such data without appropriate licenses—limiting the risk of diversion. However, security agencies give little weight to such rules and often require additional mitigation or seek to deny the deal if the technology is too sensitive—even though the security risk involved would require the foreign buyer to break the law to actually obtain unauthorized access to controlled information.

Recent CFIUS Cases: A Track Record of Increased Scrutiny

Available data on U.S. government review of foreign investments also confirms the increased CFIUS scrutiny of foreign acquisitions. Specifically, as shown on Table 77, a con-

---

[664] G. Hitt, "A Higher Bar For Foreign Buyers: Security Terms In Alcatel's Deal For Lucent Signal New Era," *The Wall Street Journal Online*, Jan. 5, 2007. Available at: http://www.financialservicesforum.org/site/apps/nlnet/content2.asp x?c=mtJ2J7MKIsE&b=1531035&ct=3356537&printmode=1.

Table 77   Recent CFIUS Review History

Year	Notifications/Reviews	Investigations	Notices Withdrawn	Presidential Decisions
1988	14	1	0	1
1989	204	5	2	3
1990	295	6	2	4
1991	152	1	0	1
1992	106	2	1	1
1993	82	0	0	0
1994	69	0	0	0
1995	81	0	0	0
1996	55	0	0	0
1997	62	0	0	0
1998	65	2	2	0
1999	79	0	0	0
2000	72	1	0	1
2001	55	1	1	0
2002	43	0	0	0
2003	41	2	1	1
2004	53	2	2	0
2005	65	2	2	0
2006	113	7	5	2
2007	147	6	5	0
2008	165	20	3	0
Total	**2,018**	**58**	**26**	**14**

Source: Department of the Treasury.

siderably larger number of acquisitions are now being reviewed by CFIUS than in the past. This does not mean there is an increase in foreign investments affecting national security. Rather, it indicates that more firms are filing cases that previously would have not been filed in light of the U.S. government's more risk-averse approach. While the number of rejections is small, there have been increases in the number of cases going to full investigation—reflective of the more robust review process. The number of mitigation agreements negotiated by CFIUS also has increased, reflecting a growing number of cases where CFIUS felt special safeguards or assurances from the foreign investor were necessary. Of the 52 mitigation agreements negotiated since 1997, when CFIUS first negotiated a mitigation measure, 34 of them were entered into in the 2005-2007 period.[665]

---

[665] U.S. Committee on Foreign Investment in the United States, Annual Report to Congress, Dec. 2008 (Unclassified Public Version). Available at: http://www.ustreas.gov/offices/international-affairs/cfius/docs/FINSA_Annual-Report.pdf.

Table 78   CFIUS Notifications and Investigations, 1988-2008

Ranking	Country	Number of Acquisitions	Percent (%) of Total Cases
1	United Kingdom	204	30
2	Canada	56	8
3	France	54	8
4	Israel	36	5
5	Australia	27	4
5	Germany	27	4
6	Japan	26	4
7	China	22	3
8	Switzerland	18	3
9	Netherlands	16	2
9	Singapore	16	2
9	United Arab Emirates	16	2

Source: U.S. Department of the Treasury.

What is missing from the data, however, and is needed to complete the picture are the acquisitions not pursued because of foreign firms' awareness of the U.S. government's policies in this arena. Anecdotally, we are aware of a number of these cases in the defense industry. In some cases, foreign firms chose not to proceed on their own in light of their awareness of restrictive U.S. policies, and in other cases informal guidance by the U.S. government caused firms not to proceed with potential acquisitions.

The more restrictive CFIUS policy is also reflected in the data on the actual foreign acquisitions of defense firms over recent years. A review of the data on Table 78 shows that there have been no sizable foreign acquisitions of U.S. defense firms, other than by UK firms, between the time the Bush Administration came to office in 2001 and the recent DRS acquisition of Finmeccanica, a leading U.S. defense firm, late in 2008. Indeed, as shown on Figure 152, nearly half of all foreign acquisitions was made by firms from the UK (approximately 47 percent). The transaction data thus reflects the reality that the investment climate in the United States under the Bush Administration has largely not been hospitable to foreign acquisitions of U.S. defense firms by firms outside the UK—i.e., from France, Germany, Israel and other U.S. Allies. An analysis of CFIUS filings over the last eight years (Table 79), which includes both defense acquisitions and acquisitions in other fields (telecommunications, information technology, other manufacturing areas, etc.), provides a similar perspective; approximately 30 percent of all filings—the most of any country—involves firms from the UK.

The one outlier in the data is the Finmeccanica transaction, at the end of the Bush Administration—the only large non-UK acquisition of a U.S. defense firm. This decision is a constructive one that reflects the deepening relationship between the United States

Table 79   European Acquisitions of U.S. Defense, Aerospace and Security Companies (Millions of Dollars—$)

Date	Company	Buyer	Country	Price	Revenue	Notes	Defense/Dual Use
Oct 2008	DRS Technologies	Finmeccanica SpA	IT	3,940.0	3,300.0	Defense Electronics	Defense
Sep 2008	M/A-COM	Cobham plc	UK	380.0	477.7	RF components	Dual Use
Aug 2008	Manitowoc Marine Group	Fincantieri	IT	120.0	321.0	Shipyard	Defense
Aug 2008	SI International, Inc.	Serco Group plc	UK	510.3	510.8	Information technology	Dual Use
July 2008	Hawker Beechcraft Svcs	BBA Aviation plc	UK	128.5	73.0	Aviation services	Dual Use
June 2008	MTC Technologies	BAE Systems, plc	UK	450.0	414.5	Intelligence support	Defense
June 2008	Sparta, Inc	Cobham plc	UK	416.0	297.3	SETA provider	Defense
April 2008	PlantCML	EADS NV	NE	350.0	NA	Emergency response	Dual Use
Jan 2008	Adv. Planning & Engineering	VT Group plc	UK	70.0	69.5	Life Cycle Support mgmt.	Dual Use
Dec 2007	Carpenter Adv. Ceramics	Morgan Crucible Co. plc	UK	147.0	91.0	Advanced ceramics	Dual Use
Dec 2007	Capco Industries, Inc.	Senior plc	UK	85.0	NA	Aircraft power systems	Dual Use
Oct 2007	NAVTEQ	Nokia	FL	8,100.0	582.0	Digital mapping systems	Dual Use
Aug 2007	Pelco, Inc.	Schneider Electric SA	FR	1,220.0	506.0	Security systems	Dual Use
July 2007	Zantaz, inc.	Autonomy Corp plc	UK	375.0	100.0	Data mining	Dual Use
July 2007	Armor Holdings, Inc.	BAE Systems, plc	UK	4,532.0	2,361.0	Armor solutions	Defense
June 2007	Teleflex Aerospace Mfg	GKN plc	UK	NA	135.0	Aircraft components	Dual Use
June 2007	K&F Industries	Meggitt plc	UK	1,800.0	424.1	Wheels and brakes	Dual Use
June 2007	webMethods, Inc.	Software AG	GE	546.0	208.8	Enterprise mgmt. SW	Dual Use
May 2007	Global Design Technologies	Bridgepoint Capital Ltd	UK	343.0	93.0	Aerospace couplings	Dual Use
May 2007	FastenTech, Inc.	Doncasters plc	UK	492.0	410.0	Aerospace fasteners	Dual Use
April 2007	ITS Corp.	QinetiQ Group plc	UK	90.0	77.5	Iinformation technology	Dual Use

Date	Company	Buyer	Country	Price	Revenue	Notes	Defense/Dual Use
March 2007	Talley Defense Systems	Nammo AS	NO	NA	62.6	Aircraft systems	Dual Use
March 2007	Analex Corp.	QinetiQ Group plc	UK	173.0	141.6	Engineering	Dual Use
Feb 2007	SFA, Inc.	Global Strategies Group	UK	NA	124.0	SETA provider	Defense
Feb 2007	MILCOM Systems Corp	VT Group plc	UK	42.5	100.0	Military communications	Defense
Nov 2006	Alcoa (Aerospace Business)	ThyssenKrupp Services AG	GE	NA	99.8	Aerospace services	Dual Use
Nov 2006	Lucent Technologies, Inc.	Alcatel SA	FR	1,340.0	9,400.0	Communications svcs	Dual Use
Oct 2006	Firearms Training Systems	Meggitt plc	UK	144.0	78.6	Training systems	Defense
Oct 2006	Aerospace Mfg. Technology	Senior plc	UK	110.0	33.6	Aerospace structures	Dual Use
Sep 2006	Stellex Aerostructures, inc.	GKN plc	UK	175.8	120.0	Aerospace structures	Dual Use
Aug 2006	Fargo Electronics, inc.	Assa Abloy	SE	300.0	81.0	Security systems	Dual Use
June 2006	Englehard Corp.	BASF AG	GE	5,000.0	4,997.0	Various technologies	Dual Use
June 2006	Deutsch Connectors	Wendel Investments SA	FR	1,040.0	55.0	Aerospace connectors	Dual Use
March 2006	Midcoast Aviation	Jet Aviation Group	SW	NA	125.0	Aircraft MROU	Dual Use
Sep 2005	Apogen Technologies	QinetiQ Group plc	UK	288.0	205.1	Information technology	Dual Use
June 2005	United Defense Industries	BAE Systems, plc	UK	4,192.0	2,292.0	Ground combat systems	Defense
April 2005	The Cube Corp	VT Group plc	UK	25.5	115.0	Facilities management	Dual Use
March 2005	Resource Consultants, Inc.	Serco Group plc	UK	215.0	256.0	SETA provider	Defense
Dec 2004	Westar Aerospace & Defense	QinetiQ Group plc	UK	130.0	140.0	Defense systems	Dual Use
March 2003	MEVATEC Corp	BAE Systems, plc	UK	82.0	120.0	Technical services	Dual Use
May 2002	Wackenhut Corp	Group 4 Falck SA	DK	573.0	2,809.0	Private security company	Dual Use

Figure 152   European Acquisitions of U.S. Defense Companies by Country

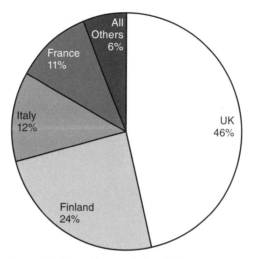

Source: Defense Mergers & Acquisitions.

and Italy, policy congruence in core areas and a level of U.S. comfort with respect to Italy's export control system. As discussed above, however, it is an ad hoc decision that does not reflect a coherent policy on supplier globalization.

Distinguishing Countries and Firms. The data also confirms that the more robust CFIUS approach under the Bush Administration also effectively draws distinctions between countries and suppliers on the basis of the country's policies and practices and the supplier's track records—which certainly is appropriate. Foreign investments from trusted suppliers in the UK pose the fewest issues. Yet, even firms located in other countries viewed as close allies have proven problematic where the country is perceived to have divergent policies on technology transfer and industrial espionage and/or the firm is not viewed as trustworthy on the basis of its business activities elsewhere, its compliance with law, its export practices and other considerations. Thus, countries like France and Israel are treated less favorably than other allies, and investments by firms in countries like China have been viewed with considerable skepticism.

A Less Open Foreign Investment Policy and Its Consequences

In sum, with the Bush Administration's more robust approach to the national security review of foreign investments, there is no doubt that the fabled "open U.S. investment policy" has now become more restrictive for any areas touching on defense and critical infrastructure and that the U.S. government will be more uneasy about investments by a broader range of buyers from a broader range of countries.

When viewed in perspective, there is no doubt that we live in an era where we are more vulnerable to existential threats such as cyberwar and attacks on our infrastructure and where there are foreign-owned or -controlled elements embedded in nearly every aspect of our economy and lives. Thus, there is a valid concern about ownership of key assets and the inherent risks. It is difficult to limit the risks of foreign intelligence penetration of and/or disruption to our infrastructure.

That said, it is doubtful that the increased costs and risks of the new and more restrictive U.S. investment policy will provide tangible security benefits—i.e., making the nation safer from terrorism and making our infrastructure more secure. For one thing, most acquisitions have little to do with Al Qaeda or Islamic Jihadism and involve sales to Western European firms with no terrorist ties. While it is certain that the more rigorous review process is likely to prevent a future case from becoming a Dubai Ports-type domestic controversy, it is far less clear that the limitations on foreign participation in our infrastructure, and the innovation, human capital, and financing such investments bring, will truly enhance our security in a globalizing economy.

The effect of the new approach is to chill foreign investment in defense and other sensitive areas; firms are aware of these policy changes and are in fact opting out. The President's 2007 Economic Report drew attention to worrying trends in this area, including declines in foreign firms' participation in the U.S. economy. Our less open investment also has adverse consequences for U.S. relations with key countries and our ability to access foreign markets. It undermines our ability to seek the establishment of open investment policies by our trading partners in critical areas like services, telecommunications, government procurement and infrastructure that have historically been closed to U.S. participation.

The Future of Foreign Investment Policy

Whether the Obama Administration will maintain this type of "risk-averse" approach to the national security review of foreign acquisitions remains to be seen. At this early juncture, several preliminary observations can be made:

- The core CFIUS processes and procedures put in place in recent years are unlikely to change under the new Administration—at least in the short term. The 2007 Act essentially requires the President and CFIUS to conduct a rigorous review of foreign acquisitions on national security grounds. Absent legislative changes, there is no walking back from the existing standards.

- The real question is how the Obama Administration will exercise its discretion in reviewing particular transactions on national security grounds. It should be noted that several key members of President-elect Obama's economic team have served on CFIUS and know the process well. Thus, if past is prologue, one can reasonably expect a more robust role for Treasury in the process and a more balanced approach.

The Role of Congress and Politics

The Dubai Ports case also symbolized and the 2007 Act reinforces the growing oversight and role of Congress in the review process. Increasingly in controversial cases, members of Congress are likely to make their views known and exert pressures on CFIUS and the White House. Some have argued that the changes made in the CFIUS process reflect less an aversion to "national security" risk than the risk that there would be domestic political controversy over an acquisition. In any event, an active role by Congress is an increasing reality—especially in more complex cases where third parties oppose the transaction and seek Congressional support.

U.S. Industrial Security Rules for Foreign-Owned Firms: Market Access Issues

The U.S. rules governing foreign ownership of firms with classified contracts can pose challenges for foreign defense firms seeking to enter and compete in the U.S. market.

The United States has one of the most developed regulatory frameworks for addressing risks associated with foreign ownership of U.S. defense firms with classified contracts. Specifically, the Defense Security Service (DSS), a separate DoD agency that reports to the Office of the Under Secretary of Defense for Intelligence, administers the National Industrial Security Program Operating Manual (NISPOM), which sets forth the framework for control of and protection against the unauthorized disclosure of classified information.[666]

The NISPOM creates a separate, and more restrictive, set of rules for U.S. companies under "foreign ownership, control or influence" (FOCI) that can significantly affect the foreign owner's ability to manage the firm. Once it is determined by DSS that FOCI exists, the U.S. firm must, in order to maintain its facility clearance, be put under one of several security arrangements that effectively limits foreign persons' level of participation in the firm's management, and establishes procedures and controls on governance of classified activities and visitation by foreign nationals. Unlike the approach prevailing in Europe (ring fencing) whereby the controls are largely focused on precluding foreign owners from access to the specific classified program, the U.S. approach focuses as well on the governance of the affected firm.

Where FOCI is found to be present, DSS then determines which of a range of protective measures established by the NISPOM are required based on: 1) the nature and degree of FOCI; 2) the foreign intelligence threat; 3) the risk of unauthorized technology transfer; and 4) the type and sensitivity of the information requiring protection.[667] These FOCI mitigation measures, which are of varying degrees of stringency, include voting trusts, proxy agreements, special security agreements, and security control agreements.[668] Significantly, in virtually all of these arrangements, the company is required to establish a Technology Control Plan (TCP) that prescribes the "security measures determined necessary to reasonably foreclose the possibility of inadvertent access by non-U.S. citizen employees and visitors to information for which they are not authorized."[669] Significantly, the TCP applies to classified as well as unclassified information subject to export controls, and is designed to ensure that access by non-U.S. citizens is strictly limited to only that specific information for which appropriate federal government disclosure authorization has been obtained (e.g., an approved export license or technical assistance agreement).[670]

---

[666] Promulgated in 1995, the NISPOM replaced a similar set of DoD rules.

[667] NISPOM, 2-302(a).

[668] Another option is a board resolution, which generally is appropriate when a foreign person owns voting stock in a company, but not sufficient stock to elect, or otherwise obtain, representation on the firm's board of directors. In such circumstances, a board resolution certifying that the foreign shareholder, among other things, shall not require, and can be effectively precluded from, access to classified and export controlled information is sufficient. NISPOM, 2-306(a). Available at: http://tscm.com/Nispom.html#linkA.

[669] NISPOM, 2-310. Available at: http://tscm.com/Nispom.html#linkA.

[670] Unique badges, mandatory escort, segregated work areas, security indoctrination schemes, and other measures shall be included, as appropriate.

Voting Trusts and Proxy Agreements

The most restrictive FOCI mitigation arrangements are voting trust and proxy agreements, substantially identical arrangements whereby the foreign owner vests his voting rights in cleared U.S. citizens (trustees or proxy holders) approved by the federal government. These trustees or proxy holders thus exercise all the prerogatives of ownership and have complete freedom to act independently. The arrangements may, however, require the trustees or proxy holders to obtain approval of the foreign owners for major decisions such as a sale of the firm's assets, mergers, etc. In short, as a practical matter, these arrangements effectively preclude foreign owners from participating in the management of the defense firms they own. In practice today, there are apparently no voting trusts in place; parties are opting for proxies for this type of arrangement.

These models and the policies underlying them are half a century old and grew out of arrangements crafted to put the Dutch holdings in the United States (Phillips) in trust to keep them from the Nazis after Germany occupied the Netherlands. Despite significant changes in the security environment, these same models have largely been used for 50 years. This approach, while used more sparingly today, has been invoked in situations involving majority foreign ownership of firms with very sensitive information, or where the firm is a services firm with access at military bases or similar sites involving sensitive classified work and it would be difficult to otherwise limit foreign access.

Special Security Arrangements (SSAs) and Security Control Agreements (SCAs)

A second set of vehicles, which are more frequently used today, are the special security arrangement and security control agreement. In contrast to the voting trust and proxy agreements, these nearly identical arrangements are less onerous; they afford foreign owners the opportunity to be represented on the firm's board of directors and to have a direct say in management while denying them unauthorized access to or decision-making regarding classified information. The SSA is generally used where a foreign person effectively owns or controls a contractor (through voting shares or otherwise); the SCA is generally used where the foreign ownership is less significant (i.e., generally a minority owner in a company majority owned or controlled by a U.S. person).

In practice, the SSA generally is a preferred choice for foreign parties acquiring a controlling interest in a U.S. defense contractor; the alternatives, proxies and voting trusts, are far less flexible and afford them virtually no control over the company.

Both the SSA and SCA include the following key features:

- The appointment of several disinterested "outside directors" to the board who are approved by and in privity with DSS; the outside directors serve on the Government Security Committee of the Board, composed only of outside directors and cleared U.S. executives who oversee classified and export control matters of the firm;

- Detailed rules on information security and physical security to protect classified and export control information; and

- Rules limiting visitations by non-U.S. citizens.

A number of the features of these arrangements impose significant costs and make it harder for foreign firms to develop synergies with their U.S. subsidiaries. Specifically:

- Visitation rules, which can be cumbersome, require advance approvals for visits to U.S. facilities by executives from the foreign parent;

- Foreign parents and their subsidiaries are only able to "share" limited "services" and as a practical matter cannot share legal, business development, most accounting and IT services. They must have separate "servers" and IT systems, and the SSA company must have its own accounting system and business development team and its own control over personnel hiring and firing. It also is difficult to obtain approvals for co-located offices;

- The U.S. firm must have separate badging for foreign visitors and employees and must utilize a variety of electronic monitoring mechanisms to ensure security; and

- Most firms under SSAs, regardless of size, are required to have three outside directors—which can be very expensive for small firms.

How much of a true impediment to market access are these rules, which plainly have legitimate security purposes?

In the late 1990s, DoD, prompted by two cases—GEC Marconi and Rolls-Royce/Allison—undertook a broad review of its industry security rules and practices. In general, DoD concluded the rules were antiquated in nature and were designed for a different era where the focus was on denial of access and not on allowing technological cooperation, rationalization of operations, or marketing and other synergies with trusted firms in coalition partner countries. For a number of reasons, significant reforms were not pursued at the time.

In the years since this review, while the NISPOM has been updated to a limited extent, the same basic rules and policies remain in place and have been strictly enforced. On one level, one might view these industrial restrictions as overly rigid, onerous and costly—and an impediment to market access. Indeed, in practice, DSS has largely been calcified in its approach—insisting on the most rigid model in circumstances sometimes not warranting it and refusing to adjust the models to twenty-first century corporate realities. In a variety of situations, DSS has declined to make reasonable, simple adjustments to the basic industrial security models and has clung rather religiously to its longstanding approaches—demanding that the language in its model agreements on its website be used verbatim. While there have been some modifications in particular situations, they have largely all been in the direction of adding additional obligations, not reducing them.

The problems are particularly acute for foreign firms that acquire U.S. firms that are primarily commercial in nature but have a modest amount of classified work. In such a scenario, the foreign firm faces difficult choices of whether to put a large U.S. business, mostly commercial, under an SSA or an SCA, with all the attendant costs and barriers that make it difficult to fully integrate the commercial business with the foreign parent, or create a separate subsidiary for classified work in circumstances where the classified work may not be sufficient to sustain a viable separate business or where employees would prefer not to work in a small classified setting—and lose the ability for collaboration and synergy with their other colleagues doing commercial work. Some firms have made business judgments to give up classified work rather than do this. Unfortunately, the current rules and models make little sense for firms that have a small amount of classified activity.

There also are a range of other problems relating to the relationship between industrial security and export controls. While the SSAs and SCAs give the authority to the Board of

Director's Government Security Committee to manage export controlled information as well as classified information, the State Department's Directorate of Defense Trade Controls in fact does not really acknowledge or value the SSA structure as a compliance tool. There is tension between these two regulatory agencies that often pose challenges for defense firms.[671]

In practice, however, for the most part foreign defense firms bent on U.S. market access have learned to live with these rules, despite their costs and limitations in terms of promoting true collaboration and integration. Indeed, foreign firms routinely have their U.S. subsidiaries seek to have these types of industrial security arrangements put in place in order to be able to compete for classified contracts. Thus, overall, however cumbersome and costly these approaches might be, foreign firms do not view them as significant market barriers as such. Given the relative size and scope of the business opportunities in the U.S. defense market, foreign firms are willing to make this trade-off.

Significant Increase in Foreign-Owned Firms Under Industrial Security Arrangements

Indeed, the fact is that there has been a significant growth of U.S. firms operating under industrial security models in the last decade. The totals have grown from 54 firms in 1994 to 94 firms in 2004 to approximately 200 today, with the large majority of firms operating under SSAs. While the majority of mitigation arrangements are with UK firms, there is an increasing number with non-UK firms as well.

The National Interest Determination: A Market Access Barrier

There is, however, one other important requirement that can be a market access barrier. Specifically, a firm operating under an SSA cannot obtain access to "proscribed information" without a "National Interest Determination"(NID).[672] Thus, in the absence of a NID, the firm would be precluded from competing for or participating in classified contracts involving proscribed information. Proscribed information includes top secret information, certain communications security information, restricted data under the Atomic Energy Act special access program information, and sensitive compartmentalized information.[673] Significantly, the NID requirement mandates a determination on a project/contract-specific basis, by a program-executive level official for the acquisition element of a particular DoD component, that the release of the requested information to the company "shall not harm the national security interests of the United States."[674]

---

[671] Of course, there are also concerns to the contrary. Critics of the NISPOM system have noted that DSS lacks the resources to meaningfully protect security. A series of GAO reports highlight "systemic weaknesses" in DSS oversight of contractors under FOCI, including DSS' failure to systemically collect and analyze information to assess the effectiveness of its operations, and its failure to analyze information on violations to determine patterns of violations or the degree of increases. According to GAO, DSS did not even know the universe of contractors operating under mitigation agreements. There is no doubt that DSS lacks sufficient resources to fully manage its function. However, part of the problem lies in the rigid, administrative models used. More streamlined models can potentially be developed that protect security and add commercial flexibility while easing DSS' administrative oversight burden.

[672] NISPOM, Section 2-303 (c)((2 & 3). Available at: https://www.dss.mil/GW/ShowBinary/DSS/isp/odaa/documents/nispom2006-5220.pdf.

[673] NISPOM, Appendix C (Definitions). Available at: https://www.dss.mil/GW/ShowBinary/DSS/isp/odaa/documents/nispom2006-5220.pdf.

[674] NISPOM, Section 2-303 (c)((2). Available at: https://www.dss.mil/GW/ShowBinary/DSS/isp/odaa/documents/nispom2006-5220.pdf.

The NISPOM has been amended in recent years to make the NID approval process less onerous and, hence, less of a market access barrier. Specifically, in 2006, DSS eliminated the requirement that: 1) there be "compelling evidence that release of such information… advances the national security interests of the United States"; and 2) the DoD component supporting the NID provide certain information on industrial policy and competitiveness that goes beyond national security (i.e., information concerning the availability of other firms with the capability to perform the contract).[675] The implications of the previous rules—which plainly had a protectionist element—was that approval of a NID was the exception to the norm and that it should be granted only if a domestic option was unavailable.

These regulatory changes were the outgrowth of ad hoc changes DoD made in the late 1990s in a series of specific cases (the GECC acquisition of Tracor, BAE's acquisition of GECC, and Rolls-Royce's acquisition of Allison Engine) as it found that the NID procedure created serious market access issues in the context of UK firms' purchases of large U.S. companies with highly classified contracts.

To be sure, the elimination of these onerous features has been salutary in nature and more NIDs have been granted than in the past. Nevertheless, the NID requirement continues to make market access difficult for firms in certain market sectors. First, whether to seek a NID is solely in the discretion of the U.S. contracting authority, and not the foreign firm; the company has no right to obtain a NID, and the contracting authority is under no obligation to pursue it unless it believes it to be warranted. Second, a senior level contracting official needs to make the determination to grant a NID. Thus, this combination of circumstances continues to make it difficult to obtain NID determinations and contracting authorities and senior officials have incentives not to seek or approve them.

In short, while improved, the NID requirement nevertheless continues to be an effective potential market access barrier for firms operating under SSAs. Indeed, a firm under an SSA may not even become aware of an opportunity to compete for a contract with proscribed data. Hence, the NID requirement does effectively limit market access for SSA firms.

As a policy tool, a NID is a blunt instrument. The categories of proscribed data for which a NID is required are not necessarily the most sensitive types of data today; they simply are separate classification categories that are administratively easy to work with. Thus, it is not at all clear that the NID focuses on the right information to control.

It is important to understand that the NID requirement does not apply to SCAs, where the foreign ownership is less pronounced, or to Voting Trusts or Proxy Arrangements, where the firm is controlled by U.S. trustees or proxy holders and, therefore, a NID requirement is not required. In effect, then, an SSA is a double-edged sword; the benefits of greater management participation by the foreign owner must be compared to the costs/risks that market access can be limited due to the NID requirement.

Thus, a foreign person seeking to acquire U.S. defense assets faces very difficult strategic choices. On the one hand, the person can establish a proxy or voting trust that allows the firm to compete fully on an equal footing with U.S. firms. However, these models preclude virtually any participation in management by the foreign owner, any technological collaboration with a foreign parent firm, or the achievement of any other rationalization of operations or business synergies. Alternatively, the foreign person can seek to utilize an SSA.

---

[675] See NISPOM (1995 edition), Section 2-309. Available at: http://tscm.com/Nispom.html#linkA.

While this allows it to participate in management and achieve some synergies and techno-logical cooperation (assuming export licenses are obtained under U.S. export control rules), the firm also potentially can be discriminated against in the U.S. market for contracts involving proscribed data. Finally, the foreign person can seek to acquire only a minority role in the U.S. defense firm, which limits its say in management and limits synergistic/rationalization opportunities but allows the U.S. firm to fully compete on an equal playing field.

Ethics and Corruption

The United States has a generally strong reputation for commitment to rule of law, ethics and corruption, with some of the most mature laws in the world and generally strong enforcement mechanisms. The World Bank's worldwide governance indicators show the United States in the 90 percent range or more for rule of law and control of corruption—among the highest scores of any major Western industrialized nation.[676] The United States also is ranked 18th in the Transparency International (TI) 2008 Corruption Perception Index. By way of comparison, France is 19th, the UK 16th and Sweden tied at 1 (with Denmark and New Zealand).[677]

Certainly, the United States has had issues with respect to procurement integrity in the past, with former government and DoD officials from time to time convicted for engaging in various types of corrupt activities. In recent years, the conviction of a former senior Air Force official over allegedly favoring Boeing in a series of competitions is illustrative. Indeed, there are recent instances suggesting too great a degree of coziness between government and industry in the contracting process—with mid-level government officials working with contractors to seek earmarks from Congress that benefitted their own organizations.[678] These cases tend to reflect the lack of sufficient checks and balances on procurement officials, who at times have been allowed to amass too much authority. Corrective actions have been taken in these situations to address these and other perceived institutional issues.

There also have been issues with respect to the misuse of "earmarks," that is, "private" amendments inserted into appropriations bills by Congressmen to benefit a particular company or individual. The most noteworthy incident was the conviction of California Congressman Randall "Duke" Cunningham, who received more than $2 million in kickbacks in return for earmarks favoring several defense companies in his district.

On balance, however, there are no overriding issues that go to the overall integrity of the procurement system. While it has it problems, there is no evidence of an overall systemic pattern of corruption where contracts are awarded on a basis other than best value. Indeed, the degree of competition in defense markets, combined with relatively transparent award criteria and a reasonable process with many people involved, mitigate against systemic procurement issues. Moreover, the United States has a series of strong laws, enforcement mechanisms, audits and other procedures that make such systemic problems unlikely.

---

[676] See World Bank Governance Indicators, 1996-2007 (Country Data Report for United States, 1996-2007). Available at: http://info.worldbank.org/governance/wgi/pdf/c228.pdf.

[677] Transparency International's Corruption Perception Index is on their website, available at: http://www.transparency.org/news_room/in_focus/2008/cpi2008/cpi_2008_table.

[678] E. Lipton, "Insider's Projects Drained Missile-Defense Millions," *The New York Times* (Oct. 11, 2008). Available at: http://coburn.senate.gov/public/index.cfm?FuseAction=LatestNews.NewsStories&ContentRecord_id=013e35d5-802a-23ad-4921-9800333ac2b7&Issue_id=.

In general, U.S. firms have a relatively strong track record of ethical conduct in third-country defense markets but there continue to be exceptions and firms still have some propensity to make illicit payments—as reflected in the sizable number of U.S. cases and investigations. The United States is, of course, a signatory to the OECD Convention on Combating Bribery of Foreign Public Officials in International Business Transactions (OECD Anti-Bribery Convention)—indeed, it was the leading force behind the negotiation of the Convention—and has long had on the books the Foreign Corrupt Practices Act (FCPA), one of the strongest laws in the world prohibiting the bribery of foreign government officials. The United States amply enforces this law and has taken numerous actions over the years, with numerous criminal convictions and civil settlements.

U.S. firms, including defense firms, do take compliance with the FCPA seriously and all major firm have detailed FCPA internal compliance programs, implementing substantial procedures, controls and audits. The firms rigorously review third-country agents and take a variety of steps to avoid liability. Most defense firms have detailed rules on making gifts of any type in third countries, paying expenses for third-country government officials, etc.

Moreover, TI's recent progress report found the United States continues to have a strong enforcement record, with considerably more prosecutions and civil actions (103) and investigations (69) in process than any other signatory to the Convention (and more prosecutions and civil actions than all the other signatories combined).[679] Indeed, over the years, the United States has prosecuted and entered into criminal plea agreements with some of the leading U.S. defense contractors with respect to illicit payments abroad, including Lockheed Martin (1995, 2003), Kellogg, Brown & Root (2004), and The Titan Corporation (2006).[680]

Yet, despite these salutary developments, there continue to be periodic allegations that U.S. defense firms have engaged in these corrupt practices in global defense markets. The United States is rated 9th in the TI Bribe Payers Index of 30 major exporting nations—suggesting that it is better than nearly all Western industrialized nations but by no means perfect.[681]

Export Controls

The United States participates in all of the leading multilateral regimes governing the export of arms and dual-use products. These include the (i) Nuclear Suppliers Group, which controls the transfer of nuclear-related materials and technologies; (ii) the Australia Group, which controls exports of chemicals and biological materials with potential for use in weapons of mass destruction and related equipment; (iii) the Missile Technology Control Regime, which controls exports of missile-related items; and (iv) the Wassenaar Arrangement on Export Controls for Conventional Arms and Dual-Use Goods and Technologies. The members of the Wassenaar Arrangement control exports of munitions and dual-use items, as well as the exchange of information about weapon transfers, in an effort to detect and prevent arms buildups that could destabilize geographic regions.

---

[679] F. Heimann and G. Dell, "Progress Report 2008: Enforcement of the OECD Convention on Combating Bribery of Foreign Public Officials in International Business Transactions," Transparency International (June 24, 2008), pp. 10, 21-22. Available at: http://www.transparency.org/news_room/in_focus/2008/oecd_report.

[680] POGO Federal Misconduct Database. Available at: http://www.contractormisconduct.org/.

[681] Available at: http://www.transparency.org/news_room/latest_news/press_releases/2006/en_2006_10_04_bpi_2006.

On one level, the United States has probably the strongest defense export control system in the world that operates to serve our national security interests. These controls appropriately help to prevent cutting-edge war-fighting technology from getting into the hands of American adversaries. On the other hand, however, the United States still has in place an antiquated Cold War system of export controls that has become rigid and calcified to the point that it is damaging American interests.

The story is not a new one—it is reminiscent of the movie "Groundhog Day." The problems have existed for years, and many of the reform proposals have been under discussion for nearly a decade. As a recent GAO report aptly put it, "[f]or over a decade, GAO has documented vulnerabilities in the export control system's ability to protect U.S. security, foreign policy, and economic interests."[682] Indeed, by various counts, there are more than 60 reports by various private and governmental groups on export controls in the period 1997-2007.[683]

The problems identified are complex and interrelated. There are longstanding questions about the effectiveness of the system in protecting key technologies; jurisdictional disputes between U.S. agencies (primarily State and Commerce), issues of enforcement, and the lack of overall assessments of the export control programs create significant uncertainty. On the other hand, many view the system as overly broad in scope. The U.S. Munitions List today applies to any product designed for use in military equipment or technical data or services related to that product. Thus, licenses must be obtained today for a range of low level subsystems and components that have little national security sensitivity—even for sale to close allies. Indeed, the U.S. Munitions List today covers spare parts on the 50-year-old C-130 engine, toilets designed for military aircraft, and a wide range of similar items that bear little on national security. Moreover, the Munitions List protects numerous products and technologies that are broadly available from other countries in a globalizing world marketplace.

In practice, the licensing process has been hindered by an increased volume of license applications beyond the capacity of a State Department staff that is too small and has serious retention problems and insufficient resources. Not surprisingly, license processing times have risen in recent years as a consequence (after an earlier period where license review times had been shrinking). Part of the problem is a licensing culture at the State Department that encourages firms to apply for narrower licenses in order to get approvals rather than "return without action" determinations. One consequence of a narrow scope license is an increased volume of new license applications to cover exports of articles, technical data and services outside the original narrow scope.

The concerns over the efficacy of the system to protect truly important technologies, skills (such as system integration) and products are directly related to concerns over the system's over-breadth. Because the State Department regulates the export of too many products and technologies that have limited sensitivity and are widely available, our limited U.S. government resources are necessarily spread too thin. Hence, we focus too much time and

---

[682] *Export Controls: Vulnerabilities and Inefficiencies Undermine System's Ability to Protect U.S. Interests*, GAO-07-1135T (July 26, 2007) (Testimony of Ann Calvaresi-Barr, Director, Acquisition and Sourcing Management, Government Accountability Office, Before the Subcommittee on Terrorism, Nonproliferation, and Trade, Committee on Foreign Affairs, U.S. House of Representatives). Available at: http://www.gao.gov/new.items/d071135t.pdf.

[683] The Center for Strategic and International Studies, Defense-Industrial Initiatives Group, has prepared a literature list that is not published.

effort in reviewing licenses (product and technical data) for unimportant things—which inevitably limits our time to focus on truly critical areas of national security.

The Underlying Philosophical Issue: What Is the Source of Our National Security?

Underlying these problems are basic philosophical questions about how to protect or enhance U.S. national security. For many years, the fundamental tenet of our export control policy has been to maintain a significant lead—even *vis-à-vis* close allies—in key enabling technologies that drive our defense, from radar and sensors to military aircraft to electronic warfare to C4ISR. This approach has largely worked. The United States has maintained a technological lead reflected in our supremacy today in conventional warfare; we have no peer competitor today and none on the very near-term horizon.

However, a number of factors suggest that this old paradigm will not operate as effectively in the twenty-first century. First, in light of the changing threats we face, we are likely to have a significant need for coalition warfare, which puts a higher priority on sharing technologies with allies than in the past in order to ensure interoperability in the struggle against terrorism and other asymmetric security threats. Second, it is likely that significant innovation will come from abroad (including from countries like India), and we need to gain access to it through collaboration with foreign firms and partners in order that our national security capabilities stay at the cutting edge.

Distinguishing Process and Technology Release Issues

Beneath the overarching philosophical issues, the problem in the export control arena is two-fold: 1) an increasingly dysfunctional licensing process (too complex and decentralized as well as under-resourced); and 2) an overly restrictive DoD technology release policy, especially since September 11.

1. Process Issues: The Licensing of Technical Data/Defense Services

Perhaps the most significant procedural impediments relate to the requirement for licensing of the "export" of "technical data" and "defense services" related to products on the Munitions List. Because the terms "technical data" and "defense services" are broadly defined, technical assistance agreements (TAAs), the authorized license for these types of exports, must be put in place before any type of meaningful cooperation or technical exchange may occur between U.S. firms and foreign firms or individuals involving ITAR-related technical data or services. Under U.S. regulations, an "export" occurs when U.S. data is released in the United States or abroad to foreign nationals (known as deemed exports), and therefore licenses must be obtained before any ITAR-controlled data can be exchanged or defense services at plant visits here or visits abroad by U.S. persons can be provided. What many people do not realize is that simple exchanges where a foreigner asks a question and a U.S. engineer answers are covered if ITAR technical data is disclosed.

The process to obtain TAAs is so complex that many U.S. firms seek to avoid collaboration with foreign firms unless absolutely necessary. Moreover, the approval time for these TAAs is long and growing, and they often are approved with conditions that can make the desired collaboration very difficult or impossible (conditions known as killer provisos).

Thus, as a practical matter, the need for licenses in advance of the collaboration can often lead both the U.S. and foreign parties to decide it is not worth the effort. Moreover, the problems inherent in the U.S. licensing system allow U.S. firms to sometimes hide behind difficult licensing requirements as the reason for not collaborating when in fact other underlying reasons may exist.

Restrictions on Academic Exchanges

In the post-September 11 environment, the requirement that TAAs must be obtained for technical data exchanges with foreign nationals and the provision of defense services has created particularly acute issues in the academic community, where many foreign students have historically participated in various research programs at the graduate and post-doctorate level. The breadth of and uncertainty surrounding the ITAR rules, combined with risk-averse decision making by the U.S. government, firms and universities, have together had the cumulative effect of chilling foreign student participation in scientific programs across the country.

2. Technology Release Issues

While the Pentagon's release policies (for the most part, not written) vary from one technology area to another, the overwhelming reality is one of limited release and greater scrutiny in the context of the war against terrorism. Fundamentally, the underlying sense is that the maintenance of technological and industrial leadership continues to be the fundamental driver of U.S. government technology "release" decisions. In one program area after another, technology release decisions are effectively precluding foreign participation in the procurement.

Reform Efforts Have Failed or Had Limited Success

While there have been efforts at defense export control reform, they have either been terminated in failure (such as the Bush Administration's National Security Policy Directive 19) or produced unexpected and counterproductive results (such as the Clinton Administration's creation of broad licenses not utilized, or shorter timelines that encouraged the use of broad and disabling provisos).

Mostly recently, in March 2007, the Coalition for Security and Competitiveness, a diverse group of leading industry associations, made a series of proposals for export control reform to the Bush Administration. After nearly a year of consideration and the raising of considerable expectations, the Bush Administration on January 22, 2008, announced a set of limited process-oriented reforms in National Security Policy Directive 56.[684] These include: more funding for the licensing function, a 60-day "default" rule for licensing decisions; enhancing the use of the electronic licensing system; some type of change on U.S. controls on exports involving dual and third-country nationals from NATO and other Allied countries; and a formal mechanism to resolve jurisdictional disputes between the Commerce and State Departments over commodity jurisdiction.[685]

---

[684] See V. Muradian, "Defense Trade Issues: Interview with Frank Ruggerio, Deputy Assistant Secretary of State for Defense Trade and Regional Security," *Defense News*, April 21, 2008.

[685] "President Issues Export Controls Directive to Reform U.S. Defense Trade Policies and Practices," U.S. Department of State Summary Sheet, Jan. 22, 2008 (unpublished).

The Old Paradigm at Work

In truth, the old paradigm is still in effect to some extent. At least in the export control community, the fundamental source of U.S. national security is perceived to be U.S. technology and industrial leadership—even *vis-à-vis* close allies. Working with allies is viewed as a "second" best way to achieve true security, and coalition warfare is given low priority in export control decision-making.

Evidence of the "old paradigm" is manifest in a variety of ways.

- U.S. armaments cooperation policy, even in a Transatlantic context, continues to be largely divorced from technology transfer policy. Technology transfer issues have continued to plague a series of major international cooperative armaments programs in which the United States and various European countries participates. This is manifest in struggles on these issues on large programs over recent years, like the F-35 Joint Strike Fighter. While we work these issues out eventually, the process is painful and the sharing is limited.

- A series of independent DoD "committees" with this risk-averse mindset have control over release policy in important technical areas. These groups have little or no significant senior oversight and procedural rigor, and effectively enable the bureaucracy to "just say no" to technology and technical information release critical to coalition war fighting. Such independent committees have jurisdiction over, among other things, low observables and counter low observables and anti-tamper devices; each of the armed services also has put in place its own oversight group.

While some of these reforms are useful and have helped to shorten the licensing process, they do not address the fundamental underlying technology release and process issues that continue to plague our export control system. The fact that formal procedures are needed to address commodity jurisdiction disputes speaks volumes about the underlying challenges in the system. The most interesting aspect of the Bush Administration package—the mention of changes in controls on third party and dual nationals long sought by European Allies—was left incomplete and unspecified.

The consequence of overly restrictive U.S. export control restrictions has been to build walls between the United States and other countries, making collaboration with even our closest allies either impossible or very difficult in key defense and related technology areas and eroding trust with our traditional partners. Indeed, as discussed in other country chapters of this study, even close allies are looking to "ITAR-free" solutions in capability areas where they want to maintain "operational sovereignty" over programs and "security of supply." Foreign industries are designing around ITAR-controlled subsystems and products, to the detriment of U.S. suppliers, to maintain the flexibility to export and meet customer needs. They also view "ITAR-free" as a marketing discriminator with foreign governments. On our current trajectory, ITAR will likely become a driver of protectionist policies aimed against us in defense trade by European and Asian Allies.

In the long term, the lack of access to foreign innovation and human capital resulting from ITAR restrictions in these areas will make it difficult for the United States—if cut off from the global market—to sustain its technological leadership in key enabling technologies related to defense, space and homeland security.

Intellectual Property Protection

The United States adheres to the major multilateral intellectual property (IP) regimes, including (i) the WTO Agreement on Trade-Related Aspects of Intellectual Property Rights, which provides core IP protection and enforcement rights (including for trade secrets); (ii) the Paris Convention for the Protection of Industrial Property, covering patents, trademarks and industrial designs; (iii) the Patent Cooperation Treaty, protecting patents; (iv) the Berne Convention, covering copyrights; (v) the Madrid Protocol, covering trademarks; and (vi) the World Intellectual Property Organization.

Generally, the United States is known to have strong laws to protect intellectual rights and enforces these rights vigorously. However, under U.S. government procurement regulations, if the United States funds the development of a defense article or technology, the U.S. government will generally require unrestricted rights in the technology or technical data related to the defense article so that the government can use the technology as it sees fit (in some cases, licensing it to other suppliers who can produce the products on a "build to print" basis). Thus, when responding to U.S. requests for proposal, both foreign and U.S. suppliers need to be vigilant in order to protect their pre-existing proprietary rights to technology—which may have been either privately developed or funded by foreign taxpayers. The Defense Federal Acquisition Regulation Supplement does allow for such protection under a specifically negotiated license agreement if the U.S. customer is willing to enter into such arrangements.

Technical Standards

The United States is a party to the WTO's Technical Barriers to Trade Agreement, which prohibits discrimination and seeks to ensure that regulations, standards, testing and certification procedures do not create obstacles to trade. However, every country has the right to adopt those technical standards that it considers appropriate in areas concerning national security. Thus, the United States has the discretion to, and has in fact put in place, its own specific technical standards for defense products that could in theory serve as a non-tariff barrier to competing foreign products.

The prospect of standards becoming trade barriers is tempered to some extent by reciprocal defense procurement agreements the United States has entered into with most of the European countries studied. In some cases, these agreements have been amended over the years to address quality assurance issues. Specifically, in the MOUs with Sweden and the United Kingdom, each party to the MOU agreed to implement procedures to ensure that defense articles and services meet mutual government acceptance. The purchasing government has the option to request that the other government independently test and provide a certification of conformity covering products manufactured by suppliers of the selling nation. These types of provisions help to facilitate mutual recognition of testing and standards and limit the prospect of arbitrary actions.

In the course of this study, we did not learn of any specific situations where techni-cal standards were used as non-tariff barriers to protect domestic producers and markets against foreign defense products.

However, the specificity of U.S. technical standards for defense products has posed chal-lenges for foreign firms seeking market entry. Specifically, the United States has devel-oped a detailed system of MIL-SPECs and MIL-STDs, which are detailed specifications and performance standards governing all aspects of the development, testing and produc-tion of U.S. military hardware and software, from resistance to vibration and temperature extremes, to the color and texture of the paint applied to the finished product.

The United States' long association with NATO means that U.S. military products are tied to NATO Standard Agreements (STANAGs) where these exist. However, the DoD has devel-oped so many product specifications and standards that are beyond the STANAG level or outside that setting that even European products meeting STANAG do not necessarily meet other U.S. standards that would allow them to readily compete in the Transatlantic market.

Some representatives of European firms interviewed for this study viewed the unique and very detailed U.S. standards as market access barriers that make it harder for them to com-pete with their products that work elsewhere in the world. They reported that because of DoD's unique specifications, they often must redesign or tailor their products in a way that works only in the United States in hopes of selling it to the United States. In some cases, for-eign developed products that have successfully operated in foreign militaries have required extensive testing and evaluation and either been found defective and/or have required sig-nificant re-engineering before they can successfully enter into the U.S. market. The Euro-pean firms interviewed perceive the necessity to tailor their products as a barrier or at least a higher cost of doing business in the United States. In practice, there have been numerous historic examples of these types of issues over many years.[686]

Nevertheless, the United States has made progress in this arena. For more than a decade, DoD has been moving away from MIL-SPEC/MIL-STD-based procurement to a greater reliance on commercial standards and specifications, augmented by military requirements only when necessary. Despite the challenges DoD faces in effectively incorporating COTS technology, the DoD nevertheless is increasingly using it in more weapon systems to reduce costs and development times and leverage commercial developments. Most of the standards that affect only superficial aspects of military systems can be waived, leaving a handful of essential performance and safety military standards in place. Computers are the most prom-inent example of the utilization of COTS, with everything from embedded microelectronic processors to "ruggedized" laptops replacing what used to be specialized MIL-STD equip-ment, which has resulted in savings measured in the thousands of dollars per unit.

---

[686] For historic examples of this kind of exclusionary behavior by U.S. development agencies, see Luttwak, *The Pentagon and the Art of War*, op. cit.